Behind the Scenes
of the New Testament

Behind the Scenes
of the New Testament

CULTURAL, SOCIAL, AND HISTORICAL CONTEXTS

EDITED BY

Bruce W. Longenecker,
Elizabeth E. Shively, and T. J. Lang

Baker Academic
a division of Baker Publishing Group
Grand Rapids, Michigan

Published by Baker Academic
a division of Baker Publishing Group
Grand Rapids, Michigan
BakerAcademic.com

Printed in the United States of America

Library of Congress Cataloging-in-Publication Data
Names: Longenecker, Bruce W., editor. | Shively, Elizabeth E., 1969–, editor. | Lang, T. J., 1980–, editor.
Title: Behind the scenes of the New Testament : cultural, social, and historical contexts / edited by Bruce W. Longenecker, Elizabeth E. Shively, and T. J. Lang.
Description: Grand Rapids, Michigan : Baker Academic, a division of Baker Publishing Group, [2024] | Includes bibliographical references and index.
Identifiers: LCCN 2024010446 | ISBN 9781540964472 (cloth) | ISBN 9781493447664 (ebook) | ISBN 9781493447671 (pdf)
Subjects: LCSH: Bible. New Testament—Criticism, etc.
Classification: LCC BS2351.L56 B34 2024 | DDC 225.6—dc23/eng/20240412
LC record available at https://lccn.loc.gov/2024010446

Cover credits: Fresco in Via Latina Catacomb, Rome, Italy, 4th century BCE and a relief portraying an official stopping place on Roman road / DeAgostini / SuperStock

Baker Publishing Group publications use paper produced from sustainable forestry practices and postconsumer waste whenever possible.

24   25   26   27   28   29   30   7   6   5   4   3   2   1

Contents

List of Illustrations   viii

Contributors   ix

Abbreviations   xii

Editors' Preface   xxii

PART ONE

Setting the Stage

I. Symbolic Worlds

1. Judaism   *Matthew V. Novenson*   5

2. Hellenization   *Carl R. Holladay*   12

3. Apocalyptic Thought   *John J. Collins*   19

4. Greek and Roman Philosophical Schools   *Te-Li Lau*   25

II. Places

5. Jerusalem, Judean Uprising, Temple Destruction   *Steve Mason*   35

6. Territories of Roman Palestine   *Jürgen K. Zangenberg*   43

7. Urban Centers of the Roman World   *Jan Rüggemeier*   51

8. The Decapolis   *Roy Ciampa*   61

9. The Synagogue in the Time of Jesus and the New Testament   *Eric M. Meyers*   68

10. Temples   *Timothy Wardle*   79

11. Greco-Roman Material Culture   *David W. J. Gill*   86

12. Houses and Meeting Places   *Richard Last*   94

PART TWO

Inhabiting the Stage

I. Scripts

13. The Septuagint and the Transmission of Jewish Scriptures   *Kristin De Troyer*   105

14. Qumran and the Context of the New Testament   *Matthew A. Collins*   113

15. Historiography   *Loveday Alexander*   122

16. Ancient Biography and the Gospels   *Helen K. Bond*   129

17. The Parables of Jesus   *Klyne R. Snodgrass*   137

18. Letters and Letter Writing   *Joshua W. Jipp*   144

19. Poetic and Hymnic Material in the New Testament   *Andrew T. Cowan and Jennifer Strawbridge*   151

20. Practices of Interpretation   *Susan Docherty*   159

21. Reading Strategies in the Greco-Roman World   *Maren R. Niehoff*   167

II. Actors

22. The Herodian Dynasty   *Morten Hørning Jensen*   179

23. Messiahs and Revolutionaries   *Max Botner*   187

24. Judean Social Classes   *Benjamin D. Gordon*   195

25. Itinerant Religious Experts   *Heidi Wendt*   203

26. Gentiles in Judean Eyes   *Hannah K. Harrington*   211

27. Judeans in Gentile Eyes   *Paul Trebilco*   219

28. Samaritans   *Magnar Kartveit*   227

29. Women in the Ancient Mediterranean World   *Susan E. Benton*   234

30. Masculinities   *Peter-Ben Smit*   241

31. Disabled Bodies   *Louise J. Lawrence*   248

PART THREE
Themes on the Stage

I. Divine Society

32. *Theos* and Theology   *T. J. Lang*   259

33. Cosmology   *Jamie Davies*   268

34. Eschatologies and the Afterlife   *Thomas D. McGlothlin*   275

35. Angels and Demons   *Robert E. Moses*   282

36. Prophecy, Divination, Oracles, and Dreams   *Jill E. Marshall*   288

37. Magic, Medicine, and Miracles   *Jennifer Eyl*   295

38. Purity and Holiness   *Matthew Thiessen*   302

39. Festivals and Feasts   *Gary M. Burge*   309

40. Imperial Devotion   *Adam Winn*   317

41. Persecution, Suffering, and Martyrdom   *Dorothea H. Bertschmann*   324

42. Mystery Cults   *Jan N. Bremmer*   331

43. Moral Transformation and Ethics   *Max J. Lee*   339

44. Sacrifice   *David M. Moffitt*   348

II. Human Society

45. The Roman Empire   *Sylvia C. Keesmaat*   357

46. Roman Law and Citizenship   *J. Brian Tucker*   365

47. Greco-Roman Associations   *Jin Hwan Lee*   372

48. Wealth and Poverty   *MiJa Wi*   380

49. Gift-Giving   *John M. G. Barclay*   388

50. Alms for the Poor   *Nathan Eubank*   395

51. Hospitality   *Andrew E. Arterbury*   401

52. Meals and Symposia   *Paul B. Duff*   408

53. Coins and Culture   *David H. Wenkel*   415

54. Race and Ethnicity   *Eric D. Barreto*   422

III. The Household

55. Household Structure   *Judith M. Gundry*   431

56. Sexuality   *William Loader*   445

57. Marriage and Divorce   *Alicia D. Myers*   452

58. Widows   *Timothy J. Murray*   460

59. Household Worship   *Caroline Johnson Hodge*   467

60. Slavery   *Katherine A. Shaner*   476

61. Literacy and Education   *Teresa Morgan*   484

62. Death and Burial Practices   *Daniel L. Smith and William L. Potter*   491

Scripture Index   499

Ancient Writings Index   509

Illustrations

6.1. Map of Roman Palestine at the time of Jesus of Nazareth, ca. 15 CE 46

8.1. The Decapolis 62

9.1. Village of Horvath Ethri 71

9.2. Ehud Netzer's proposed synagogue at Nazareth 72

9.3. Stone vessels from Shu'afat 73

9.4. Ritual bath at Sepphoris 74

9.5. Herodium and Masada 75

9.6. The Magdala Stone 76

10.1. Model of the Jerusalem Temple 80

13.1. Greek Minor Prophets Scroll from Nahal Hever 108

22.1. The coin of King Antigonus 182

32.1. *The Birth of Venus* 263

32.2. Bronze statuette of a guardian deity (*lar*) 264

32.3. Votive relief of healing 265

33.1. Cosmology: The Universe as a Tent 270

39.1. The Jewish Calendar 312

45.1. The Gemma Augustea 359

45.2. Claudius and Britannica 360

45.3. Ara Pacis altar 362

48.1. Social stratification of advanced agrarian societies 381

59.1. Terracotta figures of women praying 470

59.2. Aedicula shrine in the House of the Red Walls 472

59.3. Aedicula shrine, with figurines in situ 472

59.4. Kitchen painting in the House of Sutoria Primigenia 473

Contributors

Editors

Bruce W. Longenecker is W. W. Melton Professor of Christian Origins in the Baylor University Department of Religion.

Elizabeth E. Shively is professor of Christian Scriptures at Truett Seminary.

T. J. Lang is senior lecturer in New Testament at the University of St. Andrews.

Authors

Loveday Alexander is professor emerita of biblical studies at the University of Sheffield and an Honorary Research Fellow of the Centre for Biblical Studies at the University of Manchester.

Andrew E. Arterbury is professor of Christian Scriptures at Truett Seminary.

John M. G. Barclay is Lightfoot Professor of Divinity at Durham University.

Eric D. Barreto is Frederick and Margaret L. Weyerhaeuser Associate Professor of New Testament at Princeton Theological Seminary.

Susan E. Benton is a lecturer in religion and ministry guidance at Baylor University.

Dorothea H. Bertschmann is Honorary Fellow in the Department of Theology and Religion at Durham University and teaches biblical studies at the College of the Resurrection in Mirfield, West Yorkshire.

Helen K. Bond is professor of Christian origins at University of Edinburgh.

Max Botner is associate professor of biblical studies at Jessup University.

Jan N. Bremmer is professor emeritus of religious studies, Faculty of Religion, Culture and Society, at University of Groningen, Netherlands.

Gary M. Burge is emeritus professor of New Testament at Wheaton College and adjunct professor of New Testament at Calvin Theological Seminary.

Roy Ciampa is S. Louis and Ann W. Armstrong Chair of Religion at Samford University.

John J. Collins is Holmes Professor of Old Testament Emeritus at Yale Divinity School.

Matthew A. Collins is senior lecturer in Hebrew Bible and Second Temple Judaism at University of Chester, UK.

Andrew T. Cowan is a DPhil student at the University of Oxford.

Jamie Davies is tutor of New Testament and director of postgraduate research at Trinity College, Bristol, UK.

Kristin De Troyer is professor of Hebrew Bible at the Paris Lodron University of Salzburg, Austria. She is also the (academic) secretary of the European Academy of Sciences and Arts.

Susan Docherty is professor of New Testament and Early Judaism at Birmingham Newman University.

Paul B. Duff is professor of religion at George Washington University.

Nathan Eubank is Rev. John A. O'Brien Associate Professor of Theology at University of Notre Dame.

Jennifer Eyl is associate professor of religion at Tufts University.

David W. J. Gill is honorary professor in the Centre of Heritage, University of Kent, UK.

Benjamin D. Gordon is associate professor of religious studies and Rosenberg-Perlow Fellow in Classical Judaism at the University of Pittsburgh.

Judith M. Gundry is adjunct professor of New Testament and research scholar at Yale Divinity School.

Hannah K. Harrington is professor of Old Testament at Patten University.

Carl R. Holladay is Charles Howard Candler Professor Emeritus of New Testament at Candler School of Theology, Emory University.

Morten Hørning Jensen is professor at Fjellhaug International University College, MF Norwegian School of Theology, and University of South Africa.

Joshua W. Jipp is professor of New Testament at Trinity Evangelical Divinity School.

Caroline Johnson Hodge is professor of religious studies at College of the Holy Cross.

Magnar Kartveit is professor of Old Testament and emeritus professor at VID Specialized University.

Sylvia C. Keesmaat is founder and lead professor of Bible Remixed.

Richard Last is assistant professor of ancient Greek and Roman studies at Trent University, Peterborough, Canada.

Te-Li Lau is associate professor of New Testament at Trinity Evangelical Divinity School.

Louise J. Lawrence is professor of New Testament interpretation at University of Exeter, UK.

Jin Hwan Lee is academic supervisor at Canada School of Theology, Canada.

Max J. Lee is the Paul W. Brandel Professor of Biblical Studies at North Park Theological Seminary.

William Loader is emeritus professor at Murdoch University, Perth, Australia.

Jill E. Marshall is lead instructional designer at Artisan Learning.

Steve Mason is emeritus professor of ancient mediterranean religions and cultures at University of Groningen.

Thomas D. McGlothlin is assistant professor of systematic theology at International Christian University.

Eric M. Meyers is the Bernice and Morton Lerner Emeritus Professor of Jewish Studies and director of the Center of Jewish Studies at Duke University.

David M. Moffitt is reader in New Testament at the University of St. Andrews and extraordinary researcher in the Unit for Reformational Theology and the Development of the South African Society, Faculty of Theology, North-West University.

Teresa Morgan is McDonald Agape Professor of New Testament and Early Christianity at Yale University.

Robert E. Moses associate professor of religion at High Point University.

Timothy J. Murray is pastor of Amblecote Community Church, England.

Alicia D. Myers is associate professor of New Testament and Greek at Campbell University Divinity School and research fellow at the University of the Free State, Bloemfontein, South Africa.

Maren R. Niehoff is Max Cooper Professor of Jewish Thought at the Hebrew University of Jerusalem.

Matthew V. Novenson is Helen H. P. Manson Professor of New Testament at Princeton Theological Seminary.

William L. Potter is digital library curator at Vanderbilt University Libraries.

Jan Rüggemeier is professor of New Testament studies at University of Bonn, Bonn, Germany.

Katherine A. Shaner is associate professor of New Testament at Wake Forest University School of Divinity.

Peter-Ben Smit is professor of contextual biblical interpretation at Vrije Universiteit Amsterdam and professor (by special appointment) of ancient catholic church structures and the history and doctrine of the old Catholic churches and research associate in the Faculty of Theology at the University of Pretoria.

Daniel L. Smith is associate professor of New Testament at Saint Louis University.

Klyne R. Snodgrass is emeritus professor of New Testament studies at North Park Theological Seminary.

Jennifer Strawbridge is associate professor of New Testament studies and G. B. Caird Fellow in Theology at Mansfield College, University of Oxford.

Matthew Thiessen is associate professor of religious studies at McMaster University in Hamilton, Ontario.

Paul Trebilco is professor of New Testament studies in the Theology Programme at University of Otago, Dunedin, New Zealand.

J. Brian Tucker is professor of New Testament at Moody Theological Seminary.

Timothy Wardle is associate professor of New Testament at Furman University.

Heidi Wendt is associate professor of religions of the Greco-Roman world at McGill University.

David H. Wenkel is research fellow and affiliate faculty in New Testament at LCC International University, Klaipėda, Lithuania.

MiJa Wi is lecturer in biblical studies and global mission and director of Bridging Worlds: Centre for Asian Christianities at Nazarene Theological College, Manchester, UK.

Adam Winn holds the Louis and Ann W. Armstrong Chair of Religion and is both professor and chair for the Department of Biblical and Religious Studies at Samford University.

Jürgen K. Zangenberg is professor of the history and culture of ancient Judaism and early Christianity in the Faculty of Humanities at Leiden University, the Netherlands.

Abbreviations

General

BCE	before the Common Era
c.	century
ca.	*circa*
CE	Common Era
cf.	*confer*, compare
chap(s).	chapter(s)
e.g.	*exempli gratia*, for example
esp.	especially
frag.	fragment
i.e.	*id est*, that is
lit.	literally
no(s).	number(s)
par(r).	parallel(s)
pr.	principium
pref.	preface
v(v).	verse(s)

Old Testament

Gen.	Genesis
Exod.	Exodus
Lev.	Leviticus
Num.	Numbers
Deut.	Deuteronomy
Josh.	Joshua
Judg.	Judges
Ruth	Ruth
1 Sam.	1 Samuel
2 Sam.	2 Samuel
1 Kings	1 Kings
2 Kings	2 Kings
1 Chron.	1 Chronicles
2 Chron.	2 Chronicles
Ezra	Ezra
Neh.	Nehemiah

Esther	Esther
Job	Job
Ps(s).	Psalm(s)
Prov.	Proverbs
Eccles.	Ecclesiastes
Song	Song of Songs
Isa.	Isaiah
Jer.	Jeremiah
Lam.	Lamentations
Ezek.	Ezekiel
Dan.	Daniel
Hosea	Hosea
Joel	Joel
Amos	Amos
Obad.	Obadiah
Jon.	Jonah
Mic.	Micah
Nah.	Nahum
Hab.	Habakkuk
Zeph.	Zephaniah
Hag.	Haggai
Zech.	Zechariah
Mal.	Malachi

New Testament

Matt.	Matthew
Mark	Mark
Luke	Luke
John	John
Acts	Acts
Rom.	Romans
1 Cor.	1 Corinthians
2 Cor.	2 Corinthians
Gal.	Galatians
Eph.	Ephesians

Phil.	Philippians
Col.	Colossians
1 Thess.	1 Thessalonians
2 Thess.	2 Thessalonians
1 Tim.	1 Timothy
2 Tim.	2 Timothy
Titus	Titus
Philem.	Philemon
Heb.	Hebrews
James	James
1 Pet.	1 Peter
2 Pet.	2 Peter
1 John	1 John
2 John	2 John
3 John	3 John
Jude	Jude
Rev.	Revelation

Bible Versions

ESV	English Standard Version
LXX	Septuagint
MT	Masoretic Text
NIV	New International Version
NRSV	New Revised Standard Version
OG	Old Greek
RSV	Revised Standard Version
SP	Samaritan Pentateuch

Old Testament Apocrypha / Deuterocanonical Books

Jdt.	Judith
1–4 Macc.	1–4 Maccabees
Sir. (Ecclus.)	Sirach (Ecclesiasticus)
Tob.	Tobit
Wis.	Wisdom (of Solomon)

Old Testament Pseudepigrapha

Apoc. Ab.	Apocalypse of Abraham
2 Bar.	2 Baruch (Syriac Apocalypse)
3 Bar.	3 Baruch (Greek Apocalypse)
1 En.	1 Enoch (Ethiopic Apocalypse)
2 En.	2 Enoch (Slavonic Apocalypse)
4 Ezra	4 Ezra
Jos. Asen.	Joseph and Aseneth
Jub.	Jubilees
LAB	Liber antiquitatum biblicarum (Biblical Antiquities, or Pseudo-Philo)
LAE	Life of Adam and Eve
Let. Aris.	Letter of Aristeas
Ps.-Phoc.	Pseudo-Phocylides

Pss. Sol.	Psalms of Solomon
Sib. Or.	Sibylline Oracles
T. Ab.	Testament of Abraham
T. Benj.	Testament of Benjamin
T. Dan	Testament of Dan
T. Job	Testament of Job
T. Jud.	Testament of Judah
T. Levi	Testament of Levi
T. Mos.	Testament of Moses
T. Naph.	Testament of Naphtali
T. Reu.	Testament of Reuben

Rabbinic Literature

b.	Babylonian Talmud
m.	Mishnah
t.	Tosefta
y.	Jerusalem Talmud
Avod. Zar.	Avodah Zarah
B. Bat.	Bava Batra
Demai	Demai
Lam. Rab.	Lamentations Rabbah
Hag.	Hagigah
Menah.	Menahot
Neg.	Nega'im
Pe'ah	Pe'ah
Pesah.	Pesahim
Qidd.	Qiddushin
Sanh.	Sanhedrin
Shabb.	Shabbat
Sotah	Sotah
Sukkah	Sukkah
Ta'an.	Ta'anit
Yad.	Yadayim
Yevam.	Yevamot
Yoma	Yoma (= Kippurim)
Zevah.	Zevahim

Apostolic Fathers

Barn.	Barnabas
1–2 Clem.	1–2 Clement
Did.	Didache
Herm. Mand.	Shepherd of Hermas, Mandate(s)
Herm. Vis.	Shepherd of Hermas, Vision(s)
Ign. *Eph.*	Ignatius, *To the Ephesians*
Ign. *Magn.*	Ignatius, *To the Magnesians*
Ign. *Phld.*	Ignatius, *To the Philadelphians*
Ign. *Pol.*	Ignatius, *To Polycarp*
Ign. *Rom.*	Ignatius, *To the Romans*
Ign. *Smyrn.*	Ignatius, *To the Smyrnaeans*
Mart. Pol.	Martyrdom of Polycarp
Pol. *Phil.*	Polycarp, *To the Philippians*

New Testament Apocrypha and Pseudepigrapha

Acts Andr.	Acts of Andrew
Acts John	Acts of John
Acts Paul	Acts of Paul
Acts Paul Thec.	Acts of Paul and Thecla
Acts Thom.	Acts of Thomas
Ps.-Clem. *Hom.*	Pseudo-Clement, *Homilies*
Ps.-Clem. *Rec.*	Pseudo-Clement, *Recognitions*

Greek and Latin Works

Anonymous

Anth. Pal.	*Anthologia Palatina (Palatine Anthology)*

Appian

Mith.	*Mithridatica (Mithridatic Wars)*

Apuleius

De deo Socr.	*De deo Socratico (On the God of Socrates)*

Aristotle

An. post.	*Analytica posteriora (Posterior Analytics)*
Cael.	*De caelo (On the Heavens)*
De an.	*De anima (On the Soul)*
Eth. nic.	*Ethica nicomachea (Nicomachean Ethics)*
Gen. an.	*De generatione animalium (Generation of Animals)*
Phys.	*Physica (Physics)*
Pol.	*Politica (Politics)*

Arnobius

Adv. nat.	*Adversus nationes (Against the Pagans)*

Arrian

Epict. diss.	*Epicteti dissertations (Discourses of Epictetus)*

Augustine

Civ.	*De civitate dei (The City of God)*

Cassius Dio

Hist. Rom.	*Historia Romana (Roman History)*

Cato

Agr.	*De agricultura (Agriculture)*

Cicero

De or.	*De oratore (On the Orator)*
Div.	*De divination (On Divination)*
Fam.	*Epistulae ad familiars (Letters to Friends)*
Flac.	*Pro Flacco (For Flaccus)*
Har. resp.	*De haruspicum responso (On the Responses of the Haruspices)*
Leg.	*De legibus (On Laws)*
Nat. d.	*De natura deorum (On the Nature of the Gods)*
Prov. cons.	*De provinciis consularibus (On the Consular Provinces)*
Verr.	*In Verrem (Against Verres)*

Clement of Alexandria

Paed.	*Paedagogus (The Instructor)*
Quis div.	*Quis dives salvetur (Salvation of the Rich)*

Cornutus

Theol. Graec.	*Theologiae Graecae compendium (Compendium of Greek Theology)*

Cyprian

Eleem.	*De opere et eleemosynis (Works and Almsgiving)*

Diodorus Siculus

Bib. hist.	*Bibliotheca historica (Library of History)*

Diogenes Laertius

Vit. phil.	*Vitae philosophorum (Lives of Eminent Philosophers)*

Dionysius of Halicarnassus

Ant. rom.	*Antiquitates romanae (Roman Antiquities)*
Thuc.	*De Thucydide (On Thucydides)*

Ennius

Ann.	*Annales (Annals)*

Epictetus

Diatr.	*Diatribai (Diatribes)*

Euripides

Med.	*Medea*

Eusebius

Comm. Ps.	Commentarius in Psalmos (Commentary on Psalms)
Hist. eccl.	Historia ecclesiastica (Church History)
Praep. ev.	Praeparatio evangelica (Preparation for the Gospel)

Gaius

Inst.	Institutiones (Institutes)

Galen

Aff. dig.	De propriorum animi cuiuslibet affectuum dignotione et curatione (The Diagnosis and Treatment of the Passions of the Soul)
Alim. fac.	De alimentorum facultatibus (On the Properties of Foodstuffs)
Usu part.	De usu partium (On the Usefulness of Parts)

Gregory of Nazianus

Or.	Orationes (Orations)

Gregory of Nyssa

Beat.	Orationes viii de beatitudinibus (Homilies on the Beatitudes)

Herodotus

Hist.	Histories

Hesiod

Op.	Opera et dies (Works and Days)
Theog.	Theogonia (Theogony)

Hippocrates

Epid.	Epidemiae (Epidemics)
Genit.	Genitalia (Genitals)

Homer

Il.	Iliad
Od.	Odyssey

Horace

Carm.	Carmina (Odes)
Serm.	Sermones (Satires)

Iamblichus

Myst.	De mysteriis (On the Mysteries)

John Chrysostom

Hom. 2 Cor.	Homiliae in epistulam ii ad Corinthios (Homilies on 2 Corinthians)
Hom. Gen.	Homiliae in Genesim (Homilies on Genesis)

Josephus

Ag. Ap.	Against Apion
Ant.	Jewish Antiquities
J.W.	Jewish War
Life	The Life

Justin

Hist. Phil.	Historiae Philippicae (Philippic Histories)

Justinian

Dig.	Digesta (Digest)

Justin Martyr

1 Apol.	First Apology
2 Apol.	Second Apology
Dial.	Dialogus cum Tryphone (Dialogue with Trypho)

Juvenal

Sat.	Satirae (Satires)

Lactantius

Epit.	Epitome divinarum institutionum (Epitome of the Divine Institutes)

Lucan

Bel. civ.	De bello civili (The Civil War)

Lucian

Alex.	Alexander (Alexander the False Prophet)
Demon.	Demonax
Fug.	Fugitivi (The Runaways)
Gall.	Gallus
Hist. conscr.	Quomodo historia conscribenda sit (How to Write History)
Merc. cond.	De mercede conductis (On Salaried Posts in Great Houses)
Peregr.	De morte Peregrini (The Passing of Peregrinus)
Philops.	Philopseudes (The Lover of Lies)
Symp.	Symposium

Lucretius

Rer. nat.	De rerum natura (On the Nature of Things)

Marcus Aurelius

Med.	Meditationes (Meditations)

Martial

Epigr.	Epigrammata (Epigrams)

Minucius Felix

Oct.	Octavius

Origen

Cels.	Contra Celsum (Against Celsus)
Hom. Gen.	Homiliae in Genesim (Homilies on Genesis)
Mart.	Exhortatio ad martyrium (Exhortation to Martyrdom)

Ovid

Ars	Ars amatoria (The Art of Love)
Metam.	Metamorphoses

Persius

Sat.	Satirae (Satires)

Petronius

Sat.	Satyricon

Philo

Abraham	On the Life of Abraham
Alleg. Interp.	Allegorical Interpretation
Confusion	On the Confusion of Tongues
Contempl. Life	On the Contemplative Life
Creation	On the Creation of the World
Dreams	On Dreams
Embassy	On the Embassy to Gaius
Flaccus	Against Flaccus
Flight	On Flight and Finding
Giants	On Giants
Good Person	That Every Good Person Is Free
Heir	Who Is the Heir?
Hypoth.	Hypothetica
Moses	On the Life of Moses
Names	On the Change of Names
Planting	On Planting
Posterity	On the Posterity of Cain
Prelim. Studies	On the Preliminary Studies
QG	Questions and Answers on Genesis
Rewards	On Rewards and Punishments
Sobriety	On Sobriety
Spec. Laws	On the Special Laws

Virtues	On the Virtues
Worse	That the Worse Attacks the Better

Philodemus

Lib.	De libertate dicendi (On Frank Criticism)

Plato

Apol.	Apologia (Apology)
Crat.	Cratylus
Leg.	Leges (Laws)
Phaed.	Phaedo
Phaedr.	Phaedrus
Resp.	Respublica (Republic)
Symp.	Symposium
Theaet.	Theaetetus
Tim.	Timaeus

Plautus

Aul.	Aulularia (The Little Pot)
Mer.	Mercator (The Merchant)

Pliny the Elder

Nat.	Naturalis historia (Natural History)

Pliny the Younger

Ep.	Epistulae (Letters)

Plutarch

Alex.	Alexander
Conj. praec.	Conjugalia praecepta (Advice to the Bride and Groom)
Def. orac.	De defectu oraculorum (On the Obsolescence of Oracles)
Demetr.	Demetrius
Is. Os.	De Iside et Osiride (Isis and Osiris)
Mor.	Moralia (Moral Essays)
Quaest. conv.	Quaestiones convivales (Table Talk)
Tim.	Timoleon
Virt. mor.	De virtute morali (On Moral Virtue)
Virt. prof.	Quomodo quis suos in virtute sentiat profectus (How a Man May Become Aware of His Progress in Virtue)

Porphyry

Abst.	De abstinentia ab esu animalium (On Abstinence from Animal Food)

Pseudo-Aristotle

Physiogn.   Physiognomonica (Physiognomonics)

Quintilian

Inst.   Institutio oratoria (Institutes of Oratory)

Seneca the Elder

Contr.   Controversiae (Controversies)

Seneca the Younger

Ben.   De beneficiis (On Benefits)
Clem.   De clementia (On Clemency)
Ep.   Epistulae morales (Moral Letters)
Ira   De ira (On Anger)

Soranus

Gyn.   Gynaecia (Gynecology)

Stobaeus

Anth.   Anthologium (Anthology)

Strabo

Geogr.   Geographica (Geography)

Suetonius

Aug.   Divus Augustus
Claud.   Divus Claudius
Jul.   Divus Julius
Tib.   Tiberius

Tacitus

Ann.   Annales (Annals)
Hist.   Historiae (Histories)

Tatian

Or. Graec.   Oratio ad Graecos (Address to the Greeks)

Tertullian

Apol.   Apologeticus (Apology)
Bapt.   De baptismo (Baptism)
Cor.   De corona militis (The Crown)
Spect.   De spectaculis (The Shows)
Ux.   Ad uxorem (To His Wife)

Theophrastus

Caus. plant.   De causis plantarum (On the Causes of Plants)

Thucydides

Hist.   History of the Peloponnesian War

Valerius Maximus

Fact. et dict.   Facta et dicta memorabilia (Memorable Deeds and Sayings)

Velleius Paterculus

Hist. Rom.   Historia Romana (Compendium of Roman History)

Vitruvius

De arch.   De architectura (On Architecture)

Xenophon

Hell.   Hellenica
Oec.   Oeconomicus (Economics)

Inscriptions and Papyri

Agora 16   Woodhead, A. G. The Athenian Agora. Vol. 16, Inscriptions: The Decrees. Princeton: American School of Classical Studies at Athens, 1997

AGRW   Ascough, Richard S., Philip A. Harland, and John S. Kloppenborg. Associations in the Greco-Roman World: A Sourcebook. Waco: Baylor University Press, 2012

AM   Deutsches Archäologisches Institut. Mitteilungen des deutschen Archäologischen Instituts. Athenische Abteilung. Berlin: Deutsches archäologisches Institut, 1876–; Kyparissis, Nikolaos, and Werner Peek. Attische Urkunden. Athenische Mitteilungen 66. Tübingen: E. Wasmuth, 1941, pp. 218–39

CCCA   Vermaseren, Maarten Jozef. Corpus cultus Cybelae Attidisque. Études préliminaires aux religions orientales dans l'empire romain 50. Leiden: Brill, 1977–89

CIJ   Corpus inscriptionum judaicarum. Edited by Jean-Baptiste Frey. 2 vols. Rome: Pontifical Biblical Institute, 1936–52. Vol. 1, Europe (1936); Vol. 2, Asia-Africa (1952)

CIL   Corpus inscriptionum latinarum. Consilio et Auctoritate Academiae

	Litterarum Regiae Borussicae Editum. Berlin: Georg Reimer, 1863–74
FdD III.4	École Française d'Athènes. *Fouilles de Delphes*. Vol. 3, *Épigraphie*. Fasc. 4, Inscriptions de la terrasse du temple et la région nord du sanctuaire. Paris: de Boccard, 1954
FIRA	Riccobono, S., et al., eds. *Fontes iuris Romani antejustiniani*. 3 vols. Florence: Barbèra, 1940–41
GRA	Kloppenborg, John S., Philip A. Harland, and Richard S. Ascough. *Greco-Roman Associations: Texts, Translations, and Commentary*. Vol. 1, *Achaia, Boeotia, Macedonia, Thrace*. BZNW 181 (New York: de Gruyter, 2011); Vol. 2, *North Coast of the Black Sea, Asia Minor*. BZNW 204 (2014); Vol. 3, *Egypt*. BZNW 246 (2020)
IApamBith	Corsten, Thomas. *Die Inschriften von Apameia (Bithynien) und Pylai*. IGSK 32. Bonn: Habelt, 1987
IDelos	Roussel, Pierre, and Marcel Launey. *Inscriptions de Délos: Décrets postérieurs à 166 av. J.-C. (nos. 1497–1524); Dédicaces postérieures à 166 av. J.-C. (nos. 1525–2219)*. Académie des Inscriptions et belles-lettres. Paris: Librairie Ancienne Honoré Champion, 1937
IDelta	Bernand, A., ed. *Le delta égyptien d'après les texts grecs 1: Les confines libyques*. 3 vols. Mémoires publies par les membres de l'Institut français d'archéologie orientale du Caire 91. Cairo: Institut français d'archéologie orientale, 1970
IEph	Engelmann, H., H. Wankel, and R. Merkelbach. *Die Inschriften von Ephesos*. IGSK 11–17. Bonn: Rudolf Habelt, 1979–84
IG 1³	Lewis, David, ed. *Inscriptiones Atticae Euclidis anno anteriores* (Attic Inscriptions before the year of Eucleides). 3rd ed. Berlin: de Gruyter, 1981, 1994. Fasc. 1, *Decreta et tabulae magistratuum* (nos. 1–500)
IG 2²	Kirchner, Johannes, ed. *Inscriptiones Atticae Euclidis anno anteriores*. 4 vols. Berlin: de Gruyter, 1913–40
IG 5/1	Kolbe, W., ed. *Inscriptiones Laconiae et Messeniae*. Part 1. Berlin: Georg Reimer, 1913
IG 9/1²	Klaffenbach, Gunther, ed. *Inscriptiones graeciae septentrionalis*. 2nd ed. Berlin: de Gruyter, 1932–68. Fasc. 1, *Inscriptiones Aetoliae* (1932). Fasc. 2, *Inscriptiones Acarnaniae* (1957). Fasc. 3, *Inscriptiones Locridis occidentalis* (1968)
IG 10/2.1	Edson, Charles, ed. *Inscriptiones graecae Epiri, Macedoniae, Thraciae, Scythiae*. II: *Inscriptiones Macedoniae*. Fasc. 1, *Inscriptiones Thessalonicae et viciniae*. Berlin: de Gruyter, 1972
IG 11/4	Roussel, Pierre. *Inscriptiones Deli liberae. Decreta, foedera, catalogi, dedicationes, varia*. Berlin: Georg Reimer, 1914
IG 12/1–7	Hiller von Gaertringen, Friedrich F., W. R. Paton, J. Delamarre, and E. Ziebarth, eds. *Inscriptiones insularum maris Aegaei praeter Delum*. 9 parts (part 6 unpublished). Berlin: Georg Reimer, 1895–1915
IGR	Cagnat, R. L., J. F. Toutain, V. Henry, and G. L. Lafaye, eds. *Inscriptiones graecae ad res romanas pertinentes*. 4 vols. Paris: E. Leroux, 1911–27. Vol. 1 (nos. 1–1518) ed. R. L. Cagnat, J. F. Toutain, and P. Jouguet (1911). Vol. 2, n.p. Vol. 3 ed. R. Cagnat and G. Lafaye (1906). Vol. 4, *Asia* (nos. 1–1764), ed. G. L. Lafaye (1927)
IJO	*Inscriptiones Judaicae Orientis*. Tübingen: Mohr Siebeck, 2004. Vol. 1, *Eastern Europe*, by David Noy, Alexander Panayotov, and Hanswulf Bloedhorn. TSAJ 101 (2004). Vol. 2, *Kleinasien*, by Walter Ameling. TSAJ 99 (2004). Vol. 3, *Syria and Cyprus*, by David Noy and Hanswulf Bloedhorn. TSAJ 102 (2004)
IKios	Corsten, Thomas. *Die Inschriften von Kios*. IGSK 29. Bonn: Rudolf Habelt, 1985
IMagnMai	Kern, Otto. *Die Inschriften von Magnesia am Maeander*. Königliche Museen zu Berlin. Berlin: W. Spemann, 1900
IOlympia	Dittenberger, Wilhelm. *Die Inschriften von Olympia*. Berlin: Asher, 1896

IPergamon	Fränkel, M., ed. *Die Inschriften von Pergamon*. 2 vols. Berlin: W. Spemann, 1890–95. Vol. 1, *Bis zum Ende der Königzeit* (1890). Vol. 2, *Römische Zeit* (1895)
IPerinthos	Sayar, Mustafa Hamdi, ed. *Perinthos-Herakleia (Marmara Ereğlisi) und Umgebung. Geschichte, Testimonien, griechische und lateinische Inschriften*. Österreichische Akademie der Wissenschaften. Philosophisch-historische Klasse. Denkschriften, 269 = Veröffentlichungen der kleinasiatischen Kommission 9. Vienna: Österreichischen Akademie der Wissenschaften, 1998
ISardis I	Buckler, William H., and D. Robinson, eds. *Greek and Latin Inscriptions, Publications of the American Society for the Excavation of Sardis*. Vol. 7.1. Leiden: Brill, 1932
ISardis II	Petzl, George. *Sardis: Greek and Latin Inscriptions*. Part 2: *Finds from 1958 to 2017*. Archaeological Exploration of Sardis, Monograph 14. Cambridge, MA: Harvard University Press, 2019
ISelge	Nollé, Johannes, and Friedel Schindler. *Die Inschriften von Selge*. IGSK 37. Bonn: Rudolf Habelt, 1991
IThessN	Nigdelis, Pantelis M. Ἐπιγραφικὰ Θεσσαλονίκεια. Συμβολὴ στὴν πολιτικὴ καὶ κοινωνικὴ ἱστορία τῆς ἀρχαίας Θεσσαλονίκης. Thessaloniki: University Studio Press, 2006
IThyatiraB	Buckler, W. H. "Monuments de Thyatire." *Revue de Philologie* 37 (1913): 289–331
LSCG	Sokolowski, Franciszek. *Lois sacrées des cités grecques: Ecole française d'Athènes*. Travaux et mémoires 11. Paris: E. de Boccard, 1962
OGIS	Dittenberger, Wilhelm, ed. *Orientis graeci inscriptiones selectae: Supplementum Sylloge inscriptionum graecarum*. 2 vols. Leipzig: S. Hirzel, 1903–5; repr., Hildesheim: G. Olms, 1960
PAthen	Petropoulos, G. A., ed. *Papyri Societatis Archaeologicae Atheniensis*. Athens: Academia scientiarum Atheniensis, 1939
PBour	Collart, P., ed. *Les Papyrus Bouriant*. Paris: Honoré Champion, 1926
PCair	Spiegelberg, W., ed. *Die demotischen Denkmäler*. Vol. 2: *Die Demotischen Papyrus (nos. 30601–31270, 50001–50022)*. Part 1: *Text (Strasbourg, 1908)*. Part 2: *Plates (Strasbourg, 1906)*. Leipzig: Dragulin
PLond VII	Skeat, T. C., ed. *Greek Papyri in the British Museum*. Vol. 7, *The Zenon Archive*. London: British Museum, 1974
PMich V	Husselman, E. M., A. E. R. Boak, and W. F. Edgerton, eds. *Papyri from Tebtunis*. Part 2. University of Michigan Studies, Humanistic Series 29. Ann Arbor: University of Michigan, 1944
POxy	Handley, E. W., H. G. Ioannidou, P. J. Parsons, and J. E. G. Whitehorne, eds. *The Oxyrhynchus Papyri. LIX, Nos. 3963–4008*. London: Egypt Exploration Society, 1992
PTebt	Grenfell, Bernard P., Arthur S. Hunt, Edgar J. Goodspeed, J. G. Smyly, and C. C. Edgar. *The Tebtunis Papyri*. University of California Publications, Graeco-Roman Archaeology. London: Henry Frowde, 1902
PYadin	Lewis, N., ed. *Greek Papyri*. Vol. 1 of *The Documents from the Bar Kochba Period in the Cave of Letters*. Jerusalem: Israel Exploration Society, 1989
RICIS	Bricault, Laurent. *Recueil des inscriptions concernant les cultes isiaques*. 2 vols. Mémoires de l'académie des inscriptions et belles-lettres 31. Paris: Diffusion de Boccard, 2005
SB	Preisigke, F., et al., eds. *Sammelbuch griechischer Urkunden aus Ägypten*. Strassburg: K. J. Trubner; Wiesbanden: Otto Harrassowitz, 1915–
SEG	*Supplementum epigraphicum graecum*. Leiden: Brill, 1923–
SIG³	*Sylloge inscriptionum graecarum*. Edited by W. Dittenberger. 4 vols. 3rd ed. Leipzig: S. Hirzel, 1915–24
TAM	Österreichische Akademie der Wissenschaften. *Tituli Asiae Minoris*. 5 vols. Wien: Hoelder, Pichler, Tempsky, 1901–

Modern Works

AB	Anchor Bible
ABD	*Anchor Bible Dictionary*. Edited by D. N. Freedman. 6 vols. New York: Doubleday, 1992
AIL	Ancient Israel and Its Literature
AJEC	Ancient Judaism and Early Christianity
ANRW	*Aufstieg und Niedergang der römischen Welt: Geschichte und Kultur Roms im Spiegel der neueren Forschung.* Edited by H. Temporini and W. Haase. Berlin: de Gruyter, 1972–
ARG	*Archiv für Religionsgeschichte*
BA	*The Biblical Archaeologist*
BBR	*Bulletin for Biblical Research*
BCAW	Blackwell Companions to the Ancient World
BDAG	Danker, Frederick W., Walter Bauer, William F. Arndt, and F. Wilbur Gingrich. *Greek-English Lexicon of the New Testament and Other Early Christian Literature.* 3rd ed. Chicago: University of Chicago Press, 2000
Bib	*Biblica*
BibInt	*Biblical Interpretation*
BibInt	Biblical Interpretation Series
BJS	Brown Judaic Studies
BRLJ	Brill Reference Library of Judaism
BWANT	Beiträge zur Wissenschaft vom Alten und Neuen Testament
BZNW	Beihefte zur Zeitschrift für die neutestamentliche Wissenschaft
CBET	Contributions to Biblical Exegesis and Theology
CBQ	*Catholic Biblical Quarterly*
ConBNT	Coniectanea Biblica: New Testament Series
CP	*Classical Philology*
CQS	Companion to the Qumran Scrolls
CRINT	Compendia Rerum Iudaicarum ad Novum Testamentum
CurBR	*Currents in Biblical Research*
DCLS	Deuterocanonical and Cognate Literature Studies
DK	Diels, Hermann A., and Walther Kranz, eds. *Die Fragmenta der Vorsokratiker.* 6th ed. Vol. 1, 1–58. Berlin: Weidmann, 1951–52
DSI	De Septuaginta Investigationes
EC	*Early Christianity*
ECAM	Early Christianity in Asia Minor
EJL	Early Judaism and Its Literature

FRLANT	Forschungen zur Religion und Literatur des Alten und Neuen Testaments
Historia	*Historia: Zeitschrift für alte Geschichte*
HTR	*Harvard Theological Review*
HTS	Harvard Theological Studies
IGSK	Inschriften griechischer Städte aus Kleinasien
Int	*Interpretation*
JAJ	*Journal of Ancient Judaism*
JAJSup	Journal of Ancient Judaism Supplements
JBL	*Journal of Biblical Literature*
JECS	*Journal of Early Christian Studies*
JHS	*Journal of Hellenic Studies*
JJS	*Journal of Jewish Studies*
JQR	*Jewish Quarterly Review*
JR	*Journal of Religion*
JRA	*Journal of Roman Archaeology*
JRASup	Journal of Roman Archaeology Supplementary Series
JRS	*Journal of Roman Studies*
JSJ	*Journal for the Study of Judaism in the Persian, Hellenistic, and Roman Periods*
JSJSup	Supplements to the Journal for the Study of Judaism
JSNT	*Journal for the Study of the New Testament*
JSNTSup	Journal for the Study of the New Testament: Supplement Series
JSPSup	Journal for the Study of the Pseudepigrapha: Supplement Series
JTS	*Journal of Theological Studies*
LCL	Loeb Classical Library
LNTS	Library of New Testament Studies
LSTS	Library of Second Temple Studies
NEA	*Near Eastern Archaeology*
NICNT	New International Commentary on the New Testament
NIGTC	New International Greek Testament Commentary
NovT	*Novum Testamentum*
NovTSup	Supplements to Novum Testamentum
NTOA	Novum Testamentum et Orbis Antiquus
NTS	*New Testament Studies*
RBS	Resources for Biblical Study
RRE	*Religion in the Roman Empire*
RVV	Religionsgeschichtliche Versuche und Vorarbeiten
SBLSP	Society of Biblical Literature Seminar Papers
SNTSMS	Society for New Testament Studies Monograph Series

STAC	Studien und Texte zu Antike und Christentum	VTSup	Supplements to Vetus Testamentum
STDJ	Studies on the Texts of the Desert of Judah	WBC	Word Biblical Commentary
		WGRW	Writings from the Greco-Roman World
SUNT	Studien zur Umwelt des Neuen Testaments	WGRWSup	Writings from the Greco-Roman World Supplement Series
SVF	*Stoicorum Veterum Fragmenta*. Hans Friedrich August von Arnim. 4 vols. Leipzig: Teubner, 1903–24	WUNT	Wissenschaftliche Untersuchungen zum Neuen Testament
		YCS	*Yale Classical Studies*
TECC	Textos y Estudios "Cardenal Cisneros" de la Biblia Políglota Matritense	*ZAW*	*Zeitschrift für die alttestamentliche Wissenschaft*
TENTS	Texts and Editions for New Testament Study	*ZNW*	*Zeitschrift für die neutestamentliche Wissenschaft und die Kunde der älteren Kirche*
TSAJ	Texte und Studien zum antiken Judentum	*ZPE*	*Zeitschrift für Papyrologie und Epigraphik*

Editors' Preface

Over years of studying the New Testament, each editor of this book has come to appreciate that the interpretation of the New Testament is greatly enriched when its texts are read in relation to their historical contexts. In our experience, placing New Testament texts within the context of the ancient world and allowing the discourse of those texts to resonate within that world sharpens an appreciation of their force and significance. Sometimes first impressions about a text's meaning are corrected. Sometimes new layers of meaning become discernible. Sometimes both. While there are different ways of reading the New Testament profitably, historical study routinely sheds important light on this collection of diverse canonical texts.

The twenty-seven texts of the New Testament span a number of genres. They were written by different authors over a period of several decades, and for Christ followers in different situations. The apostle Paul, for instance, wrote letters to Christ assemblies in ways that were meaningful to those distinct audiences in their own unique circumstances, with both the author and the addressees immersed in a world that was different from ours in many respects. Without an awareness of those factors, we can too easily read our own cultural assumptions, values, and preferences into those texts, innocently but dangerously finding ourselves canonized within their pages as a consequence.

Similarly, the four canonical evangelists wrote the story of Jesus Christ with their own distinctive theological interests, often with a view to the historical and cultural realities of their world. The Gospels share a storyline about the life of Jesus Christ that the Gospel authors deemed relevant to audiences beyond their own day. But the four evangelists plotted that storyline in different ways and worked subplots along different angles, with those plot points and subplots largely taking their cues from situations, people, communities, and phenomena within the ancient world. Getting to grips with those historical and cultural data opens dimensions of the texts that would otherwise be missed.

All this is to say that the better our comprehension of the ancient world, the more intelligible the New Testament writings become within their original settings. In the process, the texts of the New Testament more readily become vehicles for conveying meanings appropriate to their original purposes; they are less readily put into the service of our own interests, identities, and agendas; and they are able to be appropriated more authentically in contexts beyond the ancient world—opening up new vistas of understanding in ways that sometimes resist the easy appropriation of domesticating interpretations.

This book (named to be paired with its Old Testament counterpart, *Behind the Scenes of the Old Testament: Cultural, Social, and Historical Contexts* [Baker Academic, 2018]) contains over sixty essays on selected aspects of the world of the New Testament. Each short essay includes some engagement with the interpretation of the New Testament. The essays fall into three parts within this book. Those in part 1 ("Setting the Stage") (1) introduce symbolic worlds that generated the larger environment of the New Testament world and (2) discuss various geographical places and situational settings of importance. The essays in part 2 ("Inhabiting the Stage") (1) highlight certain "scripts" (written discourse) that communicated meaning to people of that world and (2) provide an overview of certain "actors" of that world who are pertinent to the study of the New Testament in its original setting. The essays in part 3 ("Themes on the Stage") explore how the New Testament's theological discourse (1) shaped understandings of God in relation to practices and beliefs that were common in the ancient world, (2) spoke to sociocultural features of the age, and (3) addressed aspects of the household context, which was so formative in the construction of ancient identities. While the essays of this book are not meant to make every connection with New Testament texts, we hope they provide foundations for teachers and students to start making those connections.

The authors of these essays are recognized for their contributions to scholarship beyond the covers of this book, and they have kindly agreed to turn their expertise to the issues that they address here. They represent a multigenerational and multiethnic collection of people from different parts of the globe, and we are appreciative of their efforts. We hope readers of this book will benefit from these accessible essays, in the shared goal of discerning the message of the New Testament more competently as we learn to read its texts more proficiently and effectively.

PART ONE

Setting
the Stage

Symbolic Worlds

Judaism

MATTHEW V. NOVENSON

There is a movement afoot among some Bible scholars to replace the traditional terms "Old Testament" and "New Testament" with the terms "Jewish Scriptures" and "Christian Testament," respectively (Schüssler Fiorenza 2001, 66–67). The morally praiseworthy cause behind this proposal is to underline the fact that the Hebrew Bible was first read—and still is read—by Jews before it was ever read by Christians or anyone else. But good intentions notwithstanding, there are problems with the proposal, perhaps chief of which is this: it gives the misleading impression that the New Testament is a Christian book ("Christian Testament"), when in fact it, too, is a Jewish book! Most of the New Testament's main characters (God, Israel, Jesus, the apostles), locales (Jerusalem, Judea, Galilee, diaspora synagogues), big ideas (covenant, law, messiah, priesthood, etc.), and many, perhaps most, of its authors are Jewish. They are "Christian" only by way of theological retcon. Granted, it is Christians who *read* the New Testament as Scripture, but it was mostly Jews who *made* the texts that compose it (Levine and Brettler 2017). Hence, if we want to understand the religious context of the New Testament, then Judaism is far and away the most relevant symbolic world.

Circumscribing "Judaism"

There are other relevant symbolic worlds of the texts constituting the New Testament—in particular Hellenism (see chap. 2, "Hellenization," below) and Romanness (see chap. 45, "The Roman Empire," below). These, however, are best understood not as *competitors* with or *alternatives* to Judaism but rather as larger umbrellas subsuming Judaism and a myriad of other provincial cultures (Egyptian, Syrian, Anatolian, etc.). By the first century CE, due to the world-changing conquests of Alexander and of Augustus, the whole eastern Mediterranean world (more or less) was culturally Greek and politically Roman. (This is a generalization and exaggeration, but only a slight one.) In other words, it is a matter not of Judaism versus Hellenism, as some older books tended to put it, but rather of Judaism as one tradition among many others in the vast, Hellenism-inflected Roman Empire. To be sure, some ancient Jewish (including New Testament) texts do quarrel with Hellenism, Romanness, or both. But many ancient Jewish (including New Testament) texts do not do so; and whether they quarrel with the empire or not, they are all unavoidably part of it (Himmelfarb 1998). They are "subaltern texts" (to use the helpful language of modern postcolonial criticism), written by subject people from their respective corners of the empire, coping with the fact of empire variously: for, against, as, and otherwise (Moore 2006). We should, therefore, think of Judaism and Hellenism not as two equal and opposite forces in zero-sum competition but rather as concentric circles. Judaism is the most relevant symbolic world for the New Testament just in the sense that it is the most proximate.

The term "Judaism" is admittedly an anachronism, but there is nothing wrong with anachronism as long as we do it well. The texts that compose the New Testament, along with other texts from the early Roman Empire, do not yet have the word "Judaism." (There is one apparent, though not real, counterexample to this claim, to be discussed in a moment.) But these texts contain mountains of evidence for what we mean when we use the word "Judaism"— namely, the religion of Jewish people (Schwartz 2011). The Jerusalem temple, its priestly sacrifices, diaspora synagogues, the great annual festivals; the stories of Abraham, Moses, David, Elijah, and other heroes; customs including daily prayer, circumcision, kashrut, ritual purity, vows, tithes, marriage rites, and so on— all of this we very reasonably call "Judaism" (Sanders 1992), even if our ancient sources do not call it that. (Indeed, this is standard operating procedure with many, even *most*, modern terms of analysis: gender, ethnicity, identity, religion, economy, etc. We use our own apt terms for ancient phenomena for which ancient sources had their own, usually different, terms.)

I said that there was one apparent counterexample to my claim that New Testament and other ancient sources lack the word "Judaism." There is a rare ancient Greek word, *Ioudaismos*, which does appear twice in a single sentence in the New Testament: Galatians 1:13–14, where the apostle Paul writes to his audience of Gentile Christ believers, "You heard of my former occupation in *Ioudaismos*, how I was indicting the assembly of God severely and besieging it, and I was advancing in *Ioudaismos* beyond many of my peers among my people, being so great a champion of my ancestral traditions" (my translation, here and throughout). Because our English word "Judaism" is etymologically related to the Greek word *Ioudaismos*, many English Bible versions assume that the two words mean the same thing, and they render our verse, "You heard of my former life in Judaism . . .", as if Paul were saying that he used to practice Judaism but now practices something else instead. (Neither Paul nor any New Testament writer ever uses the word "Christianity," for the simple reason that that word did not exist yet. The Greek word *Christianismos* first occurs in the second-century letters of Ignatius of Antioch.)

But despite their surface similarity, the Greek word *Ioudaismos* and the English word "Judaism" do not mean the same thing. As I have said, "Judaism" means—in most instances and for most purposes—the religion of Jewish people, but *Ioudaismos*, in its few, rare instances in Hellenistic and Roman sources, means a particular sectarian program for the defense and promotion of Jewish customs. It is not what all pious Jews do; it is what only a radical few do. These radical few include the war-waging Maccabees in 2 Maccabees and 4 Maccabees and the young activist Paul in this reference in Galatians. As for the great mass of pious Jews, they practice what Paul here calls "the ancestral traditions" (which is what we would call "Judaism") but not *Ioudaismos*. The moral of this story is that ancient Jews, like ancient people generally, did not have a special name for their own religion. Jews had their ancestral traditions (or customs, or laws, etc.), while Greeks had theirs, Romans theirs, Gauls theirs, Egyptians theirs, and so on (Novenson 2014). Our familiar modern "-ism" words for religions (e.g., "Judaism," the traditional religion of Jewish people; "Hinduism," the traditional religion of Indian people) are artificial creations of the nineteenth-century heyday of European empires and Christian missionaries (Masuzawa 2005). They are not the natural or obvious names for these religions, and they are certainly not the ancient names.

The Sense of a Mismatch

So, then, if our word "Judaism" means the religion of Jewish people (as it does), and if the New Testament is populated largely by Jewish people doing religious things (as it is), then it follows that the New Testament attests quite a lot of Judaism—as it does (Fredriksen 2018)! And yet this claim seems strange to modern ears. Why so? One important reason is that Judaism as we know it today was decisively shaped by a cluster of events that transpired just *after* the time of the New Testament—in particular, the codification of the Mishnah and the ascendancy of the rabbis around the turn of the third century CE. Mainstream Judaism from late antiquity to the present is, in broad strokes, a form of *rabbinic* Judaism, which was not quite yet on the scene at the time of the New Testament; this accounts for at least some of the common impression of a mismatch. The Judaism of the New Testament is not yet rabbinic Judaism (Cohen 1984). Neither, on the other hand, is the Judaism of the New Testament ancient Israelite religion—that is, the religion of ancient Israelite people that we find attested (selectively, and with bias) in the Hebrew Bible (a.k.a. the Old Testament, in Christian jargon). Ancient Israel and Judah had their own monarchies, temples, panthe-

ons, schools of prophets, and so on, most of which did not survive to the time of the New Testament. The religion of Jesus and Paul differs profoundly from the religion of Elijah and Jeremiah, even if the former is a descendant of the latter.

The Judaism of the New Testament is late Second Temple Judaism (Boccaccini 1991)—that is, the Judaism of the period stretching from the late sixth century BCE to the late first century CE, during which the second temple stood in Jerusalem (the temple rebuilt under Achaemenid Persian sponsorship after the Babylonian exile). Like in ancient Israel, priests still offered sacrifices to God in Jerusalem, but unlike in ancient Israel, new classes of religious experts (e.g., Pharisees, Essenes, seers) also interpreted Torah for Jews in Judea and abroad. The New Testament falls at the very end of this Second Temple period, in the early days of the Roman Empire, roughly contemporary with the Qumran covenanters, Philo of Alexandria, Yohanan ben Zakkai, and Flavius Josephus. Its stories of Jesus and the apostles take place while the temple still stands. Thus Jesus, arrested in Jerusalem during Passover, must appear before the high priest (Mark 14:53); Paul brings a votive offering to the temple (Acts 21:23–26); and the Gospel of Matthew says that God is resident in the temple (Matt. 23:21). But most of the texts themselves were actually written after 70 CE, after Titus's Roman army had sacked Jerusalem and destroyed the temple. Thus, they sometimes betray a bit too much knowledge of how it all would end (e.g., Luke 19:43–44; 21:20–24). The New Testament is a literary artifact of this very important liminal period in Jewish history. Most of the New Testament writers know about the end of the Second Commonwealth, but they do not yet know that the rabbis will soon arise to offer a post-temple *modus vivendi* for Jews across the Mediterranean and West Asia. Like the Bar Kokhba Revolt under Hadrian (132–136 CE), the Jesus sect gives us a snapshot of a messianic movement—a direction Jewish history might have taken, which its partisans hoped it would take, but it did not. The temple was not rebuilt; the kingdom of God did not come in power. The future of Judaism lay with the rabbis; the Jesus sect, for its part, evolved into a majority Gentile religion that came to be called Christianity (Donaldson 2020).

This brings us to another reason it might seem strange to modern readers to speak of Judaism in the New Testament—namely, the presence of *anti-Judaism* in the New Testament. The New Testament is a motley collection of twenty-seven texts written by at least(!) ten different authors over the course of a century (40s to 140s CE, roughly), and so it contains multitudes. Although most of the authors of these texts were Jewish, some were Gentile. And a few of the authors (both Jewish and Gentile ones, perhaps) lash out in anger at Jews and Judaism at certain points (Fredriksen and Reinhartz 2002). For example, the author of the Gospel of John, who was possibly (though not certainly) Jewish himself, programmatically sets Jesus and his disciples against the hostile *Ioudaioi*, "Jews" (not just against the school of the Pharisees, as in Mark, Matthew, and Luke). In one heated exchange, John writes, "[Jesus said to the Jews (*Ioudaioi*),] 'I know that you are seed of Abraham, but you are seeking to kill me, because my word does not find a place in you. . . . You are from your father the devil, and you want to do his desires. He was a murderer from the beginning, and he did not stand in the truth, for there is no truth in him'" (John 8:37, 44). In this and a few other related passages, John voices what we might accurately call anti-Judaism, even though his Gospel is also a rich source for many aspects of Judaism, certainly of its characters and possibly also of its author (Reinhartz 2018).

Perhaps even more historically significant, however, are other instances where (arguably, and I think certainly) the New Testament texts themselves are not anti-Jewish but later Chris-

tian interpretation has made them so. For example, Paul, a Jewish apostle to Gentiles, and the earliest of all the New Testament writers, wrote a circular letter to Gentile Christ assemblies in Galatia (central Asia Minor) warning the men there not to convert to Judaism by proselyte circumcision. To these Gentile Christ-believing men, Paul writes, "I tell you that if you undergo circumcision, Christ will benefit you nothing. . . . [In that case] you are undone from Christ, fallen away from grace" (Gal. 5:2–4). Some later Christian interpreters, however, reinterpreted these verses to mean that *all Jews*, because their men are normally circumcised in infancy, are automatically cut off from the grace of God. Paul himself expressly rejects such an idea elsewhere (Rom. 11), but that did not stop later Christian readers from reusing his words in this way (Novenson 2022, 46–66). Another example is the Apocalypse of John (a.k.a. the book of Revelation), a late first-century CE visionary text written by a Jewish prophet from Patmos in the Aegean Sea. At one point John rages against certain anonymous people "who say they are Jews and are not but are a synagogue of Satan" (Rev. 2:9; cf. 3:9). Many later Christian readers took this phrase to be a Christian condemnation of actual Jews, involving a Christian claim to the name "Jews" and a denunciation of actual Jews as servants of Satan. But in Revelation itself, the statement has almost exactly the opposite force, condemning people who falsely appropriate the name "Jews" for themselves (as some later Christians would do!). In other words, Revelation itself is not anti-Jewish, but some later Christian interpreters took its words and made anti-Jewish meaning out of them (Marshall 2001).

Examples from the Gospels and the Letters of Paul

Precisely because there are those New Testament texts that are themselves (at least partly) anti-Jewish (e.g., John), debate over these other cases (e.g., Galatians, Revelation) continues apace. Some scholars think that Galatians and Revelation are anti-Jewish in just the way that later Christians took them to be, but other scholars (including the present writer) think not and are engaged in the complicated project of unpicking the layers of text and interpretation. To illustrate, let us consider two central examples of how Judaism functions as a symbolic world for the texts that compose the New Testament: first, the case of Jesus and ritual impurity, and second, the case of Paul and the law of Moses. In both cases, later readers would make new sense of the texts in a different, Christian frame of reference. But in their first-century context, they are Jewish texts playing by Jewish rules.

First, then, let us consider Jesus and ritual impurity. It is a commonplace in the (overwhelmingly Christian) history of research on the Gospels to say that Jesus overthrew the system of ritual purity prescribed in the Torah. According to this old saw, Jews saw menstruating women, people with skin disorders, and certain others as unclean, but Jesus chose to see them as clean, supposedly demonstrating the moral superiority of Christianity to Judaism. But as Matthew Thiessen has recently argued (Thiessen 2020, and chap. 38, "Purity and Holiness," below), this does not match up at all with what the Gospels actually say. In the stories, Jesus everywhere engages with ritually impure people (menstruating women, people with skin disorders, etc.) as if the ritual impurity does in fact exist, as the Torah says it does. What Jesus does, however, is to destroy the contaminant of ritual impurity by the power of his contagious holiness. He exercises a similar kind of purifying power to that exercised by sacrifices of purification in the temple (because he is the Messiah, the Holy One of God). Like the book of Leviticus, Jesus takes for granted that ritual impurity is a real force in the world. Like the Levitical

priests (armed with their purifying sacrificial paraphernalia), he undertakes to destroy the impurity and restore the people suffering from it to their natural, ideal state as worshipers. This whole mass of stories from the Synoptic Gospels makes sense only within a Jewish symbolic universe with a robust account of ritual impurity and the means of cleaning it (both cultic and messianic). To say that it is a Jewish system is not to say that it is not also—at a higher level of generalization— a Greco-Roman system, since most ancient Mediterranean peoples had their respective systems for cleansing ritual impurity from cultic spaces. But the particular ancient Mediterranean purity system that the Gospels assume is, naturally, the Jewish one. Later Christian interpretation of these stories played by different rules, sometimes *very* different—hence the confusion in the history of interpretation.

Second, consider Paul and the law of Moses. Here, again, the history of Christian interpretation—in this case, especially since the sixteenth-century Protestant Reformation— has wanted to say that Christianity transcends Judaism by its willingness to jettison the law of Moses and has taken Paul as biblical warrant for saying so (Novenson 2022, 180–96). As with Jesus and impurity, there is a lot of material in the letters of Paul that can be made to give this impression, but in their first-century context it is not so. For one thing, as we saw above in regard to circumcision in Galatians, there is a world of difference between opposing circumcision *for Gentiles*, as Paul does, and opposing circumcision *for all people*, which Paul emphatically does not do. (He actually praises the circumcision of Jewish men [Rom. 3:1–2], and of himself in particular [Phil. 3:5]!) Indeed, opposition to circumcision for Gentiles is a well-attested ancient Jewish view, founded on the premise that God gave the covenant of circumcision to Israel, not to everyone. So says the book of Jubilees (15.25–34), for example, and so says Paul. Paul's position on proselyte circumcision makes sense only in the context of this Jewish discourse.

Beyond the circumcision debate, however, Paul also makes some famously dismissive-sounding statements about the law of Moses *as such*. "Christ redeemed us from the curse of the law" (Gal. 3:13); "Now that faith has come, we are no longer under a custodian" (3:25); and so on. These statements, Christian readers have often thought, show that Paul must finally want to forsake Judaism for Christianity. But here, again, that is not the first-century meaning of these texts. Paul reasons, as the Torah itself reasons(!), that God gave the Torah to people who sin and die, to give them a means of restraining sin and purifying the contamination of death. The difference between Paul and Moses is that Paul believes that—because the Messiah has just risen from the dead at the end of the ages—his own generation is the last generation of mortals, that henceforth people will literally no longer sin or die. To the extent that he believes that is true, he believes that the law of Moses is transcended—*not* that people are free to disobey the commandments; Paul loudly denies that idea (Rom. 6:1–2, 15). But he thinks that he, and other people who have absorbed the *pneuma* (spirit) of God, can live a superhuman life, a life like that of the angels. Angels do not have the Torah because they neither sin nor die; so it is, too, with pneumatic people. That is Paul's position on the Torah. Paul's Christian interpreters, however—most of them—made peace with the idea that people *do* still sin and die. Hence, they reinterpreted Paul's words to make them a manifesto against Jewish law and for Christian freedom. But when Paul wrote those words, he meant them in the context of a very different, Jewish theological discourse about human mortality and its relation to divine law. Here, again, Judaism is the symbolic world within which these New Testament texts first made sense (Nanos and Zetterholm 2015; Novenson 2022).

Conclusion

If we were to follow the current fashion for calling the New Testament "the Christian Testament," we might miss the crucial fact that, in their original historical context, most of these texts were Jewish. It is only Christians, of course, who have ever read them as Scripture, which is all well and good. There is nothing inherently new about the New Testament (indeed, relative to us, it is very old!), nor anything inherently old about the Old Testament (which is why it can just as accurately be called the Hebrew Bible; see Levenson 1993, 1–32). The logic of religious communities and their canons is just different from the logic of historical description. In terms of historical description, it is not the case that—as the older textbooks often put it—Judaism is the "background" against which the New Testament stands out. On the contrary, we should think of the New Testament as one chapter in the history of ancient Judaism (Vermes 1980).

Works Cited

Boccaccini, Gabriele. 1991. *Middle Judaism: Jewish Thought, 300 BCE–200 CE*. Minneapolis: Fortress.

Cohen, Shaye J. D. 1984. "The Significance of Yavneh: Pharisees, Rabbis, and the End of Jewish Sectarianism." *Hebrew Union College Annual* 55: 27–53.

Donaldson, Terence L. 2020. *Gentile Christian Identity from Cornelius to Constantine*. Grand Rapids: Eerdmans.

Fredriksen, Paula. 2018. *When Christians Were Jews: The First Generation*. New Haven: Yale University Press.

Fredriksen, Paula, and Adele Reinhartz, eds. 2002. *Jesus, Judaism, and Christian Anti-Judaism: Reading the New Testament after the Holocaust*. Louisville: Westminster John Knox.

Himmelfarb, Martha. 1998. "Judaism and Hellenism in 2 Maccabees." *Poetics Today* 19: 19–40.

Levenson, Jon D. 1993. *The Hebrew Bible, the Old Testament, and Historical Criticism: Jews and Christians in Biblical Studies*. Louisville: Westminster John Knox.

Levine, Amy-Jill, and Marc Zvi Brettler, eds. 2017. *The Jewish Annotated New Testament*. 2nd ed. Oxford: Oxford University Press.

Marshall, John W. 2001. *Parables of War: Reading John's Jewish Apocalypse*. Waterloo, ON: Wilfrid Laurier University Press.

Masuzawa, Tomoko. 2005. *The Invention of World Religions*. Chicago: University of Chicago Press.

Moore, Stephen D. 2006. *Empire and Apocalypse: Postcolonialism and the New Testament*. Sheffield: Sheffield Phoenix.

Nanos, Mark D., and Magnus Zetterholm, eds. 2015. *Paul within Judaism: Restoring the First-Century Context to the Apostle*. Minneapolis: Fortress.

Novenson, Matthew V. 2014. "Paul's Former Occupation in *Ioudaismos*." In *Galatians and Christian Theology*, edited by Mark W. Elliott, Scott J. Hafemann, N. T. Wright, and John Frederick, 24–39. Grand Rapids: Baker Academic.

———. 2022. *Paul, Then and Now*. Grand Rapids: Eerdmans.

Reinhartz, Adele. 2018. *Cast out of the Covenant: Jews and Anti-Judaism in the Gospel of John*. Minneapolis: Fortress.

Sanders, E. P. 1992. *Judaism: Practice and Belief, 63 BCE–66 CE*. London: SCM.

Schüssler Fiorenza, Elisabeth. 2001. *Wisdom Ways: Introducing Feminist Biblical Interpretation*. Maryknoll, NY: Orbis Books.

Schwartz, Seth. 2011. "How Many Judaisms Were There?" *JAJ* 2: 208–38.

Thiessen, Matthew. 2020. *Jesus and the Forces of Death: The Gospels' Portrayal of Ritual Impurity within First-Century Judaism*. Grand Rapids: Baker Academic.

Vermes, Geza. 1980. "Jewish Studies and New Testament Interpretation." *JJS* 31: 1–17.

2

Hellenization

Carl R. Holladay

Hellenization is the process through which the language, values, and culture of ancient Greece (especially Classical Greece of the fifth and fourth centuries BCE) is appropriated by non-Greek peoples and cultures. The conquest of the eastern Mediterranean region by Alexander the Great (356–323 BCE) is usually seen as the major catalyst through which the Greek language and Greek cultural values spread to other parts of the ancient world (Walbank 1993, 29–45). For this reason, Alexander the Great marks a major point of transition in the ancient world so that scholars of classical antiquity use "pre-" and "post-Alexander" to designate two distinct historical eras.

The origin and use of the terms "Hellenize" and "Hellenization," and the related terms "Hellenism" and its adjectival form "Hellenistic," present some interpretive challenges. The ancient Greek historian Thucydides (ca. 460–400 BCE) uses the term "Hellenize" (*hellēnizein*) to mean fluency in Greek, but the context suggests that the term could also signify acquiring Greek cultural sensibilities

(*Hist*. 2.68). In 2 Maccabees 4:13 (ca. 1st c. BCE), the noun form *hellēnismos* ("Hellenization," NRSV) denotes practices typically associated with "the Greek way of life," including participating in athletic contests in the gymnasium and wearing an easily recognizable Greek hat, both of which are characterized as "foreign ways." In Acts 6:1 the dispute between "Hellenists" (*hellēnistai*) and "Hebrews" (*Hebraioi*) probably implies two competing groups who speak different languages but who also reflect different cultural values associated with those languages (cf. Acts 9:29; 11:20).

These passages suggest that "Hellenize" and "Hellenism" in the ancient context can be used in two distinct, but closely related, senses: speaking Greek and living as a Greek. In both cases, the terms imply that one actively engages in learning the Greek language and embracing Greek cultural values, and that one is similarly aggressive when urging non-Greeks to do the same. Some think Hellenization in modern usage has a negative connotation because it signifies a form of cultural domination in which one cultural system is actively imposed upon another.

The German historian J. G. Droysen (1808–84) is credited with coining the term "Hellenismus" as a way of characterizing the period from Alexander the Great to the emperor Augustus (63 BCE–14 CE). By referring to this period as the Hellenistic age, Droysen has in view not only the active spread of Greek language and culture throughout the Mediterranean world but also the fusion of Greek and non-Greek cultures. Droysen also sees the Hellenistic age as a time of energetic cultural interaction that prepared the way for the arrival of Christianity (Droysen 1952–53 [1836–43], 2012 [1833]).

Some describe the pre-Alexander period as "Hellenic" to signify its close attachment to earlier, Classical Greek culture; they refer to the post-Alexander period as "Hellenistic" in order to emphasize that the era inaugurated by Alexander the Great is still Greek, but different. One of the main differences is how the world was viewed. Alexander's sweep across the East, eventually reaching India, dramatically changed political boundaries, which resulted in the territorial expansion of Greece. These new political realities made Alexander a popular hero. His popularity is reflected in the widespread use of his image in paintings and statuary, and on coins. An entire body of literature such as the Alexander romance, a novel rehearsing Alexander's military exploits, developed around this larger-than-life military leader. Composed between the mid-second and the mid-fourth century CE, but containing stories and traditions that are much earlier, some traceable to the third century BCE, this work was extremely popular, as witnessed by its survival in eighty versions in twenty-four languages (Dowden 1989, 650). These writings broadened the geographical horizons of many readers. People became aware of countries and regions in other parts of the world in a way previously unknown.

Another innovation introduced by Alexander's dramatic rise to power related to the Greek language. Although Aramaic was the main language spoken in the eastern Mediterranean, it was eventually replaced by Greek as the lingua franca, the common language spoken by most educated people, especially court officials and the ruling classes.

With the spread of a language, now spoken by people whose own first language was different and by those speaking various dialects, changes were bound to occur. In the post-Alexander period, variations emerged in the ways Greek was spoken. New Greek words formed, sometimes as foreign words rewritten using Greek letters (*amēn*, *allēlouia*, *pascha*, *geenna*, *abba*, *maranatha*, *rabbi*). So too, common terms were used in new ways. The term *adelphos* (the word for "brother," but which could also include females, especially in the plural form; see, e.g., Luke 21:16) acquired a specialized sense, being used to designate a comember of a religious community (Rom. 8:29; 1 Cor. 5:11). Other terms acquired new meanings: for instance, *martys* (martyr; Acts 22:20; Rev. 2:13) and *metanoia* (repentance; Acts 20:21; 26:20) acquired a special religious coloring.

Along with these changes in word meaning came changes in pronunciation and patterns of inflection. This new, common Greek language came to be known as Koine ("common") Greek, a new phase of Greek clearly distinguishable from pre-Alexander Classical (Attic) Greek.

Koine Greek is widely attested during the Hellenistic-Roman period. It is found in non-literary sources, including papyri, ostraca, and inscriptions. It is also the language employed by notable Greek authors such as Polybius, Diodorus Siculus, Strabo, Plutarch, and Epictetus. Its use among Greek-speaking Jewish authors is clearly documented in the Greek translations of the Jewish Bible (Septuagint), the Letter of Aristeas, Philo of Alexandria, and Flavius

Josephus. It comes as no surprise that Koine Greek is the language found in the writings of the New Testament, which were produced in different parts of the Roman Empire between 50 and 100 CE. This is also the case with the large group of early Christian writings that appeared from the early second century onward, such as the apocryphal Acts of various apostles and other Christian leaders.

The discovery of numerous Egyptian papyri in the nineteenth century enabled scholars to see that the style of Greek found in everyday writings (such as shopping lists, school assignments, and even legal documents relating to contractual agreements of various kinds) often resembled the type of Koine Greek found in the New Testament and other early Christian writings. At an earlier period, this distinctive form of biblical Greek was sometimes referred to as "Holy Spirit Greek" as a way of accounting for its unusual grammatical and syntactical qualities. But classical scholars and linguists such as Adolf Deissmann published papyri that served as useful comparative texts for reading the New Testament (Deissmann 1978 [1911]). Through these efforts, scholars came to see that the quality and style of New Testament Koine Greek often resonated with the language found in the Greek papyri and other forms of popular Greek writing.

Those who spoke and wrote in Greek during the Hellenistic-Roman period did so at different levels and with different degrees of sophistication. Some had attended schools in which children read Classical Greek texts such as Homer and the Greek tragedians Euripides and Sophocles. These students learned to imitate these classical models and were thus able to write in a refined Classical or "Attic" style.

We see this variety within the New Testament itself. Mark's Gospel is well known for its simple, unadorned Greek and is often characterized as being written in a popular, storytelling style. The Gospels of Matthew and Luke, by contrast, display a more refined style of Koine Greek. Their vocabulary is larger than Mark's, and they often use grammatical forms that are more refined and elegant (and more correct) than the ones found in the parallel account in Mark. Luke-Acts displays a form of Koine Greek that is more typical of well-educated pagan authors such as Plutarch. The letter to the Hebrews also displays an elegant form of Greek composition, which suggests that its unknown author knew the conventions of rhetorical composition and could employ them to great effect.

Hellenization as Cultural Change

No one disputes that Hellenization, as it relates to the widespread use of Koine Greek, is present in the period following Alexander the Great. But if someone wrote in Greek as their second language, in what sense were they Hellenized? This simple act would require them to enter the world of Hellenism and to some extent embrace that world. But would the use of Greek as a second language mean that they experienced fundamental shifts in how they thought or acted?

This is where the question of "Hellenistic," and "Hellenization" as a cultural process, has been hotly contested, especially among scholars trying to ascertain the degree to which Jews became Hellenized during the period between 200 BCE and 200 CE. At one time, especially in the nineteenth century, and even earlier, it was widely assumed that Jews living in the land of Israel during this period spoke Aramaic and that Jews living in the diaspora spoke Greek. Consequently, Palestinian Judaism was equated with Aramaic-speaking Judaism, while diaspora Judaism was equated with Hellenistic, or Greek-speaking, Judaism.

Martin Hengel challenged this dichotomy in his landmark work *Judaism and Hellenism* (Hengel 1974). In this methodically argued work, Hengel showed that the Hellenization of Jews during the Second Temple period was not limited to the diaspora but characterized Palestinian Judaism. In order to support his argument, Hengel surveyed both literary and nonliterary sources from the Maccabean period. He argued that there is substantial evidence showing the widespread use of Koine Greek in Palestine during the centuries immediately preceding the time of Christ. But he also argued that the Hellenization of Palestine was deeper, that it shaped fundamental beliefs and practices of Greek-speaking Jews. Hellenization was not a surface phenomenon, limited to acquiring fluency in Koine Greek; it altered the ways Hellenistic Jews thought about their core beliefs.

One of the key figures in Hengel's reconstruction is Qoheleth, a wisdom teacher who belonged to upper-class, aristocratic circles in Judea (Hengel 1974, 1:115–30). While the dating of Qoheleth is contested, Hengel opts for 270 to 220 BCE as the probable dates for his activity. Hengel finds evidence that "the spirit and the atmosphere of early Hellenism" deeply influenced Qoheleth even though he wrote the book of Ecclesiastes in Hebrew (1:116). This is seen in the consistently critical stance of the work vis-à-vis the broader Jewish wisdom tradition. It is also reflected in Qoheleth's conception of a universal, distant God, far removed from human concerns, which Hengel thinks represents a basic theological shift toward the Greek understanding of fate. Further evidence of the Greek spirit is seen in Qoheleth's rejection of retribution, one of the pillars of Jewish belief.

While Hengel's claims about the pervasive Hellenization of Palestine in the pre-Christian era have been challenged, his book marks a turning point in the debate. After Hengel, Hellenistic Judaism could no longer be equated with diaspora Judaism, as had been the case in earlier scholarship. Even so, some scholars see Hellenism more as a veneer than as a deeply embedded cultural outlook, especially in the eastern Mediterranean.

What we mean by Hellenization has to be demonstrated on a case-by-case basis—or, perhaps, on a region-by-region basis. Philo of Alexandria serves as an illuminating example. His voluminous writings, which consist mainly of essays that comment on the Greek translation of the Pentateuch, along with a handful of thematic essays, reveal his extensive knowledge of Classical Greek literature. He frequently cites Homer, along with other Greek authors, such as Plato. He not only cites these authors, but he also knows them well. He incorporates Platonic categories relating to the ideal and real world (or, to use Philo's language, the noumenal and phenomenal world) in order to explain the two accounts of creation in Genesis 1–3. Philo writes a refined level of Greek, and his knowledge of Greek enables him to participate in philosophical discussions that typified the Middle Platonism of his time.

No one seriously doubts that Philo was thoroughly Hellenized. He wrote in Greek; he thought in Greek; there is no clear evidence that he knew much, if any, Hebrew or Aramaic. He read the Bible in Greek. For Philo, the Septuagint was the Word of God.

And yet Philo maintained certain core Jewish beliefs. He believed that God's will is revealed in the Pentateuch. He believed in the one, ineffable God and emphasized the sharp distinction between humanity and God. Like other Jewish writers at the time, he believed that the universe was populated with a diverse array of demonic powers, but he sharply differentiated them from God, "the Existent One," the One Who Is. While conceding the multiple ways in which God could be manifested, Philo remained an ardent monotheist. His conception of the Logos was novel, though not unprecedented among Jewish writers, and his conception of the Divine Logos drew on various strands of Greek philosophical thought at both scholastic and popular levels. Philo also affirmed the practice of circumcision for Jewish male infants. While he recognized the metaphorical dimensions of circumcision and saw it as an act signifying the "cutting away" of evil desires, he nevertheless upheld it. He never came close to Paul's claim that circumcision and uncircumcision are nothing (1 Cor. 7:19; Gal. 5:6). For Philo, they mattered greatly, and like other divine commands found in the Pentateuch, circumcision was part of God's ethical code, which is to be obeyed.

Philo is generally credited with developing a way of reading the Pentateuch that was philosophically compatible with Platonic thought as it was known in Alexandria at the time. He was not the first Jewish writer to engage in the sort of allegorical interpretation that one finds throughout his biblical commentaries. Aristobulus, the so-called Peripatetic philosopher, who also resided in Alexandria in the second century BCE, anticipated Philo in his use of allegory. Both were indebted to Stoicism, which had also employed allegorical interpretation to interpret Homer.

There are many ways to describe the interpretive programs of Philo and his predecessor Aristobulus, but it is appropriate to see their respective interpretations as examples of Hellenization. They were a part of Alexandrian culture, and within that setting they breathed the air of Hellenism. There is no reason to deny that they utilized the strategies of interpretation that had already been developed by Hellenistic writers. While Philo's embrace of Hellenism enabled him to synthesize biblical with Greek philosophical thought, he did not alter or abandon his core Jewish beliefs.

The Jewish historian Flavius Josephus, an equally prolific author, displays a different profile. His native language was Aramaic; Greek was his second language. In writing the *Jewish War*, Josephus used assistants whose Greek was better than his (*Ag. Ap.* 1.50). Josephus had no interest in the range of philosophical questions that intrigued Philo. But like with Philo, the Septuagint was an important source for him, although he appeared to have relied on other sources as well. The story he tells in his *Jewish Antiquities* is the biblical story, which he paraphrases, but which he extends down to his own time.

Was Josephus Hellenized? Not in the same way, or to the same extent, as Philo. But Josephus clearly saw himself as a historian of the Jewish people, writing in Greek so that he could communicate his story to the widest possible readership. There is good evidence that Josephus saw himself as a historian writing in the same tradition as Dionysius of Halicarnassus (ca. 60 BCE–7 BCE), who wrote a twenty-volume history of Rome in Greek. In this work Dionysius seeks to show that the Rome of his day (the late Republic) has noble origins that are traceable to the eighth and seventh centuries BCE. Similarly, Josephus tried to show that the Jewish people had a noble history with ancient origins comparable, even superior, to that of Rome. If this construal of Josephus's historical projects is correct, he should be seen as operating with the self-consciousness of his model, Dionysius of Halicarnassus, who wrote a history of Rome in Greek.

In the *Jewish Antiquities* Josephus does more than rehearse the story of Israel from its inception down to his own time. He also operates with theological convictions. He adheres to belief in the one God, and he even credits Abraham with formulating a teleological proof for the existence of God (*Ant.* 1.156). At times, Josephus tones down the biblical accounts of miracles, allowing his readers to judge the credibility of such accounts for themselves. In making these adjustments to the biblical story, Josephus is responding to the spirit of Hellenism.

Hellenization and the Liberal Spirit

It is sometimes assumed that Hellenization implies liberalization, a broadening of one's outlook that is somehow more universalistic and less narrow, more inclusive toward other cultures and points of view, and less exclusive of alien points of view. In some nineteenth-century scholarship (see, e.g., Harnack 1986 [1900]), Hellenization tends to signify universalism and inclusivity. It is often claimed that, as Jews became more Hellenized, they became more tolerant and less judgmental toward Gentiles. This correlation has to be examined more closely by analyzing individual Hellenistic Jewish writers.

The Jewish writer Artapanus, who flourished in Alexandria in the mid-second century BCE, wrote an account of the Jewish people in Greek. Although he is sometimes described as a historian, he should probably be seen as a writer of romantic history. His account displays an unusually strong embrace of pagan values. He portrays Moses as the teacher of Orpheus and as the founder of Egyptian religion to whom the people gave divine honor, even calling him Hermes. Some scholars find it inconceivable that Artapanus was Jewish, that someone devoted to the teachings of Moses could have said such things. But it is equally difficult to imagine a pagan writer at this time having much interest in, much less knowledge of, what Moses said or did in Egypt.

As difficult as it may seem, Artapanus was probably Jewish. And if so, his portrait of Moses can be aptly characterized as strongly Hellenized. After all, in his portrait of Moses, Artapanus is using a template found among other Hellenistic writers who were keen to present figures from their countries as cultural benefactors. Just as other figures are presented as renowned inventers, devising ingenious solutions to everyday problems, so is Moses portrayed by Artapanus as an inventor of ships, labor-saving machines, and philosophy. Artapanus's depiction of Moses follows a cultural template used by non-Jewish writers in rehearsing the exploits of such figures as the legendary Egyptian king Sesostris, among others. On any showing, Artapanus is rightly characterized as being thoroughly Hellenized. Few other Jewish writers were willing to push

the envelope the way Artapanus does (Collins 2000, 37–46; Holladay 2021, 112–14, 159–62).

At the other end of the spectrum is another Greek-speaking Jewish writer, Theodotus, an Alexandrian epic poet who flourished in the mid-second century BCE. Only short sections of his epic poetry are preserved, but the fragments focus mainly on the patriarch Jacob. Theodotus recasts the story of the rape of Dinah in Genesis 34 and reinterprets the actions of Jacob's sons Levi and Simeon in responding to Shechem's violent actions.

The poetry of Theodotus reflects close familiarity with Homeric epic and with epic poetry in general. Most agree that Theodotus is Hellenized literarily—that is, in his knowledge and use of Greek poetic style. And yet he displays little, if any, embrace of liberal, open-minded attitudes toward foreigners. Quite the reverse. Theodotus steadfastly defends circumcision as a Jewish rite that must be practiced. He also upholds endogamy by explicitly condemning intermarriage between Jews and non-Jews. Theodotus is a vivid example of what seems anomalous—a Jewish (or perhaps Samaritan) writer who is literarily Hellenized and yet who remains theologically or culturally conservative. Theodotus illustrates how someone can embrace Hellenistic style and can be thoroughly proficient in the use of a particular Greek genre, in this case Greek epic, and yet take a hard line against competing cultural values and religious beliefs. Theodotus proves that Hellenization does not necessarily mean that one is more open-minded about embracing another culture's values (Collins 2000, 57–60; Holladay 2021, 147–53).

Summary

We can speak confidently of Hellenization as a process of cultural assimilation, especially among Jews during the Second Temple period. What this actually means has to be determined within specific, well-defined parameters for judging degrees of accommodation and as- similation. That Jews adopted the Greek language as their main and, in some cases, exclusive form of communication is clear. At the level of language usage, Judaism was thoroughly Hellenized during the Second Temple period. At the level of cultural appropriation in which fundamental shifts in belief and behavior occur, we find a spectrum along which individual cases can be placed. Artapanus and Theodotus clearly represent opposite ends of that spectrum. Philo of Alexandria also illustrates a high level of Hellenization, although it takes a particular form that has to be understood within his own highly developed system of philosophical thought. Qoheleth represents another point on the spectrum, being well advanced in the direction of Hellenization, although still within the Jewish wisdom tradition.

The debate about Hellenization as it relates to early Christianity has advanced in some important ways. It is now clear that "Judaism" and "Hellenism" are not airtight categories that signify two alternative, mutually exclusive ways of thinking. Their boundaries can be fluid. When claims of Hellenization are made, we have to ask what this actually means. Is the Gospel of John Hellenized in a way that the Gospel of Matthew or Luke is not? We have also learned that Hellenization can be viewed positively or negatively. For some, it signifies openness to other points of view; for others, it threatens what is perceived as pure and undiluted.

Works Cited

Collins, John J. 2000. *Between Athens and Jerusalem: Jewish Identity in the Hellenistic Diaspora*. 2nd ed. Grand Rapids: Eerdmans.

Deissmann, Adolf. 1978. *Light from the Ancient East*. Grand Rapids: Baker. Originally published 1911.

Dowden, Ken. 1989. "Pseudo-Callisthenes: The Alexander Romance." In *Collected Ancient Greek Novels*, edited by B. P. Reardon, 650–735. Berkeley: University of California Press.

Droysen, J. G. 1952–53. *Geschichte des Hellenismus*. 3 vols. Basel: B. Schwabe. Originally published 1836–43; 3rd ed. published 1877–78.

———. 2012. *History of Alexander the Great*. Philadelphia: American Philosophical Association. Originally published 1833; 3rd ed. published 1880.

Harnack, Adolf von. 1986. *What Is Christianity?* Philadelphia: Fortress. Originally published 1900.

Hengel, Martin. 1974. *Judaism and Hellenism*. 2 vols. Philadelphia: Fortress.

Holladay, Carl R. 2021. *Hellenistic Jewish Literature and the New Testament*. Edited by Jonathan M. Potter and Michael K. W. Suh. WUNT 468. Tübingen: Mohr Siebeck.

Walbank, F. W. 1993. *The Hellenistic World*. Rev. ed. Cambridge, MA: Harvard University Press.

3

Apocalyptic Thought

JOHN J. COLLINS

The literary genre apocalypse takes its name from the opening verse of the book of Revelation in the New Testament: the revelation, *apokalypsis*, of Jesus Christ. The word is used not for just any revelation but for revelations of another world or another dimension of this world. Apocalyptic revelations assume that human affairs are heavily influenced by superhuman forces, angelic or demonic. Crucially, they assume that individuals will be judged after death and rewarded or punished forever. Belief in superhuman beings was common in the ancient world, but it is more prominent in apocalyptic literature than in other strands of Jewish thought (e.g., wisdom literature). Belief in life after death is attested sporadically in neighboring cultures but was a novelty in Judaism in the Hellenistic age. The apocalyptic worldview, however, is constituted not by any one motif in isolation but by a configuration of motifs: revelation, heavenly mysteries, angels and demons, resurrection, eternal life, and final judgment.

In 1 Corinthians 15, Paul seeks to assure his readers of the resurrection of the dead. These readers evidently accepted that Jesus had been raised, but apparently they thought of that as an exceptional event. Paul argues to the contrary: "If the dead are not raised, then Christ has not been raised" (1 Cor. 15:16). But, he insists, "Christ has been raised from the dead, the first fruits of those who have died" (15:20). He describes a fuller scenario in 1 Thessalonians: "For the Lord himself, with a cry of command, with the archangel's call and with the sound of God's trumpet, will descend from heaven, and the dead in Christ will rise first. Then we who are alive, who are left, will be caught up in the clouds together with them to meet the Lord in the air" (1 Thess. 4:16–17). In short, the resurrection of Jesus was not an isolated event but was the beginning of the end of the world as we know it. The conviction that this world was passing away and that Jesus would return to judge the living and the dead animated the early Christian movement (see, e.g., 1 Thess. 4:17; 1 Cor. 7:29; Rom. 13:11–12).

Paul here was assuming a view of the world that had developed in Judaism in the last two centuries before Christ but that was very different from the worldview of ancient Israel. In the Torah and the Prophets, the goal of life had been to live long in the land and see one's children and one's children's children. After death, good and bad alike went to Sheol, the shadowy underworld where one could not even praise the Lord. A few people (Enoch, Elijah, possibly Moses) were believed to have been taken up alive to heaven, but they were exceptions. Even when the Prophets predicted that the Lord would come in judgment, they did not suppose that the conditions of life would change radically. Qoheleth could state as undisputed fact that "the earth remains forever" (Eccles. 1:4). At the end of the book of Isaiah we find a prophecy of a new creation, in which one who died at the age of a hundred years would be considered a youth (Isa. 65:20), but even in that new creation people would still die. Another passage in Isaiah speaks of a time when God would swallow up death forever (25:8), but even that passage does not promise that the dead would be raised. One other verse in the same section of Isaiah (26:19) says to the Israelites, "Your dead shall live, their corpses shall rise," but opinion is divided as to whether that is a prophecy of resurrection or a metaphor for the restoration of Israel as in Ezekiel 37 (the valley full of dry bones).[1]

Daniel

There is only one undisputed reference to the resurrection and judgment of individuals in the Hebrew Bible. That is in the book of Daniel (12:2–3). It comes at the end of a long revelation in which the angel Gabriel discloses to Daniel what is written in "the book of truth," or what is really going on in history (Collins 1993, 361–404; Newsom 2014, 320–68). The revelation is dated to the third year of King Cyrus of Persia. Gabriel explains to Daniel that he is engaged

in combat with "the prince of the kingdom of Persia" and is aided by Michael, "one of the chief princes" (Dan. 10:13). Later "the prince of Greece" will come (10:20). "Princes" are evidently patron angels, who would have been called gods of the various nations in earlier times. Michael is "your prince" (10:21), "the protector of your people" (12:1), the patron angel of Israel. Gabriel goes on to narrate the history of the Hellenistic period, in the guise of prophecy. No names are mentioned. The king of Syria is "the king of the north," the king of Egypt is "the king of the south," and so forth (11:5–14). The prophecy culminates in the suppression of the Jerusalem cult by Antiochus Epiphanes in the years 167–164 BCE and concludes by saying that the king would meet his death in the land of Israel, "between the sea and the beautiful holy mountain" (11:45). The last prophecy was not fulfilled. Antiochus died in Persia late in 164 BCE. Already in antiquity the pagan philosopher Porphyry noted that the prophecies were accurate down to 164 and inferred that this was the time of composition (Casey 1976).[2] The accurate prophecies were composed after the fact. This inference is accepted by modern critical scholars, except in more conservative circles.

According to Gabriel's prophecy, Michael would arise in victory after the death of the king, and the resurrection would follow. "Many" would rise, not all, some to everlasting life and some to everlasting shame. The victory would be brought about not by the militant action of the Maccabees but by Michael and the angelic host. The heroes of the story are the "wise," who understand this and make the many understand. Some of them would be killed, but at the resurrection they would be exalted to shine like the stars, which is to say that they would join the angelic host. It is not clear that the world comes to an end in Daniel,

---

1. On ideas of afterlife in ancient Judaism, see Nickelsburg 2006; Collins 2015.

2. Porphyry's critique is known from Jerome's commentary on Daniel (Archer 2009).

but the goal of life is changed. It is no longer to see one's children's children but to join the angels in heaven.

Gabriel's prophecy is the last of a series of revelations in the second half of the book of Daniel. The most famous of these is chapter 7, which symbolizes the pagan kingdoms as four great beasts coming up out of the sea, a motif evocative of ancient Near Eastern myth (Collins 1993, 274–324). They are condemned in a heavenly court scene by God, represented as an ancient figure, and the kingdom is given to "one like a son of man," who comes on the clouds with the holy ones of the Most High (Dan. 7:13, 18 NIV). "Holy ones" are angels; Israel is "the people of the holy ones" (7:27). The trials of the Jewish people are seen against the backdrop of cosmic conflict, analogous to the primeval battles of gods and sea monsters in ancient myths. In the context of Daniel, the one like a son of man is the archangel Michael, leader of the heavenly host. He would later be reinterpreted as the Messiah, and in Christianity specifically as Jesus Christ.

The motif of four kingdoms, followed by a definitive fifth one, was widespread in the Hellenistic and Roman periods. (Rome was often cast as the fifth kingdom.) This was one of several ways in which history could be divided into periods. In Daniel chapter 9, the prophecy of Jeremiah that Jerusalem would be desolate for seventy years is reinterpreted to mean seventy weeks of years. In each case, the implication is that time is measured out and is near its "end." (The "end" is not necessarily absolute but marked by divine intervention and radical change.) The book of Daniel gives the number of days until the end and even gives two different numbers. According to Daniel 12:11 the time from the disruption of the cult by Antiochus Epiphanes would be 1,290 days. The following verse says, "Happy are those who persevere and attain the thousand three hundred thirty-five days." Presumably, the prophecy was updated when the first number

of days passed. Such precise prediction is exceptional in ancient apocalyptic literature, but it gave rise to numerous attempts to predict the end of the world, down to the present time (Breed in Newsom 2014, 309–20).

The view of history and human destiny in the book of Daniel is presented as revelation, transmitted to Daniel by angels. It is not something that could be learned by observation. For this reason, it is called "apocalyptic."

Enoch

The visions of Daniel are the only part of the Hebrew Bible that can properly be called apocalyptic, but Daniel was not the first apocalypse. First Enoch, which is regarded as Scripture in the Ethiopian Church, contains at least five books, several of which are older than Daniel (Nickelsburg 2001, 7–9). These books were composed in Aramaic. Fragments of most of them have been found in the Dead Sea Scrolls. (The exception is the Similitudes or Parables of Enoch, 1 En. 37–71; see Nickelsburg and VanderKam 2012.) Enoch had supposedly lived in the seventh generation from Adam. He is the subject of an enigmatic notice in Genesis 5:24: "Enoch walked with God; then he was no more, because God took him." The Hebrew word for God, 'elohim, is a plural form. In the Hellenistic period, the statement that Enoch walked with God was understood to mean that he walked with gods or angels. The statement that God "took him" was taken, reasonably enough, to mean that he was taken up alive to heaven, but because he had "walked with gods" before that, he was also believed to have made round trips to heaven, where he learned heavenly secrets and saw the heavenly tablets on which destiny was recorded. The books of Enoch purport to describe what he learned in the course of these trips.

The story of Enoch's initial ascent to heaven is told in the Book of the Watchers (1 En. 1–36). The Watchers are fallen angels (the sons of

God in Gen. 6 who lust after human women). When they are condemned, they ask Enoch to intercede for them. He goes up to heaven and sees God on his throne, described in terms very similar to Daniel 7. The petition is rejected. Enoch is told to explain to the Watchers that they have abandoned a spiritual world for the desires of the flesh. Enoch becomes the inverse of the Watchers, a human being who abandons the world of flesh for that of the spirit.

After his vision of God on his throne, Enoch is taken on a tour of places normally inaccessible to human beings. He sees the storehouses of the rain and snow but also the chambers under a mountain where the souls of the dead are kept while awaiting judgment (1 En. 22). He also sees the places that have been prepared for the final judgment. The lesson of his vision is that such places exist and that all is prepared for a final judgment. Whereas Daniel is mainly concerned with history, the Book of the Watchers is primarily concerned with cosmology. Angelic beings play a major part in both books, as does the final judgment of the dead.

Another early book of 1 Enoch, the Astronomical Book (1 En. 72–82), is concerned with the movements of the stars. Other Enochic revelations, however, deal with history. The Apocalypse of Weeks (1 En. 93 + 91.11–17) divides history into ten "weeks." An elect group emerges at the end of the seventh week. In the tenth week a new heaven will appear. After that there will be many weeks without number, but free from sin. The Animal Apocalypse in 1 Enoch 85–90 presents an elaborate allegorical review of history, in which Israel is represented by sheep and the nations by wild animals. In the postexilic period, Israel is ruled by seventy shepherds. Eventually, God comes down to judge the world. The Epistle of Enoch (1 En. 91–105) is an exhortation that encourages the righteous and promises them that they will become companions to the host of heaven (104.2, 4).

We know very little about the social location of the people who produced the books of Enoch. They repeatedly refer to the "chosen righteous," and this suggests that they may have been a distinct group, but we know nothing of their organization. Fragments of these writings were preserved in the Dead Sea Scrolls, and they were evidently translated into Greek (from which the Ethiopic was translated), so they must have circulated beyond the circles in which they were composed, but we do not know how widely they were accepted.

The books of Daniel and Enoch are usually dated to the early second century BCE. Several of them come from around the time of the Maccabean revolt, although some of the books of Enoch may be earlier. It was at this time that the apocalyptic worldview gained currency in Judaism. As can be seen from these books, the emphasis may be either on the course of history or on cosmology, but in either case human affairs are subject to the influence of superhuman powers, and human beings are liable to a judgment after death.

The Late First Century CE

Another cluster of Jewish apocalyptic writings dates from the period after the destruction of the Jerusalem temple in 70 CE (Henze 2011; Stone 1990). Two of these, 4 Ezra and 2 Baruch, were almost certainly composed in Hebrew, although they have survived only in translation (4 Ezra in several languages, including Latin and Syriac; 2 Baruch only in Syriac). Both are reflections on the problematic justice of God in light of the destruction of Jerusalem. Unlike the earlier apocalypses of Enoch and Daniel, these apocalypses are focused on the Torah and debate human waywardness in light of the sin of Adam rather than that of angels or demons (see, e.g., 4 Ezra 7.117–18; 2 Bar. 54.19). Both ultimately look to messianic deliverers. In 4 Ezra 13 the messiah is described in terms reminiscent of the one like a son of man in Daniel 7.

Other apocalypses of the period after the destruction of the temple were composed in

Greek, probably in the Egyptian diaspora. Third Baruch is preserved in Greek and Slavonic. Both versions contain Christian elements, but these differ from each other, suggesting that there were two Christian editions of a Jewish original (Collins 2019). The angel seeks to distract Baruch from his grief over the destruction of Jerusalem by showing him the mysteries of God, taking him up through a numbered sequence of heavens, where he sees the abodes of the blessed and the damned. Second Enoch also involves an ascent through a numbered sequence of heavens. It is preserved in Slavonic, and its provenance is uncertain, but it is usually thought to have been written in Greek, in Egypt in the late first or early second century CE. Apocalyptic tours of heaven were increasingly popular in early Christianity (Himmelfarb 1993).

The Dead Sea Scrolls

Before the discovery of the Dead Sea Scrolls, we had very little literature from Judea from the period between the Maccabean revolt and the destruction of Jerusalem. One notable apocalypse that probably dates from this period is the Similitudes of Enoch, which develops the son of man figure of Daniel's vision into a heavenly messiah (Boccaccini 2007). The scrolls provide a rich trove of Aramaic and Hebrew texts from precisely this period. Many of the texts are fragmentary, and we cannot be sure of their literary genre, but several contain overviews of history in the guise of prophecy, similar to what we find in Daniel and Enoch (e.g., the Aramaic Four Kingdoms text, 4Q552–53, and a few writings in the name of Daniel). It is amply clear, however, that the major sectarian scrolls were informed by what may be called an apocalyptic worldview, in which human life is shaped by angelic and demonic powers and is subject to a final judgment after death (Collins 1997).

The Community Rule (1QS) contains a remarkable passage known as the Treatise on the Two Spirits (1QS III, 13–IV, 26). God, we are told, created two spirits for humanity to walk in, one of light and one of darkness. At first the treatise seems to suggest that people are entirely ruled by one spirit or the other. Then it says that the two spirits struggle within every individual. One spirit leads to virtuous conduct, the other to vice. The destiny of the one is eternal life in the realm of light; of the other, eternal punishment in the fire of dark regions. God, we are told, has set a term for the rule of the spirit of darkness, and at the appointed time he will destroy it forever. Another text, known as the War Scroll, provides instructions for the final battle between the forces of light and darkness. The people who preserved the scrolls believed that they were living in the period called "the end of days," although some notable events, including the coming of the messiah, were yet to come.

The scrolls include copies of the books of Daniel and Enoch, so the people who preserved them were evidently familiar with belief in resurrection. Yet, remarkably, there is no clear reference to resurrection, in the sense of the dead coming back to life, in the sectarian texts. There is ample evidence for belief in some form of eternal life, differentiated as reward or punishment, but several passages suggest that members of the sectarian community had already passed from death to life and were already living with the angels. The hymnist in the Thanksgiving Hymns thanks God for purifying him from sin so that he can take his place with the host of the holy ones and enter into communion with the heavenly beings (1QH^a XI, 19–23) or become united with the sons of truth in a lot with the holy ones (1QH^a XIX, 10–14). The apocalypses of Daniel and Enoch promise fellowship with the angels after death. The Dead Sea Scrolls promise it already in this life to those who join the sectarian association and live a life of purity.

Conclusion

Apocalyptic thought is not systematic and rational in the manner of philosophy. It is a work of imagination that relies heavily on mythic symbolism. It allows for considerable variety. The dualism of the two spirits in the Dead Sea Scrolls is distinctly different from the rebellion of the fallen angels in Enoch or the beasts from the sea in Daniel. People who shared an apocalyptic worldview did not necessarily agree with each other. They might have radically different ideas about the criteria for the final judgment or about the identity of the savior figure. Underlying all this diversity, however, is an orientation to an invisible world. Salvation, as it is conceived in apocalyptic literature, is not something that can be achieved in this world as we know it. We must suppose either that the Most High has made "not one world but two" (4 Ezra 7.50) or that there will be a new creation, by which this world will be transformed.

As Paul indicates in 1 Corinthians 15, this apocalyptic worldview was an essential presupposition of the acceptance of a crucified man as Messiah. Without it there would have been no belief in resurrection of the dead and no hope that Jesus would come again as the Son of Man on the clouds of heaven. Only one book of the New Testament is structured as an apocalypse—that is, as an explicit account of revelation. That is the book of Revelation, written toward the end of the first century CE. But as in the case of the Dead Sea Scrolls, which also contain relatively few apocalypses in the formal sense, the apocalyptic worldview is pervasive in the New Testament: human life is bounded by the activity of angels and demons, and life is lived in anticipation of a final judgment, followed by everlasting rewards and punishments. As Paul wrote to the Corinthians, the present form of this world is passing away (1 Cor. 7:31). This view of the world was largely rejected by rabbinic Judaism, even as it became an essential presupposition of Christianity.

Works Cited

Archer, Gleason L., ed. and trans. 2009. *Jerome's Commentary on Daniel*. Eugene, OR: Wipf & Stock.

Boccaccini, Gabriele, ed. 2007. *Enoch and the Messiah Son of Man: Revisiting the Parables*. Grand Rapids: Eerdmans.

Casey, P. M. 1976. "Porphyry and the Book of Daniel." *JTS* 27: 15–33.

Collins, John J. 1993. *Daniel: A Commentary on the Book of Daniel*. Hermeneia. Minneapolis: Fortress.

———. 1997. *Apocalypticism in the Dead Sea Scrolls*. London: Routledge.

———. 2015. "The Afterlife in Apocalyptic Literature." In *Apocalypse, Prophecy, and Pseudepigraphy*, 198–216. Grand Rapids: Eerdmans.

———. 2019. "Pseudepigrapha between Judaism and Christianity: The Case of Third Baruch." In *The Old Testament Pseudepigrapha: Fifty Years of the Pseudepigrapha Section at the SBL*, edited by Matthias Henze and Liv Ingeborg Lied, 309–30. Atlanta: SBL Press.

Henze, Matthias. 2011. *Jewish Apocalypticism in Late First Century Israel*. TSAJ 142. Tübingen: Mohr Siebeck.

Himmelfarb, Martha. 1993. *Ascent to Heaven in Jewish and Christian Apocalypses*. New York: Oxford University Press.

Newsom, Carol A. 2014. *Daniel: A Commentary*. With Brennan W. Breed. Old Testament Library. Louisville: Westminster John Knox.

Nickelsburg, G. W. E. 2001. *1 Enoch 1*. Hermeneia. Minneapolis: Fortress.

———. 2006. *Resurrection, Immortality, and Eternal Life in Intertestamental Judaism*. 2nd ed. Cambridge, MA: Harvard University Press.

Nickelsburg, G. W. E., and James C. VanderKam. 2012. *1 Enoch 2: A Commentary on the Book of 1 Enoch 37–82*. Hermeneia. Minneapolis: Fortress.

Stone, Michael E. 1990. *Fourth Ezra: A Commentary on the Book of Fourth Ezra*. Hermeneia. Minneapolis: Fortress.

4

Greek and Roman Philosophical Schools

Te-Li Lau

Ancient Greek and Roman philosophy is different from modern philosophy. Pre-Socratic philosophers, such as Thales (ca. 6th c. BCE), were essentially cosmologists who tried to give an account of the universe. Socrates, the teacher of Plato and the primary character of the Platonic dialogues, however, shifted the focus of philosophy from the study of the natural world to that of human nature. Ancient philosophy served to equip students with the intellectual foundation and motivation to become good people and to live flourishing human lives. It was seen not so much as an abstract or theoretical system of thought as a way of life (Hadot 2002; Cooper 2012, 1–23). Xenocrates, a student of Plato, later divided philosophy into three main parts: (1) physics (including metaphysics, theology, biology, psychology, and cosmology), (2) ethics (including politics), and (3) logic (including epistemology and rhetoric). Such a division may appear strange to us today, for the modern distinction between philosophy and science was unknown to ancient philosophers. As a way of life, ancient philosophy draws on and inter-

connects its three parts. Indeed, the ethics of a philosophical school cannot be fully comprehended without also paying attention to its underpinning logic and physics. The three parts are inextricably linked (Long 1986, 118–21).

At the end of the fourth century BCE, philosophical activity was centered in Athens in the four schools founded by Plato (the Academy), Aristotle (the Lyceum), Epicurus (the Garden), and Zeno (the Stoa). In the late second and early first century BCE, the philosophical center of gravity shifted to other places, such as Alexandria, Rome, and Rhodes. By the time Athens fell to the Roman general Sulla in 86 BCE, many philosophers had already left and taken their libraries with them. This resulted in the decentralization and proliferation of small philosophical groups scattered throughout the Greco-Roman world. Lacking the dynamic dialectical interaction of the schools' original Athenian environment, these groups studied the written texts of their founders and wrote commentaries on them (Sedley 2003).

Apart from the four philosophical schools, there were two other movements: Skepticism

25

and Cynicism. These movements had no formal dogma or institutional organization, but they presented alternate ways of life (Hadot 2002, 101). In the following, I briefly describe the above four schools and two movements. I conclude with a short discussion about the relevance of ancient philosophy to the study of the New Testament.

Plato and the Academy

Plato (ca. 429–347 BCE) established his school, the Academy, in Athens. After his death, the Academy was led by various successors and passed through four main periods. The first is the Old Academy (347–267 BCE). Its leaders were Speusippus, Xenocrates, Polemon, and Crates. The codification of Plato's thought into a formal system began with Xenocrates. He was probably also responsible for the definitive edition of Plato's works. In metaphysics, the school's distinctive thought was to posit a pair of supreme principles, the Monad and the Indefinite Dyad, whose interactions produce the entire cosmos. In ethics, the school maintained that the goal of human life is to live according to nature—that is, to enjoy the gifts of nature amid a life of virtue (Dillon 2003, 27, 142, 162–63). Bodily and external goods are essential, but they are subordinated to the pursuit and exercise of virtue.

The second period is the New Academy (267–80 BCE). This period, heavily influenced by Skepticism, began when Arcesilaus assumed leadership. In response to the dogmatism of Stoic epistemology, he argued that certainty of knowledge was not possible (*akatalēpsia*); the only tenable position was to withhold assent (*epochē*) and not form any beliefs. Later scholars of the New Academy mitigated this strict Skepticism. In response to Stoic counterarguments that Skepticism rendered rational action or inquiry impossible, Carneades allowed for the possibility of various degrees of probable impressions that could serve as the foundation of rational action and theoretical inquiry. The Skepticism of the New Academy was ultimately undermined by the last scholarch (head of a school), Philo of Larissa.

The third period is Middle Platonism (80 BCE–250 CE). It began with Antiochus of Ascalon and ended with the emergence of Neoplatonism under Plotinus. Although Antiochus first espoused Skepticism, he subsequently broke with his teacher Philo of Larissa. He reinvigorated the dogmatism of Plato and augmented it with Stoic and Aristotelian thought, thereby inaugurating the period of synthesis known as Middle Platonism. There was no monolithic Middle Platonist movement (Dillon 1996, 423). Some (Eudorus, Albinus, and Atticus) were anti-Aristotelian and partial to Stoicism; others (Plutarch, Alcinous, and Galen) were anti-Stoic and partial to Aristotelianism. Nonetheless, several dominant themes stand out. First, Plato is the final and ultimate authority. Other philosophers might be consulted but only to illuminate Plato's teaching. Second, the Platonic dialogues form a coherent unity; the differences and apparent inconsistencies within them can and should be reconciled. Third, the supreme good of humanity and the goal of moral progress is to "become like God, so far as this is possible" (Plato, *Theaet.* 176b [trans. Fowler 1921, 129]). Fourth, over against the materialistic assumptions of the other major Hellenistic schools, there exists an incorporeal and transcendent God, and an immaterial world that stands as the paradigm for the material world.

The fourth period is Neoplatonism (3rd to 5th c. CE). It began with Plotinus and was continued by other significant leaders, such as Porphyry, Iamblichus, and Proclus. Despite the diversity of thought, there are some core principles (Dillon and Gerson 2004, xvii–xxii). First, the sensible world is distinct from the intelligible world; that which is available to our senses is distinct from that available to our intellect. Second, the intelligible world is hierarchical, such that the simple is prior to the complex. Third, the philosophies of Aristotle and Plato do not fundamentally conflict, for Aristotle refers to the sensible and Plato to the intelligible world. Neoplatonism heavily influenced patristic thought. Its official school in Athens was closed by Emperor Justinian in 529 CE.

Aristotle and the Lyceum

Aristotle (384–322 BCE) was born in Stagira. At the age of eighteen, he came to Athens and studied under Plato. He remained there for about twenty years until Plato died. In 343 BCE, King Philip II of Macedon summoned him to be the tutor for his son Alexander (the Great). After Alexander succeeded to the throne in 336 BCE, Aristotle returned to Athens. He opened his school in a rented gymnasium dedicated to Apollo Lyceus, from which the school derived the name of Lyceum. According to tradition, Aristotle taught while walking in a garden. Hence, the school was also known as Peripatos (Greek for walkway) and his followers as Peripatetics. When Alexander the Great died in 323 BCE, Aristotle left Athens due to the rise of anti-Macedonian sentiments. He died a few months later in 322 BCE.

Aristotle was a polymath. He wrote on biology, zoology, psychology, astronomy, mathematics, rhetoric, ethics, politics, metaphysics, and law. For example, in the area of physics, he argued that the natural world is eternal and uncreated. Its proper functioning is nonetheless dependent on an Unmoved Mover, which is itself eternal, immaterial, simple (without parts), fully actualized (without unrealized potentialities), and separate (Loux 2003, 179). In the area of ethics, Aristotle considers happiness (the good life) to be a life of rational activity according to virtue. He does not define happiness in relationship to externals. Nonetheless, one's happiness is endangered if certain goods—such as friends, children, and

health—are lacking. In this regard, Aristotle differs from the Stoics, who consider virtue to be sufficient for a happy life.

Aristotle loved Plato and wrote an elegy for him when he died. Nonetheless, he was critical of Plato's ideas even during the latter's lifetime (Shields 2008). For example, Plato held that the ultimate reality, upon which the reality of everything else is dependent, comprises eternal and changeless essences called Forms or Ideas. Aristotle, however, rejected this concept. He argued that Platonic Forms could not explain change since they are causally inert. In a more trenchant critique, he said that "the Forms may be dismissed—they are mere prattle; and even if they exist, they are irrelevant" (*An. post.* 83a34–35 [trans. Tredennick 1960, 121]). Aristotle's critique of Plato and defection from the Academy led some ancients to consider him to be the foal who kicked its mother. It may, however, be better to say that his critique was a fine example of how philosophy should be practiced in its dialectical form. Aristotle was a pupil of Plato, but he did not limit himself to preserving his teacher's doctrine. He instead sought to go beyond it in the spirit of his teacher. In this way, "Aristotle was Plato's most genuine disciple" (Diogenes Laertius, *Vit. phil.* 5.1 [trans. Hicks 1972, 445]).

When Aristotle died, the Lyceum under the leadership of Theophrastus remained a center of philosophical and scientific inquiry. The school, however, declined after Theophrastus and remained in the shadow of the Stoics, Epicureans, and Academics during the Hellenistic period. Moreover, most of Aristotle's works appear to have fallen out of circulation. The conquest of Athens by Sulla, however, proved to be beneficial to the Peripatetics, for the booty that the general took back to Rome included a library containing many of Aristotle's unpublished works. From this library, Andronicus of Rhodes in the middle of the first century BCE edited and released a systematic edition of Aristotle's works. He thus shaped and contributed to the rebirth of Aristotle's thought (Reale 1990, 15).

Within the Roman imperial period, Peripatetic scholars wrote commentaries on Aristotle's work. Foremost among these commentators was Alexander of Aphrodisias. He was appointed to a chair in philosophy, but it is uncertain whether it was one of the four chairs of philosophy that was established at Athens by Emperor Marcus Aurelius in 176 CE.

Epicurus and the Garden

Epicurus (341–270 BCE) was born in Samos. After moving to Athens around 306 BCE, he bought a house that included a garden, which became the meeting place and name for his school. The term "school" can be misleading for the Epicureans. It was not so much a formal institution as a community of like-minded philosophers who came together to live simply, unencumbered by the politics of city life. Communal life was marked by mutual friendship, goodwill, and frank speech between teachers and students. The school was also known for admitting women and slaves.

Epicurus was a prolific writer, having written more than three hundred books. Most of his writings are lost, but we do have several of his letters and portions of his major work, the collection of thirty-seven books *On Nature*. We also have a collection of his maxims (*Key Doctrines*), of which the first four are condensed as the "Fourfold Cure": (1) Don't fear the gods; (2) don't worry about death; (3) what is good is easy to get; and (4) what is terrible is easy to endure.

Epicurus considered the goal of human life to be the pursuit of pleasure, but pleasure rightly understood. He repudiated the immediate pleasures of a dissolute life that desires luxurious eating and sensual indulgences but recommended a stable or long-term pleasure that results from a body that is untroubled by physical suffering and a mind that is free from mental anguish. Epicurus therefore practiced a simple and frugal life. Moreover, he preached the importance of freeing ourselves from the fear of death or the afterlife, arguing that we cease to exist when we die. We also do not need to fear the gods, for they are unconcerned about human life and have no effect on the world or its people.

Two later noteworthy Epicureans are Philodemus and Lucretius. Philodemus (ca. 110–30 BCE) studied in the Epicurean school in Athens before moving to Italy. History knew him first as a poet until a library of philosophical texts that laid buried in the ruins of a villa in Herculaneum (now called the Villa of the Papyri), due to the eruption of Vesuvius in 79 CE, was discovered in the eighteenth century. Many of these texts were written by Philodemus. His writings and their contribution include the following: *On Frank Criticism* helps us understand the relational dynamics and structure of the Epicurean community; *On Anger* is the only substantial Epicurean treatise on an emotion; *On Piety* is an Epicurean defense against charges of atheism; and *On the Gods* rebuts divine providence and denies divine intervention in this world.

Lucretius (ca. 95–50 BCE) was a Roman Epicurean poet. His work *On the Nature of Things* is a poetic rendering of Epicurus's *On Nature*. Through his literary genius, he transformed Epicurus's dry prose into a hexameter poem. Since Epicurus's *On Nature* is fragmentary, Lucretius's *On the Nature of Things* is our primary source for understanding Epicurean physics. Lucretius's influence is extensive and his work was admired, not least by Virgil.

Zeno and the Stoa

The Stoa's history and teaching (Stoicism) can be divided into three periods: early, middle, and Roman.

Early Stoicism

Zeno of Citium (335–263 BCE) founded Stoicism. He began his philosophical training under the Cynic Crates and the Megarian Stilpo. He also attended the Academy, listening to Xenocrates and Polemo. Out of these philosophical influences, Zeno forged his own distinctive position and began teaching in a public place in Athens, the Painted Porch (*Stoa poikilē*). Stoicism derived its name from the place of teaching, as did many other philosophical schools. Zeno was succeeded by Cleanthes (331–232 BCE). He was not a creative thinker, but he did add a religious element to Stoic thought, as witnessed in his poem *Hymn to Zeus* (Thom 2005). Cleanthes was then succeeded by Chrysippus (ca. 280–207 BCE), who became the principal architect of Stoic thought such that it was said, "If there was no Chrysippus, there would have been no Stoa" (Diogenes Laertius, *Vit. phil.* 7.183 [my translation]).

Some brief remarks about the philosophical doctrines of early Stoicism are in order. In logic, especially epistemology, early Stoics affirmed that humans have the basis for true knowledge in cognitive impressions. Generally, an impression is the appearance of things as they strike us via the senses. Our reason evaluates this impression according to our beliefs, determining whether it is true or false. If we consider it to be true, we assent to the impression; if false, we reject it. Needless to say, our judgment can be flawed. Stoicism, however, also holds that there is one class of impressions (cognitive impression), which not only accurately portrays the object from which it came but does so with self-evident clarity. In assenting to such unmistakably trustworthy impressions, we grasp true knowledge.

In physics, early Stoics held to a never-ending cycle of cosmic conflagration and regeneration. The universe began with the existence of a creative fire that is sometimes identified as Zeus or god. This cosmic fire eventually condenses into a cosmogonic liquid that further transforms into air and earth, out of which develops the world in all its variety. Such a world is, however, unstable; the entire cosmos eventually bursts into flames and returns to its starting point. At this point, the entire process begins again.

In ethics, the goal of human life is to live in agreement with nature or, more specifically, to select rationally the things that accord with both cosmic and human nature. Central to achieving this goal is the therapy of one's passions. Stoics consider passions to be impulses of the soul caused by faulty judgments of a confused mind. Consequently, passions can be eliminated by correcting our false beliefs about what is good or bad. Stoicism takes a different approach than Platonism or Aristotelianism regarding the therapy of passions. Instead of moderating the passions, Stoics call for the complete extirpation (*apatheia*) of the passions. In other words, the truly wise person (the sage) will be free of passions.

Middle Stoicism

There were several scholarchs after Chrysippus, but Stoicism took a turn with Panaetius (ca. 185–109 BCE) and Posidonius (ca. 135–51 BCE). Faced with criticisms from the turn toward Skepticism within the Academy, Panaetius and Posidonius brought Platonic and Aristotelian tendencies into Stoicism. This syncretism is a hallmark of middle Stoicism. For example, Panaetius denied the periodic conflagration of the world held by earlier Stoics and instead advocated Aristotle's doctrine concerning the eternity of the world.

Roman Stoicism

Stoicism during the Roman imperial period was not centralized at an institutional school. It was a diverse movement, comprising many teachers who promoted Stoic thought.

Although a generalization, most of them emphasized practical ethics rather than logic or physics. The more notable Stoics and their significance include the following:

1. Arius Didymus was a moral adviser to Caesar Augustus. His consolation to Augustus's wife Livia on the death of their son Drusus was considered a fine example of Stoic therapy.

2. Seneca the Younger, the tutor and adviser to Emperor Nero, wrote many essays and letters that show how one should live a happy and moral life.

3. Musonius Rufus lived such an ethical life that some modern scholars consider him to be the Roman Socrates (Lutz 1947). He stressed the importance of women and family life, encouraging women to study philosophy and exhorting people to have large families rather than practice infanticide.

4. The ex-slave Epictetus reminded his listeners that their happiness was fundamentally up to them, dependent not on external circumstances but on their desires, goals, and responses to such circumstances.

5. The emperor Marcus Aurelius admired the teachings of Epictetus. In his *Meditations*, he recorded a set of Stoic doctrines by which he would live.

Skepticism

I mentioned the Skeptical tendencies of the New Academy above. Skepticism, however, began with Pyrrho (ca. 365–275 BCE). We know nothing of Pyrrho except that which comes down to us from his pupil Timon. In a highly debatable text, he said that Pyrrho considered the things of this world to be equally indifferent, unstable, and unresolved. Consequently, our sensations and opinions about them are neither true nor false. There is nothing honorable or shameful, nothing just or unjust, and nothing that is more this than that. We should therefore not be opinionated, but we should withhold judgment on all matters. While some might claim that it is impossible to live a life that is devoid of beliefs, Pyrrho contends that those who do will experience tranquility and be free from disturbance (*ataraxia*).

The Skepticism of the New Academy (Arcesilaus and Carneades) is similar to that of Pyrrho. Nonetheless, there are differences. Arcesilaus diverged from Pyrrho by not linking the suspension of judgment to tranquility. His Skepticism began as a refutation of Stoic adversaries, and he never considered his philosophical method as a way to attain happiness. Carneades's Skepticism was more moderate than that of Pyrrho. Instead of suspending all opinions, Carneades allowed for the possibility of well-grounded opinions as long as these opinions were not considered to be true knowledge.

When the Academy returned to dogmatism in Middle Platonism, Academics who were still convinced of the validity of the Skeptical position left the Academy and revived the original Skepticism held by Pyrrho. Chief among them was Aenesidemus (1st c. BCE), whose monumental contribution was his Ten Modes (ten reasons why you can never know things as they truly are). He began a new phase of Skepticism known as neo-Pyrrhonism. Another influential Skeptic in this period is Sextus Empiricus (ca. 160–210 CE). Our knowledge of Skepticism depends heavily on his writings, especially his *Outlines of Pyrrhonism*.

Cynicism

Cynicism began with Diogenes of Sinope (ca. 412–324 BCE). He was known as Diogenes the Dog (the Greek word for dog is *kyōn*, from which we get the name Cynic) because of his doggish or shameless behavior in public.

He valued freedom and flouted social conventions; any natural act (defecation, sex) was not indecent, even if it was done in public. He loved to pour scorn on his contemporaries, and his biting wit gave rise to many anecdotes. For example, it was said that when Diogenes was sunning himself, Alexander the Great stood over him and asked what favor he would like to receive. Diogenes replied, "Stand out of my light" (Diogenes Laertius, *Vit. phil.* 6.38 [trans. Hicks 1931, 41]). When a eunuch of bad character inscribed on his door the words "Let no evil enter," Diogenes asked how the master was then able to get in (6.39 [my translation]).

Diogenes did not establish a school. He did, however, have several disciples, of which the most prominent was Crates (ca. 365–285 BCE). Some of the characteristics of Cynics are as follows: They led a countercultural life; they ridiculed good birth and fame; they kept their basic needs to a minimum; they considered themselves citizens of the world rather than citizens of a particular city; and they valued self-sufficiency, self-control, indifference, and freedom of speech. Their typical attire was a begging bag, a threadbare cloak, and a staff. They did not devote themselves to the study of logic or physics but focused solely on ethics. Some of them had no formal education. Thus, many questioned whether Cynicism was really a philosophy or just a way of life (Diogenes Laertius, *Vit. phil.* 6.103).

Cynicism declined in the second century BCE. It revived in the Roman imperial period, but it was marked with significant diversity. There were austere and mild versions of Cynicism. Moreover, some philosophers merged Cynicism with other philosophical traditions. For example, Dio Chrysostom frequently used Diogenes as a model, and his discourses on kingship carry many Cynic features. He led the lifestyle of a Cynic, but he was certainly also influenced by Stoic and Platonic thought.

Conclusion

The information in this essay may appear technical and esoteric, but it is essential for studying the New Testament in at least two ways.

First, it equips us to discern how New Testament authors adopted and adapted popular philosophical arguments as they sought to persuade Hellenized Jews and Gentiles that the gospel, rather than the philosophical teachings of the various schools (Col. 2:8), represents the authentic way to live life before the one true God. For example, scholars note that Paul's rhetorical, pedagogical, and ethical strategies are similar to those of his philosophic contemporaries (Malherbe 1989; Allison 2020). This is not surprising since the author of Acts notes that Paul debated Epicurean and Stoic philosophers before the Areopagus in Athens (Acts 17:16–34). Still others observe that the New Testament uses some of the same terminology that is current in the philosophical schools: Spirit, *Logos*, freedom of speech, conscience, virtue, self-sufficiency, and self-control (Engberg-Pedersen 2017).

Second, it enables us to understand how New Testament figures and teachings might have been perceived by their contemporaries. For example, some scholars postulate that ordinary townspeople would have seen Jesus as a Cynic teacher, given the parallels between his teaching and Cynicism (Seeley 1997; Downing 2001).

In summary, knowledge of the ancient philosophical schools provides a window into the New Testament world, allowing us to understand the New Testament more clearly and fully (Sterling 1997).

Works Cited

Allison, Justin Reid. 2020. *Saving One Another: Philodemus and Paul on Moral Formation in Community.* Ancient Philosophy and Religion 3. Leiden: Brill.

Cooper, John M. 2012. *Pursuits of Wisdom: Six Ways of Life in Ancient Philosophy from Socrates to Plotinus.* Princeton: Princeton University Press.

Dillon, John M. 1996. *The Middle Platonists: 80 BC to AD 220*. Rev. ed. Ithaca, NY: Cornell University Press.

———. 2003. *The Heirs of Plato: A Study of the Old Academy (347–274 BC)*. Oxford: Clarendon.

Dillon, John M., and Lloyd P. Gerson. 2004. *Neoplatonic Philosophy: Introductory Readings*. Indianapolis: Hackett.

Downing, F. Gerald. 2001. "The Jewish Cynic Jesus." In *Jesus, Mark and Q: The Teaching of Jesus and Its Earliest Records*, edited by Michael Labahn and Andreas Schmidt, 184–214. JSNTSup 214. Sheffield: Sheffield Academic.

Engberg-Pedersen, Troels. 2017. *John and Philosophy: A New Reading of the Fourth Gospel*. Oxford: Oxford University Press.

Fowler, Harold North, trans. 1921. *Plato: Theaetetus, Sophist*. LCL 123. Cambridge, MA: Harvard University Press.

Hadot, Pierre. 2002. *What Is Ancient Philosophy?* Translated by Michael Chase. Cambridge, MA: Harvard University Press.

Hicks, R. D., trans. 1931. *Diogenes Laertius: Lives of Eminent Philosophers*. Vol. 2. LCL 185. Cambridge, MA: Harvard University Press. Originally published 1925.

———, trans. 1972. *Diogenes Laertius: Lives of Eminent Philosophers*. Vol. 1. LCL 184. Cambridge, MA: Harvard University Press. Originally published 1925.

Long, A. A. 1986. *Hellenistic Philosophy: Stoics, Epicureans, Sceptics*. 2nd ed. Berkeley: University of California Press.

Loux, Michael. 2003. "Aristotle: Metaphysics." In *The Blackwell Guide to Ancient Philosophy*, edited by Christopher Shields, 163–83. Malden, MA: Blackwell.

Lutz, Cora E. 1947. "Musonius Rufus: 'The Roman Socrates.'" *YCS* 10: 3–147.

Malherbe, Abraham J. 1989. *Paul and the Popular Philosophers*. Minneapolis: Fortress.

Reale, Giovanni. 1990. *The Schools of the Imperial Age*. Translated by John R. Catan. Albany: SUNY Press.

Sedley, David. 2003. "Philodemus and the Decentralisation of Philosophy." *Cronache Ercolanesi* 33: 31–41.

Seeley, David. 1997. "Jesus and the Cynics Revisited." *JBL* 116, no. 4: 713–19.

Shields, Christopher. 2008. "Plato and Aristotle in the Academy." In *The Oxford Handbook of Plato*, edited by Gail Fine, 645–68. Oxford: Oxford University Press.

Sterling, Gregory E. 1997. "Hellenistic Philosophy and the New Testament." In *Handbook to Exegesis of the New Testament*, edited by Stanley E. Porter, 313–58. New Testament Tools and Studies 25. Leiden: Brill.

Thom, Johan C. 2005. *Cleanthes' "Hymn to Zeus": Text, Translation, and Commentary*. STAC 33. Tübingen: Mohr Siebeck.

Tredennick, Hugh, ed. and trans. 1960. *Aristotle: Posterior Analytics*. LCL 391. Cambridge, MA: Harvard University Press.

SECTION II

Places

5

Jerusalem, Judean Uprising, Temple Destruction

STEVE MASON

The war between Judeans and Romans in 66 to 70 CE was a pivotal moment for Roman, Jewish, and Christian history. In Rome, it gave Vespasian and his son Titus, who had overseen the destruction of Jerusalem and its temple, needed justification for their violent removal of the current emperor, Vitellius. Their coup would, however, stabilize Roman governance for a century.

For Judeans, Jerusalem's destruction was a massive trauma. The temple, which had survived earlier destruction and desecration, anchored the worldwide Judean (Jewish) people. In both the Roman and Parthian empires, expatriate Judeans would send annual sums to support the routines of daily sacrifice prescribed in Moses's Torah. When possible, they would visit the temple for major festivals. With the sanctuary and great altar now destroyed, and hopes of rebuilding them faint, Judeans everywhere not only lost a primary source of identity and respect from others. The community also had to find new ways of honoring the Torah's prescriptions without animal sacrifice.

As for the rapidly growing groups of Christ followers, the Gentile majority always had difficulty explaining their relationship to Judeans. Why did they revere the Judean Jesus and yet not follow Judean law as he had done? When the temple was destroyed, forty years after Jesus's crucifixion, many Christians seized on the event as alleged proof of the end of the Torah period and the transfer of divine favor from Judeans to themselves. This justified, so they thought, the use of Judean Scripture only insofar as it pointed to Christ, without any need to follow its prescriptions in daily life.

The chasm between these last two responses to Jerusalem's fall—Christians claiming the Judean heritage even as Judeans continued to flourish while observing Moses's laws—would poison Jewish-Christian relations until recent times. Relatively few people during the intervening centuries, however, had the interest or opportunity to explore the war's real-life causes and course. Historical investigation works against any simple scheme, whether theological (e.g., "the Jews killed Christ") or political ("the Jews opposed Rome"). This essay can probe only four basic questions: (1) How did Jerusalem fare in the Roman world before 66 CE? (2) What factors contributed to the war's outbreak at that time? (3) How did the conflict take shape? (4) Who were the leading groups and personalities involved?

Before we proceed, a word about sources and methods is needed. The only contemporary account we have is Flavius Josephus's *Jewish War* (70s CE), a complex narrative that resists reduction to a single proposition. Ever more numerous archaeological finds, at locations from Jerusalem to Galilee and the desert fortresses, along with brief passages in Tacitus (*Hist.* 5.1–13), Suetonius (*Lives* of Vespasian and Titus), and Cassius Dio (*Hist. Rom.* 63–65), supplement Josephus's narrative spine. Historians must seek to understand each kind of evidence for itself (its aims, biases, and limitations) and then conjure up hypotheses about the underlying events that would explain how this evidence came to be.

Historians have taken three main approaches to this task. Social-scientific (including economic, sociological, and political) history works with models of human behavior drawn from similar situations, such as "resistance to empire" (Cline and Graham 2011; Rajak 2002, 104–43). In this kind of analysis, particular events and actors fade to the margins. Intellectual historians, by contrast, look for underlying ideas, mentalities, or ideologies, such as Jewish ideas of chosenness and covenant (Hadas-Lebel 2006; Rudich 2015; Berthelot 2021). Event-oriented historians, finally, begin with each known incident and ask about its particular context (Price 1992; McLaren 1998; Goodman 2007). Who was involved, and what were their motives? Needless to say, these approaches produce different pictures of the war against Rome. This essay takes the last road, seeking to answer the four questions mentioned above.

Jerusalem before the War

Social-scientific and intellectual history converge in supporting the most widespread perception of the war's causes: "In their native land, and especially in Jerusalem, the yoke of the Romans weighed heavily on the Judaeans, and became daily more oppressive" (Graetz 1949, 2:233). According to this view, war erupted when long-building tensions finally popped the cork, when Judea could bear Rome's alleged humiliations no more. Studying particular events of the period, however, yields a different picture.

Jerusalem, with its highland hinterland of Judea, was one of many cities in the southern half of the Roman province of Syria. Along the coast were Gaza, Ashkelon, Azotus, Jamnia, Joppa, Caesarea, Ptolemais, and Berytus; inland were Sebaste, Scythopolis, Hippos, Gadara, and Gerasa, among others. Some of these cities were thousands of years older than Jerusalem. Each had its own calendar, customs, and gods. Several hosted Judean minorities, living peacefully with the citizen majority. According to Josephus, before the explosion of tensions in 66 CE, "Our city, of all those under the Romans, managed to achieve the greatest prosperity" (*J.W.* 1.11). Why would he say that?

First, the Romans gave Jerusalem regional power, which they never thought of giving any other city. This was not for sentimental reasons but from sound strategy. Before the Roman general Pompey the Great annexed Judea to the Roman Empire in 63 BCE, the Judean priestly Hasmonean family had vastly expanded Jerusalem's territory by conquest, to include most of southern Syria. Pompey removed these acquisitions from Jerusalem's control, restoring self-governance to Judea's neighbors and winning their lasting gratitude.

Within two decades, however, the Judean-Idumean family of Herod the Great impressed a series of Roman commanders by their adaptability, loyalty, and effectiveness. Romans preferred to leave a trusted strongman in control of the region, not least as a bulwark against Parthia's incursions from the east, than to deal with the aristocracies of two dozen cities. So they made Herod a regional king (40 BCE), soon extending his realm over all of southern Syria. It took him three years to secure his throne in Jerusalem against Parthian-backed competitors. But once in power, he became Rome's capable ally for thirty-four years. He and his Roman sponsors groomed his sons as his successors. When he died (4 BCE), however, none of his surviving sons was mature enough to take over, and so the emperor Augustus divided Herod's kingdom three ways. Two sons (Philip and Antipas) ruled even longer than their father had, in Galilee and east of the Jordan River. But Archelaus, granted control over the Judean heartland, was removed in 6 CE after alienating his two main constituencies: elites in both Jerusalem and its longtime rival Samaria to the north.

Rome never abandoned its preference to keep southern Syria under a monarch in Jerusalem. Thus the emperor Claudius, after Herod's grandson Agrippa had helped him become emperor in Rome (41 CE), placed him on Jerusalem's throne with a kingdom the size of Herod's. Claudius would have liked the fifty-year-old to rule for at least a decade, until his son (Agrippa II) could succeed him. But Agrippa I died after just three years (44 CE). Since his son was only sixteen, Claudius resorted to the plan B, so to speak, that Augustus had used when he could find no monarch to trust with regional rule. When no Judean was available, the Romans did not turn to Samaria, Ashkelon, or Scythopolis for a ruler but, rather, sent their own man, of equestrian rank, to hold the fort from coastal Caesarea (6–41 and 44–66 CE), while giving Herod's heirs parts of the great king's territory outside Judea proper.

A beautiful city built by Herod on the coast, Caesarea was the best spot for such a Roman official, who would have had difficulty functioning in Jerusalem. Caesarea followed Roman customs. It boasted a temple to Rome and Augustus, along with many statues and entertainment facilities of the Greco-Roman kind. Its position on the north–south highway made for easy communication with the legate in Antioch, and it sported a superb harbor facilitating western contact. But the man holding this position (Pontius Pilate was the most famous incumbent) had a special portfolio of care for inland Judea.

Such a man was needed. Recall that the surrounding peoples and cities had lived for generations under Hasmoneans and then Herodians ruling from Jerusalem. They did not like it. Some, such as proud Gadara, whose dark basalt buildings looked down on the Sea of Galilee from the southeast, repeatedly begged Roman officials to be freed of Judean hegemony. Jerusalem's most consistent antagonist was the region of Samaria. Before the Hasmoneans, Samaria had been the military and administrative stronghold of Hellenistic rulers, and it had opposed Jerusalem's flourishing as a possible rival. After the Hasmonean John Hyrcanus destroyed Samaria's temple on Mount Gerizim, the lethal animosity with Judea left enduring marks on the pages of Josephus, the Gospels, and Tacitus.

Rome's plan B, though it highlighted their preference for Jerusalem, also created serious perils for Judea. When the seat of power shifted to Caesarea, the nature of the region's policing forces changed. The armies of Herod and his successors had included Judeans, Idumeans (who followed Judean law), and Samarians. When headquarters moved to Caesarea, Judeans and Idumeans dropped out of military service, partly because they could not observe the Sabbath or find kosher food under foreign command. When there was no monarch in Jerusalem, consequently, the "auxiliary" force commanded by the prefect in Caesarea consisted of men who had a visceral hatred of Judeans. Syria's four legions of Roman-citizen soldiers were three weeks' march away in the north and were rarely, if ever, seen in Jerusalem.

Occasional incidents, which occurred during those times when Caesarea was the seat of administration, reflected this animosity. Soon after Archelaus's removal (6 CE), for example, Jerusalem's garrison of Samarian soldiers allowed their compatriots to enter Jerusalem and scatter human bones around the temple, wrecking that year's Passover celebration by making the sacred enclosure impure (Josephus, *Ant.* 18.30). Again, when King Agrippa died in 44 CE, the Samarian soldiers erupted in exuberant and disrespectful street celebrations at Jerusalem's loss of power (19.356–59). Less than a decade later, the same soldiers tested the limits of their freedom, under the pliant prefect Cumanus, to abuse and insult Judeans (20.105–24).

Before the 60s, however, the emperor and the legate in Syria consistently protected Jerusalem in such cases. They removed the prefect who had permitted the bones episode and later also Cumanus (Josephus, *Ant.* 18.31; 20.125–36). The emperor Tiberius berated Pilate for offending Judean sensibilities (Philo, *Embassy* 299–306). When Claudius heard of the celebrations at Agrippa's death, he flew into a rage, sent a new prefect to read the riot act, and threatened to station the Samarian auxiliary in a remote province. The following prefect would be a Judean (Tiberius Julius Alexander), and the one who followed Cumanus would marry the Herodian princess Drusilla, great-granddaughter of Herod. The low-value coins produced by prefects in Caesarea, lacking human or animal images, confirm the Roman officials' deference to Judean values (Meshorer 2001, 167–76, with plates 73–76 on pp. 349–52).

In short, we can see why Josephus thought that Jerusalem enjoyed an unmatched status. That arrangement served Rome's interests. Before 66 CE, dangers came not from Rome but from Jerusalem's neighbors, in periods when the Judean capital lost its regional primacy. But

senior Roman officials were quick to stifle any expressions of that hostility.

Factors in the Uprising of 66 CE

The year 66 brought a marked change, even a reversal, in Jerusalem's position. Why? The emperor Nero was the ultimate cause. The distinctive nature and policies of each Roman emperor challenge any tendency to view "Rome" as a static entity. Gaius Caligula (ruled 37–41 CE) brought major changes after Augustus and Tiberius, but he was soon gone. Nero's impact was more profound. He came to power at age sixteen (54 CE) as a result of his mother's conniving. Although he accepted her tutelage until he was twenty-one, he then shed such constraints and had her killed. Nero broke with much imperial precedent, notably in his extended tour of Greece from mid-66 to December 67, where he competed in games and musical contests. He ostentatiously loved Greek culture. Although his wife Poppaea, whom he had killed before the Greek tour, reportedly admired Judean culture (Josephus, *Ant.* 20.195; *Life* 16), Nero showed no such interest.

Already by the time of his mother's death, Nero found his finances in dire straits. His unexpected exactions from the provinces, to meet the crisis, ignited the famous Boudica revolt in Britain (60–61 CE). Making this bad situation worse, the great fire of Rome in 64 CE burned most of the city. Nero wanted to rebuild it while creating a shining monument to himself in his unbelievably lavish Golden House: a massive private park of gardens, ponds, and innovative architecture. He ordered his equestrian governors everywhere to raid temples, to extract sums that had been deposited in them as divinely protected safes (Tacitus, *Ann.* 15.45.1–2).

This was when Nero sent Gessius Florus to Caesarea, with orders to seize funds from Jerusalem's temple. Since this temple was the only one to which Judeans the world over sent annual contributions, whereas most other temples held only local deposits, this temple was unusually wealthy. As muscle for the task, Florus could count on the auxiliary, which kept a rotating garrison in Jerusalem's Antonia Fortress. These soldiers were more than eager to march into the sacred treasury of their enemy, seize plates of gold and silver, and beat or kill any who got in their way. Josephus describes a stunned city in helpless rage as it watched even its distinguished citizens whipped or crucified (*J.W.* 2.293–329).

The big change from earlier times was that this aggression from the auxiliary now came with the emperor's backing. In the past, an emperor and his legate, in consultation with Jerusalem's leaders and Herodian royals, would check such outbreaks, even to the point of punishing a Roman commander. Those checks were now in tatters. The legate in Syria (now the seventy-year-old Cestius Gallus) was helpless to act against Nero's prefect in Caesarea. Nero had become suspicious of the senatorial class, to which Cestius belonged. He was executing senatorial governors or inviting them to kill themselves. The Herodian royals (Agrippa II and Berenice) had likewise lost their accustomed influence with this emperor and could only try to calm the Judean populace.

Jerusalem's populace reacted in the ways one might expect. Some trusted the leaders' counsel to wait and hope for a return to normal, so as to avoid provoking harsher Roman intervention. Some prayed. Some young priests defied their elders and blocked foreigners' access to the temple while halting the daily sacrifices for the emperor's well-being. Others formed armed factions under charismatic leaders to defend themselves against the auxiliary while also challenging each other for primacy. One such group besieged and massacred the auxiliary garrison, after persuading it to lay down its arms. When the legate finally brought a legion

south to restore order, he was barred from the city. As he led his army back north, to prepare a springtime campaign with a greater force, his column was attacked in the steep pass at Beit-Horon and lost many soldiers (*J.W.* 2.408–556). There had to be a reckoning.

The Developing Conflict in 67–70 CE

Jerusalem's leaders knew that their walled city of less than a square mile could never take on Rome's might. But they were in a predicament, with a furiously aggrieved population and unwilling to turn over those who had defended themselves. No one on the Roman side had the authority and willingness to work with them. This is the point at which our narrator Josephus appears. Although he was just thirty, Jerusalem's leaders sent Josephus north to Galilee. He gives conflicting accounts of his mission. In *Jewish War* he postures as a great general and claims that he trained a large defensive force. In his autobiography, a quarter century later, he more plausibly says that he went with two other priests to await the Romans' arrival and in the meantime persuade Galileans not to take up arms (*Life* 28–29). Given his lack of military expertise but rare knowledge of Rome and the Greek language, it seems likely that he went north to negotiate with the legate, whom he would have known, well before the Romans reached Jerusalem.

But the legate did not return. Nero had hit the roof when he heard of Cestius's losses near Jerusalem. He sidelined the old legate and sent Vespasian with a massive army of sixty thousand, anchored by three legions, to do whatever was needed to bring the city to heel. Vespasian was (usually) a crafty enough general to avoid entangling his legions in situations that played to enemy strengths—for example, in the alleyways of foreign cities. Exploiting his advantages, he showed dominance by having his cavalry tear across the plains and burn villages, holding his intimidating ranks of massed infantry in their shining gear for whenever a hard punch was needed. It rarely was.

Before he even arrived in Galilee, all the leaders of Judean and other cities in the region beat a path to Vespasian in Ptolemais, to assure him of their support. Judean Sepphoris, Galilee's main city, sent emissaries to request a large garrison—and forbade its citizens to involve themselves in Jerusalem's issues. Vespasian's only delay in central Galilee was at Iotapata, where he overran the city and arrested Josephus. Even still, his campaign was done by July 1, 67 CE, and he then sent the legions early to winter quarters. In the autumn he recalled them briefly to help his friend Agrippa II, whose lakeside cities resented his recent acquisition of them. Vespasian quickly assaulted the fortress town of Gamla, where Agrippa's more militant enemies had gathered.

We think of a "war" as a sustained conflict between two fighting forces. It is a stretch to call Vespasian's campaign a war in that sense. His target was Jerusalem.

When he moved south to Caesarea's winter quarters, leaders of the region's cities again came quickly to welcome him, including the Judean town of Gadara (not the more famous Gadara), leading city of the Judean territory (Perea) east of the Jordan River. He faced no resistance but continued burning villages as the Judean population surrendered, was killed in flight, or fled toward Jerusalem's walls. He established garrisons at a day's march in every direction from the Judean capital.

When Vespasian thought his preparations complete, he returned to Caesarea to plan his approach to Jerusalem that summer. While there, however, he learned of Nero's suicide in Rome (June of 68 CE). This news required him to put his plans on hold—for nearly two years as it turned out. Since Vespasian's mandate came from Nero, now deceased, he had to wait and see what the new emperor, Galba, wanted. Galba did not reach Rome until October 68. Vespasian then sent Titus to greet

him and receive instructions. But Galba was murdered (January 15, 69) while Titus was en route. Titus returned to consult with his father because two new generals, Otho and Vitellius, were contending to replace Galba. Otho won that contest, but he lasted only three months before Vitellius brought him down.

When Vespasian heard that Vitellius had prevailed, his Judean campaign had already been suspended for a year. Deciding that he would make a better emperor, and confident of having the military backing and prestige (because of success in Judea) to pull off a coup, he began planning to oust Vitellius. He personally would remain in the East until the fighting was over, however, while his generals defeated Vitellius's forces in Italy. He moved to Alexandria and sent Titus to execute his plan with Jerusalem. He must have thought the siege a manageable operation for his thirty-year-old heir. Sixty-year-old Vespasian could thus offer Rome a skilled leader in himself and a lauded general as his ready successor in Titus, thereby avoiding the succession problems that had plagued his predecessors.

So it was that Titus came to besiege Jerusalem in the spring of 70, after three years of little war fighting. Like Vespasian, he followed a cautious approach, hoping for the city's quick submission and gradually increasing the pressure. Those commanding the fighters inside would not capitulate, though many ordinary folks fled when they could. In the end, the siege took the whole fighting season (to early September) of 70, ending with the city and temple in flames. Josephus claims that the temple burned by accident, as far as human intentions went, though in reality by divine plan: to purge the sanctuary of the blood that Judean factions had shed in it.

Groups and Personalities

A major weakness of the view that the war of 66–70 was the cork popping on simmering tensions is that it steamrolls the evidence for different actors with varied motives. We close by picking apart some of that tangle.

The Romans held John of Gischala and Simon bar Giora responsible for the war, seeing the siege of Jerusalem as its main component. But John and Simon hated each other, occupied different parts of the besieged city, and eagerly killed each other's fighters. John, the wealthy strongman of his hometown in northern Galilee, had defended fellow Galileans against their neighbors' raids in 66 CE, but he had no issues with Rome. After Vespasian arrived, he remained hidden in remote Gischala. He fled to Jerusalem only because Titus visited his town in late 67.

Simon was a younger and tougher fighter, from Gerasa, but his targets had reportedly been wealthy Judeans and Idumeans. After John had worked his way to control of Jerusalem, arranging the murder of the chief priests who were thwarting him, terrified Jerusalemites begged Simon to enter the city as the only man capable of removing John. But when Simon proved unable to dislodge John from the temple heights, they were stuck with two domineering figures constantly attacking each other and the unarmed population. Many Jerusalemites who could leave had done so. It is a paradox that neither John nor Simon, whom Vespasian paraded in Rome as the enemy leaders, was from Jerusalem.

Three armed groups other than Simon's and John's followers feature in Josephus. The Latin-named *sicarii* were individuals who engaged in concealed-knife crime against fellow Judeans during the late 50s, stabbing them amid urban crowds. The only groups Josephus calls by this name had nothing to do with fighting Rome. They fled Jerusalem in 66, for Masada or Egypt. The people he calls Zealots were a new group that formed in mid-66, led by dissident priests (under Eleazar ben Simon) and based in the temple. John gradually assumed control of this group, though they sometimes fell out with him.

Idumeans, a quasi-Judean people with a strong martial tradition, are the most complicated players in Josephus's narrative. Steering clear of Jerusalem's problems, they entered the city in arms only when John persuaded them that the leading priests were planning to reach terms with Rome, a historically plausible claim. This led the Idumeans to sweep in and murder those leaders—enabling John to seize power. According to Josephus, they soon left in disgust, feeling that they had been tricked. But a year later they returned with Simon, indeed as the strongest part of his force. When their commanders later tried to reach terms with Titus during the siege, Simon's men killed the Idumean leaders.

Conclusion

In view of its huge impact on Western civilization, the conflict between Jerusalem and Rome seems to have been more of a tragedy than a war between nations. The demand for funds by young emperor Nero upset Rome's long-established arrangements in southern Syria. Jerusalem had uniquely prospered as Rome's ally but now became instantly vulnerable to local enemies who enjoyed unprecedented imperial backing. Jerusalem's understandable responses provoked an insecure emperor to catastrophic consequences.

Works Cited

Berthelot, Katell. 2021. *Jews and Their Roman Rivals: Pagan Rome's Challenge to Israel*. Princeton: Princeton University Press.

Cline, Eric H., and Mark W. Graham. 2011. *Ancient Empires: From Mesopotamia to the Rise of Islam*. Cambridge: Cambridge University Press.

Goodman, Martin. 2007. *Rome and Jerusalem: The Clash of Ancient Civilizations*. London: Allen Lane.

Graetz, Heinrich. 1949. *History of the Jews*. 6 vols. Translated by Bella Löwy and Philipp Bloch. Philadelphia: Jewish Publication Society of America. Originally published 1893.

Hadas-Lebel, Mireille. 2006. *Jerusalem against Rome*. Leuven: Peters.

Mason, Steve. 2016. *A History of the Jewish War, A.D. 66–74*. New York: Cambridge University Press.

McLaren, James S. 1998. *Turbulent Times? Josephus and Scholarship on Judaea in the First Century*. Sheffield: Sheffield Academic Press.

Meshorer, Yaacov. 2001. *A Treasury of Jewish Coins from the Persian Period to Bar Kokhba*. Jerusalem: Yad ben-Zvi.

Price, Jonathan J. 1992. *Jerusalem under Siege: The Collapse of the Jewish State, 66–70 CE*. Leiden: Brill.

Rajak, Tessa. 2002. *Josephus: The Historian and His Society*. London: Duckworth. Originally published 1983.

Rudich, Vasily. 2015. *Religious Dissent in the Roman Empire: Violence in Judaea at the Time of Nero*. London: Routledge.

6

Territories of Roman Palestine

Jürgen K. Zangenberg

The Gospel narratives on the life of Jesus might give the first impression that his world was a "small world" of farms, fields, and villages surrounding a lake dotted with the boats of hard-working fishermen. But this seemingly idyllic environment was part of the much larger, diverse, and dynamic world of Roman Palestine. Right at the beginning of Luke's two-part narrative on God's dealing with his people through Jesus and his apostles, the author draws the events of Jesus's life into the wider framework of Roman *and* Jewish political history (Luke 3:1–2). His focus cascades from imperial authorities (the emperor Tiberius) to provincial authorities (the governor Pontius Pilate), including institutions both Roman (emperor, provincial governor cooperating with regional client-rulers) and Jewish (high priests in Jerusalem). Luke was well aware of the delicate balance of power and responsibilities that had formed in the region during the decades before Jesus was born.

A Land with Many Names

"Roman Palestine" is not a New Testament term. Today's historio-geographical term "Palestine" does not exactly equal the territory of the ancient Roman province *Palaestina* or modern political or cultural conceptions of Palestine (Aharoni 1979). The name itself, however, is not alien to the region. As with the term *Iudaea*, *Palaestina* originally referred to the Phoenician-populated coastal strip. Probably derived from Aramaic *pelishta'in*, the Greek term *Palaistinē* was first used by Herodotus for the coastal strip between Lebanon and Egypt (*Hist.* 2.104; 3.91; 4.39; 7.89) and soon referred to the entire region while the older usage for the coastal region also remained in use (Pliny the Elder, *Nat.* 5.66: Syria "had a great many divisions with different names," Palestine being one of them [trans. Rackham 1942, 270–71]). For the Jewish philosopher and politician Philo, *Palaistinē* even connoted the promised land

Canaan (*Good Person* 75), while Josephus emphasizes that Jews lived not only in *Palaistinē* but also in Syria and Egypt (*Ant.* 20.259; Keel, Küchler, and Uehlinger 1984, 277–82). Jewish writers, however, almost unanimously used *Ioudaia* for what we now often call ancient Palestine, not necessarily implying any homogeneity in population but usually expressing notions of an ideal, ancestral homeland (Ben-Eliyahu 2019, 31–58). New Testament authors, if they refer to such political details at all, follow this vein, though Matthew very pointedly joins the political entities *Ioudaia* and *Galilaia* under the theologically charged term "land of Israel," thereby certainly following Jewish usage (Matt. 2:19–23).

When the Romans first began to rule over the territories between greater Syria and Egypt, they did not refer to that region as *Palaestina*. Rather, in continuation of Judean, Persian, and Hellenistic usage, they referred to it as *Iudaea*. Only after the failed and (for Rome) extremely bloody Second Jewish Revolt of 132–135/6 CE did the Romans substitute *Iudaea* as provincial name by the toponym *Palaestina*, very likely to eliminate any connotations between the land and Jews and Judaism. After Emperor Hadrian (who reigned 117–38 CE), this name remained in use despite many later administrative changes and the fundamental change of power from the Byzantines to the Umayyads ("Filastin") in the early seventh century CE.

A Region of Dynamic Change

The region referred to as Roman Palestine was in a state of constant flux, with regular border changes according to shifts in political circumstances and constellations (Jensen 2014). This included frequent change of the region's status between the end of the Seleucid period in the mid-second century BCE and late antiquity—with the region changing from a Seleucid province to an independent kingdom under the early Hasmoneans and further to a

client kingdom after Pompey and, finally, to a Roman province that changed from an administrative subunit of Syria under an equestrian *praefectus* before and to a senatorial province after the First Revolt (not to mention the brief royal intermezzo between 34/41–44 CE under King Agrippa I).

During that process, territories within the region were added or taken away. Larger units were divided up into smaller entities that received new names. The fact that political borders were not permanent did not have much effect (in one sense) on the lives of everyday people, since this was a time when Greek culture and Roman politico-military ambition sought to integrate regional diversities into an eastern Mediterranean medley in which indigenous identities were to exist alongside each other. We therefore see New Testament protagonists move freely from one region to another (e.g., Jesus from Galilee to the Decapolis and to Phoenicia; see Mark 5 and 7), though social status and cultural boundaries may have limited some people's factual mobility.

The beginning of direct Roman influence on this region dates from Pompey's reorganization of the former Seleucid territories in 63 BCE. Jews were not the only ones to have populated the region during this time. Strabo (*Geogr.* 16.2.2) simply considers the regional population as various types of "Syrians" regardless of their religious and cultural affiliation. Indeed, internal differentiation of ethnic peoples is difficult to determine. The use of different languages like Greek or Aramaic does not necessarily mark ethnic differences, and the Greek adjective *ethnikos* does not equal our notion of "ethnic," nor would the ever-changing political borders have had a deep impact on accentuating cultural differences between various population groups. Jesus's "small Galilean world on the lake" might have shown unique features compared to neighboring territories (such as its fundamentally Jewish character) while also sharing many aspects with them, like its social structure and connectedness to urban centers outside Galilee.

Tied into a Wider World

The location of "Palestine" is important in the framework of the ancient Eastern Mediterranean (Sarte 2005). While Palestine was located at the western end of the multicultural Persian Empire at the end of the Iron Age, its significance shifted when Alexander the Great incorporated it into a dynamic and diverse Mediterranean cultural sphere, where it now formed an eastern fringe of the Hellenistic world. This involved a total reversal of the region's orientation compared to the previous Persian Empire. Because of the region's prime location between the Mediterranean in the West and Syro-Arabia in the East, well-established trade routes from Egypt to Mesopotamia ran through it between the time of Alexander and Mohammed, making the region a contact zone par excellence. The fact that ancient Palestine was open to neighboring regions and was frequently traversed by armies as well as merchants provides the constant behind all of the region's minor changes, consolidations, and transformations of identities and ethnicities during these centuries. Those who considered themselves to be members of a distinctively separate culture group were able to do so only on the basis of a commonly shared world of goods, areas, and values. Ancient Palestine, therefore, needs to be seen as a place of connectivity. This may contradict a popular image of Jesus's "small world on the lake," but it is completely in line with Luke's "world historical perspective" in 3:1–2.

Internal Regional Diversity

The Coastal Strip

In terms of its terrain and climate, "Roman Palestine" was very diverse. There are various ways to describe that diversity. We could travel with the rain from west (coastal plain) to east (Transjordanian high plateau) or follow the average elevation and climate from south (low and arid) to north (mountainous and temperate). The main major landmark, the Rift Valley stretching from Syria and Lebanon down into East Africa, divides the Palestinian hill country from north to south into a western and an eastern half. With this natural division in view, my description will start in the west, with the long coastal strip extending from Mount Sinai to Mount Carmel.

At its very southern end, the northern Sinai desert and southern Negev were dominated by Nabateans and their long-distance trade, though the Hasmonean conquest of Gaza in 98 BCE brought large areas of the northern Negev at least under nominal control of the Jerusalem rulers. They must have benefited enormously by cashing in on the incense trade with Arabia. When the Romans established direct influence with Pompey's reorganization of the East and his settling of the internal rivalry in Jerusalem in 63 BCE, this sensitive area between the Mediterranean coast, the eastern bank of the Nile, and the central Palestinian land bridge became of strategic importance and consequently needed to be quiet and stable, forcing Judeans and Nabateans to overcome their traditional rivalries and obey the watchful eyes of Rome. With the end of the Roman Civil War and Augustus's rise to power, King Herod the Great and his house were responsible for regional stability to the west, while his Nabatean cousins were responsible to ensure the stability for most of the territories into the southeast of the Rift Valley.

The southern coastal strip had for centuries developed a distinctive cultural profile—being Mediterranean, cosmopolitan, and seaward oriented. Since the end of the Bronze Age, the coastal strip combining the Sharon and Shefelah plains had been settled by Philistines to the south and Phoenicians to the north, a distinction that became ever less important as time

Fig. 6.1. Map of Roman Palestine at the time of Jesus of Nazareth, ca. 15 CE

moved toward the late Iron Age and Hellenistic period. In New Testament times, this coastal strip continued to have a very colorful religious and cultural environment (as seen in the story about Philip's encounter with the Ethiopian official; Acts 8:26–40). Large, economically powerful, and culturally thriving coastal cities such as Gaza, Ashkelon, Dor, and Ptolemais/Acco had more connections overland with the Arabian Peninsula and oversea with Cyprus or the southern Asia Minor coast than with the hill country just a few miles inland. This Phoenician belt of harbor cities (using natural pockets in a coast not easily navigable) can easily be followed up beyond the Carmel and Rosh Ha-Niqra ridges into today's Lebanon (Tyre, Sidon, Beirut).

While the Hasmoneans, based in Jerusalem and the hill country, conquered the coastal cities (like in 96 BCE Gaza) and forcefully converted their inhabitants to exert control over the epic revenues of their incense trade, the Romans under Pompey were quick to liberate them again from the Hasmonean yoke and declare them "independent." Even Herod, who allegedly came from Ashkelon and was proclaimed king over Judea by the senate in Rome in 40 BCE, would not interfere in their affairs too much, supporting their cultural autonomy. In 20 BCE, he even added his own version of a coastal city in the form of Caesarea in addition to embellishing old ones. Caesarea fundamentally changed the structure of regional history. As the king's residential city second to Jerusalem, it not only boosted the trade and industry of Herod's kingdom but also added a crucial, distinctly Mediterranean component to his realm, balancing its Jerusalem-based "oriental" character. (It is very significant that the baptism of Cornelius by Peter, as described in Acts 10:23b–48, happens just here at Caesarea—a "border crossing" and "door opener" in various respects!) It is no surprise that the Roman governors used Caesarea as their prime residence once

Judea became a province in 6 CE. After 70 the city was promoted to *colonia*, even more efficiently serving as a political, administrative, and economic center and as the gateway to the wider Roman world for central *Palaestina*.

Further in the north, only Ptolemais rivaled Caesarea (although strictly speaking before 70 Ptolemais belonged to Syria, not Judea), especially after Ptolemais had been elevated to *colonia* status under Emperor Claudius in 52 or 54 CE. This step must have had a deep impact on landowners in the Acco Plain and further into Western Galilee, since the inhabitants of a *colonia* (among them likely a lot of veterans) not only were Roman citizens but also received land at the cost of the indigenous population, very likely aggravating the tensions already present shortly before the outbreak of the revolt against Rome in 66 CE. When that happened, Vespasian assembled his expedition army in Ptolemais, from where he started his invasion of rebellious Galilee and Judea, and from where he organized the supply of his huge army until the rebellion was crushed. While for the Romans Ptolemais constituted an essential element of "their" Palestine, the rabbis did not consider the city part of "Eretz Israel" and refrained from burying their dead in it.

The Central Hill Country

Just east of the coastal strip the land becomes more undulating, transforming into the central Palestinian hill country, lower in the south and rising up to eight hundred meters in the center and above twelve hundred meters in Upper Galilee. Traffic usually ran north–south along three possible routes: (1) the coast, (2) the ridge across the hills, or (3) the Rift Valley and the Transjordanian high plain further in the east. In Hellenistic and Roman times, age-old traffic routes continued to be used and were integrated into the transregional traffic network.

Much more difficult was east–west traffic. Few smaller and sometimes steep tracks crossed the central ridge, and transversal valleys were rare. Three older east–west connections were important. One route connected the Mediterranean Sea to Jerusalem and ran across the Rift Valley, ascending up to the eastern plateau via Heshbon. A second route crossed central Samaria from Caesarea by way of Wadi el-Far'ah North and the Rift Valley. The third route, which was the most important and famous one, went through the Jezre'el Valley and connected the coast and the north Transjordanian high plateau by way of Beth She'an. The Romans in particular made sure that troops and supplies could be moved quickly (1) north–south between Syria and Egypt or to the Red Sea ports and back, and (2) east–west between the Mediterranean Sea and the frontier zone facing the desert.

Jerusalem was connected to all of these roads, either directly or indirectly. During the second and first centuries BCE, this ancient royal and religious center had grown into a thriving, Judeo-Hellenized city, serving as the ceremonial and cultural capital for all Jews. A telling symbol of that role was the city's monumental, luxurious, and exotic temple. Not surprisingly, Jerusalem and the temple occupy a central role in the Gospels as a second setting of the Jesus drama, with the events recounted in the Acts of the Apostles repeatedly focusing on the city and its temple. Like anywhere else in the Roman Empire, it was possible to govern Judea effectively only if some sort of *modus vivendi* and political cooperation could be established between Roman authorities and the local population. The recognized representative body of the local Jewish population was the Sanhedrin, the assembly of priestly aristocrats under the leadership of the High Priest. Though certainly not without mutual risk and misunderstandings, the Roman and Jewish leaders were usually able to maintain the necessary political balance to help move

things along in the province and surrounding regions. If, however, mutual mistrust, incompetence, and ignorance won the upper hand, even the smallest spark could ignite the situation, with catastrophe being near—as the outbreak of the Jewish War in 66 CE shows. In the end, however, "Roman Palestine" to a very large extent was "Jewish Palestine" under Roman rule.

The southern half of the central ridge between Be'er Sheba and just north of Jerusalem had for centuries been inhabited by Judeans, while the northern part up to the Jezre'el Valley was populated by Samaritans, with their political and later cultic center at Mount Gerizim and non-Jahwistic Samaritans centering on Samaria / Herodian Sebaste. This central Palestinian mountain ridge falls into numerous smaller valleys and local plains that have been intensively used for small-scale farming and became densely populated with an increasing number of villages, towns, and cities—a situation that peaked from the first century BCE/CE to the fourth century CE.

Under Herodian and Roman rule, the distinct historical regions of Judea and Samaria became known simply as Judea, being overseen as of 6 CE by an equestrian *praefectus* under the suzerainty of the *Legatus Augusti* of Syria. The Romans took great interest in the fertile region. In 73 CE, they protected the strategically important point of passage called Flavia Neapolis (between Mount Gerizim and Mount Ebal, close to Shekhem) by means of a colony of Roman veterans.

The Jezre'el Valley

The large and extremely fertile Jezre'el Valley had for centuries been densely inhabited and used as an east–west thoroughfare between the Carmel Ridge along the northern edge of Judea and Lower Galilee. Its openness toward the Mediterranean Sea (at Ptolemais) and its access to the Jordan Valley produced a very distinctive cultural profile. Pagan sanctuaries on the Carmel Ridge during the Roman period are likely to have much older predecessors, and large Iron Age cities thrived in the Hellenistic, Roman, and Byzantine periods (Beth She'an, Tel Iztabba, Scythopolis). The agricultural plain was very likely used intensively as "royal land" and therefore had a fundamentally different profile than the more traditional village-structured economy both in Galilee and in Samaria/Judea.

Galilee

Galilee ("the circle") of course has always attracted special attention as "Jesus' own country" and "Home of the Rabbis" (Zangenberg 2021, 129–30, 143–45). We still do not know a lot about Galilee's cultural profile in the Persian and early Hellenistic periods. In general, the area seems to have been less densely populated than at other times in its history, whether before or after. In recent years, fortified hillforts from the late Hellenistic period have been excavated (at Khirbet Eikha). These excavations have revealed a material culture profile that clearly connects to the late Iron Age typologies regarding common ware and to typologies of coastal cities regarding fine wares and economy. Scattered finds demonstrate that religious affiliation with Egypt also existed, something typical for Levantine Phoenicians, who combined indigenous Semitic and Egyptian decorative elements. The so-called *emporion* at Tel Anafa in Upper Galilee illustrates how large coastal cities such as Tyre exploited their hinterland in order to extend their green belts and feed their large populations and to trade with the inhabitants further east. Sanctuaries to indigenous gods (Paneion, Dan, Omrit) attest to a lively religious life along much older lines, but the architecture and decor of those sanctuaries also attest to the importance of Hellenistic influence. In Roman times, these holy places were renovated to serve as local sanctuaries with a distinctly Roman veneer

(e.g., the Paneion at Carmel). Goods could be transported from the port city of Ptolemais through northern Lower Galilee toward Lake Tiberias (with its Hellenistic harbor at Magdala), then transported across the lake to supply the large Greco-Semitic cities at Hippos and Gadara and further into Syria beyond that. Galilee and especially the region around the lake, therefore, were sandwiched between population centers along the coast and on the Syrian high plain (Zangenberg 2019).

The apparently still quite rural world of Greco-Semites and Hellenized Phoenicians in the late second century BCE (like, e.g., at Tel Qedesh) was fundamentally transformed by the Hasmonean expansion into the north and the northeast (Perea) around the turn of the second to first centuries BCE. At that point, the prevalent Phoenicio-Semitic Hellenism was replaced by a Judeo-Jerusalemite variant, the area becoming populated by southern colonists, whose material culture carried a distinctly Jewish profile. The Hasmoneans massively invested in renovating existing infrastructure (Magdala) and building new cities (Sepphoris). In the course of the first century BCE, characteristic elements of Jewish material culture (such as square one-room synagogues with stepped benches, *miqwa'ot*, and stone vessels) spread in Galilee in a manner similar to Judea, documenting a strong Jerusalemite affiliation of the majority of inhabitants in the hill country of Upper and Lower Galilee. Quite large Jewish minorities lived in almost all of the larger Galilean cities outside the Hasmonean-controlled territory, thereby relativizing the importance of political borders and creating links between majority and minority environments in Jewish-inhabited Palestine. Until the outbreak of the First Revolt, population growth and social differentiation increased even within the Jewish population, with many Jews speaking Greek (Magdala/Tarichaea) and benefiting economically from Galilee's sandwich position between Syria and the Mediterranean Sea.

Galilee was hit hard by the devastations of the First Revolt (as evident, e.g., at Gamla), and it took a long time before Galilee began to play an important role in the reconstruction of post-70 Judaism—now along the lines of Scripture and synagogue, while the destroyed temple had become an object of pious memory and reflection instead of an active cult place.

Conclusion

While not literally mentioned in the New Testament, the term "Roman Palestine" references the geographical, historical, and sociocultural context for much that goes on within the narratives of the Gospels and Acts. It turns out to have been a region with different regional and local milieus that made it a much more diverse and dynamic area than what we might imagine when looking at only Jesus's "small world." Though predominately but not uniformly Jewish, Roman Palestine was inhabited by various population groups and connected to the wider Mediterranean world. From its geographical origins in Galilee and its strong base in Jerusalem, the earliest Jesus movement quickly found its way from Roman Palestine into the great, multicultural Roman Mediterranean. Luke is completely right when he has Paul defend the Jesus narrative by proudly proclaiming that "all these things did not happen in a corner" (Acts 26:26,

my translation). Luke thus closes a circle that he had started at the beginning of his Gospel in 3:1–2.

Works Cited

Aharoni, Y. 1979. *The Land of the Bible: A Historical Geography*. Edited and translated by A. F. Rainey. Rev. ed. Philadelphia: Westminster.

Ben-Eliyahu, E. 2019. *Identity and Territory: Jewish Perception of Space in Antiquity*. Oakland: University of California Press.

Jensen, M. H. 2014. "The Political History in Galilee from the First Century BCE to the End of the Second Century CE." In *Life, Culture and Society*, edited by. A. Fiensy and J. R. Strange, 51–77. Vol. 1 of *Galilee in the Late Second Temple and Mishnaic Periods*. Minneapolis: Fortress.

Keel, O., M. Küchler, and C. Uehlinger. 1984. *Orte und Landschaften der Bibel: Ein Handbuch und Studienreiseführer zum Heiligen Land*. Vol. 1, *Geographisch-geschichtliche Landeskunde*. Göttingen: Vandenhoeck & Ruprecht.

Rackham, H., trans. 1942. *Pliny: Natural History*. Vol. 2, *Books 3–7*. LCL 352. Cambridge, MA: Harvard University Press.

Sartre, M. 2005. *The Middle East under Rome*. Translated by Catherine Porter and Elizabeth Rawlings. Cambridge, MA: Harvard University Press.

Zangenberg, J. K. 2019. "Anchoring Ancient Galilee at the Lakeshore: Towards Re-conceptionalizing Ancient Galilee as a Mediterranean Environment." *EC* 10: 265–91.

———. 2021. "Walking along the Lakeshore (Mt 4:18): Observations on Jesus the Jew Traveling through a Changing Galilee." In *Early Christianity in Town and Countryside: Proceedings of the Conferences in Essen and Leiden*, edited by M. Tiwald and J. K. Zangenberg, 129–47. Göttingen: Vandenhoeck & Ruprecht.

Urban Centers of the Roman World

JAN RÜGGEMEIER

According to the Gospel of Mark, Jesus never entered a city during his ministry,[1] with the sole exception of Jerusalem, the place of his crucifixion. Mark's readers even get the impression that Jesus intentionally avoided cities (Mark 1:45). Not only does he not enter the Greek cities (*poleis*) of Galilee such as Tiberias, Sepphoris, Magdala, Beth She'an (Scythopolis), or Gadara (all of which are along his way), but he visits only the *vicinity* (*ta horia*) of Tyre (7:24), Sidon (7:31a; cf. 3:8), and the Decapolis (7:31b) and prefers to go to the villages (*eis tas kōmas*) around Caesarea Philippi (8:27).

Luke, by contrast, has Jesus act in an urban setting. In the Third Gospel, the urban landscapes of Capernaum (Luke 4:31), Nain (7:11–12), and Bethsaida (9:10) are emphasized, the cities of Judea (1:39; 2:4, 11) and Samaria (9:52) are brought to the reader's attention, and even Nazareth is staged as a Galilean city (*eis polin tēs Galilaias*: 1:26; cf. 2:4, 39; 4:29). According to this narrative concept, Jesus's parables are given urban flavor and are repeatedly placed in the context of urban symposia (5:29; 7:36–37; 14:1; 19:5–6; cf. Rüggemeier 2016).

How should we explain this apparent shift between Mark and Luke? Without necessarily ascribing greater historical reliability to the Gospel of Mark (since Jesus's avoidance of cities in that Gospel also might be a narrative strategy; cf. Bendemann 2012), we may assume that Luke intends to situate Jesus in an urban setting familiar to him and his readers. "Luke's own world is the city" (Goulder 1968, 53). As a Christian author of the second or third generation (Fitzmyer 1981, 35), Luke may not be able to imagine that the gospel would once have been preached in a rural or "secret place" (Acts 26:26: *ou . . . en gōnia*).[2]

---

1. This article focuses on the establishment of the early Christ movement in the urban centers of the Mediterranean. For a more general introduction to the ancient city, see Flohr 2021 and Zuiderhoek 2017.

2. Unless otherwise indicated, Scripture translations are the author's own.

Early Christian Centers

Luke's urban perspective is hardly surprising, considering the multitude of cities for which Christ groups are attested in the late first century CE. Besides Jerusalem (Acts 1–7; cf. Tiwald 2016) and Damascus (which were the starting points for Paul's mission; Acts 9; 26:20; 2 Cor. 11:32; Gal. 1:17), the New Testament makes direct or indirect reference to several provincial capitals:

> Antioch in Syria (Acts 6:5; 11–14; 15:35; 18:22, 23; cf. Zetterholm 2003)
>
> Paphos in Cyprus (Acts 13; cf. 15:39)
>
> Ephesus in Asia (Acts 18:19–21; 19:1, 8–10; 20:17; cf. Harrison and Welborn 2018; Tellbe 2009; Trebilco 2007)
>
> Thessalonica in Macedonia (1 Thess. 1:1; 2 Thess. 1:1; Acts 17; cf. Nasrallah 2010; Breytenbach 2007; Ascough 2003)
>
> Corinth in Achaia (1 Cor. 1:2; 2 Cor. 1:16, 23; 8:16–17; 12:14–18; 13:1; Acts 18; 19:1; Rom. 16:23; 2 Tim. 4:20; 1 Clem. 1; cf. Last 2016a)

Mention is also made of Paul's missionary activities in Roman military colonies, such as the following:

> Antioch of Pisidia (Acts 14; 2 Tim. 3:11)
>
> Lystra (Acts 14; 2 Tim. 3:11)
>
> Iconium (Acts 14; 2 Tim. 3:11)
>
> Derbe (Acts 14)
>
> Alexandria Troas (Acts 16:8; 2 Cor. 2:12)
>
> Philippi (Phil. 1:1; 4:10–18; Acts 16:12–40; 20:1–6; 1 Thess. 2:2; Polycarp, *To the Philippians*; cf. Öhler 2015; Ascough 2003)

Furthermore, the New Testament and early Christian writings hint at a relatively early presence of Christ groups in Tyre (Mark 7:24 par.; Luke 6:17; Acts 21:1–7) and Caesarea Maritima (Acts 18:22; 25:23), and in several cities of Asia Minor:

> Colossae (Col. 1:1–2, 7; 2:1; 4:12–13; Rev. 1:11; 3:14–16 with Col. 2:1; 4:12–13)
>
> Laodicea (Col. 2:1; 4:13, 15–16; Rev. 1:11; 3:14–22)
>
> Hierapolis (Col. 4:13)
>
> Smyrna (Rev. 1:11; 2:8–11; Ignatius, *To the Smyrnaeans*)
>
> Pergamum (Rev. 1:11; 2:12–17)
>
> Sardis (Rev. 1:11; 3:1–6)
>
> Philadelphia (Rev. 1:11; 3:7–13; Ignatius, *To the Philadelphians*)
>
> Magnesia (Ignatius, *To the Magnesians*)
>
> Tralleis (Ignatius, *To the Trallians*)
>
> Thyatira (Acts 16:14; Rev. 1:11; 2:18–29)

These writings also hint at a relatively early presence of Christ groups in the three metropolises: Athens (Acts 17:15–34; 1 Thess. 3:1), Alexandria (Acts 18:24; cf. 6:9), and Rome (Acts 18:2; 28; Rom. 1:7, 15; 16:5–17; Phil. 4:22; 2 Tim. 1:16–17; 4:21).

Urban Christianity in View of Roman Authorities and Historians

At the beginning of the second century, the early Christ movement was increasingly perceived as a major player in the city, which necessarily brings the Roman authority to the scene. For example, Pliny the Younger (ca. 62–113 CE), who toward the end of his life served as the imperial governor in *Bithynia et Pontus*, informed the emperor Trajan that in his province the Christian faith had permeated the breadth of society (cf. Öhler 2021). In particular, he worried that this new *superstitio* spreads "not only in the cities, but also across the villages and fields" (Pliny, *Ep.* 10.96.9: *neque civitates tantum, sed vicos atque agros* [my translation]). This concern seems to have been well founded, as becomes apparent by the (later) wealth of early Christian inscriptions and other material remains in Asia Minor (Mitchell and Pilhofer 2019; Pilhofer 2018).

From the Roman historians of the second century comes evidence of a Christian presence in Rome. Both Tacitus (*Ann.* 15.44.2–5) and Suetonius (*Nero* 16.2) assume that the Christians (*Chrestiani*/*Christiani*) first emerged as a unique group under Nero.[3] While Tacitus reports that the emperor blamed the fire of Rome on the Christ followers, Suetonius speaks of death sentences imposed on the capital's Christians only due to their "new and vicious superstitions" (*superstitionis novae ac maleficae*; Suetonius, *Nero* 16.2 [my translation]). Although the Neronian persecution can be denied with good reasons from a historical point of view (Shaw 2015; but see Kinzig 2021, 37–41), the statements of these two historians reveal that, in temporal proximity to Pliny's report, there was a growing awareness of Christians in Rome and in other cities. This awareness fits well with the fact that Luke, as an author at the end of the first century CE, notes that it was in the metropolis of Antioch that outsiders called the followers of Jesus "Christians" (*Christianoi*; compare with the textual variant *Chrēstianoi*) for the first time (Acts 11:26; cf. 1 Pet. 4:16).

The observation that the early Christ movement was found in all major cities of the Mediterranean within a few decades of Jesus's death raises the question of why this religious group was able to thrive so well in this specific context. In what follows, I will discuss six causes, since ultimately there is no monocausal explanation for the fact that early Christianity so rapidly became a *Städtereligion* ("city religion"; Harnack 2018 [1924], 948).

Paul's Urban Mission

Reading Luke's Acts of the Apostles, one gets the impression that the early Christ movement established itself in urban centers largely because of Paul's urban mission. Indeed, Paul obviously pursued a deliberate missionary strategy, since he preferred to stay in provincial capitals and Roman colonies (Lietaert Peerbolte 2003; Allen 1962). Simultaneously, he sought out regions that had not yet been subject to missionary activity.[4] Furthermore, we should not underestimate the role of charismatic individuals like Paul (cf. Rom. 15:18–19) and other miracle workers, philosophers (e.g., Justin Martyr), missionaries, and martyrs in the success of Christianity (Leppin 2018, 419). Nevertheless, the individual commitment of Paul cannot be the whole story, as the Christ movement was established in several cities and metropolises without Paul's engagement—for example, in Jerusalem, Antioch (see Acts 11:19), Ephesus (cf. Schnelle 2020), Colossae (Col. 1:7), Rome (Acts 28:14–16; Rom. 15:22), and Alexandria (cf. Schliesser 2021).

Urban Networks: The Strength of Occupational Ties

While Luke's basic narrative is that Paul came to a city, preached or performed a miracle, and immediately won many followers for the new faith in Jesus Christ, Paul's own reports suggest that winning new followers must have been more protracted and arduous. For example, Paul reminds the Thessalonians of his own "labor and toil," working "night and day" (1 Thess. 2:9) while preaching the gospel to them. Based on this note and Paul's later command (4:11) for his addressees also to find value and honor (*philotimeisthai*) by their work,

3. At the time of the Edict of Claudius, by contrast, the Christ followers still appear as an inner-Jewish group. See Suetonius, *Claud.* 25.44 (*Iudaeos impulsore Chresto assidue tumultuantis Roma expulit*), and for more details on this edict, see Keener 2018.

4. Some have thought this is best explained by the influence of a Jewish "table of nations" tradition (Scott 1994, 1995). Others opt for a rereading of Isa. 66:18–21 (Riesner 1998, 216–25).

Richard Ascough has argued that the Christ followers in Thessalonica began as an occupational guild (Ascough 2003; cf. Rulmu 2010). Even if the literal proximity between 1 Thessalonians 4:11 and association inscriptions remains circumstantial, a certain connection between the apostle's tradesmanship and missionary activity also becomes evident elsewhere (Acts 20:34–35; 1 Cor. 4:12). In Acts 18:1–3 Paul is portrayed as assisting Prisca and Aquila in an established awning business (*skēnopoioi*) in Corinth. Accordingly, when Paul refers to the "assembly in their house" (1 Cor. 16:19; Rom. 16:5: *kat' oikon autōn ekklēsia*), we should think of a *taberna* or workshop rather than a private house or Roman *domus* (see also Acts 16:14–15). Given the streetwise clustering of trades in an ancient city, it is reasonable to assume that such a Christian community would have used its strong ties to commercial partners in the immediate vicinity to its advantage (Reinbold 2000, 298; Dalheim 2013, 380). Such a missionary practice would find a parallel in the phenomenon of ancient neighborhood associations, though the evidence for this social form is not particularly abundant and remains largely limited to Asia Minor (cf. Kloppenborg 2019, 37–38; Harland 2014; Last 2016b, regarding 1 Cor. 14:23). We may also imagine how the advice in 1 Peter 3:15 would function well in an environment of daily work and neighborhood life: "Always be prepared to give an answer to everyone who asks you to give the reason for the hope that you have" (NIV).

Meeting Places: The (Semi-)Public Sphere of Ancient Cities

Similar to the workshop scenario just mentioned, ancient cities provided a variety of public and semi-public spaces that might have suited the needs of Christian gatherings. While earlier research assumed that Christ groups were located exclusively in the context of private homes (Filson 1939; Banks 1980; Klauck 1981), more recent studies point to a much broader variety of possible meeting places (Horrell 2004; Adams 2016; see, however, Bremmer 2020a). Already in the New Testament, religious gatherings are placed at such diverse settings as an urban garden (Luke 22:39 [*kata to ethos*]; John 18:1–2; cf. Ps.-Clem. *Hom.* 4.10; *Rec.* 4.6; 5.36), a river (Acts 16:13), a marketplace (17:17, 22–31), a school (19:9), a multistory apartment house (20:7–12), and a Roman tenement apartment (28:15, 30; see Rüggemeier 2023). Early Christian literature and archaeological remains provide further (debatable) evidence for setting religious gatherings in hotels and inns (Acts John 60–61; Ps.-Clem. *Rec.* 7.2, 38), burial sites (Acts Paul 3.23–27; Acts John 62–68), barns or *horrea* (Acts Paul 11.1; 20.9–12),[5] and other industrial premises.

The plethora of urban locations reveals a certain early Christian pragmatism in the choice of meeting places, which might be best explained by the renunciation of cultic sacrifices (Leppin 2018, 421). Yet this very pragmatism was perceived by contemporaries as a key differentiator to other religious cults and generated the accusation that Christians neglect the temples (see Tertullian, *Spect.* 13; *Apol.* 15; Minucius Felix, *Oct.* 32.1; Origen, *Cels.* 8.17.19; Arnobius, *Adv. nat.* 6.1; see also Rom. 12:1; 1 Cor. 3:16–17; 6:19–20) and propagate their false teachings on all street corners and all angles in the city (Minucius Felix, *Oct.* 8.4). Despite this hostility, the mere presence of Christianity throughout the entire city probably contributed to a phenomenon in which people of both genders and from all social or legal classes came into contact with this religious movement. Peter Oakes (2009, 94–95) vividly describes this by envisioning a workshop scenario:

5. On archaeological evidence for *horrea* structures beneath the Basilica dei Santi Giovanni e Paolo, see Snyder 2003, esp. 149.

Dark if the doors were closed, open to the street if they were open; in a very noisy environment; heavily encumbered with materials, tools and work in progress (although in this particular case, some might have been able to be sat on!); lacking in the cooking facilities and latrine that were available in the house. . . . However, the amount of space would presumably allow, say, 30 people to gather.

Conversely, for the Roman elite, a workshop as a meeting place would have been an open provocation. This is even more true for taverns or inns, which had a bad reputation (Glazebrook and Tsakirgis 2016) and yet were highly frequented by the masses.

Learning Cities: How Education Promoted Christianity

In the imperial period, education was still widely based on a private tutor system and largely provided by Greek slaves or freedmen. Ancient cities, however, provided a unique infrastructure that could indirectly serve the elementary education of the middle and even lower classes—for example by street teachers (*literati*, *grammatici*; Cribiore 1995).[6] More recent estimates suggest that in ancient cities up to 30–50 percent of the population was literate to some degree (Bagnall 2010; Johnson and Parker 2009). This assumption is supported by graffiti and inscriptions, the majority of which were addressed to members of the middle classes and were often, surprisingly, intended to appeal to a female audience or were even written by women (Benefiel and Sypniewski 2018; Benefiel et al. 2017). Other factors suggesting literacy are the libraries and book collections in local gymnasia, which contributed significantly to an increase in knowledge transfer, and the

invention of the codex, which made texts portable and storable (Martial, *Epigr.* 14.184–92) and which in turn created a new publishing sector and a profitable book market in larger cities (Pliny the Younger, *Ep.* 3.18.9; 5.10.3; Martial, *Epigr.* 1.1; 7.88; 8.3; 11.3; Josephus, *Ag. Ap.* 1.50–52).

How did this variegated field of urban education affect the early Christ movement? Scholarship no longer is constrained by the view that Christianity attracted only lower strata of society and did not maintain any viable ties to the educated elite (Deissmann 1927). The "new consensus" argues that Christ believers belonged to all social strata. Accordingly, some scholars also highlight early Christianity's affinity toward education (Söding 2016; Schnelle 2015). Early Christianity soon became a "bookish religion" (Hurtado 2016, 105–41)—that is, a movement that produced an impressive variety of literary texts serving the needs of a broad urban reading public. Not only were Paul and the author of Hebrews (Thompson 2020) familiar with the philosophy and rhetoric of their time, but to some extent the same is true for Mark (Whitenton 2016; Rüggemeier 2021) and the other Gospel writers (Becker 2017), who even created and established a new literary genre.

Early Christian Exclusivism and Egalitarianism in a Multiethnic Environment

Similar to our modern cities, ancient cities were multiethnic and multireligious. Thus, a remarkable mobility in imperial times fostered the spread of new cults. The movement of religious ideas can be traced particularly well in relation to Eastern deities (Serapis, Isis, Cybele, Mithras), which enjoyed great popularity in Greece as well as in Rome and the entire West (Moyer 2011). Some of these deities even became an integral part of Roman religion and received official devotion, such as Cybele, Rome's Magna Mater.

---

6. The elite's dismissive attitude toward such teachers is reflected in numerous comments: see, e.g., Seneca the Younger, *Ep.* 88.37; Lucillius (*Anth. Pal.* 11.154, 279); Ammianos (*Anth. Pal.* 11.156.3–4); Corpus Lucianum (*Anth. Pal.* 11.430).

Likewise, newcomers and migrants often showed a willingness for peaceful coexistence. This may be exemplified by the archaeological evidence of the Janiculum shrine in Rome, which "shows that although there were several changes to the function of the site over the centuries, the model for the relationship between the Syrian deities and other gods there should be one of co-existence rather than replacement" (Elder 2020, 278).

In contrast, early Christianity, rooted in Jewish monotheism, was exclusivist (Ehrman 2018, 120–28; Harnack 2018 [1924], 527–28), and it was precisely for this reason that it stood out in a highly pluralistic religious landscape. While the worshiping of one God offered potential for conflict within a polytheistic religious system, more educated urbanites could welcome Christianity's tendency to "reduce complexity" (Markschies 2016, 263). Thus, the first Christ followers proclaimed the one Creator God and his Son (1 Cor. 8:6), in whose death and resurrection forgiveness and eternal life are granted. It was a religious movement whose ethical guidelines were unambiguous and that offered clear orientation for daily life and for everyone.

For the middle classes, on the other hand, Christian egalitarianism would have been particularly attractive, especially in an urban universe where ethnic groups and milieus constantly clashed and competed with each other. In this respect, what is programmatic for the early Christian movement is a respective metaphorical language (Rom. 12:3–8; 1 Cor. 10:17; 12:12–27; Gal. 3:28; Eph. 5:30; Col. 3:15), the uncommon address as "brothers" and "sisters" (cf. Minucius Felix, *Oct.* 9.2), and echoes of an older civic democracy (e.g., Christ groups as *ekklēsiai*). While none of these characteristics is unique to early Christianity (cf. Kloppenborg 2019, 282–86), taken together these features provide some explanation for why early Christianity was able to establish itself across ethnic lines and across different strata of urban society.

Early Christianity and Gender Equality in Urban Contexts

Although Roman law did not grant women legal status and women were thus not allowed to vote or run for civic office, they were by no means bound to the domestic sphere only. Especially in the urban context, there are numerous examples of women's emancipation, as can be seen, for example, by the businesswoman Julia Felix of Pompeii (cf. Russell 2016) or Junia Theodora, a member of the Corinthian elite (*SEG* 18.143; Friesen 2014). Female involvement in cultic activities becomes evident in the mention of female chief priests in the cult of Artemis (cf. Kearsley 2005) or in the cult of Hestia Boulaia, where women held the influential position of prytanis (cf. *IEph* 4.1012, 1060; cf. Trebilco 1991). Participating in a mystery cult was another way for elite women but also for sub-elite women to rise to an influential religious position (cf. Browden 2010).

Despite all these examples, early Christian groups offered more extensive opportunities for female participation, and one would be hard-pressed to find "any contemporary parallel from the pagan world of such an active female presence in a religious meeting or temple" (Bremmer 2020b, 195; cf. Eckhardt and Leonhard 2018, 286). Both early Christian writings (Luke 8:2) and later inscriptions or documentary papyri bear witness that women were among the first Jesus followers and were "officeholders"—that is, they were among the apostles, patrons, benefactors, hosts, presbyters, stewards, deacons, prophets, and teachers (Eisen 2000). From the New Testament we even know the names of some of them—for example, Junia (Rom. 16:7), Lydia (Acts 16:14), Prisca (Acts 18:2–3), Chloe (1 Cor. 1:11), and Phoebe (Rom. 16:1–2).

Conclusion and Outlook

We could add more to the above-mentioned factors that favored the establishment of the early Christ movement in the urban context. Rodney Stark, for example, points to the absence of medical and social services in the ancient city, which he contrasts with a Christian "humanism" (Stark 1997, 215; similarly Veyne 2008, 27). This became particularly evident during the two great plagues, "when substantial numbers of pagans fled epidemics (while Christians stayed)" and at least *some pagans* were nursed by Christians" (Stark 1997, 91–92; italics original). Due to the Christians' intrinsically motivated love for neighbors, strangers (Luke 10:30–37), and even enemies (Matt. 5:43–44) and the unprecedented frequency of meetings and meals (1 Cor. 16:2; Rev. 1:10; Did. 14.1; Justin Martyr, *1 Apol.* 67; cf. Acts 2:46), the early Christ movement probably impressed city dwellers at earlier times as well. Given a high population density and unsanitary living conditions in most neighborhoods (Paine and Storey 2006), the mortality rate was constantly high in ancient cities, and Christians' care for one another (John 13:34–35; Acts 6:1–7; 1 Tim. 5:3–16) exceeded the social support that most other institutions provided.

Ramsay MacMullen identifies another unique selling point of the early Christ movement, postulating that contemporaries were most impressed by the experience of both individual and mass miracles (MacMullen 1986, 29). This argument may be combined with Jörg Rüpke's view that early Christianity benefited from the spiritual sterility of most traditional cults in the city (Rüpke 2015, 146). Others have diagnosed an increased consciousness of guilt in Roman society, to which Christianity simply found the appropriate theological and spiritual answers (Winkler 2009, 32). While we should be wary of such one-sided contrasts with Greco-Roman religion, these suggestions highlight that we need to consider theo-logical motives, not simply sociological factors, to explain early Christianity's rise in urban centers. This consideration includes the early Christian "rhetoric of being 'gifted,' 'filled,' 'anointed,' and 'empowered' by the Spirit of God" (Hurtado 2000, 183) and theological concern to "remember the poor" (Gal. 2:10; see Longenecker 2010). Beyond the naming of general factors, future discourse will have to focus even more on the infrastructural, ethnic, educational, social, and gender-specific characteristics of single cities. While Tralles had a well-known rhetoric school (Cicero, *De or.* 234; Strabo, *Geogr.* 12.7.18; Seneca the Elder, *Contr.* 10.5.21) and, moreover, a self-confident Jewish community (Josephus, *Ant.* 14.242), conditions in a neighboring city could look different. At the same time, cities often maintained network-like contacts with other urban centers based on shared ethnicity, trade relations, or a transfer of knowledge, with new religious ideas and beliefs then also spreading through respective channels or social relations. While in recent years the focus has been primarily on comparing early Christ groups and other quasi-institutions of the ancient city, with a particular interest in associations (Kloppenborg 2019), the diversity of individual city dwellers and subjective viewpoints on early Christianity must continue to gain currency (Rüggemeier 2020). Rather than aiming at a coherent social *history* of early Christianity, our central focus would be on the social *histories* of urban people, asking what qualities and contents of the Christian faith appealed spiritually, existentially, and socially to a Greek businesswoman in Corinth, a widow in Jerusalem, a physician in Rome, a rhetoric teacher in Ephesus, or a member of the city council in Athens.

Finally, as already indicated above with the example of Bithynia, we should take into account that urban centers do not represent an isolated entity but are always simultaneously linked to their hinterland through daily labor migration, transport of goods, traffic, family contacts, political realities, and so on (cf. Tiwald and Zangenberg 2021). Evidence of an early presence of Christianity in the countryside (Robinson 2017) inevitably challenges an overly one-sided and idealistic view of Christianity as a purely urban movement and necessitates differentiation.

All these potential future perspectives demonstrate that in the exploration of ancient cities, many paths and alleys still await discovery, some districts and neighborhoods still hold hidden corners, and quite a few crossroads need to be looked at anew when considering how the early Christ movement grew in the urban centers of the Roman world.

Works Cited

Adams, Edward. 2016. *The Earliest Christian Meeting Places: Almost Exclusively Houses?* London: Bloomsbury.

Allen, Roland. 1962. *Missionary Methods: St. Paul's or Ours?* 6th ed. Grand Rapids: Eerdmans.

Ascough, Richard S. 2003. *Paul's Macedonian Associations: The Social Context of Philippians and 1 Thessalonians*. WUNT 2/161. Tübingen: Mohr Siebeck.

Bagnall, Roger S. 2010. *Everyday Writing in the Graeco-Roman East*. Berkeley: University of California Press.

Banks, Robert. 1980. *Paul's Idea of Community: The Early House Churches in Their Historical Setting*. Grand Rapids: Eerdmans.

Becker, Eve-Marie. 2017. *The Birth of Christian History: Memory and Time from Mark to Luke-Acts*. New Haven: Yale University Press.

Bendemann, Reinhard von. 2012. "Jesus und die Stadt im Markusevangelium." In *Das frühe Christentum und die Stadt*, edited by Reinhard von Bendemann and Markus Tiwald, 43–68. BWANT 198. Stuttgart: Kolhammer.

Benefiel, Rebecca, Sara Sprenkle, Holly Sypniewski, and Jamie White. 2017. "The Ancient Graffiti Project: Geo-Spatial Visualization and Search Tools for Ancient Handwritten Inscriptions." In *DAT-eCH2017: Proceedings of the 2nd International Conference on Digital Access to Textual Cultural Heritage*, edited by Marco Büchler, 163–68. New York: ACM.

Benefiel, Rebecca, and Holly Sypniewski. 2018. "Greek Graffiti in Herculaneum." *American Journal of Archaeology* 122: 209–44.

Bremmer, Jan N. 2020a. "Urban Religion, Neighbourhoods and the Early Christian Meeting Places." *RRE* 6: 48–74.

———. 2020b. "Early Christians in Corinth (A. D. 50–200): Religious Insiders or Outsiders?" *Annali di Storia dell'Esegesi* 37: 181–202.

Breytenbach, Cilliers. 2007. *Frühchristliches Thessaloniki*. STAC 44. Tübingen: Mohr Siebeck.

Browden, Hugh. 2010. *Mystery Cults of the Ancient World*. Princeton: Princeton University Press.

Cribiore, Raffella. 1995. "A Schooltablet from the Hearst Museum." *ZPE* 107: 263–70.

Dalheim, Werner. 2013. *Die römische Kaiserzeit*. München: Oldenbourg Verlag.

Deissmann, Adolf. 1927. *Light from the Ancient East: The New Testament Illustrated by Recently Discovered Texts of the Graeco-Roman World*. Translated by Lionel R. M. Strachan. New York: Harper & Row.

Eckhardt, Benedikt, and Clemens Leonhard. 2018. *Juden, Christen und Vereine im Römischen Reich*. RVV 75. Berlin: de Gruyter.

Ehrman, Bart D. 2018. *The Triumph of Christianity: How a Forbidden Religion Swept the World*. New York: Simon & Schuster.

Eisen, Ute E. 2000. *Women Officeholders in Early Christianity: Epigraphical and Literary Studies*. Collegeville, MN: Liturgical Press.

Elder, Olivia. 2020. "Population, Migration and Language in Rome." In *Migration, Mobility and Language Contact in and around the Ancient Mediterranean*, edited by James Clackson, Patrick James, Katherine McDonald, Livia Tagliapietra, and Nicholas Zair, 268–95. Cambridge: Cambridge University Press.

Filson, Floyd V. 1939. "The Significance of the Early House Churches." *JBL* 58: 105–12.

Fitzmyer, Joseph A. 1981. *The Gospel according to Luke I–IX*. Vol. 1. New York: Doubleday.

Flohr, Miko, ed. 2021. *Urban Space and Urban History in the Roman World*. New York: Routledge.

Friesen, Steven J. 2014. "Junia Theodora of Corinth: Gendered Inequalities in the Early Empire." In *Corinth in Contrast: Studies in Inequality*, edited by Steven J. Friesen, Sarah A. James, and Daniel N. Schowalter, 203–26. Leiden: Brill.

Glazebrook, Allison, and Barbara Tsakirgis, eds. 2016. *Houses of Ill Repute: The Archaeology of Brothels, Houses, and Taverns in the Greek World*. Philadelphia: University of Pennsylvania Press.

Goulder, Michael D. 1968. "Characteristics of the Parables in the Several Gospels." *JTS* 19: 51–69.

Harland, Philip A. 2014. *North Coast of the Black Sea, Asia Minor*. Vol. 2 of *Greco-Roman Associations: Texts, Translations, and Commentary*. BZNW 204. Berlin: de Gruyter.

Harnack, Adolf von. 2018. *Die Mission und Ausbreitung des Christentums*. 4th ed. Reprint, Darmstadt: Wissenschaftliche Buchgesellschaft. Originally published 1924.

Harrison, James R., and Larry L. Welborn. 2018. *The First Urban Churches*. Vol. 3, *Roman Ephesus*. WGRWSup 9. Atlanta: SBL Press.

Horrell, David G. 2004. "Domestic Space and Christian Meetings at Corinth: Imagining New Contexts and the Buildings East of the Theatre." *NTS* 50: 349–69.

Hurtado, Larry W. 2000. "Religious Experience and Religious Innovation in the New Testament." *JR* 80: 183–205.

———. 2016. *Destroyer of the Gods: Early Christian Distinctiveness in the Roman World*. Waco: Baylor University Press.

Johnson, William A., and Holt N. Parker. 2009. *Ancient Literacies: The Culture of Reading in Greece and Rome*. Oxford: Oxford University Press.

Kearsley, R. A. 2005. "Women and Public Life in Imperial Asia Minor: Hellenistic Tradition and Augustan Ideology." *Ancient West and East* 4, no. 1: 98–121.

Keener, Craig S. 2018. "Edict of Claudius." In *Brill Encyclopedia of Early Christianity*, edited by David G. Hunter, Paul J. J. van Geest, and Bert Jan Lietaert Peerbolte. Leiden: Brill.

Kinzig, Wolfram. 2021. *Christian Persecution in Antiquity*. Translated by Markus Bockmuehl. Waco: Baylor University Press.

Klauck, Hans-Josef. 1981. *Hausgemeinde und Hauskirche im frühen Christentum*. Stuttgart: Katholisches Bibelwerk.

Kloppenborg, John. 2019. *Christ's Associations: Connecting and Belonging in the Ancient City*. New Haven: Yale University Press.

Last, Richard. 2016a. *The Pauline Church and the Corinthian Ekklēsia: Greco-Roman Associations in Comparative Context*. SNTSMS 164. Cambridge: Cambridge University Press.

———. 2016b. "The Neighborhood (*Vicus*) of the Corinthian *Ekklēsia*: Beyond Family-Based Descriptions of the First Urban Christ-Believers." *JSNT* 38, no. 4: 399–425.

Leppin, Hartmut. 2018. *Die frühen Christen von den Anfängen bis Konstantin*. Munich: Beck.

Lietaert Peerbolte, L. J. 2003. *Paul the Missionary*. CBET 34. Leuven: Peeters.

Longenecker, Bruce W. 2010. *Remember the Poor: Paul, Poverty, and the Greco-Roman World*. Grand Rapids: Eerdmans.

Macmullen, Ramsay. 1986. *Christianizing the Roman Empire (AD 100–400)*. New Haven: Yale University Press.

Markschies, Christoph. 2016. *Das antike Christentum: Frömmigkeit, Lebensformen, Institutionen*. 3rd ed. Munich: Beck.

Mitchell, Stephen, and Philipp Pilhofer, eds. 2019. *Early Christianity in Asia Minor and Cyprus: From the Margins to the Mainstream*. ECAM/AJEC 109. Leiden: Brill.

Moyer, Ian S. 2011. *Egypt and the Limits of Hellenism*. Cambridge: Cambridge University Press.

Nasrallah, Laura, ed. 2010. *From Roman to Early Christian Thessalonikē: Studies in Religion and Archaeology*. HTS 64. Boston: Harvard University Press.

Oakes, Peter. 2009. *Reading Romans in Pompeii: Paul's Letter at Ground Level*. Minneapolis: Fortress.

Öhler, Markus. 2015. "Gründer und ihre Gründung: Antike Vereinigungen und die paulinische Gemeinde in Philippi." In *Der Philipperbrief des Paulus in der hellenistisch-römischen Welt*, edited by Jörg Frey and Benjamin Schliesser, 121–51. WUNT 353. Tübingen: Mohr Siebeck.

———. 2021. "Pliny and the Expansion of Christianity in Cities and Rural Areas of *Pontus et Bithynia*." In Tiwald and Zangenberg 2021, 269–98.

Paine, Richard R., and Glenn R. Storey. 2006. "Epidemics, Age at Death, and Mortality in Ancient Rome." In *Urbanism in the Preindustrial World: Cross-Cultural Approaches*, edited by Glenn R. Storey, 69–85. Tuscaloosa: University of Alabama Press.

Pilhofer, Philipp. 2018. *Das frühe Christentum im kilikisch-isaurischen Bergland: Die Christen der Kalykadnos-Region in den ersten fünf Jahrhunderten*. Texte und Untersuchungen zur Geschichte der altchristlichen Literatur 184. Boston: de Gruyter.

Reinbold, Wolfgang. 2000. *Propaganda und Mission im ältesten Christentum: Eine Untersuchung zu den Modalitäten der Ausbreitung der frühen Kirche*. FRLANT 188. Göttingen: Vandenhoeck & Ruprecht.

Riesner, Rainer. 1998. *Paul's Early Period: Chronology, Mission Strategy, Theology*. Grand Rapids: Eerdmans.

Robinson, Thomas A. 2017. *Who Were the First Christians? Dismantling the Urban Thesis*. New York: Oxford University Press.

Rüggemeier, Jan. 2016. "Strategisches Erzählen und Strategiewechsel im Umfeld neutestamentlicher Erzähltexte: Das lukanische Gleichnis 'Vom barmherzigen Samariter' als Anschauungsbeispiel." *Diegesis E-Journal for Narrative Research* 5, no. 2: 63–83.

———. 2020. "Ein Streifzug durch Roms Gassen und Viertel: Subjektorientierte Perspektiven auf die stadtrömischen Christinnen und Christen im ersten

Jahrhundert." In *Talking God in Society: Multidisciplinary (Re)constructions of Ancient (Con)texts*, edited by Ute E. Eisen and Heidrun Marder, 307–38. NTOA 120. Göttingen: Vandenhoeck & Ruprecht.

———. 2021. "Mark's Narrative Christology following the Cognitive Turn: Developments, Implications, and Desiderata of an Interpretative Concept and Its Impact on the Analysis of Mark 1:21–28." *EC* 12: 322–45.

———. 2023. "Die römische Gefangenschaft des Paulus: Das evozierte Raumbild in Apg 28,11–31 aus erzählwissenschaftlicher und lokalgeschichtlicher Perspektive." In *Paulusmemoria und Paulusexegese: Römische Begegnungen*, edited by Jörg Frey, Jens Schröter, and Martin Wallraff, 129–64. Rom und Protestantismus Schriften des Melanchthon-Zentrums in Romans 5. Tübingen: Mohr Siebeck.

Rulmu, Callia. 2010. "Between Ambition and Quietism: The Socio-Political Background of 1 Thessalonians 4:9–12." *Bib* 91: 393–17.

Rüpke, Jörg. 2015. *Von Jupiter zu Christus: Religionsgeschichte in römischer Zeit*. Darmstadt. Wissenschaftliche Buchgesellschaft.

Russell, Amy. 2016. "On Gender and Spatial Experience in Public: The Case of Ancient Rome." *Theoretical Roman Archaeology Journal* 2015: 164–76.

Schliesser, Benjamin. 2021. "Why Did Paul Skip Alexandria? Paul's Missionary Strategy and the Rise of Christianity in Alexandria." *NTS* 67: 260–83.

Schnelle. Udo. 2015. "Das frühe Christentum und die Bildung." *NTS* 61: 113–43.

———. 2020. *The First One Hundred Years of Christianity: An Introduction to Its History, Literature, and Development*. Translated by James W. Thompson. Grand Rapids: Baker Academic.

Scott, James M. 1994. "Luke's Geographical Horizon." In *The Book of Acts in Its Graeco-Roman Setting*, edited by David W. J. Gill and Conrad Gempf, 483–88. Vol. 2 of *The Book of Acts in Its First Century Setting*. Grand Rapids: Eerdmans.

———. 1995. *Paul and the Nations: The Old Testament and Jewish Background of Paul's Mission to the Nations with Special Reference to the Destination of Galatians*. WUNT 84. Tübingen: Mohr Siebeck.

Shaw, Brent. 2015. "The Myth of the Neronian Persecution." *JRS* 105: 73–100.

Snyder, Graydon F. 2003. *Ante-Pacem: Archaeological Evidence of Church Life before Constantine*. Macon, GA: Mercer University Press.

Söding, Thomas. 2016. *Das Christentum als Bildungsreligion: Der Impuls des Neuen Testaments*. Freiburg: Herder.

Stark, Rodney. 1997. *The Rise of Christianity: How the Obscure, Marginal Jesus Movement Became the Dominant Religious Force in the Western World in a Few Centuries*. New York: HarperSanFrancisco.

Tellbe, Mikael. 2009. *Christ-Believers in Ephesus: A Textual Analysis of Early Christian Identity Formation in a Local Perspective*. WUNT 242. Tübingen: Mohr Siebeck.

Thompson, James W. 2020. *Strangers on the Earth: Philosophy and Rhetoric in Hebrews*. Eugene, OR: Wipf & Stock.

Tiwald, Markus. 2016. *Das Frühjudentum und die Anfänge des Christentums: Ein Studienbuch*. BWANT 208. Stuttgart: Kohlhammer.

Tiwald, Markus, and Jürgen Zangenberg, eds. 2021. *Early Christian Encounters with Town and Countryside: Essays on the Urban and Rural Worlds of Early Christianity*. NTOA/SUNT 126. Göttingen: Vandenhoeck & Ruprecht.

Trebilco, Paul. 1991. *Jewish Communities in Asia Minor*. Cambridge: Cambridge University Press.

———. 2007. *The Early Christians in Ephesus from Paul to Ignatius*. Grand Rapids: Eerdmans.

Veyne, Paulus. 2008. *Als unsere Welt christlich wurde (312–394): Aufstieg einer Sekte zur Weltmacht*. Munich: Beck.

Whitenton, Michael R. 2016. *Hearing Kyriotic Sonship: A Cognitive and Rhetorical Approach to the Characterization of Mark's Jesus*. BibInt 148. Leiden: Brill.

Winkler, Heinrich August. 2009. *Geschichte des Westens*. Vol. 1, *Von den Anfängen in der Antike bis zum 20. Jahrhundert*. Munich: Beck.

Zetterholm, Magnus. 2003. *The Formation of Christianity in Antioch: A Social-Scientific Approach to the Separation between Judaism and Christianity*. London: Routledge.

Zuiderhoek, Arjan J. 2017. *The Ancient City: Key Themes in Ancient History*. Cambridge: Cambridge University Press.

8

The Decapolis

Roy Ciampa

The Decapolis (lit., "ten cities") is mentioned by name in Mark 5:20; 7:31; and Matthew 4:25. Other New Testament texts refer to cities or areas that were part of the Decapolis (or were understood by some to be part of the Decapolis) at one time or another. The term refers to a geographical and cultural enclave of Greek (and then Roman) urban centers and their surrounding countryside, located mainly to the east and south of the Sea of Galilee (in modern-day Jordan, Israel, and southern Syria).

The Gospel writers mention the Decapolis in a way that might suggest they expect their readers to know something about where and what it is. Pliny the Elder, writing his *Natural History* in the 70s CE, provides a thumbnail description of the Decapolis for a readership that would include many unfamiliar with the area. Pliny tells his readers that the name is derived from the number of its towns: *deka*, meaning "ten," and *polis*, meaning "town" or "city" (*Nat.* 5.18.74). The Jewish historian Josephus, writing in the late first century CE, sometimes referred to the region as "the ten cit-

ies" (αἱ δέκα πόλεις, *hai deka poleis*) using the individual terms (Josephus, *Life* 341–42) and sometimes using the compound proper noun, "the Decapolis" (ἡ Δεκάπολις, *hē dekapolis*; Josephus, *Life* 410–11; *J.W.* 3.446–47). The distinctly Greek name, with its clear etymology, gave its meaning to the area while also clearly suggesting a Greek cultural identity.

Pliny points out, however, that not everyone had the same list of towns or cities in mind when they referred to the Decapolis. He mentions ten that he says are included in most lists: Damascus, Philadelphia, Raphana, Scythopolis, Gadara, Hippos, Dion, Pella, Gerasa, and Canatha (see fig. 8.1). But Josephus reports that Scythopolis was the largest city of the Decapolis, suggesting he did not consider Damascus a part of the Decapolis, given that the latter city was much larger than Scythopolis (Josephus, *J.W.* 3.446). A Greek inscription from 134 CE found in the region of Palmyra in Syria refers to a certain "good-messenger-Abila of the Decapolis" (Parker 1997, 128; Rey-Coquais 1992, 116), suggesting that Abila was counted as a city of the Decapolis by its

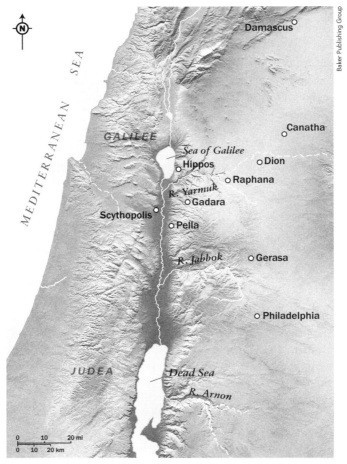

Fig. 8.1. The Decapolis

author. The second-century geographer Ptolemy provides a list that omits Raphana but adds Abila, Lysianae, and Capitolias to the others listed by Pliny. Stephen of Byzantium indicates that at one point the Decapolis consisted of as many as fourteen cities (Parker 1997, 128).

The name Decapolis may originally have referred to ten specific cities (and their surrounding areas), but over the course of its history, the number and identity of cities thought to be included varied. Lack of absolute precision in the identification of the towns thought to be included in the name did not detract from the clear identification of the region in which those towns were located. Of all the cities identified

as members of the Decapolis, only Scythopolis was situated west of the Jordan River.

The Decapolis in the Hellenistic Period

Most of the cities (including, among listed cities, Scythopolis/Beth She'an, Gadara, Gerasa, Canatha, Abila, Philadelphia [= Rabbah; Josh. 13:25], and Damascus) show evidence of occupation in pre-Hellenistic times (and well before any concept of a Decapolis). But they were all refounded in Hellenistic times. Some of the cities claimed to be founded by Alexander the Great (Parker 1997, 128; Rey-Coquais 1992, 117–18). After Alexander died in 323 BCE and his extensive empire was divided among his four top generals, the land of Judea found itself caught between the two remaining parts that dominated the eastern Mediterranean Sea: the Ptolemaic kingdom to the south with its center in Egypt, and the Seleucid kingdom to the north with its center in Syria. Evidence suggests cities of the Decapolis were founded or refounded under Ptolemaic rule (ca. 323–198 BCE). Philadelphia and Pella, for example, were refounded under the Ptolemies and given Ptolemaic dynastic names (Lichtenberger 2022, 221).

The region was a tension point in the conflicting ambitions of the Ptolemaic and Seleucid empires. In 200 BCE, at the battle of Panium (or Paneion), near Mount Hermon, as part of his conquest of Syria, southern Phoenicia, and Palestine, the Seleucid king Antiochus III the Great delivered a devastating blow to the Ptolemaic army. As a result, the whole Decapolis region came under Seleucid rule, and a number of its settlements were refounded and given Seleucid dynastic names, including Gadara, Gerasa, Hippos, and Abila (Lichtenberger 2022, 221).

Under the Seleucids, and as part of their development of the region, some towns were recognized as Greek πόλεις, cities (or semi-independent city-states), and some also received the civic and religious honor of being granted *asylia*, "inviolability" (Lichtenberger 2022, 221). Zeus Olympios, the Seleucid dynastic deity, was introduced to some Decapolis cities in this same timeframe.

During the second century and into the beginning of the first century BCE the Seleucid Empire experienced a decline that would ultimately lead to its collapse. The Seleucid king Antiochus IV Epiphanes imposed drastic Hellenizing policies, which threatened the very survival of the Jewish religion. Those oppressive measures provoked the Jewish Maccabean revolt, and its successes against the Seleucid army led to the eventual establishment of the Jewish Hasmonean kingdom as a semi-autonomous vassal of the Seleucid Empire. As the Seleucid Empire continued to weaken, the Jewish kingdom, along with the neighboring Nabatean kingdom, took advantage of the opportunities to expand into Seleucid territory. The Nabateans took possession of Philadelphia (Josephus, *J.W.* 1.129), and the Hasmonean kingdom became fully independent and grew through a series of military annexations of Seleucid territory.

Between the second century BCE and the first century CE there was constant tension regarding Jewish authority over, or ambitions regarding, the region. The territory had at one time been incorporated into the Davidic kingdom (2 Sam. 8:5–15; Josephus, *Ant.* 7.104), and David's empire may have come to set the standard for Jewish hopes and expectations (Hengel and Schwemer 1997, 55). Most of the Decapolis (including Scythopolis, Gadara, Abila, Dion, and Pella) was reconquered by the Hasmonean king Alexander Janneus, who forced the inhabitants to accept circumcision and the law of Moses or suffer the complete destruction of their cities. When the city of Pella refused to convert, it was destroyed (Josephus, *Ant.* 13.393–97; cf. 13.318).

The Decapolis in the Roman Period

The Roman general Pompey liberated the cities from Jewish and Nabatean domination when he established Roman authority over the region in 63 BCE. They were given their freedom and were attached to the province of Syria (Josephus, *Ant.* 14.74–76; *J.W.* 1.155–57). From that time until Byzantine times, most of the cities adopted their liberation by Pompey as a key theme of and the point of departure for the dating of their coins.

The region experienced a series of military conflicts in 31 BCE between the Jews and the Nabatean kingdom to their east, which had grown from a nomadic Bedouin tribe in the Arabian desert and had come to control many of the trade routes in the region (Josephus, *J.W.* 1.366–85), and in 30 BCE Augustus added Gadara and Hippos (besides Samaria and a number of coastal cities) to Herod's kingdom (Josephus, *Ant.* 15.217). This situation, which was an unhappy one for the Gadarenes (15.351–58), continued until 4 BCE, when, upon Herod's death, those cities regained their autonomy and were (re)attached to the province of Syria as they had been previously (17.320). Augustus gave Herod the Great the northern part of the Hauran (including the three provinces of Trachonitis, Auranitis, and Batanea) around 23 BCE. This area (including Canatha and Raphana) was passed on to the tetrarch Philip and then to King Agrippa I and later (after a period under Syrian administration) to the kingdom of Agrippa II until his death (ca. 93 or 100 CE).

In the first century CE there were significant Jewish communities within the cities of the Decapolis. Josephus gives evidence of both a significant level of integration of the Jewish inhabitants within the rest of society (Josephus, *J.W.* 2.463, 466–80) and also strong hostility on the part of the Gentile inhabitants toward their Jewish neighbors (1.88; 2.461, 478; 7.367; see also Kasher 1990).

At the outbreak of the First Jewish War in 66 CE, Jews attacked a number of the Decapolis cities, including Philadelphia, Gerasa, Pella, Scythopolis, Gadara, and Hippos (Josephus, *J.W.* 2.458–59). Those cities (with the exception of Gerasa) responded by slaughtering many of their Jewish inhabitants and imprisoning others (2.461–80).

A Greek inscription from the late first century mentions a Roman prefect or procurator of the Decapolis, indicating that at the time it was a Roman administrative unit attached to the province of Syria (Isaac 1981, 70–71). In 106 CE the emperor Trajan established a new province of Arabia, and the cities of the Decapolis were divided between the three provinces of Syria, Arabia, and Palestine. After that

any reference to the Decapolis could have had only geographical significance since no such political entity survived.

The Cultural and Demographic Dynamics of the Decapolis

In the past, many scholars thought that the cities of the Decapolis were part of a formal league that could address threats and opportunities with a united front (compare the Delian League of Greek city-states that Athens led to counter the Persians in the 5th c. BCE). But no evidence of such a league or confederation has been found. Many of the cities issued their own coinage, none of which refers to membership in the Decapolis, and we lack evidence that membership in the Decapolis provided any of the cities with a strong sense of group identity (Chancey 2002, 131). In the first century CE they were part of the province of Syria, and we only know of one time where they acted or were represented together: when they sent a delegation to Vespasian to petition for action against Justus of Tiberias after the latter had attacked their region during the revolt against Rome (Chancey 2002, 131). It seems the Decapolis may have had a stronger group identity in the eyes of outsiders than it did for those who lived in the region. That they lived in a region that could be distinguished by its overt identification with Hellenistic culture would have been clear to those on the inside looking out as well as to those on the outside looking in.

Externally, the cities were all perceived to share a commitment to the Hellenistic culture that distinguished them from their neighbors. They remained Greco-Roman in outwardly facing ways (coinage, architecture, inscriptions, etc.), emphasizing loyalty to their Greek and then Roman political benefactors, but they were actually much more diverse demographically and culturally below the surface. As E. M. Meyers puts it, "The oriental cities of the Decapolis and other Gentile cities should not be viewed solely as purveyors of Greco-Roman culture but rather as eastern cities with a Hellenistic overlay" (1997, 62). It was common for local deities to be given what scholars refer to as an *interpretation graeca*, a Greek name or interpretation (so Zeus Arotesios, Zeus of Dion, etc.), which makes it difficult at times to know if some Greek-labeled deity or other cultural entity reflects actual Greek cultural influence or simply a Greek veneer over an Eastern reality.

The New Testament and the Decapolis

The Gospels refer to the Decapolis (or one of its cities) in Mark 5:1–20; 7:31–37; Matthew 4:24–25; 8:28–34; and Luke 8:26–39. The earliest reference is in a passage found in all three Synoptic Gospels (Mark 5:1–20; Matt. 8:28–34; and Luke 8:26–39). Here, in what the readers are expected to understand to be predominately Gentile territory (Iverson 2007, 34), Jesus encounters a strong and terrifying man (Mark 5:2; Luke 8:27; or two: Matt. 8:28) who is possessed by a multitude of demons. In Mark's and Luke's versions, the demons identify themselves as "Legion," suggesting not only their great number but perhaps also (given the association with the legions of the Roman Empire) their status as an occupying force of overwhelming power. Those demons recognize Christ as the Son of God (Matthew; "Son of the Most High God" in Mark and Luke) and appear helpless before him. Jesus lets them enter a nearby herd of swine, which instantly runs into the sea.

While Matthew 8:28–34 and Luke 8:26–39 do not mention the Decapolis by name (only the name of one of its cities), Mark 5:1–20 tells us that after Jesus healed the demoniac, he went and "began to proclaim in the Decapolis how much Jesus had done for him" (5:20). In all three Gospels the local people are terrified by Jesus's power and ask him to leave. In all three Gospels the point seems to be that even in Gentile territory Jesus's power easily overpow-

ers a man and a multitude of demons who were perceived to be indomitable by others. Robert Gundry suggests that in Mark's narrative the reference to the proclamation in the Decapolis "serves the Christological point that Jesus' act of power inspired the ex-demoniac to exceed by far the commission that Jesus gave him" (1993, 255). Morna Hooker thinks it possible that "Mark understood the man's commission as a precursor of the mission to the Gentiles" (2001, 146; cf. France 2002, 226). Similarly, Joel Green suggests that in Luke the scene is "proleptic in its anticipation of both the power of the gospel and the opposition it will attract in the Gentile world" (1997, 336).

The Gospels of Mark and Luke indicate that this encounter took place in Gerasa (and Luke 8:26 says it was in the "country of the Gerasenes, which is opposite Galilee"), while the Gospel of Matthew indicates that it took place in "the country of the Gadarenes" (Matt. 8:28). Gerasa was located about thirty-three miles southeast of the Sea of Galilee, while Gadara was located about six miles southeast of it. Some have suggested that the region of Gadara may have actually extended to the shore of the Sea of Galilee (cf. Josephus, *Life* 42 [trans. Thackeray 1926, 19], which places villages belonging to Gadara and Hippos "on the frontiers of Tiberias and of the territory of Scythopolis," and Eisenberg's schematic map of the Decapolis region with his suggested understanding of the territory or region associated with each city in the Roman period [Eisenberg 2019, plate 10]).

Some later manuscripts of each Gospel suggest this event took place at Gergesa, a village thought to have been located at the archaeological site near the modern village of Kursi, on the shore of the Sea of Galilee. That would have been just outside the Decapolis but in Gentile territory. Origen and Eusebius think that this event took place at Gergesa (France 2002, 227). There was an impressive church there in the fifth century that was associated with this story about Jesus. Adela Yarbro Collins suggests Mark may have mistaken Gerasa for Gergesa "if Gerasa was the city of the Decapolis most familiar to [him], as possibly the most renowned of the cities of the district, and yet he was not knowledgeable of its precise location" (2007, 8). It is generally agreed that Mark located the event in Gerasa, and, as Kelly Iverson points out, "Early scribes, sensing the tension between the location and the exegetical data [that the location was too far removed from the Sea of Galilee], corrected this to Gadara and eventually to Gergesa. As the text was copied, the location gained closer proximity to a site suitable for the details of the passage" (2007, 22n4). R. T. France thinks Mark's reference to the Gerasenes probably represents "either a loose use of the term generally for the whole of the Decapolis . . . , of which Gerasa was a leading city, or simply a confusion of similar names, the better-known city substituting for the obscure Gergesa" (2002, 227).

If the event did occur at Gergesa, the Gospel writers' references to Gadara and Gerasa reflect vague or inaccurate knowledge of the area. Alternatively, it may be a matter of each author choosing to mention the nearest geographical reference point that he thinks his particular readers are likely to recognize given the vagueness of *their* knowledge of the area (Bock 1994, 783). When I was living in Ipswich, Massachusetts, and traveling internationally, I would often tell people that I lived in or near Boston or was from Boston. People were more likely to have an idea of where Boston was within the United States than to have any idea where Ipswich was located. In giving geographical information, "close enough and meaningful" is often better than "perfectly accurate but meaningless."

In Mark 7:31–37 we read about another excursion of Jesus into the region of the Decapolis. Mark tells us that Jesus cured a deaf man after returning from a trip to the region of Tyre "by way of Sidon towards the Sea of Galilee, in the region of the Decapolis" (7:31). During Jesus's first visit to the Decapolis area, as described in Mark 5:1–20, he is asked to leave; on this second visit to the Decapolis (in 7:31–37) he is asked for help. On his first visit there he is evidently unrecognized by the people and encourages his would-be disciple to proclaim the Lord's goodness to his community. On his second visit to the area, he is evidently recognized by the people (who bring the deaf man to him and ask him to lay his hands on him), and when they are told not to tell anyone about his healing of the deaf man, they proclaim it all the more (7:36).

Jesus's itinerary on this journey seems "circuitous" to most interpreters (Strauss 2014, 318). One would not normally go from Tyre to the Sea of Galilee or to the Decapolis "by way of Sidon," since Sidon is north of all of those places. Collins also suggests the problem "may lie more in the picture New Testament scholars have of the Decapolis than in Mark's text" (2007, 9). She compares Pliny's description of the Decapolis and suggests that

since the Decapolis may have been understood by Mark to include cities from Damascus in the north to Gerasa and Philadelphia in the south, his description of Jesus' route may be understood as the deliberate construction of a wide-ranging journey in a great arc, approximately 270 degrees of a rough circle. . . . Mark may simply have wanted to show that Jesus traveled in these regions, thus prefiguring, or perhaps even inaugurating, the mission to the Gentiles. (2007, 9)

In Matthew 4:23–25 we are told that after Jesus carries out a powerful ministry of teaching, preaching, and healing throughout Galilee, his fame spreads "throughout all Syria" so that people from those places also bring sick people to him. And "great crowds followed him from Galilee, the Decapolis, Jerusalem, Judea, and from beyond the Jordan" (v. 25). The fact that Jesus draws followers from such a vast area suggests his charismatic power and perhaps a subtle hint that like David's power and influence, his is also felt throughout the larger territory that was considered "biblical Israel" (Luz 2007, 167; cf. Hagner 1993, 81). The attraction of large crowds from these territories (Matt. 4:24–25; 8:34; Mark 5:14; Luke 8:35–36), the exercise of Jesus's power over Gentiles (and demons), and the acclamation of that power by Gentiles in Gentile territory (Mark 5:20; 7:37; Luke 8:39) all serve to reinforce Jesus's limitless authority and his messianic credentials. Through the demoniac(s), Jesus's messianic identity and authority are recognized even in Gentile territory (Matt. 8:29; Mark 5:7; Luke 8:28).

Paul would have passed through the Decapolis on his way to Arabia and then on his return trip to Damascus (Gal. 1:17; for Paul's ministry in Damascus, see 2 Cor. 11:32; cf. Acts 9:8–27; 22:5–11; 26:12, 20), and the Hellenistic Jewish communities there, fully embedded in a predominantly Gentile context, would have been appealing contexts for his ministry (Hengel and Schwemer 1997). According to Eusebius (*Hist. eccl.* 3.5.5), the Christians of Jerusalem fled for refuge to the countryside of Pella in the Decapolis before the fall of Jerusalem to the Romans in 70 CE (although this claim is disputed).

Works Cited

Bock, Darrel L. 1994. *Luke.* Baker Exegetical Commentary on the New Testament. Grand Rapids: Baker.

Chancey, Mark A. 2002. *The Myth of a Gentile Galilee.* SNTSMS 118. Cambridge: Cambridge University Press.

Collins, Adela Yarbro. 2007. *Mark: A Commentary.* Hermeneia. Minneapolis: Fortress.

Eisenberg, Michael. 2019. "New Discoveries at Antiochia Hippos of the Decapolis and Its Sea of Galilee Connection." *EC* 10: 363–82.

France, R. T. 2002. *The Gospel of Mark: A Commentary on the Greek Text.* NIGTC. Grand Rapids: Eerdmans.

Goodman, M. 1992. "Jews in the Decapolis." *ARAM Periodical* 4: 49–56 (vol. 4.1 of *ARAM Periodical* is dedicated to the topic of the Decapolis).

Green, Joel B. 1997. *The Gospel of Luke.* NICNT. Grand Rapids: Eerdmans.

Gundry, Robert H. 1993. *Mark: A Commentary on His Apology for the Cross.* Grand Rapids: Eerdmans.

Hagner, Donald A. 1993. *Matthew 1–13.* WBC 33a. Dallas: Word.

Hengel, Martin, and A. M. Schwemer. 1997. *Paul between Damascus and Antioch: The Unknown Years.* London: SCM.

Hooker, Morna D. 2001. *The Gospel according to St. Mark.* Black's New Testament Commentaries. London: Continuum. Originally published 1991.

Isaac, B. 1981. "The Decapolis in Syria: A Neglected Inscription." *ZPE* 44: 67–74.

Iverson, Kelly R. 2007. *Gentiles in the Gospel of Mark: "Even the Dogs Eat the Children's Crumbs."* LNTS 339. London: T&T Clark.

Kasher, A. 1990. *Jews and Hellenistic Cities in Eretz-Israel: Relations of the Jews in Eretz-Israel with the Hellenistic Cities during the Second Temple Period (332 BCE–70 CE).* TSAJ 21. Tübingen: Mohr Siebeck.

Lichtenberger, Achim. 2022. "The Decapolis." In *A Companion to the Hellenistic and Roman Near East*, edited by Ted Kaizer, 219–28. Hoboken, NJ: Wiley-Blackwell.

Luz, Ulrich. 2007. *Matthew 1–7: A Commentary.* Hermeneia. Minneapolis: Fortress.

Meyers, E. M. 1997. "Jesus in His Galilean Context." In *Archaeology and the Galilee: Texts and Contexts in the Graeco-Roman and Byzantine Periods*, edited by Douglas R. Edwards and C. Thomas McCollough, 57–66. Atlanta: Scholars Press.

Parker, S. T. 1997. "Decapolis." In vol. 2 of *The Oxford Encyclopedia of Archaeology in the Near East*, edited by E. M. Meyers, 127–30. Oxford: Oxford University Press.

Rey-Coquais, J.-P. 1992. "Decapolis." *ABD* 2:116–21.

Strauss, Mark L. 2014. *Mark.* Zondervan Exegetical Commentary on the New Testament. Grand Rapids: Zondervan.

Thackeray, Henry St. J., trans. 1926. *Josephus: The Life, Against Apion.* LCL 186. Cambridge, MA: Harvard University Press.

9

The Synagogue in the Time of Jesus and the New Testament

Eric M. Meyers

Up till very recently, the predominant thinking about the "early" synagogue, by which I mean the synagogue as it existed at the end of the Second Temple period or first century CE, was that it was primarily an all-purpose, communal institution where local and political issues were aired. It was also believed to serve some religious needs and to provide a place where the Torah could be read and studied (Ryan 2017, 13–15), though we know that this was also carried out in homes. The post-70 CE synagogue as it evolved was considered to be more a sacred place in the absence of the temple and a place where the liturgy was chanted and the Torah continued to be read and expounded (Fine and Meyers 1997). It also emerged into a designated kind of space with a special limited number of designs and ground plans. Few scholars would have said that the first-century synagogue was a specific kind of structure or designated space that was, at its very core, an institution that defined early Judaism at that time and long after 70 CE. Much of this renewed interest and confidence in the idea that the first-

century synagogue was a purpose-built structure, though different from what it becomes later, has come about because of the discovery of many new synagogues in Judea and Galilee from this period, though on this point there is not a full consensus (Levine 2005, 135–50; Adler 2022a, 182–86). In addition, there is a greater appreciation of new evidence for the practical application of Torah laws in the everyday lives of Judeans and Galileans. In this regard we have in mind the widespread observance of purity laws during this same time period that are supported by the evidence of ritual baths and stone vessels (Adler 2017; 2022a, 234–36; 2022b). Renewed interest in and research on the Theodotus inscription have also contributed to this new assessment (Kloppenborg Verbin 2000; Krause 2020, 185–86). I believe that the ongoing debate about the "late" dating of the synagogue to the Byzantine period has contributed in part to the continuing skepticism about the nature of the synagogue in this early period (Meyers and Chancey 2012, 208–33).

The idea that the Second Temple period synagogue was a central, if not key, educational institution in nascent Judaism and early Christianity is supported by literary, archaeological, and epigraphical data.[1] Much of the data indicates that this was the case both in Palestine and in the diaspora.

Literary Evidence

The testimony of Philo, Josephus, and the New Testament, as well as later rabbinic sources, provides overwhelming support for the existence of the early synagogue, or specially designated space for gathering and Torah reading and study. In most instances Philo refers to the synagogue as a place of prayer, or *proseuchē*, rather than a place of assembly, *synagogē* (*Spec. Laws* 2.62; *Moses* 2.216; *Embassy* 312). He understands the synagogue to be a place where Jews gathered on Sabbaths and holidays for reading Scripture or Torah followed by instruction and interpretation of the reading (*Good Person* 2.81–82). When Philo mentions Torah, he most certainly is referring to the Pentateuch, or Five Books of Moses. During the reading of Scripture, at appropriate points the congregations might shout out loud, "Amen," as the rabbis suggest (b. Sukkah 51b) in the great synagogue of Alexandria (Philo, *Embassy* 143). The building was so large that the sexton might have had to raise a flag to inform the congregation when to shout out a response. Philo thus assumes that synagogues were abundant in number and were part of the everyday landscape of Judean and disapora Jewish communities in his day, and there is no reason to doubt that his observations reflect reality.

Josephus provides fewer details regarding synagogues, but he recounts in several places disputes that arose in synagogues in Caesarea Maritima, Tiberius, and Dora and in passing provides some details about prayer and Sabbath worship (*J.W.* 2.285–92; *Life* 276–303; *Ant.* 19.300–311).

The New Testament, however, is full of references to synagogues and to Jesus's appearance in them (Adler 2022a, 172–74). It is impossible to include all of them here. In every instance where Jesus makes such an appearance, the day of the week is the Sabbath (Luke 4:16), as is the case at Nazareth. It is in local synagogues that Jesus also proclaims the kingdom of God (Mark 1:38–39; Matt. 4:23–25; Luke 4:14–15, 43–44; John 18:20; see Ryan 2017, 3). Apparently, after the two wars with Rome, smaller villages that could not afford a Torah scroll or synagogue building of any kind heard the Torah read on Mondays and Thursdays when markets were held outside (Safrai 1994, 239–40). Although Jesus was known to have visited synagogues in cities and villages in both Judea and Galilee, only Capernaum and Nazareth are mentioned by name (Mark 1:21; 6:1–2; Luke 7:5; John 6:59; see Ryan 2020, 204); Nazareth is where Jesus was raised (Luke 4:16) and in Capernaum Jesus "made his home" (Matt. 4:13).

We may infer from the many New Testament references to synagogues that the main purpose of the synagogue was Torah reading and learning, and so in every respect the synagogue was at its core an educational institution (Mark 1:21–22; 6:2; Matt. 4:23; 9:35; 13:54; Luke 4:15, 31–32; 6:6; 13:10; John 6:59). Perhaps the most famous case is when Jesus read to the congregation in Nazareth from a scroll of Isaiah and subsequently delivered an oral interpretation of it (Luke 4:16–30). But the incident is even better known as the place from which Jesus was rejected by the elders (Mark 6:1–6; cf. Matt. 13:53–58), which I have explained as in part arising from his strong criticism of the villagers for partaking in the rebuilding of nearby Sepphoris, where Herod Antipas was settling in with a large retinue (Meyers 2015, 91–92). This is not

---

1. This characterization of the synagogue does not eliminate the possibility that some were "associations" (e.g., Acts 6:9) such as Greco-Roman ones (Richardson 2003). Jordan Ryan adopts the term "public synagogue," which he defines as "religio-political institutions with a variety of legal-liturgical, judicial, and conciliar functions" (2017, 34).

to say that many other activities central to his ministry were not associated with or carried out in the synagogue. For example, Jesus conducted exorcisms and healings in synagogues (Mark 1:21–28; 3:1–6; Luke 6:6–11), reprimanded inappropriate behavior in synagogues (Matt. 6:2, 5), and predicted that corporal punishment would be decided in synagogues at the hands of local councils (Mark 13:9). No doubt, there were many other civic activities that are not mentioned. The use of synagogue space or other public venues, including private houses, also allowed distinguished visitors a venue for addressing the community either on Torah law or on matters of public concern or urgency. In a number of cases the person who engaged with Jesus is identified as *archisynagōgos* (Luke 13:14; see below on use of this term in the Theodotus inscription). A similar picture of teaching and preaching and other activities may be inferred from references to diaspora synagogues in Acts (9:2, 20; 13:14–15, 44; 14:1; 17:1–4, 10–12, 17; 18:4–7, 26; 19:8), including Damascus, Antioch in Pisidia, Iconium, Thessalonica, Beroea, Athens, Corinth, and Ephesus. The continuity and extensive connection between the synagogues of Jesus in Judea and Galilee and the diaspora are unmistakable: to underestimate the importance these special places had achieved in early Judaism and Christianity is to miss the most central element of these epochal times.[2]

Archaeological Evidence

Inscriptions

First and foremost we must consider the Theodotus inscription discovered in a cistern in Jerusalem in Raymond Weill's 1913–14 excavations on the eastern slope of the Ophel. Let me quote it in full:

2. It is impossible to do justice to the topic of the pre-70 diaspora synagogue in such a short treatment. Hence we have highlighted some key material, especially epigraphical data and some literary sources. The reader should see Levine 2005, 81–134.

Theodotus, son of Vettenos, priest and *archisynagogos*, son of an *archisynagogos*, and grandson of an *archisynagogos*, built the synagogue for the reading of the Law and the teaching of the commandments and [built] the guest house, and the [other] rooms, and the water fittings [installations?] for the lodging of those in need of it from abroad, [the foundations] of which were laid by his father and the elders and Simonides. (Meyers and Chancey 2012, 208; see also 312n21)

The inscription is securely dated to the first century CE, and since it was not found in situ we are not completely certain of where the original building stood, though it is hard to believe it would be far from the find spot on the Ophel. The word *synagogē* is used to denote a building with a special grouping or congregation and special functions. It is clear that the building or congregation predates the inscription by some three generations. The repeated use of the term *archisynagōgos* linking it to priestly descent, its association with a Roman background, and its location all suggest a connection with pilgrimage and ritual purity concerns. We know there are contemporary ritual baths in the area, and the inscription was found in a cistern. If there is a connection with pilgrimage, it is not too much to suggest that the water installations in the inscription may well refer to *miqwa'ot*, or ritual baths whose use was required by priests and pilgrims before entering the temple complex. Be that as it may, the most important conclusion to be drawn from the inscription is that the main purpose of this synagogue was the reading of the Law and the teaching of the commandments (Adler 2022a, 175–76). These two pillars were to define the synagogue for millennia to come but do not rule out that it was used for other purposes too (as we have already indicated). The synagogue space or rooms were also used to offer hospitality to guests—in the present instance most probably connected to pilgrimage.

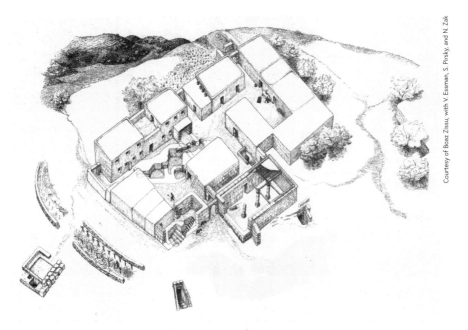

Courtesy of Boaz Zissu, with V. Essman, S. Pirsky, and N. Zak

Fig. 9.1. Village of Horvath Ethri with early synaogoue at right

Epigraphical remains from the diaspora substantiate the status of the synagogue as the central educational and communal institution of Judaism at the end of the Second Temple period, especially in the first century CE. Several inscriptions from Berenice (Cyrene) in Libya support this (Levine 2005, 96–104; Adler 2022a, 175–79; 2022b, 46). A surprising aspect of several of these inscriptions is that they refer to the synagogue using the word "amphitheater" (Levine 2005, 99), which is possibly an allusion to the oval shape of the structure. The Jewish community is referred to as the *politeuma*. The earliest inscription (end of the 1st c. BCE) honors one Decimus Valerius Dionysios, a major donor and member of the *politeuma*; it also indirectly refers to the days of assembly, interpreted to mean the Sabbath. A slightly later inscription (24–25 CE) names the leaders (or archons of the community), thanks a Roman citizen for his support of the community, and is dated to Sukkot. A third inscription from 55 CE commemorates a series of donations from eighteen individuals who made the renovations of the synagogue

possible, and in this one the term *synagogē* is used (Levine 2005, 102). In quoting Philo's *Embassy to Gaius* (155–157 CE), Levine notes that Philo's comments on the Roman Jewish community and its synagogues in the first century CE accurately sum up the situation of Jews in the diaspora: "The Jews possessed a communal building, met regularly, especially on Sabbaths, designated study as the focal liturgical activity, and sent funds (i.e., the first fruits) to Jerusalem" (Levine 2005, 106; cf. Adler 2022a, 171–72). This statement matches very well what we understand to be the message of the data from Palestine, though the terminology and degree of Hellenization are quite different.[3]

First-Century Synagogues in the Land of Israel

One of the main reasons for doubting the existence of the physical "early" synagogue in the

3. For a full discussion of the diaspora evidence, see Levine 2005, 81–134, and the entries in Olsson and Zetterholm 2003, 141–234.

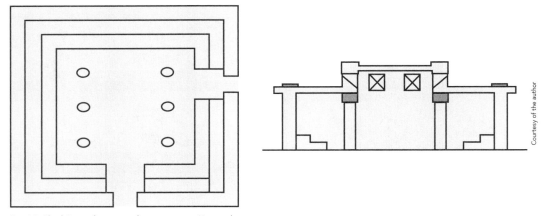

Fig. 9.2. Ehud Netzer's proposed synagogue at Nazareth

Holy Land until recently is that only a few certain examples were known. The first and perhaps best known of them was Masada, where biblical scrolls were discovered in the course of excavations led by Yigael Yadin (Yadin 1981). Gamla soon followed (Gutman 1981; Meyers and Chancey 2012, 212–14), as did Herodium (Foerster 1981, 24–29). In a recent summary of the archaeology of the first-century synagogue, Jordan Ryan lists eight "canonical" structures, by which he means those everyone can agree are early buildings (2020, 198–99), but Rachel Hachlili lists fifteen synagogues from this period, both in Judea and in Galilee (2013, 23–54). The most notable newcomers to the list would be the two found at Magdala on the Sea of Galilee, identified with Taricheae (De Luca and Lena 2015). It is important to observe that while most of the sites are in small villages, Magdala is a large town or city. While the total number might seem modest, the important literary evidence, alongside the archaeological data, makes a strong case for assuming that there were many actual synagogues. The earliest of the buildings, which date to the late Hellenistic period, are Modi'in (Umm el-'Umdan) and possibly Jericho, a hypothesis that has not won much scholarly support (Netzer 1999). Nonetheless, Netzer's identification and dating to the Hasmonean period must be taken seriously. Other

important early synagogues include Horvath Ethri, Qiryat Sefer, Tel Rekhesh, Cana, Khirbet at-Tuwana, and Khirbet Diab (Meyers and Chancey 2012, 210–22; Ryan 2020, 198–202).

The discovery of so many new synagogue structures has contributed to the consensus today that Galilee was overwhelmingly Jewish in the time of Jesus and was not devoid of Torah, or Gentile, or heavily Hellenized, as many scholars have claimed (Reed 2000, 8–12). The older view that Galilee was either Gentile or composed of Jews ignorant of the law was influenced by Yochanan ben Zakkai, who thought the area was inhabited by many poorly educated Jews: "Galilee, O Galilee, why do you hate the Torah so?" (y. Shabb. 15d).

The fact that so many excavations have been undertaken in the last twenty-five years or so is surely testimony to the interest in the newly recognized discipline of the archaeology of early Christianity (Meyers forthcoming). The south, Judea and Jerusalem, absorbed much more Greco-Roman culture at the end of the Second Temple period than Galilee in the north. This included the Greek language, arenas for sports events, hippodromes, theaters, and other enormous building projects such as the Jerusalem temple, Herodium, Sebaste, the port of Caesarea Maritima, and Masada, to mention only a few. Though Galilee lagged somewhat

Fig. 9.3. Stone vessels from Shu'afat, first century CE

behind Judea and Samaria, when Sepphoris and Tiberius were established in the early part of the first century, the region began to catch up, and Magdala (Taricheae) strongly supports the view that a Jewish urban environment was evolving. The synagogues at Magdala are proof of this, as are some of the other remains there, including ritual baths and houses that are of the highest quality and building style. In general, however, the economy and lifestyle of the Galilee region were simple and mainly agricultural. We have no evidence that Greek was spoken there in the time of Jesus. To be sure, certain local industries would greatly expand after the population explosion following the two revolts with Rome, such as pottery manufacturing, including lamps (Kefar Hananiah and Shikhin) and textiles (Sepphoris); olive oil production was always a major product of the region. The olive oil from Gush Halav (Gischala) was considered so pure and refined that the Jewish community of Tyre preferred it over oil from other suppliers, even though it was much more expensive (Longstaff 1990). Magdala was known for its salted fish (Magdala Taricheae means "Magdala of the fish salters"). One industry we know emerged in the time of

Jesus was the chalkstone vessel industry, arising from the belief that stoneware unlike ceramic vessels were impervious to contamination from an impure person. A large manufacturing center for these vessels was recently discovered near Nazareth, at 'Einot Amitai, only a few miles from Cana, and is being excavated by Yonatan Adler (2022a, 66–71; see fig. 9.3).

One of the hallmarks of Jewish observance of biblical law in the time of Jesus was the fear of bodily pollution from a menstruant, contact with a corpse or dead animal, a nocturnal emission, and so on. Ritual handwashing is associated with table fellowship. Ritual baths (or *miqwa'ot*) for complete immersion, along with stone vessels, are often found near olive presses or wine presses to ensure that the individuals working the presses are pure (Adler 2008). These stone vessels are most famously mentioned in the Gospel of John in connection with the wedding at Cana, where Jesus turned water into wine: "Now standing there were six stone water jars for the Jewish rites of purification, each holding twenty or thirty gallons" (John 2:6). Over the course of recent decades the discovery of such vessels alongside ritual baths and other items of Jewish use—such as

Courtesy of the author

Fig. 9.4. Ritual bath at Sepphoris. Reconstruction drawing by Anna Iamim.

spatulate Herodian lamps made in Judea found in Galilee, and faunal remains devoid of any pig (Grantham 2018)—has demonstrated that Jewish observance of biblical law was high in the first century CE if not a bit earlier (Adler 2017; 2022a, 234–36). At Sepphoris, just four kilometers from Nazareth as the crow flies, on the western summit, around thirty ritual baths dating to the early Roman period (i.e., 1st c. CE) have been identified (see fig. 9.4; Meyers and Gordon 2018), along with many stone vessels (Reed 2018).

Plan and Function of the Early Synagogue

Knowing the larger social and religious context for the synagogue allows us to return to our subject and ask the question: What is most distinctive about its plan and/or structure that leads us to identify or reject a building as a synagogue? The synagogue at Masada is 15 by 12 meters and includes a small room (5.7 by 3.5 meters) in the northern corner (see fig. 9.5). Five simple, undecorated columns supported the roof. Four rows of benches are attached to the surrounding walls, and one bench abuts the northern room. Yadin correctly was impressed

with its size and identified it as an assembly hall, and when scrolls of Ezekiel and Deuteronomy were recovered from the northern room it was labeled a synagogue (1966, 168–80). The northern extension room, because of the scrolls, is often associated with a genizah or scroll room. It is not to be confused with the later Torah Shrine, which became a major feature of the late Roman synagogue. There is no internal furnishing except the benches that direct focus to the center of the space. In light of the extensive literary evidence and other data to support Jewish life at this time, calling it a synagogue, a Beit Knesset, seems the correct and proper assumption. In other Judean examples, there is no evidence for sacred orientation being a defining characteristic as in the later Galilean synagogue. But the placement of the decorated stone block with menorah suggests that at Magdala orientation to the south, toward Jerusalem, was accepted practice.

In selecting an example from the north to discuss, let us look at the synagogue at Magdala with the intention of shedding further light on the nature of the early synagogue in an urban and affluent setting. First let us look

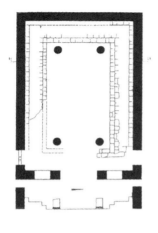
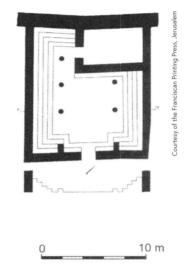

Courtesy of the Franciscan Printing Press, Jerusalem

0   10 m

Fig. 9.5. Herodium and Masada

at the plan of the synagogue. The synagogue is the northernmost building found at the site, and the structure is 120 square meters (or 1,300 square feet) (The exact length of the walls is not published in the reports, but the dimensions are about 11 by 11 meters.) The building is dated to the early or middle of the first century CE, its second phase. It is nearly square, colonnaded, and "surrounded on all four sides with a continuous aisle and benches, with portions of fine mosaic floor surviving in the eastern aisle, an entrance from the vestibule on the west (possibly used as *bet ha-midrash*), and a small room (likely a *genizah* or repository for Torah scrolls) with a mosaic floor and wall paintings in the southwestern corner" (De Luca and Lena 2015, 312; see also Aviam 2018, 128–33). It is unclear exactly when the stuccos and colorful frescoes in the Pompeian style were added. The western wall has two rows of benches. A decorated carved limestone block or pedestal (see fig. 9.6) was found in the center of the building, but whether that is its original placement cannot be determined with certainty.

Much attention has correctly focused on the limestone block, its function, and its decoration (Binder 2014; Doering 2020, 143–49; Newman

2020, 155–71). If in fact it was found more or less in its original position in the center of the synagogue, then we would think that the building was oriented south toward Jerusalem. At Gamla the main entrance is in the south and facing Jerusalem, and some scholars have suggested the row of stone pavers there mark the place for reading of the Torah (Meyers and Chancey 2012, 213). The limestone block at Magdala has four irregularly shaped small legs that suggest they were intended to be inserted into the floor. The decorations are familiar and show a strong veneration for the temple in Jerusalem, with a menorah reminiscent of the temple lampstand carved on the short front side, flanked by two ceramic vessels and two columns that suggest the temple facade. A double arcade on the two long sides also suggests the temple architectural style. A small oil lamp decorates the corners. The top of the stone is decorated with what appears to be a depiction of the showbread table. The artistic program is consistent with what we know from the temple decorations and contemporary art on ossuaries and other architectural fragments. The stone appears to be the pedestal for a table of some sort for the reading of a scroll; however, its superstructure

Fig. 9.6. The Magdala Stone

is unknown and entirely conjectural.[4] Because Magdala is associated with the twenty-four priestly courses, its elite appearance and association with wealthy priestly families are supposed (Bauckham 2018a, 2018b).

The focal point of the first-century synagogue was in most cases the center of the assembly room (Hachlili 2013, 54), and if the location of the Magdala stone discovery is its original placement, near the center of the room, the Magdala synagogue supports such a view. But the placement of the stone at Magdala also suggests, along with the possibility of a Torah Shrine at Gamla (or readers' table?), that prayer(?) and reading of Scripture were already directed toward the Jerusalem temple pre-70 CE, at least in some locations. In the

4. The discussion over the meaning of the decoration and use of the limestone block is extensive and ongoing, so much so that it is often referred to as a "stone of contention." For a full and recent discussion of the possibilities, see Aviam and Bauckham 2018.

later synagogue the Torah Shrine or fixed receptacle for the biblical scrolls becomes the focal point of worship and is usually located on the Jerusalem-facing wall.

Conclusion

Despite the relatively low numbers of physical examples of first-century synagogues in the Holy Land and in the diaspora, the evidence for assuming that they played a central role in the lives of Jews and early followers of Jesus is unmistakable. And we must not forget that many large houses had courtyards or spaces that were used for Torah study or prayer. Even our cursory examination of some key literary and epigraphical references underscores how important it was to read Scripture and interpret it, not only for proclaiming the word of God but also for educating the vast majority of the population that could not read and whose basis of learning was aurality (the shared learning of written texts communicated orally). With a relatively low rate of literacy in the Roman Empire (10–15 percent, with regional variations up to 20 percent), Jewish literacy was much lower, around 3 percent (Hezser 2001, 496).[5] I understand these low projections for Jews in Palestine to reflect the fact that the majority of the Jewish population lived in small villages and towns in Galilee and was rural in character. Most of these small settlements did not have synagogues, let alone biblical scrolls or libraries, as was common in other places in the Roman Empire. With the schools of the sages mostly located in urban areas, village life often depended on visitors to teach or tell stories from the Bible by memory or by reading from a scroll carried with them. While no other institution than the synagogue could play such a seminal role in reading, learning, and listening to the Torah proclaimed and interpreted, except the temple in Jerusalem, we may also consider the possibility that in small villages and towns (where there is no trace of a synagogue) such activity also was practiced from time to time in outdoor public spaces or in large houses. It is no wonder the evolving institution of the synagogue became the main vehicle for Jewish survival after the two wars with Rome. It allowed Judaism to prosper and survive in the homeland and in the diaspora. But it was also the church that inherited its legacy and took the message of Christianity to the entire world.

Works Cited

Adler, Y. 2008. "Second Temple Period Ritual Baths Adjacent to Agricultural Installations: The Archaeological Evidence in Light of Halakhic Sources." *JJS* 59: 62–72.

———. 2017. "Toward an 'Archaeology of Halakha': Prospects and Pitfalls of Reading Early Jewish Ritual Law into the Ancient Material Record." *Archaeology and Text: A Journal for the Integration of Material Culture with Written Documents in the Ancient Mediterranean and Ancient Near East* 1: 27–38.

———. 2022a. *The Origins of Judaism: An Archaeological-Historical Reappraisal.* New Haven: Yale University Press.

———. 2022b. "The Genesis of Judaism." *Biblical Archaeology Review* 48, no. 4: 42–49.

Aviam, M. 2018. "The Synagogue." In *Magdala of Galilee: A Jewish City in the Hellenistic and Roman Period*, edited by R. Bauckham, 127–34. Waco: Baylor University Press.

Aviam, M., and R. Bauckham. 2018. "The Synagogue Stone." In *Magdala of Galilee: A Jewish City in the Hellenistic and Roman Period*, edited by R. Bauckham, 135–60. Waco: Baylor University Press.

Bar Ilan, M. 1992. "Illiteracy in the Land of Israel in the First Centuries CE." In *Essays in the Social Scientific Study of Judaism and Jewish Society*, edited by S. Fishbane and S. Schoenfeld, 2:46–61. Hoboken, NJ: Ktav.

Bauckham, R. 2018a. "Magdala in Rabbinic Traditions." In *Magdala of Galilee: A Jewish City in the Hellenistic and Roman Period*, edited by R. Bauckham, 307–44. Waco: Baylor University Press.

———. 2018b. "Magdala in the List of the Twenty-Four Priestly Settlements." In *Magdala of Galilee: A Jewish City in the Hellenistic and Roman Period*, edited by R. Bauckham, 287–305. Waco: Baylor University Press.

Binder, D. D. 2014. "The Mystery of the Magdala Stone." In *A City Set on a Hill: Essays in Honor of James F. Strange*, edited by D. A. Warner and D. D. Binder, 17–48. Mountain Home, AR: BorderStone.

De Luca, S., and A. Lena. 2015. "Magdala/Taricheae." In *The Archaeological Record from Cities, Towns, and Villages*, edited by D. Fiensy and J. Strange, 280–342. Vol. 2 of *Galilee in the Late Second Temple and Mishnaic Periods*. Minneapolis: Fortress.

Doering, L. 2020. "The Synagogue at Magdala: Between Localized Practice and Reference to the Temple." In *Synagogues in the Hellenistic and Roman Periods: Archaeological Finds, New Methods, New Theories*, edited by L. Doering and A. R. Krause, 127–54. Göttingen: Vandenhoeck & Ruprecht.

Fine, S., and E. M. Meyers. 1997. "Synagogues." In *The Oxford Encyclopedia of Archaeology in the Near East*, edited by E. M. Meyers, 5:118–23. Oxford: Oxford University Press.

Foerster, G. 1981. "The Synagogues at Masada and Herodium." In *Ancient Synagogues Revealed*, edited by L. I. Levine, 24–30. Jerusalem: Israel Exploration Society.

Grantham, B. J. 2018. "Faunal Remains." In *Sepphoris III: The Architecture, Stratigraphy, and Artifacts of the Western Summit of Sepphoris*, edited by E. M. Meyers, C. L. Meyers, and B. D. Gordon, 871–88. University Park, PA: Eisenbrauns.

Gutman, S. 1981. "The Synagogue at Gamla." In *Ancient Synagogues Revealed*, edited by L. I. Levine, 30–34. Jerusalem: Israel Exploration Society.

Hachlili, R. 2013. *Ancient Synagogues—Archaeology and Art: New Discoveries and Current Research*. Leiden: Brill.

Harris, W. V. 1989. *Ancient Literacy*. Cambridge, MA: Harvard University Press.

Hezser, C. 2001. *Jewish Literacy in Roman Palestine*. Tübingen: Mohr Siebeck.

Kloppenborg Verbin, J. S. 2000. "Dating Theodotus (*CIJ* II 1410)." *JJS* 51: 243–80.

Krause, A. R. 2020. "The Rhetoric of Synagogue Space: Theoretical Issues in the Study of Jewish Institutions in Literary Sources." In *Synagogues in the Hellenistic and Roman Periods: Archaeological Finds, New Methods, New Theories*, edited by L. Doering and A. R. Krause, 175–88. Göttingen: Vandenhoeck & Ruprecht.

Levine, L. I. 2005. *The Ancient Synagogue: The First Thousand Years*. 2nd ed. New Haven: Yale University Press.

Longstaff, T. R. W. 1990. "Gush Halav in the Ancient Literary Sources." In *Excavations at the Ancient Synagogue of Gush Halav*, edited by E. M. Meyers and C. L. Meyers, with J. R. Strange, 16–21. Winona Lake, IN: Eisenbrauns.

Meyers, E. M. 2015. "Mark 1:39: 'And He Went throughout All of Galilee . . .'—Sepphoris and First-Century Galilee." In *The Gospels in First-Century Judaea*, edited by S. Notley and J. P. García, 88–96. Leiden: Brill.

———. Forthcoming. "New Testament and Archaeology: When and How They Developed as a Distinct Field." In *Studies in Archaeological, Historical, and Literary Context of the New Testament in Honor of the Work of James F. Strange*, edited by J. R. Strange et al. Tsemakh, Israel: Ostracon.

Meyers, E. M., and M. A. Chancey. 2012. *Alexander to Constantine*. Vol. 3 of *Archaeology of the Land of the Bible*. New Haven: Yale University Press.

Meyers, E. M., and B. D. Gordon. 2018. "The Ritual Baths: Introduction and Catalog." In *Sepphoris III: The Architecture, Stratigraphy, and Artifacts of the Western Summit of Sepphoris*, edited by E. M. Meyers, C. L. Meyers, and B. D. Gordon, 391–418. University Park, PA: Eisenbrauns.

Netzer, E. 1999. "A Synagogue from the Hasmonean Period Recently Exposed in the Western Plain of Jericho." *Israel Exploration Journal* 49: 203–21.

Newman, J. H. 2020. "Contextualizing the Magdala Synagogue in Its Place: An Exercise in Liturgical Imagination." In *Synagogues in the Hellenistic and Roman Periods: Archaeological Finds, New Methods, New Theories*, edited by L. Doering and A. R. Krause, 155–75. Göttingen: Vandenhoeck & Ruprecht.

Olsson, B., and M. Zetterholm, eds. 2003. *The Ancient Synagogue from Its Origins until 200 CE*. Stockholm: Almqvist & Wiksell.

Reed, J. 2000. *Archaeology and the Galilean Jesus: A Re-examination of the Evidence*. Harrisburg, PA: Trinity Press International.

———. 2018. "Stone Vessel Assemblage." In *Sepphoris III: The Architecture, Stratigraphy, and Artifacts of the Western Summit of Sepphoris*, edited by E. M. Meyers, C. L. Meyers, and B. D. Gordon, 749–67. University Park, PA: Eisenbrauns.

Richardson, P. 2003. "An Architectural Case for Synagogues as Associations." In Olsson and Zetterholm 2003, 90–109.

Ryan, J. J. 2017. *The Role of the Synagogue in the Aims of Jesus*. Minneapolis: Fortress.

———. 2020. "The Contributions of Historical and Archaeological Study of Early Synagogues to Historical Jesus Research." In *Synagogues in the Hellenistic and Roman Periods: Archaeological Finds, New Methods, New Theories*, edited by L. Doering and A. R. Krause, 189–214. Göttingen: Vandenhoeck & Ruprecht.

Safrai, Z. 1994. *The Economy of Roman Palestine*. New York: Routledge.

Yadin, Y. 1966. *Masada: Herod's Fortress and the Zealots' Last Stand*. London: Weidenfeld & Nicolson.

———. 1981. "The Synagogue at Masada." In *Ancient Synagogues Revealed*, edited by L. I. Levine, 19–23. Jerusalem: Israel Exploration Society.

10

Temples

TIMOTHY WARDLE

Religion in the first-century CE world touched on all aspects of family, civic, and national life, and temples were the most public place where religious activities played out. They were sacred spaces, providing access to the deities in ways unimaginable in any other location. In addition to their religious functions, temples served as economic drivers, political symbols, and a primary location for social and civic interactions. In what follows we will discuss the Jewish temple in Jerusalem before turning to a discussion of temples in the larger Mediterranean world.

Judaism and the Jewish Temple

Whereas every city of any size in the Mediterranean world had multiple Greek and Roman temples, Jerusalem was the location for the one Jewish temple. This "fact" was so well understood that Josephus could declare Jerusalem home to the "one temple for the one God" (*Ag. Ap.* 2.193 [Thackeray 1926, 371]). Josephus's statement was not altogether true—as he well knew—since he is our primary source

for the existence of other temples dedicated to the worship of the God of Israel outside of Jerusalem (Wardle 2010, 98–139). In the early second century BCE, Onias IV, a member of the high priestly family in Jerusalem, built a Jewish temple at Leontopolis in Egypt following his expulsion from Jerusalem (*J.W.* 1.31–33; 7.423–32). Similarly, a Samaritan temple dedicated to the God of Israel existed on Mount Gerizim for several hundred years before it was destroyed by John Hyrcanus in the late second century BCE (*Ant.* 11.302–47; 13.254–56; *J.W.* 1.62–63). As evidenced by Jesus's conversation with the Samaritan woman in John 4, the memory of this Samaritan temple remained strong long after its destruction. But for the vast majority of Jews in the Jewish heartland and diaspora, these two temples were of little consequence. Their temple was in Jerusalem, in the place where they believed God dwelled in a special way and the location that symbolized the connection between the God of Israel and the people of Israel.

Situated on the eastern side of Jerusalem just above the Kidron Valley and across from

Fig. 10.1. Model of the Jerusalem Temple in the first century CE

the Mount of Olives, the Jerusalem temple complex commanded the attention of anyone visiting the city. It had been this way for a long time. Solomon built the first temple dedicated to the God of Israel in this location, and following the sixth-century BCE Babylonian invasion, Jews built another temple atop the ruins of the first. But the temple that Jesus visited in the first century CE was even more magnificent than what came before (Sanders 1992, 54–69). In 20/19 BCE Herod the Great extended the temple platform and transformed the temple itself, turning an already impressive temple complex into an extraordinary one. Thirty-five acres in size and roughly 460 meters by 300 meters, Herod's Temple Mount was far bigger than any other temple precincts in Greek and Roman heartlands.

The temple area contained several courtyards of diminishing size. The Court of the Gentiles was the largest. It was surrounded by porticos on all four sides, with the most ornate, the Royal Portico, adorning the southern side, and an area called Solomon's Portico stretching along the eastern wall. Visitors would enter primarily on the southern side through double and triple gates, with some further entrances along the western side. Between this court and the next was a short wall with a notice written in Greek and Latin forbidding Gentiles from proceeding any further. Moving inward, one would pass through the Court of the Women (as far as Jewish women could go) and the Court of the Israelites (as far as nonpriestly Jewish men could go) before arriving at the innermost courtyard and altar, where only priests were allowed. Here stood the center of the Jewish religious system, for the altar was where animals were sacrificed to atone for sins and keep fellowship with the God of Israel. The temple itself, which stood just behind the altar, contained a larger chamber (holy place) and a smaller one (the holy of holies), separated by a lavishly decorated curtain. No statue of the God of Israel could be found in this temple (a fact Gentiles found strange), for the Torah proscribed the making of any images. Per Josephus, the front of the temple was covered with plates of gold, the rest with marble, and when the sun shone on the temple people had to avert their eyes (*J.W.* 5.222–23). The "one temple for the one God" was beautiful to behold.

This massive temple complex could easily accommodate all visitors on normal days (Stevenson 2001, 136–51). But during festival days, and especially pilgrimage festivals, the numbers would swell. Several hundred thousand pilgrims would gather in the city during Passover, Shavuot (Feast of Weeks), and Sukkot (Feast of Tabernacles). Those living within a few days' walk came regularly, while diaspora Jews came once or twice in their lifetime. Whatever the distance, worshipers had to undergo purification rites before entering the temple, for human impurity could not come into contact with God's holiness. Normal bodily processes, such as the emission of semen or menstrual blood, rendered a person ritually impure, as did any contact with a dead body. The type of impurity dictated the necessary purification rites, which lasted between one and seven days and usually involved immersion in water. Once a person was ritually pure, they could enter the temple courts. The pilgrimage festivals were clearly religious in nature, but they also provided an economic boon to the city. Whole industries devoted to hospitality were required to support the massive number of pilgrims, and the sheer number of sacrifices necessitated vast quantities of animals, water, firewood, and the like. Not only did pilgrims flood the city, but money did as well, and much of this money found its way to the temple. The annual half-shekel temple tax paid by all male adult Jews contributed to the temple upkeep, along with any required tithes and other gifts from visitors from as far away as Spain and Adiabene.

Priests and Sacrifices

The priests were responsible for the continuance of the proper worship of the God of Israel, and the primary way this occurred at the temple was through animal sacrifices (Sanders 1992, 77–92). Jews knew that God could be worshiped anywhere, but the Torah made clear that sacrifice could be performed only in the temple. When a Jewish worshiper came to Jerusalem, the priests would hear their confession, slaughter the unblemished animals or birds, and depending on the type of sacrifice, burn all or part of the meat. Priests also recited portions of Scripture, led prayers or other forms of public worship, and burned incense. During a major festival such as Passover, all priests likely came to Jerusalem to help perform the sacrifices. Otherwise, priests lived in various cities and towns throughout the land and followed a regular rotation for serving in the temple.

As in the Roman world, the Jewish religious system depended on animal sacrifice and other offerings (Sanders 1992, 103–18). Some sacrifices were offered on behalf of the Jewish people at large. Every morning and evening a male year-old lamb was offered as a burnt offering to atone for the sins of the Jewish people, with offerings of flour, wine, and oil accompanying the sacrifice. Individual sacrifices were also offered. Sin and guilt offerings fulfilled the rites of purification and made amends for intentional and unintentional transgressions of the Torah. Repentance and confession of sin necessarily accompanied these sacrifices, or else the sacrifice was not effective. In addition, peace offerings could be offered for the purposes of thanksgiving, fulfillment of a vow, or a freewill offering. Sacrifices occurred daily and were an integral part of the Jewish religion, but most Jews came to the temple for the purpose of sacrifice only a few times a year. The experience would likely have been equal parts awe inspiring and sobering.

Jesus and Jewish Christians

When in Jerusalem, Jesus seems to have made a habit of being in the temple area (Walker 1996, 269–89). While he could be very critical of anything that took away from the sanctity of the temple (Matt. 21:12–17; John 2:13–22) and spoke of the coming destruction of the temple and city (Matt. 24:1–4), he was not critical of Jews worshiping in the temple through prayer and sacrifice. Jesus was in the temple as an infant (Luke 2:22–38) and as a boy (Luke 2:41–51). He rode a donkey into Jerusalem in full view of the temple (Mark 11:1–11), spoke of the temple as his father's house (John 2:16), and had his disciples prepare the Passover meal, which necessitated offering a lamb in the temple as a sacrifice (Matt. 26:19). He paid the temple tax (Matt. 17:24–27), went on pilgrimage to Jerusalem and its temple numerous times (e.g., John 7:10–14), sat in the temple courtyards watching the people (Mark 12:41–44), and, when in Judea, taught frequently in the temple precincts (e.g., Luke 21:37–38). This meant that Jesus and his disciples must have performed the purification rites along with all other Jews in the temple. Jesus's earliest followers appear to have continued in the same vein, as Peter, John, and many others met daily in the temple, went up to the temple at the hour of prayer, and often congregated in Solomon's Portico (Luke 24:53; Acts 2:46; 3:1, 11; 5:12, 25, 42; cf. Skarsaune 2002, 147–59). When Paul returned to Jerusalem, he purified himself and entered the temple (Acts 21:26–30). By all accounts, the earliest Jewish followers of Jesus continued to worship in the temple until its destruction in 70 CE. For these Jewish Christians, following Jesus did not mean that they left Judaism behind. One God and one temple remained integral to their identity.

Temples in the Roman World of the First Century CE

As the Christian movement grew, it expanded beyond the Jewish world and out into a Gentile one. This movement from the monotheistic Jewish world into the polytheistic Gentile world was neither linear nor easy, and as Paul and other early Christians traveled through regions such as Cilicia, Asia Minor, Macedonia, and Achaia, they came into unavoidable con-

tact with temples dedicated to the worship of deities other than the God of Israel (e.g., Acts 14:12–13; 17:22–23; 19:23–37). From cities and villages to mountaintops and sacred groves, temples could be found nearly anywhere, especially along roads, near gates, or in city centers. While many temples were relatively small and only locally known, some—such as the temple of Zeus in Olympia, Athena in Athens, Artemis in Ephesus, Aphrodite in Aphrodisias, and Apollo at Didyma—were famous throughout the Mediterranean world (Pedley 2005, 119–34; Spawforth 2006, 98–99). Temples to deities tended to be found in areas commensurate to their specialties. For instance, temples to the gods responsible for the protection of a city, such as Zeus/Jupiter, Juno, or Minerva, were commonly built in strategically advantageous locations to oversee the city and protect it from harm, and temples dedicated to Hermes/Mercury, god of commerce and communication, were often located near the city forum (Vitruvius, *De arch.* 1.7.1; Jenkyns 2013, 26–27). Regardless of its fame, every city of any size in the ancient Mediterranean world had multiple temples. Corinth, for example, had temples dedicated to Zeus, Aphrodite, Apollo, Poseidon, Hermes, Demeter and Kore, Isis and Serapis, Asclepius, and others, with even more shrines, temples, and monuments marking the roads leading into the city (Bookidis 2005, 142–64).

Temple Layout and Activity

Greek and Roman temples differed architecturally, yet they shared enough features to be easily recognizable. Entrance to temple grounds occurred through some type of gate structure that ushered one into the larger temple complex (Pedley 2005, 57–62). These sacred precincts varied in size, with more expansive ones often containing sculptures, fountains, or buildings designated for dining, training, or theater. In the center of the sacred grounds stood the altar and temple. Temples were usually rectangular and set upon a platform, with larger ones adorned with columns either at the front or on all sides. Their primary function was to house the statue of the deity, which generally would have been visible to those outside. Some temples could be entered, but others were never open, with the altar being the closest a supplicant could come to the deity. It was enough that the deity was in the city, guarding and watching over it.

As in Judaism, the altar was the most important location in any temple, because it was here that ritual activity took place (Hubbard 2013, 111–12; Kiernan 2020, 188–95). Altars were typically situated directly in front of the temple and the image of the deity, with those bringing an offering able to simultaneously see their offering being sacrificed and the deity's image watching over the altar from inside the temple. Blood sacrifice was common, with the blood of cattle, sheep, goats, pigs, and sometimes birds offered on the altar. Depending on the type of sacrifice, meat from the sacrifice would be burned in honor of the deity, distributed to those present, or sold in markets adjacent to the temples. But not all offerings involved the death of an animal (Rives 2007, 23–28). Participants brought incense, grains, cakes, fruits, or vegetables, which were either burned as a sacrifice or left whole on an offering table, and priests poured out offerings of wine (or milk, honey, or olive oil) as libations in honor of the deity. Offerings primarily fell into three main types: to honor or thank the deity for some protection or blessing, to appease the god in cases of misfortune, or to ask for aid in a current or future situation such as before a harvest or birth of a child. Like offerings, gifts such as tables, vases, necklaces, or other jewelry could be given in return for some protection or honor the gods had given.

Divining the will of the gods through oracles, dreams, reading animal entrails, or observing the flight of birds was another important aspect of ancient religion. Some temples, such as those honoring Apollo at Delphi or Didyma, housed an oracle to which one could go for advice, wisdom, and discernment when faced with difficult decisions or situations (Naiden 2013, 47–49; Pedley 2005, 135–51). Those wishing to consult the oracle would undergo several rituals (usually involving some combination of water purification, the payment of money, and a sacrifice) before posing their question to the oracle. Priests would discern the oracle's reply and inform the supplicant of their words or directions. Temple visitors sometimes stayed the night in anticipation of having inspired dreams or being healed of various ailments.

In addition to daily sacrifices and religious activities, festivals to the various deities occurred at regular intervals, with major ones being celebrated by the entire city (Warrior 2006, 68–78). Public holidays entailed visiting temples and some combination of processions, banquets, athletic games, theatrical performances, or musical contests. On many of these occasions, the image of the deity would be taken out of the temple and paraded through the city, with processions often ending at the altar, where special offerings would be sacrificed. For example, the festival of Megalesia in honor of Cybele, known in Rome as the Great Mother, was a weeklong celebration of feasting and theatrical performances, and on the final day her image would be taken out of her temple and paraded to the Circus, where chariot races were performed in her honor (Warrior 2006, 82–85).

House of the God and Civic Responsibilities

The architecture and functions of temples tell us several things. First, temples were seen as sacred places, separate from the more profane or secular space outside of them. In moving into the temple precincts, visitors knew they had entered the dwelling of the god (Spawforth 2006, 74–88).

The Greek (*naos*) and Latin (*aedes*) terms for temples agree on this point, as both speak of temples as the "dwelling place" or "house" of the god. To physically demarcate this movement into a sacred area, participants used basins of water located at the entrance for ritual purification. Since the deity was understood to live in the temple, the closer one drew to the temple itself, the more sacred the area became. In temples that allowed visitors to enter, people would move upward (ascending stairs) and inward (past the doors and into the temple proper) before encountering the statue of the deity on the deity's home turf. Large or small, temples were understood as the home of the deity.

Second, temples provided access to the deity. Only in these spaces could the gods be approached in ways impossible elsewhere (Kiernan 2020, 190–91, 196–201). It is uncertain precisely how visitors to these temples would have understood the image of the deity before them. Was the statue of the goddess Aphrodite a physical manifestation of the goddess herself? A representation of the deity? Something else? Jews and early Christians had a common answer: these images were lifeless works created by human hands representing gods who do not exist (e.g., Wis. 13–15; Josephus, *Ag. Ap.* 2.74–75; 1 Cor. 8:4). But Gentile visitors thought differently, and many did believe the gods were somehow present in their images or that temples were places the gods could inhabit when desired. Regardless, to stand in front of the image of the god or goddess would have been an awe-inspiring experience, and everything that occurred in the temple precincts— the offerings, sacrifices, prayers, adoration of images, and dreams that people sometimes had—would have added to the temple's mystique. Here was a place special to the gods, where they could be encountered.

Third, participation in temple activities was a matter of civic responsibility (Stevenson 2001, 86–96). Veneration of the gods was incumbent upon all citizens of the city, for the gods were responsible for the protection and benefaction of the city. To not honor the gods was to betray the city. An added wrinkle to this idea arose in the first century CE as temples to the Roman emperors begin to appear. In the imperial cult, emperors were venerated in the same way as the gods, and some cities, like Pergamum, promoted loyalty to the Roman Empire by embracing the imperial cult and building temples to the emperor (Warrior 2006, 105–18). The worship of the gods had always been as much political as religious, but now it became even more so. To worship the deities and the emperor was to support the Roman Empire, as the gods blessed the empire and the emperor that governed it. To refuse to do so was a serious offense.

Temples and Early Christians

All of the above created problems for the earliest Christians. Prior to their conversion, Gentile Christians would have willingly and often participated in temple activities. But the worship of anything outside of the God of Israel, be it deity or emperor, was antithetical to Jewish and Christian monotheism, and any participation in temple functions meant continuing to inhabit an understanding of the world in which pagan deities sustained and governed the world. This may explain why Paul spent so much time talking to the Corinthian Christians about eating meat that had been sacrificed in pagan temples (1 Cor. 8–10), why Demetrius and Ephesian silversmiths were so concerned about Paul teaching against the worship of Artemis (Acts 19:23–37), or why Revelation asserted that Pergamum was the location of Satan's throne (Rev. 2:13). Paul (and other early Christian teachers) wanted early Christians to be distinct from those around them and to have their sole allegiance directed toward the God who had sent Jesus, and not toward anything else. Whatever the logic, dissociation from temple worship brought early

Christians into direct conflict with the leaders of the cities in which they lived and with the Roman Empire at large, since not venerating the gods and emperor was interpreted as opposition to the Roman order. Gentile Christians had to make a choice.

Christians also began to appropriate the language and idea of the temple (Wardle 2010, 206–23). One way they did this was to speak of heaven, the place where God now ruled, as a temple (e.g., Heb. 8:1–5; Rev. 4–5). They also adopted temple language and applied it to their own emerging Christian communities. In various writings, Paul and other early Christians described the emerging Christian communities as temples (1 Cor. 3:16–17; 2 Cor. 6:16; Eph. 2:21; cf. Ign. *Eph.* 9.1; 15.3; Ign. *Magn.* 7.2; Ign. *Phld.* 7.2; Barn. 16.1–10) or as constituent parts of the temple such as foundations (Eph. 2:20), pillars (Gal. 2:9; Rev. 3:12), and stones (1 Pet. 2:5; Ign. *Eph.* 9.1). Other early Christian documents connect the temple to individual Christians (2 Cor. 6:16) or Jesus (Mark 12:10; John 2:21). The adoption of this language signaled several things: God is present in our community, holiness must characterize the community, and all are equal participants in this communal temple.

Works Cited

Bookidis, Nancy. 2005. "Religion in Corinth: 146 B.C.E. to 100 C.E." In *Urban Religion in Roman Corinth*, edited by Daniel N. Schowalter and Steven J. Friesen, 141–64. Cambridge, MA: Harvard University Press.

Hubbard, Moyer V. 2013. "Greek Religion." In *The World of the New Testament: Cultural, Social, and Historical Contexts*, edited by Joel B. Green and Lee Martin McDonald, 105–23. Grand Rapids: Baker Academic.

Jenkyns, Richard. 2013. *God, Space, and City in the Roman Imagination*. Oxford: Oxford University Press.

Kiernan, Philip. 2020. *Roman Cult Images: The Lives and Worship of Idols, from the Iron Age to Late Antiquity*. Cambridge: Cambridge University Press.

Naiden, F. S. 2013. *Smoke Signals for the Gods: Ancient Greek Sacrifice from the Archaic through the Roman Periods*. Oxford: Oxford University Press.

Pedley, John. 2005. *Sanctuaries and the Sacred in the Ancient Greek World*. New York: Cambridge University Press.

Rives, James B. 2007. *Religion in the Roman Empire*. Malden, MA: Blackwell.

Sanders, E. P. 1992. *Judaism: Practice and Belief 63 BCE–66 CE*. London: SCM.

Skarsaune, Oskar. 2002. *In the Shadow of the Temple: Jewish Influences on Early Christianity*. Downers Grove, IL: InterVarsity.

Spawforth, Tony. 2006. *The Complete Greek Temples*. London: Thames & Hudson.

Stevenson, Gregory. 2001. *Power and Place: Temple and Identity in the Book of Revelation*. Berlin: de Gruyter.

Thackeray, Henry St. J., trans. 1926. *Josephus: The Life, Against Apion*. LCL 186. Cambridge, MA: Harvard University Press.

Walker, P. W. L. 1996. *Jesus and the Holy City: New Testament Perspectives on Jerusalem*. Grand Rapids: Eerdmans.

Wardle, Timothy. 2010. *The Jerusalem Temple and Early Christian Identity*. Tübingen: Mohr Siebeck.

Warrior, Valerie M. 2006. *Roman Religion*. Cambridge: Cambridge University Press.

11

Greco-Roman Material Culture

David W. J. Gill

Built Environment

The New Testament documents, with the exception of the Gospel narratives, are placed within the built environment of Roman cities. Paul's travels through Syria, Cyprus, Anatolia, and Greece take him through some of the major cities of the eastern Mediterranean: Antioch in Syria, Ephesus, Athens, and Corinth (e.g., Millar 1993; Mitchell 1993a; Mitchell 1993b; Gill and Gempf 1994). The letters addressed to the seven churches in Revelation (Rev. 2–3) are set in some of the key urban centers of western Anatolia: Ephesus, Smyrna, Pergamum, Thyatira, Sardis, Philadelphia, and Laodicea (Walton, Trebilco, and Gill 2017). Essentially, the cities in the eastern Mediterranean emerged from the *poleis* (cities) of the Greek world and from the spread of Greek control following the conquests of Alexander the Great and the subsequent Hellenistic kingdoms of the Attalids and Seleucids. These cities contrasted with the Roman colonies that were established as Rome's influence expanded in the eastern Mediterranean (Levick 1967). These settlements reflected the city of Rome in their culture as well as their architectural design.

The cultural settings for these New Testament narratives and epistles sometimes make specific mention of their physical settings. In some cases, however, the broader context is unmentioned but known from archaeological excavations. It is important to remember that some aspects of the material culture have survived over millennia, whereas other parts—for example, those derived from organic materials—have not. The balance can be regained from a careful reading of classical texts as well as from Greek and Latin inscriptions.

Public Spaces

The Acts of the Apostles hints at the built environment of Roman colonies. Paul arrived at the Roman colony of Philippi in Macedonia (Gill 2017), founded in the wake of the battle between Mark Antony and Octavian, and M. Iunius Brutus and C. Cassius Longinus in 42 BCE. Parts of the colony have been excavated by the French School in Athens. The main public space of the city, the *forum* (the Latin term is translated into Greek: ἀγορά, *agora*), was the setting in the Acts of the Apostles when Paul and Silas were brought before the civic magistrates (Acts 16:19). They were then placed in the civic prison (εἰς φυλακήν, *eis phylakēn*; 16:23), where they experienced a major earthquake.

At Corinth Paul was brought before the tribunal (ἐπὶ τὸ βῆμα, *epi to bēma*) to be heard by the Roman provincial governor, Gallio (Acts 18:12). This is likely to be in the area of the forum lying adjacent to the archaic temple that had survived from the Hellenistic city (Sanders et al. 2018). Both *fora* at Philippi and Corinth were dominated by temples constructed in Roman, as opposed to Greek, architectural style with distinctively high podia (Williams 1987).

The Roman *fora* at Philippi and Corinth contrast with the *agora* of the Greek city of Athens (Camp 2001, 2010). This public space to the north of the acropolis, where the main civic sanctuary was located, had developed since the archaic period. It was here that the buildings associated with the running of the democracy were located, specifically the *bouleuterion* (the council chamber) and the *prytaneion* (where the tribe in charge of the city for the month met) placed on the west side adjacent to the Kolonos Agoraios. The Stoa Basileios (Royal Stoa) was located on the north side and displayed the traditional laws of the city. In the classical period the law courts were located in the agora. The space was transformed during the Hellenistic period by the construction of a double-storied stoa (or colonnade) given to the city by the Attalid rulers from Pergamum in northwest Anatolia. During the reign of Augustus, Marcus Agrippa, the son-in-law of the emperor, presented the city with a concert hall (Odeion) that was constructed in the central open area of the agora. The agora was where Paul met with people while in Athens (Acts 17:17–18). This included engagement with Epi-

curean and Stoic philosophers: the colonnades around the agora no doubt provided suitable meeting places.

One of the main cultural structures in any city was the theater. This consisted of a stepped auditorium with a semi-circular orchestra at the bottom: by the Roman period a *skēnē* building was added. While such structures could be used for performances of plays, their capacity allowed them to be used for public gatherings. At Ephesus the riot provoked by Paul's teaching took place in the theater (εἰς τὸ θέατρον, *eis to theatron*; Acts 19:29). Other well-preserved theaters have survived at the Roman colonies of Philippi and Corinth. At Corinth, the theater was enhanced by the addition of a paved courtyard. This was the benefaction of one of the magistrates (*aediles*) of the colony whose cognomen was Erastus; this is possibly the same Erastus described with the Greek translation of the office, *oikonomos* of the city (ὁ οἰκονόμος τῆς πόλεως; Rom. 16:23). In the Gospels, Jesus uses the term "hypocrite" (ὑποκριτά, *hypokrita*; Matt. 7:5; Luke 6:42), the term for an actor in the Greek theater. A classical theater has been found at the Roman city of Sepphoris near Nazareth (Miller 1992; Netzer and Weiss 1994), and it is possible that performances here would have provided this loan word.

Stadia

Running tracks or stadia were a feature of agonistic festivals in the Greek cities of the eastern Mediterranean. Paul writes to the church at Corinth with an extended image of the stadium (1 Cor. 9:24–27): there is the *stadion* as well as boxing, plus the mention of the crowning of the athletes. Corinth was the city responsible for the Panhellenic games held at the nearby sanctuary of Poseidon at Isthmia (Broneer 1973). The prize crown that was awarded there was made of a pine wreath. At Corinth Paul joined up with Aquila and Priscilla, as they were all tentmakers (σκηνοποιοί, *skēnopoioi*;

Acts 18:3). It has been speculated that the tents or awnings were used to shield the crowds coming to view the nearby Isthmian games; the next games after Paul's visit would have taken place in 51 CE (Broneer 1962).

Harbors

The development of trade under the Roman Empire led to the creation of special harbor facilities around the Mediterranean to allow ships to be brought alongside quays to unload. Before this point, ships had invariably beached, although there were specialized harbor facilities at ports such as the Piraeus that served the city of Athens. Rome itself was served by the port of Ostia at the mouth of the Tiber. The facilities were enhanced by the emperor Claudius to ensure the security of the grain supply for the city of Rome. Corinth served as a major trading hub for the eastern Mediterranean. It had two major ports: Cenchreae on the Saronic Gulf (serving the eastern Mediterranean) and Lechaeum on the Gulf of Corinth (providing access to Italy). Parts of the harbor facilities are still visible at Lechaeum, but the ancient port of Cenchreae is now submerged (Scranton, Shaw, and Ibrahim 1978). The two harbors were separated by the Isthmus of Corinth. In the archaic period a dragway (*diolkos*) had been constructed to allow the movement of goods across this neck of land, thereby reducing the risk of sailing around the southern side of the Peloponnese; parts are still visible parallel with the modern Corinth canal. Paul used the port of Cenchreae to sail to Ephesus (Acts 18:18); the port community was also the home to a local church where Phoebe served (Rom. 16:1).

The main harbor serving the province of Judea was located at Caesarea (Vann 1992; Taylor 2017). The construction of artificial moles protected ships using the harbor; its scale may be explained in terms of Caesarea having the ambition to become the most important port in the eastern Mediterranean by eclipsing Alexandria. It was from Caesarea that Paul left for Tarsus (Acts 9:30). The harbor was dominated by the temple housing the imperial cult.

One of the great natural harbors in the Mediterranean was at Syracuse in Sicily, originally founded as a colony of the Greek city of Corinth (Wescoat and Anderson 1989). Paul's ship called here on his way from Malta to Italy (Acts 28:12). The dangerous situation caused by the lack of a safe harbor along the south coast of Crete was recognized (27:12).

Temples

Greek and Roman temples rarely feature in the New Testament documents, though their prominence in the cities as well as in the countryside would have been apparent. One of the striking images of Paul's time at Athens is his reaction to a city "full of idols" (Acts 17:16).[1] The backdrop to his discussions in the agora is the Athenian acropolis, where the main temple for the city's patron deity was located: the Parthenon, constructed in the 440s and 430s BCE (Hurwit 1999). This contained the colossal gold and ivory statue of Athena Parthenos created by the sculptor Pheidias. Immediately above the north cliffs was the Erechtheion, which marked the legendary origins of the city. To the east of the Parthenon was the temple of Roma and Augustus that served as a focus for the worship of the Roman emperor in Athens. The skyline of the acropolis was dominated by the colossal bronze statue of the Athena Promachos, probably created in the 430s BCE. At the western approach to the acropolis stood the temple of Athena Nike, a reminder that victories were brought to the city by the deity. Cut into the cliffs were a number of cult locations, including the Cave of Apollo, from where the priests would watch for lightning strikes

---

1. Scripture quotations in this chapter are from the ESV unless otherwise indicated.

to know if the city could consult the Delphic oracle. In the agora itself was the temple of Ares, moved by the emperor Augustus from a rural site in Attica (almost certainly Pallene and originally dating to the 420s BCE), as well as the sanctuary of Demeter, which was the city's location for the mystery cult based at Eleusis in Attica (Miles 1998; Stewart et al. 2019; Stewart et al. 2021). Dominating the public space of the agora, and placed above the buildings of the democracy, was the Hephaisteion, which dates to the 440s BCE (Stewart 2018). This public space was the background for Paul's comments when he was brought before the Areopagos—either the court or the physical location to the west of the acropolis—where he stated that the God whom he worshiped "does not dwell in handmade temples" (Acts 17:24, my translation).

The temple of Artemis forms the backdrop to the riot at Ephesus (Acts 19). This temple, one of the recognized wonders of the ancient world, was constructed in the sixth century BCE. The Artemision was so famous that local silversmiths, such as Demetrios, "made silver shrines of Artemis, [and] brought no little business to the craftsmen" (19:24). Presumably these were votive offerings made for those visiting the sanctuary.

One characteristic of Greco-Roman religion was the sacrifice of animals. Sacrificial cattle were presented by the priest of Zeus at Lystra (Acts 14:13). The monumental altar of Zeus at Pergamum was dedicated with colossal reliefs showing the battle between the Olympian gods and the giants. This may form the background to the statement in Revelation 2:13: "I know where you dwell, where Satan's throne is." The Pergamum altar was evoked in the design of the Altar of Peace (Ara Pacis) constructed by Augustus in Rome on the Campus Martius.

The regular sacrifice of cattle and sheep in the sanctuaries of cities meant that there was a supply of meat for the population (Jameson 1988). This is what probably lies behind the statement about "food offered to idols," an issue that emerges in the Corinthian church (1 Cor. 8:1, 4, 10). Church members were faced with the issue of eating meat that had been offered on the altars of the Roman gods and then passed into the food chain. (Although not mentioned in 1 Corinthians, the hides of sacrificed animals would have been used for leather goods in the city, as indicated by an inscription from classical Athens; *IG* 1³ 257: Lind 1985, 257–58; 1987; see also MacKinnon 2014, 224.) Paul highlights the issues to the Christian church by writing, "Eat whatever is sold in the meat market [ἐν μακέλλῳ, *en makellō*] without raising any question on the ground of conscience" (1 Cor. 10:25). The meat market or *macellum* at Corinth was located adjacent to the archaic temple that overlooked the forum (Evangelidis 2019).

Inscriptions

At Athens, Paul came across an altar dedicated to the "unknown god" (Acts 17:23). Paul's meeting at Corinth with Gallio, the governor of the province of Achaia, is fixed by the discovery of an inscription naming the governor at Delphi that can be placed in the spring or summer of 52 through the use of titles of the emperor Claudius (*FdD* III.4.286; see J. H. Oliver 1971). Inscriptions also remind us that Latin was the official language in the colonies of the Greek East: Corinth, Philippi, and Pisidian Antioch (e.g., Kent 1966). Yet graffiti scratched on Roman pottery found at Corinth indicates that Greek was in common use in these centers.

Sculpture

Public spaces and sanctuaries in the Greek world were filled with statues, often honoring civic benefactors and prominent citizens. While most of these have been lost as bronze was melted down and recycled, inscribed statue bases are a relatively common find in excavations. Moreover, for cities like Athens, the second-century CE Roman travel writer Pausanias provides an important description of public spaces and their sculptures (Habicht 1985). At Corinth, the Julian basilica contained a series of imperial marble portraits (Vanderpool 2003).

The great chryselephantine statue of Athena Parthenos that stood within the Parthenon was made from gold and ivory. A companion piece by the same sculptor, Pheidias, stood within the temple of Zeus at Olympia. These statues were intended to be awe inspiring, yet Paul reminded his audience at Athens that "we ought not to think that the divine being is like gold or silver or stone, an image formed by the art and imagination of man" (Acts 17:29). In Revelation the Gentile world continued in "worshiping demons and idols of gold and silver and bronze and stone and wood, which cannot see or hear or walk" (9:20).

Private Spaces

Roman-period housing has not always attracted archaeological investigation in the Greek East compared to the investigation of public buildings. Urban houses have been excavated in Greece at Athens and Patras, although some of the best-preserved examples date to the second century CE. Much information is derived from the well-preserved houses at Pompeii and Herculaneum that were destroyed by the eruption of Vesuvius in 79 CE. Some of the first-century CE Herodian houses in Jerusalem itself show the influence of Roman culture and taste on the Jewish elite.

At Corinth Paul stayed in the house of Titius Justus (Acts 18:7), a building that would conform to Roman norms as would befit a structure in a Roman colony. Such large houses, which would incorporate communal dining areas (*triclinia*), are likely to have served as settings for churches. At Corinth a villa has been exca-

vated at Anaploga, and examples of atrium-style houses are known. Churches were clearly meeting in private houses elsewhere, such as at Colossae (Col. 4:15; see also Philem. 2).

Roads

The Roman Empire was connected by a network of roads that allowed the swift movement of troops to the frontier regions but also facilitated the transport of foodstuffs and other goods (French 1980). The roads were carefully constructed, especially in mountainous regions, to catch available sun so that they were less liable to be blocked in harsh winters. These were paved or graveled roads with solid foundations that allowed them to be used all the year round. The routes and intermediary distances are laid out in Roman itineraries such as the Peutinger Table, a copy of which surfaced in 1508.

Roads feature in the narrative of the book of Acts. When Saul and Barnabas arrive at Salamis on Cyprus, they progress "through the whole island as far as Paphos," the seat of the provincial administration (Acts 13:5–6). The Peutinger Table provides two routes: one of 115 Roman miles, and the other of 142. The shorter southern route is attested in this period by a milestone 11 miles from Paphos (Gill 1995). This was erected after 12 BCE as Augustus was named as *pontifex maximus*.[2]

After leaving Cyprus, Saul (now renamed Paul) and Barnabas arrive at Perga on the south coast of Anatolia (Acts 13:13) and make their way toward the Roman colony of Pisidian Antioch, the family home of Sergius Paulus, the governor of Cyprus (13:7; see Mitchell and Waelkens 1998). They follow the route of the

2. The two routes started in Salamis. One headed to the north coast as far as Arsinoe (Marion) and then turned south to Paphos. The second ran along the south coast to Paphos, passing through Citium, Amathus, and Curium. One of the most useful sets of maps can be found in Cornell and Matthews 1982, 150–51.

Via Sebaste, created by the emperor Augustus in 6 BCE.

When Paul leaves Troy and arrives in Macedonia, he follows the Via Egnatia from Neapolis on the coast and then goes on to the Roman colony of Philippi (Acts 16:11–12). This road was constructed by Cnaeus Egnatius, one of the first proconsuls of the province of Macedonia. The road then headed westward, crossing the River Strymon at Amphipolis, and then passed through Apollonia arriving at Thessalonica (17:1). The road continued to the Adriatic with the two ports of Dyrrachium and Apollonia; it then connected with the Via Appia in Italy that led to Rome. Paul may have traveled this western part of the Via Egnatia in his second visit to Macedonia (20:1–2), as he mentions a visit to Illyricum (Rom. 15:19). At the end of the Acts of the Apostles, Paul arrives at Puteoli in Campania and from there travels to Rome by road (Acts 28:13–16).

Trade and Material Culture

The material finds from excavations are often dominated by pottery and fragmentary marble or stone sculpture. Organic materials rarely survive, though the excavations at Vindolanda just to the south of Hadrian's Wall in northern England have provided valuable insight into wooden and leather objects. Carbonized organic materials have also been recovered from the town of Herculaneum, destroyed by the 79 CE eruption of Vesuvius (e.g., Roberts 2013).

Because of the empire's expanse, the empire could draw on resources from across a wide region, from Syria to Spain, from Egypt to Britain. Indeed items could be brought from outside. The richness of this trade is reflected in a passage in Revelation (18:11–13): "gold, silver, jewels, pearls, fine linen, purple cloth, silk, scarlet cloth, all kinds of scented wood, all kinds of articles of ivory, all kinds of articles of costly wood, bronze, iron and marble, cinnamon, spice, incense, myrrh, frankincense, wine, oil, fine flour, wheat, cattle and sheep, horses and chariots, and slaves." It should be realized that of all these items, few are regularly found in archaeological excavations, reminding us of the gap between the world known from literary, historical, and biblical texts and the extant material culture. Of these items, wine could be identified by the presence of (empty) ceramic transport amphorae, and there are a number of small items that were cut from elephant ivory.

Gold and Silver Plate

The display of wealth in private households included the presentation of gold and silver vessels used for banquets (A. Oliver 1977). Each cup was literally worth its weight in gold or silver, and in some surviving examples small weight inscriptions have been added to the underside, no doubt as a part of a stocktaking exercise. The displays of such wealth in elite households in the Greek East is reflected in 2 Timothy 2:20: "Now in a great house there are not only vessels of gold and silver but also of wood and clay, some for honorable use, some for dishonorable."

Coinage

Coinage served as a major reminder of Roman authority (Burnett 1991). Coins were widely circulated, though individual cities were granted the right to mint coins. One of the best-known examples of coinage in the New Testament is when Jesus asks to see a coin that was used for taxation and he is presented with a denarius (Matt. 22:19–21). He specifically asks about the portrait and inscription of the emperor that are displayed on the coin. Coins also appear in the parables of Jesus, such as the story of the woman who lost one of her ten silver coins or drachmas (Luke 15:8).

Coins were used for valuation, such as when the documents used for "the magical arts" were burned at Ephesus and it was noted that the items were worth 50,000 pieces of silver—in other words, coins (Acts 19:19). Silver tridrachms minted at Ephesus under the emperor Claudius (and showing the statue of Artemis/Diana) weighed just over 10 grams, while silver denarii minted in the city under Vespasian weighed about 2.8 grams. It can be difficult to work out which unit of coinage was in use.

Jewelry and Dress

The impact of Roman imperial styles on the provinces is well documented. Honorific private portraits from the provinces reflect the styles from Rome in the choice of hairstyles (e.g., Zanker 2016). In Paul's first letter to Timothy, he urges women to "adorn themselves in respectable apparel, with modesty and self-control, not with braided hair and gold or pearls or costly attire" (1 Tim. 2:9). This position is echoed by Peter where he makes the point that while the norm in the eastern provinces was to wear elaborate jewelry, members of the church should consider their own attitudes: "Do not let your adorning be external—the braiding of hair and the putting on of gold jewelry, or the clothing you wear" (1 Pet. 3:3). Clearly some were using such ostentatious jewelry to emphasize their status. Pearls that are mentioned as part of women's adornment may, in part, have been derived from Britain. The dedication in the temple of the Divine Julius included a dedication of a cuirass made from pearls from this source, perhaps obtained during one of Caesar's invasions of Britain in 55 and 54 BCE, or perhaps subsequently (Flory 1988). A pair of pearl earrings, perhaps dating to the second century CE, are now in Toronto, though there is no information on where they were found (Kleiner and Matheson 1996, 176, cat. no. 132). Gold jewelry, though not common in the archaeological record, has survived, sometimes in graves (Kleiner and Matheson 1996, 175–80). These items were symbols of elite status, in the

scenario in which "a man wearing a gold ring and fine clothing comes into your assembly" (James 2:2), in contrast with the poor individual who is less finely attired.

Women's dress is known from visual representations in paintings, mosaics, and sculptures. Excavations at Dura Europus have found small fragments of silk that would have been brought from China via the silk route (Kleiner and Matheson 1996, 159, cat. no. 108; Hildebrandt 2017). Expensive purple dress is cited alongside adornment with gold, jewelry, and pearls (Rev. 17:4).

Works Cited

Broneer, O. 1962. "The Apostle Paul and the Isthmian Games." *BA* 25: 1–31.

———. 1973. *Topography and Architecture*. Vol. 2 of *Isthmia*. Princeton: American School of Classical Studies at Athens.

Burnett, A. 1991. *Coins*. Interpreting the Past. London: British Museum Press.

Camp, J. M., II. 2001. *The Archaeology of Athens*. New Haven: Yale University Press.

———. 2010. *The Athenian Agora: Site Guide*. Princeton: American School of Classical Studies at Athens.

Cornell, T., and J. Matthews. 1982. *Atlas of the Roman World*. Oxford: Phaidon. (Cyprus features pp. 150–51.)

Evangelidis, V. 2019. "Macella and Makelloi in Roman Greece: The Archaeological and Textual Evidence." *Hesperia* 88: 283–318.

Flory, M. B. 1988. "Pearls for Venus." *Historia* 37: 498–504.

French, D. H. 1980. "The Roman Road-System of Asia Minor." *ANRW* 2.7.2: 698–729.

Gill, D. W. J. 1995. "Paul's Travels through Cyprus (Acts 13:4–12)." *Tyndale Bulletin* 46: 219–28.

———. 2017. "Early Christianity in Its Colonial Contexts in the Provinces of the Eastern Empire." In Walton, Trebilco, and Gill 2017, 68–85.

Gill, D. W. J., and C. Gempf, eds. 1994. *The Book of Acts in Its Graeco-Roman Setting*. Vol. 2 of *The Book of Acts in Its First Century Setting*. Grand Rapids: Eerdmans.

Habicht, C. 1985. *Pausanias' Guide to Ancient Greece*. Sather Classical Lectures 50. Berkeley: University of California Press.

Hildebrandt, B. 2017. "Silk Production and Trade in the Roman Empire." In *Silk: Trade and Exchange along the Silk Roads between Rome and China in Antiquity*, edited by B. Hildebrandt and C. Gillis, 34–50. Oxford: Archaeopress.

Hurwit, J. M. 1999. *The Athenian Acropolis: History, Mythology, and Archaeology from the Neolithic Era to the Present*. Cambridge: Cambridge University Press.

Jameson, M. H. 1988. "Sacrifice and Animal Husbandry in Classical Greece." In *Pastoral Economies in Classical Antiquities*, edited by C. R. Whittaker, 87–119. Cambridge Philological Society Supplementary Vol. 14. Cambridge: Cambridge Philological Society.

Kent, J. H. 1966. *The Inscriptions, 1926–1950*. Vol. 8.3 of *Corinth*. Princeton: American School of Classical Studies at Athens.

Kleiner, D. E. E., and S. B. Matheson, eds. 1996. *I Claudia: Women in Ancient Rome*. New Haven: Yale University Art Gallery.

Levick, B. 1967. *Roman Colonies in Southern Asia Minor*. Oxford: Oxford University Press.

Lind, H. 1985. "Neues Aus Kydathen: Beobachtungen Zum Hintergrund Der 'Daitales' Und Der 'Ritter' Des Aristophanes." *Museum Helveticum* 42: 249–61.

———. 1987. "Sokrates Am Ilissos: Ig I³ 1 257 Und Die Eingangsszene Des Platonischen 'Phaidros.'" *ZPE* 69: 15–19.

MacKinnon, M. 2014. "Animals, Economics, and Culture in the Athenian Agora: Comparative Zooarchaeological Investigations." *Hesperia* 83: 189–255.

Miles, M. M. 1998. *The City Eleusinion*. Vol. 31 of *The Athenian Agora*. Princeton: American School of Classical Studies at Athens.

Millar, F. 1993. *The Roman Near East 31 BC–AD 337*. Cambridge, MA: Harvard University Press.

Miller, S. S. 1992. "Sepphoris, the Well Remembered City." *BA* 55: 74–83.

Mitchell, S. 1993a. *Anatolia: Land, Men, and Gods in Asia Minor*. Vol. 1, *The Celts in Anatolia and the Impact of Roman Rule*. Oxford: Clarendon.

———. 1993b. *Anatolia: Land, Men, and Gods in Asia Minor*. Vol. 2, *The Rise of the Church*. Oxford: Clarendon.

Mitchell, S., and M. Waelkens. 1998. *Pisidian Antioch: The Site and Its Monuments*. London: Duckworth with the Classical Press of Wales.

Netzer, E., and Z. Weiss. 1994. *Zippori*. Jerusalem: Israel Exploration Society.

Oliver, A., Jr. 1977. *Silver for the Gods: 800 Years of Greek and Roman Silver*. Toledo: The Toledo Museum of Art.

Oliver, J. H. 1971. "The Epistle of Claudius Which Mentions the Proconsul Junius Gallio." *Hesperia* 40: 239–40.

Roberts, P. 2013. *Life and Death in Pompeii and Herculaneum*. London: British Museum Press.

Sanders, G. D. R., J. Palinkas, I. Tzonou-Herbst, and J. Herbst. 2018. *Ancient Corinth: Site Guide*. Princeton: American School of Classical Studies at Athens.

Scranton, R. L., J. W. Shaw, and L. Ibrahim. 1978. *Topography and Architecture*. Vol. 1 of *Kenchreai, Eastern Port of Corinth*. Leiden: Brill.

Stewart, A. 2018. "Classical Sculpture from the Athenian Agora, Part 1: The Pediments and Akroteria of the Hephaisteion." *Hesperia* 87: 681–741.

Stewart, A., E. Driscoll, S. Estrin, N. J. Gleason, E. Lawrence, R. Levitan, R. Lloyd-Knauf, and K. Turbeville. 2019. "Classical Sculpture from the Athenian Agora, Part 2: The Friezes of the Temple of Ares (Temple of Athena Pallenis)." *Hesperia* 88: 625–705.

Stewart, A., E. Lawrence, R. Levitan, and K. Turbeville. 2021. "Classical Sculpture from the Athenian Agora, Part 3: The Pediments, Metopes, and Akroteria of the Temple of Ares (Temple of Athena Pallenis)." *Hesperia* 90: 533–604.

Taylor, J. E. 2017. "Paul's Caesarea." In Walton, Trebilco, and Gill 2017, 42–67.

Vanderpool, C. de Grazia. 2003. "Roman Portraiture: The Many Faces of Corinth." In *Corinth, the Centenary, 1896–1996*, edited by C. K. Williams II and N. Bookidis, 369–84. Vol. 20 of *Corinth*. Princeton: American School of Classical Studies at Athens.

Vann, R. L., ed. 1992. *Caesarea Papers: Straton's Tower, Herod's Harbour, and Roman and Byzantine Caesarea Including the Papers Given at a Symposium Held at the University of Maryland, the Smithsonian Institution, and the Jewish Community Center of Greater Washington on 25–28 March, 1988*. JRASup 5. Ann Arbor: Journal of Roman Archaeology.

Walton, S., P. R. Trebilco, and D. W. J. Gill, eds. 2017. *The Urban World and the First Christians*. Grand Rapids: Eerdmans.

Wescoat, B. D., and M. L. Anderson. 1989. *Syracuse, the Fairest Greek City: Ancient Art from the Museo Archeologico Regionale "Paolo Orsi."* Rome: De Luca edizioni d'arte.

Williams, C. K., II. 1987. "The Refounding of Corinth: Some Roman Religious Attitudes." In *Roman Architecture in the Greek World*, edited by S. Macready and F. H. Thompson, 26–37. Occasional Papers (New Series) 10. London: Society of Antiquities of London.

Zanker, P. 2016. *Roman Portraits: Sculptures in Stone and Bronze in the Collection of the Metropolitan Museum of Art*. New York: Metropolitan Museum of Art.

12

Houses and Meeting Places

Richard Last

Where did acts of Christ worship happen in the first century? Certainly, houses warrant first mention. On several occasions, Paul references assemblies (*ekklēsiai*) that gathered in the houses of members (*kat' oikon ekklēsia*). Hosts of these assemblies include Prisca and Aquila in Ephesus (1 Cor. 16:19) and Rome (Rom. 16:3, 5), and Archippus in Colossae (Philem. 2). In addition, the author of Colossians names Nympha as a host in Laodicea (Col. 4:15). Aside from assemblies (*ekklēsiai*) in houses, Christ worship might also be incorporated into houses through addition to a family's domestic cult. Paul knows several households (or partial households) that honored Christ somehow outside the context of *ekklēsiai*, including Stephanas and his household in Corinth (1 Cor. 1:16), as well as some members from the households of Aristobulus and Narcissus in Rome (Rom. 16:10–11). Acts provides further attestation to households whose familial religious activities included Christ worship (e.g., Acts 16:15, 29–34; 18:8), as well as to houses that were locations for ad hoc instruction and other activities for which temporary groups of Christ worshipers gathered (e.g., Acts 16:34, 40; 17:7; 18:7).[1]

There are various other, more or less nondomestic settings where Christ worship might be practiced. According to the literary record, these include a rented barn outside Rome where Paul instructed listeners (Acts Paul 11.1) and an inn where Peter provided instruction to Mattidia, mother of Clement (Ps.-Clem. *Rec.* 7.38). Other sources attest to group activities in rental rooms (Mark 14:14–15?) and burial sites (Acts John 72–86; see also *Acta proconsularia sancti Cypriani* 1.7).[2] Celsus, moreover, names shops and workshops as stereotypical places of instruction (Origen, *Cels.* 3.55).

Modeling Christ Worship: Domestic Cults and Associations

Although assemblies and households are different kinds of groupings, they are both often

---

1. Luke may also provide references to *associations* that met in houses in Jerusalem and practiced Christ worship (e.g., Acts 1:12–15; 12:10–17).

2. Overviews of non-house-based meeting locations include Adams 2013; Balch 2012; Bremmer 2020; Kloppenborg 2019, 105–6; and Sande 1999.

called "house churches" in modern scholarship so long as they incorporated Christ worship (e.g., Gehring 2004). However, instead of framing house-based Christ worship around a novel concept (i.e., the "house church"), the framework we need for single households who worship Christ is the domestic cult, and an available and appropriate model for assemblies (*ekklēsiai*) is the association.

The Domestic Cult

The domestic cult was most likely central to the very earliest practice of Christ worship in any urban setting. Paul reports that Stephanas and his *household* were the earliest worshipers of Christ in all of Achaia (1 Cor. 16:15–17; cf. 1:16). Luke also records stories of other entire households adding Christ worship to their familial religious traditions (e.g., Acts 10:1–48; 16:11–15, 25–34). Since Stephanas and his household were initially the only family who worshiped Christ in their entire city (and even region), their most readily available option was to add their new god to their ongoing domestic cult practices. Later, individual family members might expand the practice by encouraging people in their vicinity-based, occupational, and other networks to join them in worshiping Christ—whether in the context of the domestic cults or perhaps even associations.

But how, precisely, might Christ be added to the domestic religious practices of a family? A Roman family would honor generic gods, the *lar(es)*, but also other deities who could be personalized family by family—namely, the *penates*, the exact identity of whom would be determined by familial traditions and decisions (Bodel 2008).[3] The *lares* protected the physical space in which they operated, as is clear already in Ennius (*Ann.* F619) and Plautus (*Aul.* 1–39, etc.). Their role as "gods of place" is best articulated by Plautus, who assumes

that moving to a new house means worshiping the new *lar* there (Plautus, *Mer.* 834–37). Kin members of larger houses need not always have paid consistent attention to the *lares* (Flower 2017, 10–17). Since precincts for the *lares* (precincts that were later called *lararia*) are often found near or in the kitchen (Flower 2017, 48), it would seem that the *lares* were worshiped by whoever "tended the hearth, regardless of their identity, ethnicity, gender, and status" (49). In other words, *lararia* were not always managed by kin members of the household.

The cult of the *penates*, on the other hand, was supervised by kin members of the household and was found in atria and elsewhere outside kitchens and their nearest rooms. A family's *penates* included deities they deemed significant, even gods with civic cults, such as Mercury and Venus (Dubourdieu 1989; Rescigno 2000). Statuettes of these gods might be placed in the seat (*sedes*) or shrine (*aedicula, aedis*) of the *lares* but also could be situated apart from the *lararia*. The *Historia Augusta* describes the (fictional?) *lararium* of Severus Alexander as having housed statuettes of Apollonius of Tyana, Christ, Alexander the Great, and others (Scriptores Historiae Augustae, *Severus Alexander* 29, 31). These personalized combinations of gods might include the deities of state cults (e.g., Mercury, Juno, Jupiter, Minerva), Greek gods (e.g., Dionysus, Hercules), and Egyptian deities (e.g., Anubis, Isis).[4] Cicero advised that foreign and new gods should not be mixed into the rites of traditional deities (Cicero, *Leg.* 2.25). However, adding the worship of Christ to the rites of the traditional gods of a household (*lares*) might lessen any resistance Christ worshipers could otherwise face if Christ were to be worshiped separately.

It was not uncommon, moreover, for only some members of a household to adopt Christ worship (1 Cor. 7:12–16; Justin Martyr, *2 Apol.* 2). In fact, Paul rarely greets entire households

---

3. For the transformation of a single *lar* to the plural *lares*, see Flower 2017, 36–39 and 353–54.

4. For Pompeiian examples, see Huet and Wyler 2015.

when he addresses his contacts in Rome (Rom. 16:8–16). In the circumstance of a "divided" or "mixed" household, domestic cult practices might generate conflict (see Johnson Hodge 2010).

Associations

The modern concept of an "association" is suitable for any nonpublic group from antiquity that self-identifies with terminology and activities that the Copenhagen Associations Project (CAP) deem to be criteria for such a group type (https://ancientassociations.ku.dk /assoc/intro-criteria.php; see also chap. 47 in this volume). Paul pulled the word *ekklēsia* (Rom. 16:1, 3–5; 1 Cor. 1:2; Gal. 1:2; 1 Thess. 1:1), in part, from the language of ancient associations. To be sure, our incomplete evidence of ancient associations includes merely one example of *ekklēsia* (Latin: *ecclesia*) as a title (*CIL* 8.9585, see below). Other more oft-cited sources show that this term was used in reference to the *meetings* of associations.[5] Notably, moreover, some other terms used for association meetings could double as association titles.[6] In light of this evidence, it is likely that *ekklēsia* fell within the range of association vocabulary for titles.

The aforementioned association that took *ecclesia* as a title was a group of *cultores* ("worshipers," or in this case, "association members") from North Africa that predates Constantine.[7]

To be sure, this group worshiped Christ—and so conventionally would be understood as a "church" (or some synonym) instead of an "association." While the church/association dichotomy is no longer as prevalent as it was in the past, there are still a few experts on ancient associations who continue to work with it. In a recent study, for instance, the similarities between associations and Christian groups were accepted but minimized: such similarities exist, it was asserted here, only because Christian groups engaged in group practices (e.g., meals) that were relatively standardized in antiquity no matter the group, and because there were basic expectations in general (e.g., with respect to hierarchy) when it came to ancient communities, no matter the type (Eckhardt 2021, 264–65). For Benedikt Eckhardt, a more significant comparator than actual practices, one that yields apparent differences, is political disposition. To this end, Eckhardt generalizes the anti-Roman political discourse of selected Christian apologists (Paul, Tatian, Tertullian) as characteristic of Christ worshipers and sets their language apart from the civic identity and loyalty practiced by members of associations. In doing so, Eckhardt reaches the conclusion that Christian groups are best understood as something quite different from association— small communities in heaven (esp. 271–72). In summary of his overall findings, Eckhardt asserts that "the Christian organizational model claimed no 'place in Mediterranean society.' Rather, it put up with this society as a necessary evil and strived thereafter to replace it with another" (277). Even if Eckhardt's conclusions are seen as viable, it must be highlighted that he is dealing only with spokespersons of Christ worship, not actual group practices associated with Christ worship.

Unfortunately, New Testament references to house-based assembly meetings provide few details concerning the type of house and how the space was used during meetings (two exceptions are James 2:2–7 and 1 Cor. 14:23–36; cf.

---

5. For meetings, see Robert 1945, no. 73 (Sinuri [Caria] [350/344 BCE]); *IDelos* 1519, 1 (= *AGRW* 223 = CAPInv. 12; Delos [153/152 BCE]); and *IG* 12/6.1 132, 1 (= CAPInv. 1915; Samos [2nd c. BCE]).

6. The term *synodos* is used as a title and also in reference to a meeting in *IDelos* 1520 (= *AGRW* 224 = CAPInv. 9; Delos, Aegean [153/2 or 149/8 CE]). For *synagōgē* as a title, see, for example, the association of barbers from Thrace: *IPerinthos* 49 (= *GRA* 1.86 = CAPInv. 546; Perinthos-Herakleia, Thrace [1st–2nd c. CE]). For use of *synagōgē* to describe meetings and even the role of a member/official, see *SB* 22.15460 (= *GRA* 3.169 = CAPInv. 1411; Alexandria, Delta [5 BCE]).

7. *CIL* 8.9585 (Caesarea, North Africa [before 257 or 304 CE]).

Kloppenborg 2019, 118–19).[8] Even the documentary material provided by associations gives us few details about how associations used domestic space. For example, a small association (thirteen or fourteen members) of "meal companions" (*synklitai*) from Thessalonica assembled in an *oikos* (house?), but we know of them only from a gray marble slab that names the person who provided them with their meeting place: the freedman, Aulos Papios Cheilon (*IG* 10/2.1 58 [1st c. CE]). We do not know who owned the house, nor do we know Cheilon's precise role in the group. All members were sacred object carriers (*hieraphoroi*) in processions of Egyptian gods. There were likely other such *hieraphoroi* who were not members of this particular association (Steimle 2008, 185; Edson 1948, 181–88). Consequently, the inscription invites us to consider an analogous possibility: that small associations of Christ worshipers might have formed out of larger networks of Judean-deity worshipers (e.g., synagogues) or occupational guilds while maintaining connections to the larger organization—a scenario not far removed from ones Luke imagines (e.g., Acts 17:1–4; 18:1–8).

One particularly illuminating document records house meetings by seven or eight slaves of a household in Philadelphia, Egypt (*SB* 3.7182; Fayûm [2nd–1st c. BCE]). This group assembled in various locations on a farm estate: a storehouse (*SB* 3.7182, frag. 1, col. 2, line 12; frag. 4 recto, col. 3, line 62), the harness room of a stable (*SB* 3.7182, frag. 4 recto, col. 2, lines 45–46; frag. 5 recto, line 79), and in an Iseion that was perhaps outside the estate or even a domestic chapel (*SB* 3.7182, frag. 3, line 43). Perhaps this association's relationship to the owner of the estate was similar to that of a Roman *collegium* that self-presents as the

"association (*collegium*) that is in the house (*domus*) of Sergia Paullina" (*CIL* 6.10260–64; 9.9148–49 [2nd c. CE]). Both seem to have been composed of staff members of a household. The practices of this Egyptian association of slaves are well detailed and can help illuminate how assemblies of Christ worshipers funded their activities and scheduled their meetings (Last 2016, 83–113). Associations of household staff might even be behind the early assemblies of Christ worshipers to whom Paul refers as "those who belong to the family of Aristobulus" and "those in the Lord who belong to the family of Narcissus" (Rom. 16:10–11).

In the case of an association (*synagōgē*) at Stobi (Macedonia) that met in the house of Claudius Tiberius Polycharmos, a little more is known about the association's space (*IJO* 1.Mac1 = *GRA* 1.73 [2nd or 3rd c. CE]). The house was owned by Polycharmos, who is named as the father (*patēr*) of the association. His was a multistoried house, and in accordance with a vow, Polycharmos gifted the ground-level floor to the association, which included a *triclinium* room for dining and a four-column portico.

Another illuminating source is the famous stele from Philadelphia (Lydia) that is engraved with rules marking the revision or expansion of a house cult or association (*TAM* 5.1539 = *GRA* 2.117). The group stands out for its inclusive membership profile (men and women; free and slaves) as well as its focus on purity in its judicial system (Barton and Horsley 1981; Stowers 1998; Kloppenborg 2013). Members of this group apparently assembled in the house (*oikos*) of a certain Dionysios. There were altars to various gods in the house, including Greek deities such as Zeus Eumenes, Hestia, Hygieia, and Nike, as well as one non-Greek god, Agdistis (whose worship at this site predates the rites for the other gods). The cult, then (whether an element of a family's domestic religious practices or an association), illustrates by analogy how a family or association

---

8. For an overview of the debate over the types of housing used by Christ worshipers, see Kloppenborg 2019, 100–106; Last 2016, 43–62.

might incorporate the non-Greek god Christ into their long-standing religious traditions.

Several associations would have used rental domestic space for meetings, though there was usually no occasion to mention this detail in the kinds of association documents that survive—association narratives, where such information might be found are rare. But a well-known example of an association that assembled in "rented rooms" (*misthōtoi*) is the group of Egyptian migrants to Delos who worshiped Sarapis (*AGRW* 221 = *IG* 11/4 1200). It is only because the group inscribed their foundation story on a stone pillar that we learn the host of their meetings, Apollonios I, rented the group's meeting space early in the history of the association (see Last and Harland 2020, 56–59). Likewise, in Luke's narrative of Paul's stay in Rome, we find the detail that Paul rented his accommodations in the city and hosted students there (Acts 28:30). More historically verifiable are the associations (*ekklēsiai*) hosted by the leatherworkers Prisca and Aquila in Rome (Rom. 16:3–5) and Asia (1 Cor. 16:19). It is most likely that Prisca and Aquila did not own their houses, as they appear to have migrated several times throughout the 40s and 50s, and their moves included stays in Pontus, Rome, and Corinth (Acts 18:1–3), Asia (1 Cor. 16:19), and Rome again (Rom. 16:3–5). And so, two of the only known New Testament era house-based associations in which Christ was worshiped appear to have met in rental homes (i.e., Prisca and Aquila's assemblies in their Roman and Asian houses).

Nondomestic Places of Christ Worship

The evidence for ancient associations attests to a variety of meeting-venue options outside domestic space. As for Christ associations, unfortunately none of our documentary evidence for these groups mention their meeting places.[9] Celsus may have known of some such meeting places, and he caricatures the assemblies of Christ worshipers in the (rented?) workshops of woolworkers, cobblers, and fullers (Origen, *Cels.* 3.55). Edward Adams (2013) provides many other possible attestations to assemblies that met in nondomestic spaces. Since there is no New Testament evidence that any grouping of Christ worshipers came to own a clubhouse or any other property for the purpose of the group's activities, it is not necessary to review the various ways that some associations came to own such property (Last and Harland 2020, 80–89). Rather, this section will focus briefly on various kinds of space that associations *rented*.

The longest-surviving financial account produced by an association (*PTebt* 3/2 894; Tebtynis [1st c. BCE]) shows that this particular group had no stable meeting location—they moved around, assembling variously in the (rented?) shops or houses of members (e.g., frag. 2 recto, line 7) as well as in a workshop referred to simply as "the workshop" (*e[rgeutig]on*; frag. 3 verso, col. 1, line 3). If these spaces were indeed rented, then the fees were likely paid by whoever lived or worked in them, for there is no indication in this club account that membership dues were used for room rentals.

In very few known cases, an association might be itself collectively responsible for covering rental fees. This scenario was likely more common than the documentary evidence shows. As an example, a shrinking group of merchants from Tyre (Phoenicia) residing in Puteoli (Campania, Italy) encountered difficulties in affording an annual rent (*misthos*) of 250 denarii on their building complex (*statiōn*), apparently the largest one in Puteoli. They were able to stave off financial failure by success-

9. For a list of *collegia* whose members included Christ worshipers, see Last 2022, 379n7. See also the discussions in *GRA* 2.153; 3.281, 283–84.

fully appealing to the civic institutions of their homeland (Tyre) for monetary support.

It is probable that some associations rented space in large sanctuaries, such as the Sarapis sanctuary in Thessalonica (Macedonia). Here, at least three associations used the sanctuary in the first century CE: an association of banqueters (*synklitai*), the initiates of Zeus Dionysos Gongylos, and an association of Roman businessmen (*IG* 10/2.1 70 = *AGRW* 48; *IG* 10/2.1 58 = *AGRW* 47; *IG* 10/2.1 259 = *AGRW* 50; *IG* 10/2.1 33 = *RICIS* 113/0538). Although the relevant inscriptions do not mention whether any of these groups paid for using this space, it is clear that none of them owned the property (Last and Harland 2020, 78).

Finally, an illuminating private letter from early second-century CE Heptakomia (Apollonopolites) provides insights into how an association might secure rental space (*SB* 10.10278 [114–119 CE]). The letter was composed by a certain Horion, a bath assistant who agreed to lease dining rooms and storerooms (*ta symposia kai hai kellai*) from a certain Herakleios for one year. In this correspondence, he requests Apollonios's help or consent in breaking the lease agreement and explains that he has lost two hundred drachmas so far as no one was subleasing from him. Individuals such as Horion would be the contact persons for representatives of Christ worshipers looking for a short-term meeting space rental.

Conclusion

Although New Testament writers generally found no reason to detail where Christ assemblies met, it is reasonable to conclude that Christ could be worshiped in houses in the context of domestic cult activities as well as in association meetings. These contexts (domestic cult and association) are relatively well known from sources outside the New Testament, and the relevant texts (some of which have been summarized above) help to illustrate the options available to individuals for finding space, paying for it, and ultimately using it for rites in honor of Christ.

Works Cited

Adams, Edward. 2013. *The Earliest Christian Meeting Places: Almost Exclusively Houses?* New York: Bloomsbury.

Balch, David L. 2012. "The Church Sitting in a Garden (1 Cor. 14:30; Rom. 16:23; Mark 6:39–40; 8:6; John 6:3, 10; Acts 1:15; 2:1–2)." In *Contested Spaces: Houses and Temples in Roman Antiquity and the New Testament*, edited by David L. Balch and Annette Weissenrieder, 201–35. WUNT 285. Tübingen: Mohr Siebeck.

Barton, Stephen C., and G. H. R. Horsley. 1981. "A Hellenistic Cult Group and the New Testament Churches." *Jahrbuch für Antike und Christentum* 24: 7–41.

Bremmer, Jan N. 2020. "Urban Religion, Neighbourhoods and the Early Christian Meeting Places." *RRE* 6: 48–74.

Dubourdieu, Annie. 1989. *Les origines et le développement du culte des Pénates à Rome*. Rome: École Française de Rome.

Eckhardt, Benedikt. 2021. *Romanisierung und Verbrüderung: Das Vereinswesen im römischen Reich*. KLIO/Beihefte. Neue Folge 34. Berlin: de Gruyter.

Edson, Charles. 1948. "Cults of Thessalonica (Macedonia III)." *HTR* 41: 153–204.

Flower, Harriet I. 2017. *The Dancing Lares and the Serpent in the Garden: Religion at the Roman Street Corner*. Princeton: Princeton University Press.

Gehring, Roger W. 2004. *House Church and Mission: The Importance of Household Structures in Early Christianity*. Peabody, MA: Hendrickson.

Huet, Valérie, and Stéphanie Wyler. 2015. "Associations de dieux en images dans les laraires de Pompéi." In *Figures de dieux: Construire le divine en images*, edited by Sylvia Estienne, Valérie Huet, François Lissarrague, and Francis Prost, 195–221. Rennes: Presses Universitaires de Rennes.

Johnson Hodge, Caroline. 2010. "Married to an Unbeliever: Households, Hierarchies, and Holiness in 1 Corinthians 7:12–16." *HTR* 103: 1–25.

Kloppenborg, John S. 2013. "The Moralizing of Discourse in Graeco-Roman Associations." In *"The One Who Sows Bountifully": Essays in Honor of Stanley K. Stowers*, edited by Caroline Johnson Hodge, Saul M. Olyan, Daniel Ullucci, and Emma Wasserman, 215–28. BJS 356. Providence, RI: Brown Judaic Studies.

———. 2019. *Christ's Associations: Connecting and Belonging in the Ancient City*. New Haven: Yale University Press.

Last, Richard. 2016. *The Pauline Church and the Corinthian Ekklēsia: Greco-Roman Associations in Comparative Context*. SNTSMS 164. Cambridge: Cambridge University Press.

———. 2022. "Julian Christ Worshippers and Their Connection to a *Collegium* in First-Century Lyon: Reintroducing the Epitaph of Julia Adepta." In *Greco-Roman Associations, Deities, and Early Christianity*, edited by Bruce W. Longenecker, 377–96. Waco: Baylor University Press.

Last, Richard, and Philip A. Harland. 2020. *Group Survival in the Ancient Mediterranean: Rethinking Material Conditions in the Landscape of Jews and Christians*. London: Bloomsbury T&T Clark.

Rescigno, Rita. 2000. "I Penates tra Lares, Genius e Iuno." *Studi di storia e di geostoria antica* 24: 13–37.

Robert, Louis. 1945. *Le Sanctuaire de Sinuri près de Mylasa*. Mémoires de l'Institute Français d'archéologie de Stamboul 7. Bibliothèque archéologique et historique de l'Institut Français d'archéologie d'Istanbul 8. Paris: Éditions de Boccard.

Sande, Siri. 1999. "Huskirker og tituluskirker—salmer I heimen eller I badet?" *Kirke og Kultur* 104: 7–18.

Steimle, Christopher. 2008. *Religion im römischen Thessaloniki: Sakraltopographie, Kult und Gesselschaft, 168 v. Chr.–324 n. Chr.* Tübingen: Mohr Siebeck.

Stowers, Stanley K. 1998. "A Cult from Philadelphia: Oikos Religion or Cultic Association?" In *The Early Church in Its Context: Essays in Honor of Everett Ferguson*, edited by Abraham J. Malherbe, Frederick W. Norris, and James W. Thompson, 287–301. NovTSup 90. Leiden: Brill.

PART TWO

Inhabiting the Stage

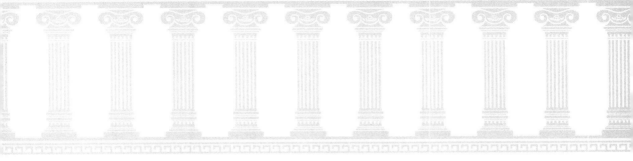

SECTION I

Scripts

13

The Septuagint and the Transmission of Jewish Scriptures

Kristin De Troyer

The study of the Old Greek text and its textual and historical data is key to understanding the transmission of the Jewish Scriptures in the Greek world from the third century BCE onward (Tov 1986; Greenspoon 1997; De Troyer 2011b, 2013a; Ross 2022). Similarly, the study of the Old Greek text is of utmost importance to that of the New Testament, as many New Testament authors cited not simply from the Hebrew Scriptures but from the Greek!

Terminology

"Septuagint" or "Septuaginta" stands for the Greek Bible and is derived from the Greek title ἡ μετάφρασις τῶν ἑβδομήκοντα (hē metaphrasis tōn hebdomēkonta), "the translation of the seventy," with the seventy being a shorthand for the seventy-two translators who, according to the Letter of Aristeas (Wright 2015; Rajak 2009; Wasserstein and Wasserstein 2006; Gruen 2016, esp. 37–40, 413–36), translated the Hebrew books of Moses into Greek. From the translation of these books, the word started to refer to the translation of the entire Bible, including the (deuterocanonical) books that were composed in Greek. Eventually, Greek translations became available in Alfred Rahlfs's two- or one-volume blue cover editions and the critical editions as produced by the (Göttingen) *Septuaginta Unternehmen* (currently continued under the auspices of the *Robert Hanhart Stiftung zur Förderung der Septuagintaforschung*), which have the word "Septuaginta" in their titles.

Origen also referred to the seventy. He used an omicron to indicate the Old Greek translation as produced by the translators who were working on Pharos. Origen, or scribes copying his work, used the reference especially in contrast to (sigla indicating) early Jewish revisers, such as Aquila (α′), Symmachus (σ′), and Theodotion (θ′).

Whereas the number seventy may have been a good way to refer to the Old Greek translation as it left the hands of the first translators, its use in "Septuaginta" to indicate a complete volume of texts may have created a difficulty, as in "the" Septuagint there are books that do *not* contain the oldest translation (e.g., the Theodotionic Daniel text) or parts of books that offer a recension of the/an original translation (e.g., the *kaige* sections in 1–4 Kingdoms).

Accordingly, many scholars use the term "Old Greek" in order to refer to the oldest translation into Greek and reserve "Septuaginta" for a collection of books, such as Codex Sinaiticus or "Rahlfs." The Old Greek (OG)[1] is used in comparison with the Masoretic Text (MT), the Vulgate (V), or the Old Latin (OL, or Vetus Latina, VL).

Location

According to the Letter of Aristeas, the OG was produced on the peninsula of Pharos near Alexandria as requested by King Ptolemy II Philadelphus (280–246 BCE) following a suggestion of his librarian, Demetrius of Phaleron. The first translation into Greek seems to have been only of the five books of Moses. Whether the entire OG was produced in Alexandria is questionable, as Greek texts have been found at Qumran and in the Cave of Horrors, which contained a revised Greek text of the Twelve Minor Prophets (see also Albrecht 2018). Whether these Greek texts were produced locally or imported is still a matter of debate.

Pluses, Minuses, and Variants

Rewriting?

When comparing the OG with the MT, one observes pluses (additions to the text), minuses (omissions from the text), and variants (changes to the text) (Pakkala 2014; Müller, Pakkala, and Romeny 2014; Müller and Pakkala 2017, 2022). Two main theories have developed to explain these phenomena. First, scholars claim that the OG is a free translation of the MT, and pluses,

---

1. When talking about the OG translators, the plural needs to be used. Most likely, every biblical book was translated by one translator.

minuses, and variants are credited to the OG translators, who added to, omitted from, or changed the text. Second, there are those who claim that the pluses, minuses, and variants stem from a different Hebrew *Vorlage* (prototype) and that the translators translated this slightly different parental text. For almost all, but especially the more text-critically complex books, scholars belonging to either category can be found.

All attempts to explain pluses, minuses, and variants point to some editorial work, which could be called "interpretation" or "rewriting" (Darshan 2023). Whether OG Isaiah interpreted the MT, or OG Esther rewrites its MT *Vorlage*, these new texts have an element of rewriting in them. There are multiple light forms of rewriting, such as reading what the Hebrew text may offer as possibilities, often done through metathesis (i.e., transposition); offering a new interpretation; or rendering explicit what was implicit (exploiting, for instance, a semantic or even syntactic possibility). This form of interpretation was inspired by the Jewish rules for exegesis (esp. the seven or thirteen rules applied in scriptural exegesis; see Safrai 1987; see also Fishbane 1985; Langer 2016).

The level of interpretation and rewriting is also dependent on the sort of literature that was being translated. The Pentateuch has minimal interpretation, even if the OG Leviticus created many new words, while the translators of the later books offered fuller interpretations, such as in OG Daniel, where texts were added (Susanna, Bel and the Dragon); similarly, OG Esther has many additions. There is also the rewritten text labeled 1 Esdras (called 3 Esdras in German-speaking countries), which most likely is a rather slavish Greek translation of a rewritten Hebrew/Aramaic *Vorlage* (De Troyer 2002).

Rewritings in all sorts and varieties can also be found among the texts of the Dead Sea Scrolls (Crawford 2008; De Troyer 2003; Zsengellér 2014; Zahn 2020) as well as in Aramaic translations of the Bible and in other rabbinic literature (Cook 1986; Smelik 2013).

Translation Technique

The question is whether the OG represents its Hebrew *Vorlage* rather slavishly or freely (Barr 1979). Translators, however, tried to translate what was in front of them (whether in manuscript or by dictation), with a view to ensuring that the audience would understand the text. Adherence to what was in front of them seems to have been greater when it came to the Pentateuch and lesser with the Writings.

The study of translation technique happens on the level of *semantics* (studying how Hebrew and Aramaic words were translated), the level of *style* (focusing on how Hebrew ways of saying things were rendered in Greek), and the level of *syntax* (researching how different Hebrew and Aramaic constructions and categories were rendered in Greek—and vice versa). The better one knows the translators and their activities and results, the more one can speak about how the underlying, parental *Vorlage* looked and whether this *Vorlage* was the MT or a Hebrew text that was slightly different. Similarly, one also develops a sense of how the translators interpreted their text.

Textual Data as Found in the Apparatus and Textual History

When studying the OG, one has to understand the data as offered in the text-critical apparatus, especially of the critical edition of the OG, whether it is the Cambridge edition (Brooke and McLean 2009 [1906]) or the Göttingen Septuagint edition (Albrecht 2021, esp. 62). A series of tools explains how the apparatus is built up (Schäfer 2012a, 2012b; De Troyer 2003).

These critical editions contain a description of the witnesses used by the editor(s), a section on the organization of the witnesses into textual families, and an explanation of how knowledge of the relationship among witnesses and the textual families aids in both reconstruction of the OG and a textual history of how the OG developed or transformed into a myriad of textual witnesses. Moreover, a critical description is offered of the daughter versions and how they help to reconstruct the OG. Next, in some editions a second apparatus offers the data of the early Jewish revisers.

This information helps to illuminate how the OG evolved from an original OG text into the text as present in many witnesses; how, in recensions, the OG was corrected with the help of the data of the early Jewish revisers, such as the Hexaplaric recension (see below); and finally how the OG was translated in other languages.

The apparatus thus offers the data from which the OG text as proposed in the text at the top of the page of a critical edition was reconstructed and in which the data of the OG text's textual development (and its versions; De Troyer 2011a) are contained. When trying to pinpoint which text a later author (such as Paul) used, one has to consider the textual development of the OG. Moreover, most texts leave traces in the textual history, and thus, when studying a quotation, it may be useful to know if a text with that quotation in it actually existed or not.

Textual Data of Actual Witnesses

The description of the actual witnesses also needs to be considered when proposing (alternative) sources as a hypothesis, especially when pointing to a possible space in which a text could have been present. For instance, when proposing a longer reading and pointing to a *vacat* (space) in a textual witness, one needs to check whether the *vacat* was truly a *vacat* or just a place in the manuscript where no text could have been written. Similarly, when reconstructing texts, it is of importance to have the actual data of a manuscript or fragment in mind. Reconstructions ought to fit within the length of a text, its width, the number of characters on a line, the number of lines of a sheet, and so on.

Recensions

When working with the OG, one cannot escape the work of Origen. One must simply understand that Origen attempted to correct the OG as he received it, with the help of the Greek texts of the early Jewish revisers, mostly Theodotion. Thus, before dealing with Origen's recensions, it is necessary to look at the early Jewish revisers. The text of the early Jewish revisers was normally printed in columns three (Aquila), four (Symmachus), and six (Theodotion) of Origen's six-column work, the Hexapla. The chronological-historical sequence is different as Theodotion was the first to stand in the *kaige*/proto-Theodotionic tradition; followed by Symmachus, who took many readings from Theodotion; and finally, Aquila, who exaggerated the endeavor and produced a very literal text. Origen used the readings of the early Jewish revisers and gave preference to the readings of Theodotion. He corrected the OG to produce a revised text, the Origenic or Hexaplaric text, with a lasting impact on other witnesses and daughter versions.

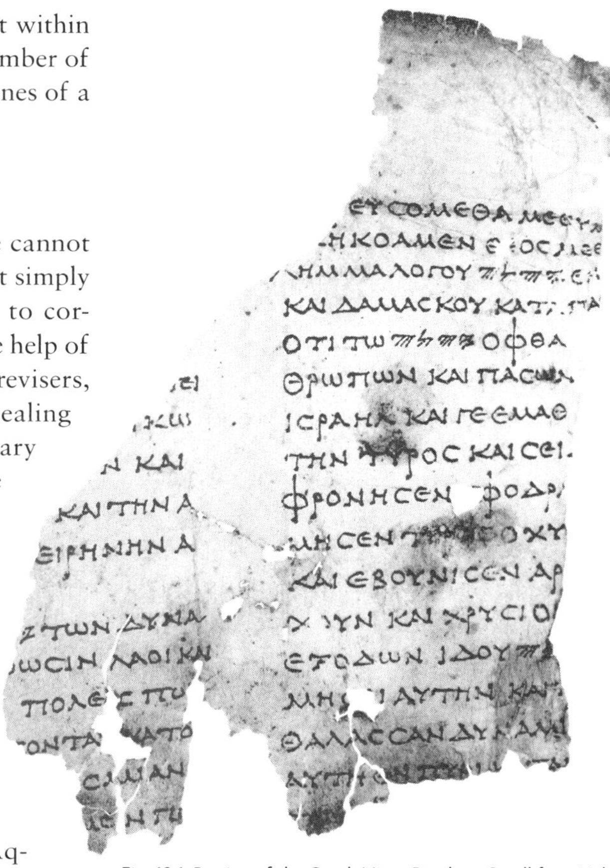

The Early Jewish Revisers

The early Jewish revisers left traces of their texts in different sorts of literature and in different places: in the margins of manuscripts (De Troyer 2006), in catena manuscripts, and in rabbinic texts.

A question remains: Did these revisers produce whole translations, whole texts, or just record variants? The evidence of the Nahal Hever Minor Prophets Scroll containing a Greek text revised according to the proto-Theodotionic/

Fig. 13.1. Portion of the Greek Minor Prophets Scroll from Nahal Hever (ca. 50 BCE–50 CE). The text is Zech. 8:18–9:7.

kaige principles points to a complete text (Tov 1990). However, there is no *kaige* evidence found for the Pentateuch, and for the book of Joshua the evidence is scant.

Another issue is when these revisions started (Aejmelaeus 2022). The *kaige* Nahal Hever text itself is dated to the late first century BCE (Aejmelaeus 2022; Parsons 1990; Alfaro and Orpana forthcoming).

Origen and His Hexapla

Origen in his Hexapla continued the tradition started by the early Jewish revisers to correct the OG and align it better with the MT. The text of the fifth column of the Hexapla is called the Hexaplaric text, which is a revised text by

Origen. Using asterisks, Origen (or his successors) indicated text elements in his fifth column that were not yet in the OG text before him and that he added to that OG text. These text elements reflected a/the Hebrew text. Origen most likely took these text fragments from the Theodotionic text of the sixth column. Also, using obelisks Origen indicated which text in his fifth column was not found in any of his sources—that is, in the texts of the early Jewish revisers. In short, variants or text marked with asterisks point to Hexaplaric corrections and alignments toward the MT; variants or texts marked with an obelisk identity the text as being OG (only). Studying the readings marked with the Aristarchian signs helps scholars understand the sort of revising Origen undertook and what the OG he had in front of him before he started the revision looked like.

The revision of Origen left a lot of traces in the textual history. For New Testament scholars, the texts and variants of Theodotion as taken up in the Hexapla are particularly important (one can, for example, consult the list of quotations and allusions in Nestle-Aland[28] [Nestle et al. 2012] under Daniel to see that this distinction is made). When Origen aligned his text toward a Hebrew text, he used especially Theodotion's text. However, some Theodotionic revisions were made by Theodotion's forebears; these readings are called *kaige* readings and were already circulating in the first century BCE (see, above, the dating of the Nahal Hever fragments). As it is often not possible to differentiate between *kaige* variants and the earliest (proto- or) Theodotionic readings, one refers to these readings as *kaige*/Theodotionic readings. Moreover, the *kaige*/(proto-)Theodotionic readings were known by the earliest scribes of New Testament texts (esp. where there was no OG available [see below], such as in 2 Sam. 11 to 1 Kings 2, leading to *kaige*/Theodotionic quotations in the letter to the Hebrews; but in Rev. 20:9 the text quoted is more a Lucianic/Antiochene text

than the *kaige*/proto-Theodotionic text [see below; see also Huotari and Kujanpää 2022; De Troyer 2013b]).

Lucian and the Lucianic Recension

Traditionally, the Lucianic recension is associated with Lucian of Antioch, a Christian theologian (240–312 CE), who is known to have produced a revision of the OG. The texts of 4QSam[a,c], however, changed that picture, as these texts were dated in the pre-Christian era and offered a Hebrew text similar to the Greek (and Antiochene) text of Lucian (Tov 1999). The relation between the so-called Lucianic text (also known as the Antiochene text) and the OG, on the one hand, and the Hebrew text, on the other, as well as its traces in many daughter versions, has been studied at length (Trebolle Barrera 2020, esp. 163–90; Torijano and Piquer Otero 2012).

Moreover, the text of 1–4 Kingdoms as found in the Rahlfs edition offers partly an OG text and partly a *kaige* text. In the *kaige* sections of these books (namely, the βγ section, that is 2 Sam. 11 to 1 Kings 2, and the γδ section, that is 1 Kings 22 to the end of 2 Kings; see Wirth 2016, 2017; Pessoa da Silva Pinto 2019; Aejmelaeus 2022), there is no OG text available but only the *kaige* text. In order to reconstruct the OG text in these sections, one has to study the Antiochene text (Fernández Marcos and Busto Saiz 1989, 1992, 1996, 2005), as this revision was most likely based on *the* OG or *an* OG.

For New Testament scholars, this means that not only the MT or "the Septuagint" needs to be taken into account when studying quotations from these books (Steyn 2011; Menken 1996) but also the Antiochene text.

Recensions, Textual History, and Dead Sea Scrolls

With texts of the Hebrew and Greek Bible increasingly becoming known through research on the Septuagint as well as the Dead Sea Scrolls, one also has to become aware that these fields of research need to be taken into account *simultaneously*. Greek *kaige* texts are found at Nahal Hever, and Hebrew texts looking like the *Vorlage* of Greek texts are found among the Dead Sea Scrolls. Scholars must thus pay more attention to the areas where Septuagint studies and Qumran studies meet (De Troyer and Herbison 2020).

The Old Greek and Its Daughter Versions

Scholars working on the Hexaplaric and Antiochene recensions as well as the *kaige* sections of 1–4 Kingdoms pay attention to the Georgian, (Old) Latin, Armenian, Coptic, Ethiopic, and other daughter versions, as these may be useful to reconstruct the OG from which they were translated. These versions thus also have to be taken into account by New Testament scholars.

The Difficult Books

There is a series of books in which most of the problems and issues mentioned above play an important role: Joshua, Judges, 1–2 Samuel, 1–2 Kings, Jeremiah, Proverbs, and Esther. These books and their textual transmission need more study, especially as there is, for instance, not yet a critical (Göttingen) edition of the books of Joshua, Judges, 1–2 Samuel, 1–2 Kings, or Proverbs.

Conclusion

The transmission of the Jewish Scriptures partly happened in Greek. There are ways to reconstruct the OG text as it left the hands of the original translators. The Göttingen critical edition is the best text to use when quoting the OG of specific books. This translation may have taken place in the Hellenistic times in Egypt and Judea. Already in pre-Christian times the OG underwent a series of revisions as it left the hands of the translators, such as can be seen in the *kaige* text of the Minor Prophets Scroll of Nahal Hever. The pre-Christian Samuel scrolls and fragments point to revised texts in Hebrew that left traces in the Greek Antiochene text, which is a recension of the OG. Also, the three early Jewish revisers, following in the footsteps of the *kaige* reviser(s), left their marks in Origen's Hexapla.

When working with the New Testament, now more than before one has to realize that there is a plethora of biblical texts, either in Hebrew or in Greek, that were available to New Testament scribes and/or authors. The study of the transmission of the Jewish Scriptures especially in the first centuries BCE and CE needs teams of scholars working together on Qumran, the Septuagint, and all daughter versions.

Works Cited

Aejmelaeus, Anneli. 2022. "The Origins of the Kaige Revision." In *Scriptures in the Making: Texts and Their Transmission in Late Second Temple Judaism*, edited by Raimo Hakola, Jessi Orpana, and Paolo Huotari, 285–311. CBET 109. Leuven: Peeters.

Albrecht, Felix. 2018. *Psalmi Salomonis*. Vol. 12.3 of *Septuaginta: Vetus Testamentum Graecum, auctoritate Academiae Scientiarum Gottingensis editum*. Göttingen: Vandenhoeck & Ruprecht.

———. 2021. "The History of Septuagint Studies: The Editions of the Septuagint." In *The Oxford Handbook of the Septuagint*, edited by Alison G. Salvesen and Timothy Michael Law, 53–70. Oxford: Oxford University Press.

Alfaro, Joshua, and Jessi Orpana. Forthcoming. *The Nahal Hever Minor Prophets Scroll and Other* Kaige *Texts: New Insights*. DSI. Göttingen: Vandenhoeck & Ruprecht.

Barr, James. 1979. *The Typology of Literalism in Ancient Biblical Translations*. Mitteilungen des Septuaginta-Unternehmens 15 / Nachrichten der Akademie der Wissenschaften in Göttingen 11. Göttingen: Vandenhoeck & Ruprecht.

Brooke, Alan E., and Norman McLean. 2009. *The Old Testament in Greek according to the Text of Codex Vaticanus, Supplemented from Other Uncial Manuscripts, with a Critical Apparatus Containing the Variants of the Chief Ancient Authorities for the Text of the Septuagint.* Cambridge Library Collection. Cambridge: Cambridge University Press. Originally published 1906.

Cook, Edward M. 1986. "Rewriting the Bible: The Text and Language of the Pseudo-Jonathan Targum." PhD diss., University of California, Los Angeles.

Crawford, Sidnie White. 2008. *Rewriting Scripture in Second Temple Times.* Studies in the Dead Sea Scrolls and Related Literature 5. Grand Rapids: Eerdmans.

Darshan, Guy. 2023. "The Quasi-Priestly Additions in MT 1 Kings 6–8 in Light of 'Rewritten Bible' Compositions from Qumran." In *The Textual History of the Bible from the Dead Sea Scrolls to the Biblical Manuscripts of the Vienna Papyrus Collection: Proceedings of the Fifteenth International Symposium of the Orion Center for the Study of the Dead Sea Scrolls and Associated Literature, Cosponsored by the University of Vienna Institute for Jewish Studies and the Schechter Institute of Jewish Studies, 10–13 April, 2016,* edited by Ruth A. Clements, Russell E. Fuller, Armin Lange, and Paul D. Mandel, 219–40. STDJ 137. Leiden: Brill.

De Troyer, Kristin. 2002. "Zerubbabel and Ezra: A Revived and Revised Solomon and Josiah? A Survey of Current 1 Esdras Research." *CurBR* 1, no. 1: 30–61.

———. 2003. *Rewriting the Sacred Text: What the Old Greek Texts Tell Us about the Literary Growth of the Bible.* Text Critical Studies 4. Atlanta: Society of Biblical Literature.

———. 2006. "The Freer Twelve Minor Prophets Codex: A Case Study; The Old Greek Text of Jonah, Its Revisions, and Its Corrections." In *The Freer Biblical Manuscripts: Fresh Studies of the Greek Biblical Manuscripts Housed in the Freer Gallery,* edited by Larry Hurtado, 75–68. Atlanta: Society of Biblical Literature.

———. 2011a. Review of *Ruth,* by Udo Quast. Vol. 4.3 of *Septuaginta: Vetus Testamentum Graecum, auctoritate Academiae Scientiarum Gottingensis editum. JSJ* 42: 423–28.

———. 2011b. "The Seventy-Two and Their Many Grandchildren: A Review of Septuagint Studies from 1997 Onward." *CurBR* 11: 1–59.

———. 2013a. "The Septuagint." In *From the Beginnings to 600 AD,* edited by Joachim Schaper and James Carleton Paget, 267–88. Vol. 2 of *The New Cambridge History of the Bible.* Cambridge: Cambridge University Press.

———. 2013b. "Quotations from the Texts of the Books of Samuel, Kings and the Minor Prophets in the New Testament." In *The Reception of the Hebrew Bible in the Septuagint and the New Testament: Essays in Memory of Aileen Guilding,* edited by David J. A. Clines and Cheryl Exum, 49–55. Sheffield: Phoenix.

De Troyer, Kristin, and David R. Herbison. 2020. "Where Qumran and Septuagint Meet: The Case of Is 40:7–8." *Textus* 29, no. 2: 156–67.

Fernández Marcos, Natalio, and José Ramón Busto Saiz. 1989. *El Texto antioqueno de la Bibla griega, 1–2 Samuel.* With the collaboration of Victoria Spottorno Díaz-Caro and S. Peter Cowe. TECC 50. Madrid: Consejo Superior de Investigaciones Científicas.

———. 1992. *El Texto antioqueno de la Bibla griega, 1–2 Reyes.* With the collaboration of Victoria Spottorno Díaz-Caro. TECC 53. Madrid: Consejo Superior de Investigaciones Científicas.

———. 1996. *El Texto antioqueno de la Bibla griega, 1–2 Crónicas.* With the collaboration of Victoria Spottorno Díaz-Caro and S. Peter Cowe. TECC 60. Madrid : Consejo Superior de Investigaciones Científicas.

———. 2005. *Indice Griego-Hebreo del Texto Antioqueno en los libros históricos.* With the collaboration of Victoria Spottorno Díaz-Caro and José Manuel Cañas Reíllo. Vol. 1, *Indice general.* Vol. 2, *Indice de nombres propios.* TECC 75. Madrid: Consejo Superior de Investigaciones Científicas.

Fishbane, Michael. 1985. *Biblical Interpretation in Ancient Israel.* Oxford: Clarendon.

Greenspoon, Leonard. 1997. "It's All Greek to Me: Septuagint Studies Since 1968." *CurBR* 5: 147–74.

Gruen, Erich S. 2016. *The Construct of Identity in Hellenistic Judaism: Essays on Early Jewish Literature and History.* DCLS 29. Berlin: de Gruyter.

Huotari, Paavo, and Katja Kujanpää. 2022. "Hebraizing Revisions in Isaiah Quotations in Paul and Matthew." In *Scriptures in the Making: Texts and Their Transmission in Late Second Temple Judaism,* edited by Raimo Hakola, Jessi Orpana, and Paolo Huotari, 313–42. CBET 109. Leuven: Peeters.

Langer, Gerhard. 2016. *Midrash.* Jüdische Studien 4675. Tübingen: Mohr Siebeck.

Menken, Maarten J. J. 1996. *Old Testament Quotations in the Fourth Gospel: Studies in Textual Form.* CBET 15. Kampen: Kok Pharos.

Müller, Reinhard, and Juha Pakkala, eds. 2017. *Insights into Editing in the Hebrew Bible and the Ancient Near East: What Does Documentary Evidence Tell Us about the Transmission of Authoritative Texts?* CBET 84. Leuven: Peeters.

———. 2022. *Editorial Techniques in the Hebrew Bible: Toward a Refined Literary Criticism.* RBS 97. Atlanta: SBL Press.

Müller, Reinhard, Juha Pakkala, and Bas ter Haar Romeny. 2014. *Evidence of Editing: Growth and Change of Texts in the Hebrew Bible.* RBS 75. Atlanta: SBL Press.

Nestle, Eberhard, Erwin Nestle, Barbara Aland, Kurt Aland, Johannes Karavidopoulos, Carlo M. Martini, and Bruce M. Metzger, eds. 2012. *Novum Testamentum Graece*. 28th rev. ed. Stuttgart: Deutsche Bibelgesellschaft.

Pakkala, Juha. 2014. *God's Word Omitted: Omissions in the Transmission of the Hebrew Bible*. FRLANT 251. Göttingen: Vandenhoeck & Ruprecht.

Parsons, Peter J. 1990. "The Scripts and Their Date." In Tov 1990, 19–26.

Pessoa da Silva Pinto, Leonardo. 2019. "The Beginning of the *Kaige* Section of 2 Samuel." *Bib* 100: 14–33.

Rajak, Tessa. 2009. *Translation and Survival: The Greek Bible of the Ancient Jewish Diaspora*. Oxford: Oxford University Press.

Ross, William A. 2022. "The Past Decade in Septuagint Research (2012–2021)." *CurBR* 21, no. 1: 293–337.

Safrai, Shmuel. 1987. "Oral Tora." In *Oral Tora, Halakha, Mishna, Tosefta, Talmud, External Tractates*, edited by Shmuel Safrai, 35–119. Part 1 of *The Literature of the Sages*. CRINT 2.3. Philadelphia: Fortress.

Schäfer, Christian. 2012a. *Benützerhandbuch zur Göttinger Septuaginta*. Vol. 1, *Die Edition des Pentateuchs von John William Wevers*. Göttingen: Vandenhoeck & Ruprecht.

———. 2012b. *Benützerhandbuch zur Göttinger Septuaginta*. Vol. 2, *Die Edition des Buches Ruth von Udo Quast*. Göttingen: Vandenhoeck & Ruprecht.

Smelik, Willem. 2013. *Rabbis, Language and Translation in Late Antiquity*. Cambridge: Cambridge University Press.

Steyn, Gert J. 2011. *A Quest for the Assumed LXX Vorlage of the Explicit Quotations in Hebrews*. FRLANT 235. Göttingen: Vandenhoeck & Ruprecht.

Torijano, Pablo A., and Andres Piquer Otero, eds. 2012. *Textual Criticism and Dead Sea Scrolls Studies in Honour of Julio Trebolle Barrera*. JSJSup 157. Leiden: Brill.

Tov, Emanuel. 1986. "Jewish Greek Scriptures." In *Early Judaism and Its Modern Interpreters*, edited by Robert A. Kraft and George W. E. Nickelsburg, 223–37. The Bible and Its Modern Interpreters 2. Atlanta: Scholars Press.

———. 1990. *The Greek Minor Prophets Scroll from Nahal Hever (8HevXIIgr)*. The Seiyâl Collection 1 / Discoveries in the Judean Desert 8. Oxford: Clarendon.

———. 1999. *The Greek and Hebrew Bible: Collected Essays on the Septuagint*. VTSup 72. Leiden: Brill.

Trebolle Barrera, Julio. 2020. *Textual and Literary Criticism of the Books of Kings*. VTSup 185. Leiden: Brill.

Wasserstein, Abraham, and David J. Wasserstein. 2006. *The Legend of the Septuagint: From Classical Antiquity to Today*. Cambridge: Cambridge University Press.

Wirth, Raimund. 2016. *Die Septuaginta der Samuelbücher: Untersucht unter Einbeziehung ihrer Rezensionen*. DSI 7. Göttingen: Vandenhoeck & Ruprecht.

———. 2017. "Dealing with Tenses in the *Kaige* Section of Samuel." In *The Legacy of Barthélemy: 50 Years after "Les Devanciers d'Aquila,"* edited by Anneli Aejmelaeus and Tuukka Kauhanen, 185–97. DSI 9. Göttingen: Vandenhoeck & Ruprecht.

Wright, Benjamin G., III. 2015. *The Letter of Aristeas: "Aristeas to Philocrates" or "On the Translation of the Law of the Jews."* Commentaries on Early Jewish Literature. Berlin: de Gruyter.

Zahn, Molly M. 2020. *Genres of Rewriting in Second Temple Judaism: Scribal Composition and Transmission*. Cambridge: Cambridge University Press.

Zsengellér, József. 2014. *"Rewritten Bible" after Fifty Years: Texts, Terms, or Techniques? A Last Dialogue with Geza Vermes*. JSJSup 166. Leiden: Brill.

14

Qumran and the Context of the New Testament

Matthew A. Collins

Between 1946/47 and 1956, the remains of over nine hundred manuscripts were discovered in a series of eleven caves in the vicinity of Khirbet Qumran, a ruined settlement near the northwestern shore of the Dead Sea, some thirteen miles east of Jerusalem. This collection of Hebrew, Aramaic, and Greek texts, popularly known as the Dead Sea Scrolls (or more specifically, the Qumran Dead Sea Scrolls), dates from the third century BCE to the first century CE and is commonly associated with a Second Temple Jewish group called the Essenes. Not only does this remarkable discovery provide us with direct access to the beliefs, practices, and concerns of another Jewish movement of the same period (as well as copies of biblical manuscripts far older than anything previously available), but it also offers an unparalleled glimpse into the very social, religious, and literary world from which the Jesus movement and the New Testament likewise emerged.

The Qumran Dead Sea Scrolls

The story of the discovery of the scrolls has often been repeated and has at times even acquired something of a mythic status. While some details remain unclear, most reports tend to agree that in late 1946 or early 1947 a Ta'amireh Bedouin shepherd, searching for a lost goat near the northwestern shore of the Dead Sea, stumbled upon a cave in which he found a number of large cylindrical clay jars, at least one of which contained several linen-wrapped scrolls. Through somewhat convoluted means, these initial discoveries eventually came to the attention of scholars at both the Hebrew University and the American School of Oriental Research in Jerusalem (Fields 2009, 23–89). Famously described by W. F. Albright in a letter of March 1948 as "the greatest manuscript discovery of modern times" (Fields 2009, 76–77), these first scrolls included two copies of the book of Isaiah (1QIsa[a] and 1QIsa[b]), a commentary/pesher on Habakkuk (1QpHab), and texts that would later become known as the Community Rule (1QS), the War Scroll (1QM), the Hodayot/Thanksgiving Hymns (1QHᵃ), and the Genesis Apocryphon (1QapGen).

Subsequent excavations by both archaeologists and Bedouin resulted in the discovery by 1956 of over nine hundred manuscripts (most of which were highly fragmentary) in a series of eleven caves near the ruined settlement of Khirbet Qumran (Fields 2009, 91–359). The scroll caves were accordingly numbered Caves 1Q–11Q, and the scrolls themselves each received a siglum denoting the location of discovery as well as a number and/or abbreviated title. (Thus, for instance, 2Q19 = 2QJubᵃ = the first of two copies of Jubilees from Cave 2Q. Similarly, 4Q267 = 4QDᵇ = the second of several copies of the Damascus Document from Cave 4Q.) Excavations at the site of Qumran itself began in 1951. A connection between the settlement and the scrolls was further reinforced by the fact that Cave 4Q, containing by far the largest cache of manuscripts (the remains of ca. 550–600 scrolls), was a manmade cave literally a stone's throw from the site, while Caves 7Q–9Q (also manmade) were within the boundary wall and accessible only through the settlement itself.[1]

The scrolls date from the mid-third century BCE to the late first century CE (ca. 250 BCE–68 CE). The majority are in Hebrew (ca. 83 percent; mainly in square script, though some in Paleo-Hebrew or cryptic scripts), with a smaller number in Aramaic (ca. 14 percent) and a few in Greek (ca. 3 percent); most are written on parchment with some on papyrus (Gzella 2019; Kottsieper 2019).

Roughly a quarter of the collection (ca. 25 percent) constitutes so-called sectarian texts. These are original compositions thought to be authored by the group or movement responsible for the collection as a whole, and as such they were previously unknown.[2] They include rule texts governing admission procedures and life in the community (e.g., the Community Rule [S] and the Damascus Document [D]), exegetical texts (e.g., pesharim/commentaries on biblical books, such as Pesher Habakkuk [pHab] and Pesher Nahum [pNah]), poetic and liturgical texts (e.g., the Hodayot, or Thanksgiving Hymns [H]), halakic texts (e.g., Miqṣat Maʿaśê ha-Torah [MMT]), and eschatological texts (e.g., the War Scroll [M]). These give us an insight into some of the specific beliefs and practices of the group behind the scrolls.

The rest of the collection (ca. 75 percent) can be categorized as "non-sectarian"—that is, compositions that originated outside the movement and were more widely known and read in the late Second Temple period. Of these, a third (roughly another quarter of the collection) constitute so-called biblical texts. Though the label is, of course, anachronistic for this period, these are copies of those texts that would later end up being included in the Jewish canon (e.g., Genesis, Exodus, etc.). The Qumran scrolls include at least one copy of every text that later made it into the Tanakh (aside from Esther), and many in multiple copies (e.g., thirty-six copies of Psalms, thirty-two copies of Deuteronomy, twenty-one copies of Isaiah; see Crawford 2019, 219–20; VanderKam 2012, 2–5). Significantly, these manuscripts are far older than the earliest extant copies previously available to us, antedating by several hundred years those of the Greek Septuagint (LXX) and by around a thousand years those of the Hebrew Masoretic Text (MT). It is no-

---

1. Cave 4Q is actually two adjacent caves, 4Qa and 4Qb. For a helpful survey of the character and contents of all of the scroll caves, see Crawford 2019, 115–65.

2. One notable exception to this is the sectarian composition the Damascus Document (4QDᵃ⁻ʰ, 5QD, 6QD), two later medieval copies of which had been previously discovered in the Cairo Genizah and published in 1910 (Schechter 1910). Following Qumran labeling conventions, these tenth- and twelfth-century "Cairo" copies (which differ slightly from each other) are now commonly referred to as CD A–B (or jointly as CD).

table that, rather than a single textual tradition, versions preserved by both the MT and LXX, as well as the Samaritan Pentateuch (SP), are all reflected in the scrolls (Ulrich 2012). This attests to the antiquity of these differing traditions, indicating further that variants found in the Greek LXX may in some cases be accurate translations of an underlying Hebrew tradition that differed from the MT. Moreover, the scrolls preserved some previously unknown readings, not found in the MT, LXX, or SP (e.g., 4QSamᵃ/4Q51, which includes an additional passage at 1 Sam. 10:27 that has since been included in the NRSV; cf. Josephus, *Ant.* 6.67–71). So-called rewritten Scriptures (e.g., 4QReworked Pentateuch A–E [4Q158, 4Q364–67], though also Jubilees, the Genesis Apocryphon, etc.) further demonstrate the fluidity and nonfixed status of these writings in the late Second Temple period (Zahn 2020), with multiple varying editions of texts found side by side among the scrolls (Crawford 2019, 219–23; Ulrich 2012; VanderKam 2012, 1–24).

The other two-thirds of these "nonsectarian" materials (roughly half of the collection) reflect the wider body of Second Temple Jewish literature circulating in this period that did not end up being included in the Tanakh. Some of these are compositions that were already well known, although significantly in several cases this included copies of texts in their original Hebrew/Aramaic that had hitherto been preserved only in translation (e.g., Tobit, Jubilees, 1 Enoch), while the vast majority were previously unknown (e.g., Apocryphon of Joshua, New Jerusalem, Testament of Qahat, Visions of Amram, Words of the Luminaries). Though some certainly appear to have been considered more authoritative than others, there is no indication of a fixed canon, with what would later be classed as "biblical" and "nonbiblical" works sitting happily alongside each other. Moreover, if use/citation in sectarian compositions and the number of copies attested are anything to go by, some of these "noncanonical" texts (e.g., Jubilees and 1 Enoch) appear to have been considered just as important and scripturally authoritative as works like Genesis or Isaiah, and more so than many of the other books that did later make it into the canon (Crawford 2019, 232–36; Ulrich 2012, 143–48).

Taken together, the collection represents a remarkable wealth of textual material from the same time and place as the early Jesus movement, providing us among other things with a window into the scribal/reading practices and scriptural fluidity of the same late Second Temple world that likewise formed the backdrop to the New Testament.[3]

The Movement behind the Scrolls

Those responsible for the Qumran collection have most frequently—and most famously—been identified with the Essenes, a Second Temple Jewish movement known to us principally from the writings of Philo (*Good Person* 75–91; *Hypoth.* 1–18), Pliny the Elder (*Nat.* 5.73), and Josephus (e.g., *J.W.* 2.119–61; *Ant.* 13.171–73; 18.18–22). A number of the beliefs and practices attributed to the Essenes by Philo and Josephus seem to be reflected in the sectarian scrolls (e.g., a lengthy multiyear admission process, shared possessions, communal meals, expulsion for major offenses, as well as specific details such as prohibition of spitting in the midst of others [Josephus, *J.W.* 2.147; cf. 1QS VII, 13]). Also, Pliny's account appears to locate them on the northwestern shore of the Dead Sea (*Nat.* 5.73), in the direct vicinity of Qumran. There are differences, to be sure (including differences between the classical accounts themselves), as indeed we

3. Introductions to key texts and genres from the Dead Sea Scrolls can be found in Brooke and Hempel 2019, and Gurtner and Stuckenbruck 2020. Transcriptions and translations for most texts are readily accessible in, e.g., García Martínez and Tigchelaar 2000, and Parry and Tov 2014.

might expect when comparing insider and outsider perspectives, and when considering a movement that existed and evolved over 150 to 200 years (cf. Josephus, *J.W.* 1.78–80; 3.11), but these are far outweighed by the notable and numerous similarities (J. J. Collins 2010a, 122–65; Crawford 2019, 269–308; Taylor 2010). Other identifications have been suggested (e.g., Sadducees, Pharisees, Zealots), normally based on one or two points of correspondence, but none of these have gained much traction or come close to accounting for the totality of evidence (Crawford 2019, 295–308; Davies, Brooke, and Callaway 2011, 54–63).

This led to the early formation of the classic "Qumran-Essene hypothesis," which posited that the Essene movement separated itself from the rest of Jewish society (in opposition to the Hasmonean high priesthood) and lived in isolation at Qumran, where they wrote and collected the scrolls. It further characterized the movement as an all-male celibate group, drawing straightforwardly on assertions in the classical sources (e.g., Philo, *Hypoth.* 14–17; Pliny, *Nat.* 5.73; Josephus, *J.W.* 2.120–21) and the lack of reference to women or children in the Community Rule (S). This position did not, however, account for the provision for marriage, women, and families in other sectarian texts, such as the Damascus Document (e.g., CD VII, 6–9; XIII, 16–18; 4Q270 7 I, 12–15; 4Q271 3 12–15) or the Rule of the Congregation (e.g., 1Q28a I, 4–13), or indeed Josephus's description of other Essenes who *did* marry and raise children (*J.W.* 2.160–61). Similarly, although Pliny significantly appears to locate (a group of) the Essenes at Qumran (*Nat.* 5.73), both Philo (*Good Person* 75; *Hypoth.* 1) and Josephus (*J.W.* 2.124; *Ant.* 18.20) describe Essenes as numbering over four thousand and living throughout the land in every town, more closely mirroring the multiple communities or "camps" envisaged in the scrolls (e.g., CD VII, 6–9; XII, 22–XIV, 19; 1QS VI, 1–8).

Closer attention to these (and other) issues has meant that, in recent decades, the Qumran-Essene hypothesis has been significantly revised. It is no longer sufficient to simplistically equate the sectarian movement reflected in the scrolls with "the Qumran community" narrowly defined (the particular group living on the northwest shore of the Dead Sea), or to consider the latter as simply synonymous with the Essenes. The current consensus (or "new perspective") instead regards the Essenes as a broader and more widespread movement, including both communities who married and were family oriented (the Damascus Document lists punishments for "murmuring" against "the fathers" and "the mothers" [4Q270 7 I, 13–15], perhaps even implying some authoritative role for women) and those who "opted for a stricter, more demanding form of community life" (J. J. Collins 2010b, 156), which may have included celibacy. Those living at Qumran may have belonged to one of the latter celibate communities (cf. Pliny, *Nat.* 5.73, and the disproportionately high number of adult male burials at the site; Crawford 2019, 209–13; Magness 2021, 200–208), but they constituted only part of "the Yaḥad" and the wider movement reflected in the scrolls (J. J. Collins 2010a, 2010b; Schofield 2009).

Khirbet Qumran itself, which may have functioned as a retreat or scribal hub/repository (Crawford 2019), appears to have been occupied in this period from about 100 BCE until its destruction by the Romans in about 68 CE (Magness 2021, 49–83). The site includes a large number of stepped pools (probable *miqwa'ot* for ritual bathing), and the complex incorporates the manmade caves 7Q–9Q (within the boundary wall) as well as the immediately adjacent manmade caves 4Q, 5Q, and 10Q. Artifacts discovered include a number of inkwells and distinctive cylindrical clay jars (of the kind known from Caves 1Q and 11Q), as well as a significant quantity of dining utensils (plates, bowls, and cups) in a pantry next to a large room usually identified as an assembly hall or communal dining room (Crawford 2019, 166–216; Magness 2021; Mizzi 2019).

The movement appears to have adopted a policy of common property (e.g., 1QS I, 11–13; V, 1–3; VI, 16–25; cf. Philo, *Good Person* 86; *Hypoth.* 4, 10–12; Pliny, *Nat.* 5.73; Josephus, *J.W.* 2.122, 127; *Ant.* 18.20), though in the Damascus Document members are required to surrender only two days' earnings each month, in order that the community might use it to look after the poor and sick (CD XIV, 12–17). They also engaged in communal meals, with a priest present to bless the bread and wine (1QS VI, 2–6; 1Q28a II, 17–22; cf. Philo, *Good Person* 86; *Hypoth.* 5, 10–12; Josephus, *J.W.* 2.129–33). The meal was only open to fully initiated members (1QS VI, 16–23; cf. Josephus, *J.W.* 2.137–39), and exclusion from the communal meal was a punishment for various offenses (e.g., 1QS VI, 24–VII, 20; cf. Josephus, *J.W.* 2.143–44).

There was a concern for ritual bathing and purification, including prior to the communal meal (e.g., 1QS V, 13–14; cf. Josephus, *J.W.* 2.129–30; 4Q213a 1 I; 4Q414; 4Q512). There is some evidence of tension with (and criticism of) the temple cult in Jerusalem (e.g., CD VI, 11–21; 4QMMT[a-f]/4Q394–99 [note 4Q397 14–21, 7–8]; cf. Josephus, *Ant.* 18.19), with the Community Rule going further still, seeming to present the Yaḥad itself as the means through which atonement for the land will henceforth be achieved, without the need for animal sacrifice (1QS VIII, 1–10; IX, 3–6). They believed in predeterminism and fate (e.g., 1QS III, 15–16; 1QH[a] IX, 7–25; CD II, 7–10; 4Q180 1 1–3; cf. Josephus, *Ant.* 13.172), and all people were considered to belong to either "the Sons of Light" or "the Sons of Darkness" (1QS III, 17–IV, 26; 4Q186), with the War Scroll envisaging a final eschatological battle between the two (e.g., 1QM I, 1–11). The movement also anticipated one or more messiahs. The Damascus Document refers to the "messiah of Aaron

and Israel" (CD XII, 23–XIII, 1; XIV, 19; XIX, 10–11) and the "messiah from Aaron and from Israel" (XX, 1), the Community Rule utilizes the plural "messiahs of Aaron and Israel" (1QS IX, 11), while the Rule of the Congregation refers to an individual "messiah of Israel" accompanied by "the priest" (1Q28a II, 11–22) (J. J. Collins 2010c; Pomykala 2019, 500–503).

Leadership of the movement included such roles as the Mebaqqer/Overseer (מבקר, *mbqr*; e.g., 1QS VI, 11–12; CD XIII, 7–13) and the Maskil/Sage (משכיל, *mskyl*; e.g., 1QS IX, 12–19; CD XII, 20–22). Various organizational units included "the council of the Community/Yaḥad" (עצת היחד, *'tst hyhd*; e.g., 1QS VI, 13–14; VIII, 1–7; 4Q171 II, 15), "the sons of Zadok" (בני צדוק, *bny tsdwq*; e.g., 1QS V, 1–3; CD IV, 3–4), and "the Many" (הרבים, *hrbym*; e.g., 1QS VI, 8–23; CD XIV, 12). A number of texts appear also to revere and look back to a foundational figure referred to as "the Teacher of Righteousness" (מורה הצדק, *mwrh htsdq*; e.g., 1QpHab VIII, 1–3; CD I, 10–11), who is presented in opposition to "the Man of the Lie" (איש הכזב, *'ysh hkzb*; e.g., 1QpHab V, 9–12; CD XX, 13–15) and "the Wicked Priest" (הכוהן הרשע, *hkwhn hrsh'*; e.g., 1QpHab XI, 4–8; 4Q171 IV, 8–10). Similar sobriquets (nicknames) are used elsewhere for other apparent opponents of the movement, such as "the Seekers of Smooth Things" (דורשי החלקות, *dwrshy hhlqwt*; e.g., 4Q169 3–4 III, 3–8; 1QH[a] X, 31–34), a group that has usually been identified with the Pharisees (Berrin 2004, 91–99; see further M. A. Collins 2009, 2017).

The discoveries from in and around Qumran thus reflect a prominent/widespread late Second Temple Jewish movement that, among other things, advocated common property and communal meals, was critical of the temple cult in Jerusalem, was concerned with the proper interpretation (and fulfillment) of Scripture, and had a complex messianic and apocalyptic outlook (believing itself to be living in and preparing for the final days). Existing both prior to and contemporaneously with the early Jesus movement, it accordingly formed a crucial part of the same cultural milieu from which the latter group sprang.

The Scrolls and the New Testament

The importance and relevance of the scrolls for New Testament scholarship began to be recognized soon after their discovery (e.g., K. G. Kuhn 1950a, 1950b), resulting in a particular flurry of scholarly activity between the 1950s and 1970s (see Brooke 2005, 3–18; Frey 2019, 529–39). The same period also saw a rise in sensationalism and speculation in the public sphere with regard to connections between the scrolls and the origins of Christianity, fueled in part by the popularizing efforts of Edmund Wilson and John M. Allegro, and delays in the publication of the manuscripts (M. A. Collins 2019, 60–61). For those interested in possible associations with the Jesus movement, the early years were spent revisiting a vast range of different New Testament texts and topics in the light of the scrolls, often with a particular focus on identifying perceived parallels (e.g., Black 1961, 1969; Braun 1966; Charlesworth 1972; Daniélou 1958; Mowry 1962; Murphy-O'Connor 1968; Sanders 1977; Stendahl 1957).

At its most extreme, the presence of ideological, theological, and terminological similarities between the movement behind the scrolls and the Jesus movement led some scholars to try to identify the two groups with each other. Robert Eisenman (1996), for instance, regarded "the Teacher of Righteousness" as James the Just, "the Man of the Lie" as Paul, and "the Wicked Priest" as High Priest Ananus, while Barbara Thiering (1992) infamously identified "the Teacher of Righteousness" with John the Baptist and "the Wicked Priest" (and "the Man of the Lie") with Jesus of Nazareth, relocating the events of the Gospels to Qumran itself! However, scientific dating of the texts alone renders all such attempts fundamentally mistaken (M. A. Collins 2009, 14–15; Frey 2019, 544–46).

José O'Callaghan (1972, 1974) and Carsten Peter Thiede (1992) even suggested that some of the tiny Greek papyrus fragments from Cave 7Q might reflect passages from the New Testament (specifically, that 7Q4 = 1 Tim. 3:16–4:3, and 7Q5 = Mark 6:52–53). However, in both cases only a few Greek letters have been preserved, and only one complete word (και, *kai*, "and")! The reconstruction would also necessitate several unlikely variants (Frey 2019, 546–50). Accordingly, the suggestion is implausible, and we can assert with some confidence that no New Testament texts have been found among the scrolls.

Similarly, the Essene movement does not appear to be mentioned in the New Testament (though compare, e.g., Matt. 5:43 and 1QS I, 9–10; Josephus, *J.W.* 2.139),[4] which is rather more focused on the Pharisees (and to a lesser extent, Sadducees). Instead, the significance of the scrolls for the New Testament lies in their shared heritage and the light this sheds on the wider late Second Temple world to which they both belonged. Areas of commonality appear to include messianic and apocalyptic concerns, criticism of the temple cult, common property (e.g., Acts 4:32–35), communal and ritual meals (e.g., Matt. 26:26–29), outlook on divorce (e.g., Mark 10:2–12; CD IV, 20–V, 6; 11Q19 LVII, 15–19), light/darkness dualism (e.g., John 12:35–36; Eph. 5:6–11; 1 Thess. 5:4–5), exorcism (e.g., 4Q242; 4Q560; 11Q11), eschatological judgment (e.g., Matt. 13:47–50; 1QS IV), anticipation of a "new Jerusalem" (Rev. 21; 4Q554–55; 5Q15; 11Q18), beatitudes (Matt. 5:3–12; 4Q525), the golden rule (Mark 12:31; CD VI, 20–21), and ritual bathing/purification.

4. See, too, Taylor 2012 (109–30) on "the Herodians" (Mark 3:6; 8:15; 12:13; Matt. 22:16); cf. Josephus, *Ant.* 15.371–79; Philo, *Hypoth.* 18.

There are also shared interests in (and approaches to) scriptural interpretation/fulfillment (e.g., Isa. 40:3 in Matt. 3:3 parr. and 1QS VIII, 12–16), drawing especially on Isaiah and Psalms (Brooke 2005, 2010; J. J. Collins 2016, 257–71), as well as shared terminology—for example, "the many"; "new covenant"; "sons of light"; "overseer" (ἐπίσκοπος, *episkopos*; מבקר, *mbqr*); "father" for God (e.g., Mark 14:36; 4Q372 1 16); "poor in spirit" (Matt. 5:3; 1QM XIV, 7); "works of the law" (Gal. 2–3; 4Q398 14–17 II, 3); "Son of God" and "Son of the Most High" (Luke 1:32–35; 4Q246); and so on. Differences of interpretation with regard to such commonality may simultaneously help signal particular areas of contention or dispute at that time (compare, e.g., Matt. 12:11–12 and CD XI, 13–14; Matt. 5:43–44 and 1QS I, 9–10; Luke 14:13–14, 21 and 1Q28a II, 3–9; and various matters concerning purity or inclusion).

Over the years, attention has also been given to questions of possible Essene influence on John the Baptist (Charlesworth 2006b; Frey 2019, 561–68; McDonald 2000; Taylor 1997), comparisons with Johannine literature (Attridge 2009; Charlesworth 1972, 2006a; Coloe and Thatcher 2011; Frey 2019, 763–90) and Pauline literature (Frey 2019, 677–762; H.-W. Kuhn 2006; Murphy-O'Connor 1968; Rey 2014; Sanders 1977), and comparative studies in areas such as messianism and eschatology (J. J. Collins 2010c; Hogeterp 2009) and wisdom (Wold 2023). While the scrolls themselves do not reflect early Christianity (contrary to some roundly debunked fringe views), they do on every count reveal plenty about the fundamentally Jewish context of both the New Testament and the Jesus movement.

Conclusion

There are other important and contextually relevant Dead Sea Scroll collections from the time of the First Jewish Revolt (66–74 CE) and the Bar Kokhba Revolt (132–135 CE) discov-

ered at Masada, Wadi Murabbaʿat, and Nahal Hever (Freund 2020; Patmore 2020; Popović 2019; Tuval 2020). However, it is the collection of manuscripts from the caves associated with Khirbet Qumran (the Qumran Dead Sea Scrolls) that is of most significance for the New Testament. Jörg Frey notes, "Before the Qumran finds, there were practically no Hebrew or Aramaic documents from Palestinian Judaism at the turn of the era" (2019, 559). We now have an abundance of them, and together they shed unprecedented light on the social, religious, and literary world of the late Second Temple period. Among other things, the scrolls contextualize and illuminate the events and concerns of the New Testament, underlining the profoundly Jewish nature of the Jesus movement and situating them both far more meaningfully within the wider Second Temple Jewish context from which they came.

Works Cited

Attridge, Harold W. 2009. "The Gospel of John and the Dead Sea Scrolls." In *Text, Thought, and Practice in Qumran and Early Christianity*, edited by Ruth A. Clements and Daniel R. Schwartz, 109–26. STDJ 84. Leiden: Brill.

Berrin, Shani L. 2004. *The Pesher Nahum Scroll from Qumran: An Exegetical Study of 4Q169*. STDJ 53. Leiden: Brill.

Black, Matthew. 1961. *The Scrolls and Christian Origins: Studies in the Jewish Background of the New Testament*. London: Nelson.

———, ed. 1969. *The Scrolls and Christianity*. Theological Collections 11. London: SPCK.

Braun, Herbert. 1966. *Qumran und das Neue Testament*. 2 vols. Tübingen: Mohr Siebeck.

Brooke, George J. 2005. *The Dead Sea Scrolls and the New Testament: Essays in Mutual Illumination*. London: SPCK.

———. 2010. "Shared Exegetical Traditions between the Scrolls and the New Testament." In *The Oxford Handbook of the Dead Sea Scrolls*, edited by Timothy H. Lim and John J. Collins, 565–91. Oxford: Oxford University Press.

Brooke, George J., and Charlotte Hempel, eds. 2019. *T&T Clark Companion to the Dead Sea Scrolls*. London: Bloomsbury T&T Clark.

Charlesworth, James H., ed. 1972. *John and Qumran*. London: Geoffrey Chapman.

———. 2006a. "A Study in Shared Symbolism and Language: The Qumran Community and the Johannine Community." In *The Scrolls and Christian Origins*, edited by James H. Charlesworth, 97–152. Vol. 3 of *The Bible and the Dead Sea Scrolls*. Waco: Baylor University Press.

———. 2006b. "John the Baptizer and the Dead Sea Scrolls." In *The Scrolls and Christian Origins*, edited by James H. Charlesworth, 1–35. Vol. 3 of *The Bible and the Dead Sea Scrolls*. Waco: Baylor University Press.

Collins, John J. 2010a. *Beyond the Qumran Community: The Sectarian Movement of the Dead Sea Scrolls*. Grand Rapids: Eerdmans.

———. 2010b. "Sectarian Communities in the Dead Sea Scrolls." In *The Oxford Handbook of the Dead Sea Scrolls*, edited by Timothy H. Lim and John J. Collins, 151–72. Oxford: Oxford University Press.

———. 2010c. *The Scepter and the Star: Messianism in Light of the Dead Sea Scrolls*. 2nd ed. Grand Rapids: Eerdmans.

———. 2016. *Scriptures and Sectarianism: Essays on the Dead Sea Scrolls*. Grand Rapids: Eerdmans.

Collins, Matthew A. 2009. *The Use of Sobriquets in the Qumran Dead Sea Scrolls*. LSTS 67. London: T&T Clark.

———. 2017. "Text, Intertext, and Conceptual Identity: The Case of Ephraim and the Seekers of Smooth Things." In *Is There a Text in This Cave? Studies in the Textuality of the Dead Sea Scrolls in Honour of George J. Brooke*, edited by Ariel Feldman, Maria Cioată, and Charlotte Hempel, 209–25. STDJ 119. Leiden: Brill.

———. 2019. "Scholarly and Popular Reception." In Brooke and Hempel 2019, 59–73.

Coloe, Mary L., and Tom Thatcher, eds. 2011. *John, Qumran, and the Dead Sea Scrolls: Sixty Years of Discovery and Debate*. EJL 32. Atlanta: Society of Biblical Literature.

Crawford, Sidnie White. 2019. *Scribes and Scrolls at Qumran*. Grand Rapids: Eerdmans.

Daniélou, Jean. 1958. *The Dead Sea Scrolls and Primitive Christianity*. Baltimore: Helicon.

Davies, Philip R., George J. Brooke, and Phillip R. Callaway. 2011. *The Complete World of the Dead Sea Scrolls*. London: Thames & Hudson.

Eisenman, Robert. 1996. *The Dead Sea Scrolls and the First Christians: Essays and Translations*. Shaftesbury: Element.

Fields, Weston W. 2009. *The Dead Sea Scrolls, A Full History*. Vol. 1, *1947–1960*. Leiden: Brill.

Freund, Richard A. 2020. "Naḥal Ḥever (Cave of Horrors and Cave of Letters)." In Gurtner and Stuckenbruck 2020, 2:534–37.

Frey, Jörg. 2019. *Qumran, Early Judaism, and New Testament Interpretation: Kleine Schriften III*. Edited by Jacob N. Cerone. WUNT 424. Tübingen: Mohr Siebeck.

García Martínez, Florentino, and Eibert J. C. Tigchelaar. 2000. *The Dead Sea Scrolls Study Edition*. 2 vols. Grand Rapids: Eerdmans.

Gurtner, Daniel M., and Loren T. Stuckenbruck, eds. 2020. *T&T Clark Encyclopedia of Second Temple Judaism*. 2 vols. London: Bloomsbury T&T Clark.

Gzella, Holger. 2019. "Languages: Hebrew, Aramaic, Greek." In Brooke and Hempel 2019, 192–203.

Hogeterp, Albert L. A. 2009. *Expectations of the End: A Comparative Traditio-Historical Study of Eschatological, Apocalyptic, and Messianic Ideas in the Dead Sea Scrolls and the New Testament*. STDJ 83. Leiden: Brill.

Kottsieper, Ingo. 2019. "Physicality of Manuscripts and Material Culture." In Brooke and Hempel 2019, 167–77.

Kuhn, Heinz-Wolfgang. 2006. "The Impact of Selected Qumran Texts on the Understanding of Pauline Theology." In *The Scrolls and Christian Origins*, edited by James H. Charlesworth, 153–85. Vol. 3 of *The Bible and the Dead Sea Scrolls*. Waco: Baylor University Press.

Kuhn, Karl Georg. 1950a. "Die in Palästina gefundenen hebräischen Texte und das Neue Testament." *Zeitschrift für Theologie und Kirche* 47: 192–211.

———. 1950b. "Zur Bedeutung der neuen palästinischen Handschriftenfunde für die neutestamentliche Wissenschaft." *Theologische Literaturzeitung* 75: 81–86.

Magness, Jodi. 2021. *The Archaeology of Qumran and the Dead Sea Scrolls*. 2nd ed. Grand Rapids: Eerdmans.

McDonald, J. Ian H. 2000. "What Did You Go Out to See? John the Baptist, the Scrolls and Late Second Temple Judaism." In *The Dead Sea Scrolls in Their Historical Context*, edited by Timothy H. Lim, 53–64. London: T&T Clark.

Mizzi, Dennis. 2019. "Archaeology of Qumran." In Brooke and Hempel 2019, 17–36.

Mowry, Lucetta. 1962. *The Dead Sea Scrolls and the Early Church*. Chicago: University of Chicago Press.

Murphy-O'Connor, Jerome, ed. 1968. *Paul and Qumran*. London: Geoffrey Chapman.

O'Callaghan, José. 1972. "¿Papiros neotestamentarios en la cueva 7 de Qumrân?" *Bib* 53: 91–100.

———. 1974. *Los papiros griegos de la cueva 7 de Qumrân*. Madrid: Editorial Católica.

Parry, Donald W., and Emanuel Tov, eds. 2014. *The Dead Sea Scrolls Reader*. 2nd ed. 2 vols. Leiden: Brill.

Patmore, Hector M. 2020. "Masada, Texts from." In Gurtner and Stuckenbruck 2020, 2:469–72.

Pomykala, Kenneth E. 2019. "Eschatologies and Messianisms." In Brooke and Hempel 2019, 496–504.

Popović, Mladen. 2019. "The Manuscript Collections: An Overview." In Brooke and Hempel 2019, 37–50.

Rey, Jean-Sébastien, ed. 2014. *The Dead Sea Scrolls and Pauline Literature*. STDJ 102. Leiden: Brill.

Sanders, E. P. 1977. *Paul and Palestinian Judaism*. London: SCM.

Schechter, Solomon. 1910. *Documents of Jewish Sectaries*. Vol. 1, *Fragments of a Zadokite Work*. Cambridge: Cambridge University Press.

Schofield, Alison. 2009. *From Qumran to the Yaḥad: A New Paradigm of Textual Development for the Community Rule*. STDJ 77. Leiden: Brill.

Stendahl, Krister, ed. 1957. *The Scrolls and the New Testament*. New York: Harper.

Taylor, Joan E. 1997. *The Immerser: John the Baptist within Second Temple Judaism*. Grand Rapids: Eerdmans.

———. 2010. "The Classical Sources on the Essenes and the Scrolls Communities." In *The Oxford Handbook of the Dead Sea Scrolls*, edited by Timothy H. Lim and John J. Collins, 173–99. Oxford: Oxford University Press.

———. 2012. *The Essenes, the Scrolls, and the Dead Sea*. Oxford: Oxford University Press.

Thiede, Carsten Peter. 1992. *The Earliest Gospel Manuscript? The Qumran Papyrus 7Q5 and Its Significance for New Testament Studies*. Carlisle: Paternoster.

Thiering, Barbara. 1992. *Jesus the Man: A New Interpretation from the Dead Sea Scrolls*. London: BCA.

Tuval, Michael. 2020. "Murabbaʿat, Wadi." In Gurtner and Stuckenbruck 2020, 2:524–26.

Ulrich, Eugene. 2012. "The Jewish Scriptures: Texts, Versions, Canons." In *Early Judaism: A Comprehensive Overview*, edited by John J. Collins and Daniel C. Harlow, 121–50. Grand Rapids: Eerdmans.

VanderKam, James C. 2012. *The Dead Sea Scrolls and the Bible*. Grand Rapids: Eerdmans.

Wold, Benjamin. 2023. *Qumran Wisdom and the New Testament: Exploring Early Jewish and Christian Textual Cultures*. Cambridge: Cambridge University Press.

Zahn, Molly M. 2020. *Genres of Rewriting in Second Temple Judaism: Scribal Composition and Transmission*. Cambridge: Cambridge University Press.

15

Historiography

LOVEDAY ALEXANDER

The war of the Jews against the Romans—the greatest not only of the wars of our own time, but, so far as accounts have reached us, well nigh of all that ever broke out between cities or nations—has not lacked its historians. Of these, however, some, having taken no part in the action, have collected from hearsay casual and contradictory stories which they have then edited in a rhetorical style; while others, who witnessed the events, have, either from flattery of the Romans or from hatred of the Jews, misrepresented the facts, their writings exhibiting alternatively invective and encomium, but nowhere historical accuracy. In these circumstances, I—Josephus, son of Matthias, a Hebrew by race, a native of Jerusalem and a priest, who at the opening of the war myself fought against the Romans and in the sequel was perforce an onlooker—propose to provide the subjects of the Roman Empire with a narrative of the facts, by translating into Greek the account which I previously composed in my vernacular tongue and sent to the barbarians in the interior.

Josephus, *Jewish War* 1.1–3
(trans. Thackeray 1927, 3, 5)

The Jewish historian Josephus wrote these words as a preface to his *Jewish War*, a detailed account in seven books of the Jewish revolt against Rome in 66–70 CE, culminating with the fall of Jerusalem. When he wrote the *Jewish War*, Josephus was living in Rome as an honored guest of the imperial family. But at the outset of the war, he was a rebel commander in Galilee, a fact that gives him a unique claim to credibility as an eyewitness reporter (*Ag. Ap.* 1.47–52). It also gives him an emotional involvement in the story he tells of his country's downfall—something that might in some eyes disqualify him from writing with the objectivity proper to a historian (*J.W.* 1.11–12).

Josephus is based in Rome, at the heart of the empire; but he writes in Greek, the language of literature and education across the eastern empire and in Rome itself. And everything he writes in this highly wrought introduction reflects a quite specific set of ambitions and expectations associated with the Greek tradition of historiography. The choice of war as a suitable subject matter for history and the claim that the war in question was superior to all other wars go back to Herodotus and Thucydides, the acknowledged classics of Greek historiography from the fifth century BCE. Josephus takes a great deal of trouble to pay homage to Thucydides, not merely in his subject matter but in the style of his writing (*Ant.* 1.7; *Ag. Ap.* 1.50). Like Thucydides (and his successor Polybius), Josephus places a high value on eyewitness reporting. And he is right to be wary of emotional involvement: Greek historians writing in Thucydidean mode claimed to avoid bias and flattery and cultivated a detached and impersonal approach to the writing of history. Even the polemical tone, which contrasts the author's work with the inferior writings of earlier historians, is a standard aspect of the distinctive persona of the Greek historian (*J.W.* 1.1–2, 6–8).

But it is equally clear from Josephus that the Greek tradition of historiography was not the only available option. He tells us that the first version of the *Jewish War* (presumably covering much the same narrative ground as the Greek) was written in Aramaic for the non-Greek-speaking inhabitants beyond the eastern borders of the Roman Empire. Though he places his work squarely within a living Greek tradition of historiography, Josephus is also a vigorous critic of Greek historians when they attempt to write the histories of the more ancient Eastern civilizations, especially the Jews (*J.W.* 1.13; *Ag. Ap.*, passim). Twenty years after the *Jewish War* he composed a much longer work in twenty books on *Jewish Antiquities*, drawing on the resources of biblical historiography and defending the superior veracity and reliability of the priestly records on which it was based. Writing in Rome at the end of the first century, Josephus is a testimony not only to the apologetic debates over the historiography of colonized peoples within the empire but also to the vigorous and varied hybrid historiographies that flourished under the empire. All of these are potentially important in assessing the historiographical scripts available to the readers and writers of the New Testament.

Greek Historiography

History is one of the most distinctive and long-lasting of Greek literary genres, a living tradition that runs from the classics of the fifth century BCE through the Roman period and beyond. Roman historiography developed from its own cultural roots but was deeply influenced by the dominant Greek tradition. In late first-century Rome, would-be historians often gave oral recitals of their work to elite audiences. There is also some evidence for the reading of history as a more popular pastime, at least for the literate few. But the nature of ancient education meant that the historians best known to the educated Greek reader in the first century CE were not recent or contemporary historians (like Polybius or Diodorus Siculus) but the classical historians who had written five hundred years earlier. Herodotus, Thucydides, and Xenophon were the historians who dominated ancient education, defining the models to be imitated and the canons of good prose (Lucian, *Hist. conscr.* 2).

Thus within the context of Greek *paideia* (elite education), the teaching of history was part of a process of creating a shared cultural heritage, a communal past that could be traced in continuous narrative right back to the Trojan War. The educated person was expected to know the stories from Greek history of the fifth century BCE, even though they might be reading in a very different place and time. This process entails an enormous effort of cultural transposition, an intensive process of cultural acclimatization reflected in the names of Attic mountains or Spartan ephors scrawled on the walls and writing tablets of school rooms around the Roman world (Marrou 1956, 233; see further Morgan 1998; Cribiore 2001). Greek historiography evokes a classical world that is distant in time and space from these later readers. Its effect is to draw readers into that distant cultural space, into a narrative world that identifies "us" as "the Greeks" (a heritage rather ambiguously adopted by the Romans) and "them" as everybody else: Persians, Egyptians, Jews, barbarians.

The predominance of the classics defines the dominant script for Greek historiography, both in style and in content. History was first and foremost a celebration of the achievements of great men and nations—*praxeis*, *res gestae*. It was a story of public heroes enacting public events, a world in which war and political life were supremely *axiologa*, worthy of speech. The subject matter of history was the public life of city-states and empires: classical historiography had little room for the private lives of individuals. The primary heroes of Herodotus and Thucydides are group characters: "the Persians," "the Athenians," "the Peloponnesians"—unlike the historical writing of the ancient Near East, which is more often structured around the exploits of the individual king or warlord (Momigliano 1993, 39–40). Under the impact of the Macedonian monarchies this focus began to change, but it was only under the Roman emperors, with the increasing domination of historical events by autocratic rulers, that this pattern of "bio-structuring" became more evident among Roman historians. In the late Roman Republic and early empire, many historians found the dominating individual a necessary strategy for "keeping the story clear, focused, and organized" (Pelling 1997, 122). Yet whether individual or collective, history's characters are public men: kings, generals and statesmen, warriors, and citizens. Women are conspicuous by their absence, unless they figure in court intrigues.

Rhetoric has a profound effect on how history is told and read in the world of the New Testament: it creates an ordered, rationalistic discourse in which debate and persuasive speech are accorded a high value and supernatural causation is bracketed or marginalized.

It is a narrative in which the rhetoric of speech plays a controlling role not only within the narrative (rhetoric on the lips of characters, rhetoric as a factor that moves events in the civic or military drama) but also on the readers. Some of the most important writings on Greek historiography are rhetorical critiques like those of Dionysius of Halicarnassus (*On Thucydides* [1st c. BCE]) and Lucian (in the satirical *How to Write History* [2nd c. CE]: both texts are available in Marincola 2017).

The style of Greek historiography was expected to match the grandeur and sublimity of its subject matter. For Dionysius of Halicarnassus history requires a style that is elevated, noble, solemn, grand, poetic, and forceful. The historian is expected to deploy the full resources of a rhetorical education, avoiding the vulgarity and inartistic simplicity of everyday speech (*Thuc.* 27–28). Lucian's ideal historian must steer a course between overuse of poetic language (which makes a history ridiculous) and the "vulgar language of the market-place" (*Hist. conscr.* 22, 44 [trans. Kilburn 1959, 59]). A soldier's campaign memoir, "completely ordinary and prosaic" while avoiding the pitfalls of overpretension, is simply the raw material of history, waiting for "some future historian of taste and ability" to "give it beauty and enhance it with the charms of expression, figure, and rhythm" (*Hist. conscr.* 48 [trans. Kilburn 1959, 61]). For Lucian, the historian, unlike the orator, is concerned not so much about *what* to say (the art of *inventio*) as *how* to say it: like a sculptor fashioning a block of marble, the historian is not "inventing" but "fashioning" his material, and his art lies in finding the right arrangement (*oikonomia*) for the material (*Hist. conscr.* 50). The historian's skill and judgment are exercised in choosing a strong organizational structure (chronological or topographical), with a clearly marked beginning and ending, including a formal *prooimion* or preface; in composing formal speeches "fitting to the occasion"; and in selecting the right episodes for detailed descriptive elaboration (*exergasia*).

But the Greek historians also had their own distinctive code of conduct, which surfaces especially in prefaces and personal digressions. Here we can discern historiographical values and aspirations that remained remarkably consistent over the length of the tradition, though enlivened by personal idiosyncrasies and variations. From this discussion emerges a strong sense of the persona of the historian, of the need to choose a "noble" subject matter, of the appropriate methods of historical inquiry, of the laboriousness of the historical task, of the importance attached to truthfulness and the avoidance of bias and myth, and of the usefulness of history for the education of the statesman. (Marincola 1997 gives an extensive account of this repertoire of historiographical themes, summarized in Marincola 2017, xxix–lxxi.)

Historiography in the Jewish World

How were the children of Jewish merchants in Alexandria or Tarsus educated in this classicizing world? Did they learn Greek from the same *grammatistai* and *rhetores* as their pagan contemporaries? If so, they could not evade the acquaintance of the ubiquitous Greek classics: Homer, Thucydides, Demosthenes, Plato. Were they simply taught from an early age, as later Christian children were, to learn the language without being contaminated by the "idolatry" implicit in the pagan texts they studied (Marrou 1956, part 3, chap. 9, pp. 419–38)? Or were they taught Greek in a parallel school system that accorded a similar "classic" status to Jewish-Greek texts? We simply do not know; we have very little information about the education systems of Hellenistic (Greek-speaking) Judaism (Heszer 2001; Vegge 2006; Hauge and Pitts 2016).

But we do know that survival for such colonized peoples (then as now) is linked inextricably to the telling of their own stories. Diaspora Judaism had its own "classic" literature, which was energetically promoted as a robust rival to the Greek classical tradition, and which provided the alternative narrative that Jews needed to sustain their identity in the Greco-Roman world (Rajak 2009). For Greek-speaking Jews, the preeminent classic text was the Greek Bible, which meant (predominantly) the Septuagint (LXX), the Alexandrian Greek translation of the Hebrew Bible that a highly educated Greek-speaking Jew like Philo revered as highly as the Hebrew text itself. This was the text that provided the gold standard for Jewish readers in all areas of literature: poetry, philosophy, law—and history. For Jews, having the Bible was like having Homer, Plato, Demosthenes, and the historians all in one volume. Philo reads the Greek Bible as a system of philosophy, matching the wisdom of Plato. Josephus reads it as the historical record of his people's past, a national history that tells the great deeds of his own people and can easily outshine those of the Greeks and other nations (*Ant.* 1.1; *Ag. Ap.* 1.1).

Josephus's *Jewish Antiquities* uses the biblical and postbiblical record as a base for a Greek-style history of the Jews. Deeply imbued with the values of Greek historiography, Josephus adapts the biblical narrative in small but significant ways to make it more palatable to Greek tastes: "In recounting the biblical story Josephus consistently dresses his narrative in Hellenistic garb. Biblical figures are given characterization through speeches and analyses of their inner motivation, and a premium is placed on emotion, pathos and suspense. Erotic and other novelistic features creep into the story at various points, . . . and biblical material is rearranged to enhance its narrative power" (Barclay 1999, 357; cf. Dormeyer 2005; Rajak 2009).

But Josephus is also deeply proud of his Jewish heritage: he insists that Jewish historiography is more reliable than the early history of the Greeks because it deploys written sources, carefully preserved by the priestly tradition, as opposed to the oral traditions on which Greek historians had to rely (Barclay 2005).

In using the tools and styles of Greek history to write and publicize the native traditions of a colonized people, Josephus exemplifies a type of "hybrid" historiography found across the Greco-Roman world (Sterling 1992). This type of historiography exploits the scientific interest in ethnography (the founding myths and customs of non-Greek peoples) that had fascinated the Greek historians since Herodotus (Bickerman 1952). But now these ethnographic histories are being written by the colonized peoples themselves, drawing on their own indigenous written sources to supplement (and sometimes to challenge) the colonial master narrative. This is what Barclay calls "autohistory"— that is, "the attempt to tell their own histories in an idiom comprehensible to the majority culture(s), but with primary reference to their own traditions and *in their own terms*" (Barclay 2005, 35, emphasis original).

Josephus's writings are clearly addressed to readers outside the community, using the discourses of Greek rationalism to assert the claims of a rival tradition (*Ant.* 1.5; Bickerman 1952). This apologetic stance is essential to understanding the rhetoric of such texts, even though they also have an important function for insiders in building up a confident sense of religious and cultural identity (Sterling 1992, 223). But not all Jewish-Greek literature is addressed to outsiders, even ostensibly: as Tessa Rajak observes, "When [Jews] adopted the common language, it was not only for conversation with others but also, and indeed even more, as a route to keeping their own traditions alive" (2009, 124). The language of the Greek Bible was "deliberately created and consciously maintained," she suggests, as "an assertion of communal independence which made it possible for the translations to serve as a vehicle for quiet cultural resistance" (Rajak 2009, 134,

158). And the effect of that language spills over into a host of related genres, deploying "a highly allusive and idiosyncratic vocabulary" that "denies easy access by virtue of its intertextuality" and "combine[s] the discourse of accommodation with the spirit of independence" (Rajak 2009, 184, 207–8).

So (as Josephus reminds us) Jews could also draw on a long tradition of Jewish historiography (prose literature about the past), both in Hebrew/Aramaic and in Greek. This includes the retellings of biblical narrative (rewritten Bible) by such writers as Demetrius, Artapanus, Eupolemus, or Pseudo-Philo (Holladay 1983; 1999; Schürer 1986 §32, §33.1; Reinmuth 1994). Jewish historians wrote historical monographs on episodes of Hasmonean history (1 Maccabees, 2 Maccabees, 4 Maccabees). Diaspora existence inspired its own novelistic narratives of crafty courtiers and faithful martyrs, whether based on characters from the Bible (Daniel, Esther, Joseph) or from Ptolemaic history (3 Maccabees). In the first century BCE and the first century CE, the Herodian court became a center of literary patronage, inspiring historical writers from Nicolaus of Damascus (Herod the Great's Greek secretary) to Josephus's rival Justus of Tiberias (Rajak 2001, 161–93). Parts of Josephus's Herodian narratives may be based on now lost biographies of Antipas and Agrippa I (Schwartz 1990, 2–38). Philo's voluminous output includes (as well as biographical narratives of biblical characters) several short (and highly partisan) historical narratives dealing with the Jewish community's relations with Roman emperors and officials (*On the Embassy to Gaius*; *Against Flaccus*; *Life of Pilate*; Sterling 2022).

Historiography in the New Testament

These alternative cultural scripts must be borne in mind when we turn to consider the historiography of the New Testament. How would the narratives of the New Testament resonate with readers whose expectations are formed by the cultural script of Greek historiography? For most readers, the most likely candidate is Luke's unique combination of Gospel plus Acts (forming roughly 25 percent of the New Testament). Many scholars have suggested that certain aspects of Luke's work, notably the prefaces and the speeches in Acts, demand comparison with the Greek historians. Unlike the other evangelists, Luke stands aside from his narrative at the start of his work to address a named reader (Theophilus) in his own voice (Luke 1:1–4). He refers briefly to his predecessors and their sources (ancient tradition based on eyewitness testimony), the motivation for his work (personal decision), his method of procedure (following everything carefully from the beginning), and his purpose (to give the reader secure and reliable knowledge). In the second volume (Acts 1:1), he addresses Theophilus again with a brief résumé of the contents of the previous book, before picking up the narrative at the point where the Gospel ends.

Yet although Luke's prefaces are *compatible* with some generic expectations for Greek history, they are not by themselves *sufficient* to identify Luke's work as "historiography." The conventions Luke employs are widespread within Greek literary culture, but they are not unique to the historians (Alexander 1993). Dedications and resumptive prefaces are very common in the Greek world, but they are actually more common on the fringes of historiography and in other genres (Alexander 1996; Marincola 1997, 52–57). Despite their superficial nods in the direction of Greek historiography, Luke's prefaces lack key generic features like the author's name, a description of the contents (a *sine qua non*, according to Lucian, *Hist. conscr.* 52), or a claim to be writing something "significant" or "useful."

And as the narrative unfolds it becomes clear that Luke is deliberately evoking a different cultural script, paying homage not to the classics of Greek historiography but to the history of an alien nation with its own prehistory and values. Rather than Thucydides and Herodotus, Luke's cultural classic is the Greek Bible (Plümacher 1972; Alexander 2004). Its impact is apparent at every level of Luke's discourse: intertextuality and allusion, diction and narrative management. The Greek Bible provides an extensive and complex prehistory that gives Luke's story its narrative depth through the speeches, sermons, and prayers that punctuate the narrative. Here the focus is not on great wars or military heroes; the politics of city and empire play a background role to the religious teachers and martyrs who make up the cast list of Acts. Unlike Josephus, Luke displays no embarrassment at Hebrew names, no need to reshape the biblical history for an audience educated in the Greek classics. Luke's language is not a classicizing Greek but an unpretentious literary Koine with a distinctively biblical flavor, a "semitizing" diction that is often *not* in his sources, prominent precisely at the start of each volume where it is most calculated to form the reader's expectations (Sterling 1992, 352–63; Alexander 2004).

For the classically trained reader, there is little sign here of a "noble" subject matter. Within the framework of Jewish diasporic historiography, however, Luke's subject makes perfect sense. He writes not of war but of salvation history, guided by the prophetic word of God (Luke 3:1–2), a tale of the tragedy of Israel's rejection of the prophetic word, and (against all odds) the surprising discovery that it is a word for the Gentiles too (Acts 10:34–11:18; 28:31). Luke's story and characters resonate with the shape of the biblical prehistory presented in the speeches of Stephen (7:2–53) and Paul (13:16–41). The Bible gives Luke his narrative framework and agenda, and above all a language for talking about God: in the bio-history of the Bible, God and the encounter with God are a necessary part of the collective memory of both past and present. The contemporary world he describes is the world of the Jewish diaspora.

His characters lead a precarious existence, acted out in the interstices of civic and imperial life, but ultimately "unstoppable" (the final word of Acts 28:31, my translation). Like Josephus (though with significant differences that also need to be explored), Luke has produced a kind of hybrid historiography, drawing on the themes and values of the dominant culture to create a narrative that challenges and subverts it.

Works Cited

Alexander, Loveday. 1993. *The Preface to Luke's Gospel*. SNTSMS 78. Cambridge: Cambridge University Press.

———. 1996. "The Preface to Acts and the Historians." In *History, Literature and Society in the Book of Acts*, edited by Ben Witherington III, 73–103. Cambridge: Cambridge University Press (also in Alexander 2006, 21–42).

———. 2004. "Septuaginta, Fachprosa, Imitatio: Albert Wifstrand and the Language of Luke-Acts." In *Die Apostelgeschichte und die hellenistische Geschichtsschreibung: Festschrift für Eckhard Plümacher zu seinem 65. Geburtstag*, edited by Cilliers Breytenbach and Jens Schröter, 1–26. Leiden: Brill (also in Alexander 2006, 231–52).

———. 2006. *Acts in Its Ancient Literary Context: A Classicist Looks at the Acts of the Apostles*. LNTS 298. London: T&T Clark International.

Barclay, John. 1999. *Jews in the Mediterranean Diaspora*. Berkeley: University of California Press.

———. 2005. "Judaean Historiography in Rome: Josephus and History in *Contra Apionem* Book I." In *Josephus and Jewish History in Flavian Rome and Beyond*, edited by J. Sievers and G. Lembi, 29–44. Leiden: Brill.

Bickerman, E. J. 1952. "Origines Gentium." *CP* 47: 65–81.

Cribiore, Raffaela. 2001. *Gymnastics of the Mind: Greek Education in Hellenistic and Roman Egypt*. Princeton: Princeton University Press.

Dormeyer, Detlev. 2005. "The Hellenistic Biographical History of King Saul: Josephus, *AJ* 6.45–378 and I Samuel 9:1–31:13." In *Josephus and Jewish History in Flavian Rome and Beyond*, edited by J. Sievers and G. Lembi, 147–57. Leiden: Brill.

Hauge, Matthew, and Andrew Pitts, eds. 2016. *Ancient Education and Early Christianity*. LNTS 533. London: T&T Clark.

Heszer, Catherine. 2001. *Jewish Literacy in Roman Palestine*. WUNT 81. Tübingen: Mohr Siebeck.

Holladay, Carl. 1983. *Fragments from Hellenistic Jewish Authors*. Vol. 1, *Historians*. Atlanta: Scholars Press.

———. 1999. "Acts and the Fragments of Hellenistic Jewish Historians." In *Jesus and the Heritage of Israel: Luke's Narrative Claim upon Israel's Legacy*, edited by David Moessner, 171–98. Harrisburg, PA: Trinity Press International.

Kilburn, K., trans. 1959. *Lucian*. LCL 430. Cambridge, MA: Harvard University Press.

Marincola, John. 1997. *Authority and Tradition in Ancient Historiography*. Cambridge: Cambridge University Press.

———, ed. 2017. *On Writing History from Herodotus to Herodian*. New York: Penguin Random House.

Marrou, H. I. 1956. *History of Education in Antiquity*. Translated by G. Lamb from the 3rd French ed. New York: Sheed and Ward.

Momigliano, Arnaldo. 1993. *The Development of Greek Biography*. Rev. ed. Cambridge, MA: Harvard University Press.

Morgan, Theresa. 1998. *Literate Education in the Hellenistic and Roman Worlds*. Cambridge: Cambridge University Press.

Pelling, Christopher. 1997. "Biographical History? Cassius Dio on the Early Principate." In *Portraits: Biographical Representation in the Greek and Latin Literature of the Roman Empire*, edited by M. J. Edwards and S. Swain, 117–44. Oxford: Clarendon.

Plümacher, Eckhard. 1972. *Lukas als hellenistischer Schriftsteller*. Göttingen: Vandenhoeck & Ruprecht.

Rajak, Tessa. 2001. *The Jewish Dialogue with Greece and Rome*. Leiden: Brill.

———. 2009. *Translation and Survival: The Greek Bible of the Ancient Jewish Diaspora*. Oxford: Oxford University Press.

Reinmuth, Eckart. 1994. *Pseudo-Philo und Lukas*. Tübingen: Mohr Siebeck.

Schürer, Emil. 1986. *The History of the Jewish People in the Age of Jesus Christ*. Vol. 3.1. Rev. Eng. ed. Edited by Geza Vermes, Fergus Millar, and Martin Goodman. Edinburgh: T&T Clark.

Schwartz, Daniel R. 1990. *Agrippa I: The Last King of Judaea*. Tübingen: Mohr Siebeck.

Sterling, Gregory E. 1992. *Historiography and Self-Definition: Josephos, Luke-Acts, and Apologetic Historiography*. Leiden: Brill.

———. 2022. "A Human *Sui Generis*: Philo's *Life of Moses*." *JJS* 73, no. 2: 225–50.

Thackeray, Henry St. J., trans. 1927. *Josephus: The Jewish War*. Vol. 1, *Books 1–2*. LCL 203. Cambridge, MA: Harvard University Press.

Vegge, Tor. 2006. *Paulus und das antike Schulwesen: Schule und Bildung des Paulus*. BZNW 134. Berlin: de Gruyter.

16

Ancient Biography and the Gospels

Helen K. Bond

Ancient biography (*bios* in Greek, *bioi* in the plural) focuses on a person's character or way of life, often presenting the hero as a model for others. It emerged in the Hellenistic era and flourished particularly in the early imperial period. Scholars commonly identify the Gospels as biographical literature. In the following essay, we will look first at the origins of biography before exploring the differences between Greek, Roman, and Jewish examples of the genre. We'll note the strong moralistic and exemplary quality of these ancient works, along with their interest in character, then turn at the end to a consideration of the canonical Gospels.

Origins

The earliest examples of what would later become biographical literature appeared in fourth-century BCE Athens: Xenophon's *Cyropaedia* (a fantastical account of the life of Cyrus the Great of Persia) and Isocrates's account of *Evagoras* (which presented the Cypriot king as a model ruler). But it was in the Hellenistic age (323–31 BCE) that biography really came into its own. This was a time of novelty, flexibility, and experimentation throughout the whole of the eastern Mediterranean—in literature as with so many other aspects of society. The creative blend of Greek and indigenous cultures that characterized this period encouraged great literary productivity. And a growing interest in other peoples, along with a greater sense of "the individual," led quite naturally to a flourishing of biographical literature (Momigliano 1971; Hägg 2012; De Temmerman 2021).

It is important to appreciate that the boundaries of biography were fluid and elastic during this period, with biography easily incorporating features of drama, *encomium* (praise), the novel, epic, apology, or any other literary genre. Authors were free to experiment and innovate, and some did so more successfully than others. The line between history and biography was particularly porous. The Greek historian Herodotus had already included several depictions of character in his works, and Theopompus's *Philippica* was a history of Greece entirely composed around the life, character, and activities of one man. In the first century BCE, Dionysius of Halicarnassus's *Roman Antiquities* contained many discussions of the lives and achievements of public figures, along with their virtues and vices. By the imperial period, the magnetic pull of the emperor meant that all history writing inevitably began to focus on one man (Shuttleworth Kraus 2005). The great biographer Plutarch suggested that history concerned itself with important actions and events, while biography was concerned with character, which is often more vividly displayed through smaller details (*Alex.* 1.1–2; Pelling 1988). The distinction is a useful one, though it was not always adhered to—even by Plutarch himself.

Greek and Roman Biography

The life that was to have the most impact on Greek biography was that of the Athenian philosopher Socrates, who was executed in 399 BCE on charges of impiety and corruption of the youth. Socrates's legacy was preserved by his students, particularly Xenophon, whose *Memorabilia* was a defense of his teacher, and Plato, whose *Phaedo* described his death. The prominence of Socrates meant that "the philosopher" was a popular biographical subject, with figures such as Plato, Pythagoras, and Diogenes the Cynic enjoying several biographies in the Hellenistic and Roman eras. Most of these no longer survive, but a good example of Greek biography comes from the hugely popular second-century CE satirist Lucian. His *Demonax* is a glowing account of his own teacher, a Cynic philosopher who lived in Athens until his death at almost one hundred years old. The work takes the form of a series of short sayings or anecdotes, designed to illustrate the character and wit of the great man. Much longer is Philostratus's third-century CE *Life of Apollonius of Tyana*. Over the course of eight books, Philostratus tells of the teach-

ing, character, and travels of the charismatic philosopher and miracle worker. At about the same time, Diogenes Laertius's *Lives of Eminent Philosophers* is not only a lengthy account of individual philosophers and their teachings but in effect a genealogy of Greek philosophy itself. It is also worth mentioning the anonymous *Life of Aesop*, a hugely popular work that circulated in several different forms. It recounts the life of the slave Aesop, who constantly outwits his master and wins his freedom, though he is eventually executed after insulting the citizens of Dephi. With its bawdy humor, simple Greek, and social satire, the *Life of Aesop* is often thought to have been written for less sophisticated audiences than the works discussed above (Grammatiki 2016). What this shows is that biography was most likely written for and enjoyed by all levels of society.

Roman biography (*vita* in Latin, *vitae* in the plural) appeared in the late Republic and tended to focus on public figures: emperors, statesmen, or generals. Closely connected with funerary orations, Latin *vitae* can be seen as an extension of the Roman interest in ancestors, public honor, and the tracking of the *cursus honorum*—the course of a man's military and political posts. Often biographies of several great men were grouped together to form collections. Our earliest surviving Latin biographies come from Cornelius Nepos and date to the first century BCE. His encyclopedic *On Famous Men* comprised at least sixteen books, though only the section "On Famous Generals" now survives (along with a handful of other lives). Nepos gathered short sketches of men from a range of backgrounds, arranging them under several headings (generals, historians, etc.), and encouraged his audience to reflect on their virtues—or vices (Stern 2012).

Although Nepos's work is not considered to have much literary merit, he may well have been the originator of the grouped political biographies that would prove so popular in the early imperial period. Suetonius's *Lives of the Caesars*, for example, recounts the lives of twelve successive Roman emperors, from Julius Caesar to Domitian, and Suetonius treats his subjects thematically to display their characters. Augustus in particular comes across as an exemplary ruler, thoroughly deserving his posthumous deification, and the yardstick by which the others are measured.

Plutarch writes about the same time, but in Greek, and his *Parallel Lives* also seems to have been influenced by Cornelius Nepos. While Nepos grouped several men together under various headings, however, Plutarch's great genius was in carefully selecting pairs of lives, typically one Roman and one Greek. And while Nepos's lives were short and superficial, Plutarch treated his subjects in some depth and detail. Plutarch's aim was to allow his readers to compare the two lives, and in so doing to reflect deeply on their respective virtues.

Morality and Character

The biographies described above differ from modern versions of the genre in several ways. Most striking is the lack of any psychological depth to the protagonists or any sense of the influence that upbringing or early experiences might have had on the heroes. Conspicuous too is the prominent display of the main character's virtues (or occasionally vices) and the strong call on the part of the audience to emulate those virtues.

Both the Greek and Roman educational systems were founded on the idea of *imitation*. This was apparent both in the sphere of literary composition, where students were encouraged to emulate great writers from the past, and in the sphere of morality, where the lives of great men served as models of moral excellence. Short stories illustrating virtue and vice (known as *exempla* in Latin and *paradeigmata* in Greek) were widely used in the training of students (Morgan 1998). In a sense, biogra-

phy was *exempla* writ large, a way of offering moral instruction through observing the lives of others. Biographers aimed not only to highlight the moral excellence of their subjects but also to present them as models for others. This moralistic agenda is very clear in Plutarch, who found it contagious: "I began the writing of my Lives for the sake of others, but I find that I am continuing the work and delighting in it now for my own sake also, using history as a mirror and endeavouring in a manner to fashion and adorn my life in conformity with the virtues therein depicted" (*Tim.* 1 [trans. Perrin 1918, 261]).

Most of Plutarch's subjects are examples of moral excellence, providing a range of examples to guide young men in public life. Some, however, serve as cautionary tales, such as the colorful but weak Antony, emasculated by his passion for Cleopatra. As Plutarch himself notes, "We will be more enthusiastic in our admiration and imitation of good lives if we examine bad and blameworthy lives as well" (*Demetr.* 1.4–6 [trans. Pelling 1988, 11]). The point was not that readers should imitate the hero's specific deeds—they were not called upon to found cities or to lead others into battle. Rather, they were to appreciate the virtues the heroes displayed while carrying out those deeds—piety, courage, moderation, loyalty, and so on—and to emulate them in their own lives (Morgan 2015).

With a few exceptions, most biographies of philosophers were written by their followers. The intention here was not only to document and remember a great life but to set out that life and teaching in such a way as to encourage others to follow the philosopher's example. Lucian makes this clear in the introduction to the biography of his teacher:

> It is now fitting to tell of Demonax for two reasons—that he may be retained in your memory by men of culture as far as I can bring it about, and that young men of good

instinct who aspire to philosophy may not have to shape themselves by ancient precedents alone, but may be able to set themselves a pattern from our modern world and copy that man, the best of all philosophers whom I know about. (*Demon.* 1–2 [trans. Harmon 1913, 143])

Lucian records little of Demonax's actual teaching; he gives no lectures or philosophical dialogues. Instead, it is his *mode of life*—presented most clearly through his freedom from ambition and boldness of speech—that would-be followers are called upon to emulate. By observing and noting Demonax's virtues, disciples could learn to live better lives themselves. Thus biographies of philosophers established a relationship between the living and the dead, allowing a revered teacher to be introduced to new audiences of would-be disciples.

At the heart of ancient biographical writing was a concern for *character*, or what Plutarch refers to as "the signs of the soul" (*Alex.* 1.3 [trans. Perrin 1919, 225]). Unlike in modern biographies, the heroes of ancient works can tend to look rather flat and lacking in development. To some degree, this was because it was assumed at the time that a person's character (or *ethos*) was largely innate, predetermined by one's ancestors and breeding (hence the interest in noting the hero's family and lineage, particularly in the case of political figures). This flatness, however, was also a result of the biographical genre itself. Biographers saw their subjects as the possessors of good or bad qualities and understood their task as one of moral evaluation in which they assigned praise or blame. Their aim was less about providing a rounded portrait of the "real" person, with all their accompanying idiosyncrasies, than it was about laying out the hero's life to scrutiny so as to expose his virtues and vices and inviting their audience to evaluate his actions and to learn from them. Biographical subjects therefore tend to be the possessors of various ethical qualities—loyalty, courage, moderation (or their opposite). Even Plutarch's lengthy biographies of hugely complex individuals tend toward the bland, with contradictory and inconsistent character traits largely ironed out in favor of flatter possessors of a range of virtues.

Of course, unlike novelists, biographers tended to focus on real, historical people who were often already well known. Their lives may well have been documented already, and competing traditions and recollections might continue to exist, outside the new account. All of this meant that biographers were not entirely free to invent their subject's character. It might be smoothed over and pared down to the basics, and a reasonable amount of fictionalization was inevitable (De Temmerman and Demoen 2016). But unless a biographer wanted to offer a radically new portrait of the subject, his work had to conform to what was generally known (Keener 2019).

Jewish Biography

The Hebrew Bible contains a number of what we might call "biographical episodes," structured around several key figures (e.g., Abraham in Gen. 12–25, Joseph in Gen. 37–50, or David in 1 Sam. 16–2 Sam. 5). Each plays their part in the wider story of God's dealings with Israel. It was once Jews came under Hellenistic influence, however, that stand-alone lives of figures from Israel's past began to emerge (Adams 2020).

Good examples of Jewish biography come from Philo of Alexandria, who wrote several lives of the patriarchs. While his works on Abraham and Joseph are marked by heavy use of the Jewish Scriptures and were probably intended for Jewish audiences, his *On the Life of Moses* is very different in style. It is clearly addressed to Gentiles (*Moses* 1.1–2) and presents an idealized account of the founding father of the Jews, presenting him as an ideal king, lawgiver, high priest, and prophet (Feldman 2007). And rather later in the first century CE, the Jewish historian Flavius Josephus rewrote the Scriptures in the first half of his *Jewish Antiquities* as a series of lives of great men. Throughout, Josephus draws on Hellenistic tropes and conventions to show that the founders of the Jewish nation—whether patriarchs, prophets, or kings—are every bit as impressive as their Greek or Roman counterparts (Feldman 1998).

As with the Greek and Roman biographies examined above, these Jewish biographies present their heroes as models to be emulated. Philo's Moses consciously sets himself up as an example to be imitated (*Moses* 1.158–59), and his remarkable career provides a model of virtue for readers. In his characteristically flowery language, Philo notes that his hero "exemplified his philosophical creed by his daily actions. His words expressed his feelings, and his actions accorded with his words, so that speech and life were in harmony, and thus through their mutual agreement were found to make melody together as on a musical instrument" (*Moses* 1.29 [trans. Colson 1935, 291]).

Similarly, Josephus's narrative frequently calls on his readers to imitate his heroes, or to avoid their excesses. Strangely, perhaps, the Witch of Endor comes over well in Josephus's retelling of the biblical tale, serving as an example to his audience to "show kindness to all who are in need" (*Ant.* 6.342 [trans. Thackeray and Marcus 1930, 499]).

We might imagine that there would be some tension between regarding a biographical subject as a unique, historically determined individual and at the same time offering that life as a paradigm for others. Yet biographers do not seem to have been worried by this, even when they lavished praise on their heroes. Both Philo and Josephus, for example, held Moses in the highest esteem, as someone chosen by God for a particular purpose. Philo presents him as the perfect man, specially loved by God, and even

calls him "God and king of the whole nation" (*Moses* 1.158 [trans. Colson 1935, 357–59]). Josephus is careful to avoid anything that looks like a deification of the patriarch, but even so he devotes three books to him, presenting him as the ideal philosopher-king and describing the wondrous circumstances that accompanied his birth and death. Despite Moses's "uniqueness," his life could still serve as a moral example for others.

The Gospels

The canonical Gospels are commonly identified as ancient biographies (Aune 1987; Dormeyer 1998; Diehl 2011; Keener 2019; Burridge 2020; Bond 2020). Although the identity of their authors is unknown, they were probably written by Jewish Christ believers, or at least people who were immersed in the thought-world of the Jewish Scriptures. And although they were written in Greek, the four works are much less indebted to Hellenistic thought and culture than are the works of Philo and Josephus noted above. They are perhaps best described as "indigenized" biographies, blending Greek biography with the more Semitic narratives of the Jewish scriptural tradition (Adams 2020).

Like Greek biographies of philosophers, the Gospels focus on the life and death of a teacher. Their structure tends to be episodic, with the narrative composed of a series of anecdotes (technically known as *chreia*, or *chreiai* in the plural; Hock and O'Neil 1986; Hock 2002; Elliott 2005). This type of structure is common in lives of philosophers, where the emphasis is on how the heroes behaved in a series of situations rather than on a formal plot. Lucian's *Demonax*, for example, is a collection of anecdotes, a series of brief stories allowing readers to admire the philosopher's wit and clever teaching. What links them all is the central place given to the hero. Similarly in the Gospels, Jesus is the central character in every scene; even when he does not appear (such as in the story of John the Baptist's death in Mark 6:14–29), the anecdote still tells us something about Jesus or draws parallels between him and others. All this means that while the Gospels undeniably have a basic plotline (Jesus incurs the jealousy of the Jewish leaders who hand him over to Rome for crucifixion), it is also important to look at how the authors have arranged their material, the grouping of scenes, and the comparisons and contrasts that emerge.

As we noted above, a key component in ancient biography is its concern with morality, its interest in holding up the hero's character and way of life as a model to be imitated. This is a striking feature of all four canonical Gospels; believers are not only to abide by Jesus's teaching but also to look to him as an example. This comes out clearly in Mark's Gospel, where Jesus continually calls on believers to "follow me" (1:17; 8:34; 10:21; cf. 10:28, 52). Moreover, this sense of imitation is woven into the structure of the Gospel: first John the Baptist comes, preaches, and is handed over (1:7, 14; 6:17–20); then Jesus comes, preaches, and is handed over; finally believers will themselves be called on to preach and be handed over (13:9–13). Mark even goes so far as to suggest that followers may need to emulate their master to the end—perhaps even to their own cross (8:34; Hurtado 1996; Capes 2003; Burridge 2007).

Not all biographies of philosophers included birth stories—disciples were usually more interested in the philosopher's early education than in details of his birth. There was, however, an assumption in the first century that the births of great men were signaled by unusual events or portents in the natural world. Both Matthew and Luke add such stories to their biographies of Jesus, drawing heavily from the Jewish Scriptures. Matthew draws on the birth of Moses in Exodus 1–2, presenting Jesus not only as a second Moses but as King of the Jews, whose birth is heralded by

a bright star and to whom Magi bring gifts (Matt. 2:1–12). Luke draws on a different set of scriptural images, modeling Jesus's birth on those of the prophets Samson and Samuel. In keeping with Luke's interest in the marginalized and those of low status, Jesus is born in a stable and visited by poor shepherds (Luke 2:1–20). Luke also provides our one canonical account of Jesus's boyhood, where Jesus is found in the temple amazing the teachers with his deep understanding (2:41–50). Such stories are common in biography, where the young child exhibits the qualities that he will later demonstrate as an adult, whether that is great learning, military tactics, or regal qualities. Josephus tells a similar story of himself in his autobiography (*Life* 8–9).

In other ways, however, the Gospels would have struck Greek and Roman readers as rather odd. Most contemporary works had a strong authorial voice, apparent from the start in the prologue. It was here that the author would introduce himself (most were men), explain his purposes, and set out his credentials. Historians were prone to lengthy and elaborate prologues. Those of biographers tended to be much shorter, but it was still usual to give an indication of the importance of the subject and the author's reasons for writing (see, e.g., Lucian, *Demon.* 1–2). Only Luke gives any kind of a prologue (Luke 1:1–4), and even this is brief and perfunctory, telling us almost nothing about the author himself. The other evangelists clearly take their cue from the Jewish tradition, where openings are often abrupt (e.g., Prov. 1:1; Ruth 1:1; Isa. 1:1) and the identity of the author is veiled. This is not to dispute that the Gospels all display a clear and omniscient narratorial voice, frequently explaining things to the audience (such as John 1:38, 41, 42, etc.), but the identity of this person is never revealed.

Ancient Greek biographers would show off their learning by quoting from earlier great writers. This was all part of the education system at the time, where students learned the art of composition by memorizing sections of Homer, Euripides, the maxims of Isocrates, and others (Morgan 1998). Instead, the Gospel writers are immersed in the story of Israel as set out in the Jewish Scriptures, and it is this body of literature that they quote from or allude to throughout. In this vein, John's poetic prologue tells us nothing about the author but instead seeks to situate the coming of Jesus within the sweep of Jewish history (John 1:1–18).

And finally, non-Jewish readers might have been a little surprised to find no physical description of Jesus. While not all biographies tell us what their subject looked like, many did (Cornelius Nepos, for example, gives a short account of each of his generals' looks). This was partly because of a long-standing assumption in Greek thought that physical appearance was closely linked to character. Thus, Plato could say that the ideal ruler should also be good looking (*Resp.* 7.535a). Conversely, ugliness was associated with low social status and dubious morals, and the ugliness of the slave Aesop marks him out as an anti-hero from the start. The reason for the Gospels' reticence, again, is likely to be because of the restraint displayed by the Jewish Scriptures, where physical description seems to be mentioned only when it is particularly relevant to the plot.

Despite these differences, the canonical Gospels are best understood in the context of ancient biographical writing. Their focus on the life and death of one exemplary teacher aligns them most closely with the lives of Greek philosophers. When the apostle Paul wrote in the 50s of the first century, the word "gospel" referred to the good news of the saving death and resurrection of Jesus. The great innovation of the evangelists was to extend what was meant by the word "gospel" to cover the *life* of Jesus too. Small wonder, then, that by the second century these works were known no longer as "lives," or *bioi*, but simply as Gospels.

Works Cited

Adams, Sean A. 2020. *Greek Genres and Jewish Authors: Negotiating Literary Culture in the Greco-Roman Era*. Waco: Baylor University Press.

Aune, David. 1987. *The New Testament in Its Literary Environment*. Philadelphia: Westminster.

Bond, Helen K. 2020. *The First Biography of Jesus: Genre and Meaning in Mark's Gospel*. Grand Rapids: Eerdmans.

Burridge, Richard A. 2007. *Imitating Jesus: An Inclusive Approach to New Testament Ethics*. Grand Rapids: Eerdmans.

———. 2020. *What Are the Gospels? A Comparison with Graeco-Roman Biography*. 3rd ed. Waco: Baylor University Press.

Capes, David B. 2003. "*Imitatio Christi* and the Gospel Genre." *BBR* 13: 1–19.

Colson, F. H., trans. 1935. *Philo: On Abraham, On Joseph, On Moses*. LCL 289. Cambridge, MA: Harvard University Press.

De Temmerman, Koen. 2021. *The Oxford Handbook of Ancient Biography*. Oxford: Oxford University Press.

De Temmerman, Koen, and Kristoffel Demoen, eds. 2016. *Writing Biography in Greece and Rome: Narrative Technique and Fictionalization*. Cambridge: Cambridge University Press.

Diehl, Judy A. 2011. "What Is a Gospel? Recent Studies in the Gospel Genre." *CurBR* 9, no. 2: 171–99.

Dormeyer, Detlev. 1998. *The New Testament among the Writings of Antiquity*. Translated by R. Kossov. Biblical Seminar 55. Sheffield: Sheffield Academic Press.

Elliott, Scott S. 2005. "'Witless in Your Own Cause': Divine Plots and Fractured Characters in the Life of Aesop and the Gospel of Mark." *Religion and Theology* 12: 397–418.

Feldman, Louis H. 1998. *Josephus' Interpretation of the Bible*. Berkeley: University of California Press.

———. 2007. *Philo's Portrayal of Moses in the Context of Ancient Judaism*. Notre Dame, IN: University of Notre Dame Press.

Grammatiki, Karla A. 2016. "*Life of Aesop*: Fictional Biography as Popular Literature?" In De Temmerman and Demoen 2016, 47–64.

Hägg, Tomas. 2012. *The Art of Biography in Antiquity*. Cambridge: Cambridge University Press.

Harmon, A. M., trans. 1913. *Lucian: Phalaris, Hippias or The Bath, Dionysus, Heracles, Amber or The Swans, The Fly, Nigrinus, Demonax, The Hall, My Native Land, Octogenarians, A True Story, Slander, The Consonants at Law, The Carousal (Symposium) or The Lapiths*. LCL 14. Cambridge, MA: Harvard University Press.

Hock, Ronald F. 2002. *The Chreia and Ancient Rhetoric: Classroom Exercises*. WGRW 2. Leiden: Brill.

Hock, Ronald F., and Edward N. O'Neil. 1986. *The Chreia in Ancient Rhetoric*. Vol. 1, *The Progymnasmata*. Atlanta: Scholars Press.

Hurtado, Larry W. 1996. "Following Jesus in the Gospel of Mark—and Beyond." In *Patterns of Discipleship in the New Testament*, edited by Richard N. Longenecker, 9–29. Grand Rapids: Eerdmans.

Keener, Craig S. 2019. *Christobiography: Memory, History and the Reliability of the Gospels*. Grand Rapids: Eerdmans.

Momigliano, Arnaldo. 1971. *The Development of Greek Biography*. Cambridge, MA: Harvard University Press.

Morgan, Teresa. 1998. *Literate Education in the Hellenistic and Roman Worlds*. Cambridge: Cambridge University Press.

———. 2015. "Not the Whole Story? Moralizing Biography and *Imitatio Christi*." In *Fame and Infamy: Essays for Christopher Pelling on Characterization in Greek and Roman Biography*, edited by Rhiannon Ash, Judith Mossman, and Francis B. Titchener, 353–66. Oxford: Oxford University Press.

Pelling, Christopher B. R., ed. 1988. *Plutarch: Life of Antony*. Cambridge: Cambridge University Press.

Perrin, Bernadotte, trans. 1918. *Plutarch: Lives*. Vol. 6, *Dion and Brutus, Timoleon and Aemilius Paulus*. LCL 98. Cambridge, MA: Harvard University Press.

———, trans. 1919. *Plutarch: Lives*. Vol. 7, *Demosthenes and Cicero, Alexander and Caesar*. LCL 99. Cambridge, MA: Harvard University Press.

Shuttleworth Kraus, Christina. 2005. "From Exempla to Exemplar? Writing History around the Emperor in Flavian Rome." In *Flavius Josephus and Flavian Rome*, edited by J. Edmondson, S. Mason, and J. Rives, 181–200. Oxford: Oxford University Press.

Stern, Rex. 2012. *The Political Biographies of Cornelius Nepos*. Ann Arbor: University of Michigan Press.

Thackeray, Henry St. J., and Ralph Marcus, trans. 1930. *Josephus: Jewish Antiquities*. Vol. 2, *Books 4–6*. LCL 490. Cambridge, MA: Harvard University Press.

17

The Parables of Jesus

KLYNE R. SNODGRASS

No one in the ancient world would have been surprised to hear a teacher use a parable. Argument by analogy is a common human strategy, and parables are *extended* analogies. Their use can be documented at least to the twenty-fourth century BCE and is evident in numerous cultures, especially among Greeks and Jews. Among Greeks (and the Romans following them) parables appear as instruction and as a form of proof by philosophers and rhetoricians (e.g., Aristotle, Epictetus, Plutarch, Seneca, and Quintilian) and as entertainment, especially with Aesop's fables. With Jews, parables are rooted in the wisdom tradition, with less emphasis, except partly for the Story of Ahiqar, on entertainment. It is especially with the prophetic writings, however, that parables become commonplace.

In the Old Testament, parables do not appear in legal material or in historical writings, except in the mouth of a prophet.[1] At least twenty-two narrative parables can be identi-fied in the Old Testament, the most obvious of which are Nathan's parable to David in 2 Samuel 12:1–7 and the parable of the vineyard in Isaiah 5:1–7. Only two of the twenty-two do not come from a prophet: Psalm 80:8–17 and Ecclesiastes 9:14–18. Some scholars list fewer or more than twenty-two parables because they use a narrower or broader definition of "parable." Some count only forms that are stories, while others include any extended comparison. One must also consider prophetic visions, such as the good and bad figs in Jeremiah 24:1–10 or the series of visions in Amos 7:1–9 and 8:1–3; dreams, such as Daniel 2:31–45; and especially acted parables by which a prophet's action mirrors Israel's fate, such as Jeremiah's ruined loincloth (Jer. 13:1–14). All such images bear metaphorical significance. In the Old Testament context, parables are primarily tools by which prophets confront, challenge, and instruct a recalcitrant people.[2]

That is precisely why Jesus adopted both the parable genre and prophetic themes for his own

---

1. There are two political, confrontational fables about trees in Judg. 9:7–15 and 2 Kings 14:9–10.

2. For further treatment of most issues relating to parables, see Snodgrass 2018.

instruction and confrontation with the nation. Whatever else he was, he presented himself as a prophet and was perceived as a prophet. For example, Matthew 13:34–35 explicitly says Jesus taught in parables to fulfill what was said by the *prophet*: "I will open my mouth in a parable," a quotation of Psalm 78:2. But Jesus brought creativity to his use of parables. He did not use them merely to confront and challenge. He also used parables as positive teaching tools to demonstrate God's character and the nature of the kingdom, both present and future, and to give ethical instruction on compassion, the use of wealth, prayer, and discipleship. The prophets did not use parables for such purposes.

People may not have been surprised to hear Jesus teach with parables, but they may have been surprised that he used so many. About one-third of Jesus's teaching in the Synoptic Gospels is in parables. People disagree on the actual number of Jesus's parables because they disagree on the definition of "parable." Mark has only four narrative parables, one of which, the seed growing secretly (4:26–29), is found only in his account. Matthew and Luke have the other three in Mark and at least six more in common.[3] Then, on the typical counting, Matthew has ten unique parables and Luke has eighteen.

The Gospel of John does not have narrative parables like those in the Synoptics, but it has numerous *meshalim* (plural of *mashal*), the broad Hebrew word covering everything from analogies, oracles, discourses, proverbs, and parables to riddles, taunts, and laments. *Mashal* can be defined as any short saying used to stimulate thought. Analogies like the "uplifted" serpent (John 3:13–14), the good shepherd (John 10), and a host of other images demonstrate the same parabolic mindset in John as is in the Synoptics.

In the New Testament, the semantic field of the Greek word *parabolē* is almost as broad as the Old Testament word *mashal* to which it corresponds. It is commonly used of parables, but in Mark 3:23–27 *parabolē* is used of a riddle and short analogies, in Mark 7:17 of a statement, and in Luke 4:23 of a proverb. Hardly anything we say about parables fits all of them or all the occurrences of the Hebrew and Greek words in question. As always, each parable needs to be examined in its own right.

That others used parabolic imagery, *meshalim*, is evident even in the New Testament. John the Baptist, for instance, says, "The axe already lies at the root of the tree" (Matt. 3:10 // Luke 3:9, my translation). Yet something is different about Jesus's parables when one considers *Jewish* parables both before and after Jesus's teaching. While the Old Testament parables clearly provide the form and the motivation for Jesus's parables, very little exists prior to his teaching that is like his narrative parables. Joachim Jeremias even argues Jesus's parables were an entirely new form of discourse (Jeremias 1972, 12). That is an exaggeration. Parabolic elements appear in a few early Jewish writings,[4] and allegorical descriptions appear in apocalyptic literature, such as the long descriptions of nations using imagery of animals in 1 Enoch 89. Most of the Mishnah, except for Pirqe Avot (Chapters of the Fathers),[5] is devoid of parabolic material. It is halakic (legal) material, not haggadah, exposition that frequently includes stories and incidents. Later rabbinic material has hundreds of parables, some very much like Jesus's in both form and content. These later rabbinic parables

---

3. A couple of other parables are similar in structure but sufficiently dissimilar in wording that they are probably different parables rather than parallels.

4. See, e.g., Jos. Asen. 12.8; T. Job 18.6–8. For other early Jewish examples, see Snodgrass 2018, 42–46. Examples closer to Jesus's parables appear in 4 Ezra and 2 Baruch, both usually dated to the end of the first century.

5. This tractate is a collection of sayings of rabbinic fathers. There are similitudes similar to Jesus's: see among others Pirqe Avot 1.3; 2.15; and 3.17. However, Avot does not use the word *mashal* and does not have narrative parables with a developed plot like those of Jesus.

are exegetical tools explaining Old Testament texts or applying Old Testament texts to problematic issues. Jesus's parables, on the other hand, *usually* are not exegetical. These rabbinic parables can illumine how parables function, but they are much later than Jesus's parables in virtually every case. Early Jewish writings and later rabbinic writings are quite distinct from each other with regard to parables, and one must not assume that rabbinic parables were present in the first century.

The early church apparently did not use parables much. The gospel required direct communication, not indirect. Analogies occur, of course, and Paul created a polemical allegory based on the story of Sarah and Hagar in Galatians 4:21–31. Most obvious is Shepherd of Hermas, which has long allegories to depict the church, its relations, and ethical teaching. None of these is close to or a continuation of Jesus's use.

The word "parable" seems so obvious to us, but a first-century person might have been surprised at the evangelists' choice of the Greek word *parabolē* to describe Jesus's analogies. This Greek word was not used frequently[6] and primarily referred merely to a comparison. Other words might have been expected, but the evangelists' choice of *parabolē* was without doubt determined by the fact that translators of the Septuagint, the Greek translation of the Old Testament, selected *parabolē* to render the Hebrew word *mashal*. They did not use it of any other Hebrew word.

The Effectiveness of Parables

Parables are effective teaching tools because they create interest with pictures and in the process create narrative worlds. They draw hearers and readers into this world and force involvement and decision. Parables are atten-

tion getters because they either explicitly or implicitly pose questions, human-interest ones, that the hearer/reader must answer. They are effective also because they are indirect communication. While direct communication may be resisted, indirect communication forces one to look elsewhere to see what one could not or would not otherwise see. This indirection removes defenses and biases and "deceives one into the truth," as Søren Kierkegaard says.[7] Parables, therefore, create an alternate world to enable sight. Finally, Jesus's parables are effective because of their subject matter, the kingdom of God and relation to God, surely topics that compel interest.

While parables are quite varied in form, some characteristics are noteworthy, enhance their effectiveness, and assist in interpretation. Parables tend to be brief and symmetrical, sometimes setting things in parallel. They do not *usually* give unnecessary details, mention unnecessary people, or explain motives. They do not focus on animals, as is the case often with Aesop's fables. They focus on anonymous humans[8] and on agricultural items like seeds and trees. They seek response, to goad people into action, and often contain elements of reversal. They make you conclude what you otherwise would not, such as, "The tax collector is the righteous person" (see Luke 18:14).

Jesus's parables were composed from common life material, and therefore, for us they provide a sociological window on the first-century world of masters and slaves/servants and all kinds of economic and social relations. Parables are not necessarily realistic or about everyday events. One does not find a treasure every day, for instance, as in the parable of Matthew 13:44, and the circumstances depicted in a parable may be an exaggeration, as in the

---

6. Josephus uses *parabolē* only twice, Philo only three times, Plato only twice, and Aristotle fourteen times.

7. Kierkegaard 1967, 288. Kierkegaard discusses indirect communication at length and frequently uses parables in his writings.

8. Only with Lazarus and the rich man (Luke 16:19–31) is someone named, in this case Abraham and Lazarus.

case of the amount of debt in the parable of the unforgiving servant (Matt. 18:24). Also unrealistic is the picture of masters and slaves that frequently emerges in Jesus's parables. No thought is given to abusive masters, for as with rabbinic parables, the master-servant parables picture the relation of God to his people—unless one accepts the sociological attempt to see Jesus's parables as depicting exploitative landowners (Herzog 1994), but that is unjustified (see Snodgrass 2018, 372–73, 585–92). Nothing in Jesus's nonparabolic teaching suggests this, and, while Jesus is very concerned about the poor and the misuse of wealth, no Amos-like rant on exploitation is found in his teaching.

Understanding the Parables

Clearly sometimes the disciples do not understand Jesus's parables and require further instruction. Mark 4:10–12 even *seems* to suggest Jesus told parables to prevent understanding, but this reading is a failure to understand Jesus, Mark, and the intent of both. Attention to the full parable discourse in Mark 4 shows that Jesus's parables were intended to elicit hearing and to deal with hardness of heart. If parables were intended to prevent understanding, it would have been easier for Jesus not to tell them and Mark not to record them. Mark 4:10–12 draws from Isaiah 6:9–10, the classic text on hardness of heart, and challenges readers not to be guilty of such hardness but to hear and be determined by Jesus's message.

The short answer to whether Jesus's hearers understood and whether we can understand the parables is "Of course they could, and so can we." Nevertheless, some parables are less obvious than others, and the history of interpretation of the parables has sometimes made things more difficult for us. Jesus's parables are among the most abused literature ever, for throughout the church's history the predominant means of interpretation was to see the parables as theological allegories. The elements in the parables were viewed as mirroring some theological reality—as, for example, the slaughtered calf in the parable of the prodigal (Luke 15:11–32) being interpreted as a pointer to Christ's atoning death. Adolph Jülicher is famous for rejecting *all* such allegorizing (and allegory) and insisting that parables can have only one point, often a simplistic moralism (1888–89). Neither allegorizing parables nor restricting their meaning to only one point works, nor do recent arguments for polyvalence, the idea that parables can have multiple and even contradictory meanings (e.g., Tolbert 1979).

Instead, we need to recognize that Jesus's parables were told into a cultural and literary context. That context frames meaning. For some parables, a specific context is given by the Gospels, but many lack such specific rootedness and have been arranged thematically by the evangelists. The majority of them are in parable collections, such as the kingdom parables in Matthew 13 and Mark 4, the parables of "lostness" in Luke 15, or parables of prayer in Luke 18. Many parables were probably told multiple times, so to ask about their *specific* context is inappropriate. Still, *Jesus's parables were told into a first-century Jewish context by a prophetic figure urging the presence of the eschatological kingdom of God.* We must not set parables in another context if we seek to understand Jesus's use of them. First-century hearers of Jesus would not be thinking about Christian theological symbols or about what polyvalent ideas they might contain, nor would they be asking what *one* point Jesus was making. They would have asked what this prophetic figure was trying to do with parables. What was their function? The questions for them and us are and must be "How does this analogy work, and to what does it refer?"

Analogies may have several connections, rather than one, with the reality they portray, because analogies require such connections to work. But correspondences are inexact, sometimes intentionally so, and sometimes they are part of the camouflage that deceives hearers into the truth. For example, in Nathan's parable to David (2 Sam. 12:1–7), the ewe lamb corresponds to Bathsheba, but it is Uriah who dies, not Bathsheba. The issue is not correspondences between image and reality but determining how the analogy works. Sometimes the meaning would not be clear until an explanation (or a *nimshal*) was given at the end—as with the parable of the wicked tenants (Mark 12:1–12 parr.), where the intent of the parable is not clear until it is explained by the addition of Psalm 118:22 in Mark 12:10. Sometimes the meaning did not require explanation, as with the kingdom being like a treasure found in a field (Matt. 13:44). And sometimes the meaning was left enigmatic until a later time, as with the parable of the sower (Matt. 13:3–9 parr.). Even then some may have grasped the point without explanation. Parables were not stories looking for a meaning or analogies Jesus told to see what people could make of them. They were told quite intentionally in the context of his kingdom ministry. We do not do justice to them unless we determine what Jesus was doing with parables and how the Gospel writers have framed them.[9] We should always ask how the analogy *functions*, rather than seeking to find correspondences between the elements in the story and reality.

In determining how an analogy functions, two items are particularly important for interpretation. First, especially with similitudes (see below), focus should be more on the *whole process* described in the parable and less on individual features. For example, with the parable of the leaven (Matt. 13:33 // Luke 13:21), the kingdom is not like a woman but like the entire process of what happens with leaven that a woman places in a large amount of

dough until the whole amount is impacted. Second, especially with narrative parables, the crucial part of a parable is the material at the end, which scholars refer to as "the rule of end stress." Here the purpose of the analogy becomes clear.

If many of Jesus's parables were told several times, a few, such as the parable of the wicked tenants (Mark 12:1–12 parr.), may have been told only once because of the events that led to their telling. Their oral recitation in the early days of the church and editorial shaping are the reasons for the Synoptic variations in wording. Therefore, for these and other reasons any thought of reconstructing an "original" form, as many attempted to do in the heyday of form and redaction criticisms, is misguided. Some thought the briefer parables in the Gospel of Thomas provided a foundation for finding an original form, but Thomas has been demonstrated to be dependent on the Synoptic Gospels (see Gathercole 2012; Goodacre 2012).

Types of Parables

Adolph Jülicher distinguished four types of parables: similitudes (an extended simile), parables, example stories (stories providing ethical examples), and allegories (although the last he rejected as artificial and illegitimate; Jülicher 1888–89, 1:49, 117). That classification system dominated for about one hundred years, but increasingly the weaknesses of the system have been voiced. The numerous attempts to distinguish parable and allegory do not work at all. Parables often have more than one correspondence between image and reality, and literary scholars question whether allegory is a separate genre or merely a way of thinking. Some, such as Craig Blomberg (2012) and John Sider (1995), are happy to call parables allegories, but by this they mean Jesus told stories with more than one correspondence between the story and reality. They are not changing the parables into theological allegories the way

---

9. To be clear, we have no other Jesus than the one the evangelists have framed.

the medieval church did. Example stories are not distinguishable from other parables on the basis of form or purpose. Many parables, such as the parable of the unforgiving servant (Matt. 18:23–35), offer examples to copy or avoid. Some people reject any classification of parables at all, but that seems shortsighted. Much can be learned by grouping similar parables together to understand how they function.

Given the breadth of the words *mashal* and *parabolē*, we should expect a broad range of forms. Some are extended comparisons and do not have plots, while longer parables have narrative plots. These longer parables tell of events and their outcome. Usually, these parables tell of a problem and how it is resolved. For example, in the parable of the prodigal (Luke 15:11–32), the dire circumstance of this son is reversed by the father's ready celebration of his return. Some parables consist entirely of a question. Some parables force the hearer/reader to make a decision, and some function differently from others with regard to the amount of indirection or the way the parable is framed.

If parables are a means of indirect communication, most of Jesus's parables are *double indirect communication*. Direct communication addresses the hearer about the subject at hand. For example, direct communication might say, "I am telling you the kingdom is worth everything you could give." Double indirect parables do not speak of the hearer/reader or the subject at hand. They in effect say, "Let me tell you about someone else and a different subject so that you can understand." The parable of the treasure in the field (Matt. 13:44) uses another person (one who finds) and another subject (the treasure) to address the hearer/reader indirectly. A few parables are *single indirect communication*. They address the hearer/reader indirectly by telling of another person, but they treat the subject at hand. The parable of the rich fool (Luke 12:16–21) addresses the hearer/reader indirectly through

the rich man, but the subject is wealth, the topic at hand.

A helpful way of categorizing these variations in parables, which also provides insight for interpretation, is as follows:

Similitudes are extended comparisons but do not have a plot. They are double indirect and tend to be briefer, as, for example, the parable of the leaven (Matt. 13:33).

Narrative parables have a plot, and most are double indirect. Jesus's longer story-type parables fit here, as, for example, the parable of the feast (Luke 14:16–24). The next two types of parables are subcategories of narrative parables.

Juridical parables are a particular type of narrative parable that forces the hearer/reader to decide about the events in the parable and in doing so judge him- or herself. The parable of Nathan to David (2 Sam. 12:1–7) is the classic example, but examples from Jesus are the parable of the two sons (Matt. 21:28–32) and Matthew's version of the wicked tenants (21:33–45).

Single indirect parables are also a particular type of narrative parable and have developed plots, but the topic of concern is not hidden in analogy. There are only five, all in Luke.[10] The good Samaritan (Luke 10:25–37) is an obvious example.

Interrogative parables do not merely contain questions, which is true of many parables, but are those with developed plots where the whole parable is a question and begins: "Who from among you . . . ?" Unfortunately, translations often lose the focus by rendering the question as

10. These include Jülicher's four example stories (the good Samaritan, the rich fool, the rich man and Lazarus, the Pharisee and the tax collector) but also the unjust steward (1888–89, 1:112).

"Suppose one of you." The answer to the question "Who from among you will do such and such" is always "No one," which is also the case with Hellenistic parables using the same form. The parable of the friend at midnight (Luke 11:5–8) is a good example. No one would fail to get up and help a friend.

"How much more" parables use a particular logic, also frequent in rabbinic parables, that argues, "If you [or some human] will do such and such, how much more will God?" The friend at midnight uses this logic. If you would provide for a friend, how much more will God?

As is evident in this classification system, attention must be given both to the particular form of a parable and to the logic by which it functions. Parables do not all function the same way. For example, contrast is often a feature in parables, sometimes explicitly setting good and bad in opposition, such as the parable of the two builders (Matt. 7:24–27 // Luke 6:47–49), and sometimes implicitly. With other parables, contrast functions in a different way to mark the difference between the image in the parable and reality. The point of the unjust judge (Luke 18:1–9) is that God is *not* like this judge. Also obvious is that parables may belong to more than one category.

With regard to focus, Jesus's parables are theocentric. They tell what God is like, what God's kingdom is like, and what human life before and with God is like. A good deal of what is known about the kingdom is given only through the parables. Rarely are the parables explicitly christological, except for the parable of the wicked tenants (Mark 12:1–12 parr.).

Some parables, such as the sower (Matt. 13:3–9 parr.) and the feast (Luke 14:16–24), implicitly point to Jesus and his role, but these are exceptions.

In sum, the purpose of parables is to engage and force response. They pose questions, provide insight, and drive one to see what is at stake, make a choice, and act. Parables are not for passive souls.

Works Cited

Blomberg, Craig L. 2012. *Interpreting the Parables*. 2nd ed. Downers Grove, IL: InterVarsity.

Gathercole, Simon. 2012. *The Composition of the Gospel of Thomas: Original Language and Influences*. SNTSMS 151. Cambridge: Cambridge University Press.

Goodacre, Mark S. 2012. *Thomas and the Gospels: The Case for Thomas's Familiarity with the Synoptics*. Grand Rapids: Eerdmans.

Herzog, William R., II. 1994. *Parables as Subversive Speech: Jesus as Pedagogue of the Oppressed*. Louisville: Westminster John Knox.

Jeremias, Joachim. 1972. *The Parables of Jesus*. Translated by S. H. Hooke. 2nd ed. New York: Scribner's Sons.

Jülicher, Adolf. 1888–89. *Die Gleichnisreden Jesu*. 2 vols. Freiburg i. B.: Akademische Verlagsbuchhandlung von J. C. B. Mohr. Vol. 1, 1888; vol. 2, 1889. (Two vols. in one; Darmstadt: Wissenschaftliche Buchgesellschaft, 1963, reprint of Tübingen: Mohr Siebeck, 1910).

Kierkegaard, Søren. 1967. *Søren Kierkegaard's Journals and Papers*. Vol. 1, A–E. Edited and translated by Howard V. Hong and Edna H. Hong. Bloomington: Indiana University Press.

Sider, John W. 1995. *Interpreting the Parables: A Hermeneutical Guide to Their Meaning*. Grand Rapids: Zondervan.

Snodgrass, Klyne R. 2018. *Stories with Intent: A Comprehensive Guide to the Parables of Jesus*. 2nd ed. Grand Rapids: Eerdmans.

Tolbert, Mary Ann. 1979. *Perspectives on the Parables*. Philadelphia: Fortress.

18

Letters and Letter Writing

Joshua W. Jipp

Given that twenty-one out of the twenty-seven writings in the New Testament take the form of a letter, it is of utmost importance that the contemporary interpreter know something of the practices, styles, and functions associated with ancient letter writing. Yet the New Testament letters are both much longer and more detailed in their argumentation than the typical ancient letter. Adolf Deissmann's *Light from the Ancient East* argues for a distinction between the letter and the epistle (see Deissmann 1908). His argument has proved influential, although it is now highly contested. Letters, Deissmann argues, were the normal, private, situational, and nonliterary way of communicating information. For instance, the remains of many letters written by the non-elite (i.e., generally not highly educated) to communicate everyday information survive. Epistles, on the other hand, were intended for a public audience and were, in some senses, a guise for the rhetorically trained to communicate their philosophical and political ideas. That is to say, there is a significant difference, for example,

between a letter from a son to his father requesting financial assistance and Epicurus's *Letter to Herodotus*, which uses the letter form as a guise for Epicurus's philosophical doctrines (Klauck and Bailey 2006, 103–82).[1] While Deissmann's distinctions between the letter (private and nonliterary) and the epistle (public and literary) have been subjected to detailed scrutiny, his work has effectively demonstrated that, while ancient authors used the letter form to communicate everyday, mundane information, most could creatively craft and shape letters to suit their particular purposes and agendas. Furthermore, one should not assume that only the highly educated and elite had familiarity with and used rhetorical conventions associated with the letter. Therefore, in what follows I will look at the format, social context, letter types, and material realities associated with letter writing in antiquity as a significant context for understanding the New Testament letters.

1. For further examples, see Cicero's *Letters*, Seneca the Younger's *Letters to Lucilius*, and the Cynic epistles.

Letters and Letter Writing in the Ancient Mediterranean World

Deissmann was right that the majority of ancient letters are simple, brief, and occasional forms of communication between absent parties. It is evident that letters functioned as a substitute for personal presence among those who were physically separated and were used in the service of a variety of social relationships. In other words, the majority of letters "functioned like phone calls, emails, and texts today. Letters were written to tell loved ones about travel plans, business, or other routine matters" (Richards 2019, 86).

Letter Format and the Social Context of Letter Writing

Occasional letters were written in stereotypical format that included

1. a letter opening or prescript, which identifies the sender and addressee (A to B), gives greetings with a wish for good health, and offers prayers for good health and well-being;

2. a body, which communicates a specific piece of information about family or business news; and

3. a closing, which may pass on further greetings and another wish or prayer for the addressee's well-being.[2]

Yet Stanley Stowers notes, "Letters were classified into types according to typical situations and social contexts of letter writing. This meant classification according to typical purposes that letter writers hoped to accomplish" (1986, 22–23). This means that the basic letter format was frequently adapted in creative ways depending on the social situation. Hans-Josef Klauck notes, however, that the private-versus-public

and literary-versus-nonliterary distinctions do not quite hold, for example, with respect to certain official correspondences—such as letters of recommendation and diplomatic letters (i.e., royal/imperial letters) (Klauck and Bailey 2006, 69–101). Rather than divide the letters into literary or nonliterary, Stowers has emphasized that it is "the activities associated with friendship, client-patron relationships, and the household that generated most of the letters which we have from antiquity" (1986, 31). Thus, depending on the particular social relationship, ancient letters are often repositories for giving honor, friendship motifs, and family and economic/business matters. One might also choose to write a letter or even send an envoy in order to respond to a difficult, embarrassing, or controversial situation (e.g., 1 Cor. 4:17; 2 Cor. 1:23–2:11; 7:5–16; see Mitchell 1992).

Types of Letters

Lists and discussions of the different letter types can be found in the essay *Epistolary Types*, attributed to Demetrius of Phaleron. His purpose is "to organize and set forth both the number of distinctions between them [i.e., the different letter types] and what they are, and [to] have sketched a sample . . . of the arrangement of each kind, and [to] have, in addition, individually set forth the rationale for each of them" (trans. Klauck and Bailey 2006, 195). Pseudo-Libanius's *Epistolary Styles* includes almost twice the number of letter types. Many of these letter types overlap with one another. A few examples include the following:[3]

1. Friendship Letters: These letters represent the primary function of ancient letters—namely, to maintain friendship between two parties. This letter type often includes friendship motifs, expressions

---

2. A helpful analysis can be found in Klauck and Bailey 2006, 9–27.

3. A helpful list that usefully synthesizes some of the letter types that overlap with one another is given in Stowers 1986, 58–173.

of affection, assertions of shared experiences, and the sharing of gifts and benefits.

2. Praise and Blame Letters: Demetrius's essay actually includes a variety of letter types that draw upon stylistic techniques such as irony, shame, invective, and warning, often to change another's course of action (e.g., letters of blame, reproach, censorship, admonishment, threat, and vituperation). Alternatively, letters of praise (such as praise of another's character or benefaction) express one's approval and legitimation of a current situation. Praise or blame (sometimes both) is used in most letters as a means of exhortation and persuasion and is found in the types of letters that follow.

3. Letters of Exhortation/Paraenesis and Advice: These types of letters may originate from ancient philosophy. Numerous philosophers used the letter as the format for converting others to a philosophical way of life, to exhort one to transform one's character, and to set forth appropriate models of virtue. In *On Style* (227), Demetrius states: "Everyone writes a letter in the virtual image of his own soul. In every other form of speech it is possible to see the writer's character, but in none so clearly as in the letter" (trans. Innes 1995, 478–81).

4. Consolation Letters: This letter (a further type of an exhortation letter) offers comfort and exhortation to those who are experiencing grief due to some type of loss. It often expresses lament in the face of fate, offers reflections on death and suffering, and calls to mind good memories and virtues of the one who has died.

Material Realities in Letter Writing

Most letters, at least during the first century, were written on parchment sheets made out of leather or papyrus.[4] Pliny the Elder gives a detailed description of how writing material was produced from papyrus that grew in and near the Nile River in Egypt (*Nat.* 13.2171–89). Both parchment and papyrus sheets could be turned into a scroll. Authors often used notebooks and tablets in order to prepare drafts, record notes from conversations, and copy passages from other works.

Both widespread illiteracy and concluding sentences indicating the presence of a secretary suggest that letters were frequently prepared through secretaries. This practice seems to have even been widespread among the lower classes when sending personal (private) letters. Letters might be produced through the process of an author dictating the contents to a secretary, perhaps (though this cannot be certain) using shorthand. A secretary also might contribute to a letter by means of style, register, syntax, and word choice. In some instances, the secretary might contribute by means of adding greetings, including a note of recommendation to receive itinerants, and even making minor editorial changes. Secretaries might even compose a letter under the guidance, direction, and approval of the so-called author. Randolph Richards notes, however, that in all these instances the authors expected the recipients to receive the letters as if they had been authored solely by the authors themselves (2004, 79). Evidently, then, the usage of a secretary in the process of letter writing was widespread, and the secretary could be used in a variety of ways under the direction of the author. As Klauck notes, there is "a scale for the secretarial role that runs from a letter that the author who lends his name to it entirely controls ('author-controlled') to a letter for which the secretary alone is basically responsible ('secretary-controlled')" (Klauck and Bailey 2006, 60).

4. For more detail on what follows in this section, see Richards 2004, 47–80; Klauck and Bailey 2006, 44–54.

Letters and Letter Writing in the New Testament

Ancient Jewish authors and communities also wrote letters as a means of addressing practical, occasional situations *and* for the purposes of sustaining group identity and cohesion among small communities.[5] Paul, among other early Christians, used the letter format for similar purposes. The letters of the New Testament can be divided into the Pauline corpus (thirteen letters ascribed to Paul) and the Catholic Epistles (James, 1 and 2 Peter, the letter to the Hebrews, 1, 2, and 3 John, and Jude). Additionally, the Acts of the Apostles contains two embedded letters (the contents of the Jerusalem council in Acts 15:23–29 and Claudius Lysias to Felix in 23:25–30), and Revelation contains the risen Christ speaking seven letters to seven churches in Asia Minor (Rev. 2:1–3:22).

The Pauline Corpus

Paul's letters (as is the case with all ancient letters) are written to bridge physical distance, having as their most basic goal the socialization of his churches into a particular way of life centered on the gospel of Jesus Christ. Through addressing the occasional situations of his churches, Paul seeks to construct "a new way of ordering experience and reality" (Lieu 2016, 170). The letters also work "to create bonds of allegiance between the readers and Paul, among the readers themselves, and between the readers and Christ" (Johnson 2020, 68). The notes of affection and consistent use of kinship language to describe Paul and his churches function to give the sense that the churches are a family. The distinction between private and public letters does not work well for understanding Paul's letters because they not only address specific communities and distinct situations but also serve as the official communication from an "apostle of Jesus Christ," to be read aloud within the public assembly (Col. 4:16; 1 Thess. 5:27).

Paul's letters are unusually long when compared to ancient Hellenistic letters, including most of the examples of literary or philosophical letters (Richards 2019, 87–89). The majority of Paul's letters follow the stereotypical format already examined, though this allows for a high level of creativity and adaptation.

1. Letter Opening: Paul's letter to the Romans, for example, begins with an opening and prescript where Paul identifies himself as the sender (Rom. 1:1) and the church in Rome as the addressees (1:7). Paul typically uses identity-shaping language to describe himself (e.g., slave of Jesus Christ [Rom. 1:1; Phil. 1:1]; apostle of Jesus Christ [1 Cor. 1:1; 2 Cor. 1:1; Col. 1:1]) and his addressees (e.g., those called by Jesus Christ [Rom. 1:6–7]; saints [Phil. 1:1]). Paul also adapts the typical term "greetings" to a benediction of "grace to you and peace" (e.g., 1 Cor. 1:3; Eph. 1:2). Most of Paul's letters also move from the greeting to an introductory thanksgiving (1 Cor. 1:4–9; Phil. 1:3–11; Col. 1:3–8; 1 Thess. 1:2–10) or prayer of blessing (2 Cor. 1:3–11; Eph. 1:3–14), and these prayers often function to highlight some of the primary themes of the letter (see Boers and O'Brien 1979). Paul's recounting of his prayers also highlights the goal of his ministry—namely, the moral transformation of his churches until the return of Jesus Christ (e.g., Phil. 1:3–6; 1 Thess. 3:11–13; see Thompson 2020, 11–13).

2. The Body of the Letter: Perhaps one of the most striking aspects of Paul as a letter writer is the remarkable length of his letters. It is generally in the body of the letter where Paul is the most verbose as well as creative. When Paul was unable

5. This is argued, and documented in great detail, in Doering 2012; see also Klauck and Bailey 2006, 229–97.

or perhaps found it unwise to further instruct, warn, and/or iron out conflicts within his churches, he responded with a letter as a substitute for his personal presence (see Funk 1967). The body of the letter, then, is where one can most clearly see the occasional nature of his letters and where Paul addresses the particular challenges and/or questions his churches are facing. Thus, Paul responds to potential objections to his gospel in Romans 1:18–4:25. He addresses conflict, division, and misunderstandings of his teachings in the Corinthian assembly in 1 Corinthians 1:18–15:58. He encourages and exhorts the Thessalonian church about how to live in a holy way with their bodies and to grieve the loss of their loved ones with hope in 1 Thessalonians 4:3–5:11.

3. Letter Closing: In his letter closings, Paul often passes on personal greetings both from himself and from members of other assemblies (e.g., Rom. 16:3–16; Phil. 4:21–22; 2 Tim. 4:19), writes letters of commendation to facilitate links between his coworkers and addressees (e.g., Rom. 16:1–2), offers notes of affection (Rom. 16:16), speaks of writing his name or a phrase with his own hand (1 Cor. 16:21; Gal. 6:11; Col. 4:18; 2 Thess. 3:17), and concludes with a final benediction (e.g., Rom. 16:25–27; Gal. 6:18; Phil. 4:23; 2 Thess. 3:18; 2 Tim. 4:22).

But can one classify Paul's letters more precisely according to the Hellenistic letter styles examined earlier? If one recognizes the multiple ways in which examples of ancient Hellenistic letters overlap and thereby avoids trying to straitjacket Paul's individual letters, one can identify similarities between Paul's letters and Hellenistic letter types. Nevertheless, it remains difficult to classify individual letters according to *one single* letter type, given that Paul draws on a variety of rhetorical conventions. For example, 2 Corinthians, Philippians, 1 Thessalonians, and Philemon all draw on aspects of the friendship letter as they exhort the community to be joined together in heart and mind (e.g., Phil. 2:1–4), communicate a longing to be physically present with one another (Phil. 1:7–8; 1 Thess. 2:17; 3:6–10), and pursue reconciliation (2 Cor. 7:5–16; Philemon).[6] While perhaps a bit of an overstatement, it has been suggested that Philippians is best classified as a letter of consolation given that Paul is addressing how his shameful imprisonment has grieved the church (Phil. 1:12–26; 2:17–19; see Holloway and Collins 2017). Some have argued that Romans is a "speech of exhortation" (i.e., a protreptic letter), as it seeks to convert its audience to a particular way of life (Aune 1991). Galatians draws on aspects of a letter of rebuke as Paul is "astonished" at their "foolish" behavior (Gal. 1:6; 3:1). Philemon is an extended letter of commendation. The Pastoral Epistles (1–2 Timothy and Titus) are closest in form to *mandata principis*—namely, letters of direction and advice given from a superior to one's delegates.[7]

I cannot address here the question of whether six (Ephesians, Colossians, 2 Thessalonians, and the Pastoral Epistles) of the thirteen Pauline epistles are pseudonymous, or some other variant thereof. But we should note that Paul does explicitly indicate his use of a scribe on occasion (e.g., Rom. 16:22) and mentions that his greetings are written by his own hand (1 Cor. 16:21; Gal. 6:11; Col. 4:18).[8] Most of Paul's letters are also coauthored (or at least cosponsored) with Timothy (2 Cor. 1:1; Phil. 1:1; Col. 1:1; Philem. 1), Silvanus and Timothy (1 Thess. 1:1; 2 Thess. 1:1), Sosthenes (1 Cor. 1:1), and "all the members of God's family" with him (Gal. 1:2) (Johnson 2020, 71–74). As Luke Timothy Johnson notes:

6. On Philippians as a friendship letter, see White 1990.
7. This is argued throughout Johnson 1996.
8. On Paul's use of a secretary, see Richards 2004, 81–94.

"The use of secretaries, co-sponsorship, the presence of social teaching practices (midrash and diatribe), and the use of prior traditions all point us to the conclusion that Paul's correspondence was both socially and literarily a complex process" (Johnson 2020, 74). Paul's letters also incorporate preformed materials—that is, early Christian tradition shared among his churches. For example, Paul's letters include shared early Christian hymns (Phil. 2:6–11; Col. 1:15–20; 1 Tim. 3:16; 2 Tim. 2:11–13), confessions and acclamations (Rom. 10:9–10; 1 Cor. 12:2–3), and gospel summaries (Rom. 1:1–4; 4:24–25; 1 Cor. 11:23–26; 15:3–8; 1 Thess. 1:9–10) (Johnson 2020, 73; Richards 2004, 95–98). While the exact details are lost to us, the evidence may move one away from a notion of Paul as a lone, individual author and toward a view that recognizes the composition of his letters took place within his larger ministry team.

Hebrews and the Catholic Epistles

Hebrews refers to itself as a "word of exhortation" (Heb. 13:22) and bears the hallmarks of an orally delivered speech or sermon.[9] It is only in its ending that there are similarities to the conclusions of ancient letters, as it provides information about Timothy's potential visit to the community, sends greetings, and concludes with a benediction (13:23–25). The letter of James begins with the following: "James, a slave of God and the Lord Jesus Christ, to the twelve tribes that are in the diaspora—greetings" (James 1:1, my translation). The letter is filled with paraenetic exhortations, metaphors, and speeches. First Peter begins: "Peter, an apostle of Jesus Christ, to the elect sojourners of the diaspora in Pontus, Galatia, Cappadocia, Asia, and Bithynia" (1 Pet. 1:1, my translation). Silvanus is spoken of as the letter carrier and perhaps also the scribe (5:12).

The letter concludes with the sending of greetings from the church "in Babylon" and from Mark (5:13). Second Peter begins, albeit a bit unusually, with many of the standard features of an ancient letter (identification of sender, audience, greetings; 2 Pet. 1:1–2), though much of its content conforms to the genre of a testament (see esp. 1:12–15). Second John, 3 John, and Jude are examples of ancient letters written to address the challenges of false teaching and the challenge of itinerant teachers.

Works Cited

Aune, David E. 1991. "Romans as a *Logos Protreptikos* in the Context of Ancient Religious and Philosophical Propaganda." In *Paulus und das antike Judentum: Tübingen-Durham-Symposium im Gedenken an den 50. Todestag Adolf Schlatters (19. Mai 1938)*, edited by Adolf Schlatter, Martin Hengel, and Ulrich Hekkel, 91–121. WUNT 58. Tübingen: Mohr Siebeck.

Boers, Hendrikus, and Peter Thomas O'Brien. 1979. "Introductory Thanksgivings in the Letters of Paul." *JBL* 98, no. 2: 303–4.

Deissmann, Adolf. 1908. *Licht vom Osten: Das Neue Testament und die neuentdeckten Texte der hellenistisch-römischen Welt*. Tübingen: Mohr.

Doering, Lutz. 2012. *Ancient Jewish Letters and the Beginnings of Christian Epistolography*. WUNT 298. Tübingen: Mohr Siebeck.

Funk, R. W. 1967. "The Apostolic Parousia: Form and Significance." In *Christian History and Interpretation: Studies Presented to John Knox*, edited by W. R. Farmer, C. F. D. Moule, and R. R. Niebuhr, 249–68. Cambridge: Cambridge University Press.

Holloway, Paul A., and Adela Yarbro Collins. 2017. *Philippians: A Commentary*. Hermeneia. Minneapolis: Fortress.

Innes, Doreen, ed. and trans. 1995. *Demetrius: On Style*. LCL 199. Cambridge, MA: Harvard University Press.

Johnson, Luke Timothy. 1996. *Letters to Paul's Delegates: 1 Timothy, 2 Timothy, Titus*. The New Testament in Context. Valley Forge, PA: Trinity Press International.

———. 2020. *The Canonical Paul*. Grand Rapids: Eerdmans.

Klauck, Hans-Josef, and Daniel P. Bailey. 2006. *Ancient Letters and the New Testament: A Guide to Context and Exegesis*. Waco: Baylor University Press.

Lieu, Judith M. 2016. "Letters and the Topography of Early Christianity." *NTS* 62, no. 2: 167–82.

---

9. On Hebrews and the Catholic Epistles, see Klauck and Bailey 2006, 334–49.

Mitchell, Margaret M. 1992. "New Testament Envoys in the Context of Greco-Roman Diplomatic and Epistolary Conventions: The Example of Timothy and Titus." *JBL* 111, no. 4: 641–62.

Richards, E. Randolph. 2004. *Paul and First-Century Letter Writing: Secretaries, Composition, and Collection*. Downers Grove, IL: InterVarsity.

———. 2019. "When Is a Letter Not a Letter?" In *Paul and the Giants of Philosophy: Reading the Apostle in Greco-Roman Context*, edited by Joseph R. Dodson and David E. Briones, 86–94. Downers Grove, IL: IVP Academic.

Stowers, Stanley Kent. 1986. *Letter Writing in Greco-Roman Antiquity*. Library of Early Christianity 5. Philadelphia: Westminster.

Thompson, James. 2020. *Apostle of Persuasion: Theology and Rhetoric in the Pauline Letters*. Grand Rapids: Baker Academic.

White, L. Michael. 1990. "Morality between Two Worlds: A Paradigm of Friendship in Philippians." In *Greeks, Romans, and Christians: Essays in Honor of Abraham J. Malherbe*, edited by David L. Balch, Everett Ferguson, and Wayne A. Meeks, 201–15. Minneapolis: Fortress.

19

Poetic and Hymnic Material in the New Testament

Andrew T. Cowan and Jennifer Strawbridge

What Do We Mean by "Poetry" and "Hymns" in the Ancient World?

Poetry and hymnody are well-attested literary genres in antiquity, from the works of Homer through the vast array of Greek poetic conventions; from cult hymnody to the literary hymns of feasts and civic occasions; from the Psalms and poetic writings of the Hebrew Bible to their noncanonical cousins in the Psalms of Solomon and Dead Sea Scrolls. Study of the New Testament has long been engaged in questions of intertextuality, influence, and background in relation to this wide range of poetic and hymnic texts and traditions.

The complexity around poetry and hymnody in the New Testament revolves around two key concerns: definition and identification. What is the difference between a poetic and a hymnic text in the New Testament? How do we identify such texts in the New Testament? To illustrate this complexity, for some scholars John 1, Philippians 2:6–11, Colossians 1:15–20, and Revelation 4–5 are exemplars of ancient hymnody; for others, these same texts epitomize New Testament poetic writings; still

for others, the distinction between hymnody and poetry is more semantic than meaningful. Similar claims are made for the infancy narrative in Luke's Gospel, where texts such as Mary's Magnificat are associated with the syntactical patterns of biblical Hebrew poetry, and because they are used as hymns from a very early period and included in the earliest collections of odes, they are identified as hymnic (see Becker 2009; Cowan 2024).

It is commonly accepted that the early Christians sang or chanted hymns in various contexts from an early stage (Acts 16:25; 1 Cor. 14:26; Col. 3:16; Eph. 5:19; James 5:13), a practice that is also attested not long afterward in Bithynia by Pliny the Younger (*Ep.* 10.96–97). Moreover, material from poetic strands of the Jewish writings (Psalms, Proverbs, Song of Songs) and from Greco-Roman poets are cited in the New Testament.

There are also frequent instances in the New Testament where "poetic" stylistic devices could be said to elevate the text, perhaps intended to stir emotion or increase memorability. Repetition, parallelism, assonance, and other such features suggest careful composition and may point to an underlying oral milieu. Whether such features constitute poetry in a stricter sense is a more complicated matter. For instance, there is no clear definition of poetry in the Hebrew Bible. While large swathes of material are regarded as poetic and might be explicitly identified within the category of song (for example), nonetheless, almost any stylistic features found in those texts are found elsewhere as well. In Greco-Roman conventions, there are much clearer rules governing poetic writing, but commonly regarded "poetic" features such as a rhythm and meter are also associated with prose writing. As noted, scholars do not always distinguish between poetry and hymnody, and when they do, some of their criteria overlap, such as parallelism, figurative language, rhythm, and known forms from Hebrew and Greco-Roman culture (see Aguilar 2014; Bailey and Vander Broek 1992). For some, a strict definition of Greek hymns similarly requires the presence of poetic meter and a tripartite structure, whereas others are content with a somewhat looser definition.

For the purposes of this discussion, it is helpful to view ancient hymns as a subset of poetic literature, with a hypothetical milieu in a cultic or religious setting. In addition, we must be alert to the potential danger of anachronism when we describe ancient texts as poetic or hymnic. It is important to indicate whether such determinations are intended to cohere with ancient definitions, are an exercise in reader response, or concern the reception or appropriation of ancient texts as poetry or hymnody in other settings.

New Testament "Hymns"

Although the New Testament refers to early Christian use of hymns, it nowhere explicitly records the textual content of such material, nor does it provide concrete parameters for identifying what is in view. For example, when

Jesus and the disciples depart the upper room in Mark 14:26 "after singing a hymn,"[1] most scholars take this as a reference to one of the Hallel Psalms known to have been used during the Passover. However, this is a reasonable conjecture rather than a certainty (see France 2002, 574). The New Testament authors nowhere signal that they are incorporating or emulating hymns in their writing, nor is any material described or introduced as "hymnic," whether in form, content, or function.[2]

However, for around a century, it has been common for scholars to refer to a range of passages in the New Testament as hymns. The set of passages in question has expanded and contracted over the years but frequently includes John 1:1–18; Ephesians 5:14; Philippians 2:6–11; Colossians 1:15–20; 1 Timothy 3:16; Hebrews 1:3; the Lukan infancy canticles; and the songs of Revelation.[3] The so-called Christ hymns of the epistles, especially Philippians 2:6–11 and Colossians 1:15–20, are often the focus, reflecting the enormous historical and theological interest they have generated in scholarship more broadly.[4]

Terminology and Methodology

While the term "hymn" has been widely adopted in the parlance of the discipline, what is actually meant by it varies. A significant number aver that the New Testament preserves portions of early Christian "hymns," meaning

---

1. Unless otherwise indicated, all Scripture translations are our own.

2. Luke does note when he is citing Psalms, but this is arguably less about genre than it is about indicating the source corpus in Scripture. The Psalms are treated almost universally by the New Testament authors in purely functional terms as prophetic literature.

3. If one were to include any material that has been described more loosely as "hymnic" in flavor, the list would expand dramatically. Ostmeyer lists a bewildering array of passages (2016, 644–45).

4. This is evident in how almost every scholarly contribution on Phil. 2:6–11 begins by channeling the despair of Qoheleth in lamenting the almost comically overwhelming mountain of secondary literature.

material that either constitutes or is representative, in form and content, of authentic "sung" material from early Christian gatherings (see R. Martin 1967; Sanders 1971). That is, what is being identified is material that satisfies expectations set by Colossians 3:16 and Ephesians 5:19 of singing "psalms, hymns, and spiritual songs." That such material might be found is not intrinsically implausible given these and other texts that refer to the practice of singing hymns in various contexts. For other scholars, "hymn" denotes material that is perceived (usually on the same methodological grounds) to be poetic in form, perhaps elevated in style and performing a literary function of praising its subject (invariably God or Jesus), but it need not necessarily presuppose the presence of preformed material, or if it does, it need not follow that it was ever actually used in an oral or liturgical setting. Still others do not define the precise sense in which these passages are to be considered hymns, but nonetheless they deploy the language when referring to them. Arguably, absent any qualification, to refer to a text as a hymn is to imply that it fulfills literary conventions that govern actual sung material. That is, within the bounded corpus of the New Testament, calling something a hymn implies correspondence to what is envisaged when the language of hymn itself occurs in that corpus (see again Col. 3:16 or Eph. 5:19).

This diversity of how "hymn" is used notwithstanding, the shared terminology implies a degree of consensus regarding the nature of these passages. This consensus derives fundamentally from earlier form-critical and philological research into the nature of the passages in question. A quest for hymns developed from German scholarship in the first half of the last century (e.g., Johannes Weiss, Eduard Norden, Ernst Lohmeyer, and Ethelbert Stauffer), itself an offshoot of an even earlier interest in possible fragments of "traditional" material in the New Testament (see historical surveys in Edsall 2012; Longenecker 1999). In short

order various form-critical criteria—such as syntax, style, linguistic usage, rhythm, and content—were routinely applied to a range of New Testament passages to determine or describe their nature as hymns, and while this methodology has evolved over time, it remains the primary means by which hymns in the New Testament have been defined and described (see, e.g., lists in Gordley 2018, 20–21; Gloer 1984; Longenecker 1999).

Potential Contributions of Hymnic Material

Where the identification of these passages as hymns (in some sense) is considered on the foregoing basis to be largely secure, the conversation has turned to the insights that their nature or contribution *as* hymns might yield (see Deichgräber 1967). In the past this led naturally to comparative studies of the New Testament passages in relation to other ancient patterns of religious thought or devotion (Sanders 1971). More recently, Matthew Gordley has focused on the didactic nature of Christian hymnody (Gordley 2011) and has compared the New Testament christological hymns with Jewish resistance poetry (Gordley 2018). Others have undertaken focused work on particular passages or sets of passages.[5]

Possible Criticisms of Hymnic Material

While the majority of New Testament scholars affirm the presence of hymns in the New Testament, recent decades have seen an increase in critical dissent. For example, Ralph Brucker (1997) famously rejected the language of hymn entirely on the grounds that none of the New Testament passages sufficiently satisfy

5. For instance, Stephen Farris (1985) on the Lukan infancy material; or Ralph P. Martin (1983) on Phil. 2:6–11; Stephen Fowl (1990) on Philippians, Colossians, and 1 Tim. 3:16; and Gordley (2007) on Col. 1. Although his work was foundational for the wider discussion, Lohmeyer's work (1928) on Phil. 2:6–11 was less interested in the form or genre of the passage.

ancient Greek hymnic conventions, particularly the requirement of poetic meter. Others have sought to nuance the discussion in other ways. For example, in an important article, Gordon Fee (1992) rejected the language of hymn for Philippians 2:6–11, preferring "exalted prose" in order to capture what he saw as the theological and literary artistry inherent in those verses.

Another problem, indicated above, is that, despite its widespread currency, there is frequently a lack of clarity over what is meant by the term "hymn." Michael Peppard (2008) cautions against the potential for unconscious anachronism when using such language. He also voices his suspicion that form-critical methodology may have emerged simply from observations drawn from the texts in question themselves and thus is ultimately circular in nature. Others have similarly questioned the validity of several of the criteria (Cosgrove 2018) or their applicability to individual passages (Balchin 1985), or noted the lack of patristic support for any of the passages in question as hymns (Edsall and Strawbridge 2015).

In defense of the dominant paradigm, Gordley (2011, 2018) has argued that such criticisms either fall short of sufficient interaction with the methodology or fail to appreciate the broader categories of hymns in the ancient world, such as that of prose hymnody. While the arguments that these passages may be better described as "prose hymns" is appealing, and more work remains to be done in this area, this position often reverts in practice to the same kinds of form-critical observations as before, and therefore still stands or falls to some degree on their validity. One intriguing recent article seeks ancient warrant for Philippians 2:6–11 as a hymn through comparison to common hymnic tropes found in ancient rhetorical handbooks, although this too could be seen as another recasting of the same methodology (Martin and Nash 2015).

So, in spite of the foregoing concerns, the tendency to refer to many passages as hymns or Christ hymns remains the dominant paradigm.

New Testament Poetry

Similar to scholars who work on hymnic material in the New Testament, those who write on poetry are quick to note the lack of agreement in how poetic forms are determined and defined. The identification of poetic passages varies widely, often depending on internal criteria such as parallelism, syntactic symmetry, style, and terseness of tone and external criteria such as comparison with and imitation of recognized odes, psalms, and contemporary Hebrew and Greco-Roman poetic writings. However, even with clear criteria and methodological precedents, scholars still reach vastly different conclusions about the presence of poetic forms in the New Testament. For example, with regard to Luke 1, Floyd Filson argues that Luke's writing is "woefully weak in parallelism," leading to questions of "whether we are dealing with poetry at all" (1948, 132). In contrast, Paul Winter contests that Luke 1 mirrors Maccabean war songs and "there is hardly a turn of speech and certainly not a single thought not to be found in older Hebrew poetry" (1954, 333). Such extremes concerning poetic identification in the New Testament have not changed significantly in the decades since Filson and Winter.

For many scholars, the identity of poetry in the New Testament is based on studies of poetry in the Hebrew Bible. Within this approach definitions of poetry often depend on so-called Lowthian principles of poetry, building on Robert Lowth's *Lectures on the Sacred Poetry of the Hebrews* (1829). In these lectures, Lowth defines poetry as more than parallelism and includes literary critical and comparative studies, as well as sensitivity to the cultures out of which the biblical corpus emerged. Timothy Decker criticizes New Testament scholarship as being too reliant on Lowthian parallelism to define poetry and argues that New Testament scholarship needs to look not to eighteenth-century literary forms but to the work of more recent scholars on Old Testament poetry, such as James Kugel, Robert Alter, and Adele Berlin (Decker 2021). For scholars who engage with New Testament poetry from other perspectives, such as Greco-Roman poetic forms or reception historical studies, a key question is whether the New Testament contains actual "poems" or simply uses language poetically in sections of narrative or prose. For still others, poetry is determined not by form or meter but as the expression of creativity and intensity in line with modern literary criticism rather than historical form (e.g., Gaebelein 1972, 247).

Terminology and Methodology

At an extreme, the whole of the New Testament—from the "hymns" of Paul's letters and Revelation to the "I am" statements in John's Gospel—is poetic, and poetic speech and narrative capture themes and images in ways that prose alone cannot (see Whitlock 2015). Such a claim is especially true in relation to divine discourse where the language of Hebrew poetry and especially that angelic speech in the Dead Sea Scrolls is mirrored in the New Testament (such as Rev. 2–3; see Mizrahi 2018), emphasizing a continuing "deep respect for the mystery of God" (Strawn 2020, 72).

As noted above, definitions of poetic forms in the Hebrew Bible vary widely, and thus it is no surprise that the identification of Hebrew poetry in the New Testament does as well. For some, the poetic material or the Hodayot from the Dead Sea Scrolls serves as a parallel or even poetic "bridge" to the New Testament (see Horgan and Kobelski 1989, passim). For others, the Old Testament psalms, such as portions of Psalms 8, 22, or 110, are poetry that have become *"prayers of Christ"* and *"prayers to Christ"* in the New Testament (Gillingham

1994, 265–66, emphasis original) and that best capture Christ's identity and ministry (Witherington 2017). Hugo Méndez (2016) focuses especially on Luke's Gospel and passages like the Magnificat (1:46–55), Benedictus (1:68–79), Gloria (2:14), and Nunc dimittis (2:29–32) as examples of Hebrew poetry in the New Testament.

Decker, who seeks to engage with Old Testament poetic forms within the New Testament, identifies five passages that best reflect such forms: the Lord's Prayer (Matt. 6:9–13); the Magnificat (Luke 1:46–55); 2 Timothy 2:11–13; 1 John 2:12–14; and the Song of the Lamb (Rev. 15:3–4). The Lord's Prayer is a specific point of contention among scholars of New Testament poetry. Michael Martin advocates for the Lord's Prayer as ancient Jewish poetry, with poetic forms generally overlooked by commentators and translators (M. Martin 2015), while Shirley Darcus Sullivan finds parallels between the Lord's Prayer's "poetic beauty" and that of classical literature, including the use of repetition, responsion, and a clear textual pattern (Sullivan 2015, 35).

A few scholars also point to the use of Hellenistic poetry in the New Testament, with possible references to texts from Epimenides in Acts 17:28 and Titus 1:12, Euripides in Acts 26:14,[6] and Menander in 1 Corinthians 15:33. Scholars such as Piotr Lorek (2021) and Clare Rothschild (2014) identify the use of the Greek sage or Cretan prophet Epimenides within the two New Testament passages just named, identifying how these texts refer to the authority of the sage, capture a nexus of traditions around this figure, and sit alongside the struggle of early Christians to reconcile apologetically the use of Greco-Roman poetic words in Christian writing. For Rothschild, the Lukan Paul uses popular religious and philosophical tools and

---

6. Bilby and Lefteratou 2022 notes the influence and use of Euripides (specifically *Iphigenia among the Taurians*) in Acts 19:21–20:1, as well.

poetic phrases, such as "In him, we live, and move, and have our being" (Acts 17:28a), to reinforce his message. Similarly, Michael Cover engages with how the comedy (and poetry) of Menander influenced Paul's rhetoric in 1 Corinthians and demonstrates a similar instance of shared topics and concerns in Paul's use of this Greco-Roman text. Cover argues that Paul's use of Menander specifically in 1 Corinthians 15:33 is an element of Paul's "larger strategy to frame the struggles in Corinth within the ambit of Greek household situation comedy" and reflects the comedy—and tragedy—of the Christ narrative (Cover 2018, 532).

Possible Contributions of Poetic Material

For a number of scholars, poetic forms in the New Testament serve to develop a writer's Christology (see Meeks 2004, 92–93, whose central example is Phil. 2:5–11). As Wayne Meeks argues, only through poetic language could the "mysterious god-equal figure" of Jesus in Philippians or Hebrews be expressed. The poetic writings within the New Testament thus communicate "the supreme model of grace, God's ultimate self-revelation" (Meeks 2004, 80). In other words, the elevated nature of poetic language, however defined, enabled the writers of the New Testament to name and describe the person of Jesus Christ more fully. One of Meeks's most significant contributions to this discussion is his challenge to the assumed divisions between "Judaism" and "Hellenism," especially in poetic form and process. Instead, he argues that poetic language allowed early Christ followers to "forge a new identity for themselves" as they tried to "solve the enigma of Jesus" (92).

Possible Criticisms of Poetic Material

One of the most significant issues with the identification of poetic forms in the New Testament (hymnic forms could also be included) concerns translation. Poetry by nature demands creativity and imagination from the reader, but such creativity and imagination push the limits of translation. To grasp such limitations, a quick comparison of different English translations of Philippians 2:5–11 or Luke 1:46–55 demonstrates the challenge translation poses to poetic forms: How are semantic symmetry, parallelism, or phonological style, for example, maintained in translation? For Ernst Wendland (2012), some languages, such as Chewa, are able to preserve the phonological poetry of texts such as the Lord's Prayer better than English. For Philip Comfort, the Greek text is essential to know, as it is there that poetic passages "stimulate our imaginations and arouse our emotions" (2010, viii). Translators also make decisions that have significant rhetorical force and influence in terms of how the text is set out once translated. Textual markers in modern translations of "poetic" passages assume that such texts are poetry with limited discussion. The translators of the Jerusalem Bible, for example, set John 1 in poetic meter, leading readers to assume such a text is poetry (see also Peppard 2008), and William Barnstone's translation sets the whole of the New Testament as free verse poetry (see Barnstone 2017, 2012). As Michael Peppard (2008) and Andrew Cowan (2024) both argue, the form of a text on a manuscript or translation—indentation, colometry, sense marks—significantly influences how New Testament texts are understood poetically. Recent work examining early biblical manuscripts challenges the assumptions of translators since few New Testament texts are set apart as poetic. Questions about what makes a New Testament text poetic thus demand further study, especially around the assumption that visual cues signal the genre of a biblical text (see Strawbridge 2023).

Conclusion

Whether or not they incorporate or preserve significant quantities of poetry and hymns, the

New Testament writers arguably display an awareness and appreciation of such material, both as prevalent literary phenomena and in relation to their devotional and didactic value. Ralph Martin's comment that "the Christian church was born in song," while difficult to illustrate by example, nevertheless remains appealingly plausible (1975, 39). The New Testament has also inspired an enduring culture of poetic and hymnic reflection through to the present day, which is a whole strand of reception worthy of attention in its own right.

Works Cited

Aguilar, Alejo. 2014. "Uso e Interpretación de la Poesía en el Nuevo Testamento." *DavarLogos* 3, no. 1: 13–22.

Bailey, James L., and Lyle D. Vander Broek. 1992. *Literary Forms in the New Testament: A Handbook*. Louisville: John Knox.

Balchin, J. F. 1985. "Colossians 1:15–20: An Early Christian Hymn? The Arguments from Style." *Vox Evangelica* 15: 65–93.

Barnstone, Willis. 2012. *The Poems of Jesus Christ*. New York: Norton.

———. 2017. *Poets of the Bible: From Solomon's Song of Songs to John's Book of Revelation*. New York: Norton.

Becker, Scot. 2009. "The Magnificat among the Biblical Narrative-Set Psalms." In vol. 2 of *Early Christian Literature and Intertextuality*, edited by Craig A. Evans and H. Daniel Zacharias, 60–73. London: Bloomsbury.

Bilby, Mark Glen, and Anna Lefteratou. 2022. "A Dramatic Heist of Epic Proportion: Iphigenia among the Taurians in the Acts of the Apostles." *HTR* 115, no. 4: 496–518.

Brucker, Ralph. 1997. *"Christushymnen" oder "epideiktische Passagen"? Studien zum Stilwechsel im Neuen Testament und seiner Umwelt*. FRLANT 176. Göttingen: Vandenhoeck & Ruprecht.

Comfort, Philip Wesley. 2010. *The Poems and Hymns of the New Testament*. Eugene, OR: Wipf & Stock.

Cosgrove, Charles H. 2018. "The Syntax of Early Christian Hymns and Prayers: Revisiting Relative and Participial Styles for Making Assertions about a Deity." *EC* 9: 158–80.

Cover, Michael. 2018. "The Divine Comedy at Corinth: Paul, Menander and the Rhetoric of Resurrection." *NTS* 64, no. 4: 532–50.

Cowan, Andrew T. 2024. "New Testament 'Hymnic' Texts in Ancient Reception and Modern Interpretation." DPhil diss., Oxford University.

Decker, Timothy. 2021. "The New Testament's Majesty of the Old Testament's Poetic Style: Interpreting New Testament Poems Stylized after Biblical Hebrew Poetry as Well as the State of Current New Testament Research." PhD diss., Lancaster Bible College.

Deichgräber, Reinhard. 1967. *Gotteshymnus und Christushymnus in der frühen Christenheit: Untersuchungen zu Form, Sprache und Stil der frühchristlichen Hymnen*. SUNT 5. Göttingen: Vandenhoeck & Ruprecht.

Edsall, Benjamin. 2012. "Kerygma, Catechesis, and Other Things We Used to Find: Twentieth Century Research on Early Christian Teaching Since Alfred Seeberg." *CurBR* 10, no. 3: 410–41.

Edsall, Benjamin, and Jennifer R. Strawbridge. 2015. "The Songs We Used to Sing? Hymn 'Traditions' and Reception in Pauline Letters." *JSNT* 37, no. 3: 290–311.

Fee, Gordon D. 1992. "Philippians 2:5–11: Hymn or Exalted Pauline Prose?" *BBR* 2: 29–46.

Filson, Floyd V. 1948. "How Much of the New Testament Is Poetry?" *JBL* 67, no. 2: 125–34.

France, R. T. 2002. *The Gospel of Mark: A Commentary on the Greek Text*. Grand Rapids: Eerdmans.

Gaebelein, Frank E. 1972. "New Testament Poetry." *Bibliotheca Sacra* 129, no. 515: 247–49.

Gillingham, Susan E. 1994. *The Poems and Psalms of the Hebrew Bible*. Oxford: Oxford University Press.

Gloer, W. H. 1984. "Homologies and Hymns in the New Testament: Form, Content and Criteria for Identification." *Perspectives in Religious Studies* 11: 115–32.

Gordley, Matthew E. 2011. *Teaching through Song in Antiquity*. WUNT 2/302. Tübingen: Mohr Siebeck.

———. 2018. *New Testament Christological Hymns: Exploring Texts, Contexts, and Significance*. Downers Grove, IL: IVP Academic.

Horgan, Maurya P., and Paul J. Kobelski. 1989. "The Hodayot (1QH) and New Testament Poetry." In *To Touch the Text: Biblical and Related Studies in Honor of Joseph A. Fitzmyer, SJ*, edited by Maurya P. Horgan and Paul J. Kobelski, 179–93. New York: Crossroad.

Longenecker, Richard N. 1999. *New Wine into Fresh Wineskins: Contextualizing Early Christian Confessions*. Peabody, MA: Hendrickson.

Lorek, Piotr. 2021. "Epimenides of Crete in the New Testament Context (Titus 1:12; Acts 17:28)." *Verbum Vitae* 39, no. 3: 849–63.

Lowth, Robert. 1829. *Lectures on the Sacred Poetry of the Hebrews*. England: Crocker and Brewster.

Martin, Michael W. 2015. "The Poetry of the Lord's Prayer: A Study in Poetic Device." *JBL* 134, no. 2: 347–72.

Martin, Michael W., and Bryan A. Nash. 2015. "Philippians 2:6–11 as Subversive *Hymnos*: A Study in the Light of Ancient Rhetorical Theory." *JTS* 66: 90–138.

Martin, Ralph P. 1967. *Carmen Christi: Philippians ii. 5–11 in Recent Interpretation and in the Setting of Early Christian Worship*. Cambridge: Cambridge University Press.

———. 1975. *Worship in the Early Church*. Grand Rapids: Eerdmans.

Meeks, Wayne A. 2004. "Inventing the Christ: Multicultural Process and Poetry among the First Christians." *Studia theologica* 58, no. 1: 77–96.

Méndez, Hugo. 2016. "Semitic Poetic Techniques in the Magnificat: Luke 1:46–47, 55." *JBL* 135, no. 3: 557–74.

Mizrahi, Noam. 2018. "The Poetics of Angelic Discourse: Revelation 2–3 and the Songs of the Sabbath Sacrifice." *JSNT* 41, no. 4: 107–23.

Ostmeyer, Karl-Heinrich. 2016. "Hymns. IV. New Testament" In vol. 12 of *Encyclopedia of the Bible and Its Reception*, edited by Dale C. Allison Jr. et al., 644–48. Berlin: de Gruyter.

Peppard, Michael. 2008. "'Poetry,' 'Hymns' and 'Traditional Material' in the New Testament Epistles or How to Do Things with Indentation." *JSNT* 30, no. 3: 319–42.

Rothschild, Clare K. 2014. *Paul in Athens: The Popular Religious Context of Acts 17*. WUNT 341. Tübingen: Mohr Siebeck.

Sanders, Jack T. 1971. *The New Testament Christological Hymns*. SNTSMS 15. Cambridge: Cambridge University Press.

Strawbridge, Jennifer. 2023. "New Testament. V. Literature." In vol. 21 of *Encyclopedia of the Bible and Its Reception*, edited by Dale C. Allison Jr. et al., 340–42. Berlin: de Gruyter.

Strawn, Brent A. 2020. "Why We Need to Read the Bible Jesus Read: The Old Testament Is Vital for Understanding the New Testament. It's Also Indispensable All by Itself." *Christianity Today* 64, no. 1: 68–73.

Sullivan, Shirley Darcus. 2015. "The Poetic Beauty of the Lord's Prayer in Greek: Reflections of a Classicist." *Crux* 51, no. 4: 28–35.

Wendland, Ernst R. 2012. "Poeticizing the Lord's Prayer for *Pronunciatio*: An Exercise in Oral-Oriented Bible Translation." *Neotestamentica* 46, no. 2: 394–415.

Whitlock, Matthew G. 2015. "Acts 1:15–26 and the Craft of New Testament Poetry." *CBQ* 77, no. 1: 87–106.

Winter, Paul. 1954. "Magnificat and Benedictus—Maccabean Psalms?" *Bulletin of the John Rylands Library of Manchester* 37: 328–50.

Witherington, Ben, III. 2017. *Psalms Old and New: Exegesis, Intertextuality, and Hermeneutics*. Minneapolis: Fortress.

20

Practices of Interpretation

Susan Docherty

The fundamental significance of the writings now termed "scriptural" for the theology, ethics, and rituals of Second Temple Judaism is universally acknowledged and is clearly demonstrated in the "Old Testament Pseudepigrapha" (for discussion of this contested designation, see Ahearne-Kroll 2019). This evidence has more recently been supplemented by the Dead Sea discoveries. These ancient manuscripts reveal the extent to which the members of the Qumran community were committed to the reading, exposition, and transmission of Israel's received traditions of law, prophecy, and wisdom (e.g., 1QS VI, 6–8). It is within this literary and religious context that the New Testament authors operated, displaying a similarly intense and wide-ranging engagement with the same authoritative texts. This chapter will begin by discussing the scope and nature of "Scripture" in this era and then consider the main ways in which it was cited and interpreted. The principal focus will be on Jewish exegetical practices, since these exerted such a profound influence on the first followers of Jesus. Neither early Judaism nor early Christianity operated in isolation from broader Hellenistic culture, however, so these methods often overlap with Greco-Roman approaches to the study of classical literature (see further Hose and Schenker 2016).

Authoritative Texts

No such entity as a definitive Bible with a fixed list of contents and a stable text existed in the early centuries BCE or CE (McDonald 2017). Nevertheless, a collection of traditional writings was beginning to attain a particular significance at this time. These works—the Pentateuch, the Psalms, and the oracles of certain named prophets—would come to form the core of what is now accepted as sacred Scripture by both Jews and Christians. Their authority can be inferred from both their level of representation among the Qumran scrolls (VanderKam 2012, 49–71) and the frequency with which they are cited and alluded to in the Apocrypha and Pseudepigrapha. It is also confirmed in occasional explicit statements about the normativity of the Law of Moses and the Prophets (e.g.,

Sir. prologue; cf. 2 Macc. 15:9; 4 Macc. 18:10; 4Q397 14–21, 10; cf. 1QS I, 2–3). The emerging scriptural status of these texts receives further support in the pages of the New Testament, as the early followers of Jesus also turned to them to explain his life and death (e.g., Luke 24:44–45; 1 Cor. 15:3–4) and to justify their beliefs and practices. They appealed most frequently to the books of Genesis, Deuteronomy, Psalms, Isaiah, and the Minor Prophets. This mirrors closely the pattern of distribution of scriptural quotations and allusions within the Dead Sea Scrolls (Brooke 1997; Evans 2015). A larger and more fluid set of other writings was also highly regarded within some Jewish circles, not all of which (e.g., 1 Enoch, Jubilees) would ultimately become canonical Scripture.

Textual Pluriformity

Many Jews would have accessed these authoritative texts only orally, through their recitation in liturgical or educational contexts (Carr 2005), but they were also physically available in a variety of modes. At Qumran, for example, in addition to copies of whole books, excerpts of different kinds were made, either of individual passages (e.g., Ps. 119 in 5Q5) or of anthologies based around a common theme, such as eschatology (e.g., 4Q174, 4Q175, 4Q176, 11Q13; see Albl 1999, 70–96). Other manuscripts present rewritten versions of large sections of the Pentateuch, in which some episodes are rearranged and additional material is included (e.g., the Temple Scroll, 11Q19–20; the Reworked Pentateuch, 4Q158, 4Q364–67; see Crawford 2008; Zahn 2020). Some books also existed in more than one literary form. The Qumran Psalms scroll (11QPs^a) differs from the Masoretic collection in its contents and ordering (Flint 1999), for instance, and Jeremiah is found in both a longer (4QJer^a, 4QJer^c; cf. MT) and a shorter (4QJer^b, 4QJer^d; cf. LXX) edition.

These writings also circulated throughout the late Second Temple period in multiple tex-

tual versions. This pluriformity is evident in the differences between the Masoretic (Hebrew) Text and the Greek translation, the Septuagint, as well as in the form of the scriptural citations in the deuterocanonical and pseudepigraphic literature. It has been further corroborated in the Dead Sea discoveries (Tov 2002). Many of these manuscripts reflect the Masoretic or proto-Masoretic Text, but some contain expansionist readings parallel to those that characterize the Samaritan Pentateuch (e.g., 4QExod-Lev^f, 4QpaleoExod^m, 4QNum^b, 4QDeut^n) or else present a Hebrew text similar to that on which the Septuagint is based (e.g., 4QExod^b, 4QDeut^q, 4QSam^a). Others diverge, in both minor and more substantial ways, from all three of these extant major text-types (e.g., 4QGen^k, 4QJosh^a). Some of the variants attested in the scrolls may have resulted from copying errors, but it is equally likely that many were deliberately introduced by scribes, who understood their role as involving not simply the transmission of the received text but also the clarification of perceived difficulties within it (Brooke 2005).

Citation Practice

A recognition of this situation of ongoing textual pluriformity is important for understanding the quotation of the Scriptures in later writings. First, their availability in a variety of forms, including excerpted and rewritten versions, helps to explain unusual readings and features of ancient citation practice such as inaccurate attribution and composite quotation (Adams and Ehorn 2016, 2018). Commentators are now expected, therefore, to investigate thoroughly the full range of extant early witnesses beyond the major Masoretic and Septuagint manuscripts before drawing conclusions about whether a citation is being deliberately modified by a New Testament author for theological purposes.

Second, and conversely, however, it is becoming more widely accepted that early Jewish scribes and interpreters were able to exercise some freedom in their re-presentation of traditional texts. The quotations within sectarian compositions at Qumran, for example, sometimes differ from all other known versions and incorporate exegetical alterations. The replacement in the citation of Habakkuk 2:15 in the Habakkuk pesher of the usual word "their nakedness" (*m'wyrhm*) with the otherwise unattested "their feasts" (*mw'dyhm*) is probably such an intentional adaptation, involving the replacement of only a single consonant (*d* for *r*) and the reordering of the letters ' and *w*. This allows the verse to be related in the ensuing commentary to the subject of the proper dating of festivals, a matter of dispute between the community and other streams of contemporary Judaism (1QpHab XI, 2–8; see Lim 2002, 54–63). This kind of editorial activity seems to be reflected in some parts of the New Testament, too, especially in the ten fulfillment quotations in Matthew's Gospel, which exhibit quite distinctive text-forms (e.g., Isa. 9:1–2 in Matt. 4:15–16; Isa. 42:1–4 in Matt. 12:18–21; see Menken 2004) and which may have emerged from within an early Christian scribal "school" (Stendahl 1954; Alexander 2000).

Third, this state of textual variety could be utilized as an exegetical technique, enabling interpreters to select from among available forms the one that most effectively supports their argument. The citation of Habakkuk 1:17 in the pesher on Habakkuk, for instance, contains the word "his sword" (*ḥrbw*), where the Masoretic Text has "his net" (*ḥrmw*). This minor consonantal difference is attested elsewhere in a Greek version (8HevXII gr), so it was not necessarily introduced by the Qumran commentator. This reading may have been preferred above others, however, as it facilitates the direct application of this verse to the contemporary Roman armies (1QpHab VI, 8–10).

The same method of textual selection may explain the occurrence of the phrase "a body you have prepared" in the quotation of Psalm 40:6 (39:7 LXX) in Hebrews 10:5–7. Two main Greek renderings of the difficult underlying Hebrew are found in the surviving manuscripts, but the one reproduced in Hebrews fits the epistle's claim that Jesus's death replaces the sacrifices required by the Mosaic law better than the more familiar form "ears you have dug" (Norton 2011, 82–87). Some commentators suggest that an author's decision to exploit a variant reading or to adapt a citation may be prompted at least in part by the desire to generate a pleasing rhetorical effect. Features like rhythm and rhyme were highly valued in both Jewish and Greco-Roman literary culture, as texts were often communicated through reading them aloud. This quotation contains the plural word "burnt offerings" (*holokautōmata*), for instance, where most extant Greek witnesses have the singular (*holokautōma*). This provides the line with an extra syllable, so that it precisely matches the cadence of the next line of the verse, thereby producing a nicer sound or "phonetic assonance" (Jobes 1992, 182).

Interpretive Techniques

Numerous techniques were used by Jewish interpreters in the Second Temple period to draw out the meaning of the authoritative texts for their audience. Space does not permit here a detailed account of all of these individual methods, but they are comprehensively described in the scholarly literature, which includes important recent studies of rabbinic hermeneutics (e.g., Bakhos 2006; Samely 2007) and the Qumran scrolls (e.g., Campbell 2004; Brooke 2006), as well as more general surveys of the field (e.g., Kugel 2010; Henze 2012). Instead, five fundamental aspects of early Jewish exegesis will be foregrounded. These are common to several different forms of interpretation (e.g., Qumranic, targumic, rabbinic) and appear to underpin the specific procedures employed within them.

Segmentation

Perhaps the most basic operation of early Jewish exegesis is the focus on short sections of text. A scriptural lemma or verse is often broken down into smaller segments, consisting of a phrase or even a single word, each of which can then be interpreted separately and without reference to its original context (Samely 2002, 31–58; 2007, 62–75). This approach is generally termed "atomistic," and it is characteristic of both rabbinic exegesis and the Qumran pesharim. A vast range of other techniques can then be applied to produce a new meaning from each unit of text. The consonants of a word can be rearranged, for instance (e.g., reading the noun "temple" [*hykl*] as the verb "he will destroy" [*yklh*] in 1QpHab XII, 16–XIII, 3; cf. Hab. 2:20), or one term can be substituted for another that looks graphically similar (e.g., the interplay between the noun *mshl* ["saying" or "taunt"] and the verb *mshl* ["to rule"], 1QpHab VIII, 6–9; cf. Hab. 2:6; for further examples, see Horgan 1979, 245–47). A similar way of reading the Scriptures is evident within the New Testament. The exposition of Psalm 95:7–11 (94:7–11 LXX) in Hebrews, for example, depends on placing interpretive stress on key individual words, like "rest" and "today" (Heb. 3:7–4:10; cf. the emphasis on "old" in Heb. 8:13; cf. Jer. 31:31–34).

Textual Juxtaposition

The second cornerstone of early Jewish interpretation is the deliberate use of one passage to illuminate another (Bernstein 2000). This practice of textual association depends on paying close and detailed attention to scriptural wording. It is exemplified particularly clearly in the rabbinic technique of *gezerah shawa*, in which verses are linked because they share a word in common. An analogical relationship between them is then inferred, so that the meaning of the key term in one location is understood as carrying over entirely to another.

This operation is especially important in legal pronouncements in the Mishnah (e.g., m. Sotah 6.3; see Samely 2002, 214–21).

This method is, though, widely employed also in other forms of early Jewish exegesis. Within the Dead Sea Scrolls, for example, texts are frequently brought together on the basis of a common theme (e.g., reasons for trusting in God in battle in 1QM X, 1–8; cf. Num. 10:9; Deut. 20:2–5) or interpreted through catchword links (e.g., "king" and "star" in CD VII, 10–20; cf. Num. 24:17; Amos 5:26–27). In his retelling of Israel's Scriptures, too, the author of the Biblical Antiquities, too, repeatedly draws out thematic connections between different episodes (Fisk 2001), such as the correspondences between the aborted sacrifice of Isaac and Jephthah's killing of his daughter in order to fulfill a vow (LAB 40.2; cf. Gen. 22:1–19; Judg. 11:29–40). In poetic and apocalyptic writings, including the Qumran Hodayot (1QH) and 1 Enoch, these intertextual relationships are usually evoked through allusion rather than direct citation. The Enochic "son of man" figure, for instance, is created out of an intricate combination of motifs and phrases drawn from across the prophetic and wisdom literature (e.g., Ps. 2:2; Prov. 8:22–31; Isa. 11:1–5; 42:1; Dan. 7:9–14; see Nickelsburg 1992).

It is not surprising, therefore, that this technique of textual juxtaposition frequently underpins the scriptural interpretation of the first followers of Jesus too. Connections between passages are forged in a variety of ways, including appeals to two supporting texts in legal debates (e.g., Matt. 12:1–8; cf. 1 Sam. 21:1–6; Hosea 6:6), quotations paired on the basis of a shared word (e.g., "son" in Heb. 1:5; cf. Ps. 2:7; 2 Sam. 7:14; "rest" in Heb. 4:4–5; cf. Ps. 95:11 [94:11 LXX]; Gen. 2:2; see especially Steyn 2011), and collections of verses sharing a common theme (e.g., "stone" in Luke 20:17–18; 1 Pet. 2:6–8). New Testament prayers (e.g., Luke 1:46–79) and apocalyptic visons (e.g., Rev. 4:1–5:14; 21:1–22:5) are, like their early Jewish counterparts, created by combining phrases drawn from numerous scriptural locations into a new composition that then resembles a mosaic or pastiche of these earlier texts (Newman 1999; Fletcher 2017).

Reapplication of Speakers

A third recurring technique across early Jewish interpretation is the provision of a new speaker, addressee, or setting for a scriptural speech. Any sentence containing a pronoun—"you" or "him," for example—is potentially ambiguous when taken out of context and so can be read as relating to a different person from the one implied in the original passage. This operation is widely utilized in the targumim and midrashim (Samely 1992, 9–31; 2002, 110–47). By this means, verses with a general meaning, especially from the Psalms, can be linked to a specific scriptural character. According to the Biblical Antiquities, for example, Hannah's rival wife Peninnah taunts her with the question put to the unnamed psalmist by his enemies: "Where is your God?" (LAB 50.5; cf. 1 Sam. 1:12; Ps. 42:3). This method also often serves to further highlight innerscriptural connections. On being told that he is to become king, for instance, Pseudo-Philo's Saul gives voice to Jeremiah's protest that he is too young to take on the task to which God has called him (LAB 56.6; cf. Jer. 1:6). This interpretive move is paralleled in the Greco-Roman practice of prosopological exegesis, in which interpreters assigned characters, or "faces" (*prosōpa*), to speakers or addressees in classical texts, to clarify their meaning and resolve any apparent difficulties within them (Bates 2015; Pierce 2020).

Scriptural words are similarly ascribed to Jesus, or to other new speakers, in the New Testament (e.g., Matt. 21:9; Luke 12:14; John 12:13; Heb. 13:6). The occasion of their utterance can also be precisely stated or recontextualized, so that they become associated with a particular event in the life of Jesus (e.g., Heb. 1:6; 10:5). Likewise, verses with a general referent can be applied to a specific person. The one whose habitation must become desolate according to Psalm 69:25 is identified as Judas in Acts 1:16–20, for example. The generic sufferings of the psalmist also become in the Gospels the concrete expression of the sufferings of Jesus, who is betrayed by false witnesses and abandoned at his death by his friends and relatives (Matt. 26:20–25, 58–60; 27:55; Mark 14:17–21, 54–56; 15:40; Luke 22:54; 23:49; cf. Pss. 27:12; 38:11; 41:9; see further Docherty 2018, 84–87).

Contemporizing Interpretation

In many forms of early Jewish exegesis, the Scriptures are understood as containing definite predictions about either the present situation or the eagerly awaited eschatological future. This heightens their direct relevance to contemporary readers. This hermeneutical approach is very visible in the Qumran pesharim, in which phrases from a quoted scriptural verse are related to known figures in the sect's past or current experience, as in this extract from the commentary on Habakkuk: "And what it says: 'Since you pillaged many peoples all the rest of the nations will pillage you [Hab. 2:8a]).' Its interpretation concerns the last priests of Jerusalem, who will accumulate riches and loot from plundering the nations. However, in the last days their riches and their loot will be given into the hands of the army of the Kittim" (1QpHab IX, 2–7 [trans. García Martínez and Tigchelaar 1997, 1:19]).

Throughout the books of the Apocrypha, too, scriptural texts are applied to both climactic moments in the history of the nation (e.g., the fall of Jerusalem to the Romans, Pss. Sol. 2.20–21; 8.14–16; cf. Isa. 3:24–26; 19:14; 51:17–23; or the slaughter of the Hasideans on the orders of the high priest Alcimus, 1 Macc. 7:16–17; cf. Ps. 79:2–3) and details in the life of an individual (e.g., Tobit's burial of the corpse of a murdered Jew, Tob. 2:6; cf. Amos 8:10; see also the faith of the Maccabean martyrs, 2 Macc. 7:6; cf. Deut. 32:36). It seems, therefore, that each verse was regarded as containing within itself an infinite number of possible meanings, so that it could be reused repeatedly and flexibly in new circumstances. The evidence of the New Testament indicates that the first followers of Jesus similarly mined the Scriptures for "prophecies," which they saw as foretelling the life and death of their founder, or events in their own community history (e.g., Matt. 1:23; 4:12–17; 8:14–17; John 2:14–22; 12:36–43; Acts 1:15–26).

Models for New Narratives

Finally, the Scriptures clearly serve as models for most of the literature produced in the late Second Temple period. Prayers and hymns (e.g., the Qumran Hodayot; see Hughes 2006) are patterned on the older Psalms, for example, and scriptural forms and language are widely adopted in new narratives. The account of the life of an early Israelite ruler Kenaz that appears in the Biblical Antiquities (LAB 25–29), for instance, appears to be created out of the traditional stories about Gideon (see Judg. 7). The author of 1 Maccabees closely follows the style of the books of the Former Prophets in recounting the exploits of the Maccabean leaders (Chester 1988), thereby portraying them as worthy and legitimate successors to the early judges and kings appointed for Israel by God (Choi 2021). Elsewhere in the deuterocanonical writings, Judith's actions in freeing her people from a foreign oppressor imitate those of scriptural figures such as Deborah (Jdt. 8:33; cf. Judg. 4:9) and Jael (Jdt. 13:18; cf. Judg. 5:24), and the characterization of Tobit combines elements of the righteous patriarch Abraham (e.g., Tob. 4:12–13; 6:9–12; cf. Gen. 24:1–67), the successful Israelite abroad Joseph (Tob.

1:13, 22; cf. Gen. 39:1–6), and the innocent sufferer Job (Tob. 1:19–2:14; cf. Job 1:1–22).

Scriptural narratives similarly provide models for the presentation of Jesus's life within the New Testament Gospels. He is presented there as a new Moses (e.g., Matt. 2:12–20; 5:1–7:29; see Allison 1993), for example, or a second Elijah (e.g., Luke 4:24–27; 7:11–17; see Brodie 2000). The opening chapters of Luke replicate scriptural language and style particularly closely, in order to set the birth of Jesus in the context of the scriptural promises of mercy and salvation (Litwak 2005, 66–115). The scholarly debate continues about the extent to which these texts reflect genuine historical memories couched in scripturally inspired language, or whether they are better described as largely fictional narratives, created to make Jesus fit with scriptural models (Vette 2022, 199–206).

Understanding of Scripture

The interpretive methods described in this chapter flow from underlying axioms about the nature of Scripture. The drive to make connections between its different sections, for instance, is prompted by a belief that it is a coherent whole, reflecting the consistency of God's speech and actions. The intense exegetical focus on small units of text illustrates the presupposition that every word of Scripture (even its individual letters) is an essential part of God's revelation, which needs to be understood. The reapplication of these scriptural words to new speakers and circumstances underscores their enduring relevance: since their message is regarded as extending far beyond the single situation in which they were first uttered, they can be addressed directly to contemporary issues. Scripture is viewed as inherently polyvalent, therefore, containing multiple meanings to be uncovered by the skilled interpreter. It is far more than simply a record of God's past dealings with Israel; rather, it serves as an ever-living divine word that continues to speak to God's people for all time.

Conclusion

Early Jewish exegetes sought to make sense of their traditional authoritative texts and to redeploy them in new compositions in a rich variety of creative ways, including through copying, rewriting, expanding, imitating, quoting, and commenting on them. New Testament interpretation of Scripture is fully understood only when placed in this context. The first followers of Jesus applied the same hermeneutical tools as other Second Temple Jews to a shared corpus of writings, albeit often reaching different conclusions about their ultimate meaning.

Works Cited

Adams, Sean A., and Seth M. Ehorn, eds. 2016. *Composite Citations in Antiquity*. Vol. 1, *Jewish, Graeco-Roman and Early Christian Uses*. LNTS 525. London: T&T Clark.

———, eds. 2018. *Composite Citations in Antiquity*. Vol. 2, *New Testament Uses*. LNTS 593. London: T&T Clark.

Ahearne-Kroll, Patricia D. 2019. "The History of the Study of the Pseudepigrapha." In *The Old Testament Pseudepigrapha: Fifty Years of the Pseudepigrapha Section at the SBL*, edited by Matthias Henze and Liv Ingeborg Lied, 103–31. EJL 50. Atlanta: SBL Press.

Albl, Martin C. 1999. *"And Scripture Cannot Be Broken": The Form and Function of the Early Christian* Testimonia *Collections*. NovTSup 96. Leiden: Brill.

Alexander, Philip S. 2000. "The Bible in Qumran and Early Judaism." In *Texts in Context: Essays by Members of the Society for Old Testament Study*, edited by A. D. H. Mayes, 35–62. Oxford: Oxford University Press.

Allison, Dale C. 1993. *The New Moses: A Matthean Typology*. Minneapolis: Augsburg Fortress.

Bakhos, Carol, ed. 2006. *Current Trends in the Study of Midrash*. JSJSup 106. Leiden: Brill.

Bates, Matthew W. 2015. *The Birth of the Trinity: Jesus, God and Spirit in New Testament and Early Christian Interpretation of the Old Testament*. Oxford: Oxford University Press.

Bernstein, Moshe J. 2000. "Interpretation of Scriptures." In vol. 1 of *Encyclopedia of the Dead Sea Scrolls*, edited by Lawrence H. Shiffman and James C. VanderKam, 376–83. New York: Oxford University Press.

Brodie, Thomas L. 2000. *The Crucial Bridge: The Elijah-Elisha Narrative as an Interpretive Synthesis of Genesis-Kings and a Literary Model for the Gospels*. Collegeville, MN: Liturgical Press.

Brooke, George J. 1997. "'The Canon within the Canon,' at Qumran and in the New Testament." In *The Scrolls and the Scriptures: Qumran Fifty Years After*, edited by Stanley E. Porter and Craig A. Evans, 242–66. JSPSup 26. Sheffield: Sheffield Academic.

———. 2005. "The Qumran Scrolls and the Demise of the Distinction between Higher and Lower Criticism." In *New Directions in Qumran Studies: Proceedings of the Bristol Colloquium on the Dead Sea Scrolls, 8–10 September 2003*, edited by Jonathan G. Campbell, William John Lyons, and Lloyd K. Pietersen, 26–42. LSTS 52. London: T&T Clark.

———. 2006. "Biblical Interpretation at Qumran." In *Scripture and the Scrolls*, edited by James H. Charlesworth, 287–319. Vol. 1 of *The Bible and the Dead Sea Scrolls*. Waco: Baylor University Press.

Campbell, Jonathan G. 2004. *The Exegetical Texts*. CQS 4. New York: T&T Clark.

Carr, David. 2005. *Writing on the Tablet of the Heart: Origins of Scripture and Literature*. New York: Oxford University Press.

Chester, Andrew. 1988. "Citing the Old Testament." In *It Is Written: Scripture Citing Scripture: Essays in Honour of Barnabas Lindars*, edited by D. A. Carson and Hugh G. M. Williamson, 141–69. Cambridge: Cambridge University Press.

Choi, Dongbin. 2021. *The Use and Function of Scripture in 1 Maccabees*. LSTS 98. London: Bloomsbury.

Crawford, Sidnie White. 2008. *Rewriting Scripture in Second Temple Times*. Grand Rapids: Eerdmans.

Docherty, Susan E. 2018. "Exegetical Techniques in the New Testament and 'Rewritten Bible': A Comparative Analysis." In *Ancient Readers and Their Scriptures: Engaging the Hebrew Bible in Early Judaism and Christianity*, edited by Garrick V. Allen and John A. Dunne, 77–97. Leiden: Brill.

Evans, Craig A. 2015. "Why Did the New Testament Writers Appeal to the Old Testament?" *JSNT* 38: 36–48.

Fisk, Bruce N. 2001. *Do You Not Remember? Scripture, Story and Exegesis in the Rewritten Bible of Pseudo-Philo*. Sheffield: Sheffield Academic.

Fletcher, Michelle. 2017. *Reading Revelation as Pastiche: Imitating the Past*. LNTS 571. London: T&T Clark.

Flint, Peter W. 1999. *The Dead Sea Psalms Scrolls and the Book of Psalms*. STDJ 17. Leiden: Brill.

García Martínez, Florentino, and Eibert J. C. Tigchelaar. 1997. *The Dead Sea Scrolls Study Edition.* 2 vols. Leiden: Brill.

Henze, Matthias, ed. 2012. *A Companion to Biblical Interpretation in Early Judaism.* Grand Rapids: Eerdmans.

Horgan, Maurya P. 1979. *Pesharim: Qumran Interpretations of Biblical Books.* Catholic Biblical Quarterly Monograph Series 8. Washington: Catholic Biblical Association of America Press.

Hose, Martin, and David Schenker, eds. 2016. *A Companion to Greek Literature.* BCAW. Oxford: Wiley-Blackwell.

Hughes, Julie A. 2006. *Scriptural Allusions and Exegesis in the Hodayot.* STDJ 59. Leiden: Brill.

Jobes, Karen H. 1992. "The Function of Paronomasia in Hebrews 10:5–7." *Trinity Journal* 13: 181–91.

Kugel, James L. 2010. "Early Jewish Biblical Interpretation." In *The Eerdmans Dictionary of Early Judaism,* edited by John J. Collins and Daniel C. Harlow, 121–41. Grand Rapids: Eerdmans.

Lim, Timothy H. 2002. *Pesharim.* CQS 3. London: Sheffield Academic.

Litwak, Kenneth D. 2005. *Echoes of Scripture in Luke-Acts: Telling the History of God's People Intertextually.* LNTS 282. London: T&T Clark.

McDonald, Lee Martin. 2017. *The Formation of the Biblical Canon.* Vol. 1, *The Old Testament: Its Authority and Canonicity.* London: Bloomsbury.

Menken, Maarten J. J. 2004. *Matthew's Bible: The Old Testament Text of the Evangelist.* Bibliotheca Ephemeridum Theologicarum Lovaniensium 173. Leuven: Peeters.

Newman, Judith H. 1999. *Praying by the Book: The Scripturalization of Prayer in Second Temple Judaism.* EJL 14. Atlanta: Scholars Press.

Nickelsburg, George W. E. 1992. "Son of Man." *ABD* 6:137–50.

Norton, Jonathan D. H. 2011. *Contours in the Text: Textual Variation in the Writings of Josephus, Paul and the Yahad.* LNTS 430. London: T&T Clark.

Pierce, Madison. 2020. *Divine Discourse in the Epistle to the Hebrews: The Recontextualization of Spoken Quotations of Scripture.* SNTSMS 178. Cambridge: Cambridge University Press.

Samely, Alexander. 1992. *The Interpretation of Speech in the Pentateuch Targums.* TSAJ 27. Tübingen: Mohr Siebeck.

———. 2002. *Rabbinic Interpretation of Scripture in the Mishnah.* Oxford: Oxford University Press.

———. 2007. *Forms of Rabbinic Literature and Thought: An Introduction.* Oxford: Oxford University Press.

Stendahl, Krister. 1954. *The School of St. Matthew, and Its Use of the Old Testament.* Acta Seminarii Neotestamentici Upsaliensis 20. Lund: Gleerup.

Steyn, Gert J. 2011. *A Quest for the Assumed LXX Vorlage of the Explicit Quotations in Hebrews.* FRLANT 235. Göttingen: Vandenhoeck & Ruprecht.

Tov, Emanuel. 2002. "The Biblical Texts from the Judaean Desert: An Overview and Analysis." In *The Bible as Book,* edited by Edward D. Herbert and Emanuel Tov, 139–66. New Castle, DE: Oak Knoll.

VanderKam, James C. 2012. *The Dead Sea Scrolls and the Bible.* Grand Rapids: Eerdmans.

Vette, Nathanael. 2022. *Writing with Scripture: Scripturalized Narrative in the Gospel of Mark.* LNTS 670. London: T&T Clark.

Zahn, Molly M. 2020. *Genres of Rewriting in Second Temple Judaism: Scribal Transmission and Composition.* Cambridge: Cambridge University Press.

21

Reading Strategies
in the Greco-Roman World

MAREN R. NIEHOFF

To appreciate the reading strategies embedded in the New Testament, it is initially important to realize that all the treatises in this collection were written in Greek, rather than in Hebrew, for example. This linguistic fact orients us toward Greco-Roman culture, which would have been familiar not only to the authors of the New Testament writings but also to their implied readers (Ehrman 2000). Given the Greek flavor of the New Testament, many scholars have adduced Greco-Roman philosophy, culture, and material evidence to understand its various texts (e.g., Malherbe 1989, 2014; Breytenbach 2015). The dimension of biblical interpretation, on the other hand, is regarded as a quintessentially Jewish activity, perhaps even *sui generis* and thus in contrast to the Greco-Roman world. Scholars therefore often contextualize early Christian interpretations of Scripture in view of Hebrew sources from the Dead Sea Scrolls and later rabbinic literature (see also chap. 20, "Practices of Interpretation," above). Such comparisons, however, must account for the cultural and linguistic gap between the New

Testament and the Dead Sea Scrolls. Yet the dichotomy between Greco-Roman and Jewish collapses if we recognize that most Jews at the time of the New Testament were Greek speakers who developed biblical interpretation along the lines of Greek reading strategies (Niehoff 2024). Greek hermeneutics, which were practiced by both pagans and Jews, therefore become relevant for understanding the New Testament. Indeed, even the assumed dichotomy between pagan and Jewish exegesis is artificial, as pagan scholars in Alexandria developed sophisticated forms of hermeneutics, which subsequently inspired pagan, Jewish, and Christian exegetes (Niehoff 2011, 2012; Schironi 2018; Paz 2022). Such contacts are not at all surprising given that the Homeric epics became the canonical text of the Greek-speaking world long before the Bible was formally fixed. Like the Jewish Scriptures, the epics provided everything from preliminary grammar to literary, religious, and philosophical foundations (Finkelberg 2012, 2020). During the time of the New Testament, additional Greco-Roman reading strategies became popular, and they, too, drew the attention of Jewish and Christian exegetes.

This essay looks behind the scenes of the New Testament by drawing attention to the diversity of Greco-Roman hermeneutics, which were well known to a broad spectrum of people in the first centuries CE, including the majority of Jews who lived in the diaspora. Most prominent among these are scholarly approaches based on grammar and systematic commentary, allegorical readings, and strategies looking for exemplary heroes who could be instantly imitated by the readers. This essay will explain each strategy in its original pagan context, then show Jewish engagements with it, and conclude by raising the question whether these strategies are also evident in the New Testament. To what extent, in other words, did early Christian interpreters of the Scriptures follow the example of their Jewish predecessors in creatively adopting pagan hermeneutics and participating in wider Greco-Roman discourses? The respective choice of reading strategies that were available also had deep cultural and even political implications: while the study of grammar and systematic commentaries was associated with the elitist environment of second-century BCE Alexandria, exemplarity became highly popular in the diverse and rather more informal discourses of imperial Rome. We can thus also ask whether early Christian interpreters favored a more traditional and secluded approach or joined widely accessible and topical trends.[1]

Grammar and Systematic Commentary

From cradle to grave, Greek speakers engaged with the canonical texts of Homer. Grammar, as Philo of Alexandria explains in a famous autobiographical passage, was the preliminary study of the poets, which ensured a correct

reading before higher goals of education, such as philosophy, could be attained (*Prelim. Studies* 74). The study of grammar and the literal text reached a peak in second-century BCE Alexandria, then an important metropolis of culture and research under the patronage of the Ptolemaic kings (Fraser 1972; Schliesser et al. 2021). Homeric scholars developed a new approach by critically studying the text according to literary methods and historical criteria. They emended the text using a system of critical signs and reconstructed Homer's epics in an authoritative way that is still accepted today (Schironi 2011; Paz 2022, 28–38). For this purpose, they carefully analyzed his characteristic style and intended message, cleansing it from later accretions. Their major achievement was the invention of systematic literary commentary, based on a line-for-line quotation, articulation of a problem or question, and its solution by scholarly techniques. Characteristic of the Alexandrian approach is also diversity of opinions. Various scholars engaged in conversation with each other, and each established his particular views in relation to his colleagues, none of whom claimed superhuman authority.

Aristarchus of Samothrace (2nd c. BCE) was the best and most influential of the Alexandrian grammarians and commentators, and his comprehensive work can be reconstructed from numerous fragments preserved in the various scholia (Schironi 2018). Inspired by the literary methods of Aristotle's *Poetics*, he produced two successive editions of the text as well as running commentaries. Critical signs in the margins of the edition alerted the reader to inauthentic lines or literary peculiarities, which were then explained in the commentary (Schironi 2012). Whether or not he ever pronounced the famous principle, preserved by Porphyry, that Homer is to be elucidated by Homer, he paid special attention to the internal coherence of the entire corpus. Assuming that Homer had authored both the *Iliad* and the *Odyssey*, Aris-

---

1. Unless otherwise indicated, translations in this chapter are my own.

tarchus inquired into his characteristic style and presentation of dramatic figures.

Issues of verisimilitude and contradictions between lines became central concerns. Insisting that Homer could not have written anything "ridiculous," Aristarchus bracketed or rejected some epic lines, because "horses do not drink wine" and "it is implausible that horses speak" (*Scholia Graeca in Homeri Iliadem* 1.100a, 19.416–17a [ed. Erbse 1969, 37; 1975, 648]). He moreover addressed problems of contradictions, often solving them by suggesting a gap in the text. In his view, the poet remains silent about certain things, which the reader must conjecture and fill in. Aristarchus dealt, for example, with a tension between two lines, one of which presents Achilles as laying down his weapon, while the other assumes that he carried it. Asking where the weapon suddenly came from, Aristarchus suggests that Achilles picked it up in the space between the lines even though the poet does not explicitly say so (*Scholia Graeca in Homeri Iliadem* 21.17a). The hallmark of Aristarchus's work is a literal approach, based on literary analysis and the search for authorial intention. In this way, a serious attempt was made to understand Homer as an author in his time.

Alexandrian Jews participated in the intellectual debates of their environment and interpreted their Scriptures in the Greek translation accordingly. They quickly became familiar with the scholarly methods of their Homeric colleagues, and lively debates seem to have emerged regarding their relevance to the interpretation of the Jewish Scriptures. Philo, the best-preserved Jewish interpreter active in the early first century CE, criticizes Jewish exegetes who compared the biblical story of the tower of Babel to a similar story in Homer and concluded that both were mythical (*Confusion* 1–15). Scattered references throughout his works moreover indicate that some Jews seem to have corrected the biblical text according to grammatical and literary criteria (Niehoff

2011, 112–30). Philo himself, as well as other Alexandrian Jews whose writings have been partially preserved thanks to later Christian authors, adopted a more conservative approach and engaged the new methods only in order to preserve the text and highlight its intact theological message.

The earliest evidence of such use is preserved in the Letter of Aristeas (2nd c. BCE), which explains the Greek translation of the Hebrew Bible as an initiative of Demetrius, the chief librarian in Alexandria. The anonymous author calls for a fixation of the text and imagines a scene of canonization in the community of Alexandria, which inverses the critical dynamics of scholarship.[2] A curse is pronounced against anyone "who will introduce an interpolation by either adding or generally transferring something of what is written or by making a deletion." Aristeas explains that this warning aimed at preserving the scrolls forever (Let. Aris. 310–11). While criticizing the application of Alexandrian scholarship to the study of the Jewish Bible, he provides a priceless window into the world of other Alexandrian Jews who seem to have marked the biblical text and corrected features they perceived to be literary flaws.

Demetrius, a Jewish interpreter active in Alexandria in the second century BCE, examines problems of contradiction and verisimilitude. Even though we possess only tiny fragments of his work, he seems to have systematically analyzed the biblical text in its Greek translation. He asks, for example, "how the Israelites had weapons, seeing that they departed from Egypt unarmed." This problem arises out of a tension between Exodus 5:3, where Moses's departure without weapons is anticipated, and 17:8–9, where the Israelites are involved in a military confrontation with Amalek. The problem is solved via Aristarchus's notion of a gap in the text, which the author left for the

---

2. For different views, see Honigman 2003.

reader to fill in. Demetrius suggests that the Israelites used the weapons of the Egyptians who had drowned in the Red Sea. Demetrius also discusses problems of verisimilitude. He asks why "Joseph at the meal gave a five-fold portion to Benjamin even though he was incapable of taking in such quantities of meat," assuming that the Bible would not suggest an unrealistic portion of food. Demetrius solves the problem by showing that Joseph was concerned about the symbolical value of the food, wishing to create an equal standing between him and his maternal brother and the rest of the brothers (fragments in Eusebius, *Praep. ev.* 9.29.16; 9.21.14).

Philo uses the Alexandrian scholarly methods in the most comprehensive manner and produces a systematic commentary on Genesis. Addressing fellow Jews in his hometown who are also versed in the Scriptures, he explicitly quotes consecutive verses, addresses specific formulations or problems in each of them, and then offers solutions, which sometimes also relate to alternative interpretations. The numerous treatises of *Allegorical Interpretation* abound with scholarly expressions relating to the literal level. Typical expressions include "let us now examine the following [phrase]," "the question next in sequence," "why [was it written]," and "one must investigate" (*Alleg. Interp.* 1.2; 1.33; 1.101; *Posterity* 32; *Worse* 32; *Sobriety* 31; 62; *Flight* 157). Philo regularly addresses problems of verisimilitude and contradictions between verses as a springboard for broader teachings, usually in allegorical style. He assumes that these "stumbling blocks" were intended by Moses, the author of the Scriptures, as hermeneutic stimulations to reach beyond the literal sense. Moses emerges as a divinely inspired author who left behind a work of unblemished literary style with sublime messages.

Looking at the New Testament from an Alexandrian perspective, one is taken by surprise. While the New Testament is replete with echoes of Scripture and sometimes even uses introductory formulas, such as "it is written," none of its texts assumes the form of a systematic commentary, which would have entailed running quotations of consecutive verses and their separate elucidation based on the identification of specific problems. No interest is explicitly articulated in the authentic version of the biblical text. Problems of contradictions between verses or cases of implausibility are not brought to the readers' attention, even though some modern scholars may be inclined to reconstruct them indirectly. Early Christian writers thus did not see themselves as systematic commentators in the Alexandrian tradition and did not adopt its well-known, highly elitist format. It is worthwhile to contemplate this insight for a moment, especially as it contrasts with later Christian traditions. The church father Origen, who was educated in third-century CE Alexandria and later transferred to Caesarea, embraced Alexandrian scholarship and inaugurated systematic commentary activities on both the Old and the New Testament writings (Neuschäfer 1987; Schironi 2012; Niehoff 2022). His scholarly style differed so much from Paul's rhetoric that he sometimes frowned on the apostle and made considerable efforts to integrate him into his own universe and that of radically changing Christian hermeneutics (Niehoff forthcoming).

Characteristic of this turn away from Alexandrian perspectives in the New Testament is Paul's highly rhetorical use of the Scriptures. As Richard Hays (1989) and David Lincicum (2020) have highlighted, Paul is not interested in understanding the Scriptures on their own terms or analyzing each of its verses, but rather he alludes to them in his argumentative strides. Tellingly, he pays little attention to Moses as the author of the Jewish Scriptures, a fact that is especially noteworthy in view of his praise of Isaiah and David as authors, whose texts, however, are also not submitted to systematic commentary (Niehoff 2020). These features resonate with the critical references in the Gospels to the grammarians, who feature next to the Pharisees as narrow-minded literalists and miss the essential points of their own Scriptures. Jesus's teaching is instead said to be based on his own authority, which instantly impresses people and has the power to drive out demons (e.g., Mark 1:22; Luke 5:30; Matt. 7:28–29). The frequent references in the New Testament to the Jewish Scriptures and the phrase "as it is written" must therefore be contextualized outside of the Alexandrian academy.

Allegory

From ancient times onward, allegory accompanied the interpretation of canonical texts, especially in cases of difficult or obscure passages (Boys-Stones 2003). The oldest available text in an allegorical mode is the Derveni papyrus discovered in modern Greece in 1962 (Tsantsanoglou, Parássoglou, and Kouremenos 2006). Dating back to the fifth century BCE, it offers an allegorical commentary on an Orphic poem, translating an enigmatic myth about the gods into philosophical language (Betegh 2004). The Stoic school subsequently became famous for allegorical interpretations of the Homeric epics, which often ignored authorial intention and instead used etymology to claim a meaning not even known to the author. While the early evidence is highly fragmentary, we possess a complete text from the first century CE—namely, the *Greek Theology* of L. Annaeus Cornutus (Boys-Stones 2018). Just to give one example, the demi-god Heracles represents in Cornutus's view "universal reason," a central pillar of Stoic ethics (*Theol. Graec.* 31).

Among Jews, Philo of Alexandria developed the allegorical method most systematically. Allegory removes "stumbling blocks" in the text and offers solutions to textual problems (*Confusion* 14). Cain's flight from God in Genesis 4:16, for example, creates an "impression greatly at variance with truth," since God is omnipresent

and flight from him impossible (*Posterity* 1). Since Moses must nevertheless have had good reasons for expressing himself thus, "nothing is meant literally," and the "path of allegory" must be chosen (*Posterity* 7). Philo concludes: "Perhaps then, as these things diverge from the truth, it is better to say allegorically that Cain intended to set up his own creed as one builds a city" (*Posterity* 49–50). Similarly, regarding the cleansing of the trees mentioned in Leviticus 19:23, Philo says that its literal meaning is "not very much in accord" and therefore an allegorical reading is required (*Planting* 113). Philo also addresses the "startling paradox" that Sarah is said to be at once sterile and exceedingly prolific (*Prelim. Studies* 3). He solves the problem by asserting that Sarah symbolizes virtue, which is barren regarding all that is bad but fruitful concerning the good (*Prelim. Studies* 3).

From an allegorical perspective, too, the New Testament holds a surprise. The Classical terms of allegory—namely, *symbolon* and *allegoria*—are not mentioned, while *hyponoia* appears only once in a nontechnical sense. Against this background Paul's single use of the verb "to allegorize" in Galatians 4:24 deserves attention. He explains here his idea of two covenants via the allegory of Abraham's two wives, Sarah and Hagar:

> For it is written that Abraham had two sons, one by a slave and one by a free woman. But the son from the slave woman was born according to the flesh, the one of the free woman through [divine] promise. These things are meant allegorically: these women are two covenants, one from Mount Sinai, bearing children into slavery—this is Hagar. For Hagar is Mount Sinai in Arabia, she resembles Jerusalem nowadays and is a slave with her children. But the Jerusalem above is free and she is our mother. (4:22–26 RSV, modified)

Paul introduces his allegory with a scriptural reference ("it is written") without, however, quoting a specific verse, as was common for ancient allegorists. While Genesis 16:15 mentions the birth of Ishmael and Genesis 21:2 that of Isaac, no verse says, "Abraham had two sons." Moreover, Paul does not tackle an obscurity in the text in order to defend the author but, on the contrary, inverts the biblical story by claiming that Ishmael persecuted Isaac, contrary to Genesis 21:9–10. This bold rereading of the biblical text under the rubric of allegory does not conform to known strategies of ancient allegory and therefore naturally aroused Origen's puzzlement. He finds it "astonishing" that the apostle "called things 'allegorical'" that are quite obviously done in the flesh (Origen, *Hom. Gen.* 7.2). He moreover questions Paul's interpretation of Ishmael's persecution: "Next, I wonder also about the Apostle who called this play [between Isaac and Ismael] a persecution . . . when certainly no persecution of Ismael against Isaac is related to have taken place" (*Hom. Gen.* 7.3). Already in antiquity it was thus recognized that Paul's interpretation of Sarah and Hagar did not conform to common practices of allegory, which usually defended a canonical text from accusations of literary flaws, and involved instead a contradiction of the biblical story, thus in a way creating problems where there had been none before. Addressing these issues, several scholars have pointed out that Paul in fact enriches the biblical plot with his own experience of persecution, as related in the opening chapters of Galatians (e.g., Standhartinger 2018). The biblical story is applied to the present situation of the interpreter and thus implies typology, which must be carefully distinguished from allegory (contrary to Martens 2008), and leads us to the third reading strategy.

Exemplarity

Canonical texts in antiquity were also accessed through the lens of exemplarity. This approach collapses the distance between the text and the reader, suggesting that literary heroes can be embraced as personal models as if they were alive here and now. The individual reader assumes center stage, selecting without further ado role models suitable to current needs. The text itself recedes into the background, and no hermeneutic strategies are required to unlock it. Remarkable license is given to individual interpreters. The school most associated with an ethics of imitation is the Cynic school, founded by Diogenes of Sinope, who became famous for mocking Plato because of his overtly theoretical approach and conventional methods of teaching in the Academy (Branham 1996). The Cynics taught in every venue of life, preferably in open marketplaces, and thus not only attracted large crowds but also reached many of the less educated (Moles 1995, 1996; Brancacci 1992a, 1992b). No expert training was necessary to follow their lectures and understand them.

In imperial Rome discourses of exemplarity became central in a wide variety of works (Langlands 2018; Roller 2018). Philo of Alexandria proves especially illuminating and offers relevant examples of reading Classical Greek literature for exemplarity. He himself spent several years in Rome as the head of the Jewish embassy and wrote many of his works in that context, addressing Greek-speaking readers in the capital of the empire (Niehoff 2018). One of his later Roman treatises, *That Every Good Person Is Free*, contains four anecdotes about Diogenes at the slave market confronting potential buyers with free speech (*Good Person* 121–24). In one of them he quotes Homer to encourage his depressed fellows:

> He [Diogenes] then received sufficient food and when he was about to be sold, together with other prisoners, he first sat down and dined most bravely, sharing also with those near him. As one of them, however, could not bear the situation and became instead very downcast, he said: "will you not stop

brooding? Make the best of the present circumstances! 'For even fair-haired Niobe thought of food, even though her twelve children perished in her halls, six daughters and six sons in their prime'" [*Il*. 24.602–4]. (*Good Person* 122)

In this anecdote Niobe, who reacted heroically to the loss of all her children, serves as a straightforward model. Diogenes encourages his comrades to embrace her virtue in their untoward situation and overcome their grief by looking at her. The canonical text is read literally and applied to the present. The next anecdote in Philo's treatise shows that Cynic hermeneutics could also be surprisingly subversive. Chaereas, an imitator of Diogenes, wittily addresses the Ptolemaic king with an emended Homeric verse:

> An imitator of Diogenes' freedom of speech was a certain Chaereas, one of the educated. For while he was living in Alexandria by Egypt, Ptolemy once became angry and threatened him exceedingly. But he considered his own innate freedom nothing inferior to the former's kingship and retorted: "rule the Egyptians, but I do not care about you, nor do I mind that you are angry" [*Il*. 1.180–81]. (*Good Person* 125)

Chaereas playfully twists the received text of the *Iliad* 1.180, replacing the Myrmidons (i.e., Achilles's men) with the Egyptians. This version bends the meter and is attested nowhere else in the extant Greek literature, including the ancient scholia (*Scholia Graeca in Homeri Iliadem* 1.180). Chaereas humorously changes the text to render it relevant to his own situation. Philo provides a unique testimony to an ancient joke, which subversively adapts the Homeric line to suit the requirements of parrhesia. Paul's interpretation of Sarah and Hagar, with the surprising twist on persecution, seems to belong to the same category. It is also based on knowledge of the canonical plot

and anticipates a smile on the part of the readers for the wittiness of the interpretation. It, too, applies an ancient text to the interpreter's immediate situation and solves a problem of difficult power relations.

Beyond the specific case of Galatians 4, the New Testament abounds with readings for exemplarity that resonate with pagan and Jewish predecessors and contemporaries. Indeed, the New Testament authors seem to be most familiar with this reading strategy, which is the most accessible and topical one at their time. Paul especially engages the Jewish Scriptures with a view to using biblical figures as role models for his readers. Not interested in scholarly commentaries or allegorical defenses of minute textual details, he instead applies a specific motive to present-day situations. The keywords are "type" and "typological," as in Romans 5:14, 6:17, and 1 Corinthians 10:6–13. The letter to the Romans prominently sets up Abraham as a role model, who is described for the sake of the readers (Rom. 4:23–24). The letter to the Hebrews similarly presents a gallery of biblical heroes who exemplify the virtues of faith and trust (Heb. 11; Alexander, forthcoming 2024).

Conclusion

Early Christian readings of the Jewish Scriptures benefit from contextualization in Greco-Roman hermeneutics, which had already been fully embraced by Greek-speaking Jewish exegetes. Rather than assuming a dichotomy between Jewish exegesis (often identified with Hebrew sources from Qumran) and Greco-Roman culture, we must look at reading strategies in Greek. These strategies were likely to be known by the authors and readers of the New Testament, which was also written in Greek. This essay has introduced the three main types of Greek hermeneutics prevalent among both pagans and Jews: scholarly interpretations based on grammar and systematic commentary, allegorical readings, and a hermeneutics of exemplarity. It has become clear that scholarly approaches associated with the highly elitist Alexandrian tradition are virtually absent from the New Testament, which shuns the format of systematic commentary. The next strategy—namely, allegory—is mentioned only once, but in a rather untypical fashion, so that Paul's allegory of Sarah and Hagar in Galatians was already noted as an exception in antiquity. The most prominent reading strategy of the New Testament is a hermeneutics of imitation, which was especially used by the Cynics in their teaching in all venues of life. This method also became popular in imperial Rome and informed the reception of the Classical Greek tradition. The New Testament authors, with Paul as their leading figure, thus inscribed themselves into the most accessible and topical approach of reading canonical texts. While Philo of Alexandria, known for his systematic, allegorical commentary of the Jewish Scriptures, shows an awareness of the attractions of exemplarity and began to partially apply it in his interpretation of the biblical patriarchs, Paul and his followers went much further and reached crowds of new dimensions.

Works Cited

Alexander, Philip. Forthcoming 2024. "Philo of Alexandria and Hebrews in the Context of the Roman Empire: Revisiting the Question of their Relationship." In *The Art of Contextualizing Philo of Alexandria*, edited by Maren R. Niehoff. Tübingen: Mohr Siebeck.

Betegh, Gabor. 2004. *The Derveni Papyrus: Cosmology, Theology and Interpretation*. Cambridge: Cambridge University Press.

Boys-Stones, George R., ed. 2003. *Metaphor and Allegory: Classical Studies in Theory and Practice*. Oxford: Oxford University Press.

———. 2018. *L. Annaeus Cornutus: Greek Theology, Fragments, and Testimonia*. Atlanta: SBL Press.

Brancacci, Aldo. 1992a. "I 'koinêi areskonta' dei Cinici e la 'koinônia' tra cinismo e stoicismo nel libro VI (103–105) delle 'Vite' di Diogene Laerzio." *ANRW* 36: 4049–75.

———. 1992b. "*Cinismo e predicazione popolare.*" In *La produzione e la circolazione del testo*, edited by Giuseppe Cambiano, Luciano Canfora, and Diego Lanza, 433–55. Lo spazio letterario della Grecia antica 3.1. Rome: Salerno.

Branham, R. Bracht. 1996. "Defacing the Currency: Diogenes' Rhetoric and the Invention of Cynicism." In *The Cynics: The Cynic Movement in Antiquity and Its Legacy*, edited by R. Bracht Branham and Marie-Odile Goulet-Cazé, 81–104. Berkeley: University of California Press.

Breytenbach, Cilliers, ed. 2015. *Paul's Graeco-Roman Context*. Leuven: Peeters.

Ehrman, Bart D. 2000. *The New Testament: A Historical Introduction to the Early Christian Writings*. New York: Oxford University Press.

Erbse, Hartmut. 1969. *Scholia Graeca in Homeri Iliadem*. Vol. 1. Berlin: de Gruyter.

———. 1975. *Scholia Graeca in Homeri Iliadem*. Vol. 4. Berlin: de Gruyter.

Finkelberg, Margalit. 2012. "Canonizing and Decanonizing Homer: Reception of the Homeric Poems in Antiquity and Modernity." In *Homer and the Bible in the Eyes of Ancient Interpreters*, edited by Maren R. Niehoff, 15–28. Leiden: Brill.

———. 2020. *Homer and Early Greek Epic: Collected Essays*. Boston: de Gruyter.

Fraser, Peter Marshall. 1972. *Ptolemaic Alexandria*. 3 vols. Oxford: Clarendon.

Hays, Richard. 1989. *Echoes of Scripture in the Letters of Paul*. New Haven: Yale University Press.

Honigman, Sylvie. 2003. *The Septuagint and Homeric Scholarship in Alexandria*. London: Routledge.

Langlands, Rebecca. 2018. *Exemplary Ethics in Ancient Rome*. Cambridge: Cambridge University Press.

Lincicum, David. 2020. "How Did Paul Read Scripture?" In *The New Cambridge Companion to St. Paul*, edited by Bruce W. Longenecker, 225–38. Cambridge: Cambridge University Press.

Malherbe, Abraham J. 1989. *Paul and the Popular Philosophers*. Minneapolis: Fortress.

———. 2014. *Light from the Gentiles: Hellenistic Philosophy and Early Christianity: Collected Essays, 1959–2012*. Leiden: Brill.

Martens, Peter W. 2008. "Revisiting the Allegory/Typology Distinction: The Case of Origen." *JECS* 16: 283–317.

Moles, John L. 1995. "Cynics and Politics." In *Justice and Generosity: Studies in Hellenistic Social and Political Philosophy—Proceedings of the Sixth Symposium Hellenisticum*, edited by André Laks and Malcolm Schofield, 129–58. Cambridge: Cambridge University Press.

———. 1996. "Cynic Cosmopolitanism." In *The Cynics: The Cynic Movement in Antiquity and Its*

Legacy, edited by R. Bracht Branham and Marie-Odile Goulet-Cazé, 105–20. Berkeley: University of California Press.

Neuschäfer, Bernhard. 1987. *Origenes als Philologe*. 2 vols. Basel: Reinhardt.

Niehoff, Maren R. 2011. *Jewish Exegesis and Homeric Scholarship in Alexandria*. Cambridge: Cambridge University Press.

———, ed. 2012. *Homer and the Bible in the Eyes of Ancient Interpreters*. Leiden: Brill.

———. 2018. *Philo of Alexandria. An Intellectual Biography*. New Haven: Yale University Press.

———. 2020. "Paul and Philo on the Psalms: Towards a Spiritual Notion of Scripture." *NovT* 62: 392–415.

———. 2022. "Origen's Commentaries on the Old Testament." In *The Oxford Handbook of Origen*, edited by Ronald E. Heine and Karen J. Torjesen, 195–210. Oxford: Oxford University Press.

———. 2024. *Judentum und Hellenismus/Hellenism and Judaism*. Lecture on the Occasion of Receiving the Lucas Prize of Tübingen University. Tübingen: Mohr Siebeck.

———. Forthcoming. "Allegory as a Contested Space in Late Antique *Palaestina*: Origen's Construction of Christian Hermeneutics amid Celsus, Philo and Paul." In *Reading across Divides: Imperial Allegory, Its Cultural Contexts and Intermedial Entanglements*, edited by Jonas Grethlein and Benedek Kruchio.

Paz, Yakir. 2022. *From Scribes to Scholars: Rabbinic Biblical Exegesis in Light of the Homeric Commentaries*. Tübingen: Mohr Siebeck.

Roller, Matthew B. 2018. *Models from the Past in Roman Culture: A World of Exempla*. Cambridge: Cambridge University Press.

Schironi, Francesca. 2011. "Alexandrian Scholarship." In vol. 1 of *The Homer Encyclopedia*, edited by Margalit Finkelberg, 30–32. Oxford: Wiley-Blackwell.

———. 2012. "The Ambiguity of Signs: Critical σημεῖα from Zenodotus to Origen." In *Homer and the Bible in the Eyes of the Ancient Interpreters*, edited by Maren R. Niehoff, 87–112. Leiden: Brill.

———. 2018. *The Best of Grammarians: Aristarchus of Samothrace on the Iliad*. Ann Arbor: University of Michigan Press.

Schliesser, Benjamin, Jan Rüggemeier, Thomas J. Kraus, and Jörg Frey, eds. 2021. *Alexandria: Hub of the Hellenistic World*. Tübingen: Mohr Siebeck.

Standhartinger, Angela. 2018. "Member of Abraham's Family? Hagar's Gender, Status, Ethnos, and Religion in Early Jewish and Christian Texts." In *Abraham's Family: A Network of Meaning in Judaism, Christianity and Islam*, edited by Lukas Bormann, 235–59. Tübingen: Mohr Siebeck.

Tsantsanoglou, Kyriakos, George M. Parássoglou, and Theokritos Kouremenos, eds. 2006. *The Derveni Papyrus*. Florence: Leo. S. Olschki Editore.

SECTION II

Actors

22

The Herodian Dynasty

MORTEN HØRNING JENSEN

Friends and Foes of Jerusalem and Rome—Now and Then

Dealing with the Herodian dynasty immediately brings us into troublesome waters with vexed navigational maps and groundswells that reverberate from our antique sources to this very day. For instance, Bible readers acquainted with the sole story in the New Testament that includes Herod the Great (i.e., the infant killings in Bethlehem in Matt. 2:1–18) might react with disgust at the mere mention of his name. Likewise, in modern Israeli history writing even the name "Herod the Great" is a point of contestation, with our man generally referred to just as "Hordus" (the Israeli version of "Herod"), not "the Great."

Despite this, the present-day visitor to Israel may well marvel over his greatness as a builder—from the temple platform in Jerusalem down to the desert fortress at Masada and out westward to the great seaport at Caesarea. This was the reaction of one of Herod's first biographers, Flavius Josephus. This first-century Jewish historian explicitly strove to reconcile the "inconsistency" in Herod's nature with his initiatives of lavish benevolence, on the one hand, and cruel brutality, on the other (*Ant.* 16.150–59).

The same complex and flatly contradictory description is found in modern-day research on Herod the Great. One trajectory paints a picture of a brutal and cruel tyrant, at times even accompanied by a psychological profile of Herod as a "malevolent maniac" (Zeitlin 1963) who suffered from "significant mental disorders" (Kasher 2007, xv).[1] Slightly less disdainful, other researchers reuse the label "half-Jewish" to capture much of Herod's identity. This label, given to him by his main contester for the throne in Jerusalem, the Hasmonean Antigonus (Josephus, *Ant.* 14.403), is presented as proof that the Herodian house not only usurped the throne from the Jewish heroes of the Maccabean rebellion (the Hasmonean dynasty) but imposed a foreign rule by an Idumean house that only paid "lip service" (Jacobson 2001, 103) to Jewish traditions. Other

1. Zeitlin pointedly concludes that Herod "attained his kingdom as a fox, ruled as a tiger and died as a dog" (1963, 1).

researchers paint a far more positive picture of Herod. They point to the stories of his successful reign, included even by Josephus,[2] and the fact that Herod managed to remain in his seat as king until his death in a period marked by a long list of tensions and political turnabouts, leading to a picture of an astute politician who "consistently morphed into the right king for the right situation" (Marshak 2015, 335). Some would even argue that Herod was driven by a positive agenda or ideology of elevating the Jewish cause within the Roman world by incorporating and merging it far more fully into the Roman world dominion (cf. Regev 2010).

In the paragraphs that follow, the task is not to solve the puzzle of Herod the Great or the Herodian house as such. Instead, alongside providing a historical overview, we will outline aspects of the Herodian dynasty that allow us to see how such different evaluations derive from the historical data. In all cases, no matter how we may judge Herod and his heirs, there is no escaping the importance of the Herodian house as the immediate political background for Jesus and his disciples and for the Jewish people of his day, noting how the Herodian house forms a bridge between the rebirth of the Jewish nation under the Hasmoneans and that nation's collapse with the destruction of Jerusalem in 70 CE.

The Prequel: From the Hasmonean to the Herodian Dynasty

When Josephus has the Hasmonean king Antigonus label Herod a "half-Jew" (ἡμιιου-δαῖος, *hēmiioudaios*) as well as a "commoner" (ἰδιώτης, *idiōtēs*; *Ant.* 14.403), he voices a concern that probably resounded through the streets of Herodian Jerusalem: How can an Idumean family from Maresha (some 50 km

south of Jerusalem) claim the throne of Jerusalem, and with it the title "king of the Jews"?

The Herodian takeover itself is surprising, considering how justified the Hasmonean family was in claiming to be the freedom fighters and liberators of the Jewish nation from the horrible Antiochus Epiphanes in 164 BCE. However, that was a century earlier, and in the meantime the Hasmonean family of freedom fighters had turned into a lineage of royalty troubled by internal factions that culminated in a bloody fight for the throne between the two sons of the wise queen Alexandra Salome (76–67 BCE)—those sons being Hyrcanus II and Aristobolus II. And this is where the Herodian house enters the story with a certain strong man from Idumea, Antipater, who strongly supported the older brother of the two, Hyrcanus. Aristobolus was more forceful and had driven his brother off the throne. But advised by Antipater, Hyrcanus decided to align his prospects with the Romans. In 64 BCE, Rome had arrived on the scene with the great general Pompey's entry into Damascus. He called both brothers to his court, but Aristobolus soon left, hoping that the other great empire of the area, the Parthians, would back his cause.

With this, the once civil fight between brothers now effectively turned into a proxy war for the hegemony of the entire area. Who was it going to be? Rome or Parthia? The early victories went decisively to Rome. In 63 BCE, Pompey took Jerusalem by force from Antigonus and installed Hyrcanus on the throne as ethnarch ("leader of a people") with Antipater as the strong man. Antipater's position at the court secured strategic positions for his sons, Phasael and Herod, and in 47 CE Herod was shipped to Galilee as commander.

But Aristobolus and his sons were not to give up their claim on the throne, despite the initial setback. To cut a long story short, Aristobolus managed to escape his imprisonment in Rome, and while he eventually was killed in the fighting (along with Herod's father, Anti-

---

2. For instance, Herod cut taxes twice, renovated the temple, and generally created a period of peace and growing prosperity. For references, see Jensen 2010, 74.

pater), Aristobulus's son Antigonus managed to make a comeback in 40 BCE with the help of the Parthians. To many Jews, this probably was a welcomed return of a strong, Hasmonean king—perhaps even dressed in biblical clothes with the Parthians resembling the Persians, another empire that had once freed Jerusalem from an oppressive empire (cf. Mason 2013). This was not good news for the Herodian house, however, and only Herod managed to escape in all haste to secure his life.

Herod the Great: King of the Jews in Rome

Seemingly deprived of his army, friends, family, and all good fortune, Herod arrived in Rome in 40 BCE with nothing much to offer. Fortunately for him, Rome was looking for a strong leader to secure its hegemony in the Judean area. With Antigonus's success, Parthia had suddenly driven a wedge between Rome's provinces in Egypt to the south of Judea and Syria to the north. Something had to be done, and it turned out that this something involved Herod. According to Josephus, it was an inflaming speech by Anthony that moved the senate to grant the title "king of the Jews" to Herod—much to his own surprise, since Hasmonean heirs were still around. In time, Herod was acclaimed king. Flanked by Anthony and Octavian, Herod ascended the steps of the great temple of Jupiter in Rome to offer sacrifice, followed by a great banquet to celebrate this new allegiance (cf. J.W. 1.282–85; Ant. 14.381–89).

There was, of course, only one problem: there already was a "king of the Jews" on the throne in Jerusalem. Moreover, that king (who, as we have seen above, was the one who scoffingly referred to Herod as a commoner and a half-Jew; Josephus, Ant. 14.403) had proudly presented himself on a newly struck coin as "king" and "high priest," together with an image of the temple menorah (see fig. 22.1). Herod, for his part, had the Romans and their

legions on his side (cf. J.W. 1.327). After a two-year military campaign, Herod was finally able to capture Jerusalem in 37 CE. But there was no Jewish welcome committee to greet the new "king of the Jews." To many Jews, this was nothing short of a state coup. It was of little comfort that, upon the massacre that followed, Herod ensured that the temple was kept free from the fighting, or that he went so far as paying Roman soldiers to stop the killing and looting when he realized that they were about to empty "the city of possessions and people," leaving him to be "king of wilderness" (J.W. 1.355 [my translation]).[3]

This entire situation from Herod's crowning as "king of the Jews" in Rome to his hostile capture of Jerusalem encapsulates the real problem of Herod's reign: Would he be able to capture the hearts of the Jews as well, or would he remain king of the Jews only in the eyes of the Romans?

It should be highlighted that Herod did everything he could to maintain his allegiance with Rome by showing his deep-seated loyalty toward his Roman patrons. Initially, this had been Anthony. But Anthony met his doom in the battle at Actium in 31 BCE against his former ally, Octavian (the later Augustus). At that point, Herod's days as king of the Jews were numbered, and his personal safety was in danger. But in a bold move, he chose to appear before the new, sole ruler of the Roman Empire, Octavian. Doing so, he approached him bareheaded, without his kingly diadem, demonstrating his loyalty toward the now deceased Anthony. Luckily for Herod, Octavian was moved by Herod's speech. Knowing the value of loyal friendship, Octavian chose to renew Herod's friendship relation with Rome and to restore Herod's kingship (cf. Josephus, Ant. 15.183–93; J.W. 1.386–90).

3. Quoting Strabo, Josephus notes that Anthony eventually beheaded Antigonus in an effort to bend the will of the Jews toward accepting their new king, so great was their fondness toward their former king (Ant. 15.8–10).

This ushered in the best years of Herod's reign. In the years to come, Herod showed his loyalty to Octavian/Augustus by building three imperial cult temples to the veneration of Augustus, as well as naming cities and buildings in the emperor's honor. In return, Augustus continually added to Herod's kingdom, which eventually grew to the size of Solomon's kingdom according to the biblical Scriptures (cf. Josephus, *J.W.* 1.396; *Ant.* 15.217). Toward the end of his life, Herod made an unusual miscalculation that upset Augustus, who punished him by stripping him of his status as "friend" of Rome (*amicus*). But even then, Herod was soon welcomed back, and trust between him and Augustus was restored (*Ant.* 16.271–94, 335–55).

It is precisely this strong affiliation with Rome that plays a crucial part in the different evaluations of Herod. Was Herod after all only "an unrepentant pagan" (cf. Jacobson 2001; Kokkinos 1998), or was he rather a skilled politician who masterfully served the Jewish cause by navigating the Roman sea (cf. Marshak 2015; Regev 2010; Mason 2013)?

Herod the Great: King of the Jews in Jerusalem

This leads us to the question of Herod's relationship with his Jewish subjects, the second main component in the puzzle of Herod and his legacy. The literary testimony of Josephus and the evidence gained from archaeological findings make clear that Herod took sizable measures to gain legitimacy in the eyes of his Jewish subjects. He married the Hasmonean princess Mariamne, securing the prospect of at least a partial continuation of the Hasmonean lineage. He also sponsored a large-scale rebuilding of the temple edifice, as well as the temple platform as such. Importantly, Herod also defended Jewish causes in the diaspora. Notice also that archaeological findings in the private residences of Herod suggest concern

American Numismatic Society / Public Domain

Fig. 22.1. The coin of King Antigonus. During his contest with Herod the Great for the throne of Jerusalem, the Hasmonean king Antigonus issued this highly symbolic coin. On the obverse side, the temple menorah is displayed alongside the Greek inscription "King Antigonus." On the reverse side, the showbread of the temple is displayed alongside the inscription "Matatya the High Priest." In this way, Antigonus communicated to the Romans that a Jewish king was already installed in Jerusalem and that the Jewish people could count on him as high priest to protect the temple.

for the observance of the Jewish lifestyle. For example, forty-one ritual baths have been discovered in the private quarters of his palaces (cf. Regev 2010, 210), which also generally lack figurative art on their walls. The argument has been made that, in these ways, Herod tried to present himself as a son of David (Marshak 2013) and perhaps as a messianic king (Horbury 2003, 91).

There is a flip side to this coin, however. Jewish sources from the Gospel of Matthew to the rabbinic writings unanimously paint a harsh picture of Herod, providing a long list of what they considered to be transgressions of Jewish law and tradition. Most telling is Josephus's latter work, *Jewish Antiquities*, in which he consistently depicts Herod as a cruel tyrant and a transgressor of the Jewish law (e.g., *Ant.* 15.267; 16.150–59).[4] Most importantly, Josephus claims that Herod planted a deep-seated hatred toward Rome in the Jewish nation, which eventually grew into the disastrous rebellion against Rome that began in 66 CE, depicting Herod as a destroyer of the temple, much like the despised Antiochus Epiphanes (cf. *Ant.* 15.281).

The brutal events that followed the death of Herod in 4 BCE remind us that his vision of a Jewish kingdom was not the kind that many Jews dreamed of (cf. Vermes 2014, 106). As a matter of fact, in the months following Herod's death, a great rebellion swirled across the whole of Judea, led by several quasi-messianic leaders. Josephus judged that "Judea was full of brigandage" in this period (*Ant.* 17.285 [my translation]; cf. *J.W.* 2.65; see also Jensen 2014, 62).

Discontent with Herod was aired in other ways in these months. It was up to Augustus to decide what to do with the land of Israel. Herod had continuously updated his will in the course of executing one son after another, and consequently three delegations departed for Rome to scramble for the land, based on different versions of his will. Interestingly, one of these delegations consisted of leading Jewish men. They requested to be free of Herodian kingship, referring to Herod's tyrannical nature and the misery he had brought to the Jewish nation that, according to them, had surpassed even all that the Jewish nation had experienced since the time of the Babylonian exile (Josephus, *J.W.* 2.86)!

The Herodian Heirs and the Battle for Kingship

In the end, Augustus did not follow the plea of the Jewish delegation. Instead he chose to follow the last of Herod's wills, with one major adjustment that in reality proved to be a portent of things to come. Rather than appointing a new "king of the Jews," Augustus only went as far as appointing Herod's main heir, Archelaus, as "leader of a people" (ethnarch)—although with the promise that Archelaus would obtain the dignity of king should he prove to be worthy of it (Josephus, *J.W.* 2.94). Neither of Herod's other two sons inherited his title. Instead, both Antipas (the full younger brother of Archelaus) and Philip received the title "tetrarch," literally meaning "ruler of a fourth" but used for rulers of principalities. Thus, Herod's kingdom was divided into three in the year 4 BCE. Archelaus ruled over Judea, Idumea, and Samaria (with an estimated revenue of 400 talents yearly); Antipas ruled over Galilee and Perea (with a revenue of 200 talents); and Philip ruled over five minor northern provinces (with a revenue of 100 talents; *J.W.* 2.95–98).

For roughly the next four decades, this tripartition would be in place, with one important alteration: in Jerusalem, it was up to Archelaus to prove his worthiness in order to gain elevation to king. Unfortunately, it seems as if he had inherited none of his father's benevolent sides but all his cruelty. After ten years, a joint delegation of Judeans and Samaritans complained to Augustus, who banished Archelaus to Vienne in Gaul (cf. Jensen 2010, 77–79).[5] From 6 BCE to 41 CE, Rome chose to rule this part of Israel directly, through a series of prefects, of which Pontius Pilate (26–36 CE) is the best known.

In Galilee, things fared better. At the very least, Antipas (or as he is known in the New Testament, "King Herod" or "Herod the tetrarch"; see the table "The Herodian Dynasty and the New Testament" below) managed to rule for more than four decades until he also

4. For a list of six such instances, see Fuks 2002. For a list of eighteen examples hereof, see Jensen 2010, 69–77.

5. His tyrannical nature is reflected in Matt. 2:22, which states that Joseph moved to Nazareth in Galilee when he heard that Archelaus ruled in Judea.

was banished to France in 39 CE (cf. Jensen 2010, 93–94). The reason for this was nothing less than the aforementioned quest for the dignity of king. After having served under Augustus and then Tiberius in ways that generally seem to have been measured (cf. Jensen 2007), Antipas made the mistake of his life by asking the new emperor in Rome, Gaius Caligula, for kingship. This was triggered by the fact that Agrippa, the brother of Herodias (Antipas's wife), had received this title against all odds in 37 CE together with Philip's old territories. Antipas decided soon after to load a ship with gifts and sail to Rome to ask Gaius for the same dignity, only to see himself completely stripped of his tetrarchy instead.

In reality, only Philip the Tetrarch ended his life on the throne. Perhaps this is because he (according to the sources we have available) did not enter into the scramble for the title "king of the Jews." Josephus goes so far as to describe him as moderate and easygoing, content with what had been allotted to him, maintaining justice by traveling around to listen to complaints and to right wrongs (*Ant.* 18.106–8). When Philip died without an heir in 33/34 CE, Tiberius did not appoint a new Jewish ruler over the four minor provinces he had overseen.

This brings us to the most noteworthy of Herod the Great's heirs, Agrippa I. Josephus provides a long and glowing description of Agrippa "the Great," as he calls him (*Ant.* 17.28). For Josephus, Agrippa preserved what was left of Hasmonean blood in the Herodian lineage, being a son of Aristobolus, one of Herod's two sons with Mariamne. But even apart from this, Agrippa's merits are notable. Despite acquiring huge debts through a youth spent in exorbitance, Agrippa had the luck or political nose to curry the favor of two soon-to-be Roman emperors in a row, both of whom lavishly repaid him for his help in the process. First, Gaius Caligula installed Agrippa as king over Philip's old territory after Tiberius's death

in 37 CE (*J.W.* 2.181). In 39 CE, he added Antipas's territory to Agrippa's domain as well. Second, when Claudius took over the emperorship after the assassination of Gaius in 41 CE, Agrippa was awarded Judea, Samaria, and Idumea as a token for his help in the process (*J.W.* 2.204–17). For the first and last time, the entirety of Herod's old kingdom (and more) was united under a Jewish king. A new golden era was about to dawn—if judged from a Judean or even Hasmonean perspective. Josephus paints a picture of Agrippa as a pious Jew who stayed in Jerusalem, kept the traditions, and fulfilled the required sacrifices, being in almost every respect the opposite of his grandfather (*Ant.* 19.328–34). This would coincide well with the description in Acts 12 of Agrippa as an active persecutor of the young church in Jerusalem.

Unfortunately for the Judean cause, Agrippa died suddenly in Caesarea in 44 CE, leaving behind a son too young to be given the kingdom by the Romans. Only later, in 53 CE, was Agrippa II appointed as a king, and only for the northern territories. Instead, Rome chose to rule Herod's old kingdom directly through prefects or procurators for the second time from 44 to 66 CE, the year war broke out. With the destruction of Jerusalem in 70 CE, an era had passed, and with it a "king of the Jews," at least in the proper sense known in the Hasmonean and Herodian periods. While Agrippa II continued to rule in the northern territories, even his throne was not upheld when he died in 100 CE.

The Herodian House and Its Legacy

The question discussed at length not only in modern research but also by our antique sources is how we should evaluate the Herodian house—not least its most important member, Herod the Great. In my opinion, caution is needed against strong and likely one-sided readings. The two extreme readings

The Herodian Dynasty and the New Testament

Name, Official Title, Tenure, and Territory	Name and Title in the New Testament
Herod the Great, king (40/37–4 BCE): Judea, Idumea, Samaria, Galilee, Perea, Iturea, Gaulanitis, Batanea, Trachonitis, Auranitis	Matthew 2:1–22—King Herod Luke 1:5—Herod, king of Judea Acts 23:35—Herod
Herod Antipas, son of Herod, tetrarch (4 BCE–39 CE): Galilee, Perea	Matthew 14:1–12—Herod the tetrarch Mark 6:14–29; 8:15—King Herod Luke 3:1, 19–20; 8:3; 9:7–9; 13:31; 23:7–12, 15—Herod the tetrarch Acts 4:27; 13:1—Herod the tetrarch
Archelaus, son of Herod, ethnarch (4 BCE–6 CE): Judea, Idumea, Samaria	Matthew 2:22—Archelaus
Philip, son of Herod, tetrarch (4 BCE–34 CE): Iturea, Gaulanitis, Batanea, Trachonitis, Auranitis	Luke 3:1—Philip the tetrarch
Herod Agrippa I, Herod's grandson, king (37–44 CE): Herod the Great's territory	Acts 12:1–23—King Herod
Herod Agrippa II, son of Agrippa I, king (53–ca. 100 CE): Herod Philip's territory	Acts 25:13–26:32—King Agrippa

are well fed by what seems at the very least to be partial aspects of the story. On the one hand, the combined achievements of Herod the Great and Agrippa I could on paper rival some of the legacy of the Solomonic kingdom (apart from the matter of political independency). On the other hand, it is also true that the policy and perhaps even Roman ideology of the Herodian rulers provoked fierce resistance among certain Jewish factions, providing support for Josephus's evaluation of a connection between the Herodian rulers and the sentiment for war against Rome (cf. Vermes 2014, 100–106). In other words, our evaluation of the Herodian house needs to be flexible enough to encompass the progress of the Jewish cause during the Herodian hegemony, evidenced not least by the rebuilding of the temple, with resistance toward the Herodian version of a "Jewish kingdom" that eventually grew into full-scale rebellion, leading to the disastrous destruction of Jerusalem and its temple in 70 CE.

Works Cited

Fuks, Gideon. 2002. "Josephus on Herod's Attitude towards Jewish Religion: The Darker Side." *JJS* 53, no. 2: 238–45.

Horbury, William. 2003. *Messianism among Jews and Christians: Twelve Biblical and Historical Studies*. London: T&T Clark.

Jacobson, David M. 2001. "Herod the Great Shows His True Colors." *NEA* 64, no. 3: 100–104.

Jensen, Morten Hørning. 2007. "Herod Antipas in Galilee: Friend or Foe of the Historical Jesus?" *Journal for the Study of the Historical Jesus* 5, no. 1: 7–32.

———. 2010. *Herod Antipas in Galilee: The Literary and Archaeological Sources on the Reign of Herod Antipas and Its Socio-Economic Impact on Galilee*. 2nd ed. WUNT 2/215. Tübingen: Mohr Siebeck.

———. 2014. "The Political History in Galilee from the 1st Century BCE to the End of the 2nd Century CE." In *Galilee in the Late Second Temple and Mishnaic Periods 100 BCE–200 CE*, edited by David A. Fiensey and James R. Strange, 51–77. Minneapolis: Fortress.

Kasher, Aryeh. 2007. *King Herod: A Persecuted Persecutor*. Berlin: de Gruyter.

Kokkinos, Nikos. 1998. *The Herodian Dynasty: Origins, Role in Society and Eclipse*. JSPSup 30. Sheffield: Sheffield Academic Press.

Marshak, Adam Kolman. 2013. "Glorifying the Present through the Past: Herod the Great and His Jewish Royal Predecessors." In *Christian Origins and Hellenistic Judaism: Social and Literary Contexts for the*

New Testament, edited by Stanley E. Porter and Andrew Pitts, 51–81. Vol. 2 of *Early Christianity in Its Hellenistic Context*. TENTS 10. Leiden: Brill.

———. 2015. *The Many Faces of Herod the Great*. Grand Rapids: Eerdmans.

Mason, Steve. 2013. "Herod's Final Curtain: What to Do for an Encore." In *The King's Final Journey*, edited by David Mevorach and Sylvia Rozenberg, 44–55. Israel: The Israel Museum.

Regev, Eyal. 2010. "Herod's Jewish Ideology Facing Romanization: On Intermarriage, Ritual Baths, and Speeches." *JQR* 100, no. 2: 197–222.

Vermes, Geza. 2014. *The True Herod*. London: Bloomsbury.

Zeitlin, Solomon. 1963. "Herod: A Malevolent Maniac." *JQR* 54, no. 1: 1–27.

23

Messiahs and Revolutionaries

MAX BOTNER

My introduction to the church came by way of two irreconcilable messages. On the one hand, I was assured by pastors and other leaders that I was "lucky" to have been born Jewish. On the other hand, those same people wanted to know why so many Jews have missed "their" messiah. Granted that it is absurd to ask a child to answer for the history of an entire people (much less a people whose history is indelibly marked by *Christian* anti-Semitism), I have nonetheless come to appreciate the question as an opportunity to reconsider popular (Christian) mental models of "messiah."

My discussion will be guided by three overarching questions. First, how should we understand the phenomenon of ancient messianism? Second, what evidence do we have for messianic movements in the first and second centuries CE? Third, how should we conceive of the relationship between messianism and Christology? What I hope to demonstrate is that ancient messianism is more complex (and indeed more interesting) than the popular iterations on offer. Jews and Christians are participants in an ongoing exegetical and discursive project about how the God of Israel rectifies and rules his good creation.

Attending Ancient Messianism: Ideas and Language

When Hermann Reimarus launched his assault on Christian origins in the mid-eighteenth century, he assumed that "messiah" meant one thing: the long-awaited Davidic king who would overthrow the Roman government and usher in the kingdom of God (1971 [1774–77], 138). Eventually, however, historians became enamored with an alternative messianic figure: the Son of Man. Jewish messianism was thus described as the product of two distinct (and often competing) strands. On the one hand, the messiah son of David represented the nationalist machinations of the Jewish masses. On the other hand, the messiah Son of Man represented the transcendent longings of an apocalyptic coterie (on Jewish apocalypticism, see chap. 3 in this volume). Not surprisingly, Protestant scholars concluded that Jesus and his followers eschewed the former in favor of the latter (e.g., Weiss 1971 [1892], 116; Bousset 1970 [1921], 31–32, 49).

The Dead Sea Scrolls changed everything. Never mind debates about the nature of *the* messiah; we now had evidence of a community that expected *two* messiahs: "the messiahs of Aaron and Israel" (1QS IX, 11; CD XII, 23). In addition, various and sundry references to "messiah(s)" in the Dead Sea Scrolls prompted debate over internal developments within Qumran messianism (summarized in Collins 2010, 84–91) as well as proposals of additional messianic models (see table 1 below).

The consensus that *diversity* characterized Jewish messianism elicited radical reappraisals of what was once supposed to be a relatively stable phenomenon. For example, in the introduction to the volume *Judaisms and Their Messiahs at the Turn of the Christian Era*, William Scott Green opines, "In early Jewish literature, 'messiah' is all signifier with no signified; the term is notable primarily for its indeterminacy" (1987, 4). And in the opening chapter of another important volume on ancient messianism, published a few years later, James Charlesworth concludes,

> The complexity of messianic ideas, the lack of coherent messianology among the documents in the Pseudepigrapha and among the Dead Sea Scrolls, and the frequently contradictory messianic predictions prohibit anything approximating coherency in early Jewish messianology. If we were statisticians, we might conclude that we should ignore Jewish messianic references because they are so meager, and when present so vague or contradictory. (1992, 28–29)

Gone, then, it would seem, are the days when we could assume what "messiah" meant.

And yet, one need not overstate the case. For it is one thing to pronounce the collapse of the "messianic idea"; it is quite another to declare that "messiah" meant anything (and

so nothing), as Green does, or to insinuate that the paucity and diversity of references to messiah(s) is evidence for the irrelevancy of messianism, as Charlesworth does. On the contrary, as Matthew Novenson argues,

> Popular hope may have been more or less current at different times and places in early Judaism, but the meaningfulness of the language is independent of the fervency of the popular hope. People could know what the words meant whether or not they shared the sentiment expressed. In short, messiah language could be used meaningfully in antiquity because it was deployed in the context of a linguistic community whose members shared a stock of common linguistic resources. (2012, 47)

Novenson makes the essential point: ancient Jews did not need to say the same things about messiah(s) to understand what their neighbors believed about messiah(s). The prerequisite of intelligible communication is a shared cultural encyclopedia (Eco 1976, 98–114), not uniform agreement on how to use it.

According to Novenson, every reference to a messiah (i.e., "messiah language") entails a "'creatively biblical' linguistic act" (2012, 53). On the one hand, ancient Jews and Christians found their messiahs in the same places in the Old Testament / Hebrew Bible: biblical phrases with the word "messiah" (e.g., "X is the messiah," "the LORD's messiah," "until the coming of the messiah," and so forth) and promises about a (future) ruler of the Jewish people (cf. Gen. 49:10; Num. 24:17; 2 Sam. 7:12–13; Isa. 11:1–2; Dan. 7:13–14; Amos 9:11). On the other hand, these writers always interpreted and configured biblical traditions based on empirical circumstances. In other words, to borrow a term from Richard Hays, ancient discourse about messiahs always involves an act of "reading backwards" (2014, 2015).

Once we appreciate that messianism "always and everywhere involves the interplay

Table 1

Messianic Model	Biblical Messiah Texts	Early Jewish and Christian References
Davidic Messiah Not all Davidic messiahs are identified as *sons* of David (Novenson 2017, 111; Botner 2019, 39–47).	Genesis 49:9–10; 2 Samuel 7:12–14; Psalm 2; Isaiah 11:1–5; Jeremiah 23:5; Ezekiel 34:23–24; Amos 9:11; Micah 5:2; Zechariah 9:9	Psalms of Solomon 17, 18; 4 Ezra 12.32; 4Q161; 4Q174; 4Q252; 4Q285; Matthew 1:1; Mark 10:47; Luke 1:32; Romans 1:3; Hebrews 7:14; Revelation 5:5; 22:16
Priestly Messiah For detailed analysis of priestly messiah traditions and traditions about Melchizedek, see Mason 2008, 64–190; summarized in Mason 2011, 60–76.	"Anointed (high) priest" (Lev. 4:3, 5, 16; Dan. 9:25–26); Melchize-dekian priest (Ps. 110:4)	Aramaic Levi; Testament of Levi 18; 11Q13 (probably an angelic priest); Hebrews 7
Priestly and Royal (Davidic?) Messiahs Scholars debate whether the "messiah of Israel" is a Davidic messiah (Schiffman 1992; Pomykala 1995, 238; Collins 2010, 81).	Pentateuchal model of leadership (Moses and Aaron); "two sons of oil" (Zech. 4:14, my translation)	1QS IX, 11; CD XII, 23; XIV, 19; XIX, 10
Prophetic Messiah This category is disputed (see, e.g., Collins 2010, 128–41).	Deuteronomy 18:15; Isaiah 61:1; Malachi 4:5	4Q521; 11Q13; Luke 4:16–21
Heavenly Messiah The most extensive discussion of this figure comes in the Parables of Enoch (1 En. 37–71), on which see Boccaccini 2007.	Daniel 7:13–14	1 Enoch 46; 4 Ezra 13; Mark 8:38 parr.; Mark 14:62 parr.; John 3:13; Acts 7:55–56; 1 Corinthians 15:24–28; Revelation 1:13

of biblical tradition and empirical circumstance" (Novenson 2017, 196), we can readily explain the diversity of messiah language (as we encounter it in early Jewish and Christian texts). Table 1 lists the major types of messiahs alongside their respective biblical traditions.

To these we may add (1) texts that anticipate a pagan deliverer (e.g., Sib. Or. 3.652–56), based on the description of Cyrus the Persian as "his messiah" (Isa. 45:1), and (2) texts that never mention a messiah (see, e.g., the "no hope list" in Horbury 2016, 64), for which there is precedent in biblical texts that navigate the Davidic interregnum (e.g., Second and Third Isaiah). Of course, the observation that most early Jewish texts (e.g., much of the Apocrypha and Old Testament Pseudepigrapha) never mention a messiah need not suggest that Jews

were largely uninterested in this figure. Silence is not necessarily rejection.

The major types of messiahs do not represent immutable or mutually exclusive categories. For example, the hackneyed dichotomy between the Davidic "national messiah" and the apocalyptic "Son of Man" (Mowinckel 2005) is not borne out in the ancient literature (Botner 2019, 48–51). Likewise, nothing would prevent a "prophetic" or "priestly" messiah from presenting as "royal" or even "Davidic." Some ancient writers insisted on the maintenance of boundaries between offices, to be sure, but their protests should not be mistaken for consensus. Quite the contrary. The various forms of messianism and concomitant structures of governance that we encounter in ancient texts are illustrative of the diverse possibilities that the Jewish Scriptures permit.

Table 2

Historical Figure	Description and Source(s)
Judah ben Heze-kiah (4 BCE)	Judas (Judah), Son of the "chief brigand" (*archilēstēs*) Ezekias (Hezekiah), organized an army at Sepphoris in Galilee. Josephus describes him as being "zealous for royal honor" (*Ant.* 17.272; *J.W.* 2.56). This Judas appears to be distinct from "Judas the Galilean," whom Josephus identifies as the founder of the "fourth philosophy" (*Ant.* 18.3–9, 23–25; *J.W.* 2.118; cf. Acts 5:37).
Simon of Perea (4 BCE)	Simon was a former slave of Herod the Great, renowned for his size and strength, who "dared to don the diadem" and was "declared king" by his followers (*Ant.* 17.273–76).
Athronges (4 BCE)	Josephus describes him as an obscure shepherd who was remarkable for his great stature and strength. The man "dared to aspire to the kingship," "put on the diadem," and held the title "king" (*Ant.* 17.278–84; *J.W.* 2.60–64). Along with his four brothers, he launched guerilla warfare against the Romans and the Herodian leadership.
The Samaritan (ca. 35 CE)	This prophetic upstart rallied his followers to Mount Gerizim, where he promised to recover the sacred vessels once deposited there by Moses. The revolt was swiftly put down by Pontius Pilate (*Ant.* 18.85–87).
Theudas (ca. 45 CE)	Josephus calls him a "sorcerer" who claimed to be a "prophet." He persuaded the masses to follow him to the Jordan River, which he claimed would part at his command (*Ant.* 20.97–98; cf. Acts 5:36).
The Egyptian (ca. 56 CE)	Josephus calls him a "sorcerer" and "false prophet." He led a large group of followers through the desert to the Mount of Olives, from which he planned to take Jerusalem by force and then set himself up as ruler of the people (*Ant.* 20.169–70; *J.W.* 2.261–63; cf. Acts 21:38).
Menahem ben Judah (66 CE)	Having raided the arsenal of Herod the Great on Masada, this son of Judah the Galilean returned to Jerusalem as a king and became the leader of the insurrection. Josephus refers to him as a "bandit" and a "tyrant," as well as a "sophist" (*J.W.* 2.433–34, 442, 445).
Simon bar Giora (68–70 CE)	Simon was a native of Gerasa and recognized for his strength and audacity. He gathered an army by proclaiming liberty for the slaves and rewards for the free, but eventually not only slaves and bandits but also well-to-do citizens became subservient to his command "as to a king." In the spring of 69 CE, he was welcomed to Jerusalem as "the savior of the people." When the city fell in the spring of 70 CE, Simon surrendered to the Romans dressed in royal attire. He was subsequently executed as the leader (king) of the Jews as part of the triumphal procession in Rome (*J.W.* 4.503–13, 574–76; 7.29–31, 36, 153–55).

Note: Translations of Josephus in this table are my own.

Revolutionary Movements and Their Messiahs

Monty Python's popular film *Life of Brian* tells the humorous tale of a fictitious character, Brian of Nazareth, an unwitting messianic pretender. The story takes a turn when our protagonist, on the run from the Roman guard, falls out of a window and into the midst of a messianic marketplace. Certain that they had found their man, the crowd pursues Brian deep into the wilderness, at which point the hapless Nazarene has no choice but to confront his would-be disciples. "I am not the messiah!" he cries out in desperation, to which one par-

ticularly enthusiastic member of the crowd responds, "I say that you are, Lord. And I should know; I've followed a few!" The line is intended to be comical, but it also reveals something of the screenwriters' historical awareness: first-century Jews knew of many (more than a few) messianic figures.

Table 2 offers a synopsis of the various revolutionaries mentioned by the Jewish historian Flavius Josephus (see further Horsley and Hanson 1999, 88–134; Collins 2010, 216–28; Novenson 2017, 141–48).

Josephus distinguishes between two classes of revolutionaries. On the one hand, he describes the movements of certain self-designated "prophets" (*prophētai*), whom he labels "sorcerers" (*goētes*) and "false prophets" (*pseudoprophētai*). On the other hand, he charts the rise of certain aspirants to the throne, whom he calls "bandits" (*lēstai*) and "tyrants" (*tyrannoi*). Perhaps, then, Josephus is working with the same categories as Jesus: "false messiahs" (*pseudochristoi*) and "false prophets" (*pseudoprophētai*) (Mark 13:22).

The issue, of course, is that Josephus never says that these "royal pretenders" claimed to be messiahs. He does, however, provide important insight into their motivations:

> But what more than all else incited them to the war was an ambiguous oracle, likewise found in their sacred scriptures, to the effect that at that time one from their country would become ruler of the world. This they understood to mean someone of their own race, and many of their wise men went astray in their interpretation of it. The oracle, however, in reality signified the sovereignty of Vespasian, who was proclaimed emperor on Jewish soil. (*J.W.* 6.312–13 [trans. Thackeray 1928, 269])

Clearly, the historian has in mind one (or more) of the Scriptures that his contemporaries interpreted messianically. Thus it seems plausible that at least some of his "diadem wearers," for example, Menahem and Simon bar Giora, were heralded as the messiah by their followers.

In fact, Simon bar Kosiba, the leader of the Second Jewish War against the Romans (132–135 CE), is the only figure (other than Jesus of Nazareth) for whom the ancient sources make an explicit messianic claim. In a famous talmudic passage, R. Akiba is reported to have expounded the passage "a star [*kokhab*] will go forth from Jacob" (Num. 24:17) as "Koziba goes out from Jacob" (y. Ta'an. 4.8 [68d; trans. Lanier 2021, 584]; cf. Lam. Rab. 2.2). Thus the man whom Akiba identified as "the king mes-

siah" (*malka meshiha*) comes to be known as Bar Kokhba, "son of the star" (cf. Justin Martyr, *1 Apol.* 31.6; Eusebius, *Hist. eccl.* 6.4.2). In the documentary sources (papyri), Bar Kokhba refers to himself as the "prince of Israel" (*nasi al yisrael*; see Yadin et al. 1963–2002), an epithet that was probably derived from Ezekiel 34:24 (cf. 1QM V, 1; CD VII, 20; 1Q28b V, 20; 4Q161 II, 15; 4Q285). He also minted coins, some of which were impressed with the image of a star (see Mildenberg 1984).

Naturally, the rabbis judged Bar Kokhba's messiahship a failure. In the talmudic tradition mentioned above, R. Yohanan b. Torta responds, "Akiva, grass will grow on your cheeks, but the son of David will not yet have come!" (y. Ta'an. 4.8 [68d; trans. Lanier 2021, 584]; cf. Lam. Rab. 2.2). Another tradition reads: "Bar Koziba ruled for two and a half years. He said to the rabbis, 'I am the Messiah.' They said to him, 'In the case of the Messiah it is written that he smells a man and judges [cf. Isa. 11:3]. Let us see whether you can smell a man and judge.' When they saw that he could not smell a man and judge, they killed him" (b. Sanh. 93b [trans. Neusner 2011, 499]). Both traditions recognize, accurately, as far as we know, that Bar Kokhba was not a descendant of David. Thus R. Yohanan b. Torta and the fictive rabbinic court argued (albeit retrospectively) that he lacked the requisite pedigree to hold the royal office.

Rabbi Akiba, by contrast, reflects the sentiments of other Jews: the messiah did not need to be a *son* of David as long as he proved to be *like* David in the ways that counted. The followers of Bar Kokhba (along with those of Judah ben Hezekiah, Simon of Perea, Athronges, Menahem, and Simon bar Giora) did not negate the David tradition. Rather, they amplified features of the tradition that their messiahs (or revolutionary leaders) met (obscure shepherd [Athronges], liberator of Jerusalem [Menahem and Simon bar Giora], victor over God's enemies [Bar Kokhba]) and attenuated features they did not—namely, ancestry. Were the followers of these movements to face the charges of our imaginary rabbinic court, they might well have responded: "David did it. Why not our man?" (Novenson 2017, 113).

Jewish Messianism versus Early Christology: What Is the Difference?

There is a long-standing assumption that discourse about Jesus Messiah is of a different nature than discourse about the other messiahs. (Even the prescriptions of the second edition of *The SBL Handbook of Style* reflect this long-standing bias: "messiah" [in general] but "Messiah" [in Christian contexts].) Christian scholars, in particular, even those who would claim the mantle of the dispassionate "historian," often feel compelled to assure their audiences that Jesus was not "merely" the messiah but the Son of God, the Second Person of the Trinity. Christology is thus permitted to enfold messianism but only in order to transcend it.

Such an arrangement may seem amicable to Christian theologians, but it hardly offers a satisfactory explanation of the historical data. First, Jesus's messianic identity is both the primary presupposition and the central message of New Testament texts (Jipp 2020). For example, the collocation Jesus Christ (or Christ Jesus), which is a commonplace in the Pauline corpus, uses *Christos* as an honorific that underscores Jesus's messianic status: Jesus *Messiah / Anointed One* (Novenson 2012, 87–97). Second, first-century discourse about Jesus Messiah plays by the same "rules" that govern discourse about the other messiahs. As Richard Bauckham notes,

> Second Temple Jewish theology, including early Christian theology, was primarily a tradition of exegesis, not a tradition of ideas passed on independently of exegesis. . . . The extent to which early Christology is novel in its Jewish context is the extent to which, in

view of the unique features of Jesus' history, it applied to Jesus a particular selection and configuration of key texts, some already well used for certain heavenly or messianic figures, some not previously so used, but *as a particular selection and configuration novel*. (2008, 174–75)

Put differently: early Christology *is* messianic exegesis (Juel 1988; cf. Novenson 2017, 274–75).

Third, then, the distinction between early Christology and Jewish messianism often boils down to whether the users of Christ language (as a species of messiah language) claimed of Jesus what no other Jews claimed of their messiahs (Bauckham 2008, 175). Yet the more one appreciates the diverse possibilities of ancient messianism, and in particular the nature of what some have called "high" messianism (Bühner 2020, 2021), the more such distinctions break down. Even when an author claims of Jesus an attribute that one might justifiably label "unique" among the messiahs (i.e., his participation in the creation of the cosmos), such constitutes not a departure from messianism but another variant of it. Or, to put it more provocatively: Jewish messianism, understood as a diverse and ever-evolving phenomenon, is able to enfold Christology.

Conclusion

Ancient messianism plays out at the intersection of exegesis and real life. Its diversity derives from the confluence of competing interpretive communities and concrete historical situations—for example, the emergence of a messianic figure, the alleged corruption of the priesthood, claims of special access to the celestial throne, and so forth. Early Christology is thus best understood as a variant of Jewish messianism.

Of course, the story does not end in the first century CE. Peter Schäfer proposes that we see "Judaism" and "Christianity" not "as static entities forever confronting each other but rather as vital, dynamic forces in constant exchange with each other" (2012, 271). An accurate appraisal of the phenomenon of ancient messianism is necessary not only to disrupt centuries of Christian anti-Judaism and anti-Semitism but also to open us to a world in which our religious differences can be rightly understood and appreciated.

Works Cited

Bauckham, Richard. 2008. *Jesus and the God of Israel: God Crucified and Other Studies on the New Testament's Christology of Divine Identity*. Grand Rapids: Eerdmans.

Boccaccini, Gabriele, ed. 2007. *Enoch and the Messiah Son of Man: Revisiting the Book of Parables*. Grand Rapids: Eerdmans.

Botner, Max. 2019. *Jesus Christ as the Son of David in the Gospel of Mark*. SNTSMS 174. Cambridge: Cambridge University Press.

Bousset, Wilhelm. 1970. *Kyrios Christos: A History of the Belief in Christ from the Beginnings of Christianity to Irenaeus*. Translated by John E. Steely. Nashville: Abingdon. Originally published 1921.

Bühner, Ruben A. 2020. *Hohe Messianologie: Übermenschliche Aspekte eschatologischer Heilsgestalten im Frühjudentum*. WUNT 2/523. Tübingen: Mohr Siebeck.

———. 2021. *Messianic High Christology: New Testament Variants of Second Temple Judaism*. Waco: Baylor University Press.

Charlesworth, James H. 1992. "From Messianology to Christology: Problems and Prospects." In *The Messiah: Developments in Earliest Judaism and Christianity*, edited by James H. Charlesworth, 3–35. Minneapolis: Fortress.

Collins, John J. 2010. *The Scepter and the Star: Messianism in Light of the Dead Sea Scrolls*. 2nd ed. Grand Rapids: Eerdmans.

Eco, Umberto. 1976. *A Theory of Semiotics*. Bloomington: Indiana University Press.

Green, William Scott. 1987. "Introduction: Messiah in Judaism; Rethinking the Question." In *Judaisms and Their Messiahs at the Turn of the Christian Era*, edited by Jacob Neusner, William Scott Green, and Ernest S. Frerichs, 1–13. Cambridge: Cambridge University Press.

Hays, Richard B. 2014. *Reading Backwards: Figural Christology and the Fourfold Gospel Witness*. Waco: Baylor University Press.

———. 2015. *Echoes of Scripture in the Gospels*. Waco: Baylor University Press.

Horbury, William. 2016. *Messianism among Jews and Christians: Biblical and Historical Studies*. 2nd ed. London: Bloomsbury T&T Clark.

Horsley, Richard A., with John S. Hanson. 1999. *Bandits, Prophets and Messiahs: Popular Movements in the Time of Jesus*. 2nd ed. Harrisburg, PA: Trinity Press International.

Jipp, Joshua W. 2020. *The Messianic Theology of the New Testament*. Grand Rapids: Eerdmans.

Juel, Donald H. 1988. *Messianic Exegesis: Christological Interpretation of the Old Testament in Early Christianity*. Minneapolis: Fortress.

Lanier, Gregory R., ed. 2021. *Corpus Christologicum: Texts and Translations for the Study of Jewish Messianism and Early Christology*. Peabody, MA: Hendrickson.

Mason, Eric F. 2008. *"You Are a Priest Forever": Second Temple Jewish Messianism and the Priestly Christology of the Epistle to the Hebrews*. STDJ 74. Leiden: Brill.

———. 2011. "Cosmology, Messianism, and Melchizedek: Apocalyptic Jewish Traditions and Hebrews." In *Reading the Epistle to the Hebrews: A Resource for Students*, edited by Eric F. Mason and Kevin B. McCruden, 53–76. Atlanta: Society of Biblical Literature.

Mildenberg, Leo. 1984. *The Coinage of the Bar Kokhba War*. Zurich: Schweizerische Numismatische Gesellschaft.

Mowinckel, Sigmund. 2005. *He That Cometh: The Messiah Concept in the Old Testament and Later Judaism*. Translated by G. W. Anderson. Grand Rapids: Eerdmans.

Neusner, Jacob, ed. and trans. 2011. *The Babylonian Talmud: A Translation and Commentary*. Vol. 16, *Tractate Sanhedrin*. Peabody, MA: Hendrickson.

Novenson, Matthew V. 2012. *Christ among the Messiahs: Christ Language in Paul and Messiah Language in Ancient Judaism*. New York: Oxford University Press.

———. 2017. *The Grammar of Messianism: An Ancient Jewish Political Idiom and Its Users*. New York: Oxford University Press.

Pomykala, Kenneth E. 1995. *The Davidic Dynasty Tradition in Early Judaism: Its History and Significance for Messianism*. EJL 7. Atlanta: Scholars Press.

Reimarus, Hermann Samuel. 1971. *Fragments*. Edited by Charles H. Talbert. Translated by Ralph S. Fraser. London: SCM. Originally published 1774–77.

Schäfer, Peter. 2012. *The Jewish Jesus: How Judaism and Christianity Shaped Each Other*. Princeton: Princeton University Press.

Schiffman, L. H. 1992. "Messianic Figures and Ideas in the Qumran Scrolls." In *The Messiah: Developments in Earliest Judaism and Christianity*, edited by James H. Charlesworth, 116–29. Minneapolis: Fortress.

Thackeray, Henry St. J., trans. 1928. *Josephus: The Jewish War*. Vol. 3, *Books 5–7*. LCL 210. Cambridge, MA: Harvard University Press.

Weiss, Johannes. 1971. *Jesus' Proclamation of the Kingdom of God*. Translated by Richard Hyde Hiers and David Larrimore Holland. Philadelphia: Fortress. Originally published 1892.

Yadin, Yigael, et al. 1963–2002. *The Finds from the Bar Kokhba Period in the Cave of Letters*. 3 vols. Jerusalem: Israel Exploration Society.

24

Judean Social Classes

Benjamin D. Gordon

In Judea around the time of Jesus, the capital Jerusalem, which was the mother city of Judeans everywhere, was expanding considerably and developing into an international pilgrimage center. The archaeological remains that have been uncovered in the past half century in the city have shown that the urban elite of the first centuries BCE and CE cultivated a luxurious consumer culture. We can assume that, in keeping with the mores of landowning Mediterranean elites of their day, many of the city's elite also enjoyed revenues in the form of rents from agricultural real estate in the hinterland. Other Judeans, meanwhile, developed resistance strategies to the disparities of wealth they were witnessing in their society. These strategies find expression in the revolutionary impulse of apocalyptic thought, for example, or in the distinctive pietism of poverty among the Essenes and the Jesus movement (e.g., Matt. 10:10 // Mark 6:8 // Luke 9:3).

Here I will expand on these phenomena in a discussion of how the growth of Jerusalem impacted Judean social classes. The significance of class and socioeconomic stratification in understanding the contexts of early Judaism and Christianity has been explored in a few recent studies (Boer and Petterson 2017; Keddie 2019, 2021; Esler 2020; Rosenfeld and Perlmutter 2020). These follow in the footsteps of a host of others on Judean social classes around the time of Jesus (e.g., Stern 1976; Fiensy 1991; Hanson and Oakman 1998; Stegemann and Stegemann 1999) or in the Roman world more broadly (e.g., Scheidel and Friesen 2009; Harris 2011, 15–26). Scholars interested in social class as a category of scholarly inquiry are aware that the category is somewhat anachronistic when applied to the ancient world because inhabitants of that world were not outwardly self-conscious of class in the way that modern people are. To some, the category is too blatantly Marxist. Regardless of how much weight we give to the category of class, it should be viewed as one of several important social distinctions at the heart of Judean society. Others include ethnic and religious identity, kinship ties, social location in an urban or rural setting, and communal or sectarian affiliation.

In the following discussion of Judean social classes, I will focus on the late Second Temple period (2nd c. BCE–70 CE) and will consider peripheral, ethnically Judean regions such as Galilee together with the Jerusalem hinterland. My approach will be gradational and will move from the ruling center of Jerusalem to the agricultural periphery, considering first the governing elites; then priests and retainer classes; then the landholding and subsistence classes, including those in a middle stratum; and finally the structurally impoverished, including the enslaved. I will draw on archaeological and textual evidence and will orient the discussion around the key assumption that the precipitous rise of Jerusalem as a pilgrimage center in the late Second Temple period accentuated disparities of wealth among Judean socioeconomic strata and contributed to class tensions around the time of the early Jesus movement in Palestine.

Governing Elites

With the demise of Greek rule in Judea in the second century BCE, two dynasties controlled the region as monarchies—the Hasmoneans followed by the Herodians—with Roman administrators becoming increasingly involved after the death of Herod in 4 BCE. As rulers of an advanced agrarian economy with vertical social stratification, these dynasts exercised the ability to control and redistribute land, and to collect agricultural surpluses in the form of taxes, utilizing a system of administrative districts called toparchies (Keddie 2019, 25–32; Esler 2020, 47). They had a council of advisers who worked under their direction in Jerusalem. This is possibly the legendary Sanhedrin in Jewish lore (Levine 2002, 267–69). Such advisers joined bureaucrats, scholars, and officials as part of the so-called retainer class, which I will discuss in the next section.

The Hasmoneans (ca. 140–37 BCE) set the stage for a number of class-related developments in Judea. Their rise to power marked the end of the attempt to establish a Greek-style citizen class in Jerusalem. It also meant the establishment of an autonomous Judean monarchy, with the local population ruled as subjects to a king. More importantly, the Hasmoneans actively promoted the Judaization of much of Palestine, including Galilee and Idumea, and spread an ethos of Torah piety in their realm (Regev 2013). This led Torah-learned scribal groups to rise in social status. The Hasmoneans also centralized the tax-collection system in Jerusalem (Tal 2009) and encouraged Jewish pilgrimage from abroad, which benefited priests and those in the city's commercial and service industries (Trotter 2019, 76–110).

The Herodians (37 BCE–44 CE) continued this investment in Jerusalem as an economic center, furthering its status as the mother city of Judeans everywhere. Herod would pay for the radical expansion of its temple to God, which was his most glorious display of piety to the divine and of patronage toward the Judean people (Rocca 2008, 291–306). Importantly, the Herodians also helped shift the orientation of the Judean elite consumer culture toward Rome (Berlin 2014). Their Romanizing lifestyle called for new entertainment venues, social bathing in heated bathhouses, and lavish feasting—all leisure activities using architectural forms new to the region.

Roman administrators and soldiers (or mercenaries) became more present with the Roman annexation of Syria in 64 BCE and the formation of the province of Judea in 6 CE, with its capital at Caesarea Maritima. Herod had founded that city as a non-Judean polis dedicated to the Roman presence in the East, and its Judean minority outwardly struggled with the city's population (e.g., Josephus, *J.W.* 2.266–70). There were similarly Hellenized environments in nearby cities such as Scythopolis, Jamnia, and Gadara. From a Judean perspective, these cities were effectively diasporic (Mason 2019). Roman efforts to revive and sustain the urban tradition on the periphery of Judea, in places the Hasmoneans had taken over, contributed a certain cosmopolitanism to the region. The Romans also introduced to Judea their distinctive system of patronage (*patrocinium*), whereby favors were exchanged between a patron of higher social status and a client of lower status. These relationships, however, appear to have remained relatively rare in Judea (Marshall 2009, 324–28; Schwartz 2010, 166–77).

Priests and Retainer Classes

Another influential social class in ancient Judea, in addition to the governing elites, was the priests. This class was clan based and hereditary—a privilege of birth and one that entitled its members to sacrificial meat and other goods offered up to the deity (Stern 1976, 561–612). While the high priest and other officials who controlled financial allocation lived year-round in Jerusalem, most priests resided in the countryside and came to Jerusalem only on special occasions (Gordon 2020, 2–4, 195–203). They were not strictly endogamous, as marrying women outside the class was allowable under Jewish law, though this was perhaps frowned upon by higher-status priests (Stern 1976, 582–83). Full priestly pedigree was a mark of honor. John the Baptist, for example, is said in Luke 1:5 to have been born into a priestly family on both his paternal and maternal sides. The wives of priests may have enjoyed elite social status, even if their status was precarious, as it could be lost through death or divorce (Schectman 2011). The Judean socioreligious group known as the Sadducees appears to have consisted largely of members of this class. They are said to have emphasized human free will over against divine providence and to have denied the possibility of bodily resurrection after death (Josephus, *J.W.* 2.164–65; Esler 2020, 55).

While some priests were obviously wealthy (Keddie 2019, 232–34; Gordon 2020, 195–98), others were so poor as to face destitution. Philo of Alexandria was aware of the existence of impoverished priests (*Spec. Laws* 1.154), as was Josephus, who recounts that some even starved to death when their holy portions were taken from them by other priests at the threshing floors (*Ant.* 20.179–81). To be sure, resentment toward the more avaricious priests runs through Judean literature (Gordon 2020, 197–98), and priestly wealth would have only increased as Jerusalem grew into a regional juggernaut.

The Levites were another sacred class, who claimed descent from the holy tribe of Levi. By the time of Jesus, their influence in Judea had long been diminished (Stern 1976, 596–600). They no longer enjoyed altar privileges, and the first tithe was no longer exclusively theirs (Udoh 2020, 244–78). Furthermore, their role in scriptural exegesis had been eclipsed by other scribal groups (Leuchter 2011). Nevertheless, as gatekeepers within the temple precinct, the Levites may have been crucial in directing pilgrims and acquainting them with the customs of the festival and, as temple singers, in creating a sacred atmosphere within the precinct through the creation of song. A comment by Josephus suggests that some lobbied the Sanhedrin to be granted the ability to be taught the musical art (*Ant.* 20.218), which suggests that Levites who were temple singers enjoyed a special status within the class.

In addition to the sacred classes, there were other groups closely tied to the institutions of power in Judea. Scribes, tax collectors, physicians, body servants, and entertainers were among some of the individuals whose personal connections to the governing elites put them in a class position above the masses. They have been called retainers (Fiensy 1991, 162–64; Stegemann and Stegemann 1999, 131–32). Among the retainer class, scribes schooled in the interpretation of Judean sacred law rose to particular prominence (Goodman 2007; Stern 1976, 619–21). Many of these retainer scribes may have formed a core component of the Pharisee movement, as has been explored in scholarship (Saldarini 1988, 42; Horsley 2022).

Landholding and Subsistence Classes

Landownership was a mark of status in ancient Judea, as elsewhere in the Mediterranean world. The best tracts of land in Judea were likely held by the ruling classes and other members of a small elite. Long before the time of Jesus, the region had seen the rise of large agricultural estates (*latifundia*), many of which practiced export-oriented monocropping (Kloppenborg 2008). Grains, olives, grapes, or other common Mediterranean crops were grown in the region. Estate owners rented out their land to a large tenant class, who in turn may have utilized day laborers; a single estate may have included plots governed by a variety of contracts (Keddie 2019, 93–101). These tenants, along with most small freeholders of land, would have lived more or less at subsistence level. In the Roman Empire, it is estimated that some 90 percent of the total population lived at such a level, with only about 1.5 percent in the aristocracy and 6–12 percent in a middle stratum (Scheidel and Friesen 2009, 84–85).

In an exegetical study of the parable of the tenants in Mark 12, John Kloppenberg discusses various kinds of agricultural tenancy. The two main forms were the fixed-rate lease and the crop-share lease. Fixed-rate leaseholders, Kloppenberg observes, would have enjoyed a higher status than crop-share leaseholders, because they were subject to less supervision (2006, 312–13). In more precarious economic positions were the day laborers, such as those described in Matthew 20:1–16. The number of laborers in Judea appears to have increased with the breakdown of traditional kinship structures in the Hasmonean and Herodian periods (Rosenfeld and Perlmutter 2020, 69–71,

87–88). The rise of tenancy also disrupted family ties to land, as did the movement of persons into cities such as Jerusalem and Sepphoris.

The breakdown of traditional kinship structures may have led many Judeans to seek out other identity groups, which can explain the rise of sectarianism in this era (Baumgarten 1996; Honigman 2021). While the Sadducean sect or philosophical school seems to have overlapped considerably with the priestly class and to have been associated with the aristocracy, the Pharisees and the Essenes appear to have drawn many of their numbers from the subsistence classes. Pharisaism was interested in imbuing everyday life with a sense of Torah-observant holiness, and it embraced the possibility of a fruitful afterlife with bodily resurrection (Josephus, *J.W.* 2.162–64; Esler 2020, 54–55). In Acts 23:6–10, Paul explicitly identifies with the group. Essenism offered an ascetic communal lifestyle marked by voluntary poverty and strict purity practices (Josephus, *J.W* 2.119–61; Esler 2020, 55–56).

As for the early Jesus movement, scholars who seek to explain the popularity of Jesus's message of social and economic justice (e.g., Horsley 1987; Fiensy 1991; Hanson and Oakman 1998), or who ground themselves in Marxist thought (e.g., Boer and Petterson 2017), tend to emphasize the power imbalance between the elite and everyone else and to assume very low rates of freeholding of land among the lower classes. The approach has struck some as hyperbolic, as Philip Esler discusses (2020, 48–49). Anthony Keddie has argued, for example, that institutional shifts in the early Roman period, such as the privatization of formerly royal land, could have benefited the lower classes, as did the overall growth of the economy (2019). And Ben Zion Rosenfeld and Haim Perlmutter have emphasized the evidence for widespread freeholding of land in the time of Jesus (2020, 116–40). Freeholding would have provided a degree of economic independence for the average family, leading Rosenfeld and Perlmutter to suggest that many Judean farmers should be classified as middle class in the Roman period.

Merchants in Jerusalem and in Galilean cities such as Sepphoris and Tiberias may have also lived quite comfortably as those cities grew, joining an empire-wide urban middle stratum that has become the subject of more recent scholarly inquiry (Scheidel and Friesen 2009, 84–85). Emanuel Mayer has even argued that Roman urbanism was shaped by the values and material culture of this class (Mayer 2012). Interestingly, Wayne Meeks has proposed that the urban communities of early Christianity were largely merchants and artisans enjoying some degree of economic independence but stigmatized in some way by their origin; their "status inconsistency" may have helped pull them together as a community (Meeks 1983, 72–73, 191).

The Judean subsistence classes would also have included those in the service industries, as well as builders, artisans, and craftsmen. By the first century CE, wealthy Jerusalemites were paying for architectural ornament in stone, stucco and plaster work, wall frescoes, and floor mosaics in their homes, as well as rock-cut facade tombs for the burial of their dead. Beyond the tombs, there are other manifestations of a growing taste among Judea's elite for finely crafted things, such as luxury table wares, jewelry, lamps, glassware, stoneware, and furnishings (Berlin 2014; Keddie 2019, 197–248). Some of these objects were locally made, though none of the Judean artisans behind them were famous enough to bear mention in the early Jewish sources (Fine 2005, 65–69). In Galilee, much of the everyday cooking and storage wares were produced at Kefar Hananya and Shikhin, demonstrating that certain village workshops could rise to positions of dominance in the local market (Rosenfeld and Perlmutter 2020, 98–99).

Sectarian texts offer critique of elite acquisitive practices, drawing on a deep corpus of biblical writings in this vein (Longenecker 2010, 29–35). For example, the apocalyptic vision of 1 Enoch 92–105 imagines a striking reversal of fortunes in a future age and can be read, among other things, as a critique of economic exploitation by the elite (Adams 2014, 196–205). The Qumran sectarians, who were probably Essene, adopted a self-consciously anti-elite lifestyle. The ceramic remains from the site are marked by a proliferation of plain dining vessels and a relative scarcity of imported and decorative table wares (Mizzi 2017, 392–95). The Essenes also eschewed many of the methods of wealth acquisition adopted by the elite. They disavowed rental income, the charging of interest, and the possession of enslaved persons. They also pooled their wealth collectively (Murphy 2002, esp. 453; cf. Acts 4:32–37). Interestingly, as tensions between the broader Judean population and the Roman administration rose in the first century CE, even the upper classes shifted to a material culture that Andrea Berlin has called anti-Roman (2002; 2014, 116–17). The archaeological record suggests a new preference for locally made pottery over against luxurious imports. Interior decor in homes became more toned down, and jewelry in fine gold-colored metals was less common.

Meanwhile, the authors of the Gospels appear to have viewed the commercial aspects of the temple as standing in blatant contradiction with its spiritual function as a place of communication with the God of Israel. Mark 11:15–17 describes Jesus as overturning the tables of the money changers and the dove sellers in the precinct and calling the place a den of thieves; similar accounts appear in Matthew 21:12–13, Luke 19:45–47, and John 2:13–16. Indeed, the temple's expansive outer court, with its porticoes and royal stoa, was open to the public and used among other things for commercial activity associated with pilgrimage (Levine 2002, 226–43). We can surmise that many of the city's aristocracy and merchant classes would have benefited financially from that activity. The Gospel accounts on Jesus's arrest in Jerusalem focus on this commercial aspect of the institution and criticize it.

The Impoverished and Enslaved

The Judean literary heritage abounds in texts calling for support of the economically vulnerable in society—orphans, widows, foreigners, the infirm, the elderly, and so on (Longenecker 2010, 109–17). This ethic of caring for the poor was seen as a religious obligation inspired by the theology of liberation in Hebrew Scripture. Certain Judeans began to adopt the trappings of an impoverished lifestyle themselves, in what Timothy Ling has called a pietism of poverty (2006). The Essenes embraced this approach, as did the early Jesus movement. Therefore, when New Testament sources mention the poor as a collective, they may be signaling communities living not in economic destitution per se but according to a pietism of poverty that was marked by asceticism, commingling of resources, and almsgiving (Ling 2006, 144–45).

Yet utter destitution was real for many, and in first-century CE Judea such hardship may have been exacerbated by the cancellation of a biblically prescribed, automatic debt remission according to the sabbatical cycle—a decree attributed to the sage Hillel and called the *prosbul* (Goodman 1982, 421–23). Seen in one light, the cancellation of periodic debt forgiveness allowed for the free flow of credit in an expanding economy by shielding creditors from loss. But in another, it removed an important safety net for those in financial trouble. Martin Goodman has argued that wealthy Jerusalemites, including priests, who had benefited from the influx of pilgrims to the city, began purchasing land from sellers in distress and investing in debt (1982, 419–21; 1987, 58–60). They issued loans even to those in acute financial difficulty, protected now from risk due to the *prosbul* and in a position to seize more property should debtors fall into arrears. The credit they offered could have been crucial for survival in periods of famine, such as the Claudian famine that swept through the Roman Empire in the 40s CE, or in times of widespread unemployment, as that described by Josephus on the eve of the war with Rome, when he claims some eighteen thousand workers were put out of work when the temple was completed (*Ant.* 20.219). Yet their credit operations also contributed to class conflict. Indeed, economic desperation coupled with anti-Roman sentiment led to a breakout of banditry in the region in the 60s CE, and one of the bandits' first acts upon entering Jerusalem in 67 CE was to burn the debt archives in the city (*J.W.* 2.247–48). This followed other instances of banditry in first-century Judea, including in Galilee, which have been seen as violent responses to the structural inequality that the impoverished faced (Horsley 1987, 86–91; Boer and Petterson 2017, 148–49). If Goodman is correct that many creditors were priests, then the debt problems that plagued the economy may have aggravated the sense that the temple was being managed by an unscrupulous group.

Finally, it must be noted that slavery was a fact of life in Judea (Hezser 2010, 227–28; Stern 1976, 624–30). Non-Judean slaves could have been purchased on the market or captured in wars led by Judean kings, while Judeans themselves may have found themselves enslaved to the Romans. One such example is the account of the burning of Sepphoris in 4 BCE by the Roman governor Varus, who is said to have taken many of its inhabitants as slaves (Josephus, *Ant.* 17.289). An ossuary of the Goliath family of priests at Jericho bears the inscription "Theodotus, freedman of Queen Agrippina" (Hezser 2010, 50), and a special synagogue of freedmen is said in Acts 6:9 to have stood in Jerusalem.

Summary

Judea's advanced agricultural economy in the second century BCE to first century CE left evidence for increased disparities of wealth as a result of economic growth under Hasmonean and Herodian rule. The rise of Jerusalem as a pilgrimage center of international importance was the main driver of this growth, and it benefited the local elite significantly. Members of the subsistence classes moved to Jerusalem and to other urban areas, such as Sepphoris, eroding traditional kinship-based ties to land in the rural sector. This process that had already been set in motion by the growth of agricultural estates in the Hellenistic period increased the size of the tenant class. Differences in class had ramifications for lifestyle too, with those in positions of power in Judea taking advantage of economic surpluses to engage in certain leisure activities and to use social capital to further entrench their status. Benefiting from revenues from the pilgrimage event and from rents from tenants on their land, many Judean elites adopted a culture of opulence. Responses to the growing disparities of wealth included apocalyptic visions with an economic dimension to them, the development of a certain pietism of poverty among sectarian groups, and even instances of outright class violence and brigandry against the rich. Many of the structural features of advanced agricultural economies had been in place for centuries in the region—the Hebrew Bible is full of texts addressing impoverishment, for instance—but the growth of the local economy in the second century BCE to first century CE only enhanced socioeconomic disparities. The social messages of the early Jesus movement developed against this backdrop. Material prosperity in the era benefited the ruling classes while leaving others with the sense that the God of Israel was soon to overthrow the current world order.

Works Cited

Adams, Samuel L. 2014. *Social and Economic Life in Second Temple Judea*. Louisville: Westminster John Knox.

Baumgarten, Albert I. 1996. "City Lights: Urbanization and Sectarianism in Hasmonean Jerusalem." In *The Centrality of Jerusalem: Historical Perspectives*, edited by Marcel Poorthuis and Chana Safrai, 50–64. Kampen: Kok Pharos.

Berlin, Andrea. 2002. "Romanization and Anti-Romanization in Pre-Revolt Galilee." In *The First Jewish Revolt: Archaeology, History, and Ideology*, edited by Andrea Berlin and J. Andrew Overman, 57–73. New York: Routledge.

———. 2014. "Herod the Tastemaker." *NEA* 77, no. 2: 108–19.

Boer, Roland, and Christina Petterson. 2017. *Time of Troubles: A New Economic Framework for Early Christianity*. Minneapolis: Fortress.

Esler, Philip F. 2020. "The Social World of Early Judaism." In *Early Judaism and Its Modern Interpreters*, edited by Matthias Henze and Rodney A. Werline, 45–68. 2nd ed. Atlanta: SBL Press.

Fiensy, David A. 1991. *The Social History of Palestine in the Herodian Period: The Land Is Mine*. Studies in the Bible and Early Christianity 20. Lewiston, NY: Mellen.

Fine, Steven. 2005. *Art and Judaism in the Greco-Roman World: Toward a New Jewish Archaeology*. Cambridge: Cambridge University Press.

Goodman, Martin. 1982. "The First Jewish Revolt: Social Conflict and the Problem of Debt." *JJS* 33: 417–27.

———. 1987. *The Ruling Class of Judaea: The Origins of the Jewish Revolt against Rome, AD 66–70*. Cambridge: Cambridge University Press.

———. 2007. "Texts, Scribes and Power in Roman Judaea." In *Judaism in the Roman World, Collected Essays*, 79–90. AJEC 66. Leiden: Brill.

Gordon, Benjamin D. 2020. *Land and Temple: Field Sacralization and the Agrarian Priesthood of Second Temple Judaism*. Studia Judaica 87. Berlin: de Gruyter.

Hanson, K. C., and Douglas E. Oakman. 1998. *Palestine in the Time of Jesus: Social Structures and Social Conflicts*. Minneapolis: Fortress.

Harris, W. V. 2011. *Rome's Imperial Economy*. Oxford: Oxford University Press.

Hezser, Catherine. 2010. *Jewish Slavery in Antiquity*. Oxford: Oxford University Press.

Honigman, Sylvie. 2021. "Social and Economic Upheavals and 'De-Traditionalization' of Judean Society in Hellenistic Times." In *Social History of the Jews in Antiquity: Studies in Dialogue with Albert Baumgarten*, edited by Michal Bar-Asher Siegal and Jonathan Ben-Dov, 67–86. TSAJ 185. Tübingen: Mohr Siebeck.

Horsley, Richard A. 1987. *Jesus and the Spiral of Violence: Popular Jewish Resistance in Roman Palestine*. San Francisco: Harper & Row.

———. 2022. *The Pharisees and the Temple-State of Judea*. Eugene, OR: Cascade Books.

Keddie, G. Anthony. 2019. *Class and Power in Roman Palestine: The Socioeconomic Setting of Judaism and Christian Origins*. Cambridge: Cambridge University Press.

———. 2021. "Introduction: The Struggle over Class in the Study of Early Christianity." In *The Struggle over Class: Socioeconomic Analysis of Ancient Christian Texts*, edited by G. Anthony Keddie, Michael Flexsenhar III, and Steven J. Friesen, 1–50. WGRWSup 19. Atlanta: SBL Press.

Kloppenborg, John S. 2006. *The Tenants in the Vineyard: Ideology, Economics, and Agrarian Conflict in Jewish Palestine*. WUNT 195. Tübingen: Mohr Siebeck.

———. 2008. "The Growth and Impact of Agricultural Tenancy in Jewish Palestine (III BCE–I CE)." *Journal of the Economic and Social History of the Orient* 51: 31–66.

Leuchter, Mark. 2011. "From Levite to Maśkîl in the Persian and Hellenistic Eras." In *Levites and Priests in Biblical History and Tradition*, edited by Mark A. Leuchter and Jeremy M. Hutton, 215–32. AIL 9. Atlanta: Society of Biblical Literature.

Levine, Lee I. 2002. *Jerusalem: Portrait of the City in the Second Temple Period (538 BCE–70 CE)*. Philadelphia: Jewish Publication Society.

Ling, Timothy J. M. 2006. *The Judaean Poor and the Fourth Gospel*. SNTSMS 136. Cambridge: Cambridge University Press.

Longenecker, Bruce W. 2010. *Remember the Poor: Paul, Poverty, and the Greco-Roman World*. Grand Rapids: Eerdmans.

Marshall, Jonathan. 2009. *Jesus, Patrons, and Benefactors: Roman Palestine and the Gospel of Luke*. WUNT 259. Tübingen: Mohr Siebeck.

Mason, Steve. 2019. "*Eretz-Israel* and Diaspora: Variations on the Category Blues." In *Tra politica e religione: I Giudei nel mondo greco-romano; Studi in onore di Lucio Troiani*, edited by Livia Capponi, 225–46. Milan: Jouvence.

Mayer, Emanuel. 2012. *The Ancient Middle Classes: Urban Life and Aesthetics in the Roman Empire, 100 BCE–250 CE*. Cambridge, MA: Harvard University Press.

Meeks, Wayne A. 1983. *The First Urban Christians: The Social World of the Apostle Paul*. New Haven: Yale University Press.

Mizzi, Dennis. 2017. "From the Judaean Desert to the Great Sea: Qumran in a Mediterranean Context." *Dead Sea Discoveries* 24: 378–406.

Murphy, Catherine M. 2002. *Wealth in the Dead Sea Scrolls and in the Qumran Community*. STDJ 40. Leiden: Brill.

Regev, Eyal. 2013. *The Hasmoneans: Ideology, Archaeology, Identity*. JAJSup 10. Göttingen: Vandenhoeck & Ruprecht.

Rocca, Samuel. 2008. *Herod's Judaea: A Mediterranean State in the Classical World*. TSAJ 122. Tübingen: Mohr Siebeck.

Rosenfeld, Ben Zion, and Haim Perlmutter. 2020. *Social Stratification of the Jewish Population of Roman Palestine in the Period of the Mishnah, 70–250 CE*. BRLJ. Leiden: Brill.

Saldarini, Anthony J. 1988. *Pharisees, Scribes and Sadducees in Palestinian Society: A Sociological Approach*. Wilmington, DE: Michael Glazier.

Schectman, Sarah. 2011. "The Social Status of Priestly and Levite Women." In *Levites and Priests in Biblical History and Tradition*, edited by Mark A. Leuchter and Jeremy M. Hutton, 83–102. AIL 9. Atlanta: Society of Biblical Literature.

Scheidel, Walter, and Steven J. Friesen. 2009. "The Size of the Economy and the Distribution of Income in the Roman Empire." *JRS* 99: 61–91.

Schwartz, Seth. 2010. *Were the Jews a Mediterranean Society? Reciprocity and Solidarity in Ancient Judaism*. Princeton: Princeton University Press.

Stegemann, Ekkehard W., and Wolfgang Stegemann. 1999. *The Jesus Movement: A Social History of Its First Century*. Minneapolis: Fortress.

Stern, Menahem. 1976. "Aspects of Jewish Society: The Priesthood and Other Classes." In *The Jewish People in the First Century: Historical Geography, Political History, Social, Cultural and Religious Life and Institutions*, edited by Shemuel Safrai and Menahem Stern, 561–630. CRINT 2. Assen: Van Gorcum.

Tal, Oren. 2009. "Hellenism in Transition from Empire to Kingdom: Changes in the Material Culture of Hellenistic Palestine." In *Jewish Identities in Antiquity: Studies in Memory of Menahem Stern*, edited by Lee I. Levine and Daniel R. Schwartz, 55–73. TSAJ 130. Tübingen: Mohr Siebeck.

Trotter, Jonathan R. 2019. *The Jerusalem Temple in Diaspora Jewish Practice and Thought during the Second Temple Period*. JSJSup 192. Leiden: Brill.

Udoh, Fabian E. 2020. *To Caesar What Is Caesar's: Tribute, Taxes, and Imperial Administration in Early Roman Palestine (63 BCE–70 CE)*. BJS 343. Providence, RI: Brown University Press.

25

Itinerant Religious Experts

Heidi Wendt

Itinerant experts were a regular feature of religious life in the ancient Mediterranean and Near East, across all periods and cultural areas. Yet the degrees of connectivity, cosmopolitanism, and demographic change achieved under the Roman Empire proved especially conducive to their activities, while encouraging types of offerings that aligned with the religious and intellectual enthusiasms of the day. The disciplined analysis devoted to these religious actors in the last two decades has yielded several clues that the earliest authorities on Christ should be counted among them. Whereas previous scholars entertained the possibility that Jesus and the apostles either were *like* the assorted holy men roving the empire's religious landscape or were themselves *mere* magicians, recent work moves beyond the limitations of such categories to approach Christ experts as regular participants in a broader and increasingly well-defined religious phenomenon.

The advantage of thus situating them is twofold: On the one hand, approaching the figures (and authors) of the New Testament and other early "Christian" sources as itinerant religious experts highlights important affinities between their practices or self-positionings and those of similar figures who were neither Jewish nor Christian. On the other, the literary record of early Christianity becomes a record of itinerant expertise more generally, one that consists of rare firsthand correspondence, redemptive historiographies, and texts utilized to lend credence otherwise to the authority or practices of aspiring authorities on Christ. Reconciling these sources with other kinds of evidence for itinerant religious experts, including writings highly critical of them, yields a striking portrait of their contributions to wider religious transformations that occurred during the Roman Empire.

Preliminary Definitions

To take "itinerant religious experts" as an object of study requires preliminary attention to each of these three terms, beginning with what makes the figures in question "religious." While scholars have become attuned to certain drawbacks in applying modern concepts of religion to antiquity, this language remains helpful as an analytical category for any social practices that involved or communicated with the gods and other divine beings (Stowers 2011; Schilbrack 2019; Rüpke 2018, 5–10). This criterion of the latter's involvement is necessary for drawing meaningful distinctions between "religious" experts and people claiming other types of expertise in the Roman world. Itinerant religious experts often strived to be jacks-of-all-trades, purveying a range of services that might be expressed in a philosophical or medical vernacular using the conventions of classical rhetoric. Likewise, philosophers espoused theological doctrines and debated the efficacy of divination and ritual.

Hence there might be considerable overlap between someone like Paul, who adopted a philosophical register, and contemporary popular philosophers (Malherbe 1989). Yet Paul did not merely theorize divine *pneuma* (usually translated "Spirit"); he also transmitted it through baptism, bestowing special abilities on those who received it (e.g., 1 Cor. 12:7–11). The role of God, Christ, and *pneuma* in Paul's practices thus places him squarely in the category of religious expert rather than that of philosopher or rhetor, even though certain of his skills or discourses were strongly associated with the latter figures.

"Itinerancy" implies constant movement or travel. Judging from Jesus's commission of the "apostles" (ones sent forth), Paul's junket, or the far-flung apostolic terrain of Acts, this condition characterized many early authorities on Christ. Aspiring experts took advantage of the Roman world's improved connectivity to stay on the move, and Christians were no exception (Marquis 2013, 2022; Nanos and Wendt 2022). Some relied on written correspondence conveyed by coworkers to communicate with clients or followers, which enabled ever more ambitious itineraries. Paul could dispatch a letter to the Romans, whom he had not met,

to cultivate a relationship on the promise of a future visit en route to Spain, though not before a stopover in Jerusalem (Rom. 15:22–29; Ehrensperger 2022). Cosmopolitan cities, especially, drew experts of all varieties and served as agonistic venues for their rivalries. Most of the places that defined the geography of early Christianity—Alexandria, Athens, Corinth, Ephesus, Rome—recur in ancient sources as attractive destinations for such figures (Wendt 2016a, 176–79). It is no accident that so many known Christian intellectuals of the second century coincided in Rome (Lampe 2003; Snyder 2020), which remained a formative hub for Christian authorities even as some fanned out in search of untapped audiences (Wendt 2016a, 202–9; 2020a; Secord 2021).

Notwithstanding, the fact of itinerancy may be less essential to this sort of religious activity than the conditions that enabled would-be experts to be transient in the first place. While many did make a habit of travel, the frequency of their movements varied considerably. Paul and his companions were always on the road, whether because their *religious* labor complemented manual labor of another form (Ascough 2000; Bell 2020) or simply to fulfill his mandate to bring the gospel to all nations (Fredriksen 2017, 21–31; Ehrensperger 2022, 295–98). In contrast, Justin Martyr, Marcion, and Valentinus permanently relocated to Rome, while Irenaeus took in its intellectual scene for a spell as he ventured forth from Smyrna to Lyons (Secord 2021).

Rather, what all itinerant religious experts (and some who were not habitually itinerant) shared was a lack of institutional affiliation. Unlike the personnel of established temples or formal religious bodies such as the Roman priestly colleges, *these* religious specialists had to generate their own authority and legitimacy. Institutional independence posed several challenges but also afforded greater opportunities for innovation and portability. An itinerant religious expert might even boast a distant institutional affiliation, but the unverifiability of such a claim abroad meant that it functioned in new contexts as a tactic of self-authorization.

The burden of constructing one's own religious authority brings us to the question of what made someone an "expert" in religion? Since itinerant specialists lacked institutional legitimacy, the burden fell on them to convince others of their authority, often through displays of knowledge and technical skills that exceeded ordinary religious competencies.[1] Institutional personnel wielded certain forms of religious specialty, but the skill associated with their roles varied with perceptions about what was required to deliver the religious services on offer. However, the cultivation of specialty for its own sake was the name of the game for itinerant religious experts, whose status as such depended on convincing audiences of not only their legitimacy but also their singularity and indispensability. Such priorities are on full display in Juvenal's sixth satire, where exotic religious experts warn Roman women of grave offenses committed unwittingly against whatever foreign gods these "priests" represent (*Sat.* 6.508–91). The latter figures also purvey exclusive remedies for the dire predicaments they diagnose. Mockable in the context of satire, the same basic scheme could describe Paul's teaching about the erstwhile estrangement of Gentiles from the Judean god, their current predicament of captivity to sin, and a forthcoming day of divine judgment (Rom. 1:18–32). Fortunately for his Gentile audience, Paul has been dispatched by this god with a special message foretelling their reconciliation through the recently revealed figure of Christ.

Tactics varied, but all would-be experts engaged in conspicuous displays of skill and proprietary wisdom. Those who could do so catered to contemporary indices of prestige

by featuring intellectual discourses and texts in their offerings (Wendt 2020b). Scholars have paid much attention to the use of "Scripture" in the letters of Paul, the Gospels, and the writings of early Christian intellectuals such as Justin Martyr, but far less so to how such appeals to "the writing" or to mysteries revealed from the law and the prophets (Rom. 16:25–27) were of a piece with how other religious experts utilized prophetic or wisdom texts in their practices (Wendt 2016b). Lucian, a second-century satirist, skewers "charlatans" for brandishing pseudo-Sibylline oracles written to presage their religious enterprises and imbue these with a sense of learned antiquity (*Peregr.* 27, 29; *Alex.* 11). But this critique may apply equally to how New Testament and early Christian authors mined Hebrew Bible texts for "oracles" mandating everything from their respective representations of Christ to their own roles and the commitments they enjoined on followers (Wendt 2022). Tellingly, several New Testament sources betray anxieties about the prospect of ongoing mythmaking, genealogical speculation, and oracular interpretation done in the service of these aims (e.g., Col. 2:4, 8, 18; 1 Tim. 1:4, 7; Titus 1:13–14; 3:9; 2 Pet. 3:15–16).

In sum, itinerant religious experts were self-authorized purveyors of myriad religious services: divination, healing, rites of initiation or purification, esoteric instruction, and spells to compel divine action, among others. Some of their claims were extraordinary even within a Greco-Roman social milieu, as Paul's promises of bodily transformation and the resurrection of the dead seem to have been for his skeptical Corinthian audience (1 Cor. 15:12–32). Operating independently of the institutional settings that naturalized both religious authority and its transactional qualities, itinerant religious actors were ever vulnerable to charges of insincerity, impropriety, or profit mongering. This is not to say that institutional independence was starkly absolute: Paul collaborated

---

1. All inhabitants of the Greco-Roman world possessed practical religious know-how as a function of acculturation, observation, and minimal (if any) active instruction (Stowers 2011, 36–41; Rüpke 2018, 11–21).

with multiple coworkers and drew legitimacy from brokered relations with the Jerusalem assembly (e.g., Gal. 2:1–10; Rom. 15:25–28), just as other such experts found advantages in networking or building alliances with one another (Nanos and Wendt 2022, 343–47). Yet institutional independence also afforded far more freedom to adapt to contemporary enthusiasms, technologies, and tokens of prestige (Rüpke and Santangelo 2017). Itinerant experts were thus well equipped to adjust and compete as they traversed the empire purveying their patent religious offerings.

"Judeans" among Itinerant Religious Experts in the Roman World

Scholarship of the last decade has endeavored to locate the protagonists of earliest Christianity (including New Testament authors such as Paul, who never identifies himself or his followers as "Christian") among a broader phenomenon of itinerant or freelance experts (e.g., Bazzana 2009, 2020; Stowers 2011; Marquis 2013; Wendt 2016a; Eyl 2019). Whereas previous generations noted affinities between early Christian leaders and other kinds of intellectuals or religious specialists in their social milieu, these scholars tended either to treat such resemblances as epiphenomenal, reifying Christianity's unique essence, or to expose Christians as some of the many charlatans that plagued the Roman world (e.g., MacMullen 1966; Smith 1978). More recent studies suspend such value judgments in favor of theorizing itinerant experts as a distinct set of religious actors that overlapped in complex ways with other sites of religious activity, such as voluntary associations or temples. As the dynamics of itinerant religious expertise have come into focus, both Christians and Jews emerge as ordinary participants therein.

The task of situating early Christians among other itinerant religious experts has been aided by arguments that some Jews (or Judeans) were

regular participants therein, acting not on behalf of a or *the* Jewish community but as self-authorized purveyors of wisdom, skills, and texts associated with the provincial territory of Judea (Wendt 2015b; 2016a, 87–107).[2] Several Roman-period authors depict Judeans behaving in this capacity. Writing in the late first century CE, the Latin poet Martial includes a Judean taught by his mother to beg among a litany of relentless beggars (followers of Bellona collecting alms, alleged shipwreck victims, and peddlers) who clutter the city of Rome at the end of the first century (*Epigr.* 12.57). Juvenal likewise treats Judeans as stock solicitors of gifts or money in exchange for religious expertise. In his third satire (*Sat.* 3.12–20), he claims that they rent out a shrine of Egeria outside the Porta Capena to beg there with special equipment, a hay-lined chest. The sixth satire places in the company of other exotic swindlers a palsied Judean woman who has abandoned her chest and now presents herself to wealthy women as an interpreter of the laws of Jerusalem—a high priestess as intermediary of the highest heaven. "She too gets her hand filled," Juvenal quips, "though with less, because Judeans sell you whatever dreams you like for the tiniest copper coin" (*Sat.* 6.542–45 [trans. Braund 2004, 285]). Judean exorcists could command a higher fee, or so Lucian claims in reprising the racket of a well-known "Syrian of Palestine" (*Philops.* 16.3–7). Judeans or their sacred texts are also implicated in expulsions, confiscations, and other punishments that regularly targeted itinerant experts (Wendt 2015a, 2015b).

While these depictions cannot be taken at face value, they offer intriguing clues about the character and reception of practices amply attested in the New Testament. The punishments and imprisonments that Paul suffered

2. There is considerable debate about how to translate the Greek term *Ioudaios* or Latin *Iudaeus*, but here "Judean" captures how these figures were perceived from a Roman perspective, as religious experts associated with a particular ethnic population or provincial territory.

have confounded scholars who resist apologetic conclusions about these incidents—that he was the victim of religious persecution by Jews and Romans—but lack an alternative historical explanation for why they occurred. Thinking of Paul, foremost, as the itinerant ambassador of an exotic Eastern deity supplies context for his ambivalent reception since the tandem qualities of itinerancy and foreignness drew suspicion in the Roman world (Marquis 2013). Moreover, by his day, there was a well-established pattern of legislative efforts being undertaken routinely against itinerant religious experts and some philosophers (Wendt 2015a; Schellenberg 2021). Some Roman authors even connect these efforts with collections undertaken by foreign "priests" for their native gods. Since collections were seen to deplete households and promulgate *superstitio*, they were tolerated only for priests of Magna Mater and only on certain days (Cicero, *Leg.* 2.22.9; 2.40.11). Josephus reports an expulsion in the reign of Tiberius that was triggered when a rogue Judean, purporting expertise in the wisdom of Moses, swindled a Roman matron out of donations intended for the Jerusalem temple (*Ant.* 18.65–84).

Judeans and Christians were not exempt from activities that piqued Roman regulatory concerns, even if the survival of their own writings offers a more redemptive picture of their motivations. Paul's collection was destined for the poor among the holy ones in Jerusalem (Rom. 15:26; 1 Cor. 16:1; 2 Cor. 9:1; Gal. 2:10), seemingly an act of charity, whereas he claims to have refrained from demanding any support in favor of working with his own hands (1 Cor. 4:12; 9:1–18; 2 Cor. 11:5–15, 27; 12:11–18). And yet, the impression that his economic practices were of a fundamentally different nature than a "con" orchestrated by the Judean swindler recounted in Josephus owes much to our possession of Paul's own writings, where he has the opportunity to frame his collection as a wholly disinterested affair. This is not to cast a shadow of suspicion over his motives, although his refus-

als of support were not absolute (2 Cor. 11:8–9; Phil. 4:15–16; Schellenberg 2018). Rather, the institutional independence of itinerant actors laid bare the economic interests and exchanges embedded in all forms of religious expertise but more easily misrecognized as such in institutional settings (Bell 2020, 435–44).

Itinerant Religious Experts and the New Testament

Paul alone confirms that itinerant religious experts supply essential context for understanding the New Testament in historical context. Indeed, in every way, including his dealings with coworkers and other apostles, he fits the part of itinerant expert in the mysteries and accompanying rites of an exotic god (Marquis 2013; Wendt 2016a, 146–89). Paul situates himself squarely within a Judean idiom, insisting that he possesses all requisite ethnic credentials (Wendt 2016a, 159–61; Eyl 2017); he presents himself as one dispatched by the Judean god with a special message for Gentiles; he anchors his teachings to events from Israelite epic and the famous Judean oracles (Wendt 2022); and he oversees a transformative initiation, "baptism," with eschatological consequences for those now "in Christ" (Johnson Hodge 2007; Stowers 2008). The agonistic dynamics between itinerant experts also account for his contentious relations with assorted rivals: philosophers, rhetors, other apostles, at times even members of the Jerusalem assembly (Nanos and Wendt 2022, 333–34, 346–47). Rivals remain an occupation of pseudepigraphic letters written in Paul's name (e.g., Eph. 5:6; Col. 2:20–23; 1 Tim. 1:3–7; 6:3–5; 2 Tim. 4:3–4), as they are of other apostolic letters (2 Pet. 2:1–3; 1 John 4:1–6; 2 John 7–9; Jude 4–16) and the letters embedded in the Apocalypse of John (e.g., Rev. 2:2, 20).

The authentic Pauline letters may be unique within the New Testament as the only writings that plainly witness an itinerant religious expert in action. Pseudepigrapha and idealizing narratives such as the Gospels and Acts contain clues that their authors were thoroughly enmeshed in this sort of religious activity, but they were written at a conscious remove from it. A good deal of Acts is devoted to negotiating the fraught terrain of itinerant expertise, and one of its main upshots is to recuperate authorities on Christ (certain ones, at least) from the unseemly associations that plagued all such experts. The Paul of Acts refrains from any practices that, in the authentic Pauline epistles, were most liable to suspicion: he lacks a collection, never writes letters, and, when he falls victim to violence or afoul of the law, these incidents are instigated by an angry mob, usually an amorphous band of roving Judeans. The apologetic aims of Acts are multiple, but this author has a prevailing interest in disentangling its protagonists from the broader phenomenon of itinerant religious expertise by placing them in the unique category of "apostle," set apart from mere "magicians" (Wendt 2016a; Patel 2021). He also trades on stereotypes about the latter in his depictions of Simon, a practitioner of magic seeking now to purchase the power of the *pneuma* (Acts 8:9–24), and a man introduced first as "a certain magician, a Jewish false prophet, named Bar-Jesus," and then as "the magician Elymas" (13:6–9).

The Gospels make varying degrees of admission to Jesus's apparent status as an itinerant religious expert. Mark and John are unabashed in portraying him as a wonder-worker who heals with "magical" techniques (Mark 8:23–25), exorcises daimons and unclean spirits, and brazenly raises the dead (Mark 5:38–43; John 11:17–44). Matthew and Luke also credit Jesus with healings, exorcisms, and restoring life to two people—the son of the widow of Nain (Luke 7:11–17) and the daughter of Jairus (Matt. 9:18–26; Luke 8:40–56), who have recently died. These scenes are subtler and less central than in the other two Gospels. These authors understand Jesus foremost as a kind of philosopher, so their narratives are dominated

instead by extensive teachings and legal debates (Stowers 2010). Still, the Synoptics portray the disciples-cum-apostles as itinerant experts in both practice and comportment when Jesus sends them forth to spread the gospel, and with explicit instructions not to accept payment or to overstay a welcome (Matt. 10:5–14; Mark 6:8–11; Luke 9:2–5).

Itinerant Experts in Earliest Christianity

Once brought into focus as such, the matter of itinerant religious expertise (both its reality and its liabilities) pervades New Testament literature. The letters of Paul indicate that this preoccupation is at least partly the result of the earliest authorities on Christ having themselves been itinerant religious experts, and unabashedly so. Subsequent New Testament authors may have been no less involved in this sort of religious activity, but their writings exhibit more apprehension about that involvement. Yet itinerant religious experts clearly remained relevant, even central, to Christian forms of religion at least through the second century, when several New Testament and early Christian sources were written.

The Johannine letters take for granted an audience that routinely receives visits from unknown teachers or prophets and offer guidelines for adjudicating their legitimacy. Third John praises its recipients for a favorable report delivered by some of the brothers, strangers to them who arrived and testified to the truth (chaps. 3–5). "John" encourages the assembly to support these brothers before sending them on their way in a manner worthy of God, since they began their journey accepting no support from outsiders (chaps. 7–8). He also vouches for one Demetrius and offers assurance that both testimonies, that of Demetrius and that of John about him, are "true." The same letter admonishes a man named Diotrephes for refusing to welcome other brothers and preventing other members from doing so (chaps. 9–12).

His circumspection is understandable, since 2 John 7–11 warns about deceivers who bear contrary teachings about Christ and must not be received or welcomed into one's house. It is striking how many facets of itinerant religious expertise converge in these brief texts: a lack of consensus about the criteria for authenticity; the power residing in a Christian group to recognize the authority of an expert; the normalcy of interaction between itinerant experts and such groups; the reality and delicacy of compensation for religious labor; and the potential of writings (particularly ones attributed to a prominent apostle) to tip the scale in favor of one expert or teaching instead of another.

Similar features coincide in other early Christian sources. Paul used letters to denounce rivals, to safeguard his legitimacy, and to recommend coworkers dispatched in his stead, among other purposes (Mitchell 1992; Marquis 2013, 87–111). They also provided ample space for him to navigate the tricky matter of receiving support in exchange for religious expertise, always affirming his entitlement to it, sometimes denying having ever commanded it, other times deflecting accusations of profitmongering, and others still acknowledging support already received. The noncanonical Didache warns about those who receive without need (1.5) and instructs Christian groups in determining the authenticity of itinerant visitors (11). Among other criteria, the "true" apostle or prophet should stay no longer than three days (11.5), should not ask for money (11.6), and will never demand money while in *pneuma* (11.12). One who violates these criteria is a "Christ monger" to be avoided (12.6).

Conclusion

The insight that the principal actors of early Christianity were itinerant religious experts should be unsurprising, since practices or groups devoted to Christ were among numerous other phenomena to arise from this form of religious activity. Itinerant experts were plentiful in the Roman world, and the intimacy of their rivalries gave rise to robust, innovative offerings with profound similarities to one another, even as patron deities, purported rewards, explanations, and mechanisms differed from one expert to the next. That the apostles and other early Christian leaders, like the groups they instituted, have appeared unique against their Greco-Roman backdrop has much to do with the richness of the Christian archive. Whereas our knowledge of most itinerant experts comes down from their harshest critics, the New Testament and early Christian literature preserve the actual writings of aspiring authorities on Christ, both authors writing plainly as such and ones who utilized texts (pseudepigrapha, apocalypses, Gospels) more covertly to scaffold their authority and teachings. Either way, such sources prime a sympathetic reading, signposting whom to view as protagonists (or antagonists) and avowing the exceptionality of the movement they attest for ancient and modern readers alike. Such prerogatives make sense as relics of itinerant religious expertise, and, restored to that context, early Christian sources contribute much to our understanding of this activity.

Works Cited

Ascough, Richard S. 2000. "The Thessalonian Christian Community as a Professional Voluntary Association." *JBL* 119: 311–28.

Bazzana, Giovanni Battista. 2009. "Early Christian Missionaries as Physicians: Healing and Its Cultural Value in the Greco-Roman Context." *NovT* 51: 232–51.

———. 2020. *Having the Spirit of Christ: Spirit Possession and Exorcism in Early Christ Groups.* New Haven: Yale University Press.

Bell, Brigidda. 2020. "The Cost of Baptism? The Case for Paul's Ritual Compensation." *JSNT* 42: 431–52.

Braund, Susanna Morton, trans. 2004. *Juvenal and Persius.* LCL 91. Cambridge, MA: Harvard University Press.

Ehrensperger, Kathy. 2022. "Romans." In *T&T Clark Handbook to the Historical Paul*, edited by Ryan S.

Schellenberg and Heidi Wendt, 289–305. London: Bloomsbury.

Eyl, Jennifer. 2017. "'I Myself Am an Israelite': Paul, Authenticity and Authority." *JSNT* 40: 148–68.

———. 2019. *Signs, Wonders, and Gifts: Divination in the Letters of Paul*. New York: Oxford University Press.

Fredriksen, Paula. 2017. *Paul: The Pagans' Apostle*. New Haven: Yale University Press.

Johnson Hodge, Caroline. 2007. *If Sons, Then Heirs: Kinship and Ethnicity in the Letters of Paul*. New York: Oxford University Press.

Lampe, Peter. 2003. *From Paul to Valentinus: Christians at Rome in the First Two Centuries*. Edited by Marshall D. Johnson. Translated by Michael Steinhauser. Minneapolis: Fortress.

MacMullen, Ramsey. 1966. *Enemies of the Roman Order: Treason, Unrest, and Alienation in the Empire*. Cambridge, MA: Harvard University Press.

Malherbe, Abraham. 1989. *Paul and the Popular Philosophers*. Minneapolis: Fortress.

Marquis, Timothy Luckritz. 2013. *Transient Apostle: Paul, Travel, and the Rhetoric of Empire*. Synkrisis. New Haven: Yale University Press.

———. 2022. "Travel and Homelessness." In *T&T Clark Handbook to the Historical Paul*, edited by Ryan S. Schellenberg and Heidi Wendt, 87–102. London: Bloomsbury.

Mitchell, Margaret M. 1992. "New Testament Envoys in the Context of Greco-Roman and Epistolary Conventions." *JBL* 111: 641–62.

Nanos, Mark, and Heidi Wendt. 2022. "Galatians." In *T&T Clark Handbook to the Historical Paul*, edited by Ryan S. Schellenberg and Heidi Wendt, 329–47. London: Bloomsbury.

Patel, Shaily Shashikant. 2021. "Notes on Rehabilitating 'Magic' in the Study of Early Christian Literature." *Religion Compass* 15 (September 1): https://doi.org/10.1111/rec3.12415.

Rüpke, Jörg. 2018. *Pantheon: A New History of Roman Religion*. Princeton: Princeton University Press.

Rüpke, Jörg, and Federico Santangelo. 2017. "Public Priests and Religious Innovation in Imperial Rome." In *Beyond Priesthood: Religious Entrepreneurs and Innovators in the Roman Empire*, edited by Richard L. Gordon, Georgia Petridou, and Jörg Rüpke, 15–48. RVV 66. Berlin: de Gruyter.

Schellenberg, Ryan S. 2018. "Did Paul Refuse an Offer of Support from the Corinthians?" *JSNT* 40: 312–36.

———. 2021. *Abject Joy: Paul, Prison, and the Art of Making Do*. New York: Oxford University Press.

Schilbrack, Kevin. 2019. "Imagining 'Religion' in Antiquity: A How To." In *Theorizing "Religion" in Antiquity*, edited by Nickolas P. Roubekas, 59–78. London: Equinox.

Secord, Jared. 2021. "Irenaeus at Rome: The Greek Context of Christian Intellectual Life in the Second Century." In *Irénée entre Asia et Occident: Actes de la journée du 30 juin 2014 à Lyon*, edited by Agnès Bastit, 141–60. Paris: Brepols.

Smith, Morton. 1978. *Jesus the Magician*. San Francisco: Harper & Row.

Snyder, H. Gregory, ed. 2020. *Christian Teachers in Second-Century Rome*. Leiden: Brill.

Stowers, Stanley. 2008. "What Is 'Pauline Participation in Christ'?" In *Redefining First-Century Jewish and Christian Identities: Essays in Honor of Ed Parish Sanders*, edited by Fabian E. Udoh, 352–71. South Bend, IN: University of Notre Dame Press.

———. 2010. "Jesus the Teacher and Stoic Ethics in the Gospel of Matthew." In *Stoicism in Early Christianity*, edited by Tuomas Rasimus, Troels Engberg-Pedersen, and Ismo Dunderberg, 59–74. Grand Rapids: Baker Academic.

———. 2011. "The Religion of Plant and Animal Offerings versus the Religion of Meanings, Essences, and Textual Mysteries." In *Ancient Mediterranean Sacrifice*, edited by Jennifer Wright Knust and Zsuzsanna Varhélyi, 35–51. New York: Oxford University Press.

Wendt, Heidi. 2015a. "*Ea Superstitione*: Christian Martyrdom and the Religion of Freelance Experts." *JRS* 105: 183–202.

———. 2015b. "*Iudaica Romana*: A Rereading of Evidence for Judean Expulsions from Rome." *JAJ* 6: 97–123.

———. 2016a. *At the Temple Gates: The Religion of Freelance Experts in the Roman Empire*. New York: Oxford University Press.

———. 2016b. "Galatians 3:1 as an Allusion to Textual Prophecy." *JBL* 135: 369–89.

———. 2020a. "Christians as and among Writer-Intellectuals in Second-Century Rome." In *Christian Teachers in Second-Century Rome*, edited by H. Gregory Snyder, 84–108. Leiden: Brill.

———. 2020b. "Intellectualizing Religion in the Cities of the Roman Empire." In *Urban Religion in Late Antiquity*, edited by Azuman Lätzer-Lasar Rubens Urciuoli in cooperation with Rubina Raja and Jörg Rüpke, 97–121. Berlin: de Gruyter.

———. 2022. "Mythmaking and Exegesis." In *T&T Clark Handbook to the Historical Paul*, edited by Ryan S. Schellenberg and Heidi Wendt, 87–102. London: Bloomsbury.

26

Gentiles in Judean Eyes

Hannah K. Harrington

The view of Gentiles through Judean eyes fluctuated during Second Temple times, depending largely on the circumstances and shifting attitudes of Gentiles toward Judeans.[1] The following guidelines form necessary parameters for a fruitful discussion of the matter. First, a fair understanding of self-identification among Judeans is essential to the task. The Torah is the wellspring for that effort since it was foundational for all Judeans in this period. Second, foreign occupation upended the political and religious stability of Judeans in this period and affected their outlook on Gentiles. In particular, the rise of Hellenism posed specific challenges. As Judeans made different decisions regarding their own identity, some insulated themselves against Gentiles, while others opened the door to conversion.

In order to organize the data clearly, I will treat Judean attitudes toward Gentiles in two categories: (1) Gentiles outside of the community and (2) Gentiles who were attracted to Judaism.

The Gentile Outsider: The Barrier between Judeans and Gentiles

The invasion and conquest of Judea by Gentile empires during the first millennium BCE formed a new reality for Judeans. Lack of autonomy, diaspora, and periods of persecution were all part of the consequences of foreign occupation. Judeans were faced with the preservation of their identity in a homeland ruled by Gentiles. As Babylonian and Persian rulers were exchanged for Greek and Roman ones, the relationship between Judeans and Gentiles became more unpredictable. The Greek king Antiochus IV, for example, sacked Jerusalem in the second century BCE and forced Jews into idolatry. But his successors restored the temple goods to the Judeans of Antioch and reinstated their citizenship rights (Josephus, *J.W.*

---

1. The term "Judeans" translates the Greek *Ioudaioi*, used in the New Testament and in other Second Temple literature to denote the people of Israel, an ethnicity with shared religious traditions and an ancestral homeland. The term was used for Judeans not only from the province of Judea but also those residing throughout the ancient world.

7.44–45). Thus, the Second Temple period was a time of fluctuation in terms of relations with Gentiles, with alternating periods of peace and panic, ending with the destruction of the Jerusalem temple by the Romans in 70 CE.

Judean attitudes toward Gentile power were mixed. When times were good, it was easier to hear the prophetic voice that Israel was meant to be a "light to the Gentiles," who would one day worship Yahweh with them (e.g., Isa. 49:6; 56:3–7; 66:23; Mic. 4:2). But under persecution and oppression, Judeans were understandably drawn to more vengeful traditions (e.g., the anticipated removal of all foreigners from the restored land of Israel [Pss. Sol. 17.28] or eschatological annihilation of all "sons of darkness" [1QM I, 9–10]). Either way, hope remained eternal that the hammer of the Gentiles would ultimately be broken either by enlightenment or by destruction. According to the Torah, Israel was required to keep non-Israelites, who followed a lifestyle of idolatry and profligate morals, outside of the community (cf. Exod. 34:15–16; Lev. 20:23–26; Deut. 7:3–4). Israel was required to maintain ethical holiness, committing themselves to a lifestyle that reflects Yahweh's character. In order to protect their status as the holy people, Israel also had to maintain a measure of physical separation from outsiders. Ancestry and ethnic traditions created a social barrier between Israel and its neighbors that protected the nation from pagan influences. During Second Temple times these barriers were quite high in many Judean communities.

Genealogy and Circumcision

In Second Temple times, genealogical lists were often produced to prove ancestry (Ezra 2; Neh. 7; 1 Chron. 1–6; CD IV, 2–6; Josephus, *Ant.* 3.276; cf. Josephus, *Ag. Ap.* 1.130–36; m. Qidd. 4.1). The genealogical lists of Ezra and Nehemiah emphasize that the whole nation, not just the priests, was linked to its

forebears and distinct from the local, mixed population (Ezra 2; Neh. 7).[2] In fact, the entire community is referred to as "holy seed" (Ezra 9:2). In a rare move, Ezra disbanded mixed marriages and expelled foreign wives and their children (Ezra 10). A certain strain of Judaism continued Ezra's attitude that all Israel is "holy seed" and must not intermarry with outsiders (see Tob. 4:12a). Ideology is malleable, but bloodline is immutable. Jubilees regards giving an Israelite child in marriage to a Gentile as committing sacrilege and violating the Molek prohibition on child sacrifice (Lev. 20:3; cf. 18:21; Jub. 30.13–15). Many authors of the Dead Sea Scrolls also deplore intermarriage, depicting it as spawning evil spirits (e.g., 4QShir, 4QIncantation), the desecration of holy seed (e.g., Damascus Document, 4QInstruction), or even as the mating of different animal species (4QMMT^b 75–76, 81–82).

The most physical ritual distinguishing Judeans and Gentiles, performed on the eighth day after birth, was the circumcision of baby boys. The point is made that the child entered into the assembly of Israel, not by choice, but by virtue of his ancestry. The indelible mark on the boy's procreative member will also remind him of his duty to raise children within the confines of Israel. This regulation also marked Israel from other forms of circumcision in the ancient world that were not practiced on babies.

Diet and Purity

One of the most distinctive rituals in Second Temple times was Israel's commitment to eating "pure" food. The Torah requires the "pure" people to eat only "pure" animals (Lev. 11). One of the Torah's dietary taboos, pork, was

---

2. According to the Torah, the priesthood was genealogically holy and protected by marriage restrictions. A priest was not allowed to marry a prostitute, divorcée, or rape victim (Lev. 21:7), otherwise he "desecrates his offspring [lit., "seed"] among his kin" (21:15, my translation).

a delectable food of the Greco-Roman world, and thus it became a significant mark of differentiation between Jews and Gentiles. Even before eating permitted foods, some Jewish sects performed ritual ablutions to maintain their purity, including the Pharisees (Mark 7:3–4; Luke 11:38; m. Hag. 2.5) and Essenes (Josephus, *J.W.* 2.129–31; cf. 4Q514 4–7).

Jewish observance of ritual purity increased dramatically during the course of this period. Purification after corpse impurity, scale disease, and sexual discharges (see Lev. 11–15; Num. 19) was often observed cross-culturally, but the Torah's laws reflect an Israelite character and significance as markers of the pure people of Yahweh (Milgrom 1991, 725, 733). Those who followed the community's version of purity were easily distinguished from outsiders, who did not. The city of Jerusalem and especially the temple were marked by purity restrictions (Let. Aris. 106; Josephus, *Ant.* 12.146; cf. 11Q19 XLVII, 3–6). Even in the diaspora, household purity was maintained (e.g., Philo, *Spec. Laws* 3.63, 205–6). According to rabbinic testimony, purity laws were taken as seriously as incest laws (t. Sukkah 4; b. Shabb. 13a; t. Shabb 1.14). The archaeological record (e.g., ritual baths, burials, and stone vessels) supports the concern for ordinary as well as temple purity in Second Temple times throughout the land of Israel (see Adler 2016; Poirier 2003).

Perhaps the most striking reaction of Judeans to foreigners among them is the ascription of ritual impurity to Gentiles (Regev 2000, 228; cf. Harrington 2019, 30–34). According to Jubilees, anyone who eats with a Gentile shares his impurity (Jub. 22.16–17; see 3 Macc. 33:3–7). Several Dead Sea Scrolls treat Gentiles as impure.[3] Herod's temple bore an inscription excluding foreigners from entering beyond

the rampart due to a "law of purification" (Josephus, *J.W.* 5.194 [trans. Thackeray 1957, 458–59]; cf. *Ant.* 12.145–46; 14.285). While Gentiles could donate a gift to the temple, they were restricted to an outer court.[4] The rabbis assign the beginnings of Gentile impurity to Second Temple times as a prevention of sexual relations leading to apostasy (b. Shabb. 17b; b. Avod. Zar. 36b; Hayes 2002, 131). Business dealings could and did occur, but intimate relations were hindered. Assimilation did occur by intermarriage in this period, but it was not widespread (Himmelfarb 1999, 3).

It was customary among many Judeans to bathe after contact with Gentiles. According to Josephus, Essenes bathed after touching junior members of the sect, "as after contact with an alien" (*J.W.* 2.150 [trans. Thackeray 1927, 381]; cf. Mark 7:4). After an epiphany, the apostle Peter says to a Gentile group, "You yourselves know that it is unlawful for a Jew to associate with or to visit a Gentile; but God has shown me that I should not call anyone profane or unclean" (Acts 10:28). Ritual ablutions biblically required of Israelites after times of impurity could also mark the transition from outsider to full member of the community, and this practice was continued in Christian baptism (see 1QS VI, 18–21; Matt. 28:19; John 4:1; m. Pesah. 8.8; Josephus, *J.W.* 2.137–38).

Sabbath

Time was treated uniquely in the Jewish week. In imitation of the Creator, Judeans were required to rest from work one day in the week, the Sabbath. Like the other particular regulations, this commitment became a mark of differentiation and contention between Judeans and Gentiles. Judeans would not work on the Sabbath, which led to accusations about their

---

3. Cf. 4Q266 5 II, 5–7; 1QS V, 14–20. The rejection of intermarriage is reinforced with specific prohibitions regarding pure food and drink (11Q19 LXIII, 10–15; 4Q251 16 2–3; 4Q13).

4. Scholars are divided on whether or not Gentiles could offer sacrifices at the temple. For the exclusivist view, see Schwartz 1992, 102–16. For a more inclusivist approach, see Donaldson 2007, 289–359.

idleness (e.g., Juvenal, *Sat.* 14.106–7). Even during times of persecution, some Judeans would not defend themselves on the Sabbath, choosing to die rather than violate the sacred law (cf. 1 Macc. 2:32–38; 2 Macc. 5:25–26; 6:11).

The Gentile Insider: Hellenism and Conversion

The empiricization of the Greeks under Alexander the Great brought cultural as well as political change. Greek philosophy, education, politics, and entertainment infiltrated local ethnic culture from Athens to India. Intermarriage between Greeks and non-Greeks was encouraged as an organic way to integrate Greek culture across the variety of the empire's subjects. This large-scale dissemination of Hellenism presented a challenge to Judeans: How to accommodate Gentiles and to what extent? On the one hand, Judeans became more differentiated as pressure mounted on them to conform to the new worldview; on the other hand, Judaism was not impervious to the influences of Hellenism. Some Judeans went so far as to attempt to hide their circumcision through surgical means in order to be accepted into the civic and athletic life of their neighbors. Walking a political tightrope to appease his Roman bosses, Herod bankrolled pagan temples and athletic games. At the same time, he was meticulous about Jewish purity laws, maintaining ritual baths in his palaces and hiring priests as masons for the temple so that its purity would not be impugned (Fredriksen 2003, 45).

Resident Alien

In light of Judeans' ancestry and ethnic practices, it would seem that there was an unbridgeable divide between Judeans and Gentiles. However, there was a biblical category of Gentiles within the community that became an important focus during Second Temple times. The Torah makes a distinction between (1) pagan non-Israelites who live in the land and follow idolatrous practices and (2) those who are content to dwell among and align themselves with Israel. While the seven Canaanite nations were slated for destruction (Exod. 34:11–17; Deut. 7:3–4) and some of Israel's immediate neighbors were prohibited as spouses (Deut. 23:3–8; but cf. 21:10–14), Gentiles who were willing to follow Israel's ways were to be treated with respect and incorporated within the community (Lev. 19:34). These Gentiles, referred to as *gerim*, "resident aliens," did not become Israelites and remained at the bottom of the social hierarchy (cf. Exod. 20:10; Deut. 14:21). Jacob Milgrom explains that although the *ger* (singular of *gerim*) was protected by the Israelite community, in terms of religious law "he was not of the same legal status; he neither enjoyed the same privileges nor was bound by the same obligations" (2000, 1496–97; cf. Lev. 17:8, 10, 13; 20:2; 22:18).

Converts and God-Fearers

With the spread of Hellenistic ideals, some Judeans developed a more open attitude toward Gentiles, many of whom were attracted to the Jewish faith. With the emphasis of a more integrative and philosophical approach toward religion in the air, Judeans began to emphasize the praiseworthy lifestyle of Judaism (Sim 2013, 12–13). In the latter half of the Second Temple period, it became possible for Gentiles who were attracted to the Jewish religion to find a place in the Jewish community and even become Jewish if they were willing to commit themselves to the Torah (cf. Josephus, *Ag. Ap.* 2.210). Josephus reports that the Judeans "were constantly attracting to their religious ceremonies multitudes of Greeks, and these they had in some measure incorporated with themselves" (*J.W.* 7.45 [trans. Thackeray 1957, 519]). Some scholars go so far as to suggest that ancestry was no longer a key factor in

Judaism, being only one of many elements of Jewish identity; however, this seems to stretch the evidence, at least for the majority of Jews (cf. Barclay 2019, 48, 53). The impact of ingrained separation in Jewish practice from the time of circumcision to marriage and beyond cannot be gainsaid.

The earliest records of a formal process of conversion to Judaism are found around the mid-second century BCE. Proselytes were required to commit themselves to the Torah, including circumcision for men. For example, Achior was circumcised as a sign of his belief in God "and joined the house of Israel" (Jdt. 14:10; cf. Josephus, *Ant.* 20.38–48). Similarly, Joseph does not consent to marry Aseneth or even acknowledge her beauty until after she has converted (Joseph and Aseneth). Further, the Greek text of Esther 8:17 explains that many Gentiles "were circumcised and judaized" out of fear of the Judeans (my translation; so also Josephus, *Ant.* 11.285). It is worthy of note that the Septuagint, produced during the Hellenistic era, translates the biblical Hebrew *ger* not as "resident alien" but as *proselytos* ("proselyte," "convert") in most cases. According to the rabbis, who later standardize the process of conversion with accompanying rituals and legislation, there were two types of *gerim*: the *ger tsedek*, the proselyte who committed to full Torah observance, and the *ger toshav*, a Gentile who lived among the Jewish community and was expected to renounce idolatry and observe a few other religious laws (b. Avod. Zar. 64b).

Judean attitudes toward proselytes show hesitation toward integrating Gentiles among the community. It does not appear that proselytes were accepted into the Qumran sect, despite the inclusion of the *ger* as a biblical category in the Damascus Document (CD VI, 21; XIV, 3–6; Gillihan 2011, 301). 4QFlorilegium bans the *ger* from the assembly (4Q174 I). The Temple Scroll includes the *ger* in theory, but only in the fourth generation (11Q19 XLIX–L). On the other hand, other Second Temple texts give evidence of Judeans who were opposed to intermarriage among priests but were open to integration of Gentiles into the rest of the nation (Hayes 2002, 59).

Generally, conversion was frowned upon in the ancient world. According to Paula Fredriksen, in the Greco-Roman polytheistic world, people could adopt other traditions as long as they remained true to their ethnic religion; to convert was to commit "cultural treason" (Fredriksen 2003, 39–42, 60). Since Judeans enjoyed exemptions granted by the early Roman emperors, many did not wish to jeopardize their status by encouraging conversion from other religions (Josephus, *Ant.* 14.213–16).[5] Imperial policy offered protection to the Judeans against any malfeasance and punishment to the offenders. Sacred money from Judeans could be sent to Jerusalem, and they were not required to appear in court on the Sabbath (*Ant.* 16.162–65).

Conversion to Judaism, although possible, was not a widespread phenomenon. In fact, earlier estimates of several millions of Judeans in the Greco-Roman world, although based on ancient sources, have come under scrutiny in contemporary scholarship (see Fredriksen 2003, 50). Furthermore, the situation of the Judeans among Gentiles was precarious, and converts would share the persecution Judeans often faced. Also, the physical regulations of the Torah (e.g., circumcision and diet) presented a serious challenge to overcome. Moreover, many Judeans rejected the possibility of conversion altogether (Schwartz 1992; Cohen 1999; Hayes 2002; Thiessen 2011). While they might agree with the prophets that Gentiles would worship Yahweh in the eschaton, commingling under current circumstances was another matter. As a matter of fact, many of the sources depict Gentiles clinging to their

---

5. The force of this exemption is felt in Gentile voices raised against it; cf. Seneca the Younger, *De Superstitione*, cited by Augustine, *Civ.* 6.11; Juvenal, *Sat.* 14.96–98.

idols right up to the end times, and even when they recognize their error, they do not become Jewish (cf. Tob. 14:5–6; Sib. Or. 3.715–24; Justin Martyr, *Dial*. 122–23; cited in Frederiksen 2003, 55).

A middle option was endorsed by Judeans for Gentiles who were attracted to the Jewish lifestyle but did not wish to convert. These people were called "God-fearers." For the polytheistic Romans, adding some foreign beliefs and exotic traditions to one's lifestyle was not a problem. Gentiles could take in as much of Judaism as they wanted, as long as they did not convert from their ancestral religion. While from the Jewish perspective one could not fully convert without renouncing other gods, God-fearers could attend synagogues and participate in Jewish life without conversion.

Jewish hesitation toward proselytes continues in rabbinic literature. The rabbis state that while the temple stood a sacrifice was used to initiate conversion, along with a commitment to the Torah, circumcision, and ritual immersion (t. Demai 2.1; Sifre Num. 108). Nevertheless, even though the full convert is said to be an equal to the native-born Jew ("like a newborn child," b. Yevam. 22a), he remains in a separate category with certain restrictions. He may not marry his daughter to a priest or perform certain judicial functions; he may marry a woman of illegitimate birth, but this will dilute his line (m. Sanh. 4.2; m. Qidd. 4.1, 6; b. Sanh. 36b; t. Qidd. 5.1).

Early Christianity

A religion rooted in Judaism but attracting large numbers of Gentiles without the barrier of difficult rituals, Christianity represented a new phenomenon in the Roman Empire. Still, while the Gospels reflect a Judeo-Christian mission to the Gentiles, a basic mistrust of them is evident in a number of passages. Some highlight the immoral behavior of Gentiles as an example of the wicked lifestyle to avoid.

These passages are presented without invective, just stating the common Jewish view that Gentiles are unholy and one should not imitate their behavior. In a particularly insulting passage, Gentiles are called pigs or dogs. Exhorting caution to avoid adversarial situations, Matthew's Jesus exhorts: "Do not give what is holy to dogs, and do not throw your pearls before swine; or they will trample them under foot, and turn and maul you" (Matt. 7:6; cf. 18:17: a believer who rebels against the church is to be treated "as a Gentile and a tax collector"). But revenge and animosity are not encouraged; instead, we find an unexpected exhortation: love your enemies. Most of these texts represent an early period in the church when there were probably very few Gentiles in the community (Tuckett 2013, 135).

Acts presents the early church's mission to Gentiles while still reflecting the Judeans' default attitude of avoiding Gentiles. Peter requires a heavenly vision to overcome his distaste for Gentiles: "You yourselves know that it is unlawful for a Jew to associate with or to visit a Gentile; but God has shown me that I should not call anyone profane or unclean" (Acts 10:28). Despite his claim that God gave "them the Holy Spirit, just as he did to us; and in cleansing their hearts by faith he has made no distinction between them and us" (Acts 15:8–9), Peter has difficulty eating with Gentile believers (Gal. 2:11–12; cf. Acts 11:2–3).

Paul pushes forward in his efforts to include Gentiles within the early church. He warns Judean Christians at Rome that physical descent in Israel does not guarantee membership in the people of God (Rom. 9:6). He points instead to the bond of believers as "one body" through the "blood" of Christ (1 Cor. 10:16–17). But Paul came under severe persecution from Judean Christians for not requiring converts to observe circumcision and other Jewish traditions (cf. Acts 22:21–22).

Some early church leaders still insisted on separation of Jews and Gentiles (e.g., Ignatius,

Marcion, and Tertullian; cf. Frederiksen 2003, 61). The members of the Didache community even considered Gentiles ritually impure and contagious (Draper 2013, 250). To share in the common meal, they had to be ritually cleansed by fasting and washing in running water or other kinds of specified water and practice appropriate ritual purity.

Conclusion

Judeans exhibit mixed views with regard to Gentiles in Second Temple times. The tension between maintaining Jewish separatist traditions, on the one hand, and the reality of living in a Gentile world, on the other hand, had to be negotiated carefully. Judeans struggled to maintain their identity in the face of anti-Semitism or assimilation. Eschatological hope for universal worship could be entertained, but this was not the only theological option. Ezra and Nehemiah advocated for an impermeable boundary between Judean and Gentile without a thought toward conversion. For most Judeans after them, holiness was restricted to those with ancestry in the people of Israel and a commitment to the Torah. Ethnic traditions—such as circumcision, purity, diet, Sabbath, and marriage restrictions—formed a unique barrier against integration of Gentiles into Jewish life.

Hellenism brought some open-mindedness toward Gentile culture: philosophy, natural science, and pursuit of virtue are ideals that the Torah was seen to promote as well. Some Judeans endorsed Hellenism and the possibility of advancement in civic and athletic life. For many others, however, idolatry and sexual license among Gentiles formed a threat to Jewish purity, and restrictions against them were increased. With the integration of different cultures in the Hellenistic world, however, a crack in the social barrier occurred in Judaism as well. Lifestyle began to play a stronger role in Jewish self-identification, and this attracted God-fearers who participated in Jewish life but did not convert to Judaism. Gentiles who wished to join the nation could follow a formal process of conversion, although they remained a distinct category within Israel.

Works Cited

Adler, Yonatan. 2016. "Between Priestly Cult and Common Culture: The Material Evidence of Ritual Purity Observance in Early Roman Jerusalem Reassessed." *JAJ* 7: 228–48.

Barclay, John. 2019. "ʼΙουδαῖος: Ethnicity and Translation." In *Ethnicity, Race, Religion: Identities and Ideologies in Early Jewish and Christian Texts, and in Modern Biblical Interpretation*, edited by Katherine Hockey and David Horrell, 46–58. London: Bloomsbury T&T Clark.

Cohen, Shaye J. D. 1999. *The Beginnings of Jewishness: Boundaries, Varieties, Uncertainties.* Berkeley: University of California Press.

Donaldson, T. L. 2007. *Judaism and the Gentiles: Jewish Patterns of Universalism (to 135 CE).* Waco: Baylor University Press.

Draper, Jonathan A. 2013. "'You Shall Not Give What Is Holy to the Dogs' (Didache 9.5): The Attitude of the Didache to the Gentiles." In *Attitudes to Gentiles in Ancient Judaism and Early Christianity*, edited by David C. Sim and James S. McLaren, 242–58. LNTS 499. London: T&T Clark.

Fredriksen, Paula. 2003. "What Parting of the Ways?" In *The Ways That Never Parted*, edited by Adam H. Becker and Annette Yoshiko Reed, 35–63. Tübingen: Mohr Siebeck.

Gillihan, Yonder Moynihan. 2011. "The *Ger* Who Wasn't There: Fictional Aliens in the Damascus Rule." *Revue de Qumran* 98: 257–305.

Harrington, Hannah K. 2019. *The Purity and Sanctuary of the Body in Second Temple Judaism.* JAJSup 33. Göttingen: Vandenhoeck & Ruprecht.

Hayes, Christine E. 2002. *Gentile Impurities and Jewish Identities: Intermarriage and Conversion from the Bible to the Talmud.* Oxford: Oxford University Press.

Himmelfarb, Martha. 1999. "Levi, Phineas, and the Problem of Intermarriage at the Time of the Maccabean Revolt." *Jewish Studies Quarterly* 6: 1–24.

Milgrom, Jacob. 1991. *Leviticus 1–16: A New Translation with Introduction and Commentary.* AB 3. New York: Doubleday.

———. 2000. *Leviticus 17–22: A New Translation with Introduction and Commentary.* AB 3A. New York: Doubleday.

Poirier, J. C. 2003. "Purity beyond the Temple in the Second Temple Era." *JBL* 112: 247–65

Regev, Eyal. 2000. "Non-Priestly Purity and Its Religious Aspects according to Historical Sources and Archaeological Findings." In *Purity and Holiness: The Heritage of Leviticus*, edited by M. Poorthuis and J. Schwartz, 223–44. Leiden: Brill.

Schwartz, D. R. 1992. *Studies in the Jewish Background of Christianity*. WUNT 60. Tübingen: Mohr Siebeck.

Sim, David C. 2013. "Gentiles, God-Fearers and Proselytes." In *Attitudes to Gentiles in Ancient Judaism and Early Christianity*, edited by David C. Sim and James S. McLaren, 9–27. LNTS 499. London: T&T Clark.

Thackeray, Henry St. J., trans. 1927. *Josephus: The Jewish War*. Vol. 1, *Books 1–2*. LCL 203. Cambridge, MA: Harvard University Press.

———, trans. 1957. *Josephus: The Jewish War*. Vol. 3, *Books 5–7*. LCL 210. Cambridge, MA: Harvard University Press. Originally published 1928.

Thiessen, Matthew. 2011. *Contesting Conversion: Genealogy, Circumcision, and Identity in Ancient Judaism and Christianity*. Oxford: Oxford University Press.

Tuckett, Christopher M. 2013. "Q and the Gentiles." In *Attitudes to Gentiles in Ancient Judaism and Early Christianity*, edited by David C. Sim and James S. McLaren, 126–37. LNTS 499. London: T&T Clark.

27

Judeans in Gentile Eyes

Paul Trebilco

Judeans in Palestine in the New Testament period lived under the power of Rome and so had a great deal of contact with Gentiles, while Judeans in the diaspora lived as minority communities in Gentile cities. Gentiles had a range of views about and reactions to Judeans and Judaism in the New Testament period ranging from sympathy and even conversion to hatred and at times violence. Gentiles wrote about Judeans in both Greek and Latin, and a range of these texts has been preserved, although often only in the works of Jewish or Christian authors. Other evidence for how Judeans were viewed by Gentiles comes from Judean sources and from inscriptions.

Here the term "Judeans" will be used as a translation of the Greek *Ioudaioi* rather than "Jews," since for modern readers when discussing the first century CE, the term "Jews" may carry a whole range of anachronistic connotations. In the first century, "Judeans" was an ethnic term, but it was used of "Judeans" who lived throughout the world and not just of those who lived in Judea. Further, since ethnicity involved a whole pattern of life, referring to people as "Judeans" included their descent, distinctive character, ancestral homeland, laws, customs, stories, and religious and political matters. Hence the term "Judeans" has a strong religious dimension too. "Judaism" will be used to refer to the practices and beliefs undertaken by "Judeans" in relation to God, but it should be recalled that, since these practices and beliefs related to all of life (including, for example, agriculture and economics, and not just what we would call "religion"), the term "Judaism" involves more than "religion," as the latter is generally understood in the contemporary world.

Gentile Authors Writing about Judeans

A number of Gentile authors wrote about Judeans, showing that they viewed them as a "foreign" nation or ethnic group with a homeland, a history, ethnic customs, and religious practices. These authors knew about a range of details, including the exodus, Moses, where Judeans lived, Judean worship of the one God at the temple in Jerusalem, that Judeans worshiped their God without fashioning any images, temple sacrifices, and Jewish practices, particularly the Sabbath, circumcision, and food laws. Gentile authors were also aware of details about the Hasmonean rulers and the Jewish War of 66–70 CE. What was said about Judeans generally came from either a distinctly positive or, more often, a distinctly negative perspective. It is also often at variance with biblical accounts.

Some Gentiles viewed Judeans positively and demonstrated both respect and admiration (see Feldman and Reinhold 1996, 105–20). The antiquity of Judean traditions could be noted positively, and Jewish monotheism and absence of images were admired (see Varro, cited by Augustine, *Civ.* 4.31; Stern 1974–84, no. 72a). Hecateus of Abdera, writing around 300 BCE, said Moses was "outstanding both for his wisdom and for his courage" (quoted by Diodorus Siculus, *Bib. hist.* 40.3.3, 6; Stern 1974–84, no. 11). Strabo, writing in the early first century CE, was also very positive about Moses, although he thought Moses was an Egyptian priest (*Geogr.* 16.2.35; Stern 1974–84, no. 115). Strabo praises imageless worship and then writes:

> [Moses] persuaded not a few thoughtful men and led them away to this place where the settlement of Jerusalem now is. . . . At the same time Moses, instead of using arms, put forward as defence his sacrifices and his Divine Being, being resolved to seek a seat of worship for Him and promising to deliver to the people a kind of worship and a kind of ritual which would not oppress those who adopted them either with expenses or with divine obsessions or with other absurd troubles. Now Moses enjoyed fair repute with these people, and organised no ordinary kind of government, since the people all round, one and all, came over to him, because of his dealings with them and of the prospects he held out to them. His successors for some time abided by the same course, acting righteously

and being truly pious toward God. (*Geogr.* 16.2.36–37; Stern 1974–84, no. 115)

Strabo does go on to note that in his view, over time, superstitious and then tyrannical people came to be in charge of the nation.

Pompeius Trogus, writing at the end of the first century BCE or the beginning of the first century CE, has a brief discussion in which he gives a reasonably favorable account of Jewish history. It is interesting for both its positive tone and its differences from the biblical account:

> [Joseph's] son was Moyses, whom, besides the inheritance of his father's knowledge, the comeliness of his person also recommended. But the Egyptians, being troubled with scabies and leprosy and warned by an oracle, expelled him, with those who had the disease, out of Egypt, that the distemper might not spread among a greater number. . . . And as they remembered that they had been driven from Egypt for fear of spreading infection, they took care, in order that they might not become odious, from the same cause, to their neighbours, to have no communication with strangers; a rule which, from having been adopted on that particular occasion, gradually became a religious institution. (Quoted by Justin, *Hist. Phil.* 36.2.11–15; Stern 1974–84, no. 137)

Here the often-made observation about Jewish exclusiveness is not seen as hatred of other ethnic groups but attributed to the Judeans' consideration for Gentiles.

Suetonius is also positive about Judeans in Rome. In connection with public mourning in the city after the murder of Julius Caesar in 44 BCE, he notes that among the many foreigners who grieved were "above all the Jews, who even flocked to the funeral-pyre for several successive nights" (*Jul.* 84.5; Stern 1974–84, no. 302).

However, many Gentile authors are very negative toward Judeans (see Schäfer 1997). Diodorus Siculus says the Judeans were driven out of Egypt because they were all leprous (*Bib. hist.* 34.1.1–2; Stern 1974–84, no. 63), and Pliny the Elder sees Moses as a magician (*Nat.* 30.11; Stern 1974–84, no. 221).

Some Jewish practices were viewed negatively. Circumcision was seen as a strange custom and was often viewed with hostility (Persius, *Sat.* 5.176–84; Stern 1974–84, no. 190; Martial, *Epigr.* 7.30, 82; 11.94; Stern 1974–84, nos. 240, 243, 245; Petronius, frag. 37; Stern 1974–84, no. 195). It tended to be seen as the key identifying mark of a Judean (Horace, *Serm.* 1.9.70; Stern 1974–84, no. 129; Petronius, *Sat.* 102.13–14; Stern 1974–84, no. 194), even though it was not exclusively practiced by Judeans. Even the emperor Augustus knew that Judeans kept the Sabbath (see Suetonius, *Aug.* 76.2; Stern 1974–84, no. 303). It was known that the Sabbath was a day of rest. This was often regarded by Gentiles as a peculiar and odd custom, and it was derided as indicating idleness or laziness (see Ovid, *Ars* 1.75–76, 413–16; Stern 1974–84, nos. 141–42; Seneca the Younger, *Ep.* 95.47; Stern 1974–84, no. 188; Martial, *Epigr.* 4.7; Stern 1974–84, no. 239; Persius, *Sat.* 5.176–84; Stern 1974–84, no. 190). Food laws were often derided, particularly the fact that Judeans did not eat pork (Juvenal, *Sat.* 6.153–60; Stern 1974–84, no. 298). The charge is also made that Judeans worshiped an ass, or that there was an ass's head in the Jerusalem temple (Mnaseas, quoted by Josephus, *Ag. Ap.* 2.112–14; Stern 1974–84, no. 28), and we also encounter the accusation of human sacrifice in the temple (Posidonius, quoted by Josephus, *Ag. Ap.* 2.79–96; Stern 1974–84, no. 44).

Judeans were often regarded as forming exclusive communities. Contributing factors to this view were that Jewish customs were perceived as quite different from those of other ethnic groups, suggesting that Judeans disliked associating with other peoples and were hostile to strangers (Diodorus Siculus, *Bib. hist.* 34.1.1; Stern 1974–84, no. 63; see Collins 2000, 10–11). Since Judeans were not involved in the worship

of pagan gods, they were also seen as despising traditional religion (e.g., Apollonius Molon, in Josephus, *Ag. Ap.* 2.148; Stern 1974–84, no. 49; see Bar-Kochva 2010, 469–516). Proselytes to Judaism were believed to have abandoned their birth families.

Some Latin authors in particular are strongly negative toward Judeans. Cicero describes Judeans as people who are "born to be slaves" (*Prov. cons.* 5.10; Stern 1974–84, no. 70), and in the context of remarks about the Judean community in Rome, he speaks of Judaism as a "barbaric superstition" and of the Jewish nation as a state "given to suspicion and calumny" (*Flac.* 28.66, 68; Stern 1974–84, no. 68). One key factor behind such negativity is that, for the Roman elite, the triumph by Pompey over the Judeans in 62 BCE showed the superiority of the Romans, their gods, and their religious system (see Gruen 2002, 19–23). In a speech delivered in 59 BCE Cicero says,

> Even while Jerusalem was standing and the Jews were at peace with us, the practice of their sacred rites was at variance with the glory of our empire, the dignity of our name, the customs of our ancestors. But now it is even more so, when that nation by its armed resistance has shown what it thinks of our rule; how dear it was to the immortal gods is shown by the fact that it has been conquered, let out for taxes, made a slave. (*Flac.* 28.69; Stern 1974–84, no. 68)

Another author who is very negative and hostile toward Judeans is Tacitus (see Gruen 2011, 179–96). Writing in the first decade of the second century CE, he introduces his account of the siege of Jerusalem in 70 CE by giving an account of the origins, customs, history, and geography of the Judean people. With regard to their departure from Egypt, Tacitus says that the king of Egypt of the time was told by an oracle "to purge his kingdom and to transport this race [of Judeans] into other lands, since it was hateful to the gods." After they had arrived in their own land, Tacitus continues,

> To establish his influence over this people for all time, Moses introduced new religious practices, quite opposed to those of all other religions. The Jews regard as profane all that we hold sacred; on the other hand, they permit all that we abhor. They dedicated, in a shrine, a statue of that creature [a wild ass] whose guidance enabled them to put an end to their wandering and thirst, sacrificing a ram, apparently in derision of Ammon. They likewise offer the ox, because the Egyptians worship Apis. They abstain from pork, in recollection of a plague, for the scab to which this animal is subject once afflicted them. . . . They say that they first chose to rest on the seventh day because that day ended their toils; but after a time they were led by the charms of indolence to give over the seventh year as well to inactivity. . . . Whatever their origin, these rites are maintained by their antiquity: The other customs of the Jews are base and abominable, and owe their persistence to their depravity: for the worst rascals among other peoples, renouncing their ancestral religions, always kept sending tribute and contributing to Jerusalem, thereby increasing the wealth of the Jews; again, the Jews are extremely loyal toward one another, and always ready to show compassion, but toward every other people they feel only hate and enmity. They sit apart at meals and they sleep apart, and although as a race, they are prone to lust, they abstain from intercourse with foreign women; yet among themselves nothing is unlawful. They adopted circumcision to distinguish themselves from other peoples by this difference. Those who are converted to their ways follow the same practice, and the earliest lesson they receive is to despise the gods, to disown their country, and to regard their parents, children, and their brothers as of little account. . . . The ways of the Jews are preposterous and mean. (Tacitus, *Hist.* 5.3.1–5.5.2; 5.5.5; Stern 1974–84, no. 281)

Political developments of the first century CE were an important factor in the negative portrayal of Judeans that we see in Latin literature in particular. Relations between Judeans and Romans had been reasonably cordial during Augustus's reign (27 BCE–14 CE), but they deteriorated in the Julio-Claudian period of 14–68 CE. Judeans were expelled from Rome in significant numbers under Tiberius in 19 CE (Suetonius, *Tib.* 36; Stern 1974–84, no. 306; Josephus, *Ant.* 18.83–84) and under Claudius, probably in 49 CE (Suetonius, *Claud.* 25.4; Stern 1974–84, no. 307; see Goodman 2007, 386–88). Roman governors struggled to keep law and order in the province of Judea during this time, leading to the Jewish Revolt (66–70 CE), which was one of the most serious revolts that the Romans faced. It is understandable, then, that as the first century proceeded, views of Judeans and Judaism held by Romans became increasingly hostile. After 70 CE the tone of Latin writings on Judeans and Judaism became even harsher, clearly because of the Jewish War. Thus, after the war, Pliny the Elder writes that the Judeans are "a race remarkable for their contempt of divine powers" (*Nat.* 13.46; Stern 1974–84, no. 214), and Quintilian, writing around 95 CE, is wholly negative toward Moses, who is said to be "the founder of the Jewish superstition," and Judeans are said to be "a race which is a curse to others" (*Inst.* 3.7.21; Stern 1974–84, no. 230).

However, many of these negative points are stock ethnic libels reflecting the racial prejudice that often characterized one ethnic group's attitude toward another; such libels were launched by Greeks and Romans against many groups.

Proselytes, God-Fearers, and Sympathizers

The genuine admiration for Judeans that we find in some literary sources and that was clearly felt by some Gentiles for Judaism could result in these Gentiles converting to Judaism as proselytes, or participating in a variety of ways in Judean communities as "God-fearers," or acting as sympathetic "friends" (see Donaldson 2007, 363–409, 469–92). These different groups clearly indicate that some Gentiles had very positive attitudes toward both Judeans and Judaism.

First, we know of proselytes who formally converted to and became exclusive adherents of Judaism, identified with the Jewish community, and in the case of males became circumcised (see Feldman 1993, 288–341; Whittaker 1994, 85–91). We learn of Achior the Ammonite who was circumcised and joined the house of Israel (Jdt. 14:10); of Izates, king of Adiabene, who converted and was circumcised on the advice of Eleazar (Josephus, *Ant.* 20.17–47); of Nicolaus, a proselyte from Syrian Antioch (Acts 6:5); and of proselytes in Rome (2:10–11) and Antioch of Pisidia (13:43). Josephus writes of the Idumeans converting to Judaism (*Ant.* 13.257–58) and of other proselytes (*Ag. Ap.* 2.123; *Ant.* 18.82), while Philo praises proselytes (*Spec. Laws* 1.51–53; *Rewards* 152; *Virtues* 102–3, 182). One of the leaders of the Jewish War of 66–70 was Simon bar Giora ("son of a proselyte"; Josephus, *J.W.* 2.521), who shows how prominent a proselyte could become at this time.

That some Gentiles became proselytes was well known among Gentiles. Juvenal writes of a father who is a God-fearer (on which see below), in that he abstains from pork and keeps the Sabbath, and whose son becomes a proselyte. Juvenal says of proselytes: "Having been wont to flout the laws of Rome, they learn and practice and revere the Jewish law, and all that Moses handed down in his secret tome, forbidding them to point out the way to any not worshipping the same rites, and conducting none but the circumcised to the desired fountain" (*Sat.* 14.96–106; Stern 1974–84, no. 301). Tacitus, as quoted above, seems to speak clearly of proselytes, saying: "Those who are converted

to their [Jewish] ways follow the same practice, and the earliest lesson they receive is to despise the gods" (*Hist.* 5.5.1–2; Stern 1974–84, no. 281). These authors, who regard conversion to Judaism as unacceptable for Romans because it involves a betrayal of Roman loyalties and values, give the impression that conversion was well known.

However, the actual number of proselytes in the New Testament period is debated. We know of very few proselytes by name (Williams 1998, 170–72). Although Tacitus (*Hist.* 5.5.1; Stern 1974–84, no. 281) and Josephus (*Ag. Ap.* 2.123) suggest there were many proselytes, it may be that the number of converts was actually reasonably small.

Second, we know about a group who are generally called "God-fearers," Gentiles who adopted some Jewish customs and beliefs and attended the synagogue but who did not formally convert and become Judeans. However, there was probably no standard set of commitments to Judaism among God-fearers.

God-fearers are referred to a number of times in Acts (10:22; 13:16, 26; 16:14; 17:4, 17; 18:7), and Josephus probably refers to this group when he writes, "But no one need wonder that there was so much wealth in our temple, for all the Jews throughout the habitable world, *and those who worshipped God*, even those from Asia and Europe, had been contributing to it for a very long time" (*Ant.* 14.110 [trans. Marcus 1933, 505]). As noted above, Juvenal writes of a father who is a God-fearer and whose son becomes a proselyte (*Sat.* 14.96–106; Stern 1974–84, no. 301), and Epictetus (quoted by Arrian, *Epict. diss.* 2.9.20; Stern 1974–84, no. 254) also seems to know about God-fearers. A second-century CE inscription from the theater in Miletus probably reads, "place of the Jews and God-fearers," indicating that a section of seats in the theater was reserved for both Judeans and God-fearers (*CIJ* 2.748 = *IJO* 2.37; Trebilco 1991, 159–62). God-fearers seemed to have become more prevalent in the third century CE and later (see Williams 2013, 17–20, 217–30, 363–81). While some scholars have doubted the existence of God-fearers, these texts and inscriptions provide strong evidence for their existence.

Third, there were "sympathizers" who can be thought of as Gentiles who supported Judean communities in some way. This might be by building a synagogue (Luke 7:2–5; also Julia Severa mentioned in a first-century CE inscription from Acmonia; *CIJ* 2.766 = *IJO* 2.168; Trebilco 1991, 58–60), by cultivating good social or political relations with the Judean community, or by being favorably inclined toward Judean customs such as monotheism and the Sabbath.

Sometimes it is difficult to know which of our three categories an author is referring to. Thus, Seneca writes, "Meanwhile the customs of this accursed race have gained such influence that they are now received throughout all the world. The vanquished have given laws to their victors" (quoted by Augustine, *Civ.* 6.11; Stern 1974–84, no. 186). Is Seneca writing about proselytes or God-fearers or sympathizers? (see also Josephus, *J.W.* 2.463; 7.45). Further, we should think not of a clear distinction between God-fearers and sympathizers but of a spectrum of ways in which Gentiles were involved in and supported Judean communities.

Positive Interactions between Judeans and Gentiles

Many Gentiles viewed Judeans favorably, as is shown by their positive interactions with Judeans. The Ptolemies encouraged Jewish immigration to Egypt, and Jewish communities were established in Asia Minor by Antiochus III in the late third century BCE as military settlements, in order to bring security to the area (Josephus, *Ant.* 12.148–53). Josephus preserves a whole range of decrees and decisions from Gentile authorities relating to Judeans (*Ant.* 12.416–19; 14.144–55, 191–98, 213–67, 306–22;

16.27–30, 162–73; on these documents see Pucci Ben Zeev 1998). These decrees show that in the first century BCE, some Judean communities in Asia Minor, as well as elsewhere, suffered harassment, but Josephus gives no evidence for this in Asia Minor from the beginning of the first century CE onward. This silence suggests that by this time, at least in Asia Minor, some sort of *modus vivendi* was established that meant there were good relations between these Judean communities and their cities (Barclay 1996, 279–81). Nevertheless, the decrees show that the Roman authorities responded to harassment that did occur by granting significant privileges and religious rights to these Judean communities, which enabled them to continue to keep their ancestral traditions and customs. These privileges included granting exemption from military service and freedom to observe the Sabbath, and the rights to assemble for religious meetings, to send their temple tax to Jerusalem, and to settle internal legal disputes within their communities.

Judeans were generally not citizens of their Greek cities, though some individual Judeans did enjoy full citizenship, including the apostle Paul, who was a citizen of Tarsus (Acts 21:39). Similarly, some Judeans were Roman citizens (such as Paul, see Acts 16:37–38; 22:25–29; 23:27; Williams 1998, 143–46). Some Judeans were local magistrates (Williams 1998, 110), although the number of Jewish magistrates increased in the third century CE onward. Some Judeans were also involved in the gymnasium (112–14). That some Judeans were citizens, held civic office, or were part of the gymnasium shows that they were viewed positively by Gentiles, or at least without overt hostility.

Hatred or Violence by Gentiles against Judeans

At times, Gentiles reacted to Judeans with hatred or violence. Starting in 167 BCE, Antiochus IV Epiphanes abolished temple sacrifices, outlawed circumcision, imposed pagan sacrifices in the temple, and killed those who resisted (1 Macc. 1:41–51; 2 Macc. 6:1–2). As noted above, Judeans were expelled from Rome in 19 and 49 CE. There was serious anti-Jewish sentiment in Alexandria, where there was a large and significant Judean community. Riots in 38 CE inflicted great trauma on the Judean community of the city (Philo, *Against Flaccus*; *On the Embassy to Gaius*), and again in 66 (Josephus, *J.W.* 2.487–98).

The Jewish War of 66–70 CE did not just impact Jerusalem, Judea, and Galilee; Josephus also writes of many Judeans of Damascus being killed in the city at the beginning of the conflict (*J.W.* 2.559–61). After the war, Judeans were ordered to pay the equivalent of the temple tax to Jupiter Capitolinus (Cassius Dio, *Hist. Rom.* 66.7.2; Stern 1974–84, no. 430). This was called the *fiscus Iudaicus* (Jewish tax). The unpopularity of Judeans with the Roman authorities at this time led to a worsening of the position of Judeans in relation to Gentiles in general. The diaspora revolt of 115–117 CE led to the decimation of Judean communities in Egypt and Cyrenaica and the complete disappearance of the community on Cyprus (Williams 1998, 132–37). After the Jewish Revolt of Bar Kokhba of 132–35 in Palestine, Hadrian transformed Jerusalem into the pagan city of Aelia Capitolina.

Conclusion

Gentiles displayed a spectrum of attitudes toward Judeans. Some Gentile authors were hostile to Judeans and to Judaism and perpetrated violence against Judeans. Such hostility could be caused by a range of factors, such as Judean religious customs being seen as strange and detestable because of Judeans' perceived social exclusivity, because of political issues connected with Jewish revolt, or because of conversion. Sometimes it was simply because of ethnic hostility. However, Judeans also evoked admiration and respect from Gentiles, and this could lead Gentiles to convert to Judaism or to become God-fearers or sympathizers. In some cities and at some times, there was active support for Judeans, who were treated well. This whole spectrum of attitudes displayed by Gentiles means that if we lack specific data about a person or place, we cannot make generalizations about their perspective. Rather, we must be careful to stay within the limits of our knowledge about a person's actual attitude toward Judeans and Judaism.

Works Cited

Barclay, J. M. G. 1996. *Jews in the Mediterranean Diaspora from Alexander to Trajan (323 BCE—117 CE)*. Edinburgh: T&T Clark.

Bar-Kochva, B. 2010. *The Image of the Jews in Greek Literature: The Hellenistic Period*. Hellenistic Culture and Society 51. Berkeley: University of California Press.

Collins, J. J. 2000. *Between Athens and Jerusalem: Jewish Identity in the Hellenistic Diaspora*. 2nd ed. Grand Rapids: Eerdmans.

Donaldson, T. L. 2007. *Judaism and the Gentiles: Jewish Patterns of Universalism (to 135 CE)*. Waco: Baylor University Press.

Feldman, L. H. 1993. *Jew and Gentile in the Ancient World: Attitudes and Interactions from Alexander to Justinian*. Princeton: Princeton University Press.

Feldman, L. H., and M. Reinhold, eds. 1996. *Jewish Life and Thought among Greeks and Romans: Primary Readings*. Minneapolis: Augsburg Fortress.

Goodman, M. 2007. *Rome and Jerusalem: The Clash of Ancient Civilizations*. London: Allen Lane.

Gruen, E. S. 2002. *Diaspora: Jews amidst Greeks and Romans*. Cambridge, MA: Harvard University Press.

———. 2011. *Rethinking the Other in Antiquity*. Princeton: Princeton University Press.

Marcus, Ralph, trans. 1933. *Josephus: Jewish Antiquities*. Vol. 6, *Books 14–15*. LCL 489. Cambridge, MA: Harvard University Press.

Pucci Ben Zeev, M. 1998. *Jewish Rights in the Roman World: The Greek and Roman Documents Quoted by Josephus Flavius*. TSAJ 74. Tübingen: Mohr Siebeck.

Schäfer, P. 1997. *Judeophobia: Attitudes toward the Jews in the Ancient World*. Cambridge, MA: Harvard University Press.

Stern, M. 1974–84. *Greek and Latin Authors on Jews and Judaism: Edited with Introductions, Translations and Commentary*. 3 vols. Jerusalem: Israel Academy of Sciences and Humanities.

Trebilco, Paul. 1991. *Jewish Communities in Asia Minor*. Cambridge: Cambridge University Press.

Whittaker, M. 1994. *Jews and Christians: Graeco-Roman Views*. Cambridge Commentaries on Writings of the Jewish and Christian World 200 BC to AD 200 6. Cambridge: Cambridge University Press.

Williams, M. H. 1998. *The Jews among the Greeks and Romans: A Diasporan Sourcebook*. Baltimore: Johns Hopkins University Press.

———. 2013. *Jews in a Graeco-Roman Environment*. WUNT 312. Tübingen: Mohr Siebeck.

28

Samaritans

MAGNAR KARTVEIT

The Samaritans have existed as a separate religious community from the times of the Bible until today. In the Gospel of Mark they are not mentioned, and the New Testament letters and the Apocalypse leave them unnoticed. In the other Gospels and in the Acts of the Apostles, they are mentioned several times, in both positive and negative terms.

The evangelist Matthew says that Jesus sends out his disciples but orders them not to go to the Gentiles or to enter any of the Samaritan villages (Matt. 10:5). This is the only time they are mentioned in this Gospel. Also, in the Gospel of Luke, there is a negative comment about them: they did not allow Jesus and his disciples to pass through their territory on the way to Jerusalem (Luke 9:51–56). The Acts of the Apostles tells about the mission to the Samaritans and about Simon, who amazed the people of Samaria (Acts 8:4–25). The description oscillates between a positive attitude toward the mission in Samaria and a negative attitude toward Simon, who offers money to the apostles if they will give him the power to provide the Holy Spirit to people.

In the other texts, the attitude toward the Samaritans is positive. A Samaritan is portrayed as an example of neighborly love in Jesus's discussion with a lawyer, so that he is the "good Samaritan" (Luke 10:25–37). The "thankful Samaritan" is the only one out of ten lepers who returns to Jesus and thanks him for the healing (Luke 17:11–19). The Gospel of John has the longest story about the Samaritans: Jesus's conversation with the Samaritan woman and the ensuing mission to the Samaritans (John 4:1–42).

How are these positive and negative attitudes explained? In order to answer this question, we have to turn to contemporary sources, first of all to the Jewish historian Josephus.

Josephus on the Samaritans

Only a few decades after the Gospels were written, Josephus in his works gives us an impression of the Jewish attitude toward the Samaritans. In the *Jewish War* he writes about the revolt that took place in 66–73 CE, and in *Jewish Antiquities* he describes the entire history of the Jewish people. His project is to present the Jewish people favorably to his Roman readers, so the Samaritans emerge in a dubious light. He attributes their origin to the situation in northern Israel after the fall of the Northern Kingdom in 721 BCE. The Assyrian king Salmanassar deported all inhabitants of Samaria to Media and Persia, and in their place he brought people from Kutha to Samaria. These new settlers are called "Kutheans" in Hebrew and "Samaritans" in Greek, according to Josephus. They were five tribes and brought their own gods with them. Plagued by a pestilence, however, they sent envoys to the Assyrian king and asked him to send back some of the captive priests from Samaria. These priests instructed them in the worship of the Most High God, so they were freed from the plague. These same rites continue in use to this day, Josephus states, and he adds that the Kutheans themselves claim descendance from Joseph, in order to appear as kinsmen of the Jews if they see them prospering. When the Jews are in trouble, however, the Kutheans say that they are not at all close to the Jews and have no claim of friendship or race, and they declare themselves to be migrants of another race (*Ant.* 9.279, 288–91; 11.341; 12.257). Josephus here describes the Kutheans in such a way that readers will think they are opportunistic.

This story is a reworking of 2 Kings 17, a narrative about the end of the Northern Kingdom. Josephus says that the situation it created lasted until his own day, and he adds the description that indicates the opportunism. According to his account, the Samaritans are foreigners who converted from their own five gods to the Most High God. Other authors later purported that they intermarried with locals. In this way, the idea of a mixed race with a mixed religion was born. Later authors used the account of Josephus to develop such ideas, although he does not speak of a mixed religion or a mixed race.

Josephus states that the Samaritans had a temple on Mount Gerizim in Samaria. He considers the construction of this temple to be the work of illegitimate priests from Jerusalem. He describes a situation in Jerusalem where Manasseh, brother of the high priest Jaddus, was sharing in the office of high priest while married to Nikaso, daughter of Samaria's satrap Sanballat. Sanballat was a Kuthean, according to Josephus (*Ant.* 11.302), just like the Samaritans, so the marriage was illegitimate. Jaddus told him to divorce or else he would lose the high priesthood. Sanballat solved the predicament by building a temple on Mount Gerizim for Manasseh (*Ant.* 11.306–12). In this way, Manasseh could stay married to Nikaso and continue as high priest. Many other Jerusalem priests who were married to non-Jewish women laid the foundation for the cult on Mount Gerizim.

This story has a biblical basis (Neh. 13:28), but it was reworked by Josephus with much new material. Even the dating is different. While the book of Nehemiah dates the incident to the time of Nehemiah, in the fifth century BCE, Josephus dates it to the last days of the Persian king Darius and Alexander the Great's invasion, in the fourth century. Many modern scholars have tried to solve this problem, by suggesting two different Sanballats, for instance—which is not impossible but is nonetheless an unlikely explanation.

For understanding the New Testament texts about the Samaritans, it is not necessary to discuss these literary and historical questions, but one should simply take note of the attitude revealed by Josephus. He states that the Samaritans were foreigners, deported to Samaria by the Assyrian king; they converted to the Most High God because of a pestilence; their temple was initiated and run by illegitimate priests from Jerusalem; and they were opportunists in their dealings with other nations.

If we assume that these sentiments lie behind the New Testament texts about the Samaritans, we can understand that Jesus concentrated on the mission of the disciples to Jews only (Matt. 10), that pilgrims on the way to Jerusalem were denied accommodation (Luke 9), and that Simon in Samaria was willing to pay for the possibility to administer the Holy Spirit (Acts 8). This background also lends force to the figure of "the good Samaritan," compared to the priest and the Levite (Luke 10), and to "the thankful Samaritan" (Luke 17). The Gospel of Luke uses the contemporary Jewish sentiments about the Samaritans as a background for understanding "Who is my neighbor?" (Luke 10) and for thankfulness across borders (Luke 17).

Jesus's conversation with the Samaritan woman according to John 4 is also significant. One topic in the conversation is the location of legitimate worship, whether that be Jerusalem or Mount Gerizim. Jesus does not arbitrate between locations but advocates a spiritual form of worship. His comment about the five previous husbands of the Samaritan woman, and her present affair with one who is not hers, alludes to the polemics found in Josephus. Josephus says that the Samaritans worshiped their own five gods but then converted to the Most High God. Texts from the period prior to the turn of the era suggest that this understanding of Samaritan worship existed for some time before Josephus. It is possible that John's Jesus translates this image of Samaritan worship into the language of marriage. The prophet Hosea speaks of religious worship in terms taken from marriage language, as does the book of Deuteronomy. In these Old Testament / Hebrew Bible texts, idolatry is described as unfaithfulness in marriage, or simply prostitution. A similar parlance may be seen in John 4. Jesus comments on Samaritan worship that "we worship what we know, for salvation is from the Jews" (v. 22).

The two missions to Samaria—conducted by Jesus and his disciples in John 4 and by Philip, Peter, and John in Acts 8—contrast with the prohibition against entering into Samaritan villages in Matthew 10. This difference may be due to developments at a later time when the gospel would be spread to the whole world (according to Matt. 28:18–20) and to all nations (Luke 24:47).

Josephus provides two important pieces of information: the Samaritans had a temple, and the origin of the Samaritans is found in the Assyrian deportation to Samaria in the eighth century BCE. Modern discoveries have modified or changed the picture he paints. But for understanding the New Testament texts about the Samaritans, his attitudes and sentiments are helpful.

Centuries later, the West would come to know of the Samaritan Scriptures, which consist of only the five books of Moses, the Pentateuch. In 1616 a manuscript of this text was brought to Paris, and in the following years it was used in polyglot Bibles in France and England. It turned out that the Samaritan text was not identical to the standard Hebrew text (the Masoretic Text) but contained expansions and changes in many instances. This was a puzzle to European scholars, and many efforts were made to explain the differences. With the discovery of the Dead Sea Scrolls in the twentieth century, scholars obtained tools to understand the phenomenon.

The Dead Sea Scrolls

In Qumran on the Dead Sea and in other locations in the wilderness of Judea, a host of manuscript fragments have been found. Bedouin, robbers, serious archaeologists, and adventurous travelers have retrieved tens of thousands of literary fragments, and among them are close to a thousand manuscripts with biblical texts in Greek, Aramaic, and Hebrew. The discoveries were made in the period from 1947 and beyond, and even today genuine ancient texts are being newly presented. Among the many surprises the biblical texts have given is a batch of texts close to the Samaritan Pentateuch. The current publication of an *editio maior* of the Samaritan Pentateuch takes all the available material into account (Schorch 2018, 2021).

The dictum of Wilhelm Gesenius in 1815 was that the Samaritan Pentateuch is of text-critical value in four instances only, where it is superior to the Masoretic Text. This dictum remained common wisdom until the discoveries from the Dead Sea. In 1955 a Qumran text was published and said to be Exodus in the Samaritan Recension. The statement was an exaggeration, but the main point is valid: the text was part of the manuscript 4QpaleoExod^m (4Q22), and it is very close to the Samaritan version of Exodus and is therefore said to be "pre-Samaritan" in character. Suddenly, it was clear that a major theory in scholarship had to be revised or abandoned. The fact that the Samaritans had only the Pentateuch was considered a critical issue for dating the split (often called the schism) between Jews and Samaritans. Scholars had often assumed that at the time of the split, only the Pentateuch was Holy Scripture, so the Samaritans brought this with them when they split off. Later, the rest of the Hebrew Bible was accorded authority and holiness among the Jewish people, resulting in a situation where the Jews ended up with a larger set of Scriptures in contrast to the Samaritans' much smaller set.

In the years after 1947, more so-called pre-Samaritan texts were discovered among the Dead Sea Scrolls, dated to the third, second, and first centuries BCE. The fact that a pre-Samaritan version of the Pentateuch was found in a group of Qumran texts proves that there was a connection between the Samaritans and the Jews until the turn of the eras. The whole Hebrew Bible existed at this time, not only the Pentateuch. The Samaritan Pentateuch cannot be used for dating a "split."

When the Samaritans added their own special texts to the Pentateuch, they used as their version a text that emerged in Jewish circles.

From the turn of the era on, they added a new tenth commandment to Exodus 20 and Deuteronomy 5, with the injunction to build an altar on Mount Gerizim. The Decalogue was rearranged so that this commandment became number ten. Also, some smaller changes were made in Exodus and Deuteronomy, all connected to the altar commandment. In the Samaritan Pentateuch, Exodus 20:24b reads, "In the place where I cause my name to be remembered I will come to you and bless you," referring to the altar on Mount Gerizim. The same sentence in the Masoretic version is "in every place where I cause my name to be remembered I will come to you and bless you," which opens up the possibility for several sanctuaries. The theory of a split also had to be abandoned in favor of a model involving a much more lengthy process.

Josephus's two stories also must be modified as a consequence. The origin of the Samaritans is not how he describes it, and the city and holy shrine are older than his dating. The reasons for this new dating are the new archaeological finds made over the last forty years.

The Excavations on Mount Gerizim

Josephus states that the Samaritans had a temple on Mount Gerizim, and the Samaritan Pentateuch contains a commandment to build an altar there. Naturally, that mountain would be of great archaeological interest. After some excavations there in the twentieth century, a major campaign was launched by Israelis after the occupation of the West Bank in 1967. Yitzhak Magen led these excavations from 1984 until 2004, and he unearthed a large city with a holy precinct in its center, dating its founding to the fifth century BCE and its total destruction to 110–108 BCE (Magen, Misgav, and Tsfania 2004). These dates are made on the basis of coins, pottery, and C14-analysis of organic material. Josephus's story of the origin of the temple is therefore wrong.

Magen did not find a temple because he did not receive permission to excavate the holy precinct where it would have been. Today, the remains of a Byzantine church stand there, but under them one can hope to find the remains of the Samaritan holy altar or even a temple. Magen considers the temple to have been destroyed by the attack in 110–108 BCE and by the Christian emperors who built a church on the site in 490–520 CE.

The fact is, however, that there was a city on the mountain a century before Josephus's dating for the construction of the temple, around 330 BCE. This city most likely had a holy shrine, so Josephus's story needs to be redated and revised.

A large surprise during the excavations was the discovery of 389 inscriptions in Aramaic and Hebrew, written in scripts from the third and second century BCE. They refer to the deity of Israel under the names "Adonay" and "Yahweh," and no other deities are mentioned, not even in the personal names, which regularly contain elements taken from names for Israel's God. If there had been Kutheans consisting of five tribes who converted to Yahweh, one might expect traces of this, but nothing indicates such a background. The place names mentioned in the inscriptions are found in Samaria around Mount Gerizim. We know from other inscriptions that they also lived on the island Delos in the Aegean Sea, and Josephus states that there were discussions in Egypt in the third century BCE between Jews and Samaritans. Inscriptions on Mount Gerizim from the fourth century CE reveal that they also lived in Caesarea Maritima on the Mediterranean Sea.

This means that the Samaritans were living in places both inside and outside Israel. They formed their own communities but lived in areas where Jews also lived. All the evidence for these places mentions Mount Gerizim as the center for Samaritans and as a topic of controversy with Jews. Josephus's story of the origin of the Samaritans is unlikely in light of the inscriptions from Mount Gerizim, from Delos, and from the history he tells.

An important piece of information in the Gerizim inscriptions is found in the phrase "before God in this place." The inscriptions use phrases typical for other inscriptions from the Hellenistic and Roman ages, but this phrase is unique, and it is found in fourteen or fifteen instances. The first part, "before God," is common, but the addition "in this place" is not found elsewhere. It seems to build on the sentence "in the place that Yahweh will choose," which is used with variations twenty-one times in Deuteronomy. It is also common in the Temple Scroll, a Qumran text created in the last half of the second century BCE, the time when the Gerizim city and sanctuary flourished. In the Hebrew Bible the "place that Yahweh will choose" is identified as Jerusalem, and this is implied in the Temple Scroll as well. Against this identification, the Gerizim inscriptions mention "this place," which can only be Mount Gerizim. This difference in interpretation of "the place that Yahweh will choose" is echoed in the two versions of the Pentateuch. The Masoretic Text uses the future tense, "will choose," but the Samaritan uses the past tense, "the place that Yahweh has chosen." The idea is that Mount Gerizim was chosen from times immemorial, and Moses in the book of Deuteronomy only refers to this fact, according to the Samaritans. The Jews, however, thought that Moses in Deuteronomy referred to the future occupation of Jerusalem by King David—therefore, the future tense.

This different interpretation had consequences. Jesus and his disciples were denied accommodation since they were pilgrims on the way to Jerusalem (Luke 9). Josephus states that Samaritans scattered dead men's bones in the temple in Jerusalem on a certain Passover. Later, Galilean pilgrims were killed by Samaritans on their way to a festival in Jerusalem. The Galileans then armed themselves and with robbers raided Samaritan villages (*Ant.* 18.29–

30; 20.118–24). Even if we should be cautious about the reliability of Josephus's account, his point about hostilities between the two groups could be correct. In the end, the Jewish ruler John Hyrcanus in Jerusalem sacked Mount Gerizim and destroyed the city completely. Magen supposes that this destruction is mirrored in the ruins he excavated, which indicate that the end came in 110–108 BCE.

The Samaritans before the New Testament

The Samaritans are not mentioned in the Old Testament. A single occurrence of the word *ha-shomronim* seems to refer to "the people of Samaria" (2 Kings 17:29). Josephus exploited the potential in the word to make 2 Kings 17 speak about the origin of the *Samaritans*, but this is much later and constitutes a polemical use of Scripture. In fact, Josephus was not the first to do this. When the syntactical features of 2 Kings 17:24–41 are taken into consideration, this last section of the chapter reveals itself as late and could well be a polemical text against the Samaritans (Kartveit 2014). Also, 2 Maccabees 6:2 (ca. 100 BCE) contains an expression that can be understood as saying that the Samaritans were strangers—but this is a possibility only, as the lexical meaning of *etynchanon* is uncertain. The Qumran text 4QNarrative and Poetic Composition[a–c] (2nd c. BCE) states that foreigners were living in the land of Joseph (i.e., Samaria). Other Jewish texts from the second century BCE are also polemical against the inhabitants of Samaria of the period, in particular Sirach 50:25–26 and the Testament of Levi (Kartveit 2009, 109–202). These texts are often neglected or marginalized in current research, with a relatively peaceful coexistence between Jews and Samaritans being assumed (Knoppers 2013, 167–78; Pummer 2016, 47–54). The fact that the archaeological remains from the period are similar in both Judea and Samaria indicates that the population of the region shared a cultural milieu, but this material cannot tell us about the feelings they harbored in relation to each other. For this information, we have to consult the texts and inscriptions mentioned above. On balance, I think the Samaritans lived under much the same cultural and political conditions as the Jews but differed markedly from them on the questions of the place for worship and of the extent and form of Scripture.

Conclusion

The group that worshiped on, or toward, Mount Gerizim shared material conditions with neighboring populations. They were also subject to the same political overlords as were Jerusalem and Galilee: the Persian kings, the Hellenistic rulers in Egypt or Syria, and the Roman conquerors. Against this background, their religious characteristics stand out, with emphasis on Mount Gerizim and on their own version of the Pentateuch. Because of the Mosaic Torah, as contained in the Pentateuch that they shared with Jerusalem, they in many issues of law and conduct had the same practice as the Jews. But in questions of the form of the Torah and the place of worship, they have a profile different from the Jews of Jerusalem. Their origin and religious profile are best sought in the development of Israel, people and land, after the exile, and not in deported peoples from the east. The animosity against them, visible in Josephus's works and earlier texts, should be kept in mind when we read the New Testament.

Works Cited

Gesenius, Wilhelm. 1815. *De Pentateuchi Samaritani origine, indole et auctoritate: Commentatio philologica-critica*. Halle: Regenerianae.

Kartveit, Magnar. 2009. *The Origin of the Samaritans*. VTSup 128. Leiden: Brill.

———. 2014. "The Date of II Reg 17, 24–41." *ZAW* 126: 31–44.

Knoppers, Gary N. 2013. *Jews and Samaritans: The Origins and History of Their Early Relations*. Oxford: Oxford University Press.

Magen, Yitzhak, Haggai Misgav, and Levana Tsfania. 2004. *The Aramaic, Hebrew and Samaritan Inscriptions*. Mount Gerizim Excavations 1. Jerusalem: Israel Antiquities Authority.

Pummer, Reinhard. 2016. *The Samaritans: A Profile*. Grand Rapids: Eerdmans.

Schorch, Stefan, ed. 2018. *Leviticus*. The Samaritan Pentateuch: A Critical Editio Maior 3. Berlin: de Gruyter.

———. 2021. *Genesis*. The Samaritan Pentateuch: A Critical Editio Maior 1. Berlin: de Gruyter.

29

Women in the Ancient Mediterranean World

Susan E. Benton

Melitine was a woman who lived in Sardis (in Asia Minor, present-day Türkiye), sometime between the first and second centuries CE. Probably younger than marriageable age, she was the daughter of Menandros, a man well known in the city for being both the director of the marketplace (*agoranomos*) and a former priest of Zeus's temple in the city.[1] Melitine herself became well known, serving as a priestess of Artemis in one of the largest temples in the city. Melitine's image was raised in statue form with a marble base inscribing her name publicly, to be witnessed by anyone passing by or entering into the temple.[2] Her appointment and public commemoration in this priestly role involved cooperation by both the religious and the civic entities of Sardis in her time. This was the case with all the young Sardian women who were able to serve in the rotation for the priesthood of Artemis.

We might be inclined to think that a young woman like Melitine, brought out of obscurity and allowed to serve publicly, was an exception in daily life of the ancient Mediterranean world. That has often been the contemporary impression of the lives of ancient women in general, fostered in part by the way that ancient male writers depicted women in their homes, with quiet lives that left the public sphere to men.[3] Yet the reality that historians increasingly recognize is far more complicated and nuanced, acknowledging a world in which ancient women often led interesting, involved, and influential lives.[4] From the late Hellenistic period (from 300 BCE to Caesar Augustus) to

---

1. We know all this from an inscription, *ISardis* II.348 (1st–2nd c. CE). The inscription is viewable online at https://sardisexpedition.org/en/artifacts/m14-348.

2. Her statue is not extant, but it probably resembled that of another priestess, Moschine, that the Sardis Expedition has documented in its collection: https://sardisexpedition.org/en/artifacts/r2-246. The priestesses were commemorated with the Lydian title *kaueis* as part of the continuation of earlier Lydian usage (Siekierka, Stebnicka, and Wolicki 2021, 879).

3. Most ancient written sources describing women are written by men, as noted by King 2014.

4. See Osiek and MacDonald 2006, 1–16. In their introduction, they helpfully outline shifts in the study of women in early Christianity.

the early Roman Empire (from Augustus to 300 CE), women's identities and roles were often dynamic, neither conforming entirely to social prescriptions nor ever completely free of them.[5] Both their geographical and social locations were significant factors shaping how a woman might be in the world. Roman Palestine might have been more conservative in regard to social expectations for women. Despite the fact that women are numbered among synagogue leaders and elders around the Mediterranean, none appear to be attested in Palestine itself (Brooten 2000, 2020; Kraemer 1986). Yet developing research exposes that even there, women owned and inherited property like the women of other regions, and they also divorced and remarried like others in the Roman world (Hylen 2018, 12).

Current Research on Women's Lives

The shift in understanding women's lives has been made possible by increased study of ancient inscriptions, like the one honoring Melitine the priestess, and other archaeological artifacts that provide reference points outside of literature. These enable historians to see how women were involved in their local communities, often in roles and activities that are left out of written sources from the same time.[6] Even though the monumental evidence still skews toward those who possessed more resources than others (and hence were able to perform the types of activities that would receive public recognition), inscriptional sources give a broader view across the ancient Mediterranean, despite very little surviving evidence about the lives of enslaved women and those among the poor in that period (Hylen 2018, 18). In the analysis

of these sources, scholars grasp some of the variety and nuance in the lives of many women.

Women in Religious, Civic, and Associational Roles

In Sardis, for example, Melitine was just one of twelve priestesses known to have served in the temple of Artemis in the first three centuries CE.[7] Cultic religious service was fairly typical for women by the imperial period. In other cities in the Greek-speaking Eastern regions and the Latin-speaking Western portions of the empire, young women were leading their communities in sanctuaries, presenting offerings on behalf of the people, and facilitating their communities' engagements with the deities both during the major festivals and in day-to-day prayers and gifts. One can imagine a situation similar to supplicants entering churches in the present day to light a candle and say prayers for loved ones; in the ancient world, a young priestess in a sanctuary could have assisted those making small offerings with their requests even as a priest in another sanctuary across town assisted there. Across the Greco-Roman world, many young women worked as religious functionaries, where they could be honored for their "service in a pious manner" to the deities.[8] A few women served as priestesses later in life also—such as Euaxis of Piraeus, who was a perpetual priestess to the Great Mother and served alongside her daughter, Metrodora (*IG* 2² 1328 = *LSCG* 48).[9]

---

5. The dynamic of reinforcing gendered expectations through participation in gendered tasks is well described in DiLuzio 2016, 10–11.

6. A recent essay collection provides a good representation of this materialist approach to history. See Ellison, Taylor, and Osiek 2021.

7. *SEG* 48.1472 (ca. 50 CE); *ISardis* I.51 (1st–2nd c. CE); *ISardis* I.206 (1st–2nd c. CE); *ISardis* I.53 (1st–2nd c. CE); *ISardis* I.54 (1st–2nd c. CE); *ISardis* I.52 (126–127 CE); *ISardis* I.44 (early 2nd c. CE); *ISardis* I.55 (125–150 CE); *ISardis* II.393 (after 212 CE); *ISardis* II.348 (1st–2nd c. CE).

8. For this wording in praise of priestesses, see Siekierka, Stebnicka, and Wolicki 2021, nos. 567.1 and 881. Other ways of identifying distinguished service appear elsewhere.

9. *AGRW* 19 = *GRA* 1.34 (online at http://philipharland.com/greco-roman-associations/19-regulations-of-the-sacrificing-associates-of-the-mother-of-the-gods/). There is not enough information to know whether she served

Serving as religious functionaries became a conventional pattern for women to participate meaningfully in community life across the ancient Mediterranean, while other opportunities were rarer (Van Bremen 1996, 28–29; DiLuzio 2016, 24–41). Certain civic offices were closed to women, from local and regional magistracies to the all-male senate that convened in Rome. Yet the Hellenistic and Roman periods witnessed women occupying more civic roles in the East, such as the *stephanophoria* (presiding annual magistracy), the *agonothetis* (funder of athletic games), the *prytanis* (civic president/magistrate), and the *kanephoros* (annually appointed priestess), roles in which they administered athletic games, city business, and other organizational matters (Van Bremen 1996, 30–34; Siekierka, Stebnicka, and Wolicki 2021, 43, 45, 714–15).[10] They may have been following in a family pattern in some of these situations, but they nonetheless became the officiants as they did so. Among the Roman populace, exemplars could be found in the women of the imperial household, like Agrippina and Livia, who helped to influence matters of state and became increasingly visible on coins and in statuary throughout the empire (Hylen 2023, 65). Their leadership helped to foster an environment where more women in the Latin West also took up responsibilities and offices in religious and civic domains (Hemelrijk 2007).[11]

Women also participated in Greco-Roman associations of the time, whether the association's type was most comparable to a club, a professional guild, or a religious fellowship.[12] People joined associations both to build connections and to undertake joint projects. Associations were places for members to enjoy belonging and increased social status in highly stratified societies. Women sometimes appear among members in local associational rosters (*alba collegii*).[13] With the other members, they shared in regular meetings and feasts and contributed annual dues to the operating budgets.[14] Additionally, women assumed positions as officers and honored leaders in their groups, providing supplementary resources for their groups' use and shaping their patterns of activity; still other women were external patrons who gave endowments and large gifts but probably did not join in any group meetings (Hemelrijk 2008). In return for women benefactors' generosity, groups often honored them in the inscriptions that endure to the present time.

Women in the Household and Industry

None of this detracts from the reality that women were central to their households, often simultaneously occupying the crucial roles of spouse, domestic administrator, mother, and

---

throughout her married life or whether she resumed her priesthood after being widowed. In other situations, priestesses are identified as married women: see Flavia Papiane of Ephesus, *IEph* 3077 (2nd c. CE), and Iulia? Menogenes of Sardis, *ISardis* II.350 (online at https://sardisexpedition.org/en/artifacts/m14-350), whose husbands are Publius Vedius Antoninus and Julius Machairion, respectively.

10. Examples are in inscriptions: *TAM* 5.2, 976 (2nd c. CE, Thyatira: *stephanophoros, agonothetis*, and *prytanis*), Iulia Menogenis, who followed after her father in these offices, and Antonia Caecilia, jointly with her husband; *IMagnMai* 117.1 (ca. 100 CE, Aphrodisias: *stephanophoros*); *ISardis* I.111 (2nd c. BCE: *stephanophoros*); *ISardis* II.350 (1st–2nd c. CE: *stephanophoros*); *ISelge* 15, 16, 17 (late 2nd–3rd c. CE: *agonothetis*); *TAM* 5.972 = *IThyatiraB* = *IGR* 4.1242 (ca. 50 CE: *agonothetis*); *IG* 2² 3457 (4th–3rd c. BCE, Athens: *kanephoros*).

11. For instance, Livia is identified as an exemplar for an Ostian woman who helped build a local sanctuary; see Hänninen 2019.

12. For profiles of these and other broad association types, see Kloppenborg 2019, 32–40.

13. See the useful appendix on "Women in Associations" in Harland and Last 2020, 189–92.

14. A few examples illustrate the broader phenomenon: *IApamBith* 35 = *CCCA* 1.252 = *AGRW* 95 = *GRA* 2.99 (119 or 104 BCE, Apameia, Bithynia), with men and women members of a cultic association. *IThessN* 2.1 (new reading and restorations) = *SEG* 56.754 (2nd–3rd c. CE, Thessalonica), with men and women in the membership and a "mother" of the group. *CCCA* 6.342 (ca. 200 CE, Serdica, Thrace), with women as members and one mother.

educator. A young woman's marriage linked her family of origin to new kinship connections, and when she was able to bear children, she provided descendants to both family lines. Inability to do either of these expected womanly functions (marriage or childbearing) might bring hardship to the woman and her birth family, a reality that appears especially harsh in light of what scientific understanding teaches us now about how a couple's infertility can result from both male and female difficulties, and the reality that many other genetic, hormonal, and physical anomalies simply resulted in women of the past being treated as "unmarriageable." For the ancients, however, theories about reproduction and infertility often placed responsibility on the women who were unable to birth live children, resulting in increased vulnerability for the already unfortunate. Elizabeth, the mother of John the Baptist, was in this sense a typical case of a woman labeled barren when a couple did not conceive (Luke 1:7, 36). Even a woman who came to carry a child might be unable to survive the difficulties of childbirth, with high mortality rates that not even access to midwifery could mitigate. Artifacts of women's offerings and prayers for safety in childbirth and for the health and well-being of young children attest the sense of precarity that accompanied the early years of trying to build a family.[15] With the help of extended family members or of household servants or slaves, women sought to create the conditions by which a family could be nurtured and protected.

When young wives were not caring for or educating their children, they were occupied with the constant household industries of generating cloth and clothing for household use, procuring and preparing food, and also contributing to their spouse's work. Recent research has dedicated more attention to understanding these elements of women's daily lives, looking at both art and figurines that depict women working looms and spinning wool, appreciating the daily lives and work of women.[16] At the same time, adjacent studies emphasize the economic value inherent in the domestic production of women.[17] While some specialization of spheres occurred in households, wives often participated in trade labor with their husbands. It was probably a common scenario to find a married couple like Prisca and Aquila working together in a common occupation (Acts 18:1–3 depicts them as tentmakers). A wife might marry a man who shared the skills of her household of origin, or she might learn her husband's trade after marriage to increase the family's economic flexibility. In many households, women oversaw the work of domestic staff and servants, keeping the daily work of the household running smoothly for everyone's sake (Hylen 2023, 25). Their manifold household obligations constituted one of the reasons that the share of women who did serve in civic, religious, and associational leadership reached nowhere near the number of their male counterparts.

Social Constraints and Expectations for Women

Notwithstanding all these ways we now understand that ancient women were acting agents in their world, the ancient Mediterranean was a patriarchal culture, and women were indeed hemmed in by social constraints and expectations. Even while they were occasionally active in religious and social leadership roles, women were still likely to receive praise in ways that reinforced traditional Greek and Roman ideals of femininity (Bain 2014;

15. See DiLuzio 2019. The Uşak Museum of Archaeology exhibits several stele with dedicatory inscriptions seeking healing; two among them name the god Men Aksittenos and "the hearing gods" in prayers for children by parents (nos. 40.1.73 and 39.6.73, respectively).

16. Examples include Dixon 2004; Caldwell 2021.
17. See examples from a number of ancient periods in Turfa and Budin 2016.

Wilkinson 2015). These were often linked to their family's social and economic positions. The priestesses like Melitine who were lauded in Sardis, for instance, received praise specifically for showing modesty and piety in their administration of the priestly offices, reinforcing two key values deemed essential for Greco-Roman women. Additionally, the titles of women contributing in their communities sometimes alluded to their domestic roles. One of the honored positions in both cities and associations was that of the "mother," and notable women were designated "daughter of the city" in places like Perge.[18] Furthermore, class distinctions created expectations for women of wealth and community renown even as their disposable funds gave opportunities for them to exert their influence.[19] For women with fewer resources, there were likely fewer constraints in terms of decorum but more limitations to the social prestige they might attain.

Regional variations might have had further impact on the range of possibilities for women's social involvement. Local traditions could mitigate the ways that women's religious leadership would be fostered or their community influence appreciated. It may have been that Jewish women navigated expectations for quiet public presence and minimal engagement with men outside their families.[20] The Judean population did not develop the habit of honoring notable female citizens with statuary, at least according to current knowledge. Similarly, the classical Athenian ideal promoted a separate

sphere of the house for women to avoid outsiders (Osiek and MacDonald 2006, 3–4). Yet even in these cases, the picture is far from clear. For instance, the book of Judith records an occasion when the widow summons two of the men who are elders of the town to come to her house and answer for their slander against her (Jdt. 8:9–11). The incident is recorded without this sounding out of the ordinary: the messengers are not scandalized, nor do the elders bat an eye. The nature of the narration would suggest that a woman might not only speak to men outside her household but also command them to come to her house and have an audience with her. Likewise, Athens's acropolis was the location of the first attested statue of a woman, and records in the community dated events according to her year of service as the *kanephoros* at the head of the festival processions (*IG* 2² 3457 [4th–3rd c. BCE]).[21]

There is still much to learn about the lives of ancient women, especially in some of the regions where women reputedly faced greater limitation. Ongoing discoveries, like the papyri of a Judean woman named Babatha, attest a mixture of local norms and Greek and Roman laws, challenging notions of a prevailing oppressive stance toward women (Hylen 2018, 76–77). Patterns of women holding property and marrying with the customs of the Hellenistic world suggest that life for women in Judean Palestine often resembled that of women in neighboring regions.

Complexifying the Picture of Ancient Mediterranean Women

In the last several decades of research into ancient Mediterranean societies there has emerged a greater appreciation for how ancient women availed themselves of opportunities to participate in the religious, social, and economic ac-

18. See *IThessN* 2.1 and *CCCA* 6.342 (as noted above in n. 14), which also attest associational mothers. My full research on associational mothers is in Benton 2023. Merkelbach 1988 features Plancia Magna, "daughter of the metropolis" in Perge; see also Boatwright 1991. *TAM* 5.2, 976 (2nd c. CE, Thyatira), celebrates a daughter of the city, Iulia Menogenes.

19. Aptly termed a situation of "class patriarchy" in Gupta 2023, 161.

20. This would be one way of understanding the aside in John 4:27, when the disciples react with surprise to Jesus's public discussion with a woman in Samaria.

21. Identified as the earliest extant in Siekierka, Stebnicka, and Wolicki 2021, 36.

tivities of their times. Even as literary sources praised long-standing ideals of secluded and quiet females, Greco-Roman women earned praise for the classical virtues while taking up responsibilities and tasks alongside men. While particularities of location and social class should always factor into consideration when imagining the cultural landscape in the New Testament world, a generalized portrait of a patriarchally conservative and disempowering society should not be the starting point. To the contrary, a more accurate characterization of women's lives in the ancient Mediterranean calls for understanding a complex social matrix in which gender was one among numerous factors that shaped people's lives. For some women, the other elements of their social profiles were weighty enough that their gender seems to have posed few limitations on their opportunities, while for those without other claims to privilege, their gender became one more factor that could not aid them in the world. When women did acquire access to greater freedom, financial resources, or status, however, the Hellenistic and Roman periods appear to have been times when women found that many options were, in fact, open to them.

Complexity when Envisioning Women of the New Testament

For New Testament research, there are several important implications of the state of current study on women in the ancient Mediterranean. First, there is greater nuance needed in discussions of the contextual backgrounds for women's lives. Patriarchy certainly did affect women's lives and experiences, but the degree to which it limited their options depended on a variety of factors, including one's region, ethnicity, social status, wealth, religious background, family, trade skills, education, and more. Whenever ancient literary sources are consulted to try to fill out the picture of society, there should be significant attempts to

balance those typically elite and male sources with material evidence that can supply additional evidence "on the ground," so to speak.

Second, moralistic and ideal representations of women from the ancient world need to be acknowledged for the opinion pieces that they are, while granting that ordinary people would have negotiated in various ways the expectations and values that existed in tension. Phoebe of Cenchreae, for example, might have both met and defied cultural expectations when she became a patron to Paul and others in her region (Rom. 16:1–2). Many wealthy women gave benefactions in their communities, and thus she exemplified Greco-Roman patronage. Yet her choice of beneficiaries—a new religious group that held little imperial status—transgressed other social ideals, and scholars have difficulty accounting for why she did so. Perhaps she was no less consistent than any other ancient person who expressed their agency with a combination of conventionality and freedom.

Third, the apparent contradictions between scriptural statements in some places (e.g., in discussions of women's participation in worship at 1 Cor. 11:1–16 and 14:34–36; or depicting Priscilla [also known as Prisca] as a teacher of "the Way of God" in Acts 18:26 in contrast to the gag order of 1 Tim. 2:11–15) might reflect a maze of conflicting expectations that ancient women were required to navigate in daily life. Perhaps it was true to life, then as now, that leaders were sometimes inconsistent or unclear about what it meant to be freed by Christ and respectful in society. If the Greco-Roman cultural milieu itself held many values in tension, maybe early Christian thinking reflected that complexity and its contradictions. While accounting for this convolution in scholarship may prove challenging, speaking accurately about the pressures of gendered expectations in ancient life is important for those who read the text as a faith resource for the challenges confronting Christian women today.

Works Cited

Bain, Katherine. 2014. *Women's Socioeconomic Status and Religious Leadership in Asia Minor in the First Two Centuries C.E.* Emerging Scholars. Minneapolis: Fortress.

Benton, Susan E. 2023. "Women Patrons and Mothers in Greco-Roman Associations and the New Testament." PhD diss., Baylor University.

Boatwright, Mary Taliaferro. 1991. "Plancia Magna of Perge: Women's Roles and Status in Roman Asia Minor." In *Women's History and Ancient History*, edited by Sarah B. Pomeroy, 249–72. Chapel Hill: University of North Carolina Press.

Brooten, Bernadette J. 2000. "Female Leadership in the Ancient Synagogue." In *From Dura to Sepphoris: Studies in Ancient Jewish Art and Society in Late Antiquity*, edited by Lee I. Levine and Zeev Weiss, 215–23. Portsmouth, RI: Journal of Roman Archaeology.

———. 2020. *Women Leaders in the Ancient Synagogue*. BJS 36. Atlanta: Scholars Press.

Caldwell, Lauren. 2021. "From Household to Workshop: Women, Weaving, and the Peculium." In *Women's Lives, Women's Voices: Roman Material Culture and Female Agency in the Bay of Naples*, edited by Brenda Longfellow and Molly Swetnam-Burland, 51–65. Austin: University of Texas Press.

DiLuzio, Meghan J. 2016. *A Place at the Altar: Priestesses in Republican Rome*. Princeton: Princeton University Press.

———. 2019. "Religion and Gender in Ancient Rome." In *Oxford Research Encyclopedia of Religion*. Oxford: Oxford University Press. https://doi.org/10.1093/acrefore/9780199340378.013.634.

Dixon, Suzanne. 2004. "Exemplary Housewife or Luxurious Slut? Cultural Representations of Women in the Roman Economy." In *Women's Influence on Classical Civilization*, edited by Fiona McHardy and Eireann Marshall, 56–74. New York: Routledge.

Ellison, Mark D., Catherine Gines Taylor, and Carolyn Osiek, eds. 2021. *Material Culture and Women's Religious Experience in Antiquity: An Interdisciplinary Symposium*. Lanham, MD: Lexington.

Gupta, Nijay K. 2023. *Tell Her Story: How Women Led, Taught, and Ministered in the Early Church*. Downers Grove, IL: IVP Academic.

Hänninen, Marja-Leena. 2019. "Religious Agency and Civic Identity of Women in Ancient Ostia." In *Gender, Memory, and Identity in the Roman World*, edited by Jussi Rantala, 63–88. Amsterdam: Amsterdam University Press.

Harland, Philip A., and Richard Last. 2020. *Group Survival in the Ancient Mediterranean: Rethinking Material Conditions in the Landscape of Jews and Christians*. London: Bloomsbury.

Hemelrijk, Emily A. 2007. "Local Empresses: Priestesses of the Imperial Cult in the Cities of the Latin West." *Phoenix* 61, nos. 3–4: 318–49.

———. 2008. "Patronesses and 'Mothers' of Roman Collegia." *Classical Antiquity* 27, no. 1: 115–62.

Hylen, Susan E. 2018. *Women in the New Testament World*. New York: Oxford University Press.

———. 2023. *Finding Phoebe: What New Testament Women Were Really Like*. Grand Rapids: Eerdmans.

King, Helen. 2014. "Women." In *The Oxford Companion to Classical Civilization*, edited by Simon Hornblower and Antony Spawforth. 2nd ed. Oxford: Oxford University Press.

Kloppenborg, John S. 2019. *Christ's Associations: Connecting and Belonging in the Ancient City*. New Haven: Yale University Press.

Kraemer, Ross Shepard. 1986. "Hellenistic Jewish Women: The Epigraphical Evidence." SBLSP 25: 183–200.

Merkelbach, R. 1988. "Die publizierten Inschriften von Perge." *Epigraphica Anatolica* 11: 97–170.

Osiek, Carolyn, and Margaret Y. MacDonald. 2006. *A Woman's Place: House Churches in Earliest Christianity*. Minneapolis: Fortress.

Siekierka, Przemyslaw, Krystyna Stebnicka, and Aleksander Wolicki, eds. 2021. *Women and the Polis: Public Honorific Inscriptions for Women in the Greek Cities from the Late Classical to the Roman Period*. Boston: de Gruyter.

Turfa, Jean Macintosh, and Stephanie Lynn Budin, eds. 2016. *Women in Antiquity: Real Women across the Ancient World*. Rewriting Antiquity. London: Taylor & Francis.

Van Bremen, Riet. 1996. *The Limits of Participation: Women and Civic Life in the Greek East in the Hellenistic and Roman Periods*. Amsterdam: Gieben.

Wilkinson, Kate. 2015. *Women and Modesty in Late Antiquity*. Cambridge: Cambridge University Press.

30

Masculinities

PETER-BEN SMIT

Most characters in the New Testament and related literature are male (and, supposedly, "straight"), yet attention to masculinity in New Testament studies often still lags behind attention to other genders (female, transgender, etc.) and nonstraight sexualities (this and the following draws on Smit 2017). This has everything to do both with emancipatory interests in the twentieth and twenty-first centuries and with a hermeneutical bias in scholarship that tends to ignore the "normal" (i.e., the normative pattern of gender: straight masculinity) and to focus on the extraordinary (everything else). Masculinities studies focuses on those patterns of behavior that are identified as "masculine" in a particular sociocultural context, without the assumption that there is something like an essential masculinity. In biblical studies at large and in New Testament studies in particular, this approach has proven very fruitful, in particular when it comes to addressing projections of contemporary, dominant ("hegemonic") forms of masculinity back into ancient texts and retrieving the strange world of ancient

discourses on and performances of masculinities. It has appeared that biblical texts engage in their own construction of masculinities, which are always part of a broader project of negotiating political, economic, and religious circumstances. The latter observation is also indicative of a key methodological conviction in masculinities studies: masculinities are always constructed intersectionally, at the crossing of multiple aspects of a person and a society, such as body, age, sexuality, ethnicity, behavior, and wealth. This chapter outlines some key dimensions of masculinities in the Greco-Roman world, as they form an important background to early Christian negotiations and constructions of masculinities. Naturally, subgroups in the Greco-Roman world, such as early Jewish and Christian communities, negotiated their own constructions of masculinities, yet this can still be plotted on the matrix of themes, topics, patterns of behavior, and ideals associated with masculinities in the Greco-Roman world at large. In this sense, early Jewish and Christian masculinities are in many ways variations on a theme.

(Ideal) Masculinities in the Greco-Roman World

Studies of masculinity/-ies in the Greco-Roman world, including early Christianity, often have as their point of departure an outline of "hegemonic" or "ideal-typical" masculinity (Asikainen 2018, 19–45). This enables one to get a good grasp of the themes and topics associated with masculinity, even if the exclusive focus on such forms of masculinity might be somewhat narrow. Notions associated with masculinity circulated around the notion of *andreia* ("manliness"; or, in Latin, _virtus_ at large), being a virtue and an aspect of gender at the same time (for this reason "feminine" is not always the antonym of "masculine" in antiquity).

The table of contents of Martin Goodman's *The Roman World* still provides an interesting starting point for a discussion of masculinity and related questions of gender ideals in the early imperial world (Goodman 1997, ix). This table of contents indicates that the book also discusses the organization of the city of Rome, listing its constituent parts as follows: imperial court, senators, *equites*, *plebs*, women, and slaves. This not only gives a good impression of a heavily stratified society but also offers an illustration of a highly hierarchical concept of masculinity, in which women also have their place. In the Greco-Roman world, a "monosexual" model was current, in which a person can be only more or less masculine and is not man or woman and hence not masculine or feminine in any essential sense. Such a concept of sex and gender may also be assumed for the world in which Paul and the Philippians lived. This hierarchy of masculinity can be described as a hierarchy of penetration. This is shorthand for a situation in which one's degree of masculinity is determined by the extent to which one penetrates others and vice versa. Even though much of the background of this image is sexual, it is of importance to note that it could be applied to all aspects of life.

In this context, concepts such as autarky (or self-sufficiency) and the control over one's own passions became closely associated with the ideal of masculinity. Jennifer Larson describes the state of affairs as follows:

> Elite males were highly conscious of the fact that each of these groups (i.e., slaves, clients, women, *pbs*) was subject to their sexual demands; their right to sexually penetrate members of these groups was a reflection of their political and social dominance. According to a celebrated saying of the advocate Haterius, "Loss of sexual virtue (*impudicitia*) is a crime in a free man, a necessity for a slave, and a duty (*officium*) for a freed-man." What was most appalling about free, elite males who played a passive role in intercourse was that they willingly surrendered the masculine prerogative, thus allying themselves with lower-status groups who were expected to conciliate, flatter, and provide pleasure to their superiors. (2004, 93)[1]

A further illustration of this state of affairs concerning gender and the construction of masculinity, with women and slaves (typically) at the bottom of the hierarchy, is the high frequency of themes such as the "clever slave" or the "dominant woman" in contemporary comedy, addressing the perpetually vulnerable masculinity of husbands and masters. Larson again helpfully summarizes the situation:

> Masculinity was viewed as an attribute only partially related to an individual's anatomical sex. Whereas breasts and womb ensured that their possessor would be viewed as essentially feminine, the same was not true for anatomical males. Because masculinity was all but identified with social and political dominance, there was no assumption that all males must be masculine. The masculinity of slaves, for example, was by definition impaired. Personal dignity, bodily integrity,

---

1. The quotation of Haterius stems from Seneca the Elder, *Contr.* 4 pref. 10.

and specific details of one's appearance were all factors in individual self-assessment and in men's evaluation of one another's masculinity. Elite men of the day were constantly concerned with the maintenance of their masculinity, because it both displayed and justified their positions of power. Unlike noble birth, which was immutable, masculinity was a matter of perception. While elites always represented their masculinity to outsiders as innate, among insiders it was implicitly recognized that masculinity was a performance requiring constant practice and vigilance. (2004, 86)

Even though various overviews of the characteristics of "hegemonic" masculinity are available, the one provided by Moisés Mayordomo Marín continues to be helpful. He mentions the following seven aspects of hegemonic masculinity: (1) The conventional Greco-Roman view of gender, sex, and body was that in reality only a "monosexual" body existed that could manifest itself as (more) masculine or (more) feminine through genitals that had either grown outwardly or inwardly. (2) Masculinity was not necessarily a fact determined by the body with which one was born but needed to be proved constantly in the public arena, through one's appearance, behavior, and performance. Everyone (male or female) could constantly become more or less masculine. (3) Masculinity was very closely bound up with the notions of activity and dominance; as Mayordomo puts it: "Being a man in antiquity was very closely linked to the role of being an active agent rather than passive. Be it in politics, in sports, in war, in rhetoric or in the vast field of sexuality, what qualified an individual as a *man* was his active control of the situation" (2006, 7). (4) Masculinity and being virtuous were closely intertwined, specifically through the cardinal virtue of *andreia* (courage, manliness, masculinity) and through the virtues in general (*virtutes*). (5) Self-control was an essential part of the aforementioned dominance: "The most

active agent would be a man who controls himself with respect to anger and all other forms of passions, especially those associated with sexuality" (2006, 8). (6) This state of affairs also meant that, *sensu stricto*, no one was really born as a man, but that even a boy needed to be educated and trained to be a proper man. (7) Finally, it should be noted that masculinity and femininity were both associated with respective social spaces—that is, outside and inside, or public and private.

As will become clear from the next section, being masculine in relation to these characteristics was a process of constant negotiation, especially if one occupied a less than elite position in society, which applied to many, if not most, early Christian personalities. To be sure, early Christians could, in this regard, also tap into the resources of (popular) philosophical discourses, such as the Stoic and Cynic ones, that were also concerned with the construction of "subhegemonic" forms of masculinity in relation to the "hegemonic" ideal, thus challenging this ideal in the process (see, e.g., Asikainen 2018, 1–18).

Greco-Roman Masculinities and Early Christian Texts

With this background, the question can be asked how early Christian masculinities relate to the ideal-typical view of masculinity in the Greco-Roman context. In order to do so, two key personalities from the early Christian world will be considered: (1) Jesus of Nazareth (as he is mainly portrayed in the canonical Gospels) and (2) Paul of Tarsus. By analyzing them, we can trace many of the central characteristics and dynamics of the early Christian discourse on masculinity.

Jesus (in the Gospels)

While the field is still in motion, some claim that Jesus represents an alternative masculinity throughout; others make the opposite claim, stating that the depiction of Jesus in the New Testament is already well on the way toward subscribing to Greco-Roman ideals of masculinity (see Conway 2008). And still others argue that it was Paul's answer to the question as to what gender differences amounted to (and where they originated from and/or were located) that also haunted the early church to such an extent that definitive answers were never given (see Dunning 2011). It is much too early to attempt to make up the balance already. Rather, some examples may be given here as to how Jesus, as a man or masculine protagonist, was and was not represented and constructed by early Christian authors. Three instances of Jesus's depiction will be considered here. First, his speech will be considered. Second, an example of a miracle story will be discussed. Third, aspects of the crucifixion and resurrection are looked at. By considering these, it will become clear how multifaceted the depiction and construction of Jesus as a man is and how this can help to explain, at least partially, the widely varying constructions of "Christian masculinities" in the aftermath of Jesus's death and resurrection.

First, one of the areas in which masculinity was to be displayed and defended was that of public debate. As Mayordomo (2006) has shown for Paul, the way in which a public speaker acted did much for the attribution of masculinity to him (or her). Paul is a somewhat conflicted figure in this respect, as his performance as a public speaker seems to have been less than spectacular—unlike his acumen in letter writing. When the depiction of Jesus as a public speaker is surveyed, however, one gets a different impression throughout. While Jesus is never depicted as writing (with the exception of the *pericopa adulterae* in John 7:53–8:11), nor are any writings by him known, he is certainly depicted as speaking, and as a superb speaker at that. He not only delivers various lengthy discourses (in the de-

piction of especially Matthew and John, that is). He also indulges in numerous instances of teaching, making use of various rhetorical techniques, not least of parables, and is presented as a superior debater, without fail putting his opponents to shame. On this basis, one might be seduced into thinking that Jesus is presented as an extraordinarily masculine person in general. However, we will see that this is not entirely correct.

Second, in miracle stories, Jesus demonstrates an extraordinary kind of authority and power, which people recognize every now and then, even though Jesus is often also depicted as being at pains to keep things quiet. This posture results in a kind of paradoxical "hypermasculine" status: one that is known to the reader but hidden from public view in the narrative itself. Nonetheless, the issue of Jesus's status and masculinity appears throughout the Gospel narratives, even in miracle stories that, at first glance, might have nothing to do with questions of masculinity, such as the miraculous feeding in Mark 6 (and parallels). However, when we read this text in its narrative context, recognizing the juxtaposition of two banqueting scenes (that of Herod's birthday and Jesus's meal in the wilderness), it appears that here two kinds of leaders are presented: one (Herod) who cannot control his feelings and descends, with his male guests, into chaos at a dinner party where the only dish mentioned contains the severed head of John the Baptist (Mark 6:21–29); the other (Jesus) maintaining perfect control over himself and others in a chaotic situation, resulting in an abundant and well-ordered meal for all (6:30–44). This development also speaks to the masculinity that Jesus and Herod embody and the "honor" they have in the eyes of contemporary society. While this applies to the Synoptic tradition, in the Gospel of John Jesus's miracles—more specifically his *semeia* (or "signs")—are explicitly related to the notion of glory or honor (i.e., *doxa*, which signifies both in Greek). Possessing *doxa* was again essential for anyone wishing to be considered truly masculine. However, in, for example, John 2:1–11 (the wedding in Cana), where Jesus acts as the stand-in patron of the wedding by providing a large amount of wine, there is something distinctly odd about Jesus's display of his power and honor: these attributes remain hidden and not publicly proclaimed. This would have been necessary for the establishment of his masculinity, given that these attributes of a person existed only when they were publicly embodied and acclaimed. A reading of this oddity relates to Jesus's remark in John 2:4 that his "hour" had not yet come. When taken as a reference to his death on the cross (which, in the Gospel of John, is also Jesus's glorification), Jesus's embodiment of masculinity must be related to the crucifixion, which is indeed a public embodiment of something—but can it be considered masculinity? This will be considered next.

Third, Jesus's death and resurrection, arguably the pivot of the early Christian story, also need to be considered from the perspective of masculinity. Whether one takes the account of any of the canonical Gospels or one of Paul's accounts (e.g., in 1 Cor. 15 or in Phil. 2:5–11), the conflicting associations that the crucifixion, death, and resurrection of Christ evoke when read against the background of Greco-Roman conventions regarding masculinity remain structurally similar. Jesus's death on the cross must be regarded as an utterly shameful death, fit for slaves, exposing, penetrating, and humiliating the body in a way that had absolutely no place in contemporary understandings of masculinity. The resurrection, soon conceptualized as a victory over death, however, must be seen as a glorious event that gave Christ a hypermasculine position and identity (according to Phil. 2:9–11, for example). Untying this knot seems to be difficult, especially as, depending on the account one takes, Jesus goes into his death willingly, thus retaining a certain amount of control over the events. One generally accepted way of conceptualizing all this would be Jesus's identity as a martyr, to whose identity a (potentially shameful) death was inherent, but Jesus, due to his faithfulness to his cause, would die an honorable death. Still, the crucifixion does not fit into this line of thought without some difficulties, shameful a death as it remained—and hence a source of some embarrassment for early Christians.

In sum, therefore, the representation of Jesus Christ's masculinity in early Christian writing is a highly unstable matter. In fact, it invites a classification as "queer," in the sense of going beyond extant categories and models—and, while there are some models that may do justice to it to a considerable extent, such as the model of the righteous martyr, some instability remains. This instability is a productive one when it comes to the reception and interpretation of Jesus traditions in subsequent discourses on human identity, specifically on masculinity.

Paul

One of the key witnesses to early Christians' attempt to come to terms with the paradoxical legacy of Jesus, as far as masculinity is concerned, is Paul of Tarsus. In his letters, Paul wrestles with the question as to what living "in Christ" means in a variety of settings and vis-à-vis a whole range of challenges. These include both reflection on Paul's experience of marginalization and the integration of the notion of being the follower (even servant) of a crucified Lord, all of which had to have an impact on his view of an appropriate performance and understanding of masculinity. The result is a rather ambiguous stance vis-à-vis generally held ideals of masculinity in the Greco-Roman world. In particular, Mayordomo has pointed out how Paul renegotiates masculinity while retaining some of its ideals. The following three of his conclusions constitute a good starting point for the line of thought followed in this note (Mayordomo 2006, 17–18):

- "As a man Paul does not question the active role of the male agent. But he makes, at least, two qualifications: A Christian male belongs as bodily person to Christ and he is morally bound to express his love towards his fellow-believers by renouncing important aspects of his male autonomy."
- "As a follower of Christ Paul clings to a system of values (or virtues) which has much in common with the Roman value system, but not all: being humble (*tapeinos*), for instance, is something which runs contrary to hegemonic forms of masculinity. On the other hand, we do not find 'courage' (*andreia*) as a virtue exposed by Paul."
- "As an unmarried Jewish man Paul limits sexuality to marriage. But even marriage is a lesser evil, because sexuality always implies a retraction from the complete rule of Christ. The most excellent form of male control is, thus, self-control."

Thus, Paul accepts generally held ideals of masculinity, such as the ideal of absolute self-control. But he also modifies them, for example, by attributing all his strength to an outside source, Christ, who himself embodies very unmanly virtues, such as humility. In this context, one can also argue that the concept of the cross and the self-identification with someone as unmanly as a crucified Messiah, while upholding the significance of true manliness, are part of the background of Paul's need to renegotiate the ideals of masculinity.

Summary

These few comments show how more generally held ideals of masculinity and emerging Christian theologizing could interact.

Especially the cross and dependence on an outward source of identity (namely, Christ), which enables a person to be in control both of himself and of whatever life and others throw at him, seem to have been important incentives for rethinking ideal masculinity. In particular, this has also been a source of inspiration for early Christian asceticism, as Mayordomo has put it: "Christian masculinity culminates in complete control over one's bodily needs for him. This anthropological choice paves the way for the latter Christian movement of celibate life. From this perspective, early ascetics and monks were not defective males but, quite to the contrary, hyper-masculine figures, able to control even the most forceful passions" (2006, 16).

Concluding Observations

At the very least, attention to the topic of masculinities makes them visible as part of the spectrum of gendered identities that can (and should) be studied when addressing questions of gender in the New Testament and early Christianity at large. This serves more than *just* understanding how gender, specifically masculinities, functions. Due to the intersectional nature of constructions of masculinities (and other forms of gender), they are also a key site for the negotiation of topics such as power and suffering (and much more). Students of the New Testament and cognate literature are well served whenever encountering a masculine figure (whether "male" or "female") to ask, What sort of masculinity is this? and, How does this position a person socially and in relation to other forms of masculinities and with what effect? The pursuit of these questions aids an understanding of both early Christian constructions of gender (esp. masculinities) and the positioning of early Christian personalities and groups in the Greco-Roman world at large (see Wilson 2015).

Works Cited

Asikainen, Susanna. 2018. *Jesus and Other Men.* Leiden: Brill.

Conway, Colleen M. 2008. *Behold the Man! Jesus and Greco-Roman Masculinity.* Oxford: Oxford University Press.

Dunning, Benjamin H. 2011. *Specters of Paul: Sexual Difference in Early Christian Thought.* Philadelphia: University of Pennsylvania Press.

Goodman, Martin. 1997. *The Roman World, 44 BC–AD 180.* New York: Routledge.

Larson, Jennifer. 2004. "Paul's Masculinity." *JBL* 123: 85–97.

Mayordomo Marín, Moisés, 2006. "Construction of Masculinity in Antiquity and Early Christianity." *Lectio Difficilior* 2: 1–33.

Smit, Peter-Ben. 2017. *Masculinity and the Bible: Survey, Models, and Perspectives.* Leiden: Brill.

Wilson, Brittany E. 2015. *Unmanly Men: Refigurations of Masculinity in Luke-Acts.* Oxford: Oxford University Press.

31

Disabled Bodies

Louise J. Lawrence

While the ancient world had no direct equivalent terminology for "disability" (a "socially constructed category of discursive investment"; Mitchell and Snyder 2002, 2), it is apparent that those bodies perceived to fall short of aesthetic ideals, or cultural values and preferences, were frequently censored and excluded: spatially, ideologically, socially, and discursively. Social constructions of disability can be understood as the degree to which an impairment (or a physical, biological, or mental state) restricts a body's social ability to fulfill certain culturally endorsed identities and functions (dis-ability). In Jewish ritual practice, based on sophisticated codes of purity and holiness, priestly functions were to be conducted by male, circumcised bodies, free of disability and disease (Lev. 21:16–23). For Greek and Roman contexts, where rhetorical ability and orality were esteemed, deafness, speech variations, or mental and intellectual differences frequently rendered such bodies as unknowing and noncommunicative. In agrarian contexts, the battlefield, or the gymnasium, where raw physical-

ity was paramount, those with "weaker" bodily forms were judged as dysfunctional and/or "invalid." In such contexts, to be a normative body (whether male, fecund, strong, symmetrical, able, and/or a persuasive communicator) was to be appropriately located, with agency and access to the centers of power. Those bodies falling short of cultural ideals were socially marginal and rendered as socially dead: outcast and driven to the peripheries of the social order. Often imagined as sinful, abject, and/or cursed, disabled bodies functioned as the foil for those "ideal" bodies that were culturally authorized and approved as whole, pure, healthy, and morally good.

Biblical studies has often overlooked sensory and affective dimensions of bodies and their movements. Yet the responses evoked by bodily performances undoubtedly played important roles in the discursive construction of social identities and affiliations. Social anthropologists reveal how bodily performances hold the power to arouse connection, identification, exclusion, and segregation by gendering, sexualizing, classing, racializing, and—crucially for our present task—disabling subjects. Such perspectives pose questions too about cultural histories of the body and its parts, and about the links between the subjective and the cultural, the individual and the social, and ideological maps of inclusion and exclusion.

Deviance and Physiognomy

Social-scientific studies of stigma and deviance provide frameworks for engaging the "disabled" body, which is categorized as "other." Sociologist Erving Goffman was sensitive to the particular ways in which perception of deviance from a norm often marked out a body as spoiled—"reduced . . . from a whole and usual person to a tainted, discounted one" (1963, 3)—and how a body's perceived otherness could leak into and subsume its entire identity through a single "deviant" trait. For a body to be stigmatized, somehow its transgression of social norms needed to be made visible or evident in its materiality, which in turn functioned as a potent surface onto which dominant social, cultural, and ethical evaluations could be projected.

The discipline of physiognomy (connecting bodily appearance with character, ethics, and morality), which was widespread in antiquity, influenced in part these common projections onto disabled bodies. Physiognomy was common within many medical and philosophical treatises and handbooks. Hippocrates is often hailed as a founder of the discipline as a science (*Epid.* 2.5.1), and major treatises on the practice include the pseudo-Aristotelian work *Physiognomonica* (3rd c. BCE) and the work of rhetorician Polemo of Laodicea *De Physiognomonica* (2nd c. CE). The technical physiognomic procedure was grounded in the confidence that bodily events and forms affected the soul, and emotions took on perceptible form in movement, stature, facial features and complexion, and associated somatic qualities.

Physiognomic comparisons between humans and animals (vipers, lambs, pigs, etc.), different races and ethnicities, different genders, different facial features (eyes, complexion, hair, shape), and bodily performances (height, gait, comportment) all became important dimensions of the evaluative process. It is unsurprising, then, that a certain physiognomic determinism frequently operated with regard to bodies perceived as disabled and became part of the apparatus by which these were rendered in both encomia and invective rhetoric as specters of stigma and deviance (Parsons 2006; Hartsock 2008; Callon 2019).

In view of such somatic reasoning, it is not surprising either that while able bodies are largely devoid of extended descriptions in New Testament traditions, disabled bodies are often bound by physiognomic commentary. Major New Testament figures and protagonists are afforded little vivid physical description (Taylor 2018), though Paul rhetorically hints at his own lack of physiognomic appeal in his letters (2 Cor. 10:10; Gal. 4:13–16), and his literary portrait is developed in extracanonical material (Acts Paul Thec. 3). In contrast, disabled bodies are "physiognomized" precisely because they are used to invoke narrative representations of disorder. Assumptions about their moral characters, made on account of physiognomic reasoning, can also be important illustrations of how conversion in early Christian discourse can lead to identity transformation.

Movement, Posture, and Gait

Emerging studies of walking cultures in antiquity have variously responded to a so-called mobility turn within the academy.[1] Jan Bremmer's work on gesture and posture in ancient Greek culture, for example, builds on Aristotelian physiognomic tracts to reveal that

---

1. Some of this section first appeared in Lawrence 2023.

the body served as an important location for self-identification and demonstration of authority. By its gait, the Greek upper-class not only distinguished itself from supposedly effeminate peoples such as Persians and Lydians, but also expressed its dominance over weaker sections of society such as youths and women. . . . [While there is no] literary evidence that slaves could not display an upright carriage either, it seems important to note that on vases and reliefs they are regularly portrayed as sitting in a squatting position or as being of a smaller stature. (Bremmer 1992, 15, 35)

The honorable and decorous citizen was unhurried and controlled in his movements. Men strode in extended steps, though women, in contrast, often adopted a diminutive tread. Walking with hips moving to and fro was frequently associated with courtesans or moral deviance (Bremmer 1992, 20). In Roman culture, too, walking involved discernment, not just movement. Gait was reflective of social status and gender: slaves harried; the elite processed honorably, admired by others; free men promenaded, but not too slowly, for fear of effeminacy (O'Sullivan 2011). In philosophy, one's gait was a visible sign of an inward composure (2011, 22). Walking was a crucial part of the philosophical formation for the peripatetic who (as their name indicates) enacted discourses while walking (Segrave 2006, 4). Cicero, too, transposed activities of the body to the mind, to illustrate character and disposition. These intellectual connections between walking and learning derived from Greek thought in which Plato and others adopted movement as a "mode of philosophical enquiry" (O'Sullivan 2011, 8, 9). Literal and metaphorical journeys also coalesced, allowing Roman elites to perform the correlation between the movement of the body and the accretion of knowledge.

In the Hebrew Bible, too, walking is often combined figuratively with a route or way to denote a moral regime. The blessed person "does not follow the advice of the wicked" (Ps. 1:1) but rather "walk[s] humbly with . . . God" (Mic. 6:8). Indeed, the term *halak* can mean simply "to walk" but also idiomatically to behave according to law or to be in right relationship with others or God. Thus, in Genesis 17:1 God commands Abraham also to walk with him and be perfect. Some modern translations regrettably substitute the material dynamism of the terminology of walking with plain terms like "live," "conduct," or "behave" (Ryken, Wilhoit, and Longman 1998, 922). The consequence is to reduce a reader's ability to see how corporeal performances function as spaces of understanding. Recapturing embodied cognition, Yael Avrahami, in surveying sensory dimensions of the Hebrew Bible, notes that walking frequently corresponds to other kinesthetic experiences: "Walking, standing, and sitting all represent here behaviour, involvement, and presence" (Avrahami 2012, 77). In the New Testament, similarly, *peripateō* is used to denote both physical walking (a use that largely dominates in the Synoptics) and a figurative walking (predominantly in John and the epistles). Paul urges converts to "walk in newness of life" (Rom. 6:4), "according to the Spirit" (Rom. 8:4) and "in faith" (2 Cor. 5:7). The Greek verb *stoicheō* (lit., "to walk in line or in a row," as in an army) is similarly employed metaphorically in Pauline epistles to link movement with robust moral insight and ethical cognition: to walk upright morally in relation to others (Rom. 4:12). Most fundamentally, indicating the status of walking and mobility to constructions of identity, the early Christians first referred to themselves as "The Way" (*hē hodos*; Acts 9:2).

If images of "upright" and "abled" walking and gait connected directly to moral perceptions of ethical practice and social hierarchies, physiognomic consciousness often projected deviant morality onto those bodies whose movement did not echo normative expectations. In Aristotelian thought the shameless man's stature and comportment were "bowed" and "not erect" (Aristotle, *Phys.* 3.807b [trans. Hett 1955, 100–101]). Such assumptions could be reflected in Jesus's command to the paralytic to "stand up and walk" and condemnation of the authorities who censor his alternative response to the man's condition: "Your sins are forgiven" (Mark 2:9 // Matt. 9:5 // Luke 5:23). While walking is at a basic level proof of a healing's veracity, many commentators also link the physical and spiritual dimensions of this man's walking. Solomon Pasala, in his exposition of the healing of the paralytic, also notes that in the *Poetics* of Aristotle walking often denotes a transformation from one stage within a drama to the converse, and additionally, "a discovery [implying] a change from ignorance to knowledge." Thus, "in getting up and walking the paralytic has manifested the discovery of truth. He begins to cross over from ignorance" (Pasala 2008, 172). Well-formed ankles and feet also denoted a certain strength of moral character, whereas those who were lame or paralyzed (Luke 5:17–26; John 5:1–16; Acts 3–4) were often understood as morally weak, passive, or effeminate. Mikael Parsons's work on the lame man in Acts 3:1–6 gives corporeal reasoning to such attitudes when he notes that feet and ankles are body parts of significant physiognomic import. Citing pseudo-Aristotle, he contends:

> "Those who have strong and well-jointed ankles are brave in character; witness the male sex. Those that have fleshly and ill-jointed ankles are weak in character, witness the female sex" (*Physiog* 810a.25–29). The lame man's weak ankles would have been viewed as an outward sign of his weak moral character. . . . The strengthening of the lower extremities would have been an outward sign of his newly found inner moral strength. (Parsons 2005, 302)

In the story of the lame man at the pool in John 5, the man is likewise portrayed as an outcast, lying for thirty-eight years at the pool (a number some have seen echoing Israel's years in the wilderness or representing long-standing spiritual weakness). Jesus's imperative command (v. 8) could be read as a call to "walk" from his thirty-eight-year exclusion from the temple (see Lev. 21:17; 2 Sam. 5:8) into temple space (John 5:14). It could also be understood as "go" or "move about," "live" or "conduct oneself," thus signaling a change of perspective regarding moral identity (see Lawrence 2019).

Stature, Size, and Skin

Physiognomic reasoning on size and stature favored those of medium height (being neither too tall nor too short), representing moderation and authenticity in demeanor and spirit. In pseudo-Aristotle's terms: "An ill-proportioned body indicates a rogue, the argument being partly from congruity and partly from the female sex. But if bad proportions mean villainy, a well-proportioned frame must be characteristic of upright men and brave; only, the standard of the right proportions must be sought in the good training and good breeding in the body, and not in the male type, as we said at the beginning" (*Physiogn.* 814a [trans. Swain 2007, 661]).

In biblical traditions, too, height is employed in characterizations of deviancy. In the Canaan conquest traditions, the formidable physiques of giants are used to exhibit the great strength of Yahweh in vanquishing them. David triumphantly kills Goliath the Gittite, who measures an imposing "six cubits and a span" (1 Sam. 17:4). Josephus's characterization of false messiahs as "tall" (*Ant.* 17.273, 278–79) could also be reflective of such aversions (Doak 2019). So, too, moral evaluations were cast on those of small stature: indeed, dwarfism is listed as a prohibitive disability for priests offering sacrifice and entering the sacred space of the holy of holies (Lev. 21:19).

The diminutive tax collector Zacchaeus (Luke 19:1–10) has also been interpreted through a physiognomic lens. His short stature, and comic performance of climbing a tree, has been read alongside Greco-Roman discourses on dwarfism and dwarfs, who often performed roles as dancers or comedians in carnivalesque forms of entertainment (Solevåg 2020). Ancient visual and material culture often display enlarged genitals on dwarf figures, which seem to point to a (sardonic) hypersexuality, or in direct contrast, an association with impotency. Aristotle, too, pictures dwarfs with large penises and makes a zoological echo of this form with donkeys, but he also notes that a beast with a long organ was "less fertile as sperm cools on its way" (Dasen 1993, 237).

In ethical and moral terms, those who were short in size and stature were also often considered "small-minded" (Parsons 2001, 53). Meanness and covetousness have been read as conceptual equivalents of this trait, which has been plotted onto ethical dimensions of Zacchaeus's occupation (tax collection was an instrument of the Roman extractive machine), accruing fraudulent material gain at the expense of others (Parsons 2001, 55). Such interpretations are reflective of the assumption that there is a direct moral dimension to his stature. Though, through his interaction with Jesus, Zacchaeus is nudged to reparative action, and presumably a "higher" moral standing.

Physiognomic conventions also often linked size and swellings with greed and wealth, or self-indulgent tyrannical rules (Hartsock 2013). At the execution of Emperor Vitellius in 69 CE, Suetonius relates how this contentious figure was not only monstrously tall but also obese, reflective of his immoderation, overindulgence, and chaotic rule (Bradley 2011). In Judges 3:12–22, the oppressor King Eglon of Moab is likewise characterized as a very fat man who has subjugated Israel for eighteen years. He is eventually subdued by being stabbed by the left-handed hero Ehud, as a result of

which Eglon's excrement and guts irrepressibly spill out (3:22). This presumably indicates a (physical) piercing of his (ideological) inflated self-importance and evokes a disgust reaction within the audience. Luke's account of a body with dropsy (Luke 14:1–6) may also be engaging this type of physiognomic commentary. This condition made the body swell up due to an unquenchable thirst and could eventually lead to gushing and explosion. Equivalent to this somatic outcome, ideologically thirsting for wealth or prestige, or a debilitating lack of self-control of the passions, could eventually destroy a person in Luke's social imaginary (Hartsock 2013). Here, as in the Zacchaeus narrative, the healing of both physical and social "dis-ease" is from self-indulgent avarice to generosity and other-regard.

Cultural histories of skin in antiquity, too, note the "strong conception of the inviolability of the body as guaranteed by the smooth and immaculate skin" (Connor 2004, 10). Breached or broken skin, in physiognomic reasoning, could also function as an indicator of the invasion of evil, transgression of social norms, and ultimately exclusion, self-mortification, and death. In the Hebrew Bible, Satan is commissioned to wreak destruction on Job's skin in his litany of tortures: "My flesh is clothed with worms and dirt; my skin hardens, then breaks out again" (Job 7:4–6). Leprosy was accordingly censored through social and religious maps of un-touch-ability and enforced isolation of the leprous body from the community (Lev. 13–14; Num. 12:15). Josephus attests the leper as corpse-like (*Ant*. 3.264). Leviticus 13 shows this graphically when it describes the disease penetrating and breaking up the skin's boundaries and, like sin, defiling and isolating its victims. Even though odor is not explicit in the representations within the Gospel stories of lepers (Mark 1:40–45 // Matt. 8:1–4 // Luke 5:12–15), nonetheless the stench (both physical and symbolic) of their bodily conditions is frequently understood to represent sin and mortality and to augment their shame and aberration.

Sight and Sense

The faculty of sight as a cipher for emotion and knowledge was also part of the physiognomic consciousness. Aristotle infers that those with red eyes are enraged in turmoil and those with blemished eyes are weak, while those with lustrous eyes are sensual and, in zoological comparison, like ravens (Aristotle, *Phys.* 6.811a). Cicero, too, notes how the eyes index emotions (*De or.* 3.221–22). The ancient optical theory of "extramission"—in which the eye was seen to emit its own particles of light, which touched the external world and accordingly facilitated sight—could lie behind Jesus's metaphorical statement that "the eye is the lamp of the body" (Matt. 6:22–23; cf. Luke 11:34–36). The corollary of an understanding of the eye as an instrument that emits light is a blinded eye that emits darkness and can cast evil on those in its sights. Evil eye is an ophthalmic phenomenon that is symptomatic of "a heart hardened and a hand shut to a neighbour in need" (Elliott 1991, 149). Lack of sight was often assumed to be the result of sin (John 9:2) or mirrors of moral aberration and/or misunderstanding. Blindness, for instance, was often related to the inability to navigate (moral) terrain. "Falling into a pit" was aligned to disorder, devastation, and the underworld (Ps. 7:15; Prov. 26:27). In this understanding, the man at Bethsaida (Mark 8:22–26) and Bartimaeus (10:46–52) have been understood to perform as interpretive ciphers exemplifying misconception (spiritual blindness) about the ideological importance of the way of the cross, and Jesus's identity known only through suffering (Lawrence 2013).

Early Christian (Self-)Depictions of Disability

Disabled bodies are often used to depict unsettling deviations from culturally accepted norms. Depictions of disability are also, however, jarringly employed as a discursive strategy to construct early Christian identity. Particularly arresting examples of such metaphorical refiguring occur in Mark's and Matthew's parallel sayings about self-dismemberment and gouging out one's eye (also cutting off one's hand or feet, or becoming a eunuch) in order to enter the kingdom (Mark 9:45–48; Matt. 5:29–30; 18:8–9; 19:10–12). Of course, somatic logic stands at the heart of the "way of the cross," which features a pierced, feminized, maimed, and ultimately lifeless body, which through discursive paradox in New Testament traditions is enabled to subvert its "stigma-tic" stereotypes (Lawrence 2019). Christian bodies navigating their own "way of the cross" are thus imaged as blinded, limbless castrates, which evocatively depict and refigure dis-ability as deviancy in early Christian imaginations.

Works Cited

Avrahami, Yael. 2012. *The Senses of Scripture: Sensory Perception in the Hebrew Bible.* The Library of Hebrew Bible / Old Testament Studies 545. London: Bloomsbury T&T Clark.

Bradley, M. 2011. "Obesity, Corpulence and Emancipation in Roman Art." *Papers of the British School at Rome* 79: 1–41.

Bremmer, Jan. 1992. "Walking, Standing, and Sitting in Ancient Greek Culture." In *A Cultural History of Gesture*, edited by Jan Bremmer and Herman Roodenburg, 15–35. Ithaca, NY: Cornell University Press.

Callon, Callie. 2019. *Reading Bodies: Physiognomy as a Strategy of Persuasion in Early Christian Discourse.* London: Bloomsbury T&T Clark.

Connor, Steven. 2004. *The Book of Skin.* London: Reaktion Books.

Dasen, Veronique. 1993. *Dwarfs in Ancient Egypt and Greece.* Oxford: Clarendon.

Doak, Brian R. 2019. *Heroic Bodies in Ancient Israel.* Oxford: Oxford University Press.

Elliott, John H. 1991. "The Evil Eye in the First Testament: The Ecology and Culture of a Pervasive Belief." In *The Bible and the Politics of Exegesis*, edited by David Jobling, Peggy Day, and Gerald Sheppard, 147–59. Cleveland: Pilgrim.

Goffman, Erving. 1963. *Stigma: Notes on the Management of a Spoiled Identity*. Englewood Cliffs, NJ: Prentice-Hall.

Hartsock, Charles. 2008. *Sight and Blindness in Luke-Acts: The Use of Physical Features in Characterization*. Leiden: Brill.

———. 2013. "The Healing of the Man with Dropsy (Luke 14:1–6) and the Lukan Landscape." *BibInt* 21, no. 3: 341–54.

Hett, W. S., trans. 1955. *Aristotle: Minor Works*. LCL 307. Cambridge, MA: Harvard University Press.

Lawrence, Louise J. 2013. *Sense and Stigma in the Gospels: Depictions of Sensory-Disabled Characters*. Oxford: Oxford University Press.

———. 2019. "Disease and Disability Metaphors in Gospel Worlds." *Int* 73, no. 4: 377–85.

———. 2023. "Take Up Your Mat and Walk: [Dis-]Abled Bodies of Communication and Early Christian Wandering." *Biblical Theology Bulletin* 53, no. 4. https://doi.org/10.1177/01461079231210849.

Mitchell, David, and Sharon L. Snyder. 2002. *Cultural Locations of Disability*. Chicago: University of Chicago Press.

O'Sullivan, Timothy M. 2011. *Walking in Roman Culture*. Cambridge: Cambridge University Press.

Parsons, Mikael. 2001. "'Short in Stature': Luke's Physical Description of Zacchaeus." *NTS* 47, no. 1: 50–57.

———. 2005. "The Character of the Lame Man in Acts 3–4." *JBL* 124: 295–312.

———. 2006. *Body and Character in Luke and Acts: The Subversion of Physiognomy in Early Christianity*. Grand Rapids: Baker Academic.

Pasala, Solomon. 2008. *The Drama of the Messiah in Matthew 8 and 9: A Study from a Communicative Perspective*. Bern: Peter Lang.

Ryken, Leland, James C. Wilhoit, and Tremper Longman III, eds. 1998. *Dictionary of Biblical Imagery*. Downers Grove, IL: InterVarsity.

Segrave, Kerry. 2006. *America on Foot: Walking and Pedestrianism in the 20th Century*. Jefferson, NC: McFarland.

Solevåg, Rebecca A. 2020. "Zacchaeus in the Gospel of Luke: Comic Figure, Sinner, and Included 'Other.'" *Journal of Literary and Cultural Disability Studies* 14: 225–40.

Swain, Simon, trans. 2007. "Appendix: The *Physiognomy* Attributed to Aristotle." In *Seeing the Face, Seeing the Soul: Polemon's "Physiognomy" from Classical Antiquity to Medieval Islam*, edited by Simon Swain, 637–61. Oxford: Oxford University Press.

Taylor, Joan E. 2018. *What Did Jesus Look Like?* London: Bloomsbury T&T Clark.

PART THREE

Themes
on the Stage

SECTION I

Divine Society

32

Theos and Theology

T. J. LANG

In spite of everything, we go on saying "God."

Williams 1986, 197

Theos is the Greek word for "God." When New Testament authors talk about God, they talk about *theos*. "Theology" is the English word for thinking about God. When it comes to God in the New Testament, whether it be one's own thoughts about God or thoughts about others' thoughts about God, the English word "theology" identifies thinking about *theos*.[1] These delineations may seem uncomplicated, but with respect to the New Testament and its context, neither the meaning of *theos* nor the domain of "theology" is straightforward.

The meaning of the word *theos* in ancient Greek sources (Christian included) is far from fixed or easily determined. As the classicist Simon Price has observed, "*Theos*, though a basic term in Greek religion, has never been given a detailed semantic study. Scholars, in their eagerness to examine what the Greeks

thought about their gods, have generally not paused to consider the prior question—what does *theos* mean?" (Price 1984, 79). This question is nowhere more vital than in the study of the New Testament. One way of reading the entirety of early Christian theology is in terms of this very question: What does one mean when one says "God"? Or as the ancient Greek poet Pindar (5th c. BCE) even more pointedly put it in a similar question half a millennium prior to the New Testament writings, "What is god?" (*ti theos?*; frag. 140d; Snell and Maehler 1975).[2]

In answering such questions, early "Christians" like Paul affirm propositions such as "one God, the Father" (1 Cor. 8:6), alluding to the Shema of Deuteronomy 6:4.[3] But

---

1. Cf. the Hebrew *'elohim* and the Latin *deus/divus*.

2. Cf. Menander as quoted by Stobaeus, *Anth.* 3.32.11: "What is a god [*ti theos*]? Ruling power."

3. The scare quotes around "Christian" signal the fact that Paul did not know he was one—that is, if by "Christian" one means something other than Jewish. Paul's ongoing loyalty to "one God, the Father" is patent evidence of his Jewish identity. The title "Christian" is a social designation that seems to have been imposed on Christ believers by outsiders, perhaps derisively. It appears only three times

alongside this and other descriptions of God, the category of "one God" is also surprisingly extended to include Christ (e.g., John 1:1–3; 20:28; Rom. 9:5; Titus 2:13; 2 Pet. 1:1). Somehow, now, the one God comprises Father *and* "the Lord, Jesus Christ," both of whom determine the "from," "for," and "through" of all existence. All of these prepositions depend on the activity of the "one God." What does this binitarian formulation mean for the meaning of "God"? What does it mean to accept some form of plurality within the identity of the "*one* God, the Father"? Early Christian theology is an extended discussion of just this question. Though often a "neglected factor" in modern study of the New Testament, the question of God is nonetheless fundamental throughout the New Testament (Dahl 1975; see also Hurtado 2010).

"Theology" is also a word with its own complications when it comes to the study of *theos* in the New Testament and its ancient context. "Theology" today designates forms of thought about the divine. Such thought ranges from the inchoate to the systematic, but "theology," like other -*ology* words, is usually associated with formal intellectual discourse. The term itself derives from the Greek word *theologia*, which would seem to be a suitable term for naming what a "theologian" (*theologos*) does. But as apt as this terminology may seem in English, it is in fact inadequate, and even distortive, when it comes to historical analysis. Whatever New Testament and other early Christian authors thought they were doing in their thinking about God, they were not doing *theologia* in the sense familiar to most ancient authors.[4] Theorizing about "god" was, in the ancient world, very much a philosophical and even a scientific activity, even while ordinary people were, of course, keen to discuss the cultic stories (or

theologia) of their associational groups. The point is that there was no segregated intellectual space named "theology." And insofar as "theology" uncouples thinking about the gods from the domains of ancient philosophical and scientific questioning, it distorts the ways in which gods belonged to a total worldview. The modern disciplinary classification known as "theology" always implicates philosophy and cosmology, and vice versa (Lang 2020).

Prior to the fourth century CE, *theologia* primarily belonged to the realm of poetry and myth. *Theologia* was the enterprise of poets, mythologists, and creative allegorical interpreters of such literary inventions (cf. Plato, *Resp.* 379a). The "theologian" (*theologos*) was thus the composer of such poetry or, alternatively, the interpreter of this enigmatically coded material about the gods. The deeper, embedded senses of poetic literature communicated profound realities about the structure of the universe, the destiny of souls, and the role of the gods therein. A "theologian" was the inspired individual capable of either composing such poetry or decoding its allegorical meanings (Lamberton 1986, 22–31). Even as later patristic authors gradually appropriated this terminology for thinking about divinity, it still more often referred generally to "speech about god" rather than systematic thought (Markschies 2015, 5–17).

"Theology" today is usually defined in such systematic terms. Intellectuals in the ancient world certainly engaged in systematic reflection on matters of divinity, but such reflection belonged to the general sphere of philosophy and so was contiguous with questions of logic, physics, and ethics. This is precisely why Cicero identifies his "theological" treatise, *On the Nature of the Gods*, as a matter of "philosophy" (*res in philosophia*) (*Nat. d.* 1.1).[5]

---

in the New Testament, and in texts likely among its later layers (Acts 11:26; 26:28; 1 Pet. 4:16).

4. The *theolog-* word group never occurs in any biblical traditions.

5. The "theological" cousin of Cicero's treatise in Greek was the *On the Gods* (*Peri Theōn*) genre, and there were a number of ancient compositions so titled.

"Theology" is not in Cicero's vocabulary. Inquiry into the gods—like inquiry into the nature of the world (physics), how one knows it (epistemology), and how one ought to live in it (ethics)—is a philosophical pursuit. Interest in the gods was, of course, not just an abstract intellectual enterprise among "philosophers." Robust conversations about divinities belonged as much to workshops and the family home or any place where interest in the divine might matter or provide entertainment. This is all important to bear in mind when reading the New Testament. Exhibit A: When the author of the Fourth Gospel identifies the "Word/Reason" (*logos*) as "God" (*theos*) (John 1:1), this author enters a long and intricate philosophical conversation, whether knowingly or not, about the nature of a divine *logos*. I have no reason to presume the author of John 1:1 had any sophisticated facility with the subtleties of Stoic or Platonic philosophies and various doctrines of a divine *logos*. But with this alignment of *logos* and *theos* ("Word" and "God") the Gospel of John enters a long-standing philosophical conversation—and even provocatively confronts long-standing debates (for John and ancient philosophy, see Engberg-Pedersen 2017). Modern interpreters of John 1:1 and all other early Christian literature are only enriched by greater familiarity with that ancient philosophical conversation (Edwards 2021).[6]

Ancient Mediterranean Gods

The historical error modern readers always risk when exploring beliefs about divinity in the ancient world is anachronism, the imposition of later ideas on earlier times. In the so-called Western world, this error most commonly occurs when Christian assumptions and modern philosophical notions about divinity are overlaid on ancient people and their beliefs about the gods. Ancient thinking about the divine population is far livelier and philosophically disorderly than tidy theological abstractions such as "monotheism" or "perfect-being theology" allow.

When the word *theos* occurs in ancient texts, it is most frequently in the plural (*theoi*). As Paul affirms, there are "many so-called gods [*theoi*], whether in heaven or on earth, as in fact there are many gods [*theoi*] and many lords" (1 Cor. 8:5, my translation). The gods in ancient Mediterranean religion belonged to a complex and ever-expanding celestial society. New gods, like international imports, could ever be acquired. Modern scholars systematize the ancient divine society with the term "polytheism" (Versnel 2011; duBois 2014; Parker 2019). This label does not always have a happy history, especially when used to demean "non-monotheistic" cultures or to deride the supposed incapacities of "pagan" thought. But, in the spirit of "an eye for an eye," in the world of the New Testament, so-called pagans had their own injurious response to the views of Christians. Early Christians were said to be "atheists" (*atheoi*). And, as such, they were a threat to proper piety (*pietas*) and thus to an empire dependent on the favor of the gods. This was not an unreasonable way of viewing the numerically minuscule and sociologically deviant collectives of people worshiping an executed Galilean peasant. Christians, in their antisocial repudiation of the gods of the Roman Empire, were indeed atheists (on ancient atheism, see Whitmarsh 2016).

Fundamental to ancient thinking about the divine population were the great works of Hesiod and Homer. Hesiod's *Theogony* (lit., "birth of the gods") recounts the origins and composition of the divine society. This society stretches from divine features in the natural world to the widely known Olympian deities. Homer's *Iliad* and *Odyssey* offer entertaining accounts of the doings of these great Greek

---

6. For the Stoic identification of *logos* and *theos*, see, e.g., Diogenes Laertius, *Vit. phil.* 7.134; Cicero, *Nat. d.* 1.39; 2.7; Cleanthes, *Hymn to Zeus*.

gods. Beyond Homer, and especially into the Roman Empire, as other deities from other cultures were absorbed within the ancient Mediterranean religious pantheon, the divine society became far more varied and complex. Given this complexity, the most salient features of "god" in ancient thought are creaturely immortality, presence and power, and personal relation.

Creaturely Immortality

The Greco-Roman gods are immortal gods. They are the "deathless [*athanatos*] gods," "deathless and ageless" (Hesiod, *Theog.* 277), "the holy race of deathless beings who always 'are'" (*Theog.* 105, my translation). The deathlessness of the gods is ubiquitous in ancient literature. But, though they are deathless, it is important to stress that the gods are not ontologically separate from the created order. Ancient Greco-Roman thinking about the gods knows no absolute Creator/creature distinction. Their immortality participates in creation. In orthodox Christian teaching, God is "other" and so is definitively distinct from creation as is entailed in the doctrine of creation as *ex nihilo* (out of nothing). Greco-Roman gods, though undying, emerge within processes of creation (see fig. 32.1).

The gods bring form and order to the cosmos, but they also intersect with it. Hesiod's *Theogony* is the most important account of creation's emergence and the "birthing" of the gods, as the Greek title of Hesiod's *Theo-gonia* clearly indicates. According to Hesiod's account, the gods are integral to the maintenance and order of the world, and they rank above humanity in the hierarchy of being, but they also still belong to the same ontological sphere of creaturely identity. The "deathless" gods are creatures who routinely mix with the rest of creation.[7] Earth, day, night, sun, stars, streams,

trees, nymphs, and a panoply of personified abstractions (such as Fortune) are all divine (or abodes of the divine), and yet they clearly belong to the ontological circle of creation (Pliny the Elder, *Nat.* 2.22). Divinity was even occasionally extended to humanity (Goodenough 1928). In the Roman experience, Julius Caesar was the first of his kind to become a god in 42 BCE. Following this, an imperial cult grew in significance (though it was not immune to mockery; see Seneca the Younger's *Apocolocyntosis*, or *The Pumpkinification of the "Divine" Claudius*). "All things are full of gods" is Thales's oft-repeated axiom and an apt summary of the Greco-Roman religious imagination (see, e.g., Aristotle, *De an.* 15.411a; Plato, *Leg.* 10.899b; the idea is developed systematically by Iamblichus, *Myst.* 1.8–9).[8] This said, there were also certainly notions of divine transcendence and an "intelligible" realm inaccessible to embodied creatures (see, e.g., Plato, *Phaedr.* 247c–248a; *Phaed.* 66c–67a). Such conceptions of divine transcendence and the absolute separation of "pure Being" from creaturely existence make texts like John 1:1–18 and the Christian commitment to the incarnation of God all the more philosophically scandalous and thought provoking.

Presence and Power

The gods in ancient religion mattered because of their presence in the world (or, at least, they mattered for people for whom gods mattered).[9] In contrast to modernity's buffered sense of selfhood, in which the self is impervious to divine intervention, personhood in the ancient world is "porous" and vulnerable to

---

7. For the veneration of natural features such as trees, caves, and rivers, see Seneca the Younger, *Ep.* 41.3.

8. What one might mean by "all things" is given some specificity in Epicurus's doctrine of *isonomia*, wherein the number of mortals must correspond precisely to the number of immortals (Cicero, *Nat. d.* 1.50). "All things," however, could certainly be interpreted in other ways.

9. "Atheists" (a complicated category; see Whitmarsh 2016) and Epicureans would presumably be exceptions to this.

Public Domain / Wikimedia Commons

Fig. 32.1. *The Birth of Venus,* by Sandro Botticelli

the doings and designs of the divine (Taylor 2007, 25–89). In most ancient senses of selfhood the gods are thus present and powerful (Rives 2007, 89–104). Offending the gods was feared, assistance from the gods desired. If you were to cross a certain stream or pass a certain cave, you best make an offering. If a morsel of food were to fall from the family table, you best offer it to the household *lar* (Pliny the Elder, *Nat.* 28.28; see fig. 32.2).[10]

As Pliny the Elder explains, "These customs were established by those of old, who believed that gods are present on all occasions and at all times" (*Nat.* 28.27 [trans. Jones 1963, 21]). Such an enchanted world is, to be sure, an anxious one but also a vibrant one (Dodds 1965). The drama of Homer's epics unfolds not simply because the gods are present, if veiled in human form, but because they have a penchant for meddling in human affairs (Cicero, *Nat. d.*

2.6; 3.5). Identifying the gods is thus a persistent matter of concern—as in Acts 14:8–18, where a miracle performed by Paul leads the Lycaonians to mistake him and Barnabas for Hermes and Zeus. The Lycaonians exclaim in their own language: "The gods have come down to us in human form!" (14:11). Alertness to gods in human guise is as old as Homer: "Gods disguise themselves as foreigners and strangers to a town, to see who violates their holy laws, and who is good" (Homer, *Od.* 17.484–87 [trans. Wilson 2018]; cf. Philo, *Dreams* 1.233; *QG* 4.2). But there is a key caveat when it comes to identifying gods: "Who can see the gods go by unless they wish to show themselves to us?" (Homer, *Od.* 10.773–74 [trans. Wilson 2018]; cf. Mark 6:48–56).

Personal Relation

The pervasive sense of divine presence and involvement in the world entailed a number of practices and institutions enabling personal

10. For further discussion of the gods and household dynamics, see Lang 2018, esp. 987–92.

interaction with the divine society. Sacrifice is at the heart of ancient religion. Temples were the officially sanctioned epicenters of sacrifice, and their prominence illustrates the concentration of the gods in everyday life. The architecture of temples and statues suffused the ancient urban landscape. This materially inscribed divinity on the cultures of these cities. Pausanias's *Descriptions of Greece*, an ancient travel guide, offers vivid depictions of how religious architecture and artifacts permeated the urban experience, providing immediate encounters with divine space.[11] Besides official cultic sacrifice, there were also numerous other "sacred disciplines" to facilitate communication with the gods (Valerius Maximus, "On Religion," in *Fact. et dict*. 1.1.1a–b). These included prayers, offerings, libations, vows, and any number of divinatory arts (Cicero, *Div.*; *Nat. d.* 3.5; see Ando 2008; Johnston 2008; Johnston and Struck 2005). Oracles were an especially important resource for accessing divine information (Plutarch, *Def. orac.*; see Parke 1967). Dreams and other visionary experiences from the gods were likewise common. Dreams and visions are also well known across the Bible. Weather and crop fertility were persistent matters of concern, and, for this, prayers were constantly expressed and offerings made. Health was another pervasive worry. Votive offerings to Asclepius (the god of healing), which depicted unwell body parts, are preserved in great numbers (see fig. 32.3). Besides depositing representations of such things as maimed limbs, desperate individuals would sometimes sleep in temples of Asclepius, hoping to be healed in some nocturnal visit from the god. In these and numerous other intimate ways, ancient "people of faith" had deeply personal relationships with their gods (MacRae 2016, 13–27).

11. Books 1 and 2 of *Descriptions of Greece* are most important for the New Testament insofar as they treat Athens and Corinth. Cf. Paul's own tour of religious architecture in Athens, as narrated in Acts 17:15–34.

Fig. 32.2. Bronze statuette of a guardian deity (*lar*) (Pompeii, 1st c. CE)

Taxonomy of the Divine Society

To speak of "the gods" as of equal status in the divine society is imprecise. The divine civilization in ancient Mediterranean religion was taxonomically diverse, teeming with genera of celestial species (Lang 2020, 514–19). "Angels" (*angeloi*) are familiar in the biblical data, and such divine "messengers" also trafficked between heaven and earth in the Greco-Roman theological cosmos (Cline 2011). Angels are not usually described as "gods" in the strict sense. They do the bidding of the gods and, in varying construals, stand metaphysically between the gods and humanity. But they are key actors in the celestial society. Akin to angels are demons (or daemons) (*daimones, daimonia*; cf. Philo, *Giants* 1.6–16; *Dreams* 1.141). Although *daimones* are usually depicted as lesser deities below the higher gods, this common noun is also used alongside *theos* for members of the divine population. Thus when Zeus returns to the Olympian deities, he returns to "the other daemons" (*daimonas allous*) (Homer, *Il.* 1.222). When one prays, one prays "to the daemons" (*daimosin*; *Il.* 6.115). In Plato *daimones* are also directly equated with the gods (*theoi*; *Apol.* 27c–d).

The English word "demon," under Christian interference, deviates from the mostly positive profile of *daimones* in the Greco-Roman world. This is why the variant spelling "daemon" is to be preferred for this class of divine species. Plutarch describes daemons as a "race" (*genos*) of species between the gods and humanity (Plutarch, *Def. orac.* 416d–f). Elsewhere they are praised for their wisdom and intelligence (Plato, *Crat.* 398a–b) and identified as guardians of humanity (Hesiod, *Op.* 122–23). Like angels, daemons are often emissaries, doing the chores of the higher gods on earth below. They also run communication between the two, such as sacrifices from earth to the gods and oracles from the gods to earth. Individuals may also have personal daemons assigned to them for matters such as personal protection (Plato, *Phaed.* 107d; *Resp.* 620e; Plutarch, *On the Sign of Socrates*; Apuleius, *De deo Socr.*; cf. Matt. 18:10).

Ancient metaphysicians of the daemonic population often ponder the materiality of these divine beings. To read the New Testament today in accord with its ancient context, it is often "very hard, [but] very important, to remember that ancient demons had bodies" (Smith 2008, 479). Ancient theorists of the divine did not confuse bodies with flesh as we might conceive it. Tatian (2nd c. CE Christian theologian) characterizes daemons as having "a spiritual structure, like that of fire or air" (*Or. Graec.* 15). As with the gods, the "spiritual structure" of daemons entails supernatural abilities, such as the capacity to change

Fig. 32.3. Votive relief of the healing of a maimed leg (or toes?). Dedicated from Tyche to Asclepius and Hygieia.

shape and appear in various forms. Porphyry (3rd. c. CE pagan philosopher) depicts daemonic shapeshifting in menacing terms: "For [daemons] are not cloaked with a solid body nor do they all have one shape, but they take many forms, . . . sometimes becoming visible, sometimes invisible, and the worst ones change their shape" (*Abst.* 2.39).[12] Porphyry further explains why daemons are associated with animal sacrifice. The smoke of sacrifice is how their "spiritual and corporeal part is fattened" (2.42). This is why early Christians urged abstention from pagan sacrifice and encouraged hostility to the demonic population (Origen,

12. Translations in this paragraph and the next are my own.

Mart. 45). As Paul advises, "No, I imply that what pagans sacrifice, they sacrifice to demons and not to God. I do not want you to be partners with demons. You cannot drink the cup of the Lord and the cup of demons. You cannot partake of the table of the Lord and the table of demons" (1 Cor. 10:20–21).

As for the domain of daemons and other "spiritual creatures," they are frequently described as belonging to the "air" or, as Philo envisions them, "flying throughout the air" (*Giants* 1.6). It is no coincidence that Paul describes Satan, or "the devil" (Eph. 4:27; 6:11), as "the ruler of the power *of the air* [*tou aeros*], the spirit that is now at work among those who are disobedient" (2:2; cf. 6:12). For Paul, Satan clearly belongs to this particular genus of aerial deities. According to the more scientific analysis of Apuleius (124–170 CE), daemons are "intermediate divine powers placed between the highest ether and the lowest earth in the region of air [*aeris spatio*]. They carry our desires and good deeds to the gods" (*De deo Socr.* 6.2–3). These daemons thus "blow about in the regions of the air that border the earth and also touch the sky" (7.4). In Apuleius's reasoning, daemons "are certainly not terrestrial, since weight would pull them down, but neither are they fiery, since heat would carry them away." They rather have bodies of an "intermediate nature . . . so that the nature of the region accords with the nature of its inhabitants" (9.1–2). Thus daemons saturate the air with their very imperceptible bodies.

Conclusion: Worship and Theology

Most religious people today usually find it easier to talk *to* God (in terms of prayer or worship) than to talk *about* god (in terms of abstract reflection). To talk *to* God requires only the presumption of communicative possibility with the entity named "God." To talk *about* that "God" requires a more complex conceptual framework. This "talking to" and "talking about" distinction is sometimes framed as "orthopraxy" and "orthodoxy"— that is, concern for *practice* versus concern for *thinking*. Although priority may be given to one or the other, in reality there is never one without the other. A worshiper may offer prayers to "God" without theorizing the ontology of that entity with methodological finesse. But still, some sense of what "God" means is required to talk to the entity so named. Setting aside *what* "God" means for the worshiper, *how* religious communities offer worship still remains integral to understanding the nature of the God they worship. As Rowan Williams explains, "The meanings of the word 'God' are to be discovered by watching what this community does—not only when it is consciously reflecting in conceptual ways, but when it is acting, educating or 'inducting,' imagining and worshiping" (Williams 2000, xii). We see this in Pauline traditions, which seamlessly juxtapose transformed thinking *about* God alongside transformed lives *for* God. As Paul states in Ephesians, "For surely you have heard about him and were taught in him, as truth is in Jesus. You were taught to put away your former way of life, your old self, corrupt and deluded by its lusts, and to be renewed in the spirit of your minds, and to clothe yourselves with the new self, created according to the likeness of God in true righteousness and holiness" (4:21–24). In this sense, Christian "theology" is the intellectual work of defining the *theos* who determines the believer's "new self"— a "new self" that ensues from the renewal of the believer's mind. On this juxtaposition of the transformed intellect, the Godward life, and the will of the *theos* Christians worship, it is appropriate to turn again to Paul and give him the final word: "I appeal to you therefore, brothers and sisters, by the mercies of God, to present your bodies as a living sacrifice, holy and acceptable to God, which is your spiritual worship. Do not be conformed to this world, but be transformed by the renewing of your minds, so that you may discern what is the will of God—what is good and acceptable and perfect" (Rom. 12:1–2).

Works Cited

Ando, Clifford. 2008. *The Matter of the Gods: Religion and the Roman Empire*. Berkeley: University of California Press.

Cline, Rangar. 2011. *Ancient Angels: Conceptualizing Angeloi in the Roman Empire*. Leiden: Brill.

Dahl, Nils A. 1975. "The Neglected Factor in New Testament Theology." *Reflections* 73: 5–8.

Dodds, E. R. 1965. *Pagan and Christian in an Age of Anxiety: Some Aspects of Religious Experience from Marcus Aurelius to Constantine*. Cambridge: Cambridge University Press.

duBois, Page. 2014. *A Million and One Gods: The Persistence of Polytheism*. Cambridge, MA: Harvard University Press.

Edwards, Mark, ed. 2021. *The Routledge Handbook of Early Christian Philosophy*. London: Routledge.

Engberg-Pedersen, Troels. 2017. *John and Philosophy: A New Reading of the Fourth Gospel*. Oxford: Oxford University Press.

Goodenough, Erwin R. 1928. "The Political Philosophy of Hellenistic Kingship." *YCS* 1: 55–102.

Hurtado, Larry W. 2010. *God in New Testament Theology*. Nashville: Abingdon.

Johnston, Sarah Iles. 2008. *Ancient Greek Divination*. Malden, MA: Blackwell.

Johnston, Sarah Iles, and Peter T. Struck, eds. 2005. *Mantikê: Studies in Ancient Divination*. Leiden: Brill.

Jones, W. H. S., trans. 1963. *Pliny: Natural History*. Vol. 8, *Books 28–32*. LCL 418. Cambridge, MA: Harvard University Press.

Lamberton, Robert. 1986. *Homer the Theologian: Neoplatonist Allegorical Reading and the Growth of the Epic Tradition*. Berkeley: University of California Press.

Lang, T. J. 2018. "Trouble with Insiders: The Social Profile of the Ἄπιστοι in Paul's Corinthian Correspondence." *JBL* 137: 981–1001.

———. 2020. "Cosmology and Eschatology." In *The Oxford Handbook of Pauline Studies*, edited by Matthew V. Novenson and R. Barry Matlock, 507–24. Oxford: Oxford University Press.

MacRae, Duncan. 2016. *Legible Religion: Books, Gods, and Rituals in Roman Culture*. Cambridge, MA: Harvard University Press.

Markschies, Christoph. 2015. *Christian Theology and Its Institutions: Prolegomena to a History of Early Christian Theology*. Translated by Wayne Coppins. Waco: Baylor University Press.

Parke, H. W. 1967. *The Oracles of Zeus: Dodona, Olympia, Ammon*. Oxford: Oxford University Press.

Parker, Robert. 2019. *Changing Names: Tradition and Innovation in Ancient Greek Onomastics*. Oxford: Oxford University Press.

Price, Simon. 1984. "Gods and Emperors: The Greek Language of the Roman Imperial Cult." *JHS* 104: 79–95.

Rives, James B. 2007. *Religion in the Roman Empire*. Malden, MA: Blackwell.

Smith, G. A. 2008. "How Thin Is a Demon?" *JECS* 16: 479–512.

Snell, Bruno, and Herwig Maehler, eds. 1975. *Pindari carmina cum fragmentis*. Pars 2, *Fragmenta*. Leipzig: Teubner.

Taylor, Charles. 2007. *A Secular Age*. Cambridge, MA: Harvard University Press.

Versnel, H. S. 2011. *Coping with the Gods: Wayward Readings in Greek Theology*. Leiden: Brill.

Whitmarsh, Tim. 2016. *Battling the Gods: Atheism in the Ancient World*. London: Faber & Faber.

Williams, Rowan. 1986. "Trinity and Revelation." *Modern Theology* 2: 197–212.

———. 2000. *On Christian Theology*. Malden, MA: Blackwell.

Wilson, Emily, trans. 2018. *The Odyssey*. New York: Norton.

33

Cosmology

Jamie Davies

The New Testament's cosmology (or cosmologies) can be usefully oriented to its use of the word *kosmos*, which broadly covers two categories of ideas. First, there is the question of *Weltbild*: the structure, order, and beauty of the universe, especially the shape of the earthly, heavenly, and subterranean realms. Second, there is the category of *Weltanschauung*: a worldview-level discussion concerning the origin and destiny of the world, divine conflict with hostile powers, and other soteriological and eschatological themes.

In the Western post-Enlightenment world, we tend to focus only on the first of these, such that cosmology is essentially the study of the structure (and perhaps the origin) of the physical universe. This reflects our separation of the science of physical cosmology from the religious claims of mythological cosmology. However, in the world of the New Testament the two were not separated in this way; questions of the shape of the cosmos, though of primary significance, were inseparable from questions of divine and human activity. *Weltbild* and *Weltanschauung* were never far apart,

and this can be seen in the earliest Old Testament traditions, and especially in the Jewish apocalyptic literature of the Second Temple period. Here, reflection on the shape of the cosmos was not esoteric speculation but had a bearing on the proper ordering of the calendar, agriculture, politics, worship, and personal destiny, as well as God's saving activity in the past, present, and future. Cosmology was, therefore, inextricably linked to theology, soteriology, eschatology, and ethics.

Though one will not find a uniform or distinctive account of cosmology in the New Testament, relevant themes and language can nevertheless be found throughout. The Gospel of Mark describes heaven being opened at the baptism of Jesus (Mark 1:10), and all three Synoptic Gospels record his discourse concerning eschatological signs in the heavens (Matt. 24:29–31 // Mark 13:24–27 // Luke 21:25–28). John, who uses the word *kosmos* more than any other New Testament writer, understands it as the system of the world opposed to Jesus and his disciples (e.g., John 7:7; 12:31; 15:18–19; 1 John 2:15–17; 4:1–5). Paul warns of enslavement to "the elements of the cosmos" (*ta stoicheia tou kosmou*; Gal. 4:3, my translation; cf. 4:9; Col. 2:8) and recounts a mystical ascent to "the third heaven" (2 Cor. 12:1–10). The letters of Peter and Jude speak of an eschatological cosmic conflagration, and there is, of course, a great deal of cosmological imagery throughout the books of Hebrews and Revelation. Despite all this evidence, however, the New Testament does not present us with a clear or systematic description of the nature of the cosmos, and thus to make sense of what we have we must turn to its broader cultural and literary world.

Weltbild: The Shape of the Cosmos

The New Testament is by no means unique in having such an interest in cosmology. Discussion of the shape of the heavens was a common concern of both Greco-Roman philosophy and Second Temple Jewish thought. Arguably the latter has more influence on the New Testament than the former, though this has long been debated, and there are strong cases for tracing Stoic cosmological themes in the Petrine letters and Platonic thought (as received by Philo) as the primary influence on the cosmology of Hebrews. As we often find, the world of the New Testament seems to have been something of a melting pot of cosmological ideas.

There is an especially rich vein of cosmological discussion in the apocalyptic literature of the Second Temple period, which is hardly surprising given their adherence to the possibility of an "open heaven" (cf. Acts 7:56; Rev. 4:1; Rowland 1982) through which a seer can encounter visions of the cosmos. The various books known collectively as 1 Enoch are perhaps the prime example, and one that is explicitly cited in the New Testament (Jude 14–15, quoting 1 En. 1.9). The Book of the Watchers (1 En. 1–36) recounts Enoch's journeys to the heavens and to the ends of the earth, during which the shape of the cosmos is carefully de-

scribed. The Astronomical Book (1 En. 72–82) is chiefly concerned, as its name suggests, with the order and movement of the celestial bodies and their relationship to the observance of a 364-day solar calendar (as opposed to the popular lunar calendar), and thus to proper observance of feasts and Sabbaths. Such a combination of cosmology and calendrical piety surfaces in many Second Temple Jewish texts (for an excellent introduction see Gurtner 2020), for example, in Jubilees (and, perhaps, in Paul's comments on the *stoicheia* and the calendar in Gal. 4:8–11).

Though there is some important variety, the basic cosmological structure assumed by 1 Enoch is one shared by much of the Old Testament and Second Temple Jewish writings. Though there is a fair amount of relevant material in the books of Hebrews and Revelation, the New Testament does not really provide an explicit and detailed cosmological description, so often we must work by inference and hypothesis. Nevertheless, this Second Temple Jewish background can reasonably be assumed to provide the basic shape of its working cosmology.

This basic shape is roughly as follows (see fig. 33.1). The cosmos is structured by the three tiers of heaven, earth, and the realm under the earth (cf. Phil. 2:10b). The middle tier of earth is understood as flat, and above it is the "firmament," which separates the heavenly realm, envisioned as a dome or canopy stretching over the earth, with gates or other openings through which celestial bodies and heavenly beings can travel. Heaven itself is, of course, the dwelling place of God, but it is also the abode of angels and other heavenly beings, as well as the storehouse for meteorological phenomena such as lightning, snow, hail, and rain (cf. Job 38, echoed by, e.g., 1 En. 41). Under the earth is found the shadowy, dusty, or watery realm of the dead, variously called "the pit" or "abyss" (e.g., Rom. 10:7; Rev. 9) or by the name Sheol (esp. in the Psalms and wisdom

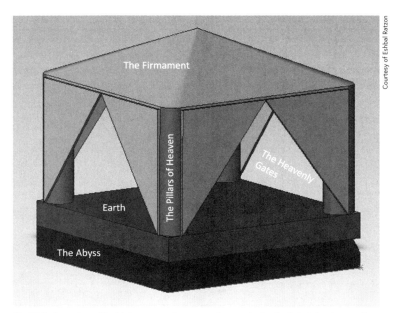

Courtesy of Eshbal Ratzon

Fig. 33.1. Cosmology: The Universe as a Tent according to the Book of the Watchers and the Astronomical Book in 1 Enoch

literature), Hades (e.g., Matt. 11:23 // Luke 10:15), or Tartarus (2 Pet. 2:4). The language used to describe this three-tiered universe is regularly that of architecture, likening the cosmos to a building or a tent (see Levenson 1984; Ratzon 2020).

Despite this shared basic cosmology, descriptions of the shape of heaven are by no means uniform in Second Temple Jewish writings or, from what we can tell, in the New Testament itself. In some texts, there is an assumption that heaven is a single, undifferentiated realm (the view that 1 Enoch and the book of Revelation appear to espouse, though this is debated). In some later apocalypses, however, we see heaven divided into a growing number of layers. The Testament of Levi, for example, speaks of three heavens of ascending importance, the third of which is God's dwelling place (T. Levi 2.7–8; 3.1–10, with later versions augmenting it to seven). The Apocalypse of Abraham has a similar view, though the number of tiers is expanded (again, likely due to the hand of a later editor) to seven "firmaments" (Apoc. Ab. 19). Other texts speak of five (e.g., 3 Baruch),

seven (e.g., 2 Enoch shorter recension), or ten (e.g., 2 Enoch longer recension) heavens.

This belief in multiple heavens, or tiers of heaven, may well be due to the common view that there was a close relationship between the shape of the cosmos and the architecture of the temple/tabernacle, a relationship that can be traced through the Old Testament. Scholars (e.g., Rowland 1982, 83–84; Levenson 1984, 283–91) regularly note that the pattern of the tabernacle shown to Moses on the mountain in Exodus 25–31 is linked to the creation account of Genesis 1–2, a connection reflected in Psalm 78:69: "He built his sanctuary like the high heavens, like the earth, which he has founded forever." The Solomonic temple's division into outer and inner houses (1 Kings 6:1–22) is perhaps reflected in the account of the shape of heaven in 1 Enoch 14. Similar discussions of the shape of heaven, and its relation to calendrical observance, can be found throughout the Dead Sea Scrolls (especially the Songs of the Sabbath Sacrifice [4Q400–407, 11Q17]; see Himmelfarb 1993, 15). Josephus, too, echoes a popular interpretation along these lines when he writes that the fabric and contents of the tabernacle were an "imitation and representation of the universe" (*Ant.* 3.179–87 [trans. Whiston 1987, 90]; cf. the similar comments about the Jerusalem temple in *J.W.* 5.184–287).

The heavens are separated from the realm of the earth by a firmament, envisioned as a tent or dome above the earth across which the celestial bodies would travel. The earth itself was understood to be flat and either circular or square in shape (indicated by the common phrase "the four corners of the earth"). Whichever shape was imagined, there was great fascination about the "ends of the earth" in Jewish thought at the time the New Testament was written. At these extremities of the earthly realm of the cosmos, one might encounter extraordinary sights, such as prisons for rebel angels, storehouses for weather, gates of access to heaven or to the underworld, the pillars that supported the firmament above, and the primordial waters or abyssal depths that surrounded the earth's expanse.

Other, more familiar, earthly locations took on cosmological significance in relation to the heavenly realm. Sites of divine action throughout salvation history indicated the ongoing commerce between the two realms. Of particular interest were mountains, repeatedly described as earthly places of divine encounter and calling, "permeated places" where heaven touches earth. The assumption of this vital connection between the two realms leads not to a strict cosmological dualism but to the recognition that commerce between heaven and earth is possible. Thus, mountains such as Sinai, Hermon, and Zion served as places where the boundary between heaven and earth was permeable and were thus described as places of revelation and divine encounter throughout the Bible. The Gospels develop the revelatory nature of this permeable cosmos in their accounts of an open heaven at Jesus's baptism (Matt. 3:13–17 // Mark 1:9–11 // Luke 3:21–22) and transfiguration (Matt. 17:1–8 //

Mark 9:2–8 // Luke 9:28–36; cf. 2 Pet. 1:16–18), and the book of Acts recounts Stephen's vision, at his moment of martyrdom, of "the heavens opened and the Son of Man standing at the right hand of God" (Acts 7:55–56).

Chief among these "holy mountains," of course, was the Temple Mount itself. The construction of the tabernacle, and then the temple, after the pattern of the heavens (discussed above) was of profound cosmological importance for the Jewish understanding of the relationship between heaven and earth. The tabernacle/temple not only was made after the model of heaven but also was this way because it is a *microcosm*, the cosmos writ small, and the cosmic central point where heaven and earth meet. Changing the metaphor to one used in some texts and in later rabbinic reflection, the temple was the *omphalos*, the "navel of the earth" (Ezek. 38:12 NRSV note; cf. Jub. 8.19 [Charlesworth 1985, 73]; see Levenson 1984, 283–84) from which the cosmos grew. In the New Testament, this vital cosmological and architectural connection between the tabernacle/temple on earth and the realm of heaven is developed christologically and theologically in the book of Hebrews especially, and in Revelation.

For John of Patmos, however, it was not simply a mountaintop experience or a vision of an open heaven that granted him cosmological revelations but also a journey into heaven, as he was summoned by the voice that called him to "come up here" (Rev. 4:1). Revelation echoes a broad prophetic and apocalyptic tradition, its roots reaching back to Isaiah 6, Ezekiel 1, and Daniel 7, of a seer experiencing an ascent to the heavenly throne room and/or temple for the disclosure of cosmological mysteries (e.g., 1 En. 14; T. Levi 1–3; cf. Rev. 11:19; 14:17; see Himmelfarb 1993). This tradition, when combined with the multitiered accounts of heaven described above, likely also forms the backdrop to Paul's account of an ascent to "the third heaven" in 2 Corinthians 12:1–10.

Many scholars have noted that the book of Revelation's account of the "new heaven and new earth" and the "new Jerusalem" draws deeply from the architectural imagery of the eschatological temple in Ezekiel 40–48, as well as similar material elsewhere in the Jewish apocalyptic tradition.

Weltanschauung: Salvation from Cosmic Forces

Mention of the eschatological new creation leads us to the second major cosmological category: worldview and divine activity. Whereas we are left with little more than tantalizing hints with respect to the shape of the cosmos, here there is an abundance of New Testament material. The cosmology of the New Testament has a lot more to say about the origin and destiny of the world (cosmogony and eschatology) than its structure, though as noted earlier these two themes are inextricably connected in the world of the New Testament (for discussion of these theological themes in Jewish apocalyptic texts, see Rowland 1982, 146–55, 160–76; for the New Testament implications, see the various essays in Pennington and McDonough 2008).

In Second Temple Jewish cosmology, there are various accounts of a broader cosmic drama in which the earth and its inhabitants are involved. In some accounts, this is understood as a primordial dualistic conflict between light and darkness, a cosmic dualism found in various expressions throughout ancient Near Eastern writings. One example of this is the Qumran Community Rule (1QS), which speaks of a primordial dualism, inherent in the created cosmos, between two spirits: one of truth (which springs from light) and one of deceit (which comes from darkness). From these sources come two cosmic actors, a "Prince of Light" and an "Angel of Darkness," who are in turn the sources of goodness and evil in the world (1QS 3–4). These two are locked in a cosmic dualistic battle, with dominion over the inhabitants of the earth resulting in a concomitant social dualism. The world is divided into "sons of light" and "sons of darkness," each living in antinomy to the other until they arrive, joined by the armies of heaven, at a final eschatological war (described in detail in the War Scroll [1QM]) between the forces of good and evil.

There are other varieties of Second Temple Jewish cosmology that develop the role of angels in a different way, ascribing the origin of evil not to a created cosmic dualism (or, primarily, to human transgression) but to a primordial angelic rebellion. Though it can also be seen elsewhere (e.g., in Jub. 4–5), the fullest account of this view is found in the Book of the Watchers (1 En. 1–36). Taking its cue from the cryptic narrative of Genesis 6:1–4, this text recounts the fall of rebel angels, the "Watchers," whose rebellion brought evil and corruption to the world, and how they and those who follow them will ultimately be overthrown, imprisoned, and judged. This is almost certainly the cosmological drama to which 1 Peter 3:18–22, 2 Peter 2:4–5, and Jude 5–7 allude in speaking of God's judgment of sinful angels and relating this to false teaching in the church. As such, the cosmological drama of angelic rebellion bears on the life of the people of God today. In the time before God's final victory over his enemies, the world will be characterized by ongoing spiritual warfare between these opposing cosmic forces, a cosmological and apocalyptic framework that, it has been argued, also appears throughout Paul's letters.

As such, the cosmological imagination of the world of the New Testament concerns not only the past but also the future, and indeed it is regularly observed that there are close connections between the cosmology of primordial time (*Urzeit*) and that of the end (*Endzeit*). Again, unsurprisingly, there is great variety in the accounts of the ultimate destiny of the cosmos. Some, as indicated above, envision a final eschatological battle (whether between the sons of light and the sons of darkness or between God and the rebel angels), leading to the judgment of God's enemies and the (re) establishment of a world of order and purity. In other accounts, the end of the world is one of cosmic de-creation, perhaps by fire, and re-creation (Adams 2000). This is a common view found in both Jewish apocalyptic thought and Stoic philosophy and may be echoed in the New Testament's description of the "passing away" of heaven and earth (e.g., Rev. 6:14; 21:1). Second Peter 3:1–13 is perhaps the clearest expression of such a view in the New Testament, as the author rebukes the "scoffers," whose cosmology seems to assume the permanence of the world, and instead speaks of heaven, earth, and the elements (*stoicheia*) all being dissolved by cosmic conflagration at the day of the Lord (though there are perhaps good reasons to read this as purgation rather than annihilation). The ultimate eschatological hope for the people of God is, unlike in Stoicism, the passing away of "this world/age" and the final renewal of the cosmos in a new heaven and new earth, in accordance with God's promises.

There are some cosmologies that develop the eschatological dissolution/re-creation theme in more specific relation to a temple-shaped cosmology, describing the end of the cosmos as a dismantling and rebuilding of the cosmic "house" (e.g., the final vision of the Animal Apocalypse [1 En. 85–90] or the Apocalypse of Weeks [93.1–10; 91.11–17]). Eschatological visions describing this "new heaven" as a new temple or new Jerusalem can be found in various places, including Ezekiel 40–48 and (after the temple's destruction) 4 Ezra 10 and 2 Baruch 4. It is regularly argued that this tradition is reflected in the final chapters of the book of Revelation, in the descent of the new Jerusalem and the eschatological hope of the cosmic union of heaven and earth. One of the standard ways of expressing this final cosmological hope in Second Temple Judaism was the phrase *kainē ktisis* (new creation), deployed twice by Paul (Gal. 6:15; 2 Cor. 5:17; cf. Jub. 4.26) to indicate, by many accounts, the final liberation of the cosmos from its bondage to decay and a cosmic renewal of all things.

Conclusion

The overall picture we find is that the New Testament is caught up in (and variously contributes to) a vibrant and diverse world of cosmological speculation, which can often only be read between the lines of the canonical texts. The Jewish apocalyptic tradition appears to have exercised a particular influence on perhaps every book of the New Testament (Pennington and McDonough 2008), but this is itself a diverse tradition without one fixed cosmological framework. In addition, there is evidence of the influence of Platonic and Stoic cosmologies in various places and to various degrees. Although we might be able to reconstruct something like a broad agreement on the shape of the cosmos, there are numerous tantalizing details and differences across the New Testament that demand our attention. More important to observe, however, is that the New Testament seems less concerned with the pattern of the cosmos than with its eschatological salvation (and, relatedly, the implications for ethical living in the meantime). Again, though, there is diversity of thought here and much to learn from observing the New Testament's varied and profound christological reworkings of Second Temple Jewish cosmological traditions.

Works Cited

Adams, E. 2000. *Constructing the World: A Study in Paul's Cosmological Language*. London: T&T Clark.

Charlesworth, James H. 1985. *The Old Testament Pseudepigrapha: Expansions of the "Old Testament" and Legends, Wisdom, and Philosophical Literature, Prayers, Psalms and Odes, Fragments of Lost Judeo-Hellenistic Works*. Vol. 2. New Haven: Yale University Press.

Gurtner, D. 2020. *Introducing the Pseudepigrapha of Second Temple Judaism: Message, Context, and Significance*. Grand Rapids: Baker Academic.

Himmelfarb, M. 1993. *Ascent to Heaven in Jewish and Christian Apocalypses*. Oxford: Oxford University Press.

Levenson, J. 1984. "The Temple and the World." *JR* 64, no. 3: 275–98.

Pennington, J. T., and S. M. McDonough, eds. 2008. *Cosmology and New Testament Theology*. LNTS 355. London: T&T Clark.

Ratzon, E. 2020. "Cosmology." In vol. 2 of *T&T Clark Encyclopedia of Second Temple Judaism*, edited by Daniel M. Gurtner and Loren T Stuckenbruck, 167–70. London: Bloomsbury T&T Clark.

Rowland, C. 1982. *The Open Heaven: A Study of Apocalyptic in Judaism and Early Christianity*. London: SPCK.

Whiston, William, trans. 1987. *The Works of Josephus: Complete and Unabridged*. Peabody, MA: Hendrickson. Originally published 1737.

34

Eschatologies and the Afterlife

Thomas D. McGlothlin

"Eschatology," from the Greek word for "last" (*eschatos*), is concerned with the final state of creation and the events leading to that final state (sometimes called the "end times"). "Afterlife" typically denotes what happens to individual humans after death. Both eschatology and afterlife are rich, complex topics. This chapter outlines key aspects of eschatology and afterlife in the Jewish and Greco-Roman environment in which the New Testament documents were written and first read.

Jewish Eschatology

Despite diversity in details, most first-century Jews shared basic hopes for the future (Sanders 1992, 289–98; Aune and Stewart 2001). These hopes can be summarized through a set of common themes rooted in Old Testament prophecies and reflected in texts from the Second Temple era, including the New Testament.

1. Reestablishment of the twelve tribes of Israel—including, in many cases, the return of the northern tribes not heard from since their deportation by Assyria many centuries before (Staples 2021; see Isa. 49:6; Jer. 31:1–22; Ezek. 37:21–22; Sir. 36:13; Pss. Sol. 11; 17; 4 Ezra 13.39–40; see also Jesus's selection of twelve disciples [Matt. 10:2–4; Mark 3:14–19; Luke 6:13–16]; Matt. 19:28; Luke 22:30; Rom. 11:26 [according to Staples 2011]; cf. James 1:1)

2. Purification or rebuilding of Jerusalem and the temple (see Ezek. 40–48 [cf. 37:26–28]; 1 En. 90.28–29; 91.13; Jub. 1.29; 4.26; Sib. Or. 3.702–4; 5.420–27; 4 Ezra 13.36; John 2:19–21; Rev. 21:9–27)

3. Conversion, subjugation, or destruction of the Gentiles (or some combination thereof), sometimes with Israel serving as judge (see Isa. 49:6; 60:1–14; 1 En. 90.19; Pss. Sol. 17; Sib. Or. 3.710–23; 1QM XII, 7; for Israel judging Gentiles, see 1 En. 91.12; 95.3; Jub. 32.18–19; in the New Testament, see Acts; Paul's ministry among the Gentiles; for God's people judging the world, see 1 Cor. 6:2)

4. Moral transformation of God's people so that they become reliably righteous and holy (see Jer. 31:33–34; Ezek. 36:25–27; 1 En. 5.8–9; 10.21; 92.4; Jub. 1.22–24; 5.12; 1QS V, 18–24; Rom. 6:1–14; 8:3–11; Col. 3:1–10)

5. Purifying renovation of the entire cosmos, whether through a dramatic renewal of the current created order or a destruction and re-creation of the cosmos[1] (see Isa. 65:17–25; 1 En. 45.4–6; 2 En. [J] 70.10; Jub. 1.29; 4.26; LAB 3.10; 2 Bar. 73; Rom. 8:18–24; Heb. 12:25–29; 2 Pet. 3:5–13; Rev. 6:12–17; 21:1)

These themes reveal a shared sense among first-century Jews of what was wrong with the world. God's people remained scattered, God's land and temple were threatened or defiled by unbelieving Gentiles and unfaithful Jews, and the cosmos was defiled or not working as designed.

Jews viewed these problems as symptoms of rebellion against their God, the creator and ruler of all. Correspondingly, running through each of these themes were political or royal questions: How will the God of Israel come to reign as king over creation in a way that is more real than it seems now? When and how will God reign over the nation of Israel as a political entity? Over the rebellious hearts of its people? Over the foreign nations that threatened and oppressed Israel and rejected its God? Over the cosmos as a whole? The language of God's kingship and the image of God's throne pervade Jewish descriptions of the eschaton from this period (1 En. 22.14; 25.1–7; 63.1–7; 84.2; T. Mos. 10; Sib. Or. 3.56;

1QM VI, 6; 2 Bar. 73.1; cf. Matt. 25:31; Rev. 4–5; 7; 20–22).

Connected to the problem of rebellion was the problem of estrangement. Text after text looks forward to the day when God will not only reign but also be present with the people, often through the temple. Then, in their fellowship with, worship of, and service to God within a creation characterized by justice and holiness, God's people will finally be able to rejoice in peace. Ultimately, this picture of intimacy, joy, peace, and service, often painted with the imagery of Eden, was the true "last thing" (1 En. 5.7–9; 25.1–7; 61.14; 105.2; 2 En. [J/A] 8–9; Jub. 1.26–27; 23.30; Sib. Or. 3.702–4; 3.781–95; 4 Ezra 7.88–99; 8.52; 2 Bar. 30.2; 73.1–74.4; cf. Isa. 65:18; Ezek. 37:26–27; Rev. 21–22; Aune and Stewart 2001, 169–73).

Note that the expectation of a Davidic messiah was not a consistent theme (Sanders 1992, 296–97; Aune and Stewart 2001, 153–58). Some texts do describe a messiah; this person usually plays the role of conquering and judging the nations (the Similitudes of Enoch [1 En. 37–71]; 4 Ezra 7; 12–13; 2 Bar. 29–30; 40; 70; cf. 1 Cor. 15:24–25). The Qumran community even expected two messiahs, a priest and a political ruler (1QS IX, 11). But other texts completely omit any mention of such a figure, even when one might be expected (the other documents comprising 1 Enoch; 2 Enoch; 3 Baruch; 1QM). These variations might be due to ambivalence about kings other than God or to a belief that God will need no human assistance.

One additional consistent theme, although not exactly a hope for the future, was the expectation that things would get much worse before they got better. The basic pattern of tribulation followed by salvation and renewal was already established by Noah's flood and the Babylonian exile. Jews therefore fully expected that a time of great conflict and hardship would precede or accompany God's final reassertion of kingship (1 En. 91.5–10; Jub. 23; 1QM I, 11–12; 2 Bar. 25–32; cf. Mark 13:1–27;

---

1. Since the latter was always understood as a re-creation out of the matter of the present cosmos rather than a re-creation out of nothing, the destruction/re-creation view did not imply a denigration of creation as such (Adams 2007, countering Wright 2003); in principle, it was no different from the resurrection of bodies that have completely decayed.

2 Thess. 2:1–12; the tribulations in Revelation). As might be expected, disagreements over what role God's people should play in that conflict (take up arms to trigger it? join God or God's messiah in fighting it? passively wait and watch God win the conflict?) had important political implications (Sanders 1992, 279–89).

Jewish Afterlife

Although Second Temple Jews shared many hopes for the future of the cosmos, they were divided on the afterlife of the individual. Some denied that there would be any afterlife at all. This perspective appears in Ben Sira (Sir. 17:27–28) and underlies the Sadducees' objection to the resurrection of the dead (Josephus, *J.W.* 2.14; *Ant.* 18.4; Matt. 22:23; Acts 23:8). Proponents of this view rejected any notion of a conscious afterlife; consequently, they also rejected any notion of postmortem rewards or punishments for deeds in this life—except a good name in posterity or perhaps calamity falling on one's descendants (Sir. 41:5–13).

Many have noted that this view seems to match the perspective of most of the Old Testament. Several cultures surrounding Old Testament Israel, such as Egypt, had robust views of a personal afterlife with rewards and punishments. Moreover, regular prohibitions of necromancy suggest that many Israelites believed in a personal afterlife and were tempted to try to contact the dead (Lev. 19:31; 20:6, 27; Deut. 18:11; Isa. 8:19; cf. 1 Sam. 28:3–25; Friedman and Overton 2000). Yet the Old Testament in general is remarkably reluctant to discuss the afterlife. The psalmists cry out to God for salvation from impending death by pointing out that the dead do not praise God (e.g., Pss. 6:5; 30:9; 88:10–12; 115:17; Goldingay 2000). The dead simply go down to Sheol, a place of shadowy nonlife comparable to the Homeric portrayal of Hades (Isa. 14:9–11; Homer, *Od.* 11). This fate awaits all, regardless of their deeds in this life (with the exception of Enoch

and Elijah; see Gen. 5:24; 2 Kings 2:3–12). The prospect of reuniting with loved ones in Sheol was not a source of joy (Gen. 37:35).

During the Second Temple period, however, many Jews came to hold much more detailed beliefs about what would happen after death. These views developed within the eschatological framework of God's kingship described above. The righteous would be rewarded and the wicked punished in the afterlife because the God of Israel would finally dispense justice as a righteous king (cf. Ps. 11:4–7). The wicked would be banished from the earth and the righteous would finally take up their proper places and roles within creation because that is what it means for all to be well in the kingdom of the Creator.

By the time of Jesus, many Jews believed in a future resurrection of the dead, an expectation that does not appear to have been widely presupposed in earlier generations. The clearest witness to this belief within the Old Testament is Daniel 12:2: "Many of those who sleep in the dust of the earth shall awake, some to everlasting life, and some to shame and everlasting contempt." This important text takes up motifs of rising from the dead, already found in Isaiah 26:19–21 and Ezekiel 37. Although resurrection is clearly a metaphor for national renewal in Ezekiel, and the same might be true in Isaiah, Daniel 12 looks forward to the future resurrection of individual people. In a similar way, the Book of the Watchers (1 En. 1–36) allusively employs language from Isaiah 65–66 to describe the eschatological resurrection (Elledge 2017, 67–78). Modern scholars continue to debate the source of resurrection belief, whether Zoroastrianism (Boyce and Grenet 1991, 389–436) or the deep conviction within the theology of preexilic Israel that the creator God promises life (Levenson 2006). Yet to those first-century Jews who believed in the resurrection of the dead, such as the Pharisees, it was simply biblical.

It is important to pause and note that future bodily resurrection was not the only option for Jews who wanted to affirm a conscious afterlife (against the Sadducees). Some, such as Philo of Alexandria and the author of 4 Maccabees, spoke freely of the immortality of the soul without ever mentioning resurrection. It is difficult to know the relative popularity of these views on the ground. Many have argued that resurrection was by far the most popular option in the first century (Bauckham 1998; Wright 2003), although important objections have been raised (Vermes 2008; cf. Elledge 2017, 9–13). It is certainly the case, however, that Josephus presents the Pharisees' views on the afterlife as most persuasive to the people (*J.W.* 2.14–15; cf. *Ag. Ap.* 2.218), and resurrection is very well represented in the Second Temple texts that survive.

Even within texts that affirm or seem to allude to resurrection, though, there is remarkable diversity or lack of clarity on a range of questions. Some of those questions include the following:

1. Does "resurrection" or "rising up" necessarily mean the return to life of dead corpses, leaving graves empty (Matt. 27:51–54; 1 En. 25.6; Sib. Or. 4.181–82; 4 Ezra 7.32; 2 Bar. 50.2; LAB 3.10)? Or might a different kind of return to life be in view, perhaps involving a completely different body—or no body at all (as some read 1 En. 104.1–6 and Jub. 23.30–31)? Consequently, is it safe to assume that references to "rising up" or "resurrection" necessarily entail the emptying of graves, even when those resurrected bodies are not "flesh and blood" but rather "spiritual" (1 Cor. 15:44, 50)? (Wright 2003 argues that the assumption is safe, but Nickelsburg 2006 disagrees.)

2. What will be the form of resurrected bodies, and where will they live? Several texts describe a transformation at or shortly following the resurrection (Dan. 12:3; 1 En. 61.14–16; 104.2; 4 Ezra 7.97;

2 Bar. 51.1–12; cf. 1 Cor. 15:35–49 and appearances of the resurrected Jesus). What is the meaning of the astral and angelic imagery frequently found in these contexts? Will the resurrected righteous actually live in the heavens as stars (1 En. 104.2), or will they dwell on the earth (45.5; 51.5)? Given the common opinion that stars were living (Scott 1991), and the view that some stars have rebelled against their God-given responsibility to help rule over creation (18.13–16; cf. Gen. 1:16–18), the possibility that astral imagery in any given text is to be taken literally cannot be dismissed out of hand.

3. Will all people be raised to face judgment (4 Ezra 7.32–38; 2 Bar. 50–51) or only some (1 En. 22.13; 2 Macc. 7:14; Josephus's descriptions of the Pharisees in *J.W.* 2.14 and *Ant.* 18.3)? And if only some, who, and for what purpose (McGlothlin 2018, 18–27)?

4. Will the resurrected live forever (1 En. 58.3; 4 Ezra 7.97) or only for a long time, as in the era before Noah's flood (1 En. 25.6; cf. Isa. 65:20)?

Expectation of a future resurrection raises the question of what the dead will be doing in the meantime, and many texts address this issue directly. Here, from the earliest texts to the latest, the answer is remarkably consistent: they will be kept in holding places (cf. Isa. 24:21–23; 26:20–21), enjoying rewards or suffering punishments that anticipate the verdict they will receive at the great, final judgment connected to the resurrection (1 En. 22; 2 En. [J/A] 40.13; 61.2–3; 4 Ezra 7; 2 Bar. 30). (Rebellious angels are also being held for judgment; see 1 En. 10; cf. 1 Pet. 3:19–20.) Then, at that great judgment, the books in which every person's sins have been recorded will be opened (1 En. 98.7–8; 104.7; 2 En. [J/A] 53.2; 2 Bar. 24.1; T. Ab. 12; cf. Rev. 20:12). Descriptions of what will happen to the wicked, both before and after the great judgment, are sometimes quite graphic, frequently featuring fire (e.g., 1 En. 103.8; 2 Bar. 44.15; cf. Isa. 66:15) and sometimes complete with angels brandishing instruments of torture (e.g., 1 En. 53.3–5; 2 En. [J/A] 10.1–3; see Himmelfarb 1983).

These common eschatological and afterlife themes are scattered across Jewish texts, sometimes in fragmentary form. But several apocalyptic texts lay out fully developed eschatologies, complete with a tribulation (including signs of its impending arrival), a messiah (sometimes), a differentiated intermediate state for the righteous and the wicked, a bodily resurrection, judgment, and cosmic renewal. Examples include the Book of the Watchers (1 En. 1–36), the Similitudes of Enoch (1 En. 37–71), 4 Ezra, and 2 Baruch. These texts are obviously important for any student of the New Testament, but they should be used with care. It is very tempting to read one eschatological framework, conclude that it represents "the" Jewish eschatological or afterlife framework of the day, and attempt to use it as a key to interpreting anything found in the New Testament. This temptation should be resisted. There are too many variations on too many details for a framework extracted from any one text to function as "the" Jewish eschatology lying "behind" the New Testament. A more profitable approach is to read as many texts as possible (as wholes, rather than through excerpts of eschatological passages) in order to gain a clearer sense of the context and contours of Jewish eschatology. This will equip readers to turn to the New Testament and see how the same themes are supplemented, developed in distinctive ways, or sometimes dramatically reinterpreted.

Greco-Roman Eschatology

Among Greco-Roman philosophers, the future fate of the cosmos as a whole was a point of some disagreement. Aristotle affirmed the eternal existence of the cosmos (*Cael.* 1.10–12). Platonists agreed, but Epicureans and Stoics did not (Adams 2007, 107–26). For Epicureans, the world we inhabit is just a temporary conglomeration of indivisible particles. Like an organism, it grew when it took in more particles than it lost; but now the opposite is happening, and the remaining particles will soon disperse (Lucretius, *Rer. nat.* 2.1105–72; 5.91–109, 235–415). Stoics believed that the cosmos would be engulfed in a great, purifying fire at some time in the future. Yet this fire, precisely as a purifying fire, would not actually cause the cosmos to pass out of existence. Rather, it would end the cosmos as we currently know it, only to make possible a new cycle that would eventually end in yet another purifying conflagration (Lapidge 1978; Long 2006, 256–82).

The question of the future of the cosmos, then, was approached more as a physics problem than as a theological problem (to use a distinction that would have been foreign to Greco-Roman philosophers). To find out what would happen to the cosmos in the future, one needed to consider the material composition of the cosmos, not inquire after the will of the gods.

Greco-Roman Afterlife

The basic, popular view of the afterlife in the Greco-Roman world was that the dead entered Hades, where they were divided up according to their ethical merits. The wicked suffered painful punishments for their deeds in an unpleasant space often called Tartarus, while the righteous enjoyed delights in paradisiacal meadows called the Elysian Fields (Cumont 1922, 34). Most (but not all) believed these spaces for postmortem punishment or reward existed under the surface of the earth. (Hades had not always been divided up in this way. In *Odyssey* 11, there is no distinction between the righteous and the wicked in their nonlife as shades in Hades; all are unhappy. Yet in Virgil's renarration of the visit to the underworld in *Aeneid* 6, Hades has ethical categories [Segal 2004, 242–44].)

Philosophers argued over the location of these spaces and whether the dead would remain in them forever, and their conclusions largely depended on their respective understandings of the universe and the nature of the soul (Cumont 1922; Segal 2004, 204–47). As with questions concerning the fate of the cosmos, questions about what happens to individuals after death were approached by at least some people as what many moderns might consider to be "science" questions.

According to neo-Pythagoreans—for whom the human soul is related to God yet is entombed in the body during this life—all souls ascend after death. Souls of the criminal and impious fall short of the moon and are trapped in the lower air, only to be reincarnated, while souls of sages ascend to the moon before pure reason rises back to the sun itself. Plato's dialogues, by contrast, have some suffering subterranean punishments and others enjoying rewards in the heavens before both are reincarnated (*Phaedr.* 249; *Resp.* 10.614–15). Aristotelians either accepted the survival only of the reasoning faculty of a soul (without any individual personality) or denied survival of any part of the human soul after death. Stoics saw the human soul as the spark of divine fire pervading the entirety of the human body, just as that divine fire pervades the entire cosmos and gives it its order. Correspondingly, as fire, the soul—if it survives the death of the body in an individuated form at all—must rise upward (Cumont 1922, 12–17). Hades, therefore, was the sublunar sphere (above the surface of the earth, not below it, as assumed in most mythological accounts). Epicureans flatly rejected the idea of a conscious postmortem existence on the basis of their view that the human soul is simply a collection of atoms that, at death, will be dispersed like the wind (Lucretius, *Rer. nat.* 3.455–58).

Conclusion

Jewish views on eschatology and the afterlife were not sealed off from Greco-Roman thought (Glasson 1961). This is clear even in terminology: in many Jewish texts, Sheol became Hades (Sir. 14:12; Wis. 1:14; 4 Ezra 4.41; cf. Matt. 11:23; Luke 16:23; Rev. 1:18), and the place of postmortem punishment could be called Tartarus (1 En. 20.2; Sib. Or. 4.186; 2 Pet. 2:4). God's creation of the new heavens and new earth could be described in ways remarkably similar to the Stoic conflagration (2 Pet. 3:10–12). Yet even if terminology, imagery, and natural mechanisms (like fiery conflagration) echoed Greco-Roman culture and philosophy, a deep difference remained.

For most Greco-Roman philosophers, there is no one Creator whose will is the key to the future of the cosmos. For Jews, by contrast, the Creator, the God of Israel, is the king of creation. The creator God is the cause of its beginning and therefore could be the cause of its end, if it will have an end, and will definitely be the cause of any radical transformation. As God declared to Ezra, "I planned these things, and they were made through me alone and not through another; just as the end shall come through me alone and not through another" (4 Ezra 6.6). The material composition of creation might be relevant for thinking about how that creator God will accomplish those eschatological purposes, but such considerations were never decisive. Notwithstanding terminological and "scientific" borrowings from the Greco-Roman world, the New Testament's eschatological perspective is decidedly Jewish: "The time is fulfilled, and the kingdom of God has come near" (Mark 1:15).

Works Cited

Adams, Edward. 2007. *The Stars Will Fall from Heaven: Cosmic Catastrophe in the New Testament and Its World*. London: T&T Clark.

Aune, David E., and Eric Stewart. 2001. "From the Idealized Past to the Imaginary Future: Eschatological Restoration in Jewish Apocalyptic Literature." In *Restoration: Old Testament, Jewish and Christian Perspectives*, edited by James M. Scott, 147–77. JSJSup 72. Leiden: Brill.

Bauckham, Richard. 1998. "Life, Death, and the Afterlife in Second Temple Judaism." In *Life in the Face of Death: The Resurrection Message of the New Testament*, edited by Richard N. Longenecker, 80–95. Grand Rapids: Eerdmans.

Boyce, Mary, and Frantz Grenet. 1991. *A History of Zoroastrianism*. Vol. 3, *Zoroastrianism under Macedonian and Roman Rule*. Handbuch der Orientalistik. Section 1, Der Nahe und der Mittlere Osten. Leiden: Brill.

Cumont, Franz. 1922. *After Life in Roman Paganism*. New Haven: Yale University Press.

Elledge, C. D. 2017. *Resurrection of the Dead in Early Judaism, 200 BCE–CE 200*. Oxford: Oxford University Press.

Friedman, Richard Elliot, and Shawna Dolansky Overton. 2000. "Death and Afterlife: The Biblical Silence." In *Death, Life-after-Death, Resurrection and the World-to-Come in the Judaisms of Antiquity*, edited by Alan J. Avery-Peck and Jacob Neusner, 35–60. Part 4 of *Judaism in Late Antiquity*. Leiden: Brill.

Glasson, T. Francis. 1961. *Greek Influence in Jewish Eschatology*. London: SPCK.

Goldingay, John. 2000. "Death and Afterlife in the Psalms." In *Death, Life-after-Death, Resurrection and the World-to-Come in the Judaisms of Antiquity*, edited by Alan J. Avery-Peck and Jacob Neusner, 61–86. Part 4 of *Judaism in Late Antiquity*. Leiden: Brill.

Himmelfarb, Martha. 1983. *Tours of Hell: An Apocalyptic Form in Jewish and Christian Literature*. Philadelphia: University of Pennsylvania Press.

Lapidge, Michael. 1978. "Stoic Cosmology." In *The Stoics*, edited by John M. Rist, 61–85. Berkeley: University of California Press.

Levenson, Jon D. 2006. *Resurrection and the Restoration of Israel: The Ultimate Victory of the God of Life*. New Haven: Yale University Press.

Long, A. A. 2006. *From Epicurus to Epictetus: Studies in Hellenistic and Roman Philosophy*. Oxford: Clarendon.

McGlothlin, Thomas D. 2018. *Resurrection as Salvation: Development and Conflict in Pre-Nicene Paulinism*. Cambridge: Cambridge University Press.

Nickelsburg, George W. E. 2006. *Resurrection, Immortality, and Eternal Life in Intertestamental Judaism and Early Christianity*. Expanded ed. HTS 56. Cambridge, MA: Harvard University Press.

Sanders, E. P. 1992. *Judaism: Practice and Belief, 63BCE–66CE*. London: SCM.

Scott, Alan. 1991. *Origen and the Life of the Stars: The History of an Idea*. Oxford: Clarendon.

Segal, Alan. 2004. *Life after Death: A History of the Afterlife in the Religions of the West*. New York: Doubleday.

Staples, Jason A. 2011. "What Do the Gentiles Have to Do with 'All Israel'? A Fresh Look at Romans 11:25–27." *JBL* 130: 371–90.

———. 2021. *Israel in Second Temple Judaism: A New Theory of People, Exile, and Israelite Identity*. Cambridge: Cambridge University Press.

Vermes, Geza. 2008. *The Resurrection: History and Myth*. New York: Doubleday.

Wright, N. T. 2003. *The Resurrection of the Son of God*. Christian Origins and the Question of God 3. Minneapolis: Fortress.

35

Angels and Demons

Robert E. Moses

Angels and Heavenly Beings in the Hebrew Bible

The context for the presentation of angels and demons in the New Testament must begin with the Hebrew Bible. The Hebrew word *mal'ak* and the Greek *angelos* denote a messenger—a *human* messenger commissioned by a person or God to deliver a message (e.g., Gen. 32:3; Num. 20:14; Josh. 7:22; Mark 1:2–3; Luke 7:24; 9:52) or a *transcendent being* with intellect and will sent by God. The Septuagint (LXX) and Old Greek (OG) consistently translate the Hebrew word *mal'ak* with *angelos*. In the Hebrew Bible, angels are part of the heavenly court (e.g., Gen. 28:12; Ps. 148:2) and are sent to earth to carry out God's will, assist humans (e.g., Gen. 24:40; 32:1; Exod. 14:19; 23:20–23; Num. 20:16; Ps. 34:7), and intercede on their behalf (e.g., Zech. 1:12). Angels serve as conveyors of divine revelation (e.g., Zech. 5:1–11; 6:1–8) and also serve, at times, as agents of divine wrath (e.g., Exod. 33:2; Num. 22:22–23; 2 Kings 19:35; 1 Chron. 21:15–16; Pss. 35:6; 78:49; 91:11; Isa. 37:36). Angels in the Hebrew Bible are overwhelmingly portrayed in a posi- tive light; they are so aligned with the will of God that, on occasion, the manifestation of "the angel of the Lord" seems interchangeable with the manifestation of God (e.g., Gen. 16:7– 14; 22:15–19; Exod. 3:1–6; Judg. 6:11–27).

The Hebrew Bible's depiction of angels is, however, complicated by two stories: the de- scent of the sons of God in Genesis 6:1–4 and the depiction of the Satan figure in the book of Job. In Genesis 6:1–4, the "sons of God" (*bene ha'elohim*) take wives among mortals and bear children with them, resulting in the birth of "the Nephilim" (*hanepilim*) (see further dis- cussion in Auffarth and Stuckenbruck 2004; Harkins, Bautch, and Endres 2014; Wright 2015; Götte 2016; Doedens 2019). The Sep- tuagint translator makes a translation decision that exemplifies the ambiguous treatment that angels receive in the Second Temple and New Testament period: the translator renders the Hebrew "sons of God" as *hoi angeloi tou theou* (the angels of God). And in a move that will foreshadow the treatment of this story in Jew- ish Pseudepigrapha, the Septuagint translator of Genesis renders the Hebrew "Nephilim" as *hoi gigantes* (the giants; cf. Num. 13:31–33). Having narrated these events, the author of Genesis immediately proceeds to tell of the proliferation of wickedness among humans (Gen. 6:5–8), which results in God sending the great flood to cleanse the earth (6:9–22). The author of Genesis does not explicitly connect these events; however, as we shall see shortly, later Jewish writers made the explicit connection between the descending "angels" and the proliferation of evil among humankind that results in the great flood.

Another important development in the Hebrew Bible is the presentation of the "Satan" figure in the book of Job (see Clines 1989, 19–20). The Hebrew author presents the Satan as part of the "heavenly beings" (lit., "sons of God" [*bene ha'elohim*]; Job 1:6; 2:1), which seem to compose a divine council that convenes before God. This figure's task seems to be to scout out the earth for human wrongdoing and bring accusations against humans before God. The Satan plays a similar role in Zechariah 3:1–5; and the apostle Paul alludes to the Satan's accusing role in Romans 8:33, when he asks, "Who will bring any charge against God's elect? It is God who justifies" (see also Jude 9). The Satan in Job seems to be a benign figure whose duties support the maintenance of cosmic justice.[1] However, as the narrative progresses, the reader discovers that the figure has overstepped his bounds and is manufacturing evidence. The figure is not bringing evidence against Job but is torturing Job in order to produce evidence against him (Job 1:12–21; 2:7–10). The Old Greek translator of Job, working independently of the Septuagint translator of Genesis, also renders the heavenly council in Job as *hoi angeloi tou theou* (the angels of God; Job 1:6; 2:1); and the translator renders the Satan as *ho diabolos* (the Adversary or the Devil). These translation

decisions are important, for they foreshadow some of the ambiguous treatment of angels that one encounters later: if the Satan was initially part of the angelic council of God, then it follows that some angels can become hostile and dangerous to humans. It foreshadows later claims that some angels are in partnership with Satan (e.g., *angelos satana* [angel of Satan] in 2 Cor. 12:7).

Angelic Figures in Second Temple Literature

Second Temple Jewish literature shows a more studied interest in angelic figures and beings that occupy the heavenly realm than one finds in the Hebrew Bible and the New Testament (for further discussion, see Reed 2020). Here one finds detailed accounts of the creation of the angels and their different ranks and functions before God (e.g., Jub. 2.1–4). In these accounts, angels are often identified by name (e.g., 1 En. 6.7). One also encounters details about the angels' lust for women on earth. Acting on their lust, some of the angels descend to earth, mingle with humans, and procreate with mortal women (e.g., 1 En. 6.1–8; 7.1–6). The foundation for this development can be found in Genesis 6:1–4. The Jewish historian Josephus offers a similar interpretation of the Genesis 6 story as the Septuagint translator by identifying the Nephilim as "angels of God" and their offspring with mortal women as resembling "giants" (Josephus, *Ant.* 1.73 [trans. Thackeray 1998]). Importantly, Josephus refers to this information as "tradition" (*paradidontai*), cementing this as an established reading of the Genesis story. The descent of the angels to mingle with mortals is variously condemned in the literature. Some authors view the descent of the angels as the cause of wickedness among humans, as the angels pass on corrupting knowledge and eternal secrets to humans (1 En. 8.1–3; 9.6; Jub. 7.21). Other authors condemn the crossing

---

1. For detailed discussions on the figure of Satan, see Forsyth 1987; Pagels 1995; Wray and Mobley 2005.

of sexual boundaries between heavenly beings and earthly beings (T. Naph. 3.2–3). The corrupting influence of the descending angels (sometimes called Watchers) becomes the prelude to the great flood that God sends upon the earth to cleanse it (Jub. 7.21–25; Josephus, *Ant.* 1.73–76; cf. Gen. 6:5–7). God also dispatches the angels Michael, Gabriel, and Raphael to punish the corrupt angels and bind them for eternal judgment (1 En. 10.1–22). The union between the descending angels and humans begets giant offspring who later become evil spirits wreaking evil upon the earth (1 En. 15.8–12). The writer of Jubilees seems to imply that the Watchers themselves are the demons (Jub. 7.27) leading humans astray to commit evil acts.

The angels Michael and Gabriel are named in the Old Testament and New Testament (e.g., Dan. 8:16; 9:21; 10:13, 21; 12:1; Luke 1:19, 26; Jude 9). Second Temple literature, however, represents a major shift, not only in the detailed interest in the origins, names, ranks, and functions of angels, but also in its attribution of the cause of evil and wickedness on earth. Erring angels who abandoned the heavenly court to mingle with humans are to blame. In other words, while the Hebrew Bible largely paints angels in a positive light, the period leading up to the writing of the New Testament saw views develop wherein some angels serve the divine purpose while others seek to thwart the divine purpose and afflict humans. And these views were derived from interpretations of the Hebrew Bible, especially the roles played by the sons of God in Genesis 6 and the Satan in Job. The Satan in Job is a member of the divine council who is on his way to becoming evil because he manufactures evidence against Job in order to afflict him. Nevertheless, the Satan in Job is still allowed to appear before God. Second Temple Jewish literature depicts evil angels who are not only banished from the heavenly court but also condemned to eternal judgment.

The documents from Qumran also portray good angels who serve God's purposes and evil angels who oppose them. The well-known doctrine of the two spirits depicts opposing spirits that govern spheres in which humans must exist: the spirits of injustice and truth (see further discussion in Davidson 1992; Vanderkam 2010, 101–7). The spirits of injustice are ruled by the Angel of Darkness (1QS III, 15–24; 1QM XIII, 1–5). The Angel of Darkness and the spirits of injustice lead humans astray into sin, iniquities, and unlawful deeds. They are also the cause of miseries that humans experience. On the other side of this fierce battle is the Angel of Truth / Prince of Light, who rules the spirits of light and together with them aids the sons of light against the schemes of the Angel of Darkness (1QS III, 25; 1QM XIII, 10–15). Within the Qumran documents the satanic figure named here as the Angel of Darkness is often referred to as Belial (e.g., 1QM I, 1–5; XIII, 10–15; 1QS I, 18; II, 4–5). But he is also at times referred to as the Prince of Darkness (1QM XVII, 5–6), the Angel of Malevolence (1QM XIII, 10–15), and the Spirit of Deceit (1QS IV, 9). The spirits of injustice are also at times equated with angels, such as the War Scroll's assertion that all the spirits of Belial's lot are the "Angels of Destruction," who walk in the realm of darkness (1QM XIII, 10–15). A variation of the name for the Satanic figure Belial—that is, Beliar—can be found in 2 Corinthians 6:14–7:1. The name Beliar is attested also in Jubilees (1.20; 15.33) and the Testaments of the Twelve Patriarchs (T. Reu. 4.8; T. Levi 18.12; T. Jud. 25.3; T. Dan 5.10–11; T. Benj. 6.1; 7), where he is presented as a prince of demonic forces.

Angels and Demons in the New Testament

The New Testament depiction of angels largely follows the Hebrew Bible's positive portrayal of these supernatural beings. Here also angels are part of the heavenly court (e.g., Matt. 18:10;

Mark 8:38; 13:32; Luke 12:8–9; 15:10; John 1:51; 1 Pet. 3:22; Rev. 5:11–12). They bring messages to God's children (e.g., Acts 10:3–8; 11:13; Heb. 2:2) and especially announce the good news of Jesus's birth (e.g., Matt. 1:18–25; Luke 1:26–38; 2:8–20) and resurrection (e.g., Matt. 28:5; John 20:12). They warn God's children about impending danger (e.g., Matt. 2:13–15) and deliver them from danger (Acts 5:19–20; 12:7–11). They minister to Jesus in a time of great need (e.g., Matt. 4:11; Mark 1:13). They are conveyors of divine revelation (e.g., Rev. 1:1; 22:16), and they will serve as agents of God's wrath on sinners and God's deliverance of the saints at the eschaton (e.g., Matt. 13:36–43; 16:27; 24:29–31; Mark 13:27; 1 Thess. 4:13–18; 2 Thess. 1:6–10; Rev. 7:1–2, 11; 8:2–13).

However, the New Testament also contains traces of angels' ambiguous character that we find in both the Hebrew Bible and Second Temple Judaism. The writings of the apostle Paul provide good illustrations of the ambiguous treatment angels receive. Paul's letters show awareness of good angels who are part of the heavenly court (e.g., Gal. 1:8; 2 Thess. 1:7). But Paul is also aware that angels can work against God's purposes (e.g., 2 Cor. 11:14). He implies that Satan has his angels (2 Cor. 12:7), a view similar to one encountered in the Gospels, where the Devil is said to have his angels who are condemned to eternal judgment (Matt. 25:41).

In the book of Revelation war breaks out in heaven between Michael and his angels and the great dragon and his angels (Rev. 12:7; see further discussion in Beale 1999, 638–40). The great dragon is also called "the ancient serpent," "the Devil and Satan" (12:9). Satan and his angels are defeated and cast out of heaven (12:8). In another vision, John sees an angel coming down from heaven who seizes the Satan, binds him, and locks him in the bottomless pit for a thousand years (20:1–3). He will be released after the thousand-year reign of Christ to deceive the nations for battle but will be thrown into the lake of fire for eternity (20:7–10). The book of Revelation seems to allude to the tradition found in 1 Enoch, where God sends the angels Michael, Gabriel, and Raphael to bind the Watchers for eternal judgment (1 En. 10.1–22). The author of 2 Peter also echoes the story of the Watchers when he warns those who persist in sin of coming judgment:

> For if God did not spare the angels when they sinned, but cast them into hell and committed them to chains of deepest darkness to be kept until the judgment; and if he did not spare the ancient world, even though he saved Noah, a herald of righteousness, with seven others, when he brought a flood on a world of the ungodly; . . . then the Lord knows how to rescue the godly from trial, and to keep the unrighteous under punishment until the day of judgment. (2 Pet. 2:4–9; cf. Jude 6)

Overall, then, the New Testament presentation of angels situates these supernatural beings on a moral spectrum from good to evil. In addition, on several occasions Paul presents angels as morally neutral (e.g., 1 Cor. 4:9; 6:3; 11:10; 13:1). The latter view may be compared with Greco-Roman portrayals of angels and demons. Greco-Roman authors for the most part viewed angels and demons as intermediaries between a supreme, inaccessible God and humans (see further discussion in Vos and Otten 2011; Lange, Lichtenberger, and Römheld 2003; Brisson, O'Neill, and Timotin 2018). These beings were not necessarily entirely good or evil; they were mercurial at best, and humans could experience them as either good or evil. These beings represented a kind of divinity, at times distinct from the gods or at times equated with the gods (see, e.g., Plutarch, *Is. Os.* 25 [*Mor.* 360e], 26 [*Mor.* 361a–c]; Plato, *Symp.* 201e–204a). "Demons" in the Greek tradition could even refer to the souls or spirits of the deceased (e.g., Hesiod,

Op. 121–29). The Hebrew Bible and the New Testament equate the gods of Gentiles with demons. For example, the author of Deuteronomy equates the gods of the nations with demons: "They made him jealous with strange gods, with abhorrent things they provoked him. They sacrificed to demons, not God, to deities they had never known, to new ones recently arrived, whom your ancestors had not feared" (Deut. 32:16–17; cf. Ps. 96:5 MT [95:5 OG]). Paul quotes this passage in 1 Corinthians 10:20 in his warning to the Corinthians to refrain from eating food sacrificed to idols.

It may be important at this point to highlight that while angels receive an ambiguous treatment in the New Testament, demons do not. An important difference between Greco-Roman views of demons and the New Testament view is that demons in the New Testament are not harmless; they represent an evil force in the cosmos. The early Christian writer Origen expresses this difference lucidly in his rebuttal of the anti-Christian, Greek philosopher Celsus (see Origen, *Cels.* 3.37). Celsus wants to preserve the Greek distinction that allows for some good demons, but Origen demurs, claiming that all demons are evil:

> In the same way, all angels are not said to be angels of God, but only those that are blessed: those that have fallen away into sin are called "angels of the devil," just as bad men are called "men of sin," "sons of perdition," or "sons of iniquity." Since, then, among men some are good and others bad, and the former are said to be God's and the latter the devil's, so among angels some are angels of God, and others angels of the devil. But among demons there is no such distinction, for all are said to be wicked. (Origen, *Cels.* 8.25 [trans. Crombie 1885, 649])

Origen acknowledges that some angels belong to God and others to the Devil. However, no such distinction exists among demons. In an allusion to the Gospel accounts, Origen reminds

his audience that the demons do not belong to God, for their prince is Beelzebul (Matt. 12:24; Luke 11:15). It seems fair to say that Origen accurately captures the New Testament depiction of demons, which, unlike its Greco-Roman context, views demons as purely evil.

In the Gospels, demons are responsible for all kinds of physical ailments—such as muteness (Matt. 9:33; Luke 11:14), epilepsy (Matt. 17:14–18), and mental illness (Luke 8:26–39). They are unclean spirits that possess humans (Mark 7:24–30; Luke 4:31–37, 41; 8:2; 9:37–43; see further discussion in Wahlen 2004). Demons are part of Satan's kingdom and the old age. A sign of the ushering in of God's kingdom and the new age is the casting out of demons (Matt. 12:22–32). In the words of Jesus, "If it is by the Spirit of God that I cast out demons, then the kingdom of God has come to you" (12:28). As already noted, for Paul, the Greco-Roman gods are not benign or benevolent beings; they are demons (1 Cor. 10:20–21). Any union with these gods would nullify a believer's participation in Christ. And at the end of the age, demons will be associated with Satan's deceitful works and leading people astray into idolatry (Rev. 9:20; 16:14).

The New Testament authors are not interested in the names, origins, ranks, and functions of various angels and demons as one discovers in Second Temple Jewish literature (see further discussion in Arnold 1992). This is because, for the New Testament authors, Satan and his angels and demons all represent the same phenomenon: guardians of an old age that is passing away. God's inbreaking revelation through his Son Jesus Christ has ushered in a new age. In the words of Paul, Satan is "the god of this age" (2 Cor. 4:4, my translation) and together with his minions forms "the rulers of this age" (1 Cor. 2:6, 8). And yet believers are also reminded that the present form of this age is passing away (1 Cor. 7:31). Satan and his angels and demons are aligned on the opposite (and wrong) side of the battle line against God and Christ. They remain a real threat to the children of God and should not be taken lightly. However, believers should not be preoccupied with Satan and his angels and demons, for they have been dealt a fatal blow at the crucifixion of Jesus (cf. 1 Cor. 2:8; Col. 2:14–15; see the detailed discussion in Moses 2014). Satan and his angels and demons are still at work in the world. But believers live in the light of the victory that the cross of Christ has achieved, foreshadowing the ultimate judgment of Satan and his angels and demons. For now, believers dwell within the space of the already but not yet. Satan and his minions have already been defeated, but their final defeat will not happen until the eschaton, when they are cast away for eternity.

Works Cited

Arnold, C. E. 1992. *Powers of Darkness: Principalities and Powers in Paul's Letters*. Downers Grove, IL: InterVarsity.

Auffarth, C., and L. T. Stuckenbruck. 2004. *The Fall of the Angels*. Themes in Biblical Narrative 6. Leiden: Brill.

Beale, G. K. 1999. *The Book of Revelation: A Commentary on the Greek Text*. NIGTC. Grand Rapids: Eerdmans.

Brisson, L., S. O'Neill, and A. Timotin, eds. 2018. *Neoplatonic Demons and Angels*. Leiden: Brill.

Clines, D. J. A. 1989. *Job 1–20*. WBC 17. Dallas: Word Books.

Crombie, F. 1885. *Ante-Nicene Fathers*. Vol. 4, *Tertullian, Part Fourth; Minucius Felix; Commodian; Origen, Part First and Second*, edited by A. Roberts, J. Donaldson, and A. C. Coxe. New York: Christian Literature Publishing Company.

Davidson, M. J. 1992. *Angels at Qumran: A Comparative Study of 1 Enoch 1–36, 72–108 and Sectarian Writings from Qumran*. JSPSup 11. Sheffield: JSOT.

Doedens, J. 2019. *The Sons of God in Genesis 6:1–4: Analysis and History of Exegesis*. Oudtestamentiche Studiën 76. Leiden: Brill.

Forsyth, N. 1987. *The Old Enemy: Satan and the Combat Myth*. Princeton: Princeton University Press.

Götte, M. E. 2016. *Von den Wächtern zu Adam: Frühjüdische Mythen über die Ursprünge des Bösen und ihre frühchristliche Rezeption*. WUNT 2/426. Tübingen: Mohr Siebeck.

Harkins, A. K., K. C. Bautch, and J. C. Endres. 2014. *The Watchers in Jewish and Christian Traditions*. Minneapolis: Fortress.

Lange, A., H. Lichtenberger, and K. F. D. Römheld, eds. 2003. *Die Dämonen: Die Dämonologie der israelitisch-jüdischen und frühchristlichen Literatur im Kontext ihrer Umwelt = Demons: The Demonology of Israelite-Jewish and Early Christian Literature in Context of Their Environment*. Tübingen: Mohr Siebeck.

Moses, R. E. 2014. *Practices of Power: Revisiting the Principalities and Powers in the Pauline Letters*. Minneapolis: Fortress.

Pagels, E. 1995. *The Origin of Satan*. New York: Random House.

Reed, A. Y. 2020. *Demons, Angels, and Writing in Ancient Judaism*. Cambridge: Cambridge University Press.

Thackeray, Henry St. J., trans. 1998. *Josephus: Jewish Antiquities*. Vol. 1, *Books 1–3*. LCL 242. Cambridge, MA: Harvard University Press.

Vanderkam, J. C. 2010. *The Dead Sea Scrolls Today*. 2nd ed. Grand Rapids: Eerdmans.

Vos, N., and W. Otten, eds. 2011. *Demons and the Devil in Ancient and Medieval Christianity*. Supplements to Vigiliae Christianae 108. Leiden: Brill.

Wahlen, C. 2004. *Jesus and the Impurity of Spirits in the Synoptic Gospels*. WUNT 2/185. Tübingen: Mohr Siebeck.

Wray, T. J., and G. Mobley. 2005. *The Birth of Satan: Tracing the Devil's Biblical Roots*. New York: Palgrave Macmillan.

Wright, A. T. 2015. *The Origin of Evil Spirits: The Reception of Genesis 6:1–4 in Early Jewish Literature*. Rev. ed. Minneapolis: Fortress.

36

Prophecy, Divination, Oracles, and Dreams

JILL E. MARSHALL

Early Christian authors and interpreters of early Christian texts inherited the distinction between "prophecy" and "divination" from the Hebrew Bible (Deut. 18:9–22; see Hilber 2018, 368). In Deuteronomy, this distinction is primarily polemical: prophecy is true and is what the in-group ("we") does, while divination is illegitimate and is what other peoples do. Later Christian traditions, often including modern New Testament scholars, have continued with this polemical definition: prophecy was good and a biblical inheritance, while divination was bad and what Greek polytheists did.

But if we delve further into the Greek linguistic and cultural milieu in which New Testament authors like Paul and Luke wrote, we find a much thinner line between "divination" and "prophecy." The Greeks used terms derived from the verb *prophēteuō* (to speak forth, prophesy, or interpret the gods) to describe what went on in divinatory or oracular temples, such as the famous temple of Apollo in Delphi. Plato calls the priestess at Delphi (who received and spoke messages from the god) a *prophētis* (Plato, *Phaedr.* 244a), the feminine version of the term used by Paul and other New Testament authors for figures like Isaiah, Moses, or Jeremiah. Plato and other Greek authors also use terms related to the verb *manteuomai*, "to divine or prophesy," to describe divinatory and prophetic rituals at oracular temples (Plato, *Apol.* 22b–c), including *mantis* (seer or prophet) for the Delphic prophetess and *mantikē* (divination).

In essence, then, "divination" and "prophecy" describe similar religious activities for ancient Greek speakers: knowing the will of God/the gods and communicating it to a human audience. Philosophical texts in Greek and Latin are particularly preoccupied with the two sides of this communication chain—from god to human prophet and from prophet to other humans. Divination/prophecy was central to the religious worldview of the ancient Mediterranean because it addressed the question of how the divine interacts and communicates with humanity.

Inspired and Technical Divination

Greeks and Romans distinguished two means by which gods communicated to humans. Divination was either (1) inspired, caused by direct communication of the god or spirit with the human, or (2) technical, provided through natural signs or patterns that trained priests or priestesses could interpret.

Inspired divination was the more dramatic of the two and provided indelible images of raving prophets for poets to spice up their epics and tragedies and for polemicists to cast aspersion upon. The Greek term for inspiration is *enthousiasmos* (god within), from which the English term "enthusiasm" derives. Plutarch, a priest at the oracular temple of Delphi, wrote about the theories for how the prophetesses at Delphi were able to enter into the state of inspiration and share the god's messages with priests and inquirers. He emphasizes the rituals that take place at the temple that allow the prophetess to enter into a suitable mental state to accept the entrance of the spirit of the god. At the same time, though, the mental capacity of the woman is not shut off when the god enters; rather, she must make sense of the images the god places in her mind and put them into human language for her audience.

Plutarch emphasizes the nontechnical nature of this activity at Delphi. The prophetess, in his telling, is uneducated, which is preferable because it allows the god to enter her and communicate unfiltered. This insistence, however, contradicts his view of the woman prophet as using her mind to interpret and translate divine images and messages, and it is likely a convenient fiction to support the Delphic institution against its critics.

The Delphic institution, like other oracular temples, also housed technical divination in the form of lots. Petitioners who may not have had the means to ask the inspired oracle a question could have asked a yes/no question in another part of the temple complex, and a priest or priestess would have drawn a token to answer the question (much like flipping a coin today). This method was used for personal and familial questions (e.g., Will my wife give birth to a son?), while the inspired oracle gave political prophecies to elites (Should I attack the Persians?).

Other forms of technical divination include interpreting the natural signs available in the flight of birds (augury), the entrails of sacrifices (haruspicy), and the movements of the stars (astrology). Technical forms of divination became popular during the Roman Republic, and Cicero wrote a dialogue that debated the validity of divination, especially these technical methods (*On Divination*). The idea underlying technical divination is that God/the gods are active and influential in the whole cosmos, so any observable part of the world can be mined for divine messages.

Cicero considers dream divination a form of inspired divination, but it included elements both inspired and technical. Greek temples housed incubation rituals, in which a person slept inside the temple to allow a divinity to enter their consciousness in their dreams. In some cases, the purpose of incubation rituals was healing; at temples of the healing god Asclepius, people with injuries, ailments, or infertility slept so that the god would visit, give them a message, and heal them during sleep. A message in a dream could then be interpreted by a professional trained in the art of interpreting dreams. Artemidorus's *Oneirocritica*, or *The Interpretation of Dreams*, a second-century CE, five-volume treatise on signs and symbols in dreams, is an ancient text that witnesses to the complex art of dream interpretation and pervasive belief that dreams allowed the divine to communicate the future to human beings.

Evidence for Divination and Prophecy

Texts

A number of texts written in the centuries around the New Testament texts discuss divination or prophecy as a central topic. Across the cultural categories of Greek, Roman, and Jewish, there are commonalities in how authors address divination based on the genre they are writing and their purpose in discussing divination. In other words, a Jewish author writing in a philosophical mode may have more in common with a Greek philosopher than he does with a Jewish poet. This means that it is important to be cognizant of genre and literary conventions when analyzing any portrayal of ancient diviners or prophets. Three literary traditions provide evidence for divination and prophecy: philosophical, poetic, and oracular.

In philosophical literature, the central concern is interrogating how gods communicate with humans. Philosophical writers were interested in categorizing and rationalizing the prophetic process and making sense of the body-soul connection that enabled a god to speak through a prophet.

Many of the texts mentioned thus far fall into the philosophical category, most notably Cicero's *On Divination* and Plutarch's dialogues on Delphi (*On the Obsolescence of Oracles* and *The Oracles at Delphi No Longer Written in Verse*). These authors were influenced by earlier philosophical discussions of prophets, especially the historian Herodotus and the philosopher Plato. Herodotus records one of the first literary portrayals of the Delphi priestess, who is rational and composed when receiving the spirit of god and when challenged by men who do not like the oracles they received (*Hist.* 1.91). For Herodotus, the concern is to show how gods work within history through prophecy. While in Herodotus's portrayal the prophet is not out of her mind, in Plato's portrayal the concept of madness, or *mania*, is philologically related to *mantikē* (divination).

Plato discusses madness in contrast to philosophical rationality and categorizes three types of *mania:* the poetic, prophetic, and Dionysian (wine induced).

Both Herodotus and Plato discuss prophets and divination in passing. Plutarch and Cicero wrote entire treatises on the topic and were close to the religious practices they described. Cicero used the dialogue form to question the possibility of human-divine communication in *On Divination*, written around 44 BCE. This dialogue was the sequel to the three-volume *On the Nature of the Gods*. Cicero's interlocutor in the dialogue, Quintus, suggests at the beginning that Cicero overlooked divination in his former treatises and that the topic is central to any consideration of Roman *religio*: "If there are gods, there is divination" (*Div.* 1.10 [trans. Falconer 1923, 415]). Cicero introduces the topic by noting the various Greek philosophical stances toward divination, including Plato's view of mantic madness. Throughout the dialogue, he gives philosophical arguments for and against the efficacy of various technical and inspired forms of divination, and he seeks to separate practices that can allow for communication between gods and humans from practices that are mere superstition.

In two late first-century CE dialogues, Plutarch argues for the efficacy of prophecy at Delphi and blends different philosophical perspectives to validate a ritual form of communication with the gods in light of the new social, cultural, and political situation under Roman imperial rule (see Marshall 2019). Plutarch was responding to cultural changes and what many people saw as a decline in the importance of the ancient, revered institution of Delphi. In *No Longer in Verse*, he addresses the question of the change in oracular form from verse to prose, a discussion that leads to philosophical arguments about language and the mechanics of *enthousiasmos* (god within) in prophecy. In *The Obsolescence of Oracles*, he addresses complaints that the Delphic oracle is in decline and gives possibilities for why the prophets receive fewer or incorrect messages from the gods. Again, the mechanics of prophecy is key: the possibilities include that the gods now refuse to give messages, population decline necessitates less divine interaction, or the demigods or winds that mediate between gods and humans have changed or disappeared. When approaching Plutarch's eclectic texts, written in philosophical dialogue form, it is important to keep in mind his distinct situation between philosophical rationalizing (he was a philosopher) and religious institution (he was a priest). This position shapes his interpretation of what went on in the oracular cavern. Moreover, his historical position at a time of cultural change influences his arguments.

While Plato established the terms for prophetic madness that philosophers then discussed at length, Greek and Latin poets portrayed that madness using prophetic characters. Three tendencies arise in poetic images of prophets and divinatory practices: poets (1) imagined prophets as frenzied and mad, which created interpretive problems for the prophet's audience; (2) depicted possession as violent and showed the prophet enduring violence from gods and men; and (3) used sexualized language to describe the process by which prophets received messages from the gods. As with philosophical texts, it is important to recognize the literary conventions and rhetorical purposes of a text before accepting a dramatic portrayal as a historically sound representation of how divination actually happened.

Since classical Athenian drama thrived on miscommunication and missed connections for its tragic and comedic moments, the often ambiguous speech of prophets fits the genre perfectly. In Sophocles's *Oedipus the King*, the Delphic prophet's oracles cause the dramatic twists and turns, and the legendary blind male prophet Teiresias clarifies the oracles, even as he probes questions about divine communi-

cation, clarity of oracles, misunderstandings, and riddles. Euripides set *Ion* at the Delphic temple complex and provided glimpses into the inner workings of the temple at that time. Perhaps most significant is Aeschylus's portrayal of Cassandra in *Agamemnon*. Cassandra, the captured priestess of Athena from Troy, prophesies the murder of Agamemnon and cannot control the frenzied, painful state that prophecy sends her into. Inspiration is for her a volatile storm that throws her body around, an effect of how clear and violent her visions are. But the chorus refuses to understand her and insists that her language is ambiguous, even as she speaks clearly.

We can trace this frenzied, violent image of prophets into Latin epic poetry. In Virgil's *Aeneid*, the Sibyl, an ancient Greek prophet adopted by both Roman and Jewish traditions, leads Aeneas to the underworld and experiences frenzied, uncontrolled inspiration, much like Aeschylus's Cassandra. Ovid too includes the Sibyl in his *Metamorphoses* and emphasizes her extreme old age and sexual relationship with Apollo, understood to be the mechanism of her inspiration. Finally, in *The Civil War*, an epic poem about Julius Caesar's rise, the poet Lucan includes an extended scene in which the Delphic priestess is driven completely mad by prophecy. The god's spirit "plunge[s] flames into her guts," and she "boils with a mighty fire" (*Bel. civ.* 5.173–75 [trans. Braund 2008, 89]). She whirls around in frenzy but is still able to produce a prophecy, even if it is ambiguous. Lucan's depiction of prophecy aligns with his overarching message of the violence of war, the insistence of fate, and the futility of divine communication. Even if humans can receive a god's message, they are unable to do anything to change their fate.

All of these poetic images of prophets, usually women, are tendentious, and readers should not accept them uncritically as historical reality. New Testament commentators have often prooftexted Lucan's prophetess to describe the differences between Paul's prophecy and speaking in tongues (1 Cor. 14). This is an error, and the historian must weigh these exaggerated poetic images against other depictions of the prophet as calm, composed, and ritualistic. The rhetorical purpose of any text, inside and outside the New Testament, should always be identified in order to avoid oversimplifying the evidence.

Finally, by oracular literature I mean written collections of oracles or prophetic statements, whether in poetry or prose. This form of literature was more important in Roman and Jewish contexts than in the Greek context. Readers of the Hebrew Bible are particularly familiar with the oracular genre: books like Isaiah and Jeremiah are composite collections of messages from God to God's people via a prophet. Isaiah's oracles are political and given in the first-person voice of God. At points throughout the collection, historical narration situates an oracle (e.g., Isa. 7:1), and the prophet describes how he received the prophecy, or the mechanics of his inspiration (e.g., 8:1).

In the Greek- and Latin-speaking worlds, oracular collections of sayings by famous seers (such as the Sibyl, Bacis, and Musaeūs) circulated, and wandering oracle interpreters (*chrēsmologoi*) consulted them on behalf of inquirers. These collections were popular and practical, not high literary or aesthetic art. The Romans especially came to use the Sibylline books in ritual. During the Republican period, the state began collecting Sibylline writings, and by Cicero's time the priestly college of the *quindecimviri* interpreted the books, essentially becoming institutional *chrēsmologoi* (*Har. resp.* 13). When Caesar Augustus took power, he collected and inspected all prophetic books in circulation, burned dubious ones, and kept the authentic books in the Temple of Apollo on the Palatine in Rome (Suetonius, *Aug.* 31.1). These oracular collections became central Roman religious and political institutions.

These two literary-cultural traditions (Hebrew prophetic collections and Roman Sibylline books) come together in the Sibylline Oracles, a composite text written in different Jewish diasporic locations (from Italy to Asia Minor to Egypt) and in different centuries (2nd c. BCE to 2nd c. CE and beyond). The voice is that of the Greek (and therefore "idolatrous") prophet the Sibyl, but she articulates Jewish (and in later strata, Christian) monotheism, ethics, and eschatology. The rhetorical power of the oracles lies in this juxtaposition: a legendary non-Jewish prophet, often associated with Apollo's inspiration, is actually inspired by the one "Great God" and has been prophesying in line with the Jewish worldview for centuries.

The image these texts produce is of a Sibyl who is depicted much like the Greek and Latin poetic representations of prophets. Her inspiration is internal and physical, and God places words and visions into her breast, heart, or mind. She shakes and burns when she sees the future. This image is distinct from portrayals of male prophets in the Hebrew Bible, who receive prophecy on their lips or mouths. This distinct image of the Sibyl stems from the melding of two cultural traditions: that of the raving Greek/Roman prophet and that of the übertextual Hebrew prophet.

Archaeology

Literature is not the only witness to prophecy and divination in the world around the New Testament. Archaeology also lends texture to our understanding of the ritual communication between gods and humans. Many of the great oracular temples have been extensively excavated. Excavations at Delphi produced an immense amount of treasure and gifts given to the temple throughout history, reinforcing the image of the temple's political importance in producing divine guidance to city-states. The path up the hill to the temple was lined with treasuries from different cities, which housed the gifts, and inscriptions to the god thanking him for oracles and for freedom from enslavement. The Doric temple itself is massive, with underground passages and caverns.

The temples of Apollo at Claros and Didyma in western Asia Minor have also been excavated and have features similar to Delphi—most notably, caverns or rooms obscured from view where the prophetic ritual took place. Secrecy was important to divinatory rituals, and the architecture at these temples reflects this. Both Claros and Didyma also have sacred wells or water sources, indicating that imbibing holy water may have been part of the prophetic ritual.

Finally, Dodona was an oracular temple in the northern part of Greece that was distinct from the other temples mentioned here in that it was an oracle of Zeus rather than Apollo. Dodona's ritual revolved around an oak tree, and scholars have suggested that the priestesses' divination was primarily technical: they interpreted movements of birds and the wind in the trees. Since the means and setting of prophecy seem to have been outside in nature, archaeologists have found little evidence for structures. They have found, however, a cache of strips of metal that were inscribed with questions, most of which were yes/no questions. This archaeological evidence supports the idea that multiple means of divination took place at the same temple complex and provides examples of the kind of questions that people sought to answer via divination. (For the archaeological evidence for these temples and divination more broadly, a good place to start is Johnston 2008).

Implications for New Testament Studies

Prophecy was mysterious and dramatic and touched on the essential question of how humans can know the future or god's will. Because of the secrecy revolving around prophecy, the literary and archaeological evidence is fragmentary and tendentious. Students and scholars of the New Testament, therefore, must be discerning in how they use the evidence and what questions they ask. I have cautioned against prooftexting, reading a depiction of a prophet as unequivocally historical, and considering Greek and Roman ritual as negatively "other" compared to Jewish or biblical practices. The antidote to these errors is to consider the rhetorical purpose of any text that describes prophecy or divination. What was the author trying to do with the mention or image of a prophet?

One detail you may have noticed as you read about the definitions, different methods, and evidence of prophecy/divination is that women often played the role of prophet in Greek and Roman traditions. Even the Jewish and early Christian traditions adopted a female prophet, the Sibyl. This is in contrast to the Hebrew Bible, which mentions only a few women prophets (Miriam, Deborah, Huldah) and instead designates prophecy predominantly to the realm of men. The gender dynamics of prophecy/divination in the world around the New Testament may have affected how early Christian authors addressed the topic. Consider Paul's arguments about prophesying and praying in tongues in 1 Corinthians 12–14. Those arguments are introduced and concluded by statements about women's speech in the church (11:2–16; 14:33–36). Might ideas about women prophets have influenced his conclusions? Similarly, Luke-Acts and Revelation mention women prophets, sometimes in a negative light (Acts 16:16–19; Rev. 2:20–23). Is the gendered polemic at play in these texts informed by divination in Greek or Roman contexts?

In the ancient Mediterranean world, divination probed eternal questions of how God/the gods communicated with humans and how humans can know their future. Since religious practices were not separate from social and cultural expectations of men and women, gender dynamics influenced how the rituals took place and how authors understood them. The eternal and timeless is always housed in the particular and embodied.

Works Cited

Braund, Susan H., trans. 2008. *Lucan: Civil War*. New York: Oxford University Press.

Falconer, W. A., trans. 1923. *Cicero: On Old Age, On Friendship, On Divination*. LCL 154. Cambridge, MA: Harvard University Press.

Hilber, John W. 2018. "Prophecy, Divination, and Magic in the Ancient Near East." In *Behind the Scenes of the Old Testament: Cultural, Social, and Historical Contexts*, edited by Jonathan S. Greer, John W. Hilber, and John H. Walton, 368–74. Grand Rapids: Baker Academic.

Johnston, Sarah Iles. 2008. *Ancient Greek Divination*. Malden, MA: Wiley-Blackwell.

Marshall, Jill E. 2019. "Paul, Plutarch, and the Gender Dynamics of Prophecy." *NTS* 65, no. 2: 207–22.

37

Magic, Medicine, and Miracles

JENNIFER EYL

In chapter 7 of the Gospel of Mark, Jesus encounters a deaf man who also suffers from a speech impediment. He takes the man aside and places his fingers in the man's ears. He then spits and touches the man's tongue. Jesus looks toward heaven and says, "Ephphatha," which the reader is told means "Be opened." Immediately, the man's "ears were opened, his tongue was released, and he spoke plainly" (Mark 7:34–35). In the Gospel of Luke, Jesus instructs the representatives of John the Baptist (who have come to inquire about his identity), "Go and tell John what you have seen and heard: the blind receive their sight, the lame walk, the lepers are cleansed, the deaf hear, the dead are raised, the poor have good news brought to them" (Luke 7:22). In the Gospel of John, Jesus magically turns water into wine (John 2:3–11), transforms five loaves of bread and two fish into such an abundance that they feed over five thousand followers (6:5–14), and miraculously walks on water (6:16–20). Readers are told that crowds followed Jesus everywhere because "they saw the signs that he was doing for the sick" (6:2).

Jesus performs numerous kinds of "signs and wonders" (many of which pertain to healing, but many of which have nothing to do with healing at all) in the Gospels, as do Jesus's immediate disciples in the Acts of the Apostles, and Paul in his own letters.[1]

How are we to understand the sudden disappearance of deafness and resolution of speech impediments, or the transformation of five loaves of bread and two fish into enough food to feed thousands? More shockingly, how ought a reader to understand the reanimation of a dead body (Mark 5:21–43; John 11:38–44)? Are such events magic? Are they miracles? Are the healings related to medicine, or are they at odds with practices of medicine? Where does medicine end and miracle begin? What is the role of magic in medical healing? How can the reanimation of a dead body be anything but horrifying and contrary to everything people know about death? What is the relationship between all of these things and deities or, even

1. See, e.g., Acts 3:1–10; 5:12; 8:13; 9:17–18, 32–35; 13:4–12; 19:11–12; 20:7–12; 28:7–9; Rom. 15:18–19; 1 Cor. 12:4–11, 27–31; 2 Cor. 12:12.

more broadly, religion? In this chapter we will consider how these practices fit into the larger cultural landscape of ancient Mediterranean life, while we also explore the complicated overlap between the categories we use to describe such practices. The chapter will demonstrate that categories we take for granted, such as magic, medicine, and miracles, are sometimes laden with ideological approval or disapproval by those using the terms. Furthermore, we will see that Paul was not unique in making such claims about himself, nor were Gospel authors unique in making such claims about Jesus. Perhaps most importantly, we will find that, while we have distinct categories such as religion,[2] science, magic, and medicine, such categories were far from clear for inhabitants of the ancient Mediterranean world.

Magic

Let us start with magic. *Mageia*, the Greek root for "magic," initially referred to astrological expertise in the region of ancient Chaldea-Babylon. A *magos* (magician), then, was a highly skilled divination specialist whose expertise pertained to reading the stars. We see this sense retained by the author of the Gospel of Matthew when he indicates that *magoi* (Eastern astrologers; plural of *magos*) view a special star in the sky that announces the birth of a significant king. They travel all the way to Jerusalem to pay homage to this new king but manage to rankle Herod in the process (Matt. 2:1–16). In English translations, the *magoi* are often referred to as "wise men," but the term actually points to such Eastern

astrology specialists. The author of Matthew draws on their reputation for predictive and astrological interpretive skill to authorize the significance of Jesus's birth. That is to say, if multiple *magoi* travel so far to offer homage to the newborn Jesus, the significance of his birth must be monumental.

By the first century, when most New Testament documents were written, *mageia* had taken on an additional sense that suggested nefarious intentions at worst, and private, selfish intentions at best. That is to say, *mageia* was perceived to be socially oppositional in the sense that magical practices sought to harness and direct the power of gods, spirits, or *daimonia* (low-level deities) for some kind of personal gain. Archaeologists have excavated innumerable potsherds, lead tablets, and inscriptions from the ancient Mediterranean world with incantations manufactured to curse other people, cast spells on them, or petition a deity for some kind of personal win. Such things include causing someone to fall madly in love with you, to die, or to lose their fortune, or petitioning to win a bet on the local horse race or to be cured of some illness. For these reasons, *mageia* was frowned on, and the accusation of *magos* could get a person thrown out of town, arrested, or beaten.

Mageia and *magos* appear in only two texts of the New Testament: the Gospel of Matthew and the Acts of the Apostles. In Matthew, as we have seen, the *magoi* are respected and skilled interpreters of the stars. The author of Acts uses *mageia* terminology in the suspicious, derogatory, and oppositional sense. The most famous case is that of Simon Magus (or Simon the Magician) in Acts 8:9–13:

> Now a certain man named Simon had previously practiced *mageia* in the city and amazed the people of Samaria, saying that he was someone great. All of them, from the least to the greatest, listened to him eagerly, saying, "This man is the power of God that is

2. To be clear, the ancient Hebrew, Greek, and Latin languages do not have a word for "religion." Thus, scholars have long debated the merits of applying the word "religion" to ancient Mediterranean practices. Indeed, many modern readers would be surprised to learn that the word "religion" appears nowhere in the Bible—neither the Hebrew Bible nor the New Testament. I use the term here in a minimalist sense, to denote practices and ideas that pertain to gods.

called Great." And they listened eagerly to him because for a long time he had amazed them with his *mageia*. But when they believed Philip, who was proclaiming the good news about the kingdom of God and the name of Jesus Christ, they were baptized, both men and women. Even Simon himself believed. After being baptized, he stayed constantly with Philip and was amazed when he saw the signs and great miracles that took place.

In Acts 13:4–8, we again encounter a *magos*:

So, being sent out by the Holy Spirit, they went down to Seleucia; and from there they sailed to Cyprus. When they arrived at Salamis, they proclaimed the word of God in the synagogues of the Jews. And they had John also to assist them. When they had gone through the whole island as far as Paphos, they met a certain *magos*, a Jewish false prophet, named Bar-Jesus. He was with the proconsul, Sergius Paulus, an intelligent man, who summoned Barnabas and Saul and wanted to hear the word of God. But the *magos* Elymas (for that is the translation of his name) opposed them and tried to turn the proconsul away from the faith.

In each of these cases, the apostles wield the power of a legitimate deity, and the *magos* (Simon and Bar-Jesus/Elymas) wields illegitimate power. Indeed, in the case of Simon, the magician quickly drops his charade and becomes a follower of the apostle Philip. Philip's astonishing feats, which amaze Simon and others, are not described as *mageia*, even though they might be classified as such, but instead are called "signs" and "wonders." This terminology (signs and wonders) is found earlier in the fourth-century BCE Greek philosopher Theophrastus, as well as in letters of Paul and in the Septuagint.[3] In the case of Bar-Jesus,

Paul afflicts the magician with sudden blindness, which inspires the proconsul to become a follower of the apostle.

The dynamic relationship of "apostle" versus "magician" is a contest of one-upmanship that finds its most extended description in the apocryphal Acts of Peter. In this text, which dates to approximately 150 CE, the apostle Peter and Simon Magus go head to head in magical feats until the apostle finally wins. This scenario is reminiscent of the scene in Exodus when Pharaoh's magicians compete with Moses and Aaron over the superiority of their wonder-working skills, which is, by default, a contest over the superiority of the gods who empower them. Needless to say, the Israelites and their deity win (Exod. 7:1–13).

Indeed, although references to *mageia* or *magoi* occur in only two New Testament texts, the kinds of practices that might qualify (to an outsider) as *mageia* occur repeatedly. For that reason, avoidance of the term *mageia* appears intentional in most of these texts. The apostle Paul, for example, refers to a host of unnamed wonders, powers, and signs in his letters. In addition to the unnamed events and abilities, Paul also identifies some wondrous feats such as miracle healings and speaking in tongues (1 Cor. 12–14). Paul even facilitates the material transformation of the bodies of his faithful followers into divine eternal bodies (15:50–52). This transformation is made possible through the ritual of baptism, in which initiates receive the divine material "spirit" of Christ (Eyl 2019, 129–36). Does Paul call this wondrous transformation "magic"? Absolutely not. Yet, if we step back and examine such a claim in the larger context of ancient Mediterranean religious practices, we would likely refer to such a ritual as a "magical" one. Paul's practice of baptism for the dead (15:29)

---

3. The Septuagint is the Greek translation of the Hebrew Bible. For the phrase "signs and wonders," see Theophrastus, *Caus. plant.* 5.4.3, 4. It appears eighteen times in the Septuagint, including Exod. 7:3; 11:9; Deut.

29:3; and Isa. 8:18. Paul uses the phrase in Rom. 15:19. Gospel authors also adopt the terminology: for example, Mark 13:22; Matt. 24:24; John 4:48; and Acts 5:12.

perhaps provides us with another meaningful example. His followers are ostensibly using their own bodies as a stand-in, so as to extend the benefits of baptism to those who have already died. Such a ritual is what anthropologists call "sympathetic magic," whereby one object or body is manipulated so as to affect the body or object it represents.[4]

Medicine

Ancient Mediterranean medicine was, in many ways, woefully insufficient compared to today's modern medicine. But in some ways, it was strikingly adept: people commonly concocted healing poultices and salves; the healing properties of hot springs and methods of recuperation were widely acknowledged; and minor surgeries were regularly practiced, including tooth extraction, sutures, and amputations. Ancient physicians produced medical manuals on such topics as fractures, gynecology, chronic diseases, hemorrhoids, and epidemics. As for physical explanations for disease, the Greek physician Hippocrates and his followers believed that an imbalance of the humors (bodily fluids) was often responsible. Hippocrates's approach to diagnosis and treatment relied on the innovative strategy of observation and evidence. Indeed, medical manuals from Hippocrates dominated medicine in Europe, Byzantium, and the Arab world until the seventeenth century. Although the Hippocratic Corpus (that is, the entire collection of medical treatises attributed to Hippocrates and his followers) is more extensive than other ancient medical collections, Hippocratic medicine was significantly more rudimentary. It would not be until the Hellenistic period (323 BCE–31 CE) that physicians could study, through autopsy, the circulatory system, the valves of the

heart, and the network of nerves throughout the body.[5]

Despite the ubiquitous existence of local physicians and midwives in antiquity, healing and sickness were widely attributed to the power of the gods. That is to say, regardless of ethnicity, class, or geographic location, people in the ancient Mediterranean routinely believed that both sickness and healing came from a divine source. Sickness, for example, was often viewed as a punishment or sign of abandonment by a god.[6] Apollo sends a ten-day plague to afflict Greek warriors in book 1 of the *Iliad*. Many assumed the plague that decimated Athens in 448 BCE was divine punishment (Mitchell-Boyask 2008). Likewise, the God of Israel sends a plague to afflict the Egyptians in Exodus (Exod. 7:14–11:10).[7] These examples are entirely in keeping with how many ancients conceptualized the origin of illness and the role of deities.[8]

Healing from illness or disability was widely thought to be bestowed by a god or by a person empowered by a god. In Exodus, the God of Israel promises the Israelites that he

4. On sympathetic magic, see Alvar Nuño 2014; Faraone 1990; Franek and Urbanová 2019.

5. While Hippocrates may be the most famous physician from antiquity, he was hardly alone. We have a good amount of evidence from other physicians, such as Herophilus of Chalcedon, Erasistratus of Ceos, Asclepiades of Bithynia, Soranus of Ephesus, and Galen.

6. For example, abandonment by the God of Israel is Paul's explanation for why Gentiles were so sick and depraved in Rom. 1:18–32.

7. Numerous examples demonstrate this throughout the Hebrew Bible / LXX, but none as succinct as God's declaration in Deut. 32:39: "I kill and I make alive; I wound and I heal."

8. In the case of Greek and Roman polytheism, the role of healing was associated with specific deities. In the case of "monotheism," the assigned roles for specific gods are reassigned to a single mega-god. Thus, the one god becomes the god of war *and* peace, the god of sickness *and* health, the god of life *and* death. Because of the mono-deity traditions of Israel/Judea, the deity espoused by Paul and the Gospel authors inflicts disease and brings healing in equal measure. In some instances, however, that "mega-god" steps back and permits afflictions to occur through other agents, rather than inflicting them himself (Job 2, for example).

will not afflict them as he has the Egyptians, provided they listen to his voice, do what is right in his eyes, and keep his commandments. "For," he states, "I am the LORD who heals you" (Exod. 15:26). Likewise, in Sirach readers are told to value and respect physicians, but they are also told: "Healing comes from the Most High" (Sir. 38:2); "pray to the Lord, and he will heal you" (38:9); and "recovery lies in the hands of physicians, for they, too, pray to the Lord that he grant them success in diagnosis and in healing, for the sake of preserving life" (38:13–14).

The notion that gods played a role in healing could sometimes be at odds with the view of physicians who sought other explanations for disease and its resolution. Indeed, tension sometimes existed between those trained as physicians and those who offered to facilitate divine aid. For example, in his first-century treatise *De Medicina*, the Roman author Celsus observes that, prior to his own day, "diseases were then ascribed to the anger of the immortal gods, and from them help used to be sought" (*Prooemium* 4 [trans. Spencer 1971, 5]). Celsus understands the advancements of medicine by his day to look for physical, rational explanations. He overestimates the degree to which divine explanations had changed by the early empire; regardless of the flourishing of more "official" physicians, the vast majority of people assumed that God(s) played a role in both sickness and its resolution.

Evidence demonstrates that many physicians saw themselves as working in conjunction with a deity, and even diagnosing and prescribing treatments at dedicated healing shrines. The most widespread of these were shrines and compounds to the healing god Asclepius, whose symbol (a snake winding its way up the god's healing staff) persists as the symbol of the American Medical Association to this day (Wickkiser 2009). Across the Mediterranean, people afflicted with illnesses, injuries, and disabilities would travel to such shrines, where they would spend time engaged in therapeutics that blended what we would call medicine and "divine healing" from the god.[9] The patient would sleep in a room called an *abaton*, hoping to be visited with a vision of the god, who would then heal the ailing body part. The patient would also, in gratitude, offer an effigy of the body part in question; archaeologists have discovered hundreds of such offerings: terracotta figurines in the shape of legs, arms, breasts, ears, eyes, lungs, and so on (compare fig. 32.3 this volume; see also Oberhelman 2013, 2014). Such figurines point to medical healing and divine healing simultaneously.

Thus, when a figure such as Jesus heals blindness, paralysis, or a prolonged hemorrhage, ancient readers would not have found this especially unusual. In the New Testament, Paul discusses divine healings in 1 Corinthians 12:9 and 12:28 and includes healing practices in the list of *pneumatic*/spiritual gifts that faithful followers may be able to cultivate.[10] Indeed, for Paul, healing ranks second only to "deeds of power" (1 Cor. 12:28).[11] In the canonical Gospels, Jesus heals numerous people from illnesses, blindness, paralysis, and even demonic possession. As we saw earlier, in Mark, Jesus uses his own spit to heal a man from deafness and a speech impediment. Throughout the canonical Gospels, Jesus performs dozens of healings and exorcisms. Such claims are no stranger than what adherents of Asclepius assume from the god.

9. The most famous of these was located at Epidaurus in Greece. But archaeologists have found over three hundred shrines to Asclepius across the Greek and Roman world, including Pergamum, Athens, the island of Kos, the Tiber Island in Rome, and at Messene.

10. Such gifts include the abilities to prophesy, to heal, to work miracles, to discern various sorts of spirits, to channel divine speech (tongues), and to interpret such speech.

11. This passage ranks people (apostles, prophets, and then teachers) and then miraculous powers (deeds of power, healing, etc.).

Miracles

The word "miracle" comes from the Latin *miraculum*, which means "object of wonder." The closest Greek equivalents would be *thauma*, which refers to something that strikes wonder or bewilderment, or *teras*, which is also a terrifying or wondrous thing. Because the New Testament texts are written in Greek, *miraculum* does not appear, but we do encounter *thauma* and *teras* frequently. *Thaumata* and *terata* (the plural form of both words) were often associated with gods in antiquity and could include things such as divine earthquakes, sudden eclipses, the birth of twins, a statue that weeps, or perplexing things that people found difficult to believe as true. Such things could defy the assumed laws of nature but did not have to. Furthermore, "objects of wonder" could be construed as magic (if performed by a person) or simply as evidence of the divine power of gods.

"Miracles" or "wonders" abound in the New Testament, just as they abounded in the wider culture that produced the New Testament. Recall examples from the beginning of this chapter: Jesus turns water into wine; he multiplies bread loaves so as to feed thousands of people; he brings people back from the dead; he walks on water; and so on. But they also include many things Paul claims to have performed among his followers and abilities that they themselves may receive: the ability to heal, to channel divine voices, to discern whether a possessing spirit is a "good" one or "bad" one (see 1 Cor. 12). Paul even refers more generically to divine "signs and wonders" (*sēmeia kai terata*; Rom. 15:19) that he has performed, although he does not articulate what that includes. Presumably, his intended readers would recall. Such miracles are used as evidence in persuading outsiders to become followers and to bolster the conviction of those who have already become followers. The author of John, for example, calls such feats *sēmeia*, which means "signs" and "evidence" in Greek. It is clear the author means both simultaneously, as when Jesus raises Lazarus from the dead and indicates that he does so for the sake of the crowd so that they will be persuaded that he is sent from God (John 11:38–44). Immediately afterward, his detractors (in this case, the Pharisees) decide to kill him because he continually performs such miracles (*sēmeia*, signs), which undermine them and will bring the wrath of Rome on Judea (11:47–50).

Conclusion

Today, we use categories like magic, medicine, and miracles as though they are distinct and have clear boundaries. But this was not the case in antiquity: the boundaries between medicine and magic were often unclear; healing was typically a combination of therapeutics and religious rituals. The distinction between magic and what we call miracles could come down simply to who is participating—a human practitioner or an immediate divine entity. Regardless of the ancient vocabulary pertaining to signs, magical powers, or wonders, the modern word "miracle" tends to emphasize the divine origin of an inexplicable event or feat. Unlike "magic," which implies the presence of a practitioner or specialist who facilitates a supernatural event or feat, "miracle" can remove the practitioner from the equation. In this sense, "miracle" can misguide the modern reader of the New Testament insofar as its "miracle workers" claimed proficiency in a range of powers and abilities (Eyl 2019). For the ancient reader who was not a follower of Jesus, the feats performed by him (or by others in his name) would likewise be understood in terms of human wonderworking channeling the power of a particular deity—that is, magic.

Works Cited

Alvar Nuño, Antón. 2014. "Sympathetic Magic and Magic-Religious Mentality from Antiquity to the Modern World: A Longstanding Mental Structure?" *Dialogues d'histoire ancienne* 40, no. 1: 147–62.

Eyl, Jennifer. 2019. *Signs, Wonders, and Gifts: Divination in the Letters of Paul*. New York: Oxford University Press.

Faraone, Christopher. 1990. "Molten Wax, Spilt Wine and Mutilated Animals: Sympathetic Magic in Near Eastern and Early Greek Oath Ceremonies." *JHS* 113: 60–80.

Franek, Juraj, and Daniela Urbanová. 2019. "'May Their Limbs Melt, Just as This Lead Shall Melt . . .': Sympathetic Magic and Similia Similibus Formulae in Greek and Latin Curse Tablets (Part 1)." *Philologia Classica* 14, no. 1: 27–55.

Mitchell-Boyask, Robin. 2008. *Plague and the Athenian Imagination: Drama, History and the Cult of Asclepius*. Cambridge: Cambridge University Press.

Oberhelman, Steven M., ed. 2013. *Dreams, Healing, and Medicine in Greece: From Antiquity to the Present*. Burlington, VT: Ashgate.

———. 2014. "Anatomical Votive Reliefs as Evidence for Specialization at Healing Sanctuaries in the Ancient Mediterranean World." *Athens Journal of Health* 1, no. 1: 47–62.

Spencer, W. G., trans. 1971. *Celsus: On Medicine*. Vol. 1, *Books 1–4*. LCL 292. Reprint, Cambridge, MA: Harvard University Press. Originally published 1935.

Wickkiser, Bronwen. 2009. *Asklepios, Medicine, and the Politics of Healing in Fifth-Century Greece*. Baltimore: Johns Hopkins University Press.

38

Purity and Holiness

Matthew Thiessen

In Leviticus 10:10, God tells Israel's priests: "You are to distinguish between the holy and the profane, and between the impure and the pure" (my translation; cf. Ezek. 22:16; 44:23). This job of making proper distinctions among these four categories was central to the priestly role and necessary for Israel to dwell in proximity to their God. Yet modern readers, be they clergy, laity, or even scholars, have often failed to distinguish accurately among these four categories, leading to various misunderstandings of biblical and nonbiblical texts.[1]

The Binaries of Holy and Profane, Pure and Impure

First, modern readers must recognize that these four categories are separate. Contrary to many interpreters, the words "holy" and "pure" are not synonymous, and neither are the words "profane" and "impure." Each category refers to something distinct. The word "holy" relates to that which is set apart for special use. For Israel, that which is holy is connected to Israel's God (e.g., Lev. 20:7, 26; 22:32). Since Israel's God dwells in the tabernacle and later the temple, they too are holy (e.g., Exod. 31:14; Ps. 11:4), as are the various instruments and furniture connected to these structures. Likewise, time can be holy, set apart for the special use of resting from one's labors. And both Israel's priests and Israel itself are set apart to God and are therefore holy (e.g., Ps. 106:16; Lev. 11:44–45).

The *holy* forms one important binary with the category of the *profane*. All things can be divided into these two categories: an object, a building, a period of time, or a person is either holy or profane. And *almost* everything is profane. In contrast to modern English usage, in which the word "profane" refers to something bad (e.g., profane language), in an ancient context what is profane relates only to that which is not set apart for special, cultic use. It is normal or regular and can be used for a broad variety

---

1. The work of Jacob Milgrom is foundational to modern scholarship on this topic. See especially his encyclopedic three-volume commentary (1991–2001), as well as his abbreviated and more accessible commentary (2004), in the works cited list below.

of things. The first six days of the week, for instance, are profane: they are perfectly good and can be used to do work. A field outside of Jerusalem or a building unrelated to the tabernacle or temple is profane and can be used without concern for one's ritual status. Ultimately, the category of the profane marks the absence of something: the absence of the status of holiness. There is nothing intrinsically wrong or sinful with being profane, but one must distinguish and keep it separate from the holy. If one does not do this accurately, or if something profane enters holy space, negative consequences result. To treat as profane something that is holy (like the Sabbath or the temple) is to fail to distinguish properly between the holy and the profane. To do so is a cultic offense.

There is yet one more binary that divides the world according to Israel's priests and in relation to God's tabernacle or temple: the pair created by that which is *pure* and that which is *impure*. Again, all things are in either a state of ritual purity or a state of ritual impurity. First, ritual impurity is a condition that arises in relation to three physical sources: genital discharges of blood and semen (Lev. 12; 15), a series of apparently minor skin conditions referred to as *tsara'at* in Hebrew or *lepra* in Greek (Lev. 13–14), and corpses (Num. 19). Second, ritual impurity is a state that excludes one from approaching holy space (the tabernacle or the temple). For instance, anyone who is ritually impure from particularly potent sources of ritual impurity (corpses, *tsara'at*, irregular genital discharges) cannot dwell in the wilderness camp (Num. 5:1–4). Similarly, Israel's priests were permitted to eat food connected to sacrifices and therefore the altar only if they were ritually pure (18:11–13).

Sources of Ritual Impurity

Genital Discharges

Genital discharges of blood or semen make one ritually impure (Lev. 12; 15). This category of impurity can be further divided into normal and abnormal discharges. Normal discharges include sex, nocturnal emissions, menstruation, and childbirth. People experience a one-day impurity after sex or nocturnal emissions. Menstruation results in a seven-day impurity. Childbirth impurity is a bit more complicated. The birth of a boy results in an initial seven-day period of impurity, followed by a lesser state of impurity for an additional thirty-three days. In contrast, the birth of a girl results in an initial fourteen-day impurity, followed by a lesser state of impurity lasting sixty-six days.[2] At the end of these respective periods, the woman is required to bring both a burnt offering and a purification offering (Lev. 12:8). Abnormal discharges, on the other hand, pertain to genital discharges of blood or semen that are unrelated to normal bodily functions and have no clearly defined end. These seem to overlap with what we would consider medical conditions. No remedy is prescribed for such conditions, but if and when they cease, the person continues to be impure for seven additional days and then must offer both a burnt and a purification offering.

Lepra

Another source of ritual impurity is a skin condition referred to as *tsara'at* and translated into Greek as *lepra*. Whatever the condition or variety of conditions included within this category, it is almost assuredly not leprosy (that is, Hansen's disease), despite a long translation history. We know this for several reasons. First, there is no evidence that leprosy occurred in the ancient Mediterranean world at the time of the composition of Leviticus 13–14. In fact, the first evidence of leprosy comes from India in the sixth century BCE, and only in the second century BCE do we begin to find corpses with leprosy in Egypt (Mark 2002). So Leviticus cannot be referring

---

2. For the embryological reasoning behind this legislation, see Thiessen 2018.

to this medical condition. Second, the series of descriptions Leviticus provides of *tsara'at* do not match how leprosy manifests itself. Third, in addition to infecting people, *tsara'at* can also infect clothing and buildings (Lev. 13:47; 14:34), something that leprosy does not do. Fourth, Greek and Roman medical writers never refer to leprosy with the Greek word *lepra*, the word that the Septuagint translator uses to translate *tsara'at*. Instead, they use words such as *elephantiasis*, *elephus*, or *elephus morbus* when they speak of leprosy. In contrast, they use *lepra* to refer to a variety of relatively minor skin conditions (conditions akin to, if not necessarily the same as, psoriasis or eczema). Whatever the identity of this skin condition, Leviticus provides no means to remove it. Instead, Leviticus describes a seven-day purification process one needs to follow once a priest has determined that *tsara'at* has left the person's body (Lev. 14).

Corpses

Finally, the most severe ritual impurity arises in relation to corpses, which are permanently impure and contagious (cf. Num. 19:11–20). Even after burial, corpses continue to emit impurity, making anyone who walks over a place of interment impure. People or objects that come into direct contact with corpses are impure for a seven-day period. Unlike other sources of impurity, corpses also contaminate people and objects within an enclosed space (e.g., a tent or building), without direct contact. To further underline the strength of corpse impurity, corpse-contaminated people and objects become not only impure but also contagious, conveying a one-day, noncontagious impurity to anyone they touch. Those who endure a seven-day impurity remove this contracted impurity by washing in a mixture of water and the ashes of the red heifer on the third and the seventh day (19:1–12).

Summary

These three sources of impurity were naturally occurring and would have been encountered at various points throughout one's life. Israelites inevitably contracted ritual impurity, and such impurity was neither forbidden nor sinful for Israelites. Two exceptions to this rule are worth noting. According to the Holiness Code, Israel's priests were forbidden to contract corpse impurity from any corpse apart from a close relative (Lev. 21:1–4), while the high priest was not permitted to contract corpse impurity even from close relatives. Further, the person who had taken a Nazirite vow was also forbidden to contract corpse impurity (Num. 6:6–7). While most people were not prohibited from contracting ritual impurity, a ritually impure person was temporarily prohibited from accessing holy space and partaking in food connected to holy space.

Dietary versus Moral versus Ritual Impurity

Somewhat confusingly, Leviticus uses the language of impurity to refer to a number of different things: impure animals, ritual impurity, and immoral actions. While the language is shared, the things referred to are distinct. Impure animals do not convey impurity in the same way that ritual impurity is conveyed. They also are irrevocably impure—born impure, living impure, giving birth to impure offspring, and dying impure. The impurity of such animals only becomes activated, though, at the point of death. Consequently, Israel must not eat impure (nonkosher) animals and must take care to purify themselves when disposing of their carcasses.

The impurity associated with immoral behavior also differs from ritual impurity. Unlike ritual impurity, moral impurity does not exclude one from holy space, nor is it contagious in the same way that ritual impurity is. Unlike contact with a ritually impure person, contact with those who are morally impure does not make a person morally impure (Klawans 2000; Hayes 2002, 19–24). Unfortunately, people frequently conflate these forms of impurity, leading to numerous interpretive errors, such as suggesting that Jews thought it was sinful to touch a corpse or a ritually impure person (e.g., Mark 1:41). Setting aside a consideration of impure, or nonkosher, animals, ritual and moral impurity are understood in almost entirely different ways, as the following comparison demonstrates:

Ritual Impurity	Moral Impurity
Unavoidable	Avoidable
From a natural substance	From an action
Contagious	Noncontagious
Bathed away	Atonement/punishment
Not an abomination	An abomination
Not sinful	Sinful

This comparison illustrates important differences between moral impurity and ritual impurity. Moral impurity is inherently sinful, while ritual impurity is fundamentally a cultic state of being. When modern readers unknowingly conflate moral and ritual impurity, they break down important distinctions that help make sense of ancient Jewish purity systems. To be sure, there are times when these two categories, ritual and moral impurity, bleed into each other. For instance, when a person does not remove a ritual impurity using the prescribed method at the prescribed time, it can lead to moral impurity—sin.

Impurity and the Realm of the Holy

The category of the holy is not synonymous with the category of the pure; neither is the category of the profane synonymous with the category of the impure. Consequently, both holy and profane things are also simultaneously either pure or impure. These four separate categories result in four possible states of being:

- Holy and pure
- Holy and impure
- Profane and pure
- Profane and impure

These four categories relate to Israel's God, who has chosen to make God's dwelling among humans, first in the tent in Israel's wilderness camp, and then, ultimately, in the temple in Jerusalem. Because God dwells in the wilderness tent and then the temple, these spaces are holy or sacred. As the Holy One of Israel and the source of all holiness, God's presence infects the wilderness tent and temple with holiness (e.g., 1 Sam. 2:2; 2 Kings 19:22; Pss. 71:22; 78:41; Isa. 1:4; Ezek. 39:7). Where God's glory (Hebrew *kavod*) rests, there holiness dwells. And because the Holy One of Israel chooses to dwell in these spaces, they must be treated with great care and approached in the right ritual state: purity.

Consequently, the wilderness tent or temple functioned as a protected area with different barriers erected around it to guard against unqualified entrance. Those who were not set apart (made holy) could not enter holy space. Those who were set apart but were in a temporary state of ritual impurity also were not permitted entrance into holy space. Thus, the wilderness tent and temple were surrounded by an outer courtyard, while the tent or building itself was divided into two rooms, with the inner room cordoned off by an inner curtain. These three spaces became progressively more holy and therefore progressively more difficult to enter, with the holy of holies being entered only once a year, on the Day of Atonement (Lev. 16), and then only by the high priest. According to Ezekiel and later traditions, the Levites were appointed to guard the sacred space so that no one encroached on holy space where they were not allowed.

God's holy presence requires that humans approach God carefully. Only certain people, and only when they are in a state of ritual purity, can come near to God's *kavod* or glory. To do so in the wrong state or in the incorrect way was to endanger both God's presence among Israel and one's own life. The barriers around the temple and the requirement that one must be ritually pure to enter were intended not only to safeguard God's presence but also to protect God's people from the consequences of wrongly approaching God. Compassion animates the Jewish purity system; it was a protective and benevolent system intended to preserve God's gracious presence among Israel, a presence that could be of considerable danger to humans if they approached God wrongly.

Leviticus provides us with an example of qualified people who approach God in the wrong way—not because they are in a state of ritual impurity but because they come before God with the wrong cultic materials (Lev. 10). Nadab and Abihu come to God with a fire burning with materials that God did not sanction. This strange fire results in their deaths. Similarly, when an unqualified person, such as Uzzah, touches the ark of the covenant, the result is again immediate death (2 Sam. 6). Introducing ritual impurity into holy space, therefore, was a potentially dangerous situation, as Leviticus 15:31 nicely summarizes: "Therefore, you shall separate the people of Israel from their impurity, so that they do not die by their impurity by defiling my tent which is in their midst" (my translation; cf. Num. 19:13, 20). Care around holy space was necessary so that God would continue to dwell with Israel and so that Israel would continue to live safely in such proximity to a holy God.

These ritual requirements meant that Israelites needed to keep a safe distance from God when they were ritually impure. If Israel allowed impurities to accumulate in God's earthly dwelling, God would abandon it. The boundaries around the tent or temple protected both the inside (God's presence) and the outside (any Israelite in a state of impurity) from the havoc that impure forces could cause. Such cultic thinking was common in the ancient Mediterranean world (Frevel and Nihan 2013). As Paula Fredriksen puts it, ancient "gods tended to be emotionally invested in the precincts of their habitation, and they usually had distinct ideas about the etiquette they wanted observed when humans approached them there" (2005, 56).

The Logic of Ritual Impurity

Jacob Milgrom (1993) has argued that an underlying logic connects the three sources of ritual impurity: death. Corpses most obviously relate to death. But a number of ancient texts also depict the skin condition of *tsara'at* as looking corpse-like, with white, flaky skin (Num. 12:12; 2 Kings 5:7; Job 18:13; cf. Josephus, *Ant.* 3.264), and therefore connect this condition to death. Finally, since blood is associated with life (Gen. 9:4; Lev. 17:11, 14), and since semen was thought to be connected to blood, the loss of genital blood or semen might be associated with the loss of life force. From this observation, Milgrom concludes that in Jewish thinking ritual impurities represent the forces of death.

Some scholars have questioned this association of ritual impurity with death. After all, does it make sense to connect things like sexual intercourse and birth, events connected to genital emissions, with death?[3] And if the loss of genital blood or semen represents the loss of life force, which thereby explains its impurity, then would it not make sense that any loss of blood should result in someone

---

3. For instance, Frymer-Kensky 1983; Maccoby 1999; and Feder 2022. Other ancient Near Eastern cultures also associated birth with death, an association that makes sense in a world where the process of childbirth could frequently result in the death of the infant, the mother, or both.

becoming ritually impure (Maccoby 1999, 49)? Such scholars argue that ritual impurity is connected to mortality more broadly. In this sense, humans, being mortal, differ from the holy God, who is immortal, and therefore unborn and undying. The fact that Israel's holy God must be kept separate from the impure suggests that the holy and the impure are *functional* opposites. Thus if impurity is associated with death and mortality, then holiness must be associated with life. Whatever the precise logic, ritual impurity underlines the ontological gap between humans (as well as the rest of creation) and Israel's God. Since Israel's God chooses to dwell in the midst of Israel, the wilderness tent and later the temple cult apparatus set up boundaries to keep the holy and the impure separate.

The New Testament

Although it is common in Christian interpretation to conclude that Jesus overturned or rejected laws related to purity, at times based on Mark 7,[4] the Gospels continue to work with these central categories of holiness and profaneness, impurity and purity.[5] For instance, Luke depicts Jesus's family observing the purification rites required after Jesus's birth (Luke 2:22). And the Synoptic Gospels depict Jesus, who both Mark and Luke call the Holy One of God, interacting with people who are ritually impure: people with *lepra*, a woman with an abnormal genital hemorrhage, and corpses. At the end of each encounter, the source of the ritual impurity no longer afflicts the person. And Jesus's own death, and thus his own corpse impurity, is overcome in the resurrection (see also Shively 2020). Paul too contrasts the powers of impurity and holiness, although his

primary focus is on the moral purity required of non-Jewish followers of Jesus now that they have become worshipers of the living and holy God and dwelling places of the Holy Spirit. In Romans 6, for instance, Paul contrasts a life devoted to sin (moral impurity) that leads to death with a life devoted to righteousness that leads to holiness and, ultimately, life. And the letter to the Hebrews concerns itself with how Jesus's resurrection culminates in the resurrection of all his followers. This resurrection life transcends the mortal condition characterized by birth, death, and impurity and thereby permits Jesus's followers to enter unhindered into the heavenly tent where God dwells. A similar depiction of the eschaton occurs in Revelation 21–22, where the author envisages a new Jerusalem that no longer contains a temple building. Such a vision, though, does not undermine or reject the temple cult and the ritual requirements for safe entry. Rather, because nothing impure will ever enter the city and since those who live in it will no longer be subject to death, no ritual impurity will exist. This eschatological conclusion enables the immortal, holy God to dwell in an unmediated way with the immortal and perpetually pure faithful who participate in this new city.

Works Cited

Feder, Yitzhaq. 2022. *Purity and Pollution in the Hebrew Bible: From Embodied Experience to Moral Metaphor*. Cambridge: Cambridge University Press.

Fredriksen, Paula. 2005. "Compassion Is to Purity as Fish Is to Bicycle and Other Reflections on Constructions of 'Judaism' in Current Work on the Historical Jesus." In *Apocalypticism, Anti-Semitism and the Historical Jesus: Subtexts in Criticism*, edited by John S. Kloppenborg and John W. Marshall, 55–67. JSNTSup 275. London: T&T Clark.

Frevel, Christian, and Christophe Nihan, eds. 2013. *Purity and the Forming of Religious Traditions in the Ancient Mediterranean World and Ancient Judaism*. Dynamics in the History of Religion 3. Leiden: Brill.

Frymer-Kensky, Tikva. 1983. "Pollution, Purification and Purgation in Biblical Israel." In *The Word of the Lord Shall Go Forth: Essays in Honor of David*

---

4. For an alternate reading of Mark 7 that does not see Jesus abandoning laws about impure (nonkosher) food, see Furstenberg 2008.

5. As has been argued by Kazen 2002, 2010; Wassen 2016a, 2016b; Shively 2020; and Thiessen 2020.

Noel Freedman in Celebration of His Sixtieth Birthday, edited by Carol L. Meyers and M. O'Connor, 399–404. Winona Lake, IN: Eisenbrauns.

Furstenberg, Yair. 2008. "Defilement Penetrating the Body: A New Understanding of Contamination in Mark 7.15." *NTS* 54: 176–200.

Hayes, Christine E. 2002. *Gentile Impurities and Jewish Identities: Intermarriage and Conversion from the Bible to the Talmud*. New York: Oxford University Press.

Kazen, Thomas. 2002. *Jesus and Purity Halakhah: Was Jesus Indifferent to Impurity?* ConBNT 38. Stockholm: Almqvist & Wiksell.

———. 2010. *Issues of Impurity in Early Judaism*. ConBNT 45. Winona Lake, IN: Eisenbrauns.

Klawans, Jonathan. 2000. *Impurity and Sin in Ancient Judaism*. New York: Oxford University Press.

Maccoby, Hyam. 1999. *Ritual and Morality: The Ritual Purity System and Its Place in Judaism*. Cambridge: Cambridge University Press.

Mark, Samuel. 2002. "Alexander the Great, Seafaring, and the Spread of Leprosy." *Journal of the History of Medicine and Allied Sciences* 57: 285–311.

Milgrom, Jacob. 1993. "The Rationale for Biblical Impurity." *Journal of the Ancient Near Eastern Society of Columbia University* 22: 107–11.

———. 1991–2001. *Leviticus: A New Translation with Introduction and Commentary*. AB 3–3B. New York. Doubleday.

———. 2004. *Leviticus: A Book of Ritual and Ethics*. Continental Commentary. Minneapolis: Fortress.

Shively, Elizabeth E. 2020. "Purification of the Body and the Reign of God in the Gospel of Mark." *JTS* 71: 62–89.

Thiessen, Matthew. 2018. "The Legislation of Leviticus 12 in Light of Ancient Embryology." *Vetus Testamentum* 68: 297–319.

———. 2020. *Jesus and the Forces of Death: The Gospels' Portrayal of Ritual Impurity within First-Century Judaism*. Grand Rapids: Baker Academic.

Wassen, Cecilia. 2016a. "Jesus' Work as a Healer in Light of Jewish Purity Laws." In *Bridging between Sister Religions: Studies of Jewish and Christian Scriptures in Honor of Prof. John T. Townsend*, edited by Isaac Kalimi, 87–104. BRLJ 51. Leiden: Brill.

———. 2016b. "The Jewishness of Jesus and Ritual Purity." *Scripta Institute Donneriani Aboensis* 27: 11–36.

39

Festivals and Feasts

GARY M. BURGE

The purpose of every ritual observance in Second Temple Judaism was to shape the worldview of the Jewish community and remind them that they were an uncommon people, separated from the rest of the world, belonging by covenant to the God of Israel. This would fulfill the exhortation of Exodus 19:5 that all Israel would become a "kingdom of priests" and "a holy nation." Obedience to the law, participation in the synagogue, and sacrificial worship at the Jerusalem temple each reinforced the singularity of this identity. Literacy came through study of Torah; meals were carefully prescribed; clothing had rules—in all, according to some rabbis writing after the New Testament period, there were 613 such laws, 365 prohibitions and 248 positive exhortations. Three ritual symbols served as reminders as well: the tzitzit (the tassels or fringes on garments; Num. 15:38; Deut. 22:12), the mezuzah (the scroll box fitted to the right-hand doorframe of a house; Deut. 6:9; 11:20), and the tefillin (the phylacteries or straps worn by males during prayer; Exod. 13:9; Deut. 11:18).

Time was likewise subsumed within this comprehensive ritual expectation. The Israelite calendar was organized around twelve lunar months. Each month was understood to begin when the first sliver of a new moon appears (the waxing crescent) and to end when the moon moves through its cycle and a last sliver disappears (the waning crescent). The calendar year was further organized around a series of festivals, some major, some minor, each reminding Israel of its history with God and Israel's obligations. The New Testament is fully aware of these festivals and presupposes that we too understand their rhythms and symbols.

Sabbath

The primary festival of Israel is not annual but weekly. In the Roman world, alongside circumcision, Sabbath observance was a well-known identifier of Jewish culture. The term *shabbat* (Sabbath) is Hebrew and designates the number seven—a number significant not only throughout the Old Testament but in the duration of the pilgrimage festivals. In Exodus

20:8–11 Israel is commanded to rest from work on the seventh day, as God did following creation. Since this was a day lived in imitation of God, it could also be viewed as God's own day and thus holy, set apart for him alone. Sabbath observance also was a signal to Israel that it had a covenant with God, belonged to God, and found its holiness in God alone (Exod. 31:12–17). The importance of this can barely be underestimated. Refusal to obey Sabbath law was punishable by death (31:14).

In the Second Temple era the importance of Sabbath was reinforced. The book of Jubilees underscores how Sabbath observance marks Jewish life and serves as a sign of Jewish identity in the world (Jub. 2.17–22). Leading teachers (often scribes or Pharisees) in this period defined what this obedience looked like. The idea of "rest" is more difficult than it first appears. Engaging in routine labor on the Sabbath was prohibited, but what about carrying things? Or gathering firewood? Or collecting water? Or boiling it? How much weight can someone lift, and how far can someone walk, before violating the Sabbath rule of rest? The Hebrew Bible provides some direction (fires could not be lit, Exod. 35:3; water could not be boiled, nor could food be baked, Exod. 16:23). But when we learn that "burdens" could not be carried (Jer. 17:21–24), we might wonder, How much is a burden? In this period, case law developed, clarifying what wrongful "work" might entail. Both Jubilees (2.29–30; 50.8) and the Mishnah (m. Shabb. 8) outline answers. Even though the Mishnah was compiled 150 years later, most scholars believe that its tractate Shabbat gives us a fair window into Sabbath life in the mid-first century. The Mishnah defines thirty-nine types of work that are forbidden (reaping, plowing, tying knots), but then we wonder, How much reaping is too much? This is where interpretation and application were debated. We even see this in Matthew 12:2 when Jesus and his disciples pluck grain for food on the Sabbath. A few stringent Pharisees are quick to condemn this work that is (according to them) against the law. In fact, violating the Sabbath appears to be one of Jesus's signature deeds to require people to rethink how Sabbath law had expanded unreasonably. We can imagine the controversy that followed Jesus's saying, "The Sabbath was made for man, not man for the Sabbath" (Mark 2:27 NIV).

This strict observance of Sabbath may seem odd to modern readers, but its motivations stemmed from a deep desire to honor God, set apart sacred time, and reflect on the One who created the world. Sabbath obedience was an orienting expression of piety, grounding the first-century Jews in their identity with God. Jews would meet in synagogues if they were available (or homes or set places, Acts 16:13) to listen to the Scriptures, pray, and hear teachings. In the New Testament, if Jesus wants to find a crowd gathered from a village (e.g., Mark 3:1), the synagogue is the perfect venue (see also Paul, such as in Acts 17:10). As a teacher with a wide reputation, Jesus or Paul might well be invited to choose a Scripture and give an interpretation (Luke 4:16–30).

The Sabbath also became a platform that Jesus could use to declare his identity and question the detailed enforcements of some Jewish leaders. When Jesus heals the man with the disabled hand (Mark 3:1–6), the moment evolves into an opportunity for Jesus to show his real authority and to provoke the Pharisees to think about Sabbath "work." John 5 is a crucial passage where Jesus heals a paraplegic man at the Bethzatha pools in Jerusalem and tells the man to pick up his pallet and then walk. Jesus is immediately accused of inspiring work on the Sabbath (5:10), but this too evolves: authority over the Sabbath belongs to the Father, and Jesus is working *as the Father works*. According to John, this ignites a theological controversy that lays the groundwork for Jesus's eventual persecution and death (5:18).

Three Pilgrimage Festivals

The Sabbath cycle of seven days provided the basic structure for the three major annual feasts (2 Chron. 8:13). The festival cycle ends on the seventh month. As an agrarian society, Israel followed the rhythms of the harvest closely, and these feasts would punctuate the harvest season (Lev. 23). But also Israel found in them reminders of Israel's own redemptive story. All circumcised men were expected to attend and join the celebrations centered at the Jerusalem temple (Deut. 16:16).

The first festival marked the beginning of new growth (in the flock and in the field) and celebrated God's springtime provision. The first "sheaf" of the cereal (or wheat) crop along with a newborn lamb would be sacrificed at the temple. The second festival marked the conclusion of the cereal harvest (now barley) seven weeks after the earlier sheaf offering. And the third festival, in the seventh month of the year, marked the gathering in from tree and vine (grapes, olives, pomegranates). This concluded the harvest year and ended with joyous celebration and rest because Israel's food supply was secure for another year. But also, it was a time of worship and thanksgiving, crediting God for his generous provision to his people.

These three festivals enjoyed significant attention during the Second Temple period (see Jubilees or the Mishnah). The annual rhythms also came to represent three steps in the great redemptive story of God with his people. The first, Passover, recalled Israel's dramatic departure from Egypt and salvation marked by the sacrifice of a lamb. The second, Weeks (later Pentecost), continued this story and recalled the gathering of Israel at Sinai and the giving of the law. The third, Tabernacles (or Booths), retold the story of Israel's wandering in the wilderness after Sinai. Of course, Israel had its own Hebrew names for these three festivals: Pesach (passing over), Shavuot (weeks), and Sukkot (booths). But in each festival, the historical recollection of redemption was triggered by some feature of the feast. Newborn lambs each spring recalled the lambs sacrificed in Egypt. Shelters built for the olive harvest recalled the wilderness shelters used for forty years.

Passover (Pesach)

The religious calendar began in spring with the first Jewish month called Nisan. Passover began on the first full moon following the spring equinox, thus anchoring it to celestial movements and making its date flexible (Exod. 12:1–13; Lev. 23:4–14; Deut. 16:1–8). A second festival, the weeklong Feast of Unleavened Bread, followed Passover, and the two feasts virtually merged in the popular imagination (Mark 14:1). Thus, in the Jewish ceremonies attention is given both to the lamb sacrifice and to the removal of leaven (yeast) from homes (m. Pesah. 1–3). The Mishnah provides detailed descriptions of both the sacrifice (m. Pesah. 4–6) and the meal itself (m. Pesah. 10). Scholars debate, however, how many of these details idealize the ceremony and how many actually represent first-century practices.

As the Hebrew Bible directs, this was a sacrificial festival celebrating the new growth of springtime. Lambs were being born, and cereal crops (the mainstay of Israel's diet) were emerging. These offerings were gifts of thankfulness. The sacrificial ceremonies at the temple took place on the thirteenth day of Nisan, and after sundown on that day, on the fourteenth day of Nisan, a Passover meal began for a gathering of at least ten persons (m. Pesah. 7.13–8.8). The fourteenth of Nisan could thus be on any day of the week. The feast would close with the waving of a sheaf (or bundle) or the first wheat to emerge from the fields, which held the promise of a good grain yield yet to come.

But Passover was also a well-known anniversary of God's dramatic defeat of Pharaoh and the rescue of Israel from Egypt. The sacrifice of

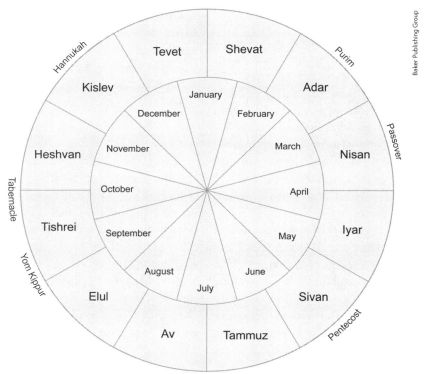

Fig. 39.1. The Jewish Calendar

Baker Publishing Group

lambs at the temple evoked ideas of redemptive sacrifice. The Mishnah tells us that Jews living in the Second Temple period would ordinarily travel to Jerusalem, sacrifice their own lamb or one purchased at the temple, and then on Nisan 14 begin the feast (m. Pesah. 1–5). Meals were held within the walled city of Jerusalem, people remained in or near Jerusalem all night, the city gates were left open, and their activities followed ritual formulas to recall the departure from Egypt. The meal included lamb, unleavened bread, and bitter herbs (recalling life in Egypt). Four cups of diluted wine also punctuated the service (m. Pesah. 10.1–7). The Passover story was retold, the Hallel Psalms were sung, and all would disperse in revelry (10.8).

We know that the early Christians used and shaped the Jewish meal, imitating Jesus's final meal in the upper room (Mark 14:17–25). Paul can even recite the liturgy of this meal to the Corinthians (1 Cor. 11:23–32), which means it

was in wide use. The meal was so well known that in 1 Corinthians 10 Paul can contrast the holiness of the Lord's Supper with inappropriate idol worship (1 Cor. 10:14). In 1 Corinthians 10:16 he even gives us a provocative hint that the sacred cup of our Lord's Supper was "the third cup" of the Pesach, the "cup of blessing."

Passover is the most commonly cited feast in the New Testament. Sometimes the reference is indirect, such as when Paul refers to Christ's resurrection as the "firstfruits" (1 Cor. 15:20–23; Rom. 8:23), hinting at the waving of the firstfruits of the spring harvest ceremony (Lev. 23:9–11). The annual festival is also mentioned in the Gospels. John refers to Passover three times (John 2:13; 6:4; 11:55), and these references are often used to determine the duration of Jesus's ministry (three years). The Synoptics point to it once during the passion story. When Jesus travels to Jerusalem at the end of his life, it is Passover season (Mark 14:1). However, the

Gospels are likely not comprehensive about the number of times Jesus celebrated any of the feasts, and their recorded number should not be used to determine the length of Jesus's public ministry.

In many respects, as the Passover is the defining redemptive event for the Old Testament, so too the Passover *as appropriated by Jesus* is the defining redemptive event for the New Testament. Here we have descriptions of Jesus's final meal in a Passover setting, as well as references to Passover lambs, whose death is parallel to the death of Jesus. In John, when Jesus is on the cross, the Passover imagery is explicit. When Jesus thirsts, Passover hyssop is used to give him sour wine (John 19:28–30; Exod. 12:22; Ps. 69:21). When a soldier pierces him, blood flows from him, just as flowing blood was required of any Passover lamb. When Jesus eats his final meal with his disciples and refers to his body broken and blood spilled (with bread and wine), he has taken an ancient remembrance and reappropriated it for his followers to have a perpetual ceremonial ritual.

Scholars debate whether Jesus's final meal was a Passover meal as the Synoptics indicate (Mark 14:12). If this meal was on Nisan 14, then Jesus died on that day (the next day was a continuation of the previous evening). John suggests that Jesus died when the Passover lambs were killed (John 19:14, 31), which means his death was on Nisan 13, making the previous night's meal something other than Passover. Many scholars believe this is a misreading of John. John says that Jesus dies "on the day of preparation" ("Passover" does not appear in 19:31). John is likely referring to "preparation for the Sabbath" in 19:14, which, in this year, followed Passover. His body is removed from the cross not out of concern for the Passover but due to the upcoming Sabbath. This means that both the Synoptics and John could be in one accord. Either way, it was Passover season, and the texts want us to identify Jesus as "the Lamb" of God—an unmistakable link to the Passover feast (John 1:29, 36). Paul can say, "Clean out the old yeast so that you may be a new batch of dough, as you really are unleavened. For our paschal lamb, Christ, has been sacrificed" (1 Cor. 5:7).

Pentecost (Shavuot)

The second major feast in the Jewish pilgrimage season was the Pentecost festival. The Old Testament does not indicate the duration of the feast, but likely it lasted one week in imitation of Passover and Tabernacles. This festival occurred seven weeks after Passover, concluded the grain harvest, and was a time of celebration and worship at the temple (Exod. 34:22; Lev. 23:15–21; Deut. 16:9–12). Recall that Passover anticipates this second celebration by the waving of the sheaf as Passover closes. Pentecost begins seven weeks after the sheaf is waved (Lev. 23:15).

Its Hebrew name was Shavuot (or Weeks), which was translated in the Septuagint to Pentecost (for "fifty" days; see Lev. 23:16). Once again pilgrimage was required (23:21), but the temple ceremony was far simpler than at Passover. Two newly baked loaves of leavened bread, made with the grain of the new harvest, were presented to the Lord in sacrifice (along with other sacrifices; 23:17). No work was done during the festival (the field work had been completed), and Israel rejoiced in the bounty of this harvest.

During this festival, Israel was also reminded that the goodness of the harvest was linked to their redemption and God's good favor in his covenant. Hints of Passover reemerge here (Deut. 16:9–12) so that Israel's covenant status was reinforced. But the links to the biblical salvation narrative are far weaker with this feast. In the Second Temple era, however, symbolic interest in Pentecost grew, and before long (Jub. 1.1–26) its connection with the giving of the law at Sinai was common. In Jubilees connections generally between covenant making and

Pentecost are frequent, and such connections are even more explicit in the much-later Babylonian Talmud (b. Shabb. 86b).

The New Testament provides limited interest in Pentecost and mentions it in passing when, for instance, Paul is trying to arrive at a destination in time for the feast (Acts 20:6; 1 Cor. 16:8). Its chief appearance is in Acts 2 when Jews are crowded into Jerusalem to celebrate the feast. Here in Luke's narrative we have a montage of imagery echoing numerous Old Testament motifs. Here the anticipated Spirit is given, fulfilling the promises of the prophets (Joel 2:28–32), and the gift of languages reverses the confusion of Babel. This holy fire that descends on the church is reminiscent of the fire from Sinai (or from the tabernacle or temple) when the law was given and Israel's covenant nationhood with God began. For some scholars, the same is happening here. If in the Second Temple era Shavuot recalled the giving of covenant and law to Israel (i.e., Israel's covenant birth), then Acts 2 may be pointing to the birth of a new Israel, the church. Temple fire, once lit to remind Israel of the presence of God, now has settled on a new community, which has been filled by God's promised Spirit.

Tabernacles (Sukkot)

The Feast of Tabernacles was the third and final festival of the agricultural year. Cereal grains had been harvested before the dry summer began. Then some months later in the autumn, a final ingathering would commence. Crops that came from "tree and vine"—including grapes, olives, pomegranates, figs, and dates—were now collected and stored or prepared. This was a joyous seven-day festival in Jerusalem (Lev. 23:33–43) that concluded Israel's agrarian year. It began on the fifteenth day of the seventh month (Tishri).

"Tabernacles" is a translation of the Hebrew name *Sukkot*, which means "booths" or "dwellings." Thus, the festival could also be called the Feast of Booths (Lev. 23:34) or even the Feast of Ingathering (Exod. 34:22). Here the historical recollection and the agricultural practice merge again. Temporary dwellings were often kept in the fields while the harvest was underway—for convenience, but also to protect the crop, whose value was considerable. But these dwellings recalled the temporary dwellings used in the wilderness for forty years following the exodus. Thus, Leviticus says, "You shall live in booths for seven days; all who are native-born in Israel shall live in booths, so that your generations may know that I made the Israelites live in booths when I brought them out of the land of Egypt: I am the LORD your God" (Lev. 23:42–43). Since this was also a time to remember Israel's covenant (Neh. 8:18), every seventh year the covenant was read aloud. However, use of this festival seems to have lapsed during Israel's monarchy and was revived with Ezra. The feast was reintroduced (Neh. 8:13–18), and its celebration continued through the New Testament period.

The Second Temple era drew marked attention to the festival. The Ezra reforms describe the festival shelters, whose roofs consisted of a loose collection of branches from the field: willow, palm, and myrtle (Neh. 8:15; see Lev. 23:40; also LAB 13.7). The Mishnah gives exacting details for how the *sukkah* (shelter) could be built (m. Sukkah 1.1–3.4), saying, for instance, that it could not be built indoors or under a tree but required a loose thatch. (The later Jerusalem Talmud adds that the night and its stars must be visible through the roof; t. Sukkah 2.3). During the ceremonies, people tied up bundles of willow, myrtle, and palm branches (called a lulav), and these were waved along with a citron fruit (Heb. *'etrog*; m. Sukkah 3.8–16) during the Sukkot ceremonies.

Most ancient civilizations in the northern hemisphere marked the slow decrease in sunlight each autumn (or "the dying of the sun"), and this in Judaism introduced a light festival on the final day of Tabernacles. There was dancing and flute playing in the temple courtyards, and trumpet blasts were heard throughout the city. Levites would build four large stands; each held four bowls of oil. Each bowl was given a wick and was lit (m. Sukkah 5.2). The Mishnah describes the festivities and says that anyone who has never seen this has failed to see a true wonder in their life. When we imagine the nighttime darkness of ancient cities, we can understand the drama of this light festival. The key text used for the festival was Zechariah 14 and its promise of eschatological light that is never extinguished (14:7). The festival thus became a prayer for light, which would return in the spring.

Zechariah also makes reference to water. In the late autumn, drought threatens the entire Middle East, and prayers for rain were common. A water festival accompanied the feast. Each day priests would walk to the Gihon Spring and carry a pitcher of water to the temple altar while chanting Isaiah 12:3: "With joy you will draw water from the wells of salvation." On the final day, seven water processions brought seven pitchers to the altar, showing the temple to be the source of divinely given water (Ezek. 47:1; Zech. 14:8). Throughout these ceremonies the people would wave the lulav and citron and sing from Psalms 113–18.

Tabernacles is vitally important to the New Testament. Some scholars wonder if Jesus's triumphal entry to Jerusalem (Mark 11:1–11) may have been at Tabernacles. This is because in the Gospel story the people are using leafy branches and palms to celebrate Jesus's entry (11:8). Jesus's actions in the temple, calling for its purity, may also link to Zechariah (see 14:21). John's Gospel is the only Gospel to refer explicitly to Tabernacles (John 7:2). Here the narrative is given in three stages (7:1–13; 7:14–36; 7:37–8:20) and climaxes with Jesus's remarkable twin announcements: "Let anyone who is thirsty come to me" (7:37) and "I am the light of the world" (8:12). Both of these are set in Tabernacles and signal that what Jerusalem sought in its water and light ceremonies is now satisfied in Christ.

Other Holy Days

While the three pilgrimage festivals anchor the Jewish year, other festivals were held in Jerusalem. A few of the most prominent include the following.

The Festival of Purim was celebrated one month before Passover (Adar 14–15) and recalled the story of Esther's defeat of Haman (the fourteenth is called Mordecai's Day). Keeping the festival is commended in Esther (9:20–22). This defeat of Israel's enemies was soon linked to the success of the Maccabees, and the day before Purim, Adar 13—the day before Mordecai's Day—was used to recall victory over the Greeks in the second century BCE (2 Macc. 15:36). The New Testament does not refer to Purim.

The Day of Atonement (Yom Kippur) was held just before Tabernacles on the tenth day of the seventh month (Tishri). It was given to Israel at Sinai (Exod. 30:10; Lev. 23:26–31), where Aaron was directed to host an annual sacrifice of atonement for the nation's sins. Its detailed instructions are in Leviticus 16:1–28. This continued through the New Testament period. Acts 27:9 likely refers to it (see "the fast"). Scholars debate if this feast is assumed in Hebrews 9. A full explanation is provided in the Mishnah (m. Yoma).

The Festival of Hanukkah (or Dedication) was a late feast celebrated on the twenty-fifth day of the ninth month (Kislev) to recall the Maccabean victories, the corruption of the temple's leadership, and the rededication of the temple (2 Macc. 10:6–8). Ezekiel 34 was a central text because it describes the bad shepherds that led Israel astray. John picks up on this theme in John 10 when Jesus appears during the festival (10:22) and describes himself as the good shepherd who is unlike the failed shepherds of Ezekiel 34.

Festival Life

Every culture creates festivals to commemorate great events or remind each new generation about its cultural or religious legacy. Second Temple Judaism brought these forward from the Hebrew Bible and shaped them to serve new generations. Images, metaphors, stories, readings, and ceremonies each solidified a person's identity in the larger story of God with his people. Such festival images or codes are presupposed in cultures, which is why it is so difficult for us to read the New Testament if we fail to grasp commonly understood cultural symbols. The Passover lamb, the Tabernacles lulav, and the stories of Hanukkah are hidden in the background of the world of the New Testament.

Further Reading

Bokser, B. M. 1992. "Unleavened Bread and Passover." *ABD* 5:755–65.

Chilton, B. 2000. "Festivals and Holy Days: Jewish." In *Dictionary of New Testament Background*, edited by C. Evans and S. Porter, 371–78. Downers Grove, IL: InterVarsity.

Hasel, G. F. 1992. "Shabbat." *ABD* 5:849–76.

Herr, M. D. 1976. "The Calendar." In vol. 2 of *The Jewish People in the First Century: Historical Geography, Political History, Social, Cultural and Religious Life and Customs*, edited by S. Safrai and M. Stern, 834–64. 2 vols. Philadelphia: Fortress.

Isaacs, E. D., and J. B. Payne. 1982. "Feasts." In vol. 2 of *The International Standard Bible Encyclopedia*, edited by G. Bromiley, 292–96. 4 vols. Grand Rapids: Eerdmans.

Olsen, M. 1992. "Pentecost." *ABD* 5:222–23.

Safrai, S. 1976. "Religion in Everyday Life." In vol. 2 of *The Jewish People in the First Century: Historical Geography, Political History, Social, Cultural and Religious Life and Customs*, ed. S. Safrai and M. Stern, 793–833. 2 vols. Philadelphia: Fortress.

Sanders, E. P. 1992. *Judaism: Practice and Belief, 63 BCE –66CE*. Esp. "The Common People: Daily Life and Annual Festivals" (pp. 119–45) and "Observing the Law of God I: General Characteristics, Worship and Sabbath" (pp. 195–211). Philadelphia: Trinity Press International.

Vanderkam, J. 1992. "Calendars: Ancient Israelite and Early Jewish." *ABD* 1:814–20.

40

Imperial Devotion

Adam Winn

Ancient Mediterranean peoples perceived the gods to hold tremendous power over world affairs. At the will of the gods, storms raged or ceased, crops flowered or withered, women were fertile or barren, children thrived or died, armies won or lost, business ventures boomed or busted, and empires rose or fell. The will of the gods could be fickle, but mortals were not without recourse. The pious could find favor in the eyes of the gods, and the most pious could experience tremendous divine blessing, even divine status themselves. A significant aspect of piety involved showing proper honor to those who deserved it. People honored the gods by constructing temples, offering prayers, and giving generous sacrifices. They also honored those who represented the gods, such as priests, rulers, and social superiors (e.g., patron, father, husband). Moreover, piety involved the display of virtues, such as justice, prudence, truth, faithfulness, courage, and modesty. Thus, those who both properly recognized the divinely orchestrated hierarchy of their world and displayed great virtue could find significant favor

with the gods. One cannot understand Rome's empire or the ubiquitous devotion granted to it apart from these deeply held convictions. The threads of these convictions were woven together to create the fabric of the narrative Rome continuously told and retold to both explain and legitimize its imperium over the world. It is this Roman imperial narrative that generated and required the devotion of the empire's inhabitants. Here we trace the formation of that narrative and the expressions of devotion it both demanded and produced.

Roman Religious Devotion and Virtue as the Basis for Its Imperium

Drawing on the widespread beliefs of the Mediterranean world outlined above, Rome's imperial narrative boldly proclaimed Roman imperium as the result of divine favor—favor that resulted from Rome's superior religious devotion and virtue. Cicero writes about the gods' reciprocation of Rome's devotion, "I have held the conviction that Romulus by his auspices and Numa by his establishment of our ritual laid the foundations of our state, which assuredly could never have been as great as it is had not the fullest measure of divine favour been obtained for it" (*Nat. d.* 3.2.5 [trans. Rackham 1933, 291]). And similarly, "in piety, in devotion to religion, and in that special wisdom which consists in the recognition of the truth that the world is swayed and directed by divine disposal, we have excelled every race and every nation" (*Har. resp.* 9.19 [trans. Watts 1923, 341]). Horace also declares the gods' role in Rome's greatness: "'Tis by holding thyself the servant of the gods that thou dost rule; with them all things begin; to them ascribe the outcome" (*Carm.* 3.6.5 [trans. Rudd 2004, 163]). Finally, Cicero reflects on the connection between Roman virtue and its success: "No man should complain that character counts for more than anything in Rome, when it is character that makes Rome the mistress of the world" (*Verr.* 2.4.81 [trans. Greenwood 1928, 383]).[1] Thus, Rome presented itself as a devoted and virtuous people whom the gods chose to rule the world. The gods confirmed their choice over and over again by military conquest, for in the ancient world, no one was victorious in battle without divine favor.[2] The implications of this divine mandate are far from subtle. If the gods had chosen Rome to rule the world, then those they rule had little choice but to succumb to that rule and devote themselves to their divinely chosen overlords. To do otherwise would be a futile attempt to resist the will of the gods.

The Blessings of the Roman Imperial Order as a Basis for Imperial Devotion

Military might by divine right was not the totality of Rome's narrative, nor was Rome's self-understanding of its own rule the sole

basis for soliciting devotion from its imperial subjects. Rome depicted its virtue both as a basis for obtaining its great empire and as the reason for its ongoing success. As a part of its narrative, Rome paraded its virtue as a blessing for all who found themselves under its rule. Rome's imperial system displayed virtues of justice, faithfulness, mercy, and prudence. The fruits of these virtues were peace, security, and prosperity for all who lived under the provision of Rome's empire and were faithful to it. Inherently, the Roman narrative asked, "Was your life better prior to Roman rule?" and then answered with a resounding, "No!" The Roman historian Marcus Velleius Paterculus clearly explains this aspect of Rome's grand narrative (19 BCE–31 CE):

> Justice, equity, and industry, long buried in oblivion, have been restored to the state; the magistrates have regained their authority, the senate its majesty, the courts their dignity; rioting in the theatre has been suppressed; all citizens have either been impressed with the wish do right, or have been forced to do so by necessity. Right is now honored, evil is punished; the humble man respects the great but does not fear him; the great has precedence over the lowly but does not despise him. When was the price of grain more reasonable, or when were the blessings of peace greater? The peace of Augustus, which has spread to the regions of the east and west and to the bounds of the north and the south, preserves every corner of the world safe from the fear of brigandage. . . . The cities of Asia have been restored; the provinces have been freed from the oppression of their magistrates. Honor ever awaits the worthy; for the wicked punishment is slow but sure. (*Hist. Rom.* 2.126.1–4 [trans. Shipley 1924, 317, 319])

The philosopher Seneca the Younger echoes the same sentiments:

> To-day your subjects one and all are constrained to confess that they are happy, and,

---

1. For further discussion on the role of virtue in Rome's greatness, see Lind 1972.

2. For discussion on the role of military victory and the will of the gods, see Fears 1981.

too, that nothing further can be added to their blessings, except that these may last. Many facts force them to this confession, which more than any other a man is loath to make: a security deep and abounding, and justice enthroned above all injustice; before their eyes hovers the fairest vision of a state which lacks no element of complete liberty except the license of self-destruction. (*Clem.* 1.1.8 [trans. Basore 1928, 361, 363])

Thus, according to Rome's imperial narrative, these great blessings of peace, security, and prosperity should produce instant devotion from those under its rule. Such devotion was both expected and cultivated.

Structures for Cultivating Roman Imperial Devotion

While Rome acquired its vast empire by military conquest, it did not maintain it through the same means. In the years of the early empire (ca. 14 BCE–100 CE), Roman military presence was sparse and hardly of the size necessary to quell a rebellion in a major city or region. To be sure, all inhabitants knew that Roman military force could and would be called on should rebellion break out, but due to the success of nonmilitary measures such rebellions were rare. Rome maintained peace and stability through the promise of advancement in honor, wealth, and prosperity to provincial and municipal elites. Rome and its emperors functioned as generous patrons to the elites of cities like Ephesus, Antioch, and Ancyra. They gave these elites positions of honor, such as political offices and priesthoods, and established profitable business arrangements and certain protections or benefits related to taxation. Through such patronage, the elites of these cities not only maintained but also grew their honor and wealth under Roman imperium. Rome's patronage, however, came with strings attached. For their benefits, the empire's provincial and municipal elites became clients of Rome and the emperor, who expected loyalty and mutual blessing. The elites of these cities showed their loyalty by promoting the Roman imperial cult—that is, the state religion requiring people to worship the goddess Roma as well as living and dead Roman emperors. Elites showed their loyalty by constructing temples, erecting altars and statues, and multiplying honorific inscriptions. Additionally, festivals or games put on at the expense of the city or its wealthy citizens were held to honor the goddess Roma and/or the current living emperor. Finally, elites ensured that Rome benefited from the wealth of the city, that taxes would be adequately rendered, and that citywide loyalty to Rome was maintained.[3]

Beyond such actions, the elite (and others) expressed loyalty by taking oaths of allegiance to Rome:

> I swear to Zeus, Earth, Sun, all the gods and goddesses, and to Augustus himself, that I will be loyal to Caesar Augustus, his children, and descendants all through my life, both in word, deed, and thought, holding as friends those they [i.e., the imperial family] hold as friends and considering those as enemies whom they judge to be such, that with regard to things that concern them I will not be sparing of my body or my soul or life or children, but will face every peril with respect to things that affect them. If there is anything that I should recognise or hear as spoken, plotted, or done contrary to this, I will report this and be an enemy of the person speaking, plotting, or doing any of these things. Whomever they judge to be enemies, I will pursue and defend against them by land and sea with arms and steel. If I should do anything contrary to this oath or fail to follow up what I have sworn, I impose a curse on myself encompassing the destruction and total extinction of my

3. For discussion of Rome's use of civic elites to cultivate devotion and maintain imperial stability, see Gleason 2006.

body, soul, life, children, my entire family, and everything essential down to every successor and every descendant of mine, and may neither earth nor sea receive the bodies of my family and descendants nor bear fruit for them. (*OGIS* 532 [trans. Parkin and Pomeroy 2007, 9])

At the very least an oath of this nature reflects the seriousness with which civic and provincial elites took their allegiance to their Roman patrons and quite likely the allegiance those patrons expected in return for their beneficence.

Such loyalty to Rome did not end with the provincial and civic elites. These elites were themselves patrons, having clients under them, and those clients were patrons to yet more clients. Thus, the system of patronage between Rome and the elites of the empire was replicated throughout Roman provinces and cities and became a successful way of establishing widespread allegiance and devotion to Rome. Each set of clients was expected to show the same loyalty to Rome as that shown by their patrons. As one moved down the patron-client pyramid, the means by which one showed loyalty changed. For example, some at the top might be able to fund the building of a temple, while those below might only be able to fund a regular sacrifice or contribute certain elements to a regular festival. Regardless of degree and scope, however, all in the pyramid were expected to demonstrate actively their loyalty to Rome and its emperor.

Not all inhabitants of the empire were part of the patron-client system. Quite often over half a city's inhabitants would fall outside of this system, since those at the bottom of society simply did not have the resources both to support their patrons and to take on clients of their own. Other means for showing imperial devotion were cultivated among those who fell outside the patron-client system. One means was the promise of social advancement for those who, for example, regularly participated in religious festivals or offered incense at an altar to the emperor's *genius* (divine life force). Those who neglected to honor Rome would be unlikely to find someone willing to take them on as a client. Thus, for any who sought social advancement, offering one's allegiance and devotion to Rome was nonnegotiable.

A second means by which Rome secured devotion from those outside the patron-client system was by linking the traditional expressions of Greek religious devotion with the imperial cult. For example, Rome placed imperial altars and inscriptions in the temples of traditional gods and depicted emperors as embodiments of traditional gods.[4] By blending the Roman imperial cult with traditional Greek religion, Rome was able to draw on a fundamental aspect of ancient Mediterranean culture to secure loyalty and devotion from the common inhabitant of its empire. As stated at the outset, people of the ancient Mediterranean world perceived the gods and other supernatural forces to have tremendous power over their lives. Thus, people were deeply committed to honoring these gods through temples, altars, sacrifices, and prayers for the sake of their security and prosperity. By co-opting the religious institutions to which people attached their hope of divine security, Rome found a way to cultivate imperial devotion from a captive audience.

A third means of securing devotion was through gifts granted by Rome (often through civic elites in the name of Rome) that would benefit an entire city. Such gifts included architectural improvements, grand festivals, Olympic-style games, gladiatorial games, and even generous gifts of money and food. These types of benefaction from Rome or Roman representatives drew in the common inhabitants of the empire who otherwise would not benefit from the patron-client system. The expected

4. For discussion and further examples, see Strait 2019, 69–118.

response to such benefaction was loyalty and faithfulness to Rome and its rulers.

Besides the patron-client system, trade guilds cultivated and manifested Roman imperial devotion. These guilds were formal associations of people connected with a particular trade such as merchants, scribes, masons, metalworkers, or woodworkers. While trade guilds would often be led by the wealthier and more honorable members of the city, they would have likely included people across the socioeconomic strata. The degree to which these guilds sought to advance the success of the trade itself is uncertain, and to a large degree it seems they functioned to enhance the social status of their members. Like most institutions in the ancient world, they were closely tied to religious devotion, with participation in the guild requiring devotion to the guild's patron god or goddess. While traditional deities were often the objects of a guild's devotion, they could incorporate devotion to Roma or the Roman emperor. This devotion could come through blending the imperial cult with the cult of the traditional deities (see discussion above) or through explicit commitment of the guild to an expression of imperial cult. Thus, through these guilds Rome was able to further intertwine one's socioeconomic advancement with imperial devotion.

In sum, one's response to the means by which Rome cultivated imperial devotion was not optional. Failure to participate in the various expressions of imperial cult or properly honor the emperor in one's home could be perceived as a sign of disloyalty or dangerous sedition. If brought to the attention of the powerful, such failures could result in punishments, including imprisonment, exile, or even execution.[5]

---

5. Some emperors were more sensitive to loyalty concerns than others, and thus, punishments in response to perceived disloyalty might vary in frequency and severity depending on the emperor in power. Yet, a certain level of loyalty and devotion to Rome would have been expected

Forms of Roman Imperial Devotion

Numerous means of imperial devotion have been noted above, but here they will be outlined more fully. The most obvious expression of imperial devotion came in the form of Roman imperial cults. Temples and altars to the goddess Roma and both living and dead emperors were ubiquitous throughout the empire. Each temple had its own set of priests and officiants, usually composed of private citizens who all had different levels of honor and responsibility (e.g., some to pay for upkeep, some to provide sacrifices, some to put on games and festivals, some to perform regular rites, some to sing hymns). In these temples, sacrifices, prayers, and hymns were offered as signs of devotion to Rome and the imperial family. These temples also provided space for elites to hold meals or games and festivals for the entire city. As noted above, in addition to cultic worship offered to Rome in these dedicated temples, such worship was also offered to Rome through traditional cults of traditional deities. Beyond the temples, devotion to Rome was also expressed through independent altars and shrines. In many Roman cities, one would find public shrines or altars to the emperor's *genius*, or the living emperor himself. At these shrines and altars, some of which stood at the intersection of two city streets, people could express their devotion by offering incense or libations of wine.

People also expressed imperial devotion through inscriptions that could be found throughout Roman cities. Two such inscriptions to Augustus are illustrative. The first, found in the city of Olympia, praises him for his restoration of the cities of Asia Minor: "The Emperor Caesar, son of God, god *Sabastos* has by his benefaction to all people outdone even the Olympian gods" (*IOlympia* 53 [trans. Hardin 2008, 28]). The second comes

---

by all Roman emperors, and failure to meet such expectations would have had consequences. For discussion, see Strait 2019, 138–43.

from the city of Priene but would have been replicated throughout the cities of Asia Minor. The inscription reflects the successful efforts of the cities of Asia Minor to establish Augustus's birthday as the first day of the calendar year (a significant act of imperial devotion in its own right). A sampling of this inscription and the imperial devotion expressed in it follows:

> Since providence, which has ordered all things and is deeply interested in our life, has set in most perfect order by giving us Augustus whom she filled with virtue that he might benefit humankind, sending him as a savior, both for us and for our descendants, that he might end war and arrange all things, and since he, Caesar, by his appearance excelled even our anticipations, surpassing all previous benefactors, and not even leaving to posterity any hope of surpassing what he has done, and since the birthday of the god Augustus was the beginning of the good tidings for the world that came by reason of him. (*OGIS* 458 [trans. Evans 2000, 69])

Finally, people expressed private devotion. As noted above, some took oaths of allegiance to the Roman emperor and his family. Private homes often had shrines devoted to the goddess Roma or the emperor, where inhabitants could offer incense and libations of wine. Evidence also shows that before meals, the host would pour out a libation of wine to the Roman emperor while saying a prayer to him (see Gradel 2002, 207–21).

Roman Imperial Devotion and the Early Christian Movement

Rome's grand imperial narrative and the imperial devotion it demanded were significant components of the ancient Mediterranean matrix from which early Christianity emerged. This Roman narrative stood in sharp contrast to the narrative of early Christians, a narrative that proclaimed an entirely different Lord

and empire. Thus, every early Christian and expression of Christian faith would have had to negotiate the realities of imperial devotion required by Rome's narrative. While there was likely diversity in Christian attitudes regarding participation in such devotion, it is probable that most Christians would have regarded full participation as unacceptable. Religious devotion could be granted only to the creator God and his Messiah, Jesus. As a result, most Christians would adopt the Jewish approach to imperial devotion. While Jews offered prayers and sacrifices to their God *on behalf of* Rome and its emperor, they refused to offer anything resembling cultic worship *to* Roma or a Roman emperor. This Jewish refusal was permitted by Rome as a special dispensation for the Jews and the Jews alone. All other inhabitants of Rome's empire were expected to show their faithfulness to Rome and its divinely ordained imperium. Christians fell under this special dispensation as long as Rome perceived them as Jews. Whenever and wherever Christians were distinguished from Jews, however (a problem that likely faced many Gentile converts to the Christian movement), no dispensation was granted to those Christians. In such situations, Christians experienced social and political pressure to participate in the various forms of imperial devotion. These pressures and the ways that Christians negotiated them can be found throughout the New Testament. Some examples are obvious and easily discernible, such as Paul's teaching on Christian engagement with the government in Romans 13 or Revelation's prophetic visualization of Rome's destruction (Rev. 18). Other examples are more subtle, particularly to the modern reader, such as Paul's claim that destruction will fall quickly on those who proclaim "peace and security" (1 Thess. 5:3), a common mantra of Rome's narrative that proclaimed its promised blessings to the faithful. Might Mark's account of Jesus defeating a legion of demons have Roman imperial implications (Mark 5:1–20)?

Might Luke's placement of Jesus's birth during the Augustan census reflect a clash between competing imperial narratives? Awareness of Rome's imperial narrative and the devotion it required offers a crucial context for understanding the early Christian movement and the writings of the New Testament that it produced.[6]

Works Cited

Basore, John W. 1928. *Seneca: Moral Essays.* Vol. 1. LCL 214. London: William Heinemann.

Evans, C. A. 2000. "Mark's Incipit and the Priene Calendar Inscription: From Jewish Gospel to Greco-Roman Gospel." *Journal of Greco-Roman Christianity and Judaism* 1: 67–81.

Fears, J. R. 1981. "Theology of Victory at Rome: Approaches and Problems." *ANRW* 2.17.2: 736–826.

Gleason, M. W. 2006. "Greek Cities under Roman Rule." In *A Companion to the Roman Empire*, edited by D. S. Potter, 228–49. Malden, MA: Blackwell.

Gradel, Ittai. 2002. *Emperor Worship and Roman Religion.* Oxford Classical Monographs. Oxford: Oxford University Press.

Greenwood, L. H. G., trans. 1928. *Cicero: The Verrine Orations.* Vol. 1. LCL 221. Cambridge, MA: Harvard University Press.

Hardin, Justin K. 2008. *Galatians and the Imperial Cult.* WUNT 2/237. Tübingen: Mohr Siebeck.

Lind, L. R. 1972. "Concept, Action, and Character: Reason for Rome's Greatness." *Transactions and Proceedings of the American Philological Association* 103: 235–83.

Parkin, T., and A. Pomeroy. 2007. *Roman Social History: A Sourcebook.* London: Routledge.

Rackham, H., trans. 1933. *Cicero: On the Nature of the Gods, Academics.* LCL 268. Cambridge, MA: Harvard University Press.

Rudd, Niall, trans. 2004. *Horace: The Odes and Epodes.* LCL 33. Cambridge, MA: Harvard University Press.

Shipley, Frederick W., trans. 1924. *Velleius Paterculus: Res Gestae Divi Augusti.* LCL 152. Cambridge, MA: Harvard University Press.

Strait, D. J. 2019. *Hidden Criticism of the Angry Tyrant in Early Judaism and the Acts of the Apostles.* New York: Lexington Books / Fortress Academic.

Watts, N. H., trans. 1923. *Cicero: Pro Archia, Post Reditum in Senatu, Post Reditum ad Quirites, De Domo Sua, De Haruspicum Responsis, Pro Plancio.* LCL 158. Cambridge, MA: Harvard University Press.

Winn, Adam, ed. 2016. *An Introduction to Empire in the New Testament.* RBS 84. Atlanta: SBL Press.

---

6. For an introduction to the way in which the writings of the New Testament engage and negotiate Roman imperial realities, see Winn 2016.

41

Persecution, Suffering, and Martyrdom

Dorothea H. Bertschmann

In 197 CE the Christian apologist Tertullian wrote: "If the Tiber rises as high as the city walls, if the Nile does not send its waters up over the fields, if the heavens give no rain, if there is an earthquake, if there is famine or pestilence, straightway the cry is, 'Away with the Christians to the lion!'" (Tertullian, *Apol.* 40 [trans. Thelwall 1926, 47]).

Tertullian's words reflect a time when the church took shape in the crucible of opposition and persecution prior to the emperor Constantine's policy of toleration of the Christian church (ca. 313 CE). Scholars disagree on the severity and frequency of state-led persecution.[1] The experience of persecution was likely local, sporadic, and spontaneous with the exception of more-centralized waves during the reigns of Decius in the third century CE and Diocletian in the early fourth century CE.[2]

Suffering as persecution is already an important topic in the New Testament, though most of its writings were penned some time before Christians perished in gruesome public spectacles, such as the waves of persecution in the third and fourth centuries (e.g., under the emperors Decius and Diocletian). The first bout of persecution under the emperor Nero in the mid-sixties only affected the Christians in Rome. The oldest document in the New Testament, 1 Thessalonians (ca. 49–51 CE), mentions "tribulation" or "pressure" (*thlipsis*) in 1:6 and 3:3–4. Paul frequently talks about his manifold sufferings in his role as apostle to the Gentiles, most prominently in his lists of sufferings in 2 Corinthians 11:23–33.

The book of Acts, which narrates the fate of the two first Christian martyrs, Stephen (6:8–7:60) and James (12:1–2), and which tells us of the manifold sufferings of Paul on his mission trips, ends on a tantalizing note of suspense: we see Paul in Rome under house arrest (28:30–31) but learn nothing of his fate. Acts

---

1. For the classic view of frequent and intense state persecutions of Christians *qua* Christians, see Frend 2008. Moss 2013 is representative of a revisionist and minimalist approach. For a balanced evaluation, see Middleton 2021.

2. For concise introductions to the phenomenon of martyrdom in different religious contexts, see Mitchell

2012; Middleton 2011. For a theological-biblical account from the majority world, see Lee 2022.

does not narrate the emperor Nero's brutal lashing out at Roman Christians in 64 CE when Paul lost his life, according to later tradition. Even Revelation, which expects near-universal martyrdom for the believers, does not report many concrete killings.[3]

What, then, was the nature of persecution? Jesus repeatedly warns his disciples of being dragged before courts and kings (Mark 13:9 parr.) and of being hated by all (13:13 parr.). We hear of imprisonments (e.g., Acts 8:3; 12:3; Phil. 1:13; Col. 4:18; Philem. 1; Heb. 13:3), beatings and floggings (e.g., Acts 5:40; 2 Cor. 11:23–25), and the confiscation of goods (Heb. 10:34). Even where there was no physical violence involved, varying degrees of social shunning and ostracizing could quickly lead to economic hardship.[4] The early followers of Jesus suffered at the hands of both Jewish and "pagan" neighbors (1 Thess. 2:14). But what caused the hostility?

From a Jewish perspective, followers of Jesus were watering down the Torah, generating a conflict already visible in Jesus's interactions with the Pharisees and later in Paul's clashes with Jerusalem and diaspora Jews. Acts describes how the Roman authorities would intervene during such clashes, sometimes benevolently, sometimes more heavy-handedly, though not with a view to singling out Christians *qua* Christians. Rather, such interventions were intended to uphold law and order (e.g., Acts 21:35). From a pagan perspective, the opting out of the polytheistic fabric of society, which included forms of emperor worship, could undermine the pillars of society. Later, Christians were accused of "atheism" by their pagan neighbors for the startling move of abandoning the traditional gods, on whose benevolence the welfare of a city depended (see Mart. Pol. 3.2). Tacitus accused Christians of *odium humani generis*, of "hatred of the human race" (Tacitus, *Ann.* 15.44). Around 110 CE, Pliny the Younger, governor of an Eastern province, was concerned that Christians would refuse even simple gestures of loyalty such as offering sacrifices and worship to the image of the emperor (Pliny, *Ep.* 10.96). Overall, Christ believers were a new religion with no "natural allies" (Middleton 2011, 31). This made them an ideal group for singling out and scapegoating.

In the face of such hostility, some robust theological reflection and reasoning was needed in order to make sense of suffering and persecution, whatever the external reasons. In doing so, the earliest believers in Christ could build on motifs and theological *topoi* already expressed in the Hebrew Bible and greatly elaborated on in Jewish writings to narrate and evaluate a period of fierce persecution during the Seleucid reign in the second century BCE.

In the following sections I shall look into this kind of theological meaning-making and its roots in the beginnings of Jewish and Christian martyrology, mostly focusing on 2 and 4 Maccabees. I shall distinguish the (intimately related) aspects of the *cause* of the suffering from its *purpose* and *transformation* in God's greater economy.

The Cause of Suffering "for" and "on behalf of" God

In the Hebrew Bible suffering is regularly framed as divine punishment. Especially in what scholars call the Deuteronomistic history, collective and individual sufferings, not least the disaster of exile, are seen as a direct result of human disobedience and sin.[5] Within the

---

3. We see "the souls of those who had been slaughtered" under the altar (Rev. 6:9) and the whore of Babylon who is "drunk with the blood of the saints and the blood of the witnesses to Jesus" (17:6) but learn of only one named martyr (Antipas in 2:13).

4. See Oakes's imaginative and informed reconstruction of such persecution scenarios in Oakes 2001, 89–90.

5. This is aptly summed up in passages such as Deut. 30:11–20.

framework of the covenant, the human partner is held to account and punished if necessary. Later writings reflect on such punishments as having a disciplinary quality with the goal of restoration, not destruction (cf. Wis. 11:9–10).

In the Psalms we encounter the voice of the "righteous sufferer," who cries out to God in great distress, protesting their innocence. The cry for relief from what is undeserved suffering can take on a note of "suffering for God," such as, "for your sake . . . I have borne reproach" (Ps. 69:7) or "because of you we are being killed all day long" (44:22). Many of the preexilic prophets are portrayed as suffering persecution from evil kings and religious leaders, a tradition well known to New Testament writers (e.g., Luke 11:47; 1 Thess. 2:15). Thus, different perspectives on human suffering stand side by side in the Hebrew Bible, planting important seeds for understanding suffering as a badge of righteousness.

This notion of suffering on behalf of God's cause rises to new intensity and prominence during the time of the Maccabean uprising in the mid-second century BCE. The first and second books of Maccabees describe how embracing the process of Hellenization by some leading, assimilating Jews in Jerusalem triggers God's judgment in the form of a military attack on the city by the Seleucid king Antiochus IV Epiphanes (cf. 1 Macc. 1:20–23; 2 Macc. 4:11–17). A ruthless campaign of forced Hellenization follows.[6] The pagan overlord not only brings Hellenistic culture to the heart of the holy city of Jerusalem but also plunders and defiles the temple in 167 BCE (1 Macc. 1:20–23; 2 Macc. 5:15–21). As part of the campaign, circumcision, Sabbath, and kosher eating are outlawed, and the population has to sacrifice to pagan deities in order to show their loyalty

(1 Macc. 1:41–64; 2 Macc. 6:1–11; 4 Macc. 4:15–26).

The resistance takes two forms: one military and one martyrological. Under the leadership of the priest Mattathias and his five sons, especially Judas Maccabeus (1 Macc. 1:1–5), the rebels in Judea take up arms and gain some military victories, which result in the rededication of the temple (1 Macc. 4; 2 Macc. 10). Others pay a heavy price for their refusal to break the Torah, in particular its food taboos. Second Maccabees relates the story of an old scribe, Eleazar, who would rather endure torture and death than taste pork (2 Macc. 6:18–31). Straight after that incident we hear of another martyrdom, where seven brothers are gruesomely tortured to death for a similar refusal, fired up by their mother. Fourth Maccabees elaborates the story of their martyrdom. It is "the oldest Jewish text which is devoted to martyrdom in its entirety" (van Henten 1997, 58)[7] and is more a philosophical treatise than history, showing how "devout reason is sovereign over the emotions" (4 Macc. 1:1). The authors stress that this kind of suffering is "for the sake of God's laws" and "because of their allegiance to God." The Maccabean martyrs are dying "for his laws" (2 Macc. 7:9; cf. 6:28; 7:37), "because of his laws" (7:11), and "for the sake of his laws" (7:23; cf. 4 Macc. 6:27, 30), or "for the sake of virtue" (4 Macc. 7:22). In a time of crisis and all-pervasive evil, suffering and death are seen as a badge of honor, not a sign of divine displeasure; that is, it is a consequence and corollary of their faithfulness to God.

Martyrdom as Hidden Power: Purpose

Suffering for the right reason is nothing to be ashamed of but fulfills an important purpose. This purpose can be summed up as bearing

---

6. Unlike 1 Maccabees, 2 Maccabees was likely written in Greek possibly shortly after the events it describes around 124 BCE (see van Henten 1997, 17–57).

7. The work is commonly thought to have been written around 100 CE in Asia Minor.

witness, which is the original meaning of the Greek word *martys* (witness) or *martyria* (testimony). The term has its *Sitz im Leben* in a courtroom situation, where the testimony of trusted witnesses helps to establish the guilt or innocence of the accused and more broadly to establish the reliability or factuality of certain events. In a secondary meaning, witnesses can testify to the strength of their own convictions no matter what the consequences are. Those who stand firm in this way become an embodiment of the truth they embrace by being unyielding to the end.[8]

The use of *martys* as a technical term for somebody who suffers a cruel death rather than abandoning their convictions is largely absent from 2 and 4 Maccabees. But the concept is fully spelled out and serves as a template in later postbiblical Christian martyr texts.[9]

The Maccabean martyrs refuse to heed a royal decree that would compromise their faith even if the consequence is a brutal death. Before their death they interpret their deeds in dialogues with the evil king, especially in 4 Maccabees. Contrary to what meets the eye, the martyrs are the stronger party. Their deaths are *exemplary* and *noble* and even have *atoning* power. The old scribe Ezra is offered an escape from torture by only pretending to eat unclean food (2 Macc. 6:21–22). He straightaway turns this proposal down. He needs to "leave to the young a noble *example* of how to die a good death willingly and nobly for the revered and holy laws" (6:28).

The goal of martyrdom is therefore not simply about preserving one's personal integrity but also about being truthful in the eyes of all who are watching, both friend and foe.[10] This public and visual aspect of martyrdom is cru-

cial, just like the element of freedom.[11] The martyrs always have a choice of action presented to them, though from their perspective it is, by default, an impossible choice. This gives the narrative an element of suspense. After six brothers have been butchered to death, the seventh and youngest is offered limitless wealth and power by the king but coldly turns it down (2 Macc. 7:24; 4 Macc. 12:3–5). The martyrs thus die freely, compelled by their loyalty to the ancestral traditions alone, not by the hand of the king. Their example of loyal endurance and steadfast courage brings them into close proximity to the many tales of *noble and heroic deaths* in the Greco-Roman world. Like Socrates, they refuse to betray their convictions, and as in Iphigeneia's case, their deaths are interpreted as a sacrifice, which changes the course of history.[12]

The Maccabean martyrs act as *representatives* of their people and stand in solidarity with them. The narrator of 2 Maccabees repeatedly assures the readers that though terrible calamities have befallen the nation on account of its sins, "these punishments were designed not to destroy but to discipline our people" (2 Macc. 6:12; cf. 5:17). As a collective, Israel had betrayed God and was being duly punished. The martyrs' faithfulness not only contrasted with this mass apostasy but also redressed the balance, in the eyes both of the wider world and of God. The martyrs accepted their suffering as a consequence of human sin in solidarity with the wider people. As the sixth brother explains: "For we are suffering these things on our own account, because of our sins against our own God" (2 Macc. 7:18; similar 7:32). Moreover, they intercede for the disobedient people by asking God to credit their faithfulness to the wider people and "through me and my brothers to bring to an end the

8. For a thorough analysis of the terminology prior to and within the New Testament, see Trites 1977.

9. See the Martyrdom of Polycarp with its dialogue between the martyr and the proconsul in chaps. 9–12.

10. Even the torturers marvel at the courage and endurance of the seven brothers (4 Macc. 1:11).

11. The fifth brother thanks the tyrant for "an opportunity to show our endurance for the law" (4 Macc. 11:12).

12. For a concise overview with samples from sources, see van Henten and Avemarie 2002, 9–41.

wrath of the Almighty that has justly fallen on our whole nation" (4 Macc. 7:38). By far the most striking instance is found in 4 Maccabees, where Eleazar prays: "Be merciful to your people, and let our punishment suffice for them. Make my blood their purification, and take my life in exchange for theirs" (6:28–29). This is further emphasized by the frequent use of cultic language—the martyrs are bringing the ultimate sacrifice of their own bodies in a time when the temple has been desecrated and the cult has come to a halt (e.g., 17:22).

Victory and Vindication: Transformation

Throughout the showdown between the evil king and the seven brothers, the martyrs in 4 Maccabees show themselves to be invincible, because the king in all his might is unable to make them obey his commandment: "By their endurance they conquered the tyrant" (4 Macc. 1:11). The scribe Eleazar says it with great pathos: "You may tyrannize the ungodly, but you shall not dominate my religious principles, either by words or through deeds" (5:38; cf. 8:2). The martyrs are invincible, *aniketoi* (9:18; similarly in 11:21, 27).

Though this show of strength and endurance validates the suffering of the martyrs, they are further spurred on by the hope of vindication beyond the grave. The second of the seven brothers says to the king, "You accursed wretch, you dismiss us from this present life, but the King of the universe will raise us up to an everlasting renewal of life, because we have died for his laws" (2 Macc. 7:9). His brothers express similar hopes of having their limbs restored (7:11) and enjoying the "resurrection to life" (7:14). The mother of the seven expresses the fervent hope that the God who created her sons in her womb will restore them after their voluntary death (7:23, 29). A similar resurrection hope, which is not expressed with this clarity in the Hebrew Bible apart from Daniel 12:2, motivates Razis in his dramatic suicide to

escape the hands of his pagan enemies (2 Macc. 14:46).[13]

The martyrs shall "live to God" (4 Macc. 16:25) and be in heaven (17:5). The prize for endurance is "immortality [*aphtharsia*] in endless life" (17:12). The hope of vindication of the righteous goes hand in hand with the expectation of the punishment of the wicked, who will get their just deserts.[14] In 2 Maccabees 9 we learn about how Antiochus IV is at last visited by God's judgment and suffers torments that match the pain he inflicted on others. His late (and in his case futile) acknowledgment of the God of Israel (9:13–18) is an important *topos* in persecution literature.[15] It is narrated in the book of Daniel, which tells the story of four steadfast Hebrew youths, Hananiah, Mischael, Azariah and Daniel, set at the time of the Babylonian exile.[16] They refuse to follow a law that corrupts their religious identity and are willing to pay the ultimate price. Their miraculous rescue from death in the fiery furnace or the lions' den (Dan. 3 and 6) brings about a change of heart in the king (3:28–30; 6:25–28).

Martyrdoms are not least seen as a kind of irresistible proclamation of or even propaganda for the God of the martyrs. Though the Maccabean martyrs die, their deaths have immediate and positive consequences by enabling a series of military victories of Judas Maccabeus (2 Macc. 8). Their sacrifice has led to reconciliation with God (5:20) and the restoration of the Jewish nation. The author of 4 Maccabees dwells a lot less on the political consequences of the martyrdoms but calls their

13. On suicide and its overlap with martyrdom, see Droge and Tabor 1992.
14. A neat summary is in 4 Macc. 9:8–9: the martyrs "shall be with God," whereas the tyrant will undergo "eternal torment by fire." See also 2 Macc. 9:24b–25, 32; 12:11–18; and many more.
15. Cf. a similar story about Heliodorus's conversion in 2 Macc. 3:35–40.
16. The stories of these four Hebrew youths are referenced in, e.g., 4 Macc. 16:21.

deaths an "atoning sacrifice" (*hilastērion*) that purifies the land (17:22).

Next to sacrificial language we find athletic metaphors in the martyrdom stories in 2 and 4 Maccabees: Eleazar is gasping and sweating under torture "like a noble athlete" and thus victorious (4 Macc. 6:10–11). Theirs is a struggle (*agōn*) in the "arena of sufferings" (11:20; see also 12:14; 17:11–12). Joy and gladness accompany the suffering because it is a joy coming from virtue (9:31; cf. 10:20). Eleazar says with his dying breath, "I am enduring terrible sufferings in my body under this beating, but in my soul I am glad to suffer these things because I fear him" (2 Macc. 6:30).

Echoes of Martyrdom Literature in the New Testament

The Maccabean martyrs have an important afterlife in the Christian church, venerated as saints and prototypes of the Christian martyrs. The "playbook" of their deaths is repeated over time with Christian believers boldly resisting an imperial order even if the consequence is a violent death. In contrast, the New Testament does not yet explicitly reference these texts or people but shares and develops a number of motifs and *topoi*.

Christian suffering of persecution is qualified, too, as "suffering on behalf" (*dia* or *heneka*), though it is for the sake of or because of Christ, not the law (e.g., Matt. 5:10; John 15:20–21; 2 Cor. 4:11). The sufferings Christians endure are part of their discipleship and its cost. The author of 1 Peter 4:16 reassures its readers that suffering *hōs Christianos* (as a Christian), as opposed to suffering for a crime, carries no shame. Christian suffering is suffering dishonor "for the sake of [*hyper*] the name," as Luke puts it in Acts 5:41.

Though no atoning power is ascribed to the believers' suffering, they are bearing witness to the truth in the footsteps of Jesus, who stood firm during his trial and willingly gave his life.

In particular, the Gospel of John emphasizes the witness character of Jesus's entire ministry (e.g., 18:37) and the uncoerced nature of Jesus's death: "No one takes [my life] from me, but I lay it down of my own accord" (10:18).

In Acts, the apostles are commissioned to be Jesus's witnesses to the ends of the earth (1:8). The apostolic witness is understood in its original sense as an eyewitness to crucial events, in this case Jesus's resurrection. This witness can involve being on trial before Jewish and Gentile authorities, such as in Stephen's case (Acts 7). When Paul speaks of how "the blood of your witness [*martys*] Stephen was shed" (22:20), the theological-juridical concept of *martys* is for the first time combined with the violent end of such a witness. The aspects of being a witness and suffering are further drawn together in the book of Revelation, where the Christians are called to patient endurance for the testimony (*martyria*) of Jesus (Rev. 1:9), who is himself the "faithful and true witness [*martys*]" (3:14).

Christian suffering is suffering in the footsteps of Jesus, following his example (1 Pet. 2:21–23). It means carrying one's cross (cf. Matt. 16:24) and suffering in communion with Jesus (Rom. 8:17). This christological configuration of the martyrdom *topoi* puts the emphasis on assurance: Christ has already overcome suffering and death and will share his present glory with those who presently suffer for him and in him. If anything, notions of joy and victory intensify and dominate the picture, though the cry for vengeance and punishment of the oppressors has not completely disappeared.[17]

Those who suffer for the sake of righteousness are called blessed (Matt. 5:10). Suffering for Christ is a gracious gift (Phil. 1:29),

---

17. Cf. Rev. 6:9–10, where the martyrs under the "souls of those who had been slaughtered . . . for the testimony they had given" cry out with a loud voice: "How long will it be before you judge and avenge our blood?" See also 2 Thess. 1:8–9.

and Paul rejoices even as he is in chains (Phil. 4:4), just as the apostles rejoice because they have been deemed worthy to suffer dishonor for the sake of the name (Acts 5:41). There is a struggle (*agōn*) to be fought (Phil. 1:30) and a race to be completed (Phil. 3:13–14)—but the prize is the crown of life (James 1:12; Rev. 2:10). Paul sounds the highest note of victorious reassurance in his all-encompassing enemy taunt: "We are more than conquerors [*hypernikōmen*] through him who loved us" (Rom. 8:37).

Works Cited

Droge, A. J., and J. D. Tabor. 1992. *A Noble Death: Suicide and Martyrdom among Christians and Jews in Antiquity*. San Francisco: HarperSanFrancisco.

Frend, W. H. 2008. *Martyrdom and Persecution in the Early Church*. Cambridge: James Clarke. Originally published 1965.

Lee, Ch.-Ch. 2022. *When Christians Face Persecution: Theological Perspectives from the New Testament*. London: Apollos.

Middleton, P. 2011. *Martyrdom: A Guide for the Perplexed*. London: T&T Clark.

———. 2021. "Were the Early Christians Really Persecuted?" In *Tolerance, Intolerance and Recognition in Early Christianity and Early Judaism*, edited by O. Lehtipuu and M. Labahn, 229–50. Early Christianity in the Roman World 2. Amsterdam: Amsterdam University Press.

Mitchell, J. 2012. *Martyrdom: A Very Short Introduction*. Oxford: Oxford University Press.

Moss, C. R. 2013. *The Myth of Persecution: How Early Christians Invented a Story of Martyrdom*. New York: HarperOne.

Oakes, P. 2001. *Philippians: From People to Letter*. SNTSMS 110. Cambridge: Cambridge University Press.

Thelwall, S., trans. 1926. "The Apology." In *Ante-Nicene Fathers*. Vol. 3, *Latin Christianity: Its Founder, Tertullian*, edited by A. Roberts, J. Donaldson, and A. C. Coxe, 17–60. New York: Charles Scribner's Sons.

Trites, A. A. 1977. *The New Testament Concept of Witness*. SNTSMS 31. Cambridge: Cambridge University Press.

van Henten, J. W. 1997. *The Maccabean Martyrs as Saviours of the Jewish People: A Study of 2 & 4 Maccabees*. Leiden: Brill.

van Henten, J. W., and F. Avemarie. 2002. *Martyrdom and Noble Death: Selected Texts from Graeco-Roman, Jewish and Christian Antiquity*. New York: Routledge.

42

Mystery Cults

JAN N. BREMMER

Until about the last decades of the twentieth century, it was thought that at the time of the New Testament there was a strong competition between emerging Christianity and the so-called mystery religions, especially the one of Mithras (Lannoy and Praet 2023). It was Walter Burkert (1931–2015), the leading expert of Greek religion of the time, who persuasively argued in a small book on the mysteries (Burkert 1987) that these latter were not religions but normal cults, that they were more directed to this life than to the one hereafter, and that they were no competition for Christianity. These insights, which were new at the time, have since been generally accepted and will be the starting point for this contribution.

In modern parlance, "mysteries" always suggests something mysterious, a puzzle to be solved or a detective story. That was not quite how the term came into being. Originally, *Mystēria*, "Mysteries," was the name of a local festival in Eleusis, where an important sanctuary of the goddess Demeter and her daughter Kore (Persephone) was located. As is normal with other Greek festivals, such as the Anthesteria or Thesmophoria, the name appears in the plural, and the Romans, consequently, translated it as *Initia*, which eventually gave rise to the English word "initiation," just as the Roman translation *mysterium* gave rise to "mystery." Fairly soon other terms also became current for the festival. Given that the ritual of the Eleusinian Mysteries led up to a kind of climax, Greek *telos*, it is perhaps not surprising that from the fifth century BCE onward we also find a more generic term, *teletē*, "initiation, mystery cult," and even *orgia*, which gave rise to our "orgy" but in antiquity meant something like "secret rites" and was used first in connection with the Eleusinian Mysteries.[1]

According to Burkert, the mysteries were "initiation rituals of a voluntary, personal, and secret character that aimed at a change of mind through experience of the sacred" (1987, 11).

---

1. For all evidence on the Eleusinian, Samothracian (§1), Orphic-Bacchic (§2), Mithraic, and Dionysiac mysteries (§3), see Bremmer 2014, with very full primary and secondary sources. I limit, therefore, my references mostly to literature that has appeared later or that I had overlooked.

Yet the postulated change of mind is hard to prove, and we have simply no idea of the impact of the mysteries on the individual participants, the *mystai*. We have even less an idea of the impact of the mysteries on participants because, unlike most civic festivals, the mysteries were open to everybody at this time: locals and strangers (as long as they could speak Greek), free and slave, men and women.

In this brief overview, it is of course impossible to give a detailed survey of the Greek mysteries. I will not touch on mysteries that became more important from the later decades of the second century CE onward, such as those of Isis, Attis, and Cybele, but will limit myself here to the most prominent ones, those of Eleusis and Samothrace, then the Bacchic and Orphic ones as well as those of the Roman Empire, before coming to the New Testament and early Christianity.

Prototypical Mysteries

It is not easy to say when the mysteries started to emerge in Greece, but the phenomenon must have occurred pretty early, as we hear of quite a few in Arcadia and the rest of the Peloponnese (Graf 2003), areas that were more conservative in religious respect than the larger cities of the Greek world, be it on the mainland or in Ionia and Southern Italy. However, our information about these other ones is nearly always quite late and often mentioned first by the second-century CE traveler Pausanias. Yet the overall picture strongly suggests that mysteries were an ancient institution.

However many there were, there can be no doubt that the most famous and respected mysteries were those of Eleusis, whose fame will have been helped by the proximity to Athens and their being praised in the *Homeric Hymn to Demeter* (7th/6th c. BCE). There were various stages preceding the initiation, which are, however, rather poorly documented (Patera 2020). The yearly initiation started in the middle of September with the coming together of the crowd of prospective initiates and their accompanying friends in the agora of Athens, where they heard the pronunciation that excluded from participation those who were not Greek or who had blood on their hands. The next day they all went to the sea to purify themselves and their sacrificial victims, as they had to bring everything necessary for the initiation themselves—which must have prevented the very poor from joining in. After a rest of three days, the participants went to Eleusis, which is roughly fifteen miles from Athens, in a long procession; in its heyday about three thousand people may have participated. At the front, there were the Eleusinian dignitaries dressed in full regalia, followed by the priestesses with the sacred objects and, in later times, the ephebes, the Athenian male youths. After them, there must have been an endless stream of people, some in coaches but most of them on foot, singing and dancing in the hot sun. It took a day before they finally reached the sanctuary of the goddesses. The night fell early, and the flickering of thousands of torches must have resulted in a kind of psychedelic experience.

The next day, sometime after sunset, the prospective initiates gathered in the *telestērion*, a square or rectangular building, which contained a kind of chapel, the *anaktoron/anaktora*, in its center. It must have been part of the specific character of the mysteries that people gathered indoors for this religious ritual, as normally the interior of a temple was closed to the public and the main activities took place at the altar in front of a temple. The initiation proper was divided into two stages, taking place over two consecutive nights. The first stage seems to have centered on the kidnapping of Persephone by Hades. The main roles must have been acted out by the Eleusinian clergy, but we cannot say anything about its actual performance. However, we know that the initiates went out to look for the goddess, and when she was found, although we have no idea how, the ritual came to an end with "rejoicing and brandishing of torches," as the Christian author Lactantius (*Epit.* 38.7) tells us.[2] As the recovery of Demeter's daughter in the *Homeric Hymn* ends the drought and allows again the fertility of the land, the original meaning of this stage may well have been a connection with agricultural wealth.

The second stage, called *epopteia*, literally "viewing," which was performed the second night, was accessible only to those who had passed through the first stage in previous years. Most of our information derives from Christian authors who may or may not have tinkered with our evidence. However, not all our information is from Christian sources, and the comparison with mysteries that were clearly modeled on those of Eleusis, those of Isis (Bremmer 2014, 110–25), and those designed by Alexander of Abunoteichos (Bremmer 2014, 15, 155) enable us to be relatively certain in our reconstruction.[3] It is clear that there were allusions or performances of a sexual nature, singing of hymns, and terrifying of the audience by the appearance or suggestion of a monster. The climax came with the display of an ear of corn in a blazing light, while the high priest announced the birth of a boy, probably Ploutos, the personified agricultural wealth.

Was the goal of the Eleusinian mysteries, then, the promotion of fertility? At first sight this seems to be the case, since nothing of the ritual that we know of points to an eschatological aspect, and neither do the many visual representations of, or allusions to, the Eleusinian mysteries on Greek vase paintings (Mitsopoulou 2021; Patera 2021; more in general, Belayche and Massa 2021). Yet literary texts often speak of the eschatological hopes that await the initiates or of the punishments awaiting noninitiates. This difference between the ritual and its interpretation remains difficult to understand. It may well be that in the course of time Eleusinian clergy tried to make the mysteries more attractive by introducing eschatological promises, which presumably were explained to the prospective initiates in the preliminary stages of the initiation. The *Homeric Hymn to Demeter* (lines 480–83) says only this about the afterlife: "Blessed is he of men on earth who has seen them, whereas he that is uninitiated in the rites [. . .] has another lot wasting away in the musty dark." That is all, and the other, older texts with this promise are equally vague. In the end, we must confess that we cannot really lift the veil of these ancient mysteries.

There is one last point to make in this respect. In his dialogues, Plato often uses metaphors or alludes to the *epopteia*, especially in the *Phaedrus* and the *Symposium*. Given his enormous influence on the succeeding centuries, it is no wonder that we find mystery terminology not only in many pagan authors but also in Philo (a somewhat older contemporary of Paul) and Clement of Alexandria (Riedweg 1987; Lang 2015).

After Eleusis, the most famous mysteries in Greece were those of the island of Samothrace (Bremmer 2014, 21–54; Clinton 2017, 2021). We know even less of them than of Eleusis, but a comparison with the Eleusinian mysteries shows that the Samothracians had modeled their own mysteries to a significant extent on those of Eleusis. I will limit myself to noting three important differences. First, unlike Eleusis, there was no single occasion for initiation, as it was possible to become initiated all through the sailing season, from April to November. Second, the main aim of the initiation was to acquire safety at sea, and, third, the main gods were the Kabeiroi, divinities with an Anatolian background.

2. Unless otherwise indicated, all translations are my own.

3. This is insufficiently taken into account by Belayche 2021.

Private Mysteries

The Eleusinian and Samothracian mysteries were firmly established in the local civic cultic scene, but this was different in some other cases. From the late sixth century BCE onward, we start to hear of private religious entrepreneurs who offered initiations into mysteries to private, surely well-to-do clients. Our oldest source is the famous, albeit obscure, philosopher Heraclitus of Ephesus (ca. 500 BCE), mentioned in a well-known fragment (DK B 14). There Heraclitus is shown to threaten various groups (among whom he mentions *mystai*) with a fiery punishment after death; in the same fragment we also find the Greek term *mystēria* for the very first time. At about the same time, at the other end of the Greek world, in southern Italy and Sicily, we witness the emergence of an alternative religious movement, generally called Orphism, which not only promoted a distinct lifestyle with vegetarianism but also offered initiations into private mysteries. Our knowledge of these Orphic-Bacchic mysteries (as they are often called these days) has been greatly increased by several discoveries in the last fifty years, in which we see the prominence of Dionysos Bakchos: (1) the so-called Gold Leaves, some kind of passports to the underworld; (2) the publication of vase paintings from Apulia with representations of the afterlife; and (3) the finding of one of the oldest European books, the Derveni Papyrus (Kotwick 2017; Santamaría Álvarez 2019), containing a commentary on the oldest Orphic theogony, written in Athens at the end of the fifth century BCE (Bremmer 2019).

Orphism as a whole still poses many problems.[4] Yet it is generally agreed that its mysteries promised the initiates a high status in the hereafter and a blissful afterlife, whereas it predicted a really bad one for the nonini-

tiates. This distinction was never so clear in traditional Greek religion, in which the afterlife plays only a relatively minor role. In this respect, Orphism would exert an important influence on early Christianity, as we can see especially in the early apocalypses (Bremmer 2017, 269–345; more generally, Herrero de Jáuregui 2010). Unfortunately, we know little about the performance of the Orphic-Bacchic mysteries. There was ecstatic dancing, and the initiates were crowned with the twigs of a white poplar. More importantly, though, whereas the Eleusinian mysteries were without cognitive contents and stressed the visual aspect, the Orphic mysteries contained, in all probability, the telling of the murder of Dionysos and the incest of Zeus with his daughter, and perhaps also some "information" about the afterlife. It may well be that because of growing literacy in the Greek world the simple display of an ear of corn had become less satisfactory for a number of Greek men and women (the latter being an important part of the Orphic clientele), which led to a more discursive content of the Orphic-Bacchic mysteries.

Mysteries in the Roman Empire

In the first centuries of the Roman Empire, we witness a proliferation of mysteries, although there is a clear distinction between East and West. The most popular ones in the West were the Mithraic mysteries, which were long seen as strong competition for emerging Christianity,[5] and the Dionysiac ones in the East. We will concentrate here on these two types of mysteries.

Regarding Mithras, our earliest testimony is found in the Roman poet Statius's epic *Thebaid* (1.719–20), dating from the late first century

---

4. For the bibliography until 2014, see Bremmer 2014, 55–80; see also Edmonds 2013; Meisner 2018.

5. For sources and bibliography until 2014, see Bremmer 2014, 125–41. Since then, there has been a steady stream of publications on Mithras, but see especially the most recent ones: McCarty and Egri 2020; Bricault and Roy 2021; and Bricault, Veymiers, and Amoroso 2021.

CE, and it still seems plausible, albeit by no means certain, that the cult originated in the Roman capital. From there, it spread extremely fast, and around 100 CE we already find various Mithraea (sanctuaries of Mithras) in Germany, Bulgaria, and Austria. Even though more recent discoveries have also brought to light Mithraea in the East, the main center of the cult was clearly in the West.

A great problem, though, is that almost all of our Mithraic evidence is archaeological, whereas, in contrast, the evidence for the only slightly earlier emerging Christianity is mostly textual. This makes the reconstruction and interpretation of the cult extremely difficult and contested. As Richard Gordon (perhaps the greatest living expert of Mithras) formulates the matter: "If the sheer diversity of the archaeological material suggests a great deal of local, even personal, initiative, interpretation and understanding within a broadly conceived tradition, can the modern scholar actually write that diversity?" (Gordon 2017, 669). The same problem is of course at stake in a description of emerging Christianity. However, as scholars, we cannot do otherwise than to simplify and generalize, even though we have to take into account the local diversities as much as we can.

What can we say when taking into account more recent scholarship? Here we may limit ourselves to five aspects in particular. First, there was no unified cult in which everybody followed the same script. Yet the fact that a Mithraeum is fairly easy to recognize (since they all display a similar structure) suggests that we also should not overemphasize the differences. Second, in the late twentieth century it was fashionable to ascribe deep philosophical ideas to the cult and even all kinds of astronomical speculations. Neither of these fashions has stood the test of time, but it is not impossible that there was "a good deal of intellectual speculation, especially in large cities such as Rome and Alexandria" (Gordon 2017, 669). However, as we have only snippets left of those speculations, there is not much we can say about them. Third, in the last century it was generally believed that in every local cult there was a strict system of initiatory grades. Yet it is now recognized that the further away from Rome, the less individual grades are being heard of, and it seems more likely that the grade system was flexibly applied, depending on local circumstances.

Fourth, it used to be thought that the military constituted the main group of worshipers; more recent studies have shown that the social composition was rather varied, but neither too high nor too low. Participants could not have been poor since the cult required investments of money, but neither were they usually rich: the faunal deposits of some Mithraea have shown that the worshipers dined on small animals like chickens and piglets but not on an expensive bull, as used to be believed on the basis of the bull-stabbing Mithras, the required statue in every Mithraeum. Fifth, like emerging Christianity, there was a certain community that performed the mysteries and functioned also outside the performance of the mysteries. This is an important aspect, as Eleusinian and Samothracian initiates did not constitute a community, and we cannot be certain about the Orphics. However, there was a limit to the size of the community, given the small space of a Mithraeum. Women were excluded, and there was no close cooperation between the various Mithraic communities. These conditions made them more vulnerable to economic and personal hazards, and we can see a decline of Mithraea already in the third century.

In the East (especially in Asia Minor), the Dionysiac mysteries were by far the most popular (Bremmer 2014, 101–9). The early history of these mysteries is very complicated and is still in need of a thorough investigation. It is sufficient to note here that from the second half of the first century CE onward we can see an increasing growth of mysteries and groups of *mystai* that all drew on the

Dionysiac tradition, be it female, male, or just mythical, and with considerable local differences. Unlike the Mithraic ones, the Dionysiac mysteries were of a mixed character, with women often occupying the more religious functions, whereas males dominated the administrative ones. However, about their contents we are not well informed, and it seems likely that there was even more diversity in their rites than is nowadays claimed for the Mithras cult.

The actual initiation often took place in a cave, was biennial, and, as with all mysteries, was secret. Since these Dionysiac mysteries were not as ancient as those of Eleusis and Samothrace, they were not equally respectable. As in Eleusis, with its two-stage initiation, there probably was a similar system, but as in the case of Mithras, it will have depended on the size of the association that performed the mysteries. Typically in Dionysiac mysteries there was dancing, perhaps the performance of a play; there were threatening figures, a winnowing fan, and a phallus, and a snake in the so-called *cista mystica*; and there must have been some kind of grand finale, perhaps the display of a statue of Dionysos. But the place of all these elements in the whole of the Dionysiac mysteries is completely unclear, and we are unable to reconstruct even a plausible order of events. We do know, though, that after their initiation participants became a member of a Dionysiac association, which feasted and dined often in idyllically landscaped grottoes or halls.

Our understanding of the mysteries in the earlier Roman period is made more complicated by the fact that from the second half of the first century CE onward all kinds of cults took on mystery-like aspects. Scholars even speak of a "mysterification" of religion in Asia Minor so that we also find mysteries in connection with the imperial cult (Bremmer 2016). It seems that the local elites used this development to intensify their contacts with the emperor and the imperial administration and thus also to distance themselves from the social layers below them.[6]

The New Testament, Early Christianity, and the Mysteries

Christianity, then, emerged in a world in which the ancient mysteries of Eleusis and Samothrace were seen as highly respectable, but in which there were also many other mystery associations. They were even on the rise in Asia Minor, as we just saw. There can be no doubt, then, that the authors of the early Christian writings will have known of the mysteries and that some might even have been initiated themselves before their conversion. Yet the vocabulary of the mysteries is rare in the New Testament.

The oldest passages occur in the writings of the apostle Paul, who only occasionally uses mystery terminology, but sometimes at key points in his letters (Lang 2015). In 1 Corinthians he uses *mystērion* for his message to them (2:1), and he compares himself and the apostles to the stewards of the *mystēria* (4:1). In Romans (11:25) he even uses *mystērion* for the heart of his message, the key to understanding God's plan. In the later Gospels, the most interesting passage is Mark 4:11, where Jesus says to his disciples about the parable of the sower, "To you has been given the secret [*mystērion*][7] of the kingdom of God, but for those outside, everything comes in parables." Jesus apparently compares his message to a hidden meaning as revealed in the mysteries to the initiated but not to outsiders. Scholars sometimes see a connection with the Hebrew/ Aramaic *raz* (mystery) (Brown 1968), but the

6. For this development, see the fundamental study of Eckhardt and Lepke 2018; note also Belayche, Massa, and Hoffmann 2021.

7. The parallel passages of Matt. 13:11 and Luke 8:10 have the plural, *mystēria*, and are closer to Greek linguistic usage.

association with an in/out group rather points to the Greek mysteries (Riedweg 1987, 89n69; see also Rescio and Walt 2021). Still, as Arthur Darby Nock (1902–63) saw long ago, mystery terminology is as good as absent from the New Testament (Nock 1972; Bremmer 2014, 147–54; Longenecker 2020).

This near absence makes it all the more intriguing that already in the second century Christians started to comment on the supposed similarity of their rituals with those of mysteries. Thus, around 150, Justin Martyr comments in his *First Apology* (66.4) regarding the Eucharist: "This is exactly what the wicked demons have handed down by imitation in the mysteries of Mithras, viz. that bread and a cup of water are placed with certain formulas in the mystic rites of the initiate." Interestingly, Justin clearly presupposes that his readers know of the mysteries of Mithras, even though not that many Mithraea would have existed in Rome at that time. Evidently, Justin was worried by the perceived similarity of the Christian Eucharist and the Mithraic initiation. Half a century later, Tertullian (*Bapt.* 5.1) compares baptism to rites of the mysteries.

Yet it was not only Christians who saw similarities. The pagan philosopher Celsus, who wrote a treatise against the Christians around 180, also compared the Mithraic initiation with the Christian initiation (*teletēn* [see my introduction to this chapter]; Origen, *Cels.* 6.24).[8] Apparently, some Christian Gnostic groups had appropriated elements of the mysteries, especially from the Orphic-Bacchic ones, but this is a scholarly minefield that need not concern us here (Thomassen 2010; Lang 2022). However, when Christianity became better known in the third century and several mysteries started to lose some of their glory, the perceived threat posed by the pagan mysteries began to recede. And after Constantine's rise to power, Christian intellectuals amazingly quickly incorporated some of the terms and elements of the age-old pagan mysteries of Eleusis and Samothrace (Bremmer 2014, 161–64). But that is another story.

Works Cited

Belayche, Nicole. 2021. "Percer la loi du silence? Les 'nuits illuminantes' à Éleusius au iie siècle." In Belayche, Massa, and Hoffmann 2021, 25–53.

Belayche, Nicole, and Francesco Massa, eds. 2021. *Mystery Cults in Visual Representation in Graeco-Roman Antiquity*. Leiden: Brill.

Belayche, Nicole, Francesco Massa, and Philippe Hoffmann, eds. 2021. *Les mystères au IIe siècle de notre ère: un tournant*. Turnhout: Brepols.

Bremmer, Jan N. 2014. *Initiation into the Mysteries of the Ancient World*. Boston: de Gruyter.

———. 2016. "Imperial Mysteries." *Mètis* 14: 21–34

———. 2017. *Maidens, Magic and Martyrs in Early Christianity*. Tübingen: Mohr Siebeck.

———. 2019. "The First Columns of the Derveni Papyrus and Polis Religion." *Eirene* 55: 127–41.

———. 2021. "Early Christianity and the Pagan Mysteries: Esoteric Knowledge?" In *Apocryphal and Esoteric Sources in the Development of Christianity and Judaism*, edited by Igor Dorfmann-Lazarev, 88–104. Leiden: Brill.

Bricault, Laurent, and Philippe Roy. 2021. *Les cultes de Mithra dans l'Empire romain: 550 documents présentés, traduits et commentés*. Toulouse: Presses universitaires du Midi.

Bricault, Laurent, Richard Veymiers, and Nicolas Amoroso, eds. 2021. *The Mystery of Mithras: Exploring the Heart of a Roman Cult*. Morlanwelz: Musée royal de Mariemont.

Brown, Raymond E. 1968. *The Semitic Background of the Term "Mystery" in the New Testament*. Philadelphia: Fortress.

Burkert, Walter. 1987. *Ancient Mystery Cults*. Cambridge, MA: Harvard University Press.

Clinton, Kevin. 2017. "Two Buildings in the Samothracian Sanctuary of the Great Gods." *Journal of Ancient History* 5: 323–56.

———. 2021. "Athens, Samothrace, and the Mysteria of the Samothracian Great Gods." In *Sidelights on Greek Antiquity: Archaeological and Epigraphical Essays in Honour of Vasileios Petrakos*, edited by Konstantinos Kalogeropoulos, Dora Vassilikou, and Michalis Tiverios, 17–44. Boston: de Gruyter.

Eckhardt, Benedikt, and Andrew Lepke. 2018. "Mystai und Musteria im kaiserzeitlichen Westkleinasien." In *Transformationen paganer Religion in der römischen*

8. Bremmer 2021; see also Massa and Belayche 2021.

Kaiserzeit, edited by Michael Blömer and Benedikt Eckhardt, 39–79. Boston: de Gruyter.

Edmonds, Radcliffe G., III. 2013. *Redefining Ancient Orphism: A Study in Greek Religion*. Cambridge: Cambridge University Press.

Gordon, Richard. 2017. "Mithraic Ideas and Reflections." *JRA* 30: 666–69.

Graf, Fritz. 2003. "Lesser Mysteries—No Less Mysterious." In *Greek Mysteries*, edited by Michael B. Cosmopoulos, 242–62. New York: Routledge.

Herrero de Jáuregui, Miguel. 2010. *Orphism and Christianity in Late Antiquity*. New York: de Gruyter.

Kotwick, Mirjam E. 2017. *Der Papyrus von Derveni*. Boston: de Gruyter.

Lang, T. J. 2015. *Mystery and the Making of a Christian Historical Consciousness from Paul to the Second Century*. Boston: de Gruyter.

———. 2022. "Mystery Cults and Christian Associations in Early Alexandrian Theology: The Case of Clement of Alexandria." In *Greco-Roman Associations, Deities, and Early Christianity*, edited by Bruce W. Longenecker, 417–34. Waco: Baylor University Press.

Lannoy, Annelies, and Danny Praet, eds. 2023. *The Christian Mystery: Early Christianity and the Ancient Mystery Cults in the Work of Franz Cumont and in the History of Scholarship*. Stuttgart: Steiner.

Longenecker, Bruce W. 2020. *In Stone and Story: Early Christianity in the Roman World*. Grand Rapids: Baker Academic.

Massa, Francesco, and Nicole Belayche, eds. 2021. *Les philosophes et les mystères dans l'empire romain*. Liège: Presses Universitaires de Liège.

McCarty, Matthew, and Mariana Egri. 2020. *The Archaeology of Mithraism: New Finds and Approaches to Mithras-Worship*. Leuven: Peeters.

Meisner, Dwayne A. 2018. *Orphic Tradition and the Birth of the Gods*. Oxford: Oxford University Press.

Mitsopoulou, Christina. 2021. "Faisceaux et guirlandes, entre iconographie et réalité: Images, gestes, rites et finances éleusiniennes." In *Rituel en image—Images de ritual*, edited by Anne-Françoise Jaccottet-Muller, 133–54. Bern: Peter Lang.

Nock, Arthur D. 1972. "Hellenistic Mysteries and Christian Sacraments." In vol. 2 of *Essays on Religion and the Ancient World*, edited by Zeph Stewart, 791–820. 2 vols. Oxford: Clarendon. Originally published 1952.

Patera, Ioanna. 2020. "Individuals in the Eleusinian Mysteries: Choices and Action." In *Religious Individualisation*, edited by Martin Fuchs, Antje Linkenbach, Martin Mulsow, Bernd-Christian Otto, Rahul Bjørn Parson, and Jörg Rüpke, 679–94. Boston: de Gruyter.

———. 2021. "'Heureux qui possède, parmi les hommes de la terre, la vision de ces Mystères': La vue et les autres sens dans les Mystères d'Éleusis." In *Rituels religieux et sensorialité (Antiquité et Moyen Âge): Parcours de recherche*, edited by Beatrice Caseau Chevallier and Elisabetta Neri, 105–17. Milan: Silvana Editoriale.

Rescio, Mara, and Luigi Walt. 2021. "The Esoteric Rule on Parables: Mark 4:10–12 and Its Earliest Reception History." *Humanitas* 76, Suppl. 1: 86–107.

Riedweg, Christoph. 1987. *Mysterienterminologie bei Platon, Philon und Klemens von Alexandrien*. New York: de Gruyter.

Santamaría Álvarez, Marco Antonio, ed. 2019. *The Derveni Papyrus: Unearthing Ancient Mysteries*. Leiden: Brill.

Thomassen, Einar. 2010. "Orphics and Gnostics." In *Myths, Martyrs and Modernity: Studies in the History of Religions in Honour of Jan N. Bremmer*, edited by Jitse Dijkstra, Justin Kroesen, and Yme Kuiper, 463–73. Leiden: Brill.

43

Moral Transformation and Ethics

MAX J. LEE

Defining Moral Transformation and Its Integrated Processes

Moral transformation is the comprehensive process by which a person's emotions and ethical actions are reoriented from vicious tendencies to virtuous modes of conduct. It is the reconstitution of the self from a condition of vice to virtue. Or, in the language of early Christian discourse, it is the radical change from the old into a new creation.

More than just a *topos* or "commonplace" topic among the variegated ethical traditions of the Mediterranean world, moral transformation functioned during the Greco-Roman era as an organizing principle for ancient ethics.[1] While rival philosophical schools disputed with one another on a range of ethical issues (including the degree to which the mind's rational faculties play a role in moral transformation;

Nussbaum 2009, 81–93; Lee 2020, 66–67), they nevertheless generally agreed that the formation of the virtuous person necessitated three integrated subprocesses: (1) self-mastery over emotions, (2) ethical action and habit, and (3) the cultivation of virtue.

Philosophical systems (whether Platonist, Stoic, Epicurean, or Peripatetic) also took into consideration the contributing role of external agents. Philosophical trainees experienced moral progress with the support of mentors who acted as both frank critics and exemplars. In some systems, God or deities played an important function in a person's moral development by modeling a divine standard of virtue for humanity to imitate (cf. Eph. 5:1–2). Not only do New Testament authors speak on all these subprocesses of moral transformation as individual *topoi*, but some authors (especially the apostle Paul) attempt to offer their own configuration of how self-mastery, ethical action, and virtue formation interrelate with one another to change the person once dominated by sin and

---

1. The key to mapping the moral universe of the Greco-Roman world is to discover the conceptual interconnectedness between various ethical *topoi* (Thom 2003, 569–70). Moral transformation is one such framework of interconnectedness (Lee 2020, 486–87).

vice into a moral agent of godly character (Johnson 2009, 64–78).

Mastering Emotions in the Greco-Roman World and Early Christianity

The first process of moral transformation is the management of emotions, or what philosophers called "self-mastery" (in Greek, *enkrateia*) over the passions of the soul. Emotions or passions (*pathē/pathēmata*) can be dangerous (Diogenes Laertius, *Vit. phil.* 7.110–11; Lee 2020, 184–86)—especially desire (*epithymia*), fear (*phobos*), grief (*lypē*), and pleasure (*hēdonē*). As the name *pathos* implies, emotions were experienced in the Greco-Roman world as powerful motivating forces from which a person "suffered" psychological conflict. Many Euripidean tragedies tell the tale of how heroes and heroines (in the heat of anger, grief, fear, lust, and other passions) made irrational choices that led to their own self-destruction (Nussbaum 2001, 1–22; Lee 2020, 33–37).

The most notorious example was Medea, who, out of vengeance against her former husband, Jason, later murdered their own children when he abandoned her for another woman. Medea justified her irrational behavior with the infamous line: "I realize well the evil things I'm about to do, but passion overpowers my reasoning" (Euripides, *Med.* 1078–79).[2] Medea, over time, became a fabled example among the masses on the dangers of *akrasia*. This was Aristotle's term for "weakness of the will" or the loss of self-control—that is, the psychological phenomenon whereby a person irrationally acts against what has been reasoned to be good (Destrée 2007). Much of Greek ethics is dedicated to solving the problem of *akrasia*

2. Unless otherwise noted, all English translations of Greek and Latin sources, including the New Testament, are my own.

and managing emotions well (Stowers 2016, 270–78).

How emotions can be controlled was the subject of intense debate among various philosophical schools. The Platonists and Peripatetics, for example, argued for the "moderation of emotions" (*metriopatheia*) and that emotions could be channeled, if guided by reason, as positive motivating impulses toward ethical action. Anger, according to Theophrastus, was necessary for justice since a good person raged against wicked deeds (Seneca the Younger, *Ira* 1.14.1). Plato's favorite metaphor likened self-mastery to the actions of a charioteer who bridled the fierce power of horses—that is, the rational mind had the means to rein in and redirect wild passions toward a beneficial end (Plato, *Phaedr.* 246a–b; Lee 2020, 63). Similarly, the Epicureans asserted that anger is "natural" (*physikē*) to the human disposition and that any emotion, if "reasonable" (*eulogos*), contributes to virtue (Philodemus, *Lib.* col. 20.24–25; 36.20; Armstrong 2008, 93–101).

The Stoics were the most radical in their theory of self-mastery. They argued that emotional control was a matter not of redirecting the passions but of eliminating them altogether. They aimed for the complete "extirpation of the passions" (*apatheia*). Seneca warns: "A passion is as bad a subordinate as it is a leader. Therefore, reason will never accept the help of a shortsighted, violent impulse over which it has no authority. . . . May virtue be spared the dilemma of having reason ever retreat to vice for help!" (*Ira* 1.9.4–1.10.1 [trans. Basore 1928, 131, modified]). Stoicism acknowledges some "good emotions" (*eupatheiai*)—including joy (*chara*), caution (*eulabeia*), and volition (*boulēsis*). These, however, are not motivating impulses but *resultant* cognitive states that stem from rational actions (Diogenes Laertius, *Vit. phil.* 7.116; Lee 2020, 201–2).

The New Testament gives a prominent place for emotions in human moral psychology. The position of early Christian authors regarding emotion was more akin to the *metriopatheia* of Aristotle and the Middle Platonists than the *apatheia* of the Stoics. While aware that the passions can dangerously mislead people toward vice (Rom. 1:26; Gal. 5:16–25; James 1:14–15; Thompson 2011, 136–49), New Testament writers nevertheless recognized the positive role of emotions in the Christian life and integrated them as essential mechanisms for ethical practice (McClure 2019, 50–56).

Anger, for example, can motivate Christian activism against injustice (Edwards 2020, 91–106). In Ephesians 4:26, Paul exhorts the church: "Be angry and do not sin" (*orgizesthe kai mē hamartanete*). The church was commanded to be angry but not in an unfocused way, which leads to vicious behavior. If anger is excessive, it becomes evil (*perisseian kakias*; James 1:19–21; Jackson-McCabe 2019, 56). It spirals into revenge and undermines unity (Rom. 12:17–19; Eph. 4:26–27; 1 Pet. 3:9; Barton 2015, 31–34). What is crucial for Christian practice is not just the *degree* but the *object* of anger. If directed toward evil, anger can unite the church to confront the misuse of power. Jesus himself displayed anger whenever the marginalized were mistreated (e.g., Mark 3:1–6; Spencer 2021, 43–70). During the temple cleansing (John 2:14–22), Jesus's zeal along with his prophetic act of overturning merchant tables functioned as a display of divine anger targeted against the commercialism of the cult (Snodgrass 2009, 464, 469–71).[3]

If the object of anger has to be evaluated and redirected, anger cannot simply be a physical sensation. Anger and other emotions must contain a cognitive component as part of their composition (Inselmann 2016, 548–54). In 1 Thessalonians 4:13, believers are *not* told to never grieve; they are told not to grieve like nonbelievers who have no hope. Believers are admonished to evaluate the source of their grief from an eschatological perspective and to understand that any loss of possessions, social position, or life itself are outweighed by the promise of renewal at Christ's *parousia* (Barton 2011, 581–91). Paul further explains how godly sorrow (*lypē kata theon*) can direct someone to repentance (2 Cor. 7:9–10; Welborn 2011, 565–70), and pain appropriately accompanies a burden and love for others (Rom. 12:15; 2 Cor. 11:28–29; White 2020, 158–66).

Even fear plays a role in discipleship. The Gospel of Mark's engagement with fear is complex. Fear can interfere with faith (5:15, 36; 6:20; 11:18, 32), but, in the form of reverent awe, fear is also an interim step toward faith, especially during a theophanic event that reveals Jesus's divine origin (4:41; 6:50; 16:8; Lincoln 1989, 286–87; Aernie 2016, 790–91). So the New Testament engages anger, grief, fear, and other passions and argues not for their extirpation but for their redirection as positive motivating forces. It also celebrates positive emotional states—especially joy (Dinkler 2017, 269–70; Jew 2021, 88–99).

Ethical Action, Virtue Formation, and Divine Agency

The New Testament affirms the following general pattern of moral psychology: *what we do* determines *what we become*, and *what we are* affects *what we do* (Johnson 2009, 158–71; Lee 2020, 41–43; cf. Aristotle, *Eth. nic.* 1104a33–b1). In James 1:14–15, the author highlights the dangerous progression from wrong desire to evil actions: "But each person is tempted by one's own desire as if being dragged and lured away by it. Next, as desire [*epithymia*] is conceived, it gives birth to sin [*hamartian*]." Self-control over desire is the moral key to prevent sinful, erroneous, and vicious actions. In philosophical discourse, *hamartia* is a technical term used to describe an "error" of judgment

---

3. Jesus's overturning tables at the temple demonstrated anger—following ancient "display rules" (i.e., facial expressions or body language that express emotions; Inselmann 2016, 554). Note that divine zeal was often accompanied by divine wrath or anger (Ortland 2012, 36).

and action that produces vicious behavior (Plutarch, *Virt. mor.* 451e–f; Diogenes Laertius, *Vit. phil.* 7.108), but here James uses it in a nontechnical way to denote all immoral activities (Cheung 2006, 217–18).

Believers are not immune to the dangers of wrong desire. James calls the believer who experiences internal conflict "doubled minded" or "two-souled" (*dipsychos*)—that is, the soul is divided against itself (1:8; 4:8; cf. Plato's description of *diplous tis* in *Resp.* 554d–e; Jackson-McCabe 2019, 57–58). He warns that this state of mind can become so "unstable" (*akatastatos*) it causes a person to doubt and act contrary to faith (James 1:6–8).

Paul describes in Galatians 5:16–21 a similar psychological conflict between competing desires. Believers can either follow the "desire(s) of the flesh" (*epithymian sarkos*; 5:16), which prompt the "works of the flesh" (*erga tēs sarkos*; 5:19) and their attendant vices—including self-indulgence (*aselgeia*), jealousy (*zēlos*), irascibility (*thymos*), greed (*pleonexia*), and the like (*ta homoia toutois*; 5:19–21; Col. 3:5; Thompson 2011, 142–44).[4] Or, believers can choose what "the Spirit desires against the flesh" (*to de pneuma* [*epithymei*] *kata tēs sarkos*; Gal. 5:17; cf. Rom. 8:5) and carry out actions that result in the "fruit(s) of the Spirit" (*karpos tou pneumatos*; Gal. 5:22). The reference to spiritual fruit is part of a complex horticulture metaphor used by Paul, Jesus, and philosophers alike to describe human nature and the cultivation of moral virtues (cf. Matt. 7:15–20; Galen, *Aff. dig.* 7.30.16–31.6; Lee 2020, 166–67)—including joyfulness (*chara*), self-control (*enkrateia*), honesty (*chrēstotēs*; Gal. 5:22–23), but also temperance (*sōphrosynē*; Acts 26:25; 1 Tim. 2:9; cf. Mark 5:15; 1 Tim. 3:2), piety (*eusebeia*; 1 Tim. 6:11; 2 Pet. 1:6), courage (*andreia*; cf. 1 Cor. 16:13), justice (*dikaiosynē*;

Phil. 1:11; Eph. 5:9), and other qualities (*tis aretē*; Phil. 4:8).[5]

Both James 1:6–8 and Galatians 5:17–21 address the problem of *akrasia*. Human desire stands in tension between two different ethical poles. One pathway leads to virtue, the other vice. Yet, the passions of the flesh can prevent believers from doing what they wish (*hina mē ha ean thelēte tauta poiēte*; Gal. 5:17). In 1 Corinthians 7:2–6, Paul exhorts Christian spouses not to deprive one another of conjugal pleasures "because of *akrasia*" (*dia tēn akrasian*) and the dangers of immorality (*porneias*; Thompson 2011, 141–42).

The most detailed description of *akrasia*, however, is found in Romans 7:14–25, a passage whose interpretation is vigorously debated. Whether the passage describes a Christian struggle (Osborne 2011; van Kooten 2008, 379–83), an *akratic* Gentile proselyte (Stowers 1994, 258–84), or Paul's postconversion retrospective view of his previous Jewish life under the Torah (Chester 2011; Moo 2018, 434–90) matters not for this article's thesis. The interpreter need not depend on Romans 7 to argue for the *Christian* experience of *akrasia* since it is addressed directly in other passages analyzed above.

Nevertheless, Romans 7:14–25 adds a degree of complexity to our understanding of *akrasia* by describing sin as an intruding agent in human moral psychology. Paul explains: "For I don't know what I am doing, since I don't practice what I will [*ou gar ho thelō touto prassō*] but do the very thing that I hate. . . . Yet really it's no longer I who does the work [*ouketi egō katergazomai*] but sin which dwells within me" (7:15 [cf. v. 19], 17). Here the "I" (*egō*) of Paul's speech-in-character (*prosōpopoiia*) is voiced by a *persona* (henceforth "the lamenter") whose struggle and cry of desperation ("Wretched

---

4. For other vice lists, see Rom. 1:29–31; 1 Cor. 5:9–11; 6:9–10; 2 Cor. 12:20–21; Eph. 4:31; Porter 2016, 376–81.

5. For other virtue lists, see Rom. 5:3–5; 2 Cor. 6:4–8; Gal. 5:22–23; Phil. 2:2–4; 4:8; Porter 2016, 374–76. Note that *chara* can denote both the emotion "joy" and the disposition "joyfulness" (Graver 2016).

person that I am!"; 7:24) find compelling analogs with such tragic figures as Medea in Greco-Roman literature (Euripides, *Med.* 1074–80; Thiessen 1987, 211–21; Stowers 1994, 260–64) and Eve in Second Temple Jewish texts (Philo, *Creation* 157–70; LAE 19.3; Jos. Asen. 6.2–8; Elder 2018, 746–62). The lamenter is a fusion of these traditions such that the *prosōpon* or face of Eve in Romans 7 represents tragic female characters as a whole, including Medea, Antigone, Phaedra, and the like who all faced disaster and death (Elder 2018, 755–59).

The lamenter describes her *akratic* struggle in the context of a divided self. While her entire inner person delights in God's commandment (*tō nomō tou theou*; Rom. 7:22), nevertheless there is a civil war within. She claims: "I see a different operating principle [*heteron nomon*] waging battle with the operation of my mind [*tō nomō tou noos*] and taking me captive to the rule of sin [*tō nomō tēs hamartias*] among my members" (7:23). The lamenter here expresses not a Platonic contest of competing faculties in the soul (contra Wasserman 2008, 114–16) but a cognitive dissociation with the self (Engberg-Pedersen 2008, 239–46).

Emma Wasserman (2008, 98–103) objects to the *akratic* reading of Romans 7 in favor of interpreting the condition of the soul not as struggling *but as dead*—that is, not *akrasia* but *akolasia*. Yet, these need not be competitive states and should be viewed on a continuum (Lee 2020, 38–42). Romans 7 at least begins with *akrasia* since the soul is alive and fighting (*antistrateuomenon*) to do what is right (7:22–23), and only later does the struggle bring the lamenter to the verge of despair and death (7:24), anticipating a rescue from God (7:25–8:2).

The work of the Spirit is therefore the New Testament's solution to the problem of *akrasia*. Human volition requires divine empowerment both "to will and to act" (*to thelein kai to energein*) according to God's purposes (Phil. 2:13). In Romans 1:28–32, Paul challenges phi-losophy's boast that the rational mind can sufficiently choose and perform right actions. For Paul, the mind (*nous*) is not Marcus Aurelius's invincible citadel (*akropolis*; *Med.* 8.48) imbued with an incorruptible divine presence (as the Stoics so claimed; Ware 2008, 276–78), but rather it has been breached by sin so that people do inappropriate deeds (*poiein ta mē kathēkonta*; Rom. 1:28; cf. Diogenes Laertius, *Vit. phil.* 7.108; Lee 2020, 263–64). The *nous* has been made unfit (*adokimos*; Rom. 1:28) to recognize evil and instead approves of ungodly behavior as normative practice (1:32; Keener 2016, 1–30). Therefore, the mind must be transformed (*metamorphousthe*) by the Spirit so that the person can do what pleases God (Rom. 12:2).

Moral transformation requires human participation. The work that believers do ("work out [*katergazesthe*] your salvation") is embedded in the work of the Spirit ("for God is at work [*ho energōn*] within you"; Phil. 2:12–13). Both divine and human agents participate in moral progress but through an uneven relationship, where God is the principal actor (Barclay 2006, 152; Rabens 2014, 171–202). Thus, Paul paradoxically claims, "While I labored [*eko-piasa*] more intensely than all of them [i.e., other apostles], it was not I [*ouk egō*] but the grace of God [*hē charis tou theou*] that is with me" (1 Cor. 15:10; cf. Gal. 2:20). God operates through the labor of Paul in such a way that human actions are made to correspond with divine activity (Barclay 2006, 151).

The Moral Logic of Progress and Perfection

More important than the individual *topoi* addressed in the New Testament is how these cohere together in one system of thought. The New Testament provides enough data to reconstruct the moral logic of at least one of its authors: Paul. Among the philosophical systems of his day, Paul's moral logic finds its best analog with Stoicism. The all-or-nothing logic of early Stoic perfection and the efforts of neo-Stoicism to accommodate the stages of moral progress within it provide points of comparison with how Paul ties progress and perfection together.

Concerning the Stoics, Diogenes Laertius reports: "It is a tenet of theirs that there is no middle ground [*metaxu*] between virtue and vice [*aretēs kai kakias*], whereas according to the Peripatetics there is something intermediate between virtue and vice: namely, moral progress [*prokopēn*]" (*Vit. phil.* 7.127 [trans. Hicks 1991, 231, modified]). The Peripatetics (and the Middle Platonists) understood moral transformation as a *gradual* process whereby a person progresses in wisdom and character over a lifetime (Lee 2020, 83–85). The Stoics disagreed. For them, there was no mediating position. A person was either completely virtuous or completely vicious, either the perfect sage or wholly the fool.

It is not that the Stoa did not have some concept of progress. They did (see, e.g., Seneca the Younger's three stages of progression in *Ep.* 75.8–16). But all progressors, even those who were nearly perfect, were considered fools. The Stoa insisted that moral transformation was *instantaneous*, like the flash of the Phoenix reborn (*SVF* 3.658). Regardless of what progress is made, even the progressor remains in a state of vice until perfection is reached. Progress, at best, is a kind of preparation for a more radical, sudden transformation (*metabolē*; Plutarch, *Virt. prof.* 76e–f; Lee 2020, 236–42, 351–56).

Likewise, there is no mediating category of vice and virtue for Paul. Paul, like his Stoic contemporaries, would simply call the entire space "vice," or to use Pauline language, all humanity lives "under sin" (*hypo [tēn] hamartian*; Gal. 3:22; Rom. 7:14). No matter what virtuous qualities people may cultivate, they are subject to sin's dominion and power. For Paul, the total transformation of the believer from vice to virtue takes place at the resurrection, when "in a flash . . . we will be changed" (*en atomō . . . allagēsometha*; 1 Cor. 15:52). Paul recognizes that human beings do noble deeds randomly as a "law to themselves" (Rom. 2:14), but they are not free. It is only by participating in the life of God, or what Paul calls "being in Christ," that humanity can experience freedom from sin's reign (8:5–9; Campbell 2012, 176–90). So rather than a "self-determining self" kind of logic (*pace* Engberg-Pedersen 2008), Paul's moral logic depends on a coagency of divine power and human action.

Human participation is not just individual but corporate. Early Christian communities provide the social context for moral transformation. Mature believers act as moral mentors to new converts and aid the latter in their spiritual growth through frank criticism and exhortation. These mentors model what virtues and godly practices their disciples should imitate (1 Cor. 4:13–21; Lee 2014).

Believers are being transformed (*metamorphoumetha*) daily by God into Christ's image (2 Cor. 3:18), but they are still progressing to what they should be. They are in process but not yet there. They have not reached perfection. Paul confesses: "I want to know Christ and the power of his resurrection. . . . *Not* that I have already received this *nor* have I already perfected it [*ouch . . . ēdē teteleiōmai*], but I press on to grasp it" (Phil. 3:10–12). Paul is not Stoic, but Stoicism provides categories for understanding the paradoxical relationship between progress and perfection characteristic of Paul's thought.

Moral transformation is constituent of a larger event whereby the self is reconstituted into a new creation (2 Cor. 5:17; Gal. 6:15; cf. Rev. 21:5). This newly created self stands in the eschatological tension between the "already" and "not yet." The formation of virtue under the agency of the Spirit is evidence for the former, but the unrealized goal of perfection until the resurrection is evidence for the latter

(Ladd 1993, 522–23; Pitts and Pollinger 2012, 174–76).

Conclusion

New Testament descriptions of moral transformation are best situated within their Greco-Roman philosophical milieu (Johnson 2009, 46–47, 64–65). Yet, Christian writers do not necessarily draw on any single ethical tradition but engage various philosophies depending on the *topos* of moral inquiry. Theirs is not an uncritical eclecticism either. Rather, New Testament interactions with philosophical schools were complex—ranging from an irenic appropriation of moral traditions that support apostolic teaching to a competitive adaptation of a rival sect's linguistic inventory for the purposes of redefining concepts for Christian instruction (Lee 2021, 4–7). It is therefore no surprise that New Testament authors describe moral transformation as an integrated process of emotional management, ethical action, and virtue. What made Christianity distinct, however, among its fellow philosophical contemporaries was its insistence that transformation necessitated the dual agency of human action in correspondence with divine power. Moral progress functions as a demonstration of the Spirit's present work in the conduct and life of the believer, but complete transformation is future oriented when all old things pass away and only the new endures.

Works Cited

Aernie, Jeffrey W. 2016. "Cruciform Discipleship: The Narrative Function of the Women in Mark 15–16." *JBL* 135, no. 4: 779–97.

Armstrong, David. 2008. "'Be Angry and Sin Not': Philodemus versus the Stoics on Natural Bites and Natural Emotions." In *Passions and Moral Progress in Greco-Roman Thought*, edited by John T. Fitzgerald, 79–121. New York: Routledge.

Barclay, John M. G. 2006. "'By the Grace of God I Am What I Am': Grace and Agency in Philo and Paul." In *Divine and Human Agency in Paul and His Cul-* *tural Environment*, edited by John M. G. Barclay and Simon J. Gathercole, 140–57. LNTS 335. New York: T&T Clark.

Barton, Stephen C. 2011. "Eschatology and the Emotions in Early Christianity." *JBL* 130, no. 3: 571–91.

———. 2015. "'Be Angry but Do Not Sin' (Ephesians 4:26a): Sin and the Emotions in the New Testament with Special Reference to Anger." *Studies in Christian Ethics* 28, no. 1: 21–34.

Basore, John W., ed. and trans. 1928. *Seneca: Moral Essays*. Vol. 1. LCL 214. Cambridge, MA: Harvard University Press / London: William Heinemann.

Campbell, Constantine R. 2012. *Paul and Union with Christ: An Exegetical and Theological Study*. Grand Rapids: Zondervan.

Chester, Stephen. 2011. "The Retrospective View of Romans 7: Paul's Past in Present Perspective." In *Perspectives on Our Struggle with Sin: 3 Views of Romans 7*, edited by Terry L. Wilder, 57–103. Nashville: B&H Academic.

Cheung, Luke Leuk. 2006. *The Genre, Composition and Hermeneutics of the Epistle of James*. Paternoster Biblical Monographs. Eugene, OR: Wipf & Stock.

Destrée, Pierre. 2007. "Aristotle on the Causes of *Akrasia*." In Akrasia *in Greek Philosophy: From Socrates to Plotinus*, edited by Christopher Bobonich and Pierre Destrée, 139–66. Philosophia Antiqua 106. Leiden: Brill.

Dinkler, Michal Beth. 2017. "Reflexivity and Emotion in Narratological Perspective: Reading Joy in the Lukan Narrative." In *Mixed Feelings and Vexed Passions: Exploring Emotions in Biblical Literature*, edited by F. Scott Spencer, 265–86. RBS 90. Atlanta: SBL Press.

Edwards, Dennis R. 2020. *Might from the Margins: The Gospel's Power to Turn the Tables on Injustice*. Harrisonburg, VA: Herald.

Elder, Nicholas. 2018. "'Wretch I Am!' Eve's Tragic Speech-in-Character in Romans 7:7–25." *JBL* 137, no. 3: 743–63.

Engberg-Pedersen, Troels. 2000. *Paul and the Stoics*. Louisville: Westminster John Knox / Edinburgh: T&T Clark.

———. 2008. "The Logic of Action in Paul: How Does He Differ from the Moral Philosophers on Spiritual and Moral Progression and Regression?" In *Passions and Moral Progress in Greco-Roman Thought*, edited by John T. Fitzgerald, 238–66. New York: Routledge.

Graver, Margaret R. 2016. "Anatomies of Joy: Seneca and the *Gaudium* Tradition." In *Hope, Joy, and Affection in the Classical World*, edited by Ruth R. Caston and Robert A. Kaster, 123–42. New York: Oxford University Press.

Hicks, Robert D., ed. and trans. 1991. *Diogenes Laertius: Lives of Eminent Philosophers*. Vol. 2. LCL 185. Cambridge, MA: Harvard University Press / London: William Heinemann. Originally published 1925.

Inselmann, Anke. 2016. "Emotions and Passions in the New Testament: Methodological Issues." *BibInt* 24: 536–54.

Jackson-McCabe, Matt. 2019. "The Letter of James and Hellenistic Philosophy." In *Reading the Epistle of James*, edited by Eric F. Mason and Darian R. Lockett, 45–72. Atlanta: SBL Press.

Jew, Ian Y. S. 2021. *Paul's Emotional Regime: The Social Function of Emotions in Philippians and 1 Thessalonians*. LNTS 629. New York: T&T Clark.

Johnson, Luke Timothy. 2009. *Among the Gentiles: Greco-Roman Religion and Christianity*. Anchor Bible Yale Reference Library. New Haven: Yale University Press.

Keener, Craig S. 2016. *The Mind of the Spirit: Paul's Approach to Transformed Thinking*. Grand Rapids: Baker Academic.

Ladd, George Eldon. 1993. *A Theology of the New Testament*. Revised and edited by Donald A. Hagner. Grand Rapids: Eerdmans.

Lee, Max J. 2014. "Ancient Mentors and Moral Progress according to Galen and Paul." In *Doing Theology for the Church: Essays in Honor of Klyne Snodgrass*, edited by Rebekah A. Eklund and John E. Phelan Jr., 55–70. Eugene, OR: Wipf & Stock.

———. 2020. *Moral Transformation in Greco-Roman Philosophy of Mind: Mapping the Moral Milieu of the Apostle Paul and His Diaspora Jewish Contemporaries*. WUNT 2/515. Tübingen: Mohr Siebeck.

———. 2021. "A Taxonomy of Intertextual Interactions Practiced by New Testament Authors." In *Practicing Intertextuality: Ancient Jewish and Greco-Roman Exegetical Techniques in the New Testament*, edited by Max J. Lee and B. J. Oropeza, 3–16. Eugene, OR: Cascade Books.

Lincoln, Andrew T. 1989. "The Promise and the Failure: Mark 16:7, 8." *JBL* 108, no. 2: 283–300.

Marquardt, Ioannes et al., eds. 1967. *Claudii Galeni Pergameni Scripta Minora*. Vols. 1–3. Amsterdam: Adolf M. Hakkert. Originally published 1884–93.

McClure, Barbara J. 2019. *Emotions: Problems and Promise for Human Flourishing*. Waco: Baylor University Press.

Moo, Douglas J. 2018. *The Letter to the Romans*. 2nd ed. Grand Rapids: Eerdmans.

Nussbaum, Martha C. 2001. *The Fragility of Goodness: Luck and Ethics in Greek Tragedy and Philosophy*. Rev ed. Cambridge: Cambridge University Press. Originally published 1986.

———. 2009. *The Therapy of Desire: Theory and Practice in Hellenistic Ethics*. Repr., Princeton:

Princeton University Press. Originally published 1994.

Ortlund, Dane C. 2012. *Zeal without Knowledge: The Concept of Zeal in Romans 10, Galatians 1, and Philippians 3*. LNTS 472. New York: T&T Clark.

Osborne, Grant. 2011. "The Flesh without the Spirit: Romans 7 and Christian Experience." In *Perspectives on Our Struggle with Sin: 3 Views of Romans 7*, edited by Terry L. Wilder, 6–48. Nashville: B&H Academic.

Pitts, Andrew W., and Seth Pollinger. 2013. "The Spirit in Second Temple Jewish Monotheism and the Origins of Early Christology." In *Christian Origins and Hellenistic Judaism: Social and Literary Contexts for the New Testament*, edited by Stanley E. Porter and Andrew W. Pitts, 135–76. Vol. 2 of *Early Christianity in Its Hellenistic Context*. TENTS 10. Leiden: Brill.

Porter, Stanley E. 2016. "Paul, Virtue, Vices, and Household Codes." In vol. 2 of *Paul in the Greco-Roman World: A Handbook*, edited by J. Paul Sampley, 369–90. 2 vols. New York: Bloomsbury T&T Clark.

Rabens, Volker. 2014. *The Holy Spirit and Ethics in Paul: Transformation and Empowering for Religious-Ethical Life*. 2nd rev. ed. Minneapolis: Fortress.

Snodgrass, Klyne R. 2009. "The Temple Incident." In *Key Events in the Life of the Historical Jesus: A Collaborative Exploration of Context and Coherence*, edited by Darrell L. Bock and Robert L. Webb, 429–80. Grand Rapids: Eerdmans.

Spencer, F. Scott. *Passions of the Christ: The Emotional Life of Jesus in the Gospels*. Grand Rapids: Baker Academic, 2021.

Stowers, Stanley. 1994. *A Rereading of Romans: Justice, Jews and Gentiles*. New Haven: Yale University Press.

———. 2016. "Paul and Self-Mastery." In vol. 2 of *Paul in the Greco-Roman World: A Handbook*, edited by J. Paul Sampley, 270–99. 2 vols. New York: Bloomsbury T&T Clark.

Thiessen, Gerd. 1987. *Psychological Aspects of Pauline Theology*. Translated by J. P. Galvin. Philadelphia: Fortress.

Thom, Johan C. 2003. "The Mind Is Its Own Place: Defining the *Topos*." In *Early Christianity and Classical Culture: Comparative Studies in Honor of Abraham J. Malherbe*, edited by John T. Fitzgerald, Thomas H. Olbricht, and L. Michael White, 555–73. NovTSup 110. Leiden: Brill.

Thompson, James. 2011. *Moral Formation according to Paul: The Context and Coherence of Pauline Ethics*. Grand Rapids: Baker Academic.

van Kooten, George H. 2008. *Paul's Anthropology in Context: The Image of God, Assimilation to God, and Tripartite Man in Ancient Judaism, Ancient*

Philosophy and Early Christianity. WUNT 2/232. Tübingen: Mohr Siebeck.

Ware, James. 2008. "Moral Progress and Divine Power in Seneca and Paul." In *Passions and Moral Progress in Greco-Roman Thought*, edited by John T. Fitzgerald, 267–83. New York: Routledge.

Wasserman, Emma. 2008. *The Death of the Soul in Romans 7: Sin, Death, and the Law in Light of Hellenistic Moral Psychology*. WUNT 2/256. Tübingen: Mohr Siebeck.

Welborn, L. L. 2011. "Paul and Pain: Paul's Emotional Therapy in 2 Corinthians 1.1–2.13; 7.5–16 in the Context of Ancient Psychagogic Literature." *NTS* 57, no. 4: 547–70.

White, B. G. 2020. "The Varieties of Pain: Re-examining the Setting and Purpose of 2 Corinthians with Paul's *lyp-* Words." *JSNT* 43, no. 2: 147–72.

44

Sacrifice

David M. Moffitt

Sacrifice was a common religious practice in the ancient world. We meet it in texts as diverse as the *Iliad* and Leviticus and in artifacts as different as the Altar of Peace in Rome and the ancient horned altars found throughout the Levant.

Given the ubiquity of sacrifice in the past, we might be surprised to learn that many of our contemporary conceptions about the practice are mistaken. Consider one example: many today imagine that when Jews sacrificed animals in the temple in Jerusalem, they placed the animals on the altar to kill them. Popular art and online videos illustrating biblical sacrifice often reinforce this picture. Killing an animal on an altar is sometimes assumed to be the definition of "sacrifice." This is completely wrong. The altar in the courtyard of the temple was *not* the place where animals were killed. Careful attention to Leviticus and to descriptions of sacrifice at the temple in Jerusalem show that *animals were not killed on any of the temple's altars*. This example may prompt us to wonder what other mistaken notions we hold about sacrifice.

This essay offers an introductory survey of the large and complex subject of sacrifice. Since the authors of the New Testament assumed that appropriate sacrifice could be given only to the God of Israel, sacrifice at the temple in Jerusalem will occupy most of our attention. We will only look briefly at Greco-Roman sacrifice. We consider first the basic kinds of Jewish sacrifices. We then address some concepts that were associated with elements of sacrifice. Finally, we explore some ways in which the New Testament draws on sacrificial practice to reflect on the person and work of Jesus.

Jewish Sacrifices

Leviticus 1–7 introduces five kinds of sacrifice. Our descriptions basically follow Leviticus and include some details we know from sources nearer to the time of Jesus. Leviticus 1 introduces the whole burnt offering. This sacrifice could make atonement (1:4), fulfill a vow, or be a freewill offering of thanksgiving to God (22:18). The offerer could bring an animal to the temple, but sheep, goats, cattle, and birds were available there for purchase.[1] As with all animal sacrifices, the burnt offering had to be unblemished (1:3). As part of the transfer of the animal to God, the offerer laid both hands on its head and gave an explanation for the offering. This would involve confession of sin if the sacrifice was for atonement (t. Menah 10.12), a declaration of the fulfillment of one's vow for a votive offering, or a declaration of one's innocence and worthiness to give the offering if it was given in thanks (Philo, *Spec. Laws* 1.197–99). A Levite or a priest typically cut the animal's throat (1.199), but only a priest could collect its blood in a bowl. Bulls were slaughtered "before the LORD" (Lev. 1:5)—that is, in the courtyard in front of the bronze altar. Flock animals were killed in a special space to the north side of the altar (1:11). The animal was butchered, and certain parts were washed and salted (Josephus, *Ant.* 3.227; see also Ezek. 43:23–24). A priest took the bowl containing the blood and dashed the blood on each of the four sides of the altar (Lev. 1:5). A priest also laid the pieces of the animal on the altar, where they were entirely burned. The smoke rose from the altar as "an offering by fire of pleasing odor to the LORD" (1:9).

A number of elements just described were common to all animal sacrifices (i.e., laying hands on the head of the animal, cutting its throat, a priest collecting the blood in a bowl, applying the blood to the altar, washing and salting parts of the animal, burning parts of the animal upon the altar, the smoke ascending as a pleasing odor) and will not be treated in detail below.

Leviticus 2 describes the grain offering. This sacrifice functioned in many ways like the whole burnt offering and could be given if a person could not afford to offer an animal (e.g., Lev. 5:11–13; see also Philo, *Names* 234; m. Menah. 13.11). An offerer usually brought flour (Lev. 2:1), baked loaves (2:4–7), or parched grain (2:14) to a priest. As with animal offerings, the priest took some of the offering to the outer altar and burned it, creating a pleasing odor for God (2:2). The rest belonged to the priest to eat (2:3).

Leviticus 3 details the peace or well-being offering. This sacrifice was offered to give thanks (cf. 7:12–15), fulfill vows or be a freewill offering (7:16–17), and celebrate (Num. 10:10). The offerer laid hands on the animal (m. Menah. 5.7), which was killed in the courtyard (Lev. 3:2).[2] The blood was dashed, and some parts were burned (3:2–5). While some of the sacrifice was given to the priest to eat (7:28–36), the rest was eaten by the offerer. All consumption occurred within a stipulated period of time (7:15–16). Notably, the peace offering was the only kind of sacrifice that lay offerers could eat.

Leviticus 4:1–5:13 describes the sin offering. Unlike the burnt, grain, and peace offerings, this sacrifice could not be given to fulfill a vow, as a freewill offering, or in thanksgiving. It was offered only to make atonement for sins committed unwittingly or for the purification of certain impurities. The offerer probably confessed the sin or declared the impurity requiring the sacrifice while laying hands on the animal (5:5; see also m. Menah. 9.7–8). Flock animals were slaughtered to the north of the altar (Lev. 4:24). Bulls were slaughtered in the courtyard (4:4). The blood was handled differently from the other sacrifices. In some cases, a priest took the bowl containing the blood into the temple. He sprinkled blood from the bowl in the holy place and applied some to the four horns of the inner altar of incense (4:5–7). When not taken into the temple, blood was applied instead to

---

1. When the Gospels describe Jesus driving out of the temple those changing money and selling doves (Matt. 21:12–13 // Mark 11:15–17 // Luke 19:45–46) or selling sheep and cattle (John 2:15–16), they are referring to animals being bought and sold in order to be offered as sacrifices to God.

2. The Mishnah states that individual peace offerings were killed in the courtyard, while peace offerings for the whole congregation were killed in the space to the north side of the altar (m. Zevah. 5.5, 7).

the four horns of the outer altar (4:25). The blood remaining in the bowl was not dashed around the sides of the altar but poured out—that is, shed—at its base (4:7, 18, 25, 30, 34; see also 8:15; 9:9). Parts of the animal were also burned (4:10). In cases where blood went into the temple, the rest of the sacrifice was not burned on the outer altar but taken to a pure place "outside the camp" and burned there (4:11–12; 6:30). In cases where blood was applied only to the outer altar, the priests ate the rest of the animal (6:26).

The fifth sacrifice detailed in Leviticus is the guilt offering (Lev. 5:14–6:7; 7:1–7). This was given to make atonement for sin knowingly committed (esp. 6:1–7).[3] The sacrifice typically consisted of a ram plus a financial penalty (5:16; Num. 5:5–8). The offerer had to confess the sin (Num. 5:7), likely when laying hands on the animal (m. Menah. 5.7; 9.7; Neg. 14.8). The animal was killed in the space to the north of the altar (Lev. 7:1–2). Unlike with the sin offering, a priest dashed the blood around the sides of the altar (7:2). Parts were burned on the altar (7:3–5), while the rest was eaten by the priest (7:6).

Wine, oil, incense, and lifting up or waving elements were sometimes part of the sacrificial process. The golden altar in the holy place was also a place of offering. While blood was applied to its horns as part of certain sin offerings, the only thing burned on it was a special incense sacrifice (Exod. 30:7–10).

These basic sacrifices were combined in certain ways to form central elements of daily and annual sacrifices and festivals. They were, as Kathryn McClymond (2008, 39) observes, "the basic building blocks, either performed independently or combined with one another to create more complex rituals." A few of these more complex rituals deserve mention.

Twice daily, once in the morning and once in the late afternoon, a lamb was offered as a whole burnt offering (Exod. 29:38–42). This was known as the *tamid* (meaning "continual") sacrifice. Incense was also offered on the inner altar as part of this sacrifice (30:7–8). The *tamid* was understood to make regular atonement for the nation (Jub. 6.14). Prayer and sacrifice were always closely related, but people would especially pray when the *tamid* was offered.

Every spring the annual Passover festival was celebrated to commemorate the exodus from Egypt. At this festival offerers most likely slaughtered their own animals (Philo, *Spec. Laws* 2.145; m. Pesah. 5.5–6), though in Jerusalem priests collected the blood and dashed it around the outer altar (2 Chron. 35:11). The animals, typically lambs, were then eaten by the offerers. Thus, the Passover sacrifice appears to be a kind of peace offering (Anderson 1992, 878). It was not an atoning sacrifice. After Passover the Festival of Unleavened Bread was celebrated for seven days (Lev. 23:6–8). Fifty days after Passover came the Festival of Firstfruits, also called Pentecost. The grain sacrifice was an especially important element of this feast (23:9–14).

Two noteworthy fall holidays were held. First came the Day of Atonement on the tenth day of the seventh month (Lev. 16; 23:26–32). This involved national fasting and prayer, as well as special sin offerings in which the high priest offered incense and blood in the most special room in the temple, the holy of holies. This was the space where God's presence most fully dwelled on earth. Since the blood of these sin offerings went into the temple, the bodies of the animals were taken out of the temple and burned, in keeping with the directives of 4:11–12 and 6:30. Five days later the seven-day Festival of Booths was celebrated to commemorate the giving of the covenant and law at Sinai (23:33–36). In addition to various sacrifices, this weeklong festival involved a unique ritual

3. Philo (*Spec. Laws* 1.227, 234–37) and Josephus (*Ant.* 3.230–32) both describe the guilt offering as a kind of sin offering given for intentionally committed sins.

in which water was poured out on the altar (m. Sukkah 4.9–10).

Important Sacrificial Concepts

The preceding descriptions of Jewish sacrifice illustrate a number of significant points about the practice. First, sacrifice involved several different steps. For various reasons (sometimes rejoicing, sometimes guilt, sometimes bodily purification, and so on) an offerer would bring grain or select or buy an animal and bring it to a priest at the temple. If the sacrifice was an animal, the offerer laid hands on its head and likely said something about why it was being offered. The animal was then taken to the appropriate place and slaughtered, and its blood collected in a bowl. Several things were done to various parts of the animal, depending on the sacrifice. The blood was always applied to the outer altar in some way. Sometimes blood was taken into the temple building. Taking blood from a bowl and applying it to the altar (especially the base of the outer altar) is how sacrificial blood was "shed" at the altar; the language of "shedding blood" in relation to sacrifice does not denote slaughtering an animal but denotes "pouring out" its blood from the bowl. At least a part of every sacrifice was burned on the outer altar. The altars, in other words, were the main places where sacrifices were burned and to which blood was applied.

Four important points can be deduced from this summary. First, sacrifices were offered for different reasons. Many involved atonement, but many did not. Second, sacrifice was a process involving a sequence of activities. Third, the altars were the places where the sacrifice was given to God, not least by burning, so that the smoke could rise into his presence (a perpetual fire was to be kept burning on the outer altar; Lev. 6:9), and only priests could take the elements of the sacrifice (often blood and flesh) to the altars. These facts suggest that the activities at the altars were the most important parts of the process. Fourth, sacrifice moved in a particular direction—from an offerer to a priest to an altar and then into God's presence.

The preceding four points correlate with three important concepts sometimes missed in modern thinking. First, Jewish sacrifice was relational, a constitutive aspect of worship. It was fundamentally about *giving a gift to God*. Leviticus 7:37–38 even describes all the sacrifices as gifts (i.e., offerings) brought to God. Modern notions of sacrifice that think primarily of "giving something up" belie an anthropological focus that would have been foreign to ancient worshipers. For the latter, sacrifice had a theologically oriented focus: while something was given up by an offerer, sacrifice was primarily oriented toward the act of *giving something to* God. Second, since sacrifice involved a process, the verb "to sacrifice" does not mean "to slaughter" or "to kill" something. Not all sacrifices were slaughtered (e.g., grain, wine, oil, incense). When sacrifices were slaughtered, many other things happened before they were brought to the altar and burned. It is a mistake to reduce the act of sacrifice to that of slaughter, an act that did not occur on the altars. Third, the noun "sacrifice" refers to the actual item given as a gift to God—a lamb, a bull, grain, incense, and so on. While the language of sacrifice could be used metaphorically (e.g., Ps. 51:17), a sacrifice at the temple was not about an abstract idea like suffering or death; it was an item given as a gift to God.

Two other concepts deserve mention: blood and atonement. Leviticus 17:11 explains that blood is able to make atonement because blood contains the life of the animal (in the sense of its life force). Applying blood to the altars is probably associated here with returning the life of an animal to God. Blood applied to the altar is neither a symbol for life nor a symbol for death. Rather, that animal's life is *in* the blood and, God has said, applying this life to an altar makes atonement for his people. But what is atonement?

The word "atonement" originally meant "reconciliation." In the sixteenth century William Tyndale used atonement language to translate some instances of the Hebrew verb *kipper*. In sacrificial context, this verb denoted a mechanism for removing some hindrance between God and his people so that reconciliation could subsequently occur. Tyndale's translation substituted this mechanism with the idea of reconciliation itself. When we today speak of a sacrifice making atonement, we sometimes miss that this involves removing an impediment between God and an offerer *before* they were reconciled (Gane 2005, 194). We also tend to miss the fact that atoning sacrifices were not just about helping solve problems created by sin or moral faults but also about solving problems created by ritual impurities (e.g., childbirth in Lev. 12; recovering from certain skin diseases in 14:1–32; see also chap. 38 in this volume). By removing a stain or impurity, sacrifice contributes to reconciliation between God and an offerer, not least because God condescends to extend forgiveness to the offerer when sin created the impediment.

Sacrifice and the New Testament

Jewish sacrifices and festivals show up in various ways in the New Testament. Jesus spoke of sacrifices in terms of giving God gifts at the altar (Matt. 5:23–24). Zechariah offered incense in the holy place as part of the *tamid* sacrifice (i.e., making atonement for the nation) while the people gathered at the temple prayed outside (Luke 1:5–22). Acts describes Peter and John going to the temple at the hour of afternoon prayer (Acts 3:1), which corresponded with the afternoon *tamid* sacrifice. In John, the Lamb of God language (John 1:29; see also Rev. 5:6–14) likely evokes both Passover and the *tamid*. When Jesus declares during the Feast of Booths that he is the source of living water (John 7:37–39), he probably alludes to the festival's unique water ritual. Jesus was also

crucified at Passover. John associates this with the time when the offering of the lambs was occurring at the temple (John 19:14). His death is also fittingly described in terms reminiscent of the redemption and liberation from slavery that occurred at the exodus and first Passover (e.g., Mark 10:45; Heb. 2:14–16).

The larger Hellenistic context in which Jesus's early followers lived also influenced the ways they thought and spoke about Jesus and sacrifice. When, for example, Paul speaks about Jesus dying "for us," the ideas he draws on do not come from the conceptual realm of Jewish sacrifice. Isaiah 53 was certainly an important influence (see 1 Cor. 15:3), but when Paul spoke to Gentiles, he must have known that this kind of language would relate to ideas widely known in Greco-Roman culture about one person dying as a sacrifice to save the many from evils such as plagues (Hengel 1981). On the other hand, his references to the Passover lamb being slaughtered and his emphasis on subsequently keeping the feast (1 Cor. 5:7–8) focus on the importance of maintaining purity during the Jewish Feast of Unleavened Bread after Passover.

While not denying the importance of Hellenistic ideas or the significance of Jesus's death, the rest of this essay focuses on a few New Testament texts that indicate that Jesus's sacrificial work extends beyond his death to include his ascension into God's presence, where he performs his ongoing high priestly ministry.

The epistle to the Hebrews is the only New Testament book that explicitly identifies Jesus as a high priest. Hebrews also explains Jesus's sacrifice in ways that closely align with some of the concepts discussed above. Hebrews describes Jesus's ascension in terms of his "pass[ing] through the heavens" (4:14) to enter the heavenly tabernacle and appear in God's presence (9:24–25). This is how he offers God "the sacrifice of himself" (9:26). Jesus's death is certainly part of his sacrifice (9:28). But just as Jewish sacrifice was a process in which a priest brought a gift into God's presence, so Hebrews naturally argues that Jesus died, rose, and then ascended so that, as the great high priest, he could enter God's heavenly presence and offer himself to God there. He now perpetually intercedes on behalf of his siblings, ensuring their complete salvation (7:25). Hebrews draws sustained analogies between the ongoing ministry of the ascended Jesus and the high priest's annual ministry on the Day of Atonement. Like the high priest who moved into God's presence in the holy of holies on the Day of Atonement to offer blood to sanctify the people (9:7; 13:11), Jesus, after his death and resurrection, ascended into the heavenly holy of holies to offer himself to God and minister there for the sanctification of his people (4:14–16; 6:20; 9:24–26; 10:19–20). From the perspective of Jewish sacrifice, Hebrews appropriately connects the culmination of Jesus's atoning work with his entrance into the heavenly tabernacle, appearance before God to offer himself as a sacrifice, and ongoing high priestly intercession for his people. This is an essential part of how he makes their full salvation possible (for more detailed discussion, see Moffitt 2022, esp. 135–80).

A similar idea appears in 1 John. The author clearly speaks in sacrificial terms in 1:7–9 when he stresses the purifying effects of Jesus's blood and the importance of confession of sins as prerequisite to forgiveness and purification from unrighteousness. He implies in 2:1–2 that forgiveness is an ongoing reality because Jesus is now both the advocate "with the Father" and the atoning sacrifice. Both Jesus's location and his identity as advocate and atoning sacrifice suggest that he is the sacrifice now located in God's presence. First John alludes to Jesus's death in sacrificial terms in 4:9–10, where the author says that God's love is clearly seen by the fact that he sent his Son as an atoning sacrifice. Together, 1:7–2:2 and 4:9–10 indicate that 1 John thinks about sacrifice along the lines discussed above—as a process that moves

from the death of the victim to the transferal of the gift into God's presence. The Father sent his Son into the world as an atoning sacrifice, and the Son has returned to be with the Father as an atoning sacrifice. This epistle does not explicitly identify Jesus as a high priest, but the idea of Jesus as the sacrifice who advocates for his people in God's presence comes very close conceptually to the account of Jesus's person and work found in Hebrews (Moffitt 2022, 156n47, 194).

Conclusion

Jewish sacrifice was a multistep process whereby a gift moved from an offerer to a priest to an altar and then into God's presence. While the New Testament shows the influence of wider cultural ideas about sacrifice when reflecting on Jesus's death, it also contains theological claims about Jesus's person and work that correlate his ascension with the larger process of giving a gift to God. By way of analogies drawn from the practice of sacrifice, both Jesus's death and his ascension can be seen in the New Testament to contribute to how he makes sacrificial atonement for his people.

Works Cited

Anderson, Gary A. 1992. "Sacrifice and Sacrificial Offerings (OT)." *ABD* 5:870–86.

Gane, Roy E. 2005. *Cult and Character: Purification Offerings, Day of Atonement, and Theodicy.* Winona Lake, IN: Eisenbrauns.

Hengel, Martin. 1981. *The Atonement: The Origins of the Doctrine in the New Testament.* Translated by John Bowden. London: SCM.

McClymond, Kathryn. 2008. *Beyond Sacred Violence: A Comparative Study of Sacrifice.* Baltimore: John Hopkins University Press.

Moffitt, David M. 2022. *Rethinking the Atonement: New Perspectives on Jesus's Death, Resurrection, and Ascension.* Grand Rapids: Baker Academic.

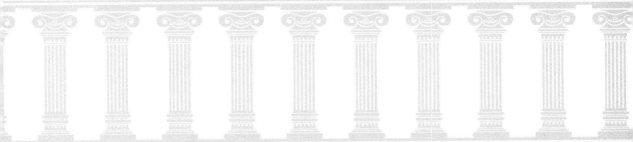

Human Society

45

The Roman Empire

Sylvia C. Keesmaat

It is not that difficult for most of us to imagine a world where almost everyone has access to the same images and stories, especially now, when the internet, social media, and quick air travel facilitate the widespread sharing of movies, advertising, and songs. It is more difficult for us to believe that even without these conveniences in the first century, the Roman Empire dominated the imaginative world of people from Britain to Spain, across Europe to the Middle East, and south to North Africa. Under Caesar Augustus, who was the first emperor (27 BCE–14 CE), the story of the Roman Empire spread with startling success (Zanker 1988; Price 1984). This story emphasized the importance of Rome's culture, the power of its military, the justice of its laws, and the (almost) divine character of the emperor. At the time when Jesus lived, and during the years that his followers were writing the oral traditions that became the Gospels and the letters that became the rest of the New Testament, this narrative about Rome and its rulers was the pervasive cultural context in which the early Jesus followers struggled with what it

meant to follow a Messiah who had died and been raised to new life.

Not only did the symbols, images, and narratives of Augustus continue to shape how subsequent emperors portrayed themselves; they also defined the way that the average person imagined imperial rule.[1] This was partly because many of the military exploits and actions of the emperors were immortalized through statues, carvings on buildings, coins, and the paintings that adorned walls in the theater, shops, and homes (Nasrallah 2010, 1–17; Maier 2013, 1–62). These artifacts often blended the stories of the emperor with those of the Roman (and Greek) gods and goddesses. This, along with the fact that statues and carvings endure for decades, meant that there was a timeless quality to the stories—the victories of Augustus were reinforced by the victories of Claudius and Nero. And all their victories were

---

1. The emperors of note who succeeded Caesar Augustus in the first century were Tiberius (14–37 CE), Caligula (37–41 CE), Claudius (41–54 CE), Nero (54–68 CE), Vespasian (69–79 CE), Titus (79–81 CE), and Domitian (81–96 CE).

part of a larger narrative of the gods' blessing on the Roman Empire (Shaner 2017, 350–53).

This narrative was celebrated throughout the empire during the frequent feasts and festivals that marked Roman military victories. Sacrifices and praise for imperial rulers also prefaced all events in the theater, as well as meetings of associations. The stories of the empire were told with such regularity that the imperial imagination permeated daily life.

The result was a remarkably consistent narrative about Roman rule, not only across the geographical spaces of the empire, but also temporally throughout the first century, when Jesus and his first followers were alive. If we could sum up this story with one word, it would be "power." Roman power legitimated military violence, reinforced the hierarchical structure of Roman society, justified violence against women and slaves, and demanded the aggressive altering and exploitation of the physical landscape. We will first explore how this power was seen by the privileged in Roman society and then consider how this power may have been experienced by those who suffered under imperial rule.

Imperial Depictions of Power

Power Bestowed by the Gods

Sometime between the years of 10 and 20 CE, a cameo called the Gemma Augustea was carved for circulation around the provinces of the Roman Empire (see fig. 45.1). Those provinces included early Christian communities that we know of in Corinth, Thessalonica, Philippi, Colossae, Ephesus, Smyrna, Laodicea, Thyatira, Hierapolis, Pergamum, Sardis, Philadelphia, and Antioch. This cameo contains in a remarkably compact format the most important features of the first-century Roman imperial worldview.

On the Gemma Augustea, the goddess Roma sits next to the emperor Augustus.

Augustus is being crowned by another goddess, Oikoumene, representing the whole of the inhabited world. A sea god looks on from the extreme right, alongside a goddess representing the earth. The eagle under the throne represents the god of the sky, Jupiter (known as Zeus in the Greek East), the god with whom the imperial rulers were most closely identified (Long 2013, 139–47). On the far left, Victoria (the goddess of Victory) holds the reins of a chariot. The message is clear: the gods not only surround Rome's ruler but grant him his power, approve of his rule, and ensure his victories in battle.

Power Rooted in Military Violence

Military symbols permeate the Gemma Augustea. Augustus is sitting on the throne with his feet on a shield, holding the augur by which he discerns whether to go into battle. The goddess Roma, representing Rome itself, rests her feet on the armor of the conquered. She has a spear in one hand, while her other hand rests on the hilt of her sword. The chariot on the far left, driven by the goddess Victoria, has likely just returned from battle (although there is a sense that it may take off for another one shortly). Augustus's son Tiberius is descending from the chariot, wearing the laurel leaves of the victor. A sword, shields, a spear, a chariot: the power granted to Rome by the gods is tightly bound to military might (Fischer 2024, 72–94).

On the lower left part of the cameo are Celtic or German prisoners of war, and soldiers raising a cross on which they have put the breastplate and helmet of those they have conquered (usually called a trophy). Other figures are engaged in subduing their enemies, including in one case by dragging them by their long, loose hair—a symbol of the wild and uncontrollable nature of barbarians. The two levels of the cameo are meant to be read together: military conquest of the barbarians underlies orderly rule and civilization.

James Steakley / Wikimedia Commons / CC BY-SA 3.0

Fig. 45.1. The Gemma Augustea (measures 7.5 inches by 9 inches)

The narrative conveyed in this image was common throughout the empire: Rome's power was granted by the gods and made possible by military violence. By forcibly subduing his enemies, who were unruly and wild barbarians, the emperor was honored by all of the inhabited world. This was an empire that used its authority to civilize the whole world, and it did so by means of violence and war.

Power over the Uncivilized and Barbarian "Other"

The images on the Gemma Augustea were rather common throughout the empire (although care was taken not to portray the emperor as divine in Rome itself). In fact, the Romans seemed to enjoy picturing defeated peoples in various postures of submission and humility. Defeated peoples, usually with hands tied behind their backs, were depicted on coins, the sides of public buildings, on altars, and in temple complexes. They were everywhere.

One such temple complex was found in Aphrodisias, not far from the early Christian communities of Colossae and Laodicea (in modern-day Turkey). This temple demonstrates how those who belonged to the elite class of society sought to emphasize their own importance in their communities and in the eyes of the empire by creating buildings (and sponsoring events) that would honor the emperor. In this way, they also accelerated the spread of the stories and symbols of Rome throughout the empire.

The temple complex in honor of Aphrodite in Aphrodisias included a long, three-story colonnade that functioned like an avenue in the town. With shops below, the top two stories contained sculptures and reliefs that depicted scenes not only of Roman imperial power but also of Greek mythology, reinterpreted to fit in with Roman history.

In addition, the colonnade included a striking array of statues and reliefs portraying fifty peoples (*ta ethnē*) that the Romans had conquered or subdued.[2] Each ethnic group was represented by the statue of a woman standing on a pedestal. Each pedestal had a man's head carved below the name of the people that the man and woman represented. The women are portrayed as exhibiting varying levels of civilization, indicated by their dress and hair. Those who had modest clothing and hair that was orderly and restrained were on their way to being "civilized." Those with loose, flowing hair and less modest clothing were peoples more in need of Rome's civilizing influence. These images were standard copies of statues that had originally been carved in Rome and which were "exported" and copied throughout the empire as a way to reinforce Rome's message about how the empire had united all the peoples, tribes, and nations under its benevolent rule (Smith 1988, 75–77; Lopez 2010, 52). The reach of Rome was seen to encompass the whole world; all peoples were now part of one body politic, Rome, with the emperor as its head.

There were also more evocative depictions of Rome subduing the nations in Aphrodisias. In one relief the emperor Claudius, naked except for a cape and scabbard, is kneeling on a stricken, fallen woman who represents Britain (see fig. 45.2). Her head is pulled back, her expression tortured as she waits for the death blow from the weapon that we can no longer see (Shaner 2017, 358). She is weak and powerless. His calm demeanor radiates power and control. While the nakedness of the emperor

Dosseman / Wikimedia Commons / CC BY-SA 4.0

Fig. 45.2. Claudius and Britannica

was an heroic indication of his divinity, the woman's long hair and half-clothed body demonstrate her shameful and uncivilized character. She needs to be dominated and subdued by the serene and culturally superior Claudius. By picturing defeated nations as women, images like this emphasized the weakness and irrationality of the conquered peoples. They also legitimated violence against women and slaves (Shaner 2017, 357–58; Lopez 2010). These images of defeat, along with depictions of prisoners with their hands bound behind their backs awaiting death or slavery, communicated a powerful message to other peoples: humiliation, servitude, and death await those who resist the power of Rome.

Power over the Natural World

Not only did imperial power provide benefits for other peoples, but carvings throughout the empire also depicted the new age of fertil-

2. It should be noted that the Greek *ta ethnē*, usually translated as "Gentiles" in the New Testament, is often more accurately translated as "the peoples." For most people in the first century, the usual contrast would have been not between Judeans and the peoples (or, more commonly, Jews and Gentiles) but rather between *Rome* and the peoples—in all of their diversity (Keesmaat 2021).

ity and abundance that the emperor Augustus, and later Nero, brought to the world. Augustus was the lord of all creation; his rule brought rich crops and the peace necessary for those crops to flourish. But the reminder was never far away: this, too, was rooted in the power of Roman military violence. Consider the Ara Pacis, the altar of peace in Rome. On one side is a detailed portrayal of the goddess of Peace, sitting in the midst of children, animals, and bountiful fruit and grain (see fig. 45.3). On another side is an image of Roma seated on a pile of armor. The two images were meant to be read together—as people walked around this altar, the pictures would have been mutually reinforcing (Zanker 1988, 175; Beard, North, and Price 1998, 83–85). Peace and abundance were made possible by the power of Roman conquest and military violence; weapons were necessary for peace and security.

All of the images I have described reinforced a narrative that was nurtured by the imperial rulers and promoted by the ruling elite. In that narrative, Augustus, and those emperors who followed him, were hailed as "savior" and "son of God." They were the ones whose military victories were celebrated as "good news" (*euangelion*, the same word in Greek that is translated as "gospel" in the New Testament). The Roman Empire brought justice, piety, and peace (the Greek words for "justice" and "piety" [*dikaiosynē* and *pistis*] are translated as "righteousness" and "faithfulness" in the New Testament). What is more, this narrative had worldwide significance. This was the empire that the gods had blessed to rule the whole world, to bring justice and peace to all peoples. Caesar was the savior and lord, descended from the gods, and the one through whom the gods rule (Keesmaat 2019, 7–22).

Experiencing Roman Power "from Below"

Power to Crush

This story of Roman power, as inescapable as it was in the first century, was promoted and nurtured primarily by those with wealth and privilege throughout the empire. Those who had the leisure and learning to write histories of the empire or those who could afford to sponsor temple complexes or to commission altars, statues, and paintings controlled the story. However, this Roman story in all its aspects (i.e., the blessing of the gods, the abundance that empire promised, the civilizing effects of Roman military control, and the stability of Roman law and justice) was experienced in a vastly different way for those who inhabited the lower echelons of the hierarchical Roman social structure.

Depending on where one lived, the assurances of abundance, stability, and peace that Roman power promised could seem a little hollow. For those in Galilee, Samaria, and Judea during the first century, the Roman Empire was experienced as an increasingly oppressive power. Pompey's devastating victory over the area in 63 BCE resulted in the enslavement of part of the population. The Jewish community in Rome, some of whom heard Paul's letter to the Romans, was descended from freed slaves who had been captured by Pompey (Bradley 2004).

When the Galilean town of Sepphoris rebelled against the rule of Herod (known as a friend of the Romans) around 4 BCE, the inhabitants of the town were killed or enslaved, and the town was rebuilt as a Roman administrative center and resettled with people from other parts of the empire. Roman elites controlled the fishing industry at the Sea of Galilee and, in addition to Sepphoris, built Tiberius as an important administrative center for the area. Throughout both Galilee and Judea, imperial representatives appointed tax collectors, who were adept at collecting both tolls and head taxes and encouraged the expansion of large estates for export crops such as wine and olive oil, all at the expense of local villagers. Imperial representatives also ensured that those who rebelled against their rule were brutally

Fig. 45.3. Ara Pacis altar

stamped out. Pontius Pilate, the Roman governor, was particularly adept at this.

It was no surprise, therefore, that the simmering tensions that the occupation created erupted into a full-scale rebellion in 66 CE, resulting in the destruction of Jerusalem by Titus and the removal of its inhabitants in 70 CE. The event was commemorated on coins with the heading *Iudaea Capta* (Judea Conquered), often with a weeping bound woman (or, occasionally, a bearded man) representing Judea, sitting under a palm tree. These coins were issued and circulated throughout the empire for the next twenty-five years, reinforcing the power of Rome over those who resisted its rule and the defeated character of the Judeans throughout the empire.

This pattern of imperial control in Galilee and Judea was not unique. Other towns, too, over the long history of Rome, were completely destroyed by the Romans and resettled with new populations. Corinth was one such town

that we know of from the New Testament. Destroyed by the Romans in 146 BCE and refounded as a Roman colony in 44 BCE, it was resettled by freed slaves from other parts of the empire. Philippi, also important in the New Testament, was the scene of the last battle of the Roman civil war. It was named a Roman colony and settled with veteran soldiers on the land of its original inhabitants, who were still there (Shaner 2017, 358–59). Rome excelled in severing people from their land and their history.

Power to Enslave

The resettlement of rebellious peoples and the awarding of land to soldiers were only part of the reason why the empire was characterized by the mass relocation of people. By far the largest movement of people under Rome was that of the slave trade. Captured peoples were brought in chains to be paraded through the streets of Rome as symbols of imperial victory. Those not killed were sold as slaves. Later, as outright warfare became less common, many slaves were trafficked from the outskirts of the empire. The connection between military violence and slavery, however, was never lost: the violence celebrated on imperial statues against "barbarians" (i.e., those who were not "civilized") was often enacted by masters on their slaves, who were not "people."

Power for Destruction

The devastating impact of imperial power was also evident in the effect that Roman rule had on the land and the waterways. Under imperial rule, water became polluted and land became less fertile. As the growing city of Rome demanded more food, the fertility of the land in Italy plummeted due to deforestation and erosion. This hastened the clearing of land in North Africa to grow wheat and in Spain to cultivate olives and grapes for wine, all of which were sent to Rome. The pressure of Rome was also felt at the far reaches of the empire. The army alone had enormous needs: leather for tents and clothing; grain for the animals who ultimately were turned into leather; metal for nails, weapons, armor, and fastenings; wood for building, cooking fires, and baths. Mining demanded large amounts of wood for reinforcing the mines and smelting the metals. Wood was also needed for ships to move goods quickly and easily to the heart of the empire, and for baths in Rome. As the Roman Empire moved northward, soldiers cleared forests for an endless supply of wood (Hughes 2014, 70–76, 110–20, 124–26).

Waterways were polluted by mining and smelting, and harbors silted up with erosion after trees were cleared, increasing mosquito habitat and unleashing malaria on local populations. Animals were killed by the hundreds every week in Rome alone, never mind other cities, as part of imperial gladiatorial games.

The first extinctions in Europe were caused by the Romans (Hughes 2014, 104). In addition, exotic spices, unusual fruits, fine woods, jewels, linens, silk, ivory, marble, and precious metals were brought from the far reaches of the empire for the consumption of the elite in Rome.

Perhaps the most effective symbol of Roman environmental destruction is the Roman road. Forty feet wide, with deep foundations, Roman roads cut off streams, flattened hills, cut down forests, and created erosion (Hughes 2014, 180). An environmental disaster, these roads have been praised throughout history as the ultimate symbol of Roman engineering, since they made it possible to move troops, people, and goods to and from Rome. The cry of the earth was drowned out by an ongoing fascination with progress even then.

Power Subverted?

So pervasive were the messages of Roman power, divine authority, and military might and control that it might come as a surprise that local customs, languages, and religions still flourished throughout the empire. This was partly because Rome simply did not have the troops or administrators to directly control much of the empire. As a result, Greek, not Roman Latin, continued to be the dominant official language in the Roman East, with many ethnic groups throughout the empire still speaking their own languages in nonofficial contexts (Strelan 2011). Rome's easy identification of Roman gods with local deities meant that traditional religious practices and worship continued to flourish in most places in happy harmony with the worship of imperial deities. The exceptions were the Judeans and Christians, whose refusal to worship Roman divinities alongside their own god and messiah was for many a puzzling stance.

And, of course, the infrastructure of the empire itself made possible the sharing of narratives that challenged the official stories of power. Roman roads, for instance, provided relatively easy travel for the members of the early Christian communities and their enslaved servants who carried the letters that Paul and others wrote to small communities of Jesus followers across the empire. On those roads Paul himself rubbed shoulders with tradespeople, teachers, merchants, those who were homeless, and those who were enslaved. Some engaged in legitimate business, while others were on the run. On those roads Paul heard the stories of his fellow travelers, which would have included stories of struggle, capture, violence, hunger, and homelessness (Tamez 1993, 48–53). And on those roads Paul shared the story of another kind of power and the hope of another kind of empire.

For most inhabitants of the empire, however, the all-encompassing nature of Roman power, divinely ordained, violently reinforced, and powerfully upheld by the dynamics of honor and shame, was something that could never be changed. The best one could do was either engage in small acts of resistance or seek to move up to a position of higher honor and power oneself. It was in this overarching story of divine power, violence, and control that the New Testament offered an alternative story, one that would challenge the power of Rome in revolutionary ways.

Works Cited

Beard, Mary, John North, and Simon R. F. Price. 1998. *The Religions of Rome*. Cambridge: Cambridge University Press.

Bradley, Keith R. 2004. "On Captives under the Principiate." *Phoenix* 58, nos. 3–44: 398–418 (see plates on pp. 374–90).

Fischer, Julia C. 2024. *Power and Propaganda in the Large Imperial Cameos of the Early Roman Empire*. London: Routledge.

Hughes, J. Donald. 2014. *The Environmental Problems of the Greeks and Romans: Ecology in the Ancient Mediterranean*. Baltimore: Johns Hopkins University Press.

Keesmaat, Sylvia C. 2019. *Romans Disarmed: Resisting Empire, Demanding Justice*. Grand Rapids: Baker Academic.

———. 2021. "Citizenship and Empire: A Missional Engagement with Ephesians." In *Cross, Participation and Mission*, edited by Christopher W. Skinner, Nijay K. Gupta, Andy Johnson, and Drew Strait, 240–59. Grand Rapids: Eerdmans.

Long, Frederick, J. 2013. "Roman Imperial Rule under the Authority of Jupiter-Zeus: Political-Religious Contexts and the Interpretation of 'The Ruler of the Authority of the Air' in Ephesians 2:2." In *The Language of the New Testament*, edited by S. E. Porter and A. W. Pitts, 113–54. Leiden: Brill.

Lopez, Davina C. 2010. *Apostle to the Conquered: Reimagining Paul's Mission*. Minneapolis: Fortress.

Maier, Harry O. 2013. *Picturing Paul in Empire: Imperial Image, Text and Persuasion in Colossians, Ephesians and the Pastoral Epistles*. New York: Bloomsbury T&T Clark.

Nasrallah, Laura S. 2010. *Early Christian Responses to Roman Art and Architecture*. London: Cambridge University Press.

Price, Simon R. F. 1984. *Rituals and Power: The Roman Imperial Cult in Asia Minor*. Cambridge: Cambridge University Press.

Shaner, Katherine A. 2017. "Seeing Rape and Robbery: ἁρπαγμός and the Philippians Christ Hymn (Phil. 2:5–11)." *BibInt* 25: 342–63.

Smith, R. R. R. 1988. "*Simulacra Gentium*: The *Ethnē* from the Sebasteion at Aphrodisias." *JRS* 78: 50–77.

Strelan, Rick. 2011. "The Languages of the Lycus Valley." In *Colossae in Space and Time: Linking to an Ancient City*, edited by Alan H. Cadwallader and Michael Trainor, 77–103. NTOA 94. Göttingen: Vandenhoeck & Ruprecht.

Tamez, Elsa. 1993. *The Amnesty of Grace: Justification by Faith from a Latin American Perspective*. Translated by Sharon H. Ringe. Nashville: Abingdon.

Zanker, Paul. 1988. *The Power of Images in the Age of Augustus*. Ann Arbor: University of Michigan Press.

46

Roman Law and Citizenship

J. Brian Tucker

The question of what made Roman society Roman is not simple to answer, because the term "Roman" includes complexity in what it signifies (Lavan 2020). Nonetheless, despite the unique character of local expressions of Roman identity, the term "Roman" tends to signify a shared social identification as a citizen community that valued Roman citizenship (*civitas Romana*) and adherence to Roman "civic law" (*ius civile*). Roman citizenship, from the middle Republic onward, provided a means for maintaining control over an immense amount of territory. Roman citizens inhabited diverse regions in which they possessed a recognized juridical social identity that provided status in all the territories under the power of Rome (Cecchet 2017, 8–9). When contrasting Roman law with the "law among the other nations," Cicero concludes: "For it is incredible how disordered, and wellnigh absurd [*ridiculum*], is all national law [*ius civile*] other than our own" (*De or.* 1.44.197 [trans. Sutton and Rackham 1942, 137]). Roman civic law comprised "the norms which were exclusively applicable to Roman

citizens and to them alone," stemming "from customary practices, from statues, or from juristic interpretation" (Schiller 1978, 525). While these norms extended specific rights to Roman citizens, they also came with certain duties that at times could form Roman citizens into a discernible social group. Many of these duties could be traced back to the Twelve Tables, a fifth-century BCE manual of Roman law, which continued to provide autochthony for local expressions of Roman social identity in the first century CE.

Roman writers were confident in the practical wisdom of Roman law, believing that it produced a superior way of ruling and living. Gaius, a second-century CE Roman jurist, similarly extols the unique supremacy of Roman civic law, especially as it relates to the "power of a father" (*patria potestas*): "This right is peculiar to Roman citizens; for scarcely any other men have over their sons a power such as we have" (*Inst*. 1.55 [trans. De Zulueta 1946, 17]; Gaius acknowledges, however, that the "Galatians" have a similar law). Noting this and other rights of Roman citizens enabled Gaius to strengthen the connection between Roman citizenship and its juridical identity. Roman civic law helped to construct a distinct Roman social identity, even as it encompassed aspects of laws from other nations. Ulpian, another Roman jurist who wrote a few decades after Gaius, claims that Roman civic law "is that which neither wholly diverges from *jus naturale* [natural law] or *jus gentium* [nations' law]" and notes that "whenever . . . we add anything or take anything away from" the civic legal corpus "we make a law special to ourselves" (Justinian, *Dig.* 1.1.6 pr. [trans. Watson 2009, 2]). The aggregation of these indigenously configured laws is one way in which Roman civic law took shape and allowed Rome's interests to be perpetuated around the Mediterranean basin (Girdvainyte 2014, 8, 10). This is the social context for much that occurs in the New Testament, with its depictions of people navigating Roman rule in the Roman province of Judea and of the Christ movement's leaders being subjected to legal rulings or norms informed by Roman "ancestral customs" (*mos maiorum*) in areas far beyond Judea.

Roman Citizenship

Roman citizenship, which conferred political and legal privilege (and therefore excluded enslaved persons), was a complex and multifaceted phenomenon in the early centuries of the Common Era. Often citizenship was inherited, for those whose parents were Roman citizens. But it could also be bestowed on individuals by generals and emperors. For instance, Tacitus records a decree by the Roman emperor Otho (who reigned for three months in 69 CE) in which he "bestowed . . . on the entire people of the Lingones the privileges of Roman citizenship" (*Hist.* 1.78 [trans. Church and Brodribb 1864, 53]). The example of Otho only repeats what had been occurring for several hundred years, as grants of citizenship on the Italian peninsula were targeted to include some people

further west as well. Cassius Dio records the way the emperor Claudius "granted citizenship to others quite indiscriminately, sometimes to individuals and sometimes to whole groups," adding that indiscriminate granting and purchasing of citizenship "cheapened" its currency so much that a saying developed that you could buy citizenship "by giving the right person some bits of broken glass" (*Hist. Rom.* 60.17.5–6 [trans. Cary and Foster 1924, 411]). Nonetheless, the granting of citizenship by imperial decree was usually restricted "to particular individuals, often members of local elites, whom it was valuable to have as Roman allies" (Walton 2017, 242). Conversely, many enslaved people gained Roman citizenship upon manumission (if their former enslavers were themselves Roman citizens), with the expectation that they would now act on their own agency as responsible members of Roman society. In some instances, former enslaved persons who gained their freedom before the age of thirty were deemed "Junian Latins," who could enjoy only a limited form of citizenship until they could prove certain credentials over a limited period of time, at which point full citizenship opened up to them (for an example, see Longenecker 2020, 19–20). There were, then, a diversity of ways in which individuals could obtain the status of Roman citizenship. For Dionysius of Halicarnassus, these various ways of securing citizenship resulted in Rome emerging "from the smallest nation to the greatest and from the most obscure to the most illustrious" (*Ant. rom.* 1.9.4 [trans. Cary 1937, 31]).

Roman citizenship conferred certain kinds of privileges and protections. In some contexts, Roman citizens were shielded against legal charges being brought against them by noncitizens. If legitimate charges were brought against them, they were entitled to a trial and the privilege of appealing to the emperor if their case did not end in a favorable result. If found guilty of a serious offense, citizens would be protected from the more severe types of punishments. Citizens were able to vote in Roman elections, and those whose citizenship had not been tarred by previous enslavement could run for political office. Citizens may also have been exempted from paying certain taxes. They could execute a Roman marriage contract or engage in adoption. Citizens were extended certain protections in relation to commercial pursuits, along with various property and inheritance activities (Jeffers 1999, 198–99). In the Republican period, there was "the duty of military service," but by the time of the Principate this duty had been removed "from the list of essential characteristics of the citizenship" (Sherwin-White 1973, 266). This demonstrates that the privileges and duties of citizenship could change at various times.

Freedpersons, Jews, and Women

We have seen that it was possible for a former enslaved person to acquire citizenship through manumission in accordance with Roman law (Gaius, *Inst.* 1.1.16–21). If the enslaver was a Roman citizen, the enslaved person would receive citizenship upon their manumission; if the enslaver was a "resident alien" (*peregrinus*), they would not. Even if people were granted Roman citizenship upon manumission, they enjoyed fewer freedoms than those in possession of Roman citizenship by birth. The former enslaved person still had obligations to their former enslaver, though from an economic perspective they could still surpass a poor "freeborn person," especially if they had been an imperial enslaved person (*ingenuus*; Pliny the Elder, *Nat.* 33.134–35). Those freedpersons who were skilled and educated in civic jobs had an existing social network by which to establish a means of economic advancement. Even though their juridical social identity had changed, they often maintained a lack of social acceptability found among multigenerational Roman citizens (Horace, *Serm.* 1.6; *CIL* 10.846).

The fact that freedpeople carried their identity as former enslaved persons with them is evidenced in the reference to "those who belonged to the synagogue of the Freedmen" (*libertinōn*) in Acts 6:9. This synagogue was constituted by former enslaved persons who likely had become Roman citizens (Gaius, *Inst.* 1.12). The plausibility of this is strengthened by a first-century inscription that describes "Theodotus, son of Vettenos, priest and synagogue chief," as an individual who remodeled a pre-70 CE synagogue in Jerusalem that had been built previously by his grandfather (*CIJ* 2.332–35 §1404). Theodotus's father, Vettenos (a Latin name), was likely a freedperson from the family of Vettius who had migrated back to Jerusalem from Rome.

The background to this probably lies in the enslavement of Judeans by the Roman general Pompey in 63 BCE, who forced them to migrate to Rome. Some of these people were eventually manumitted and remained in Rome, living together across the Tiber River and establishing synagogues there (Philo, *Embassy* 155–56). As long as those Jews married within the community of Roman citizens, their children maintained their Roman citizenship, shedding the "freedperson" title and status in the process. Some of these Jews with Roman citizenship then traveled from Rome to reside in other parts of the empire, including Judea (Keener 2020, 230; Josephus, *Life* 13).

The fact that Jewish Roman citizens were living in Judea raises questions with regard to the way Roman law was enforced in that Roman province, especially in light of the existing laws found in Israel's scriptural tradition, which Josephus characterizes as an "all-encompassing legal tradition" (Josephus, *Ag. Ap.* 2.173–74). This is one example of a larger challenge Rome faced as it navigated the way Roman law applied to citizens and the way local laws continued to apply to noncitizens. Extant sources do not provide extensive evidence for the way Roman law preserved rights for Jews, though even after direct Roman rule from 6 CE on there is still a "lack of uptake of Roman legal practices" (Czajkowski 2020, 96). For instance, Julius Caesar declared in 47 BCE that "if . . . any question shall arise concerning the Jews' manner of life, it is my pleasure that they shall have the decision" (Josephus, *Ant*. 14.190–95; see Ben Zeev 1998, 1). This would come to mean that Jews were able to maintain key aspects of their administrative and monetary structures, assemble and debate, celebrate feasts and communal meals, and observe Sabbath and other of their ancestral traditions (*Ant*. 14.213–16, 225–27, 241–46, 256–67). These brief examples are not unique to Jews but were part of the way Rome negotiated and maintained its empire (Appian, *Mith*. 6.39).

By the first century CE, women who were Roman citizens had notable legal privileges, although not to the same extent as men. They could register legal charges against others and could appear in court, though there were restrictions associated with these actions. Gaius records that women were required to have a legal guardian in court regardless of their age or status (*Inst*. 144, 190–91). According to one inscription (*IG* 5/1 1208), a female Roman citizen by the name Phaenia Aromation gave a significant donation of money to supply oil for those in Gytheion. She wanted this to be recognized legally in view of Roman law, so she executed a document in court in the presence of her guardian (P. Ophellius Crispus), as required by Roman law. She also sought protection for her freedpersons by appealing to a local law in the province of Achaia. This inscription is a good example of the interplay between Roman law and local law, as well as the political savviness of Phaenia in navigating financial, manumission, and guardian legal issues (Girdvainyte 2020, 231).

Noncitizen women might also interact with Roman law. An example of this is the archive of documents from the early second century CE pertaining to a woman named Babatha, who lived in an Arabian town on the southeastern end of the Dead Sea (see further Oudshoorn 2007; Esler 2017). This Jewish woman secured access to a Roman court and brought with her a guardian, as required by Roman law. One document from this archive is written in Aramaic, Greek, and Latin, highlighting the contextual application of Roman law in the provinces (*PYadin* 16). Babatha's copies of the court rulings were crucial for her continued protection of her child's interests (*PYadin* 28–30, *actio tutelae*; Girdvainyte 2020, 231). Both of these examples remind us of the diverse ways various groups of people experienced Roman law, both as citizens and as noncitizens within the provinces.

Paul's Citizenship

With various ways of possessing Roman citizenship, people in the Greco-Roman world were conscious that there were certain status differentials in play with regard to citizenship (Longenecker 2020, 17–18). There was, for instance, a binary opposition between citizens and noncitizens. This is illustrated in the exchange between Paul and the magistrates in Philippi, who would have treated Paul differently had they known of his Roman citizenship. Members of the Roman colony of Philippi accuse Paul and Silas of advocating anti-Roman practices. Then "the crowd joined in attacking them, and the magistrates had them stripped of their clothing and ordered them to be beaten with rods" (Acts 16:22). Later they are thrown into jail without a trial (16:37). When it was discovered that Paul and Silas were Roman citizens, "the magistrates . . . were afraid" (16:38). Although they had mistreated Paul and Silas for putative anti-Roman activities, it now becomes evident (ironically) that the Roman provincial officials themselves were implicated for such activities in their treatment of Paul and Silas.

If there was a binary relationship between citizens and noncitizens, there were also "variables even within citizenship status" (Longenecker

2020, 17), as in the following exchange: "The tribune [Claudius Lysias; Acts 23:26] came and asked Paul, 'Tell me, are you a Roman citizen?' And he said, 'Yes.' The tribune answered, 'It cost me a large sum of money to get my citizenship.' Paul said, 'But I was born a citizen'" (Acts 22:27–28). This amounts to a challenge-and-riposte encounter. The Roman tribune Lysias seeks to belittle Paul by minimizing his citizenship status. In the end, his assumption that Paul had purchased his citizenship cheaply (the point made by Cassius Dio, *Hist. Rom.* 60.17.5–6, as noted above) or by being manumitted turns out to be mistaken. Paul's status as a citizen ran deeper than Lysias's, being by birth rather than any other means.

Scholars sometimes debate whether Paul was actually a Roman citizen or if this was crafted by Luke for rhetorical affect, especially since Paul never says this about himself in his letters (cf. Stegemann 1987; Keener 2020, 415–17), even in contexts where we might expect him to have done so (e.g., Phil. 3:2–11). But if it were merely a Lukan literary invention, the narrative implications are significant since the appeal to the emperor as the means by which Paul arrives safely in Rome (though in custody) is predicated on his Roman citizenship (Acts 25:10–12; cf. Phil. 4:22; Adams 2008, 315). If invented, this narrative feature would place Luke's plot in jeopardy for those who knew otherwise (see further Christensen 2018, 63–74).

Two points should be mentioned that are in the background of Luke's narrative regarding Paul's Roman citizenship. First, the various protections and privileges afforded to a Roman citizen did require some means by which to determine whether a claim was legal and legitimate. There were harsh punishments for those who falsely claimed to be in possession of this (Epictetus, *Diatr.* 2.24.41; Suetonius, *Claud.* 25.3). For those born into citizenship, a record of this status was recorded in the archive for that city or colony. This was to occur within thirty days of the birth, at which point

the father would have been given a wooden diptych that functioned as a birth certificate and proof of citizenship (Walton 2017, 243). This then would have been kept in the possession of any citizen who was traveling as proof of their status. If for some reason this was unavailable, witnesses could be called to attest to a person's Roman citizenship.

The second point is that in late Republican Rome dual citizenship was not allowed. However, by the first century CE this had changed. Roman citizenship could be added to an existing citizenship without relinquishing the original status (Walton 2017, 244; White 2021, 59). The existence of dual citizenship "was thoroughly established about the reign of Claudius" (Rapske 1994, 83, quoting *FIRA* 1.55, 68). In Acts 21:39, Luke recounts one of Paul's speeches, "I am a Jew, from Tarsus in Cilicia, a citizen [πολίτης, *politēs*] of an important city"; later, in 22:3, he exclaims, "I am a Jew, born in Tarsus in Cilicia." This civic status exists alongside Paul's Roman citizenship (although the Greek word πολίτης can also signify someone who is merely a resident of a city, in which case the citizenship relationship shifts; see BDAG 846).

Cosmopolitanism and Heavenly Citizenship

Some Roman citizens wanted to think of themselves as citizens of the world rather than simply as citizens of the most powerful city in that world. They saw themselves as members of a cosmopolis. Ovid could exclaim, "The circuit of Rome is the circuit of the world" (*Fasti* 2.684 [trans. Frazer 1987, 107]). Cosmopolitanism has been defined as "a complex of practices and ideals that enabled certain individuals not only to cross cultural boundaries, but to establish an enduring normative framework across them" (Lavan, Payne, and Weisweiler 2016, 1). This idea, and the practices that were embedded within it, allowed Rome to maintain juridical control over vast territories.

The Jewish philosopher Philo of Alexandria had his own conception of cosmopolitanism, in which people would "marvel at the might of God as the creator and father of all" (*Creation* 7 [Yonge 1993, 3]). For Philo, the universe is ordered by Torah instead of Roman law (*Creation* 3, 142–43). As a Roman citizen living in Egypt, Philo found himself in a liminal space in relation to two competing ideas of cosmopolitanism— much like some early Christ followers.

In the New Testament, citizenship language occurs especially in Philippians, where Paul draws from the social encyclopedia of citizenship on two occasions. In Philippians 3:20 he writes: "But our citizenship [πολίτευμα, *politeuma*] is in heaven, and it is from there that we are expecting a Savior, the Lord Jesus Christ." The indigenous Greeks and Thracians living in the Roman colony of Philippi were restricted from positions of political power if they were not also Roman citizens. The civic structures of Philippi (and beyond) "were in the hands of Roman citizens" (Ehrensperger 2019, 29). Political power had coalesced around a small group of Roman citizens, while the majority of the population was left without significant agency. In that setting, Paul, as one familiar with the discourses of Roman citizenship, construes a social identity for the local Christ group as "citizens of heaven," a pattern of belonging that finds its social identification in another realm rather than with one ordered by Roman law and citizenship expectations (Thompson and Longenecker 2016, 49–51). Roman citizens who found their identity in this heavenly citizenship may have experienced an "attendant loss of identity and status" within that broader culture (White 2021, 60–61; see also Flower 2011, 2–3).

In Philippians 1:27, Paul writes to these Greek and Thracian "citizens of heaven" in this fashion: "Only, live your life [πολιτεύεσθε, *politeuesthe*] in a manner worthy of the gospel of Christ." Here Paul uses a Greek verb that can signify "to be a citizen" (BDAG 846;

Acts 23:1). He does this to encourage the group to root their sense of belonging in the realm from above, to which they now belong. Kathy Ehrensperger (2019, 43) sees Paul fashioning a "Jewish small-world network cosmopolitanism" that will result in human flourishing even amid "their everyday concerns and pressures." They are then to form an "alternative colony," one that will inevitability be in conflict with the Roman colony in Philippi (Thompson and Longenecker 2016, 51).

Conclusion

An understanding of Roman law and society is crucial for interpreting the New Testament in its historical context. The importance of Roman citizenship and adherence to Roman "civic law" in forming local expressions of the social identity of the Roman citizen community cannot be overstated. New Testament texts reflect this societal and legal framework in a myriad of ways, from Paul's use of legal language to describe the believer's relationship with God to the portrayal of Jesus's trial and crucifixion (Hunt 2019). Therefore, an appreciation of the nexus between Roman law, citizenship, and society is necessary for a nuanced understanding of the New Testament and the world in which it was written.

Works Cited

Adams, Sean A. 2008. "Paul the Roman Citizen: Roman Citizenship in the Ancient World and Its Importance for Understanding Acts 22:22–29." In *Paul: Jew, Greek, and Roman*, edited by Stanley E. Porter, 309–26. Leiden: Brill.

Ben Zeev, Miriam Pucci. 1998. *Jewish Rights in the Roman Word: The Greek and Roman Documents Quoted by Josephus Flavius*. Tübingen: Mohr Siebeck.

Cary, Earnest, trans. 1937. *Dionysius of Halicarnassus: Roman Antiquities*. Vol. 1. LCL 319. Cambridge, MA: Harvard University Press.

Cary, Earnest, and Herbert B. Foster, trans. 1924. *Dio Cassius: Roman History*. Vol. 7. LCL 175. Cambridge, MA: Harvard University Press.

Cecchet, Lucia. 2017. "Greek and Roman Citizenship: State of Research and Open Questions." In *Citizens in the Graeco-Roman World: Aspects of Citizenship from the Archaic Period to AD 212*, edited by Lucia Cecchet and Anna Busetto, 1–30. Leiden: Brill.

Christensen, Daniel K. 2018. "Roman Citizenship as a Climactic Narrative Element: Paul's Roman Citizenship in Acts 16 and 22 Compared with Cicero's *Against Verres*." *Conversations with the Biblical World* 38: 55–75.

Church, A. J., and W. J. Brodribb, trans. 1864. *The History of Tacitus: Translated into English*. Cambridge: Macmillan.

Czajkowski, Kimberly. 2020. "Law and Romanization in Judaea." In *Law in the Roman Provinces*, edited by Kimberly Czajkowski, Benedikt Eckhardt, and Meret Strothmann, 84–100. Oxford: Oxford University Press.

De Zulueta, Francis, trans. 1946. *The Institutes of Gaius*. Part 1, *Text with Critical Notes and Translation*. Oxford: Clarendon.

Ehrensperger, Kathy. 2019. "The Politeuma in the Heavens and the Construction of Collective Identity in Philippians." *Journal of the Jesus Movement in Its Jewish Setting* 6: 22–45.

Esler, Philip. 2017. *Babatha's Orchard: The Yadin Papyri and an Ancient Jewish Family Tale Retold*. Oxford: Oxford University Press.

Flower, Harriet I. 2011. *The Art of Forgetting: Disgrace and Oblivion in Roman Political Culture*. Studies in the History of Greece and Rome. Chapel Hill: University of North Carolina Press.

Frazer, J. G., trans. 1987. *Ovid: Fasti*. Rev. ed. Revised by G. P. Goold. LCL 253. Cambridge, MA: Harvard University Press.

Girdvainyte, Lina. 2014. "Roman Law, Roman Citizenship, Roman Identity? Interrelation between the Three in the Late Republic and Early Empire." MA thesis, Leiden University.

———. 2020. "Law and Citizenship in Roman Achaia: Continuity and Change." In *Law in the Roman Provinces*, edited by Kimberly Czajkowski, Benedikt Eckhardt, and Meret Strothmann, 210–42. Oxford: Oxford University Press.

Hunt, Laura J. 2019. *Jesus Caesar: A Roman Reading of the Johannine Trial Narrative*. WUNT 2/506. Tübingen: Mohr Siebeck.

Jeffers, James S. 1999. *The Greco-Roman World of the New Testament: Exploring the Background of Early Christianity*. Downers Grove, IL: InterVarsity.

Keener, Craig. 2020. *Acts*. New Cambridge Bible Commentary. Cambridge: Cambridge University Press.

Lavan, Myles. 2020. "Beyond Romans and Others: Identities in the Long Second Century." In *Literature and Culture in the Roman Empire*, edited by Alice König, Rebecca Langlands, and James Uden, 37–57. Cambridge: Cambridge University Press.

Lavan, Myles, Richard E. Payne, and John Weisweiler. 2016. "Cosmopolitan Politics: The Assimilation and Subordination of Elite Cultures." In *Cosmopolitanism and Empire: Universal Rulers, Local Elites, and Cultural Integration in the Ancient Near East and Mediterranean*, edited by Myles Lavan, Richard E. Payne, and John Weisweiler, 1–28. Oxford: Oxford University Press.

Longenecker, Bruce W. 2020. *In Stone and Story: Early Christianity in the Roman World*. Grand Rapids: Baker Academic.

Oudshoorn, Carolien. 2007. *The Relationship between Roman and Local Law in the Babatha and Salome Komaise Archives: General Analysis and Three Case Studies on Law of Succession, Guardianship and Marriage*. STDJ. Leiden: Brill.

Rapske, Brian. 1994. *The Book of Acts and Paul in Roman Custody*. Grand Rapids: Eerdmans.

Schiller, A. Arthur. 1978. *Roman Law: Mechanisms of Development*. New York: Mouton.

Sherwin-White, A. N. 1973. *The Roman Citizenship*. 2nd ed. Oxford: Clarendon.

Stegemann, Wolfgang. 1987. "War der Apostel Paulus ein römischer Bürger?" *ZNW* 78, nos. 3–4: 200–229.

Sutton, E. W., and H. Rackham, trans. 1942. *Cicero: On the Orator, Books 1–2*. LCL 348. Cambridge, MA: Harvard University Press.

Thompson, James W., and Bruce W. Longenecker. 2016. *Philippians and Philemon*. Paideia Commentaries on the New Testament. Grand Rapids: Baker Academic.

Walton, Steve. 2017. "Heavenly Citizenship and Earthly Authorities." In *The Urban World and the First Christians*, edited by Steve Walton, Paul R. Trebilco, and David W. J. Gill, 236–52. Grand Rapids: Eerdmans.

Watson, Alan, trans. and ed. 2009. *The Digest of Justinian*. Vol. 1. Philadelphia: University of Pennsylvania Press.

White, Adam G. 2021. *Paul, Community, and Discipline: Establishing Boundaries and Dealing with the Disorderly*. Paul in Critical Contexts. New York: Lexington Books/Fortress Academic.

Yonge, C. D., trans. 1993. *The Works of Philo: Complete and Unabridged*. New updated ed. Peabody, MA: Hendrickson.

47

Greco-Roman Associations

Jin Hwan Lee

The Greco-Roman world was largely institutionalized—from the family (the smallest unit of society) to the *polis* as a whole. Each unit had its own system of social relations and boundaries, cultic operations, and benefits for its members (Kloppenborg and Ascough 2011, 1). Encompassing the family and the *polis* was another ubiquitous, unofficial institution that provided social activities in the private realm.[1] It had various nomenclatures, such as *collegium*, *sodalitas*, *cultores*, or *familiae* in Latin, and ὀργεῶνες (*orgeōnes*), θίασος (*thiasos*), ἔρανος (*eranos*), κοινόν (*koinon*), or σύνοδος (*synodos*) in Greek. These Latin and Greek words are generally translated as "association." Dennis Smith correctly defines the association as "an enlarged family" and "a miniature *polis*" because associations provided social benefits to their members similar to those of the family and the *polis* (2003, 96; see also Nock 1924; Dill 1904, 263, 280). While membership in these two institutions was automatically granted by birth, membership in associations was generally less restricted. Because of this character, associations were sometimes called "voluntary associations," but "private associations" is a better term and widely accepted in scholarship today, since not all associations practiced open membership (Wilson 1996, 1; Arnaoutoglou 2003; Kloppenborg 2019, 23).

Scholarship in the late nineteenth century classified associations in three types based on their functional purposes: cultic, funerary, and professional (Waltzing 1895, 1:46; Kornemann 1900, 388). Such a taxonomy, however, has been problematized. This is because epigraphic evidence simply does not verify any association that existed solely for the purpose of burial (Kloppenborg 1996, 20–22; Ausbüttell 1982, 22–23; Ascough 2003, 21; Harland 2003, 28–29). In fact, every association commonly had cultic and burial practices, demonstrating considerable overlaps in a functional point of view. Hence, scholarship today classifies associations in five types based on either membership profile (Kloppenborg 2006, 323–24)

1. There were several official ones sanctioned by the state for governing purposes; see Kloppenborg 1996, 16–17.

or social networks (Harland 2003, 25–53): household, cultic, professional, ethnic, and neighborhood groups.

Associations are known from before the sixth century BCE. We find the first literary evidence regarding associations from the law of Solon (Bonfante 1960 [*Digesta Iustiniani Augusti* 47.22.4]). Archaeological evidence from the acropolis also proves the same (Ferguson 1944, 68). However, it is after the time of Alexander the Great that we see a notable rise in the existence of associations, with many associational inscriptions coming from the fourth century BCE and onward (Kloppenborg 1996, 17). Current association studies, therefore, rely mainly on those inscriptions in an attempt to figure out the social practices of associations. Association data not only reveal detailed ancient in-group praxis and ethos but also help us to grasp a balanced understanding of the Greco-Roman world. Inscriptions cited below are only selective for exemplary purpose. There are indeed numerous inscriptions from a range of time periods verifying similar practices in associations.

Associations and Social Engagement

Private associations promoted substantial social engagement for members in two ways. First, besides professional guilds such as artisans in trades (which were normally male dominated; Whelan 1993, 75–76), most associations had removed gender and status as hindrances to membership. For example, in *IG* 2² 1297 (= *GRA* 1.24 [3rd c. BCE]), we find fifty-eight names inscribed, of which twenty-one are female and thirty-seven are male. *TAM* 5.539 (= *GRA* 2.117 [100 BCE]) reveals various status profiles of its members: men, women, free people, and even slaves. Such heterogeneous membership profiles in terms of gender and status can be observed in later associations as well (*IEph* 20 = *GRA* 2.127 [54–59 CE]; *SEG* 46.800 = *GRA* 1.72 [250 CE]), demonstrating that associations were generally practicing open membership.

Second, associations provided social benefits to members—which individuals particularly in lower social strata generally could not afford for themselves, such as burial and a funeral ceremony (*IG* 2² 1275 = *GRA* 1.8 [325–275 BCE]; *IG* 2² 1327 = *GRA* 1.35 [178/177 BCE]; *IG* 2² 1368 = *GRA* 1.51 [164/5 CE]). Other benefits that associations provided were financial support, emotional support in the case of a loss of loved ones (*IPergamon* 374 = *GRA* 2.111 [129–138 CE]; *PCair* 30606 = *GRA* 3.191 [158/157 BCE]), and the offsetting of homesickness for those who had to move to different regions for the purpose of their professions or trades.

Perhaps the most astonishing benefit that associations provided to members was a chance to elevate their personal status in a corporate context. Associations elected their functionaries (such as priests, treasurers, secretaries, and so forth) for the purpose of effective governing. These positions, however, were not permanently given to the elected members but only temporarily entrusted to them. Associations periodically convened a meeting for voting on new functionaries. Casting a lot seemed a proper mode for electing functionaries in associations (*IG* 2² 1369 = *GRA* 1.49 [2nd c. CE]; *IG* 2² 1368 = *GRA* 1.51 [164/5 CE]; *SEG* 31.122 = *GRA* 1.50 [2nd c. CE]) as it was widely practiced in ancient Greece (Avasthi 1958, 276). Some associations appointed their functionaries simply according to their membership lists (*CIL* 14.2112 = *AGRW* 310 [136 CE]) or directly by their functioning priest (*eukosmos*, "charge of order," in *IG* 2² 1368, 136–39). Complying to the one-year incumbency of various magistrates under the empire (Vishnia 2012, 106), many associations also established one-year terms of service (*IG* 2² 1369; *AM* 66, 228 no. 4, plates 75, 76 = *GRA* 1.39 [138/137 BCE]; *SEG* 2.9 = *GRA* 1.21 [243/242 BCE]). Depending on a group's situation, however, there could be different terms of service. The Iobakchoi group elected their treasurer every two years (*IG* 2² 1368, 146–47; other roles were one year), and other groups had terms as short as a month (*IKios* 22 = *GRA* 2.101) or even a day (*SEG* 31.122, 31–32).

Authoritative positions in associations were basically rotated from time to time, allowing all members, even in a lower social stratum, the chance to become a functionary. Of course, such a given status was fictive, valid *only* in that group. Because of this so-called flat hierarchy, many people from lower social strata were drawn to associations, allowing them to enjoy an elevated status within a corporate context (Kloppenborg 1996, 18).

"Life with status" in associations was certainly attractive. At least two social phenomena are worth noting. First, serving as a functionary itself was a benefaction to the group a person was involved in. Associations counted not only monetary support but also nonmaterial support such as appropriate administration and virtuous disposition as important benefactions (Lee 2018, 69). In return, associations honored their benefactors in public by inscribing their benefactions and names on steles, announcing and crowning them at communal gatherings, and so forth. Hence, by serving their group as a functionary, he or she could enjoy honorable rewards because reciprocity was at the core of benefaction practice in associations. For example, some associations *guaranteed* to return counterbalancing favor to every benefactor (*IG* 2² 1301 = *GRA* 1.25 [219/218 BCE]; *IG* 2² 1262 = *GRA* 1.10 [300/299 BCE]).

Second, although meals in associations were generally simple and not at all luxurious (mostly with bread and wine, as in *IPergamon* 374; *CIL* 5.7920; *CIL* 11.6033; Kloppenborg 2016, 176; Lee 2018, 97–100), functionaries had the chance to receive more food than other ordinary members at their communal gatherings. We often find peculiar measurements in food distribution in association data, such as a

"double portion" (*IDelta* I 446, 39–41 = *GRA* 3.160 [67–63 BCE]; *SEG* 31.122; *SEG* 40.688; *CIL* 14.2112), "a share and a half portion" (*CIL* 14.2112), and "a half amount" (*Agora* 16.161 = *GRA* 1.14 [early 3rd c. BCE]). Adding to these, we also find another measurement, a "given portion" (*SEG* 58.1640 = *GRA* 2.149 [150–100 BCE]). These data provide reasonable clues that associations had portioned meals (cf. Plutarch, *Quaest. conv.* 2.10.2) based on geometric distribution. That is to say, functionaries or benefactors received greater portions than other ordinary members, yet whose portions ("given portion") were nonetheless guaranteed at communal meals (Lee 2018, 93–97). In fact, such a hierarchical aspect embedded in geometric food distribution was widely practiced outside of associations in a sense of "equality" (D'Arms 1990, 318). However, external social ranks remained unchangeable; the change occurred only *within* associations, thus allowing members from lower social strata to temporarily experience a life with status.

Associational Meals, Fees, and Fines

Meal practices in associations are worth further discussion. Along with financial relations, association meals were at the center of an association's social activities. Meals and financial tasks were closely related since the meal in associations was not free. Although we do see a few cases demonstrating that a member or a patron/patrona of a group provided free meals for the group (*IG* 2² 1343 = *GRA* 1.48 [36 BCE]; *IDelos* 1520 = *AGRW* 224 [153/152 BCE], respectively), such cases occurred only irregularly and were regarded as noncontinuing benefactions. Instead, most communal meals were run based on members' assigned dues per meal, which were part of membership obligations. For example, the Iobakchoi group (*IG* 2² 1368) collected fifty denarii and a libation as a membership fee (lines 37–38) and fixed monthly dues (for wine) for official monthly gatherings (lines 42–47). We find a number of inscriptions verifying such fee collecting cases for periodic communal meals (Lee 2018, 133–34). These membership dues seemed crucial for provisioning a communal meal, since associations levied fines for those who did not fulfill their obligations (*IG* 2² 1339 = *GRA* 1.46 [57/56 BCE]; *SEG* 31.122). The Iobakchoi group even banned any member who could not make the payment from joining the communal gatherings (*IG* 2² 1368, 48–49 = *GRA* 1.51).

Not only did associations make much of dues for meals, but they also put a premium on creating a specific atmosphere while having communal meals. Many inscriptions demonstrate multiple table etiquette rules associated with fines and/or penalties. Quite frequently we find regulations against fighting (*IG* 2² 1368; *IG* 9/1² 670 = *GRA* 1.61 [mid-2nd c. CE]; *IG* 2² 1369; *SEG* 31.122; *PLond* VII 2193 = *GRA* 3.199 [69–58 BCE]), insulting (*IG* 2² 1368; *IG* 9/1² 670; *PMich* V 243 = *GRA* 3.206 [14–37 CE]; *PCair* 30606), and acting disorderly, including blows (*IG* 2² 1368; *IG* 9/1² 670; *IEph* 215 = *GRA* 2.125 [2nd–3rd c. CE]; *PLond* VII 2193). Associations assigned seats according to the internal status of members, which possibly caused many problems, particularly from the side of ordinary members whose actual social status was higher than those who held an internal status of authority. Rules against taking someone else's seat (*IG* 2² 1368; *PMich* V 243) and drunkenness (*PMich* V 243; cf. *SEG* 31.122) bolster the claim that associations directed their communal meetings to be as orderly and neat as possible by reducing the chances of such misbehavior. The Iobakchoi group even banned singing and speaking loudly at communal gatherings. The members were only able to sing and speak upon the priest's permission; otherwise, they were liable to pay fines of thirty drachmas (*IG* 2² 1368, 107–10 = *GRA* 1.51).

Absenteeism was also a crucial regulation in associations. Members were supposed to participate in every official meeting unless he or she had particular reasons, such as illness or travel. Fines for being absent without reason were normally higher than for other types of misbehavior. In the case of the Iobakchoi group, fines were doubled for absenteeism, up to fifty drachmas, while other misbehavior was fined at twenty-five drachmas. The same ratio is found in the Egyptian group (*PMich* V 243); this group charged one drachma (= six obols) for absenteeism when meeting in the village, while only collecting three obols for reclining on another member's seat. This group, particularly when having a meeting in the city, charged four drachmas for absenteeism, demonstrating how the group put a premium on solidarity in the communal gatherings. The group of *PCair* 30606 warned its members against absenteeism with the threat of curses by the god Sobek (lines 11–12). One of the reasons for levying higher fines for absenteeism, as well as collecting different amounts of fines depending on venues, must have been related to the meeting place settings. When associations gathered in nondomestic settings such as *tabernae*, warehouses, or rentable dining halls called *hestiatoria*, private meetings became no longer fully private but were often semi-public (cf. Dunbabin 2003, 72). Outsiders or passersby could see what a group of people was doing and possibly judge the group's standing by their attendance and table etiquette, which made associations manage misbehavior more strictly while holding periodic communal meals (Lee 2018, 76–83).

The Common Fund

Membership fees, internal and external monetary benefactions (*sportulae*; ἐνθήκη, *enthēkē*), assigned dues for meals, and collected fines—these all contributed to the common fund (κοινόν, *koinon*; ἔρανος, *eranos*) that each group had, which was managed by its treasurer (Harland 2015, 5–19). Depending on the availability of properties, some associations lent their temples or dining areas and expanded their common fund. The group of *IG* 2² 1361 (= *GRA* 1.4 [330–324/323 BCE]) had a house (οἶκος, *oikos*) that was utilized at the same time as a sanctuary. This group generated additional income by renting out the sanctuary along with water use (lines 8–12). The income was to be used for the repair and maintenance of the property. The Sobek temple found in Tebtynis had at least four dining areas, one of which was inside the temple, while the other three were located on the public road (*dromos*) leading to the vestibule of the temple. *PCair* 30606 reveals that these dining spaces were rented out for an agreed period of time, with rental dues payable every month. Some associations made use of their common fund to invest additional income. Members of some associations made lump sum endowments at the beginning. For instance, the association founded by a man named Marcus Aemilius Eucharistos (*SEG* 31.122) expanded the fund with membership dues and made loans from it (lines 42–43). Its functioning treasurer was not to draw from the principle but could utilize interest fees within three hundred drachmae limits (lines 9–13) for its periodic meetings. The association founded by a man named Symmasis (*SEG* 58.1640) also utilized interest from the common fund (which was not supposed to be used except for loans) for the yearly sacrifice meeting and the Founder's Day (lines 6–14 in face C). Both groups seriously penalized financial misappropriation by levying a burden of fines against those who misused the common fund (*SEG* 31.122: three times more than what was taken; *SEG* 58.1640: twice more than what was misused). Generally speaking, such strict management and auditing of financial transactions and tasks were common to all associations. As the Greek word *koinon* bears a sense of partnership, associations called *all* members to piously perform in every aspect of their social practices whatsoever related to the common fund, whether it be management of the fund or fulfillment of membership obligations.

Public Projects and Performance

Associations sometimes participated in a public project of the *polis*, such as the construction/repair of sanctuaries or public buildings, sacrifices and religious festivals, the purchase of grain, and so forth (Kloppenborg 2019, 248). Associations made monetary contributions for which they ran a collection project (ἐπίδοσις, *epidosis*). Such a fiscal practice was outside of regular membership obligations, but when they decided to undertake an *epidosis*, associations expected their members to properly perform their part in the additional expense as well as their other regular contributions.

Some peculiarities of the ways in which associations organized *epidosis* are worth noting. First, associations set a certain period of time for running a collection project, such as a year or so. Adding to this, some projects of the *polis* required a particular payment structure: a certain amount at the time of signing, the next after six months, and finally the balance at the completion date (*SEG* 50.1050). Second, each member could voluntarily set the amount of contributions according to the limits of the minimum and/or maximum amounts dictated by a project. For example, the project revealed in *SEG* 50.1050 set a thirty-drachmae minimum with no limits on maximum contributions, but others seem often to have had limits of both a minimum and a maximum (*IG* 2² 791; *IG* 2² 2332). More significant than the amount contributed was whether a person participated in an *epidosis* project that a group decided to operate. Since the treasurer recorded who paid and how much they paid, and finally publicized these amounts, those who did not make any contribution were naturally revealed and humiliated. Third, anyone could make a promise for future contributions and fulfill them later on before the due date of a project. However, associations were critical of whether the pledge was actually fulfilled or not, since some individuals could renege on their promises even after their names and promised amounts were already inscribed on a stele (Gygax 2016, 26). Hence, by following up with inscribing the "payment" for the promises, associations could report full participation in an *epidosis* (Kloppenborg 2019, 251).

Overall, social practices in associations were performative. Voting for functionaries, making decisions, handling duties/services, fulfilling membership obligations with regard to communal meals, proper table etiquette, and many other association practices altogether contributed to what it meant to be counted as a "member" of a group. That is to say, associations were supposed to be run not by a limited contingent of members with power but by the collective actions of all members. The proper performance of each member was *the* way he or she could be treated honorably, and associations were always ready to compensate for proper performance with counterbalancing favor.

Associations and Early Christianity

In recent years, association studies have contributed to the study of early Christianity in many ways. Though such scholarship traces back to the nineteenth century (Foucart 1873; Heinrici 1876; Hatch 1881), its influence was limited. Since the late 1990s, however, scholarly attention to associations has grown, impacting wider scholarship on early Christianity. This includes the important work of John Kloppenborg (1993, 1996, 2006, 2019), Richard Ascough (2000, 2003, 2006, 2022a, 2022b), and Philip Harland (2003, 2014). These scholars have also translated numerous inscriptions from Greco-Roman associations with helpful commentaries (see their six-volume *Greco-Roman Associations* series [GRA]; also Ascough, Harland, and Kloppenborg 2012), giving other scholars

greater access not only to the association data but also to the social and cultural worlds of associations (see, e.g., the contributions in Longenecker 2022). Their contributions extend to a greater understanding of the very concept of "associations," often treated in the past as separate entities parallel with Jewish groups, philosophical groups, and even Christ groups (cf. Meeks 2003, 74–84; Gager 1975, 132–40; Stegemann and Stegemann 2001, 251–87). However, the term is now understood more comprehensively—that is, all sorts of social groups in the Greco-Roman world were considered "associations" (Ascough 2015, 235–36; cf. 2000), and terms that we group under the umbrella term "association" were never used in an exclusionary way in the Mediterranean world (Kloppenborg 2019, 18–19). Based on this new understanding of associations, new insights have been introduced with regard to the formative social aspects of early Christ groups, such as membership size (Kloppenborg 2013; Last 2016), communal meals and meeting places (Kloppenborg 2016; Adams 2016; Last 2016; Lee 2018), elections (Last 2013; Lee 2020), collection projects (Kloppenborg 2017; Lee 2022), and the Thessalonian Christ group identity (Ascough 2000, 2014). Data from associations are surely vivid and heuristic, providing practical solutions to many questions one might have on the social movements of early Christ groups.

Works Cited

Adams, Edward. 2016. *The Earliest Christian Meeting Places: Almost Exclusively Houses?* Rev. ed. LNTS 450. London: T&T Clark.

Arnaoutoglou, Ilias. 2003. *Thusias Heneka Kai Sunousias: Private Religious Associations in Hellenistic Athens.* Athens: Academy of Athens.

Ascough, Richard S. 2000. "The Thessalonian Christian Community as a Professional Voluntary Association." *JBL* 119, no. 2: 311–28.

———. 2003. *Paul's Macedonian Associations: The Social Context of Philippians and 1 Thessalonians.* Tübingen: Mohr Siebeck.

———. 2006. "Voluntary Associations and the Formation of Pauline Christian Communities: Overcoming the Objections." In *Vereine, Synagogen, und Gemeinden im kaiserzeitlichen Kleinasien*, edited by Andreas Gutsfeld and Dietrich-Alex Koch, 149–83. Tübingen: Mohr Siebeck.

———. 2014. "Re-Describing the Thessalonians' 'Mission' in Light of Greco-Roman Associations." *NTS* 60, no. 1: 61–82.

———. 2015. "What Are They Now Saying about Christ Groups and Associations?" *CurBR* 13, no. 2: 207–44.

———. 2022a. *Early Christ Groups and Greco-Roman Associations: Organizational Models and Social Practices*. Eugene, OR: Cascade Books.

———. 2022b. *Christ Groups and Associations: Foundational Essays*. Waco: Baylor University Press.

Ascough, Richard S., Philip A. Harland, and John S. Kloppenborg, eds. 2012. *Associations in the Greco-Roman World: A Sourcebook*. Waco: Baylor University Press.

Ausbüttell, Frank M. 1982. *Untersuchungen zu den Vereinen im Westen des römischen Reiches*. Kallmünz: Michael Laßleben.

Avasthi, Rajendra. 1958. "Elections and Electioneering in Ancient Greece." *Indian Journal of Political Science* 19, no. 3: 276–81.

Bonfante, Pieto. 1960. *Digesta Iustiniani Augusti*. Mediolani: Formis Societatis Editricis Librariae.

D'Arms, John. 1990. "The Roman *Convivium* and the Idea of Equality." In *Sympotica: A Symposium on the Symposion*, edited by Oswyn Murray, 308–20. Oxford: Oxford University Press.

Dill, Samuel. 1904. *Roman Society from Nero to Marcus Aurelius*. London: Macmillan.

Dunbabin, Katherine M. D. 2003. *The Roman Banquet: Images of Conviviality*. Cambridge: Cambridge University Press.

Ferguson, William Scott. 1944. "The Attic Orgeones." *HTR* 37, no. 2: 61–140.

Foucart, Paul. 1873. *Des associations religieuses chez les Grecs: Thiases, éranes, orgéons, avec le texte des inscriptions rélatives à ces associations*. Paris: Klincksieck.

Gager, John G. 1975. *Kingdom and Community: The Social World of Early Christianity*. Englewood Cliffs, NJ: Prentice-Hall.

Gygax, Marc Domingo. 2016. *Benefaction and Rewards in the Ancient Greek City: The Origins of Euergetism*. Cambridge: Cambridge University Press.

Harland, Philip A. 2003. *Associations, Synagogues, and Congregations: Claiming a Place in Ancient Mediterranean Society*. Minneapolis: Fortress.

———. 2014. *North Coast of the Black Sea, Asia Minor*. Vol. 2 of *Greco-Roman Associations: Texts, Translations, and Commentary*. BZNW 204. Berlin: de Gruyter.

———. 2015. "Associations and the Economics of Group Life: A Preliminary Case Study of Asia Minor and the Aegean Islands." *Svensk Exegetisk Arsbok* 80: 1–37.

Hatch, Edwin. 1881. *The Organization of Early Christian Churches*. London: Rivingtons.

Heinrici, Georg. 1876. "Die Christengemeinden Korinths und die religiösen Genossenschaften der Griechen." *Zeitschrift für Wissenschaftliche Theologie* 19: 465–526.

Kloppenborg, John S. 1993. "Edwin Hatch, Churches, and *Collegia*." In *Origins and Method: Towards a New Understanding of Judaism and Christianity; Essays in Honour of John C. Hurd*, edited by Bradley McLean, 212–38. JSNTSup 86. Sheffield: JSOT Press.

———. 1996. "Collegia and Thiasoi: Issues in Function, Taxonomy and Membership." In *Voluntary Associations in the Graeco-Roman World*, edited by John S. Kloppenborg and Stephen G. Wilson, 16–30. London: Routledge.

———. 2006. "Associations in the Ancient World." In *The Historical Jesus in Context*, edited by Amy-Jill Levine, Dale C. Allison Jr., and John Dominic Crossan, 323–38. Princeton: Princeton University Press.

———. 2013. "Membership Practices in Pauline Christ Groups." *EC* 4, no. 2: 183–215.

———. 2016. "Precedence at the Communal Meal in Corinth." *NovT* 58, no. 2: 167–203.

———. 2017. "Fiscal Aspects of Paul's Collection for Jerusalem." *EC* 8, no. 2: 153–98.

———. 2019. *Christ's Associations: Connecting and Belonging in the Ancient City*. New Haven: Yale University Press.

———. 2020. *Ptolemaic and Early Roman Egypt*. Vol. 3 of *Greco-Roman Associations: Texts, Translations, and Commentary*. BZNW 246. Berlin: de Gruyter.

Kloppenborg, John S., and Richard S. Ascough. 2011. *Attica, Central Greece, Macedonia, Thrace*. Vol. 1 of *Greco-Roman Associations: Texts, Translations, and Commentary*. BZNW 181. Berlin: de Gruyter.

Kornemann, Ernst. 1900. "Collegium." In vol. 4 of *Paulys Real-Encyclopädie der classischen Altertumswissenschaft*, edited by G. Wissowa and W. Kroll, 380–479. Stuttgart: Metzler and Druckenmüller.

Last, Richard. 2013. "The Election of Officers in the Corinthian Christ-Group." *NTS* 59: 365–81.

———. 2016. *The Pauline Church and the Corinthian Ekklēsia: Greco-Roman Associations in Comparative Context*. New York: Cambridge University Press.

Lee, Jin Hwan. 2018. *The Lord's Supper in Corinth in the Context of Greco-Roman Private Associations*. Lanham, MD: Lexington Books / Fortress Academic.

———. 2020. "Reading 1 Cor 11:19 in Light of Election Practices in Private Associations." *Journal of Early Christian History* 10, no. 3: 29–43.

———. 2022. "The Benefaction-Reward Convention in Greco-Roman Private Associations and Paul's Jerusalem Collection." In Longenecker 2022, 348–58.

Longenecker, Bruce W., ed. 2022. *Greco-Roman Associations, Deities, and Early Christianity*. Waco: Baylor University Press.

Meeks, Wayne A. 2003. *The First Urban Christians: The Social World of the Apostle Paul*. 2nd ed. New Haven: Yale University Press.

Nock, A. D. 1924. "The Historical Importance of Cult-Associations." *The Classical Review* 38, no. 5: 105–9.

Plutarch. 1870. *Plutarch's Morals: Translated from the Greek by Several Hands*. Corrected and revised by William W. Goodwin. Vol. III. Boston: Little, Brown, & Co.

Smith, Dennis Edwin. 2003. *From Symposium to Eucharist: The Banquet in the Early Christian World*. Minneapolis: Fortress.

Stegemann, Ekkehard, and Wolfgang Stegemann. 2001. *The Jesus Movement: A Social History of Its First Century*. Translated by O. C. Dean. Minneapolis: Augsburg Fortress.

Vishnia, Rachel Feig. 2012. *Roman Elections in the Age of Cicero*. New York: Routledge.

Waltzing, Jean-Pierre. 1895. *Étude historique sur les corporations professionnelles chez les Romains depuis les origines Jusqu'à la chute de l'Empire d'Occident: Mémoire couronné par l'Académie royale de Belgique*. Leuven: Peeters.

Whelan, Caroline F. 1993. "Amica Pauli: The Role of Phoebe in the Early Church." *JSNT* 15, no. 49: 67–85.

Wilson, Stephen G. 1996. "Voluntary Associations: An Overview." In *Voluntary Associations in the Graeco-Roman World*, edited by John S. Kloppenborg and Stephen G. Wilson, 1–15. London: Routledge.

48

Wealth and Poverty

MiJa Wi

The issues of wealth and poverty in the first-century Greco-Roman world and Roman Palestine within which the New Testament writings emerged cannot be discussed apart from religious, social, and political factors. Wealth and poverty were not purely economic matters. Complex factors, such as health conditions (disability), age (children and elderly), legal status (free or slave), social relations (foreigners or recent immigrants), and gender (women and widows) determined one's economic reality in ancient societies. Despite challenges involved in mapping wealth and poverty in the first-century world today, it was the disparity between rich and poor that captured ancient minds most vividly. A good example is Luke's story of the rich man and Lazarus, whose lives were starkly contrasted in terms of their places of dwelling, clothing, health condition, food consumption, and burial (Luke 16:19–22).

The first-century Greco-Roman world was an agrarian society whose economy was largely based on land and its produce (Finley 1992, 89–91; Garnsey and Saller 1987, 64). Land was the principal source of wealth both for the empire and for personal fortunes. Land belonged to the elites, and the possession of land was closely linked to status, while the majority of the population who worked on the land lived at subsistence level. The profile of rich and poor in broad terms could thus be determined by one's access to sufficient land. As in other preindustrial ancient societies, wealth was viewed as a limited good alongside status, honor, and power, all of which existed in finite quantities. Hence in limited good societies, one's accumulation of wealth was at the expense of others. The distribution of wealth was unequal, and redistribution only expanded the gulf between landlords and peasants, tenants, and hired workers.

Landownership connected directly to wealth, food, and clothing. These were often indicators of wealth in ancient Roman society. With whom one banquets, what one eats, and what one wears mark one's power, status, and wealth. As eating and fine clothing were markers of wealth, so were hunger and nakedness markers of poverty. As we examine wealth and

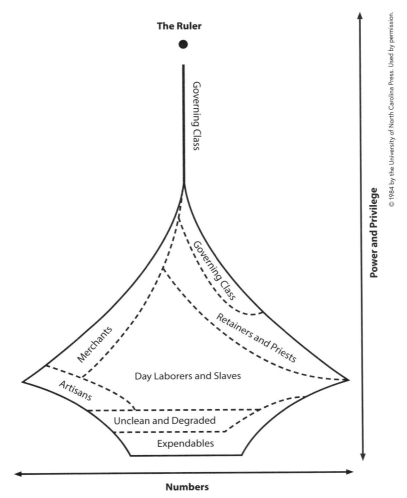

Fig. 48.1. Social stratification of advanced agrarian societies

poverty in the Roman Empire in general and the New Testament in particular, three key issues will be addressed: (1) the poverty scale in the Roman Empire, (2) poverty and the profile of the poor in rural and urban settings, and (3) the lived experience of poverty in hunger and indebtedness.

The Poverty Scale

How does one measure wealth and poverty in Roman society in general and among early Christians in particular? The concentration of wealth to a few elites was a given, but were

there middle groups? Was the society made up of a few extremely rich with the majority of the population at subsistence level? What might be economic profiles of early Christians in the Roman Empire? To answer these questions, Gerhard Lenski's diagram (1984, 284; see fig. 48.1) and Steven Friesen's Poverty Scale (PS) (see the following table) are apposite.

Lenski's diagram depicts a thin line at the top for the small number of persons in the governing class and at the lower center shows the large number of day laborers, with artisans next to them. Jesus, as a carpenter, could have belonged to this group. Retainers and priests

Poverty Scale for the Roman Empire

Scale	Description	Includes	Percent
PS1	Imperial Elites	Imperial dynasty, Roman senatorial families, a few retainers, local royalty, a few freedpersons	.04 percent
PS2	Regional or Provincial Elites	Equestrian families, provincial officials, some retainers, some decurial families, some freedpersons, some retired military officers	1 percent
PS3	Municipal Elites	Most decurial families, wealthy men and women who do not hold office, some freedpersons, some retainers, some veterans, some merchants	1.76 percent
PS4	Moderate Surplus	Some merchants, some traders, some freedpersons, some artisans, and military veterans	*7 percent?*
PS5	Stable Near Subsistence Level	Many merchants and traders, regular wage earners, artisans, large shop owners, freedpersons, some farm families	*22 percent?*
PS6	At Subsistence Level	Small farm families, laborers, artisans, wage earners, most merchants and traders, small shop/tavern owners	40 percent
PS7	Below Subsistence Level	Some farm families, unattached widows, orphans, beggars, disabled, unskilled laborers, prisoners	28 percent

Source: Friesen 2004, 341.

are located in between the governing class and peasants. This is particularly helpful in evaluating ambiguous positions of the priestly groups, scribes, and lawyers mentioned in the Gospels in their relation to the rulers and to the ruled. Moreover, there is ample evidence from Josephus about the great riches of the high priestly families (see Josephus, *Ant.* 20.205–7) as they were close allies of the rulers. The most marginalized (unclean and degraded, expendables) are placed at the bottom of the diagram. In the Gospels, they are the ones to whom the good news is proclaimed in Jesus's ministry: the disabled, the captives, the oppressed, the lepers, and the poor (e.g., Matt. 11:4–5; Luke 4:18–19; 7:22; 14:21).

While Lenski's diagram offers social stratification of advanced agrarian societies, Friesen's Poverty Scale offers an economic profile of the Roman Empire, drawing from quantifiable financial resources, such as the amount of money needed to buy food or to pay tax and the estimated income in Roman urban settings. This Poverty Scale ranges from PS1 to PS7. The top three (PS1–PS3) include elites, composing less than 3 percent of the whole population.

Some large-scale merchants and military veterans may fall into PS4 with a moderate surplus, composing 7 percent. While about 90 percent of the population in the Roman Empire lived near, at, or below subsistence level (PS5–PS7), shop owners and farm families with relative stability consisted of 22 percent (PS5). This leaves about 68 percent of the population in the Roman Empire at or below subsistence level (PS6–PS7). Most likely early Christians, including Paul and his congregations, belonged to PS6 or 7, with few exceptions who might have had a moderate surplus to offer their houses for gathering places (PS4 or PS5). For instance, Philemon and Phoebe, whose houses were used as house churches, might have belonged to this group. But Paul, who worked as an itinerant artisan, lived a life near or at subsistence, similar to those in most of his congregations, who could be located in PS6 (or PS7) as typical urban poor in the Roman Empire. Nevertheless, Paul's letters frequently speak of the collection for the poor Jerusalem saints (e.g., Rom. 15:14–32; 1 Cor. 16; 2 Cor. 8–9; cf. Acts 11:27–30; Gal. 2:10), who fell into a dire situation and lived below subsistence (PS7). Paul encouraged the congregations in Corinth and elsewhere, many of whom most likely belonged to PS6, to give generously. This in fact might have meant to give not from their surplus, of which there was hardly any, but from what they had for their own survival. Moreover, Paul's commendation of the churches in Macedonia who gave generously out of their destitution appears to be on the mark (2 Cor. 8:1–2).

As seen from both Lenski's diagram and Friesen's Poverty Scale, the majority of the population in the Roman Empire and early Christians in particular lived near, at, or below subsistence level. Hence a profile of those who made up about 90 percent of the population of the Roman society and who included most if not all early Christians merits further discussion.

Poverty and the Profile of the Poor

The wealthy in the Roman Empire by default were the owners of large estates, from the emperors to local aristocrats (Wi 2019, 29–35). They lived in urban centers, while leaving their land to the labor of tenants, hired workers, and slaves. As in the parable of the tenants (Matt. 21:33–46; Mark 12:1–12; Luke 20:9–19), an absentee landowner who leased his vineyard to the tenants would send his slaves to collect its produce when the harvest time came. While the parable was spoken against the chief priests and the elders (in fact, they were most likely absentee landowners themselves who owned sizable estates surrounding Jerusalem), common practices of absentee landowners and antagonistic relations between landowners and tenants in the Roman society are well reflected in the parable (Kloppenborg 2006, 279). Whether living in rural areas or in urban settings, those who worked with their hands belonged to the unprivileged and the poor. The realities of their living conditions were harsh, precarious, and often at the mercy of others. But what can be said further about the poor

who covered the majority of the population of the empire? A brief profile of the poor in rural and urban areas may be helpful.

Peasants, Tenants, Hired Workers, Debt Slaves in Rural Areas

In traditional agrarian societies, there were a small number of large landowners who took the yield and profited from land and many peasants who worked their land for daily survival. Peasants owned small plots of land that would produce barely enough food to feed their family, and if weather remained favorable to them, their income could be supplemented by selling any surplus they produced. But they were extremely vulnerable to unpredictable weather conditions. Even with as few as two years of drought, there would be little chance for peasants to secure their small plot of land to feed their families and to pay taxes. In many cases, peasants temporarily became tenants of their own land due to debts, or their land would eventually be absorbed into nearby large estates when debts could not be repaid in due course (Gil 2006, 306). Hence peasants constantly lived on the verge of becoming landless. Archaeological surveys during this period also point to the possible increase of large landholdings at the expense of the small landowners and the increase of tenancy (Reed 2002, 87–88). For instance, there was a rise of specialization in crops such as viticulture, which was both capital and labor intensive (see the landowner of the vineyard hiring a good number of day laborers in Matt. 20:1–16, as noted below). But it was the most profitable crop in the Roman Empire (Duncan-Jones 1982, 39).

Once peasants lost their plot of land, they were left with only a few options. Some left for cities to take menial work; others remained to work the land as tenants or hired workers. In some extreme but not uncommon cases, they would live as fugitives to avoid debts. While tenancy farming was common during this period (well attested in the Gospels), tenants were under the burden of paying a fixed percentage of harvest in rent. Considering what little surplus they would yield (still depending on favorable weather conditions), the increased tension between absentee landowners and tenants was not surprising when the harvest time came. Those who could not fulfill the contract of tenancy offered themselves as day laborers. Waiting all day (from early morning to evening) at the marketplace to be employed for a day's work was the reality vividly portrayed in the parable of the workers in the vineyard (Matt. 20:1–16). Regardless of how hard they worked, precarious living conditions were the daily experiences of peasants, tenants, and hired workers, who could easily fall into the trap of debt and whose family members could become debt slaves of large estates (Hanson and Oakman 1998, 75, 111).

Artisans, Craft Workers, Semi-Skilled/ Unskilled Workers in Urban Settings

An illuminating depiction of the typical lives of semi-skilled or unskilled workers is reflected in the writings of Lucian, a second-century CE Greek satirist. Micyllus, a cobbler, in Lucian's *Gallus*, worked from early morning barely to earn his daily bread. Hunger was his usual experience, and it was only in his dreams that he could find refuge from the life of poverty (Lucian, *Gall.* 1). In another writing, Lucian describes the subsistence lifestyle of artisans and craftsmen, whose toil from morning to night was rewarded only with a starvation wage, in contrast to the lavish lifestyle of philosophers (*Fug.* 13, 17). Hence small business traders (e.g., vegetable or salt fish sellers), tanners, cobblers, tentmakers, and casual laborers (e.g., building workers) were typical urban poor who filled the Roman cities. Lucian's portrayal of the harsh life of manual workers in urban settings was strikingly similar to that of Paul, a tentmaker, who worked day

and night not to burden others (1 Thess. 2:9), who grew weary from working hard for a living, and who nevertheless experienced hunger, nakedness, and homelessness regularly (e.g., 1 Cor. 4:11–12; 2 Cor. 11:27). On top of that, high rent (particularly in Rome) was another factor that made the life of the urban poor more vulnerable to indebtedness (see Juvenal, *Sat.* 3.166).

While peasants and artisans were typical of those who lived near or at subsistence level, widows, orphans, recent immigrants, fugitives, and those who lived outside of city walls— namely, the disabled, beggars, prostitutes, and lepers—were destitute in first-century Roman society, where there was no so-called welfare provision (Rohrbaugh 1991, 133–36). They were particularly vulnerable to unpredictable circumstances, such as diseases, food crises, political instabilities, and indebtedness, which could easily take their life to deprivation. It is particularly illuminating to see early Christian concerns for the care of orphans and widows (e.g., Acts 6:1; 1 Tim. 5:3–16; James 1:27), and the inclusion of those who were commonly excluded or considered as the invisibles in the Roman Empire in Jesus's ministry (e.g., Matt. 11:4–5; 21:32; Luke 4:18–19; 7:22; 14:21). While vulnerability may well encapsulate the life of the ordinary poor and the destitute in the Roman society, both in rural and urban settings, it was through the support of those who were relatively poor with a minimum surplus (PS5–PS6) that relief was offered in times of need and economic crisis.

Lived Experiences of Poverty: Hunger and Indebtedness

Two key issues need further discussion in relation to the lived experiences of poverty— namely, common experiences of hunger and indebtedness, both of which defined the life of the poor in the first-century Greco-Roman world. Unpredictable factors, such as bad weather conditions (droughts), natural disasters (earthquakes), or wars, frequently caused a period of food shortages or food crises and at times catastrophic famine. Between 27 BCE and 68 CE, there were ongoing severe food crises in the Roman world (Garnsey 1988, 2). The funerary inscription of Augustus recorded his relief work for the entire city of Rome when the city suffered food shortages (Augustus, 63 BCE–14 CE, *Res Gestae Divi Augusti*; see Wallace 2000). In fact, this relief was free grain distribution (grain dole), provided most likely for Roman citizens, not the destitute or the poorest among the poor. We hear of an empire-wide famine in Acts 11:28, which took place during the reign of Claudius (41–54 CE), according to Agabus's prophecy (see Josephus, *Ant.* 3.320; Tacitus, *Ann.* 12.43). In response, the believers in Antioch determined to send relief to those who suffered from it in Judea. Also, Jesus mentioned the worldwide famine in the time of Elijah (Luke 4:25) and told the story of the prodigal son, who was in great need due to a severe famine (15:14–16).

Both the rural and urban poor profiled above were particularly vulnerable to food shortages, not to mention others who did not have any support networks in times of crisis. Food crises not only caused the rise of the price of grain but also further worsened indebtedness, malnutrition, and disease among the poor (Galen, *Alim. fac.* 6.749). Food was scarce for the majority, and hence the experience of hunger was common. Jesus, his disciples, and many in the New Testament were familiar with hunger. Hunger was a prominent motif, especially in the Gospels. Although not always linked to poverty, Jesus was hungry after forty days of fasting and tempted to change stones to loaves of bread (Matt. 4:2–3; Luke 4:2–3). Jesus's disciples were hungry and ate heads of grain on the Sabbath (Matt. 12:1). Jesus promised to those who were hungry that they would be fed (Luke 6:21), and he filled the hungry crowd with food until they were full (9:17). Hunger

and thirst were part of Paul's life realities as a manual worker in Roman cities (1 Cor. 4:11; 2 Cor. 11:27). On the other hand, hoarding grain in storage was a habitual practice of large landowners, either for plain necessity or for profitable sale (Garnsey 1988, 75–76). The story of the rich landowner (Luke 12:16–18) reflects this practice. When his land produced abundantly, he was worried about how to store all the grains and goods he had, and he decided to build new and larger storages for them. Yet his thoughts of hoarding were sharply criticized by Jesus with the pronouncement of his sudden demise. Jesus taught his disciples to pray for daily bread (Matt. 6:11; Luke 11:3) and not to worry about what to eat but to share what little they have with others in times of scarcity (Luke 12:22, 33).

Indebtedness is another salient factor that marked economic realities of peasants and the urban poor in first-century Roman society. It is not surprising that the Gospels express overriding concerns for debts and release of debts. Frequent crop failures and subsequent food shortages caused the poor to easily fall into the vicious cycle of debts, which led them to be tenants of their own land, to be sold into debt slavery, or to live the life of a fugitive (Wi 2019, 41). But what worsened the situation of indebtedness of the poor was the heavy burden of taxation that fell across the population. The Roman Empire imposed various taxes on its subjects. A poll tax was imposed on each person, and a land tax was imposed on agricultural produce. In addition, there was local taxation, a temple tax for the Jews, and various tax on goods. In the Gospels, whether it was legal to pay taxes to the Roman authorities or not was a controversial question brought to Jesus (Matt. 22:15–22; Mark 12:13–17; Luke 20:20–26). On another occasion, Peter was challenged by the tax collectors about whether Jesus paid the temple tax (Matt. 17:24). In both incidents, neither Jesus nor Peter had the money needed at hand. This was not unusual for many, considering the produce or income of many, which was barely enough to feed them. Hence paying taxes in normal times was challenging, not to mention in times of crisis. Also, oppressive and corrupt practices of tax collection are reflected in John the Baptist's teaching to the tax collectors who came to be baptized when he told them not to collect more than what was prescribed (Luke 3:13; cf. 19:8).

This heavy burden of taxation in addition to frequent crop failures worsened the problem of debt and indebtedness of both rural and urban poor. The debtors could be sold into slavery if they were not able to pay the money back. The Gospels portray the possibility of losing all one's possessions in the process of settling the debts or of imprisonment or debt slavery even of family members (Matt. 18:23–25). While debts in ancient society often hampered the peasants' sustainability, the forgiveness of debt was disdained by the privileged as a revolutionary slogan of the poor (Oakman 2008, 13). Josephus's account testifies to this point when he states that it was to cause a rising of the poor that the rebels burned the archives where the moneylenders' bonds and the records of debts were kept during the Jewish War (66–70 CE; see *J.W.* 2.427). In contrast, the Gospels demand the cancellation of debts. The Lord's Prayer intertwines forgiveness of debts with that of sins (Luke 11:4). Elsewhere, the creditor's gracious acts of canceling debts were analogously used for God's acts of forgiving sins (Matt. 18:23–35; Luke 7:41–43). The Gospels are keenly aware of the problem of debt and the affliction of the poor it caused. Debt was indeed a dividing marker between the rich and the poor. It was debt that kept the poor under the power of the rich. Hence the burden of debt repayments with taxes and rents controlled the lives of peasants, tenants, and the urban poor.

Conclusion

To the ears of first-century Roman dwellers, the saying "blessed are the poor" (Luke 6:20; cf. Matt. 5:3) must have sounded absurd. They lived in a society where the lives of the poor were entrapped in an oppressive cycle of indebtedness, and in a culture where poverty brought nothing more than shame. Life was marked by hunger and hardships. These harsh realities affected the majority of people in the Roman Empire, whose lives hinged on the uncertainties of food shortages, diseases, and frequent wars. The threat of falling into debt was always lurking below the surface. Wealth was accumulated at the expense of the very existence of the poor, and exploitative systems favored the rich and the powerful. But Jesus's pronouncement of blessings on the poor and the hungry was a reminder that God's justice could redress their afflictions.

The general attitude toward wealth in the New Testament, therefore, is that of disapproval, if not hostility. It warns that great riches hinder one from entering the kingdom of God (Matt. 19:23–24; Mark 10:23–25; Luke 18:24–25; cf. 19:1–10). The desire to be rich draws one away from faith and leads to self-destruction. Earthly riches are associated with the powers of evil (e.g., 1 Tim. 6:10; Rev. 18:3–5). It is mammon (or "riches") that easily takes the place of God and makes one enslaved to it (Matt. 6:24; Luke 16:13). But at the same time the New Testament affirms that fiscal means are necessary for one's subsistence. Such means are to be used and shared for that purpose (e.g., Acts 4:32–37). Hence the New Testament calls God's people to respond to God's grace with the cancellation of debts, the sharing of possessions, and the generous giving out of one's own scarcity, even in times of crises.

Works Cited

Duncan-Jones, Richard. 1982. *The Economy of the Roman Empire: Quantitative Studies*. 2nd ed. Cambridge: Cambridge University Press.

Finley, Moses I. 1992. *The Ancient Economy*. 2nd ed. London: Penguin.

Friesen, Steven J. 2004. "Poverty in Pauline Studies: Beyond the So-Called New Consensus." *JSNT* 26, no. 3: 323–61.

Garnsey, Peter. 1988. *Famine and Food Supply in the Graeco-Roman World: Response to Risk and Crisis*. Cambridge: Cambridge University Press.

Garnsey, Peter, and Richard Saller. 1987. *The Roman Empire: Economy, Society and Culture*. London: Duckworth.

Gil, Moshe. 2006. "The Decline of the Agrarian Economy in Palestine under Roman Rule." *Journal of Economic and Social History of the Orient* 49, no. 3: 285–328.

Hanson, Kenneth C., and Douglas Oakman. 1998. *Palestine in the Time of Jesus: Social Structures and Social Conflicts*. Minneapolis: Fortress.

Kloppenborg, John S. 2006. *The Tenants in the Vinyard*. WUNT 195. Tübingen: Mohr.

Lenski, Gerhard E. 1984. *Power and Privilege: A Theory of Stratification*. Chapel Hill: University of North Carolina Press.

Oakman, Douglas. 2008. *Jesus and the Peasants*. Eugene, OR: Cascade Books.

Reed, Jonathan L. 2002. *Archaeology and the Galilean Jesus: A Re-Examination of the Evidence*. Harrisburg, PA: Trinity Press International.

Rohrbaugh, Richard L. 1991. "The Pre-Industrial City in Luke-Acts: Urban Social Relations." In *The Social World of Luke-Acts: Models for Interpretation*, edited by Jerome Neyrey, 125–49. Peabody, MA: Hendrickson.

Wallace, Rex. 2000. *Res Gestae Divi Augusti: As Recorded in the Monumentum Ancyranum and the Monumentum Antiochenum; Introduction, Grammatical Notes, Historical Commentary, Facing Vocabulary*. Wauconda, IL: Bolchazy-Carducci.

Wi, MiJa. 2019. *The Path to Salvation in Luke's Gospel: What Must We Do?* LNTS 607. London: T&T Clark.

49

Gift-Giving

JOHN M. G. BARCLAY

The giving of gifts was a pervasive feature of social relations in the Greco-Roman world, complex in practice and highly varied in form. We may define "gift" broadly as any kind of benefit or favor (social, economic, political, or personal) that takes place within social relationships, in the family, among friends and neighbors, in business relations, between political allies, or between patrons and clients. Gifts operate within *voluntary* and *personal* relations; they are characterized by *goodwill* in the conferring of some *benefit*; and in the ancient world they are assumed to elicit some form of *reciprocal return* that is both obliged and voluntary. Gifts either initiate or (more often) continue a social relationship, and the return (whether in the form of gratitude alone, or gratitude expressed in some counter-gift) is necessary for the continuation of the relationship.

A rich variety of terms may be deployed in this context, at least as varied and as nuanced as our distinctions between a donation, a present, an honorarium, a favor, and a bribe. In Greek, *didōmi* and its various compounds are common in this connection, alongside a set of cognate nouns (*dosis, doma, dōrēma, dōron,* etc.). *Charis,* whose meaning ranges from "charm" to "benevolence," "gift," and "gratitude," is frequently deployed to indicate the agreeableness of the relationship. In Latin, there is a subtle range of meaning between words from the *do-* root (*do, donum,* etc.) and terms such as *beneficium, munus,* and *gratia* (Barclay 2015, 575–82). There is no standard form of a gift: its content is defined by its social context, its meaning is negotiated between the partners involved, and its practice is governed by a complex etiquette concerning the "proper" form of gift, its giving, receipt, and return.

Contexts and Expectations for Gift-Giving

While modern, Western society has generally limited the legitimate use of gift-giving to the private sphere (thereby banning gifts, as "bribes," from political or commercial domains), in the Greco-Roman world gifts pervaded politics, were basic to the understanding of religion, and routinely penetrated commercial, market relationships. Politicians expected financial "kick-backs" and assistance from those they favored, as well as the honor they craved from as wide a circle as possible. The divine and human spheres were bound together by ties of gift—divine aid being sought or gratefully acknowledged with human gifts of sacrifice, praise, and honorific donations. Commercial relationships could be theoretically distinguished from gifts, in that sales and purchases were calculable in value, legally regulated, and relatively impersonal. But they were often, in fact, permeated by personal ties and relationships of favor—the employment of household members, special deals for friends, and favorable rates of interest. It is a modern mistake to imagine that there was a "gift-economy" separable from, even opposite to, market exchange. While gift-giving and gift-reciprocity defied financial calculation, stood outside the law, and extended over long periods of time, they often provided the frame and influenced the terms of more calculable forms of exchange that took place in markets, contracts, loans, and business relations. Because they were personal and selective, gift-relations were imbued with a high moral tone: it mattered ethically what you gave, to whom you gave it, and how you conducted the gift-relationship. The moral character and the honor of both giver and recipient were always at stake.

Modern developments in Western society, economy, and philosophy have led scholars to imagine the "pure" gift as completely disinterested, carrying no expectations of return, imposing no obligations (no strings attached), and, by some definitions, ideally anonymous (for analysis, see Barclay 2015, 51–63; Leithart 2014). To impose such expectations on ancient gift-giving would be misleading. Since gifts were designed to create or maintain social relationships, the "strings" were essential to the practice of the gift. Anonymous gifts could be justified only in exceptional circumstances. The ideal gift was not unilateral but reciprocated, because its return showed that the relationship was acknowledged, appreciated, and likely to continue. That "return" could take many different forms, depending on the nature of the relationship: in an unequal relationship, gratitude, honor, and a comprehensive attitude of goodwill might be what the more powerful giver most wanted and expected. If there was a counter-gift, it might be of a very different kind, and it might come after some interval of time. But whatever their form, gifts were understood to express an ongoing relationship of exchange. As the philosopher Chrysippus once put it, good gift-giving was like a ballgame of throw and catch, where one gave gifts precisely so that they could be well caught (received and acknowledged) and well returned (in gratitude or counter-gift; see Seneca the Younger, *Ben.* 2.17).

In his famous anthropological analysis of gift-giving, Marcel Mauss has identified three obligations in gift-giving: to give, to receive, and to return the gift (Mauss 1990). The same three dimensions of the gift were represented by the famous Greek image of the Three Graces (*Charites*), in which three young women dance in a ring, symbolizing giving, receiving, and giving back (Seneca, *Ben.* 1.3). The sense of obligation did not negate the fact that gift-giving was still, in important senses, voluntary and "free." The radical modern polarity between freedom and obligation is foreign to antiquity, where it was possible to choose more or less enthusiastically to do what was also socially obliged. Another modern dichotomy should also be scrambled: that between a disinterested (or altruistic) gift, on the one hand, and the performance of actions for self-interested (or selfish) reasons. Such a polarity depends on a radical disjunction between the interests of the self and the interests of others; but that does not account for the possibility of a form of friendship, hailed in antiquity, where the interests of the self were entwined, even identical, with the interests of another. To be sure, it was recognized in antiquity, as today, that gifts could be manipulative or degrading to the recipient, given ostensibly for the benefit of the recipient but really (in intention or result) *only* for the utility of the giver. But it was not necessary to reverse the polarity, making the gift *only* for the benefit of the recipient *and not at all* for the benefit of the giver. It was possible to imagine (and to practice) gifts of *conjoined* benefit, where the interests of the giver and of the recipient were shared to such an extent that the benefit to one was also, at the same time and even to the same degree, a benefit to the other. Thus, gifts in antiquity could be both disinterested and self-interested: if we find this confusing or nonsensical, the problem lies with us.

Because gifts were intended to create a social relationship, it mattered to whom you gave them, and why. Coins might be tossed, in a chance encounter, to an importunate beggar, but such occasional or indiscriminate forms of "almsgiving" could hardly be characterized as a gift-relationship. Gifts entailed a personal relationship of goodwill, so they generally presupposed some prior knowledge of the recipient, sufficient to know what would be to their benefit. Moreover, one would not wish to give to those unlikely to be grateful or those unable to offer any worthwhile form of return, nor would one wish to tie oneself in a gift-relationship to unfitting recipients who would degrade one's honor. Thus in describing gift-giving, our sources frequently mention the "worth" of the recipient, measured by various criteria: social status, intellectual capacity, ethnicity, or moral character. Indiscriminate giving, which to our minds might seem the most noble, could be considered in antiquity both foolish and immoral. If the gods give certain gifts indiscriminately (rain or sunshine), it is only because they cannot channel such gifts in a more discriminate way (Seneca, *Ben.* 4.28).

Gifts among Equals and in Asymmetrical Relationships

The multiple forms of gift-giving could be divided, structurally, between gifts among "horizontal" equals and gifts within an asymmetrical ("vertical") relationship; in the latter category, gifts between unequal humans can be distinguished from gifts between humans and the (even more unequal) divine.

"Horizontal" Relationships

Gifts among (more or less) equals took place all the time in the Greco-Roman world, though they are less easily evidenced than the spectacular gifts by the super-rich that were memorialized in inscriptions and celebrated in literature. When a guest arrives unexpectedly, and you don't have bread to feed him, you ask a friend to help you out (Luke 11:5–8), on the understanding that you would do the same in return, when required. The advice of Hesiod (7th c. BCE) was still quoted in the Roman era: "Invite your friend, but not your enemy, to dine; especially be cordial to your neighbor, for if trouble comes at home, a neighbor's there, at hand. . . . Measure carefully when you must borrow from your neighbor, then, pay back the same, or more, if possible, and you will have a friend in time of need" (Hesiod, *Op.* 342–51 [trans. Wender 1973, 69, slightly modified]). What is assumed here is that a favor in one direction will be (and will need to be) repaid in return: "Give something and get something" (Epicharmus, DK 30); "one favor always begets another" (Sophocles, *Ajax* 522).

There are two interconnected reasons for this assumption of reciprocal return. First, since the majority of the population of the Greco-Roman world lived, in fluctuating conditions, near the edge of survival, it was extremely likely that one would need help from others on numerous occasions. Many kinds of personal and economic shock could precipitate a crisis: an accident, illness, sudden loss of employment, the death of a family member, or a rise in food prices caused by poor harvests, hoarding, or social unrest. Those who lived at or only just above subsistence level needed to cultivate networks of trust and loyalty with people who could be counted on for support (in the form of food, cash, loans, or practical assistance) when the chips were down. And as Hesiod advises, one way to cultivate those networks was to assist others, where possible, when they were in need. Such swapping and sharing need not be precisely calculable, but they created social debts that could be called in when required (Schellenberg 2018).

Second, dignity required that in this constant dance of give and take, one would not wish to be—or to be seen to be—the person who always receives and never gives. The most depressing social feature of poverty in the Greco-Roman world was that the poor appeared ever dependent on others. The beggar on the street (who had lost all normal networks of support) was the most dramatic example of this shameless condition, to be avoided if at all possible: "I am too ashamed to beg," says the crisis-hit steward in Jesus's parable (Luke 16:3, my translation). Beggars vividly encapsulated the fears of all those living on the edge of survival: just as frightening as their physical vulnerability was their social degradation. "I hate poor people," says a graffito from first-century Pompeii. "If anyone wants something for nothing, he should pay for it" (*CIL* 4.9839b, my translation). For the sake of honor, everyone wanted to be able to give, self-sufficient enough to be able to share what they had with others. As Jesus was remembered as saying, "It is more blessed to give than to receive" (Acts 20:35). That did not mean that one only ever gave and never received; only the super-rich were that secure. But it meant that giving and sharing were crucial to one's honor, as well as constituting a vital form of social insurance.

"Vertical" Relationships, Both Human and Divine

Every form of giving involves an imbalance of power, since the giver places the recipient in an indebted position. Among those of similar economic and social levels, where giving runs both ways, an imbalance in one direction would soon be equalized by an imbalance in the other. But some gift-relationships were permanently unequal, where a wealthy benefactor gave benefits or favors, often ostentatiously, to those of an inferior rank. Such benefactions might be one-off or intermittent, as when a civic magistrate paid for a new building or a civic feast, in a system of political benefaction we call "euergetism" (Veyne 1990). Although the super-rich elite were small in number (less than 3 percent of the population), their wealth was hugely disproportionate to the resources of the ordinary population, and they were tolerated only if they were seen to be generous—as publicized by inscriptions, statues, crowns, and wreaths (Harrison 2003). But where a benefactor-beneficiary relationship took the form of an enduring, selective, and personal relationship across a large difference in status, we may speak of a form of *patronage*. These long-term relations, sometimes inherited over generations, could become exploitative, but they could also be valued by both parties. The "clients" (usually called "friends" to preserve their dignity) gained special access to power, while "patrons" (whether styled as such or not) gained an appreciative chorus who ensured good publicity and enhanced the patron's influence. Gifts of many sorts sustained such relationships, although in such unequal relationships the superior party could dictate the terms.

Gifts circulating between humans and divine powers are a more extreme example of asymmetrical gift-giving. The cycle of reciprocity is basic to both Greek and Roman religion: as benefactors (to nations, cities, associations, families, or individuals), the gods distributed their favors with appropriate discrimination (choosing, where possible, worthy recipients), while humans offered worship, prayer, dedicatory gifts, and sacrifices in return (Parker 1998). It was not always clear where the cycle began: sacrifices could be seen as return gifts (for benefits already received), as inducements (for benefits requested), or as both at once. It is common to represent Greek and Roman religion as structured by the motto *do ut des* ("I give that you may give"). That correctly identifies the reciprocity ethos of ancient religious practice, but it wrongly puts one-sided stress on the human giver as the initiator of the cycle. Each side in this relationship might wish to position themselves as taking the initiative. There is nothing necessarily crude or transactional about this relationship; the reciprocal exchange of gifts is a noble activity, and not every form of exchange is commercial.

The Jewish religious tradition participates in similar gift-dynamics, with some distinctive features.[1] Here religious narratives and motifs were embedded within the ethical concerns of the Jewish tradition, such that the benefactions of God (in the gifts of the land and the exodus from slavery) are cited as a model for human benefaction (e.g., Lev. 25:35–38). There are also repeated instructions to support even the lowliest members of society. Against the obvious objection that the poor had little with which they could reciprocate, Jewish texts invoke God as the ultimate, and most trustworthy, guarantor of a return: "Do good to the devout, and you will be repaid—if not by them, certainly by the Most High" (Sir. 12:2). During the Second Temple period, the expectation of a divine, this-worldly return was joined, and sometimes replaced, by the hope of an eschatological reward. Giving can rescue

from death (Tob. 12:9), not just in keeping you alive (by human gifts of assistance in a time of need), but by God bringing you, through death, to an eternal recompense (Anderson 2013). That notion is basic to Jesus's teaching in the Gospels, where what is advocated is not a unilateral, no-return gift but a gift spread with risky generosity that may receive no human recognition or reward but will elicit a definitive return at a future time and from a better source, God (e.g., Matt. 6:1–4; Luke 14:12–14).

The Etiquette of Gift-Giving

As a structural feature of everyday life, operative in so many contexts and at all social levels, gift-giving followed the rules of a complex etiquette, attuned to the status of the different parties and the power relationship between them. The fullest analysis of gifts that has survived from antiquity is Seneca the Younger's *On Benefits*, which both describes common features of ancient gift-giving and offers distinctively Stoic solutions to its well-known problems.[2] Seneca makes clear the difficulty in deciding whom to benefit, in what form, and in what manner. It was important to give to fitting recipients, but by what criteria should one determine their worth, and would too much discrimination limit one's reputation for generosity? If the recipients showed no gratitude, and failed to make a return, should one interpret that as hostility, indifference, or shame? Should one keep giving even in the face of ingratitude? With regard to the benefit itself, were some gifts wholly unfitting—too large, too mean, or simply inappropriate to the status and capacity of the recipient? Should one always give what the recipient requested, or was one entitled to choose a different, more "appropriate" gift?

1. Schwartz has argued that the Jewish tradition is founded on a "rejection of reciprocity" (2010, 5). For a critical response, see Barclay 2015, 39–45.

2. For a recent translation, see Griffin and Inwood 2011; for analysis, see Inwood 1995; Griffin 2003; Engberg-Pedersen 2008; Barclay 2015, 45–51.

Multiple errors could accompany the act of giving. One could give too slowly and thereby humiliate the recipient, who had to make a request more than once. One could give with evident reluctance and thus undercut the spirit of goodwill supposed to accompany the gift. One could give so many times in quick succession that the recipient was left scrambling to know how to reciprocate and to restore their honor. There could be faults also on the side of the recipient: they could fail to be grateful or to show gratitude in appropriate ways; they could be slow in offering a return; they could try too hard to outdo the initial gift and thus humiliate the initial giver. There is endless scope here for competition, misunderstanding, resentment, and disgrace.

As a Stoic philosopher, Seneca offers numerous solutions to the possible dysfunctions of gift-giving, in accordance with his Stoic theory of value: what counts is not the thing (*res*) but the spirit (*animus*) in which it is given, not the content but the goodwill. Thus he insists that givers should give close attention to the manner of their giving but should then pay no regard to whether they receive a return. The one thing they should care about is gratitude, the social virtue intended by the gift. Hence they should do all they can to ensure that the gift is well placed and is capable of being well received, so that the recipient is not crushed or annoyed by the gift but is able to express genuine appreciation. For the beneficiary, the best way to avoid resentment or despair at the inability to return is to focus on the essential thing: gratitude. That gratitude can, of course, be accompanied by a return gift, in due course and in some form, but what is sought by goodwill is the return of goodwill, not a constant state of indebtedness. Thus Seneca deploys a famous paradox: the benefactor should immediately forget the gift, while the beneficiary should always remember it (*Ben.* 2.10.4).

Since the language of "obligation" and "debt," ubiquitous in ancient gift-giving, could make this relationship appear *nothing other than* a form of financial accounting, Seneca seeks always to draw gift-relationships away from the terrain of money lending (which he considers dishonorable); but he does not shun the language of "debt" so long as what is owed is defined in moral, rather than material, terms. And for all the extremes in his Stoic conceptualization of the gift, he never idealizes the one-way, unreciprocated gift. Since the whole system of gifts is "the chief factor in tying human society together" (*Ben.* 1.4.2, my translation), its proper expression is (a refined form of) reciprocal exchange.

Gift-Giving in the New Testament

A number of scholars have recognized the importance of ancient gift-giving for the interpretation of the New Testament (see, e.g., Peterman 1997; deSilva 2000; Joubert 2000; Harrison 2003; Downs 2008; Briones 2013; Barclay 2015; Blanton 2017). Jesus's ministry is replete with benefactions (not always acknowledged; Luke 17:11–19), his parables recount many forms of extreme beneficence (e.g., 15:11–32), and he interprets the law with special focus on an extension of generosity that is not limited by the requirement of a human return (Matt. 5:38–48).

Paul negotiates the fact that he did not request financial support at the earliest stages of his mission—a fact that he interpreted as noble generosity but that his critics took to signal his inferior status (1 Cor. 9:1–18; 1 Thess. 2:1–12). His collections for Jerusalem, on behalf of his churches in Galatia, Macedonia, and Achaia (Rom. 15:25–32; 1 Cor. 16:1–4; 2 Cor. 8–9), required extreme delicacy. Such a gift and his own role in its administration were easily misconstrued, and honor was at stake on all sides; he was even unsure if the gift would be accepted (Rom. 15:31). But here and elsewhere Paul places human gifts in the context of divine self-giving, using the common language of *charis* (grace, gift) to link human generosity with the benevolence of God and specifically "the grace [*charis*] of our Lord Jesus Christ" (2 Cor. 8:9 ESV).

In Paul's theology, this definitive gift of "the Son of God, who loved me and gave himself for me" (Gal. 2:20), provides not just a model to imitate but a transformative momentum through which the gift is passed on to others. Even here reciprocity is important, in the return of the transformed self to the divine benefactor (Rom. 12:1–2; 2 Cor. 8:5) and in the mutual giving and receiving that takes place within the body of Christ (1 Cor. 12:12–26; 2 Cor. 8:13–15). Where Paul is a recipient, if he cannot himself return a gift, God can and will (Phil. 4:10–20).

In the interpretation of such texts, modern, Western concepts of gift easily lead us astray. The modern moral horror at placing people under "obligation," our (theoretical) preference for the one-way gift, and our anxiety to "purify" gifts of any element of self-interest—all these lead to anachronistic expectations or misinterpretations of the New Testament. A better-informed understanding of the normal patterns of gift-giving in the Greco-Roman world is therefore vital, not least where it demonstrates some significant early Christian modifications to the typical gift-giving rules.

Works Cited

Anderson, G. A. 2013. *Charity: The Place of the Poor in the Biblical Tradition*. New Haven: Yale University Press.

Barclay, J. M. G. 2015. *Paul and the Gift*. Grand Rapids: Eerdmans.

Blanton, T. R., IV. 2017. *A Spiritual Economy: Gift-Exchange in the Letters of Paul of Tarsus*. New Haven: Yale University Press.

Briones, D. E. 2013. *Paul's Financial Policy: A Socio-Theological Approach*. London: Bloomsbury T&T Clark.

deSilva, D. A. 2000. *Honor, Patronage, Kinship, and Purity: Unlocking New Testament Culture*. Downers Grove, IL: InterVarsity.

Downs, D. J. 2008. *The Offering of the Gentiles: Paul's Collection for Jerusalem in Its Chronological, Cultural, and Cultic Contexts*. Tübingen: Mohr Siebeck.

Engberg-Pedersen, T. 2008. "Gift-Giving and Friendship: Seneca and Paul in Romans 1–8 on the Logic of God's χάρις and Its Human Response." *HTR* 101: 15–44.

Griffin, M. 2003. "*De Beneficiis* and Roman Society." *JRS* 93: 92–113.

Griffin, M., and B. Inwood. 2011. *Seneca: On Benefits*. Chicago: University of Chicago Press.

Harrison, J. R. 2003. *Paul's Language of Grace in Its Graeco-Roman Context*. Tübingen: Mohr Siebeck.

Inwood, B. 1995. "Politics and Paradox in Seneca's *De Beneficiis*." In *Justice and Generosity: Studies in Hellenistic Social and Political Philosophy*, edited by A. Laks and M. Schofield, 241–65. Cambridge: Cambridge University Press.

Joubert, S. 2000. *Paul as Benefactor: Reciprocity, Strategy, and Theological Reflection in Paul's Collection*. Tübingen: Mohr Siebeck.

Leithart, P. 2014. *Gratitude: An Intellectual History*. Waco: Baylor University Press.

Mauss, M. 1990. *The Gift*. Translated by W. D. Halls. London: Routledge. Originally published 1925.

Parker, R. 1998. "Pleasing Thighs: Reciprocity in Greek Religion." In *Reciprocity in Ancient Greece*, edited by C. Gill, N. Postlethwaite, and R. Seaford, 105–25. Oxford: Oxford University Press, 1998.

Peterman, G. W. 1997. *Paul's Gift from Philippi: Conventions of Gift-Exchange and Christian Giving*. Cambridge: Cambridge University Press.

Schellenberg, S. 2018. "Subsistence, Swapping, and Paul's Rhetoric of Generosity." *JBL* 137: 215–34.

Schwartz, S. 2010. *Were the Jews a Mediterranean Society?* Princeton: Princeton University Press.

Veyne, P. 1990. *Bread and Circuses*. Abridged and translated by B. Pierce. London: Penguin.

Wender, D., trans. 1973. *Hesiod and Theognis*. London: Penguin.

50

Alms for the Poor

NATHAN EUBANK

The English word "alms" (or "almsgiving") is derived from the Greek ἐλεημοσύνη (*eleēmosynē*), a word that means "mercy" but that also came to refer to charitable giving—either to the act of giving or to the thing given. The word appears just over a dozen times in the New Testament, all of which occur in Matthew or Luke-Acts (Matt. 6:2–4; Luke 11:41; 12:33; Acts 3:2–10; 9:36; 10:2–4, 31; 24:17). The reality of almsgiving, however, appears much more often than the occurrence of this word. For example, Matthew's famous portrayal of final judgment of the nations on the basis of various acts done for the needy (25:31–46) never uses the word "alms," but the passage obviously describes various charitable deeds.[1]

Alms in Jewish Tradition

Across all the major parts of the Hebrew Bible, the right treatment of the poor and vulnerable is held up as a solemn duty and a means of serving God, though "alms" in the sense of charity from one individual to another does not became a major concern until the Second Temple period. The Torah prescribes a range of practices designed to protect the poor and prevent the unchecked accumulation of wealth. For instance, the edges of fields were to be left unharvested so that immigrants, orphans, and widows would have food (Lev. 19:9–10; Deut. 24:19). Every seven years all debts owed by fellow Israelites were to be forgiven (Deut. 15:1–5). Deuteronomy warns that it is forbidden to refuse to lend when this "sabbatical year" approaches (15:7–11), despite the near certainty that lenders would receive nothing in return. Kindness to the needy is based on YHWH's own character. YHWH provides for orphans, widows, and foreigners, so the Israelites, who were themselves foreigners in Egypt, are to do likewise (10:18–19). It is unclear to what extent these laws were observed, and indeed the laws concerning sabbatical years are often labeled "utopian." Nevertheless, the belief that Israel's God loves the poor would exercise a

---

1. Some ancient readers of Matthew used the word ἐλεημοσύνη (*eleēmosynē*) to describe these deeds. See, e.g., John Chrysostom, *Hom. Gen.* 5.4; Clement, *Paed.* 3.12.93.

strong pull on the imagination of later Jews and Christians.

The prophetic books of the Old Testament consistently condemn what might be called a lack of "social justice"—that is, the oppression of the poor and vulnerable instead of the fair distribution of resources. Isaiah, for example, pronounces doom on those who acquire excess property and thereby leave insufficient resources for others (5:8–9). Amos lambasts the Northern Kingdom of Israel for abusing the poor by selling "the righteous for silver, and the needy for a pair of sandals" (2:6)—that is, selling insolvent debtors into slavery. Activities such as feasting, drinking, and listening to music are repeatedly condemned (Isa. 5:11–13; Amos 6), apparently not because they are problematic per se but because it seems wrong to luxuriate while neighbors lack basic resources. Another consistent refrain in the prophets is the claim that ritual observances in the absence of justice are an abomination to God. "I hate, I despise your festivals," God says in the book of Amos (5:21), declaring preference for justice and righteousness (5:24). According to Isaiah 58, the people fast and perform ritual displays of humility, but God would prefer that they share their bread with the hungry, their homes with the homeless, and their clothes with the naked (58:1–7). Similarly, Ezekiel declares that the righteous person is one who "gives his bread to the hungry and covers the naked with a garment, [and] does not take advance or accrued interest" (18:7–8).

As noted above, individual acts of almsgiving increase in importance in the Second Temple period. One possible reason for this shift in emphasis is the presence of many Jews in cities in the diaspora. The book of Tobit, which was written in the second or third century BCE, addresses this new situation by portraying its eponymous main character as an exile living in the city of Nineveh after the Assyrian destruction of the Northern Kingdom. When he lived in Israel, Tobit had faithfully worshiped in Jerusalem (1:6–8), but when he was forced to live elsewhere he focused on performing acts of charity (1:3). Tobit thus portrays alms as a way of remaining faithful to God even in a foreign city (Anderson 2013, 18–19). The book of Sirach (2nd c. BCE) has a similar understanding of almsgiving but speaks to an audience that still has access to the temple in Jerusalem. The author, Ben Sira, advises fidelity to the temple cult and its priests as well as kindness to the poor (Anderson 2013, 20–22). It was during this period that a distinctive terminology for alms began to emerge in Hebrew and Aramaic. Sirach uses a Hebrew word that would normally be translated "righteousness" (צְדָקָה, tsedaqah) to refer to almsgiving (3:30; 7:10; 12:3; 40:2), and both Tobit and the book of Daniel use the Aramaic cognate צִדְקָה (tsidqah) in the same way (Tob. 4:7–8; Dan. 4:27), perhaps because almsgiving was seen as a righteous deed par excellence (Gregory 2010, 172–79). This becomes the ordinary way of referring to almsgiving in rabbinic Judaism (Gray 2019, 1–32), the earliest literature of which was compiled around the beginning of the third century CE. The New Testament occasionally uses the Greek word δικαιοσύνη (dikaiosynē, righteousness) in similar ways.[2]

One other persistent feature of almsgiving in Jewish tradition is worth noting. In all the literature mentioned here, almsgiving involves three main parties: the giver, the recipient, and the deity. Instead of almsgiving being an exchange simply on the horizontal plane, the Hebrew Bible and later traditions under its influence tend to claim that God is in some sense the unseen recipient of alms and that God will reward those who are generous or punish those who are not. Those who help the poor will be helped by God (e.g., Prov. 19:17). Those who give away their possessions store

2. See 2 Cor. 9:9. Matthew 6:1–18 discusses three acts of δικαιοσύνη (dikaiosynē), the first of which is ἐλεημοσύνη (eleēmosynē).

up treasure in heaven, which is more reliable than earthly treasure (Tob. 4:9–10; 12:8; Sir. 29:11–12; t. Pe'ah 4.18). Conversely, those who ignore the poor will be ignored by God (e.g., Prov. 21:13). As gifts to God, alms were often described as having a sacral quality (Deut. 14:28–29; 26:12–15; Sir. 35:3–4; Anderson 2013, 26–28).

Alms in the Wider Greco-Roman World

Outside of Judaism and Christianity there is much less evidence of care for the poor. Indeed, faced with the undeniable importance of almsgiving in Judaism and Christianity and the relative lack of evidence of almsgiving among pagans, it has been alleged that only Jews and Christians tried to help the poor or even that the bishops of the ancient church "invented the poor" (Brown 2002, 8), in the sense of making them visible to the wealthy for the first time. This claim is exaggerated, but it is based on some truth. To be sure, the Greco-Roman world was obsessed with generosity, but the evidence suggests that relatively few people were particularly concerned with generosity to those in need. Instead, far more attention was given to acts of generosity to those higher up the socioeconomic ladder, those with the resources to give something back. Gifts of money or other resources were often meant at least in part to strengthen relationships by creating an ongoing exchange.[3] For the first-century CE Roman philosopher Seneca the Younger, a well-placed gift should trigger a cascade of gifts and counter-gifts, a back-and-forth of exchanges that is the basis of friendship (*Ben.* 2.18.5). Gifts to social and economic inferiors were also meant to spark an exchange. Patrons assisted clients in exchange for loyalty. The wealthy often gave large gifts to cities to finance building projects or festivals in return

for public honors, a phenomenon that scholars call "euergetism" from the Greek εὐεργέτης (*euergetēs*, benefactor). In short, at the risk of oversimplification, one might say that Jewish tradition emphasized care for the needy that is rewarded by God, whereas the wider Greco-Roman world tended to emphasize gifts to those who could reward the giver themselves.

Despite the relative lack of evidence of pagan almsgiving, it would be a mistake to conclude that almsgiving was unknown outside of Judaism and Christianity. There is good evidence that begging was quite common in the ancient world, and the very existence of beggars suggests that people sometimes offered them assistance (Parkin 2006, 66). Moreover, beggars sometimes showcased their disabilities to passersby or even feigned disability or intentionally mutilated children to make them more successful beggars. None of this activity would make sense unless passersby were moved by the appearance of suffering to offer assistance (70–71). There are, moreover, scattered anecdotes of instances of pagan almsgiving, such as the account of the philosopher Musonius Rufus tossing a coin to a beggar despite the objections of his companions (Longenecker 2010, 84–85).

Comparison with Jewish tradition also raises the question whether pagans gave to the needy as a way of serving the gods. There are hints that some pagans may have seen almsgiving as a religious duty, something done in imitation of the gods or at their behest. Seneca the Younger claimed that those who give gifts are like gods (*Clem.* 2.6.3), and Musonius Rufus said that Zeus desires all people to be generous (Longenecker 2010, 102–3). Hospitality, though not identical with almsgiving, was sometimes imagined as a duty required by the gods, and there are stories of gods taking human form and rewarding those who showed them hospitality (Ovid, *Metam.* 8.626–724; cf. Gen. 18; Heb. 13:2). Beggars were known to frequent temples, which could suggest that they

---

3. For more on gift-giving, see Barclay's chapter in this volume (chap. 49).

hoped to receive assistance from worshipers (Longenecker 2010, 97–98). While giving to the poor out of deference to God or the gods is not unique to Judaism and Christianity, it should be admitted that scholarly attention to pagan almsgiving and its possible religious motivation derives not so much from the study of Greco-Roman sources themselves but by comparison with Judaism and Christianity. In other words, the emphasis on alms in communities influenced by the Bible is so great that it raises the question whether and to what extent generosity to the poor existed outside of that influence. Scholarly investigation of generosity in the wider Greco-Roman world typically and rightly focuses on practices other than almsgiving, such as euergetism and patronage.

The New Testament and Early Christianity

On the subject of almsgiving, the New Testament and early Christian literature are very much at home in the wider Jewish tradition. Care for the poor is often described as an important duty for Jesus followers (e.g., James 2:14–17; 1 John 3:17) or even as a strict requirement without which it is impossible to belong to the people of God or to enter eternal life (e.g., Matt. 25:31–46; Clement, *Quis div.* 32). Often it is said that God is the unseen recipient of alms and that God, not the poor, will pay the giver back (e.g., Luke 14:12–14). Gifts to the needy are also described as worship or compared to sacrifices to God (e.g., Heb. 13:16; James 1:27). Early Christians also claimed that possessions given to the poor paradoxically fund a more reliable treasure in heaven (e.g., Luke 12:13–34). In all these ways the New Testament and other early Christian literature stand in the same stream of tradition as Tobit, Sirach, and the later rabbis. The chief difference is the early Christian habit of reorienting everything around Jesus. A few examples from the Synoptic Gospels illustrate the point.

In Mark's Gospel, selling one's possessions and giving to the poor to earn treasure in heaven are linked with being willing to give up one's life to follow Jesus (see Mark 10:17–31). Matthew and Luke retain this idea while greatly expanding the importance of almsgiving. For Matthew, care for the hungry, thirsty, stranger, unclothed, sick, and incarcerated is held up as the decisive action that determines whether one will enter into eternal life or eternal punishment (25:31–46; Eubank 2013, 103–4). The same passage also describes Jesus as the unseen recipient of these deeds, giving him the role ordinarily played by God in the Bible. Matthew also stresses the importance of giving alms privately so that repayment comes from God rather than in the form of praise from humans (6:1–4; Eubank 2014). Luke places even greater emphasis on the importance of renouncing one's possessions and on helping the poor, describing these as acts of repentance that prepare one to meet the Lord or that bring salvation (3:7–14; 19:1–10; Giambrone 2017) or that render the giver pure (Luke 11:37–41; Downs 2016, 125–29). The book of Acts describes the earliest Christians sharing their possessions and says that the first Gentile convert was singled out by God because of his prayers and alms (Acts 2:43–47; 4:32–35; 10:1–4, 30–31). At the same time, Luke describes the poor themselves as God's people, beginning with Jesus's family (Luke 1:46–53; 2:7, 22–24; cf. Lev. 12:8). Luke heralds a reversal of fortunes, wherein the poor are blessed and lifted up, while the rich are punished (Luke 1:52–53; 6:20–21, 24–25; 16:19–31). Luke also explicitly attacks central features of ordinary reciprocal generosity in the Greco-Roman world, claiming that one must not invite people to dine who can return the invitation. Instead, one should invite the destitute, who can offer no repayment, and then repayment will come from God (14:12–14; cf. Matt. 6:1–4). The Lukan Jesus also tells the disciples that, unlike Gentile authorities, they are not to be lauded as benefactors (εὐεργέται, *euergetai*) but are instead to behave like servants in imitation of Jesus himself (Luke 22:24–27).

Almsgiving plays a less obviously prominent role in some New Testament texts, most notably John's Gospel and Paul's letters. John's Gospel contains little in the way of explicit ethical teaching. Alms for the poor are presumed to be important (12:4–6; 13:29), but Jesus never says anything on the topic. Note, however, that 1 John claims that members of the community must share their possessions with the needy if the love of God is to abide in them (3:17). The context in 1 John also suggests that sharing possessions is a way of imitating the self-gift of Jesus on the cross (see 3:16).

Scholars have often claimed that Paul's letters evince little interest in the poor, sometimes alleging that Paul's expectation that the world would shortly come to an end precluded any serious interest in material prosperity. Paul's letters do contain scattered references to generosity (e.g., Rom. 12:8) and to his collection of money for the church in Jerusalem (Rom. 15:25–29; 1 Cor. 16:1–4; 2 Cor. 8–9), but it has not been obvious to scholars, especially in previous generations, that these passages evince a consistent ethic of almsgiving similar to what is found in the Synoptic Gospels. Nevertheless, there is good reason to believe that Paul shared the broader early Christian belief in the vital importance of almsgiving and that he contributed to it with his characteristic creativity.

Paul's habit of mentioning the importance of generosity in passing even while discussing other issues (e.g., Rom. 12:8; 1 Cor. 12:28) suggests that sharing possessions was an essential part of Pauline catechesis. Moreover, like the authors of the Synoptic Gospels and others in the biblical tradition, Paul taught at least some of his congregations that gifts to the needy are gifts to God that God will repay (2 Cor. 9:6–11; Phil. 4:10–20; Eubank 2015). He also labeled the Corinthian congregation's mistreatment of the poor during the Lord's Supper an "un-worthy" use of "the bread" and "the cup of the Lord" that would incur divine judgment (1 Cor. 11:17–34), which shows that the well-being of the less prosperous members of the congregation was a concern.

The relevance of the Jerusalem collection for almsgiving is difficult to ascertain because Paul explains its significance in different ways, some of which have little if anything to do with helping the poor (e.g., Rom. 15:27). At least some passages discussing the Jerusalem collection, however, explicitly link the collection to a general obligation to be generous. Second Corinthians 9 is replete with indications that the Corinthians should be sharing their possessions regularly with "all people" (see especially 9:13 but also 9:8–11). In 2 Corinthians 8, which may have originally belonged to a different letter than 2 Corinthians 9, Paul appeals to the example of Christ, who "though he was rich, yet for your sakes he became poor, so that by his poverty you might become rich" (8:9). Paul also argues that giving to the collection is necessary to correct a current imbalance between those with much and those with little, thereby achieving equality (8:13–14). Galatians 2:10 states that Paul agreed with the Jerusalem apostles that his Gentile congregations must "remember the poor." This is often assumed to be a reference to the Jerusalem collection rather than "the poor" in general (though see Longenecker 2010, 157–206). Even if this assumption is correct, the fact that the recipients of the collection are described simply as "the poor" arguably suggests a concern for the poor outside of Jerusalem (cf. Gal. 6:7–10; Eubank 2015, 183–85).

Finally, it is worth noting that care for the poor is a major concern of 1 Timothy, a letter with instructions on how to care for widows (5:3–16), warnings about the love of money (6:3–10), and instructions to the rich on how to "take hold of true life" by sharing their possessions (6:17–19, my translation; see Eubank 2012). Though most scholars believe 1 Timothy was written by someone other than Paul, these passages show that Paul was remembered as someone who made care for the poor an important part of his message.

In the centuries that follow, ancient Christians continued to be enthusiastic advocates of almsgiving, explaining the importance of this practice by employing all of the biblical themes described above (e.g., Cyprian, *Eleem.*), not infrequently using biblical texts in ways that mirrored contemporaneous rabbinic discussions of alms (e.g., Ps. 112:9 in b. B. Bat. 10b; Eusebius, *Comm. Ps.* 23.597; John Chrysostom, *Hom. 2 Cor.* 61.533; Gregory of Nyssa, *Beat.* 44.1208; Basil the Great, *Destruam horrea mea* 3.30; Gregory of Nazianzus, *Or.* 8.12). Fourth- and fifth-century preachers such as Basil the Great, Ambrose, John Chrysostom, and Augustine regaled and cajoled their congregations with biblical arguments regarding the absolute necessity of giving to the poor (Brown 2012). The late ancient Christian emphasis on the poor, combined with the growing cultural and political power of Christians, resulted in almsgiving and other acts of generosity to the needy coming to be regarded as important religious and civic duties for centuries.

Works Cited

Anderson, Gary. 2013. *Charity: The Place of the Poor in the Biblical Tradition*. New Haven: Yale University Press.

Brown, Peter. 2002. *Poverty and Leadership in the Later Roman Empire*. Hanover, NH: University Press of New England.

———. 2012. *Through the Eye of a Needle: Wealth, the Fall of Rome, and the Making of Christianity in the West, 350–550 AD*. Princeton: Princeton University Press.

Downs, David J. 2016. *Alms: Charity, Reward, and Atonement in Early Christianity*. Waco: Baylor University Press.

Eubank, Nathan. 2012. "Almsgiving Is 'the Commandment': A Note on 1 Timothy 6.6–19." *NTS* 58: 144–50.

———. 2013. *Wages of Cross-Bearing and Debt of Sin: The Economy of Heaven in Matthew's Gospel*. BZNW 196. Berlin: de Gruyter.

———. 2014. "Storing Up Treasure with God in the Heavens: Celestial Investments in Matthew 6:1–21." *CBQ* 76: 77–92.

———. 2015. "Justice Endures Forever: Paul's Grammar of Generosity." *Journal for the Study of Paul and His Letters* 5: 169–87.

Giambrone, Anthony. 2017. *Sacramental Charity, Creditor Christology, and the Economy of Salvation in Luke's Gospel*. WUNT 2/439. Tübingen: Mohr Siebeck.

Gray, Alyssa M. 2019. *Charity in Rabbinic Judaism: Atonement, Rewards, and Righteousness*. New York: Routledge.

Gregory, Bradley C. 2010. *Like an Everlasting Signet Ring: Generosity in the Book of Sirach*. DCLS 2. Berlin: de Gruyter.

Longenecker, Bruce W. 2010. *Remember the Poor: Paul, Poverty, and the Greco-Roman World*. Grand Rapids: Eerdmans.

Parkin, Anneliese. 2006. "'You Do Him No Service': An Exploration of Pagan Almsgiving." In *Poverty in the Roman World*, edited by M. Atkins and R. Osborne, 60–82. Cambridge: Cambridge University Press.

51

Hospitality

ANDREW E. ARTERBURY

Though no ancient author provides an overview of the custom of hospitality as this essay seeks to do, we nevertheless encounter glimpses of ancient hospitality as we read the diverse literature of antiquity. Notably, these references to or depictions of the custom of hospitality appear in writings from most of the ancient cultures of the Mediterranean basin. As a result, the best way to learn about the historical practice of this custom is to read ancient literature while taking note of the hospitable practices that are commonplace therein.

Defining Ancient Hospitality

At its most basic level, ancient hospitality, or Greek *xenia*, referred to the practice of hosting travelers whenever those travelers were away from their home region (see, e.g., Arterbury 2005; Bolchazy 1977; and Herman 1987). Essentially, anything that takes place "from the moment a visitor approaches someone's house until the moment he departs" can be accurately described as an outgrowth of either inhospital-

ity or hospitality (Reece 1993, 5; see also Arterbury 2005, 51). Unlike contemporary travelers, who often seek out "hospitality industry" businesses to meet their needs, ancient travelers more often relied upon individuals or families to care for them temporarily while they were away from their homes. Inns existed, but they were frequently associated with questionable activities and less-than-ideal conditions. For instance, regarding inns in antiquity Everett Ferguson (2003, 89) writes, "Their reputation (in quality and morals) was notorious. The wine was often adulterated . . . , sleeping quarters were filthy and insect and rodent infested, innkeepers were extortionate, thieves were in wait, government spies were listening, and many were nothing more than brothels." As a result, most travelers preferred to seek out and forge hospitality relationships with respected householders in whatever region they visited.

The relationships that were forged within a hospitality context in antiquity were often temporary relationships that revolved around meeting the immediate needs of the wayfarer. These temporary relationships might last only as long as it took to prepare and eat a meal together (e.g., Homer, *Od*. 1.102–324; Gen. 18:1–16; Luke 24:13–35), or perhaps the guests might sleep at least one night in their host's home (e.g., Homer, *Od*. 3.487–93; Luke 10:5–7; Acts 21:3–6; 28:13–14). On other occasions, however, the encounter between the host and the guest morphed into lengthy visits and permanent bonds known as "guest-friendships" or "fictive kinships." These guest-friendships were often depicted as relationships that transcended the boundaries of region, culture, and time. In fact, at times, these permanent hospitality relationships or guest-friendships were passed down from generation to generation as a two-party covenant or alliance that outweighed even one's loyalty to the members of one's home region. Additionally, while two individuals or two groups most often established these guest-friendships, at times individuals or groups established a hospitality relationship with a city or nation, thereby making the characteristics of an alliance or covenant relationship even more evident (e.g., Herodotus, *Hist*. 1.27.50; 1.69.3; and Xenophon, *Hell*. 6.1.2–4). When Paul instructs Philemon to prepare a guest room for him, it suggests that the two had previously established a guest-friendship (Philem. 22). Similarly, Peter's lengthy stay in Cornelius's house suggests that they too forge a fictive kinship (Acts 10:48).

Perhaps the most famous example of the enduring quality of guest-friendships in antiquity involves Glaucus and Diomedes in Homer's *Iliad* (6.137–282). Despite the fact that Glaucus fights alongside his fellow Trojans and Diomedes fights alongside his fellow Greeks in the Trojan War, when Diomedes hears Glaucus invoke the name of Glaucus's grandfather, Diomedes immediately stops fighting and announces that his grandfather forged a permanent hospitality relationship or guest-friendship with Glaucus's grandfather. As a result, even as the fighting rages around them, the two men reach a truce, exchange armor

(as an act of gift-giving), and go off to fight other Trojans and Greeks respectively. In other words, the permanent hospitality relationship forged by their grandfathers still functions as a sacred covenant two generations later. The guest-friendship takes precedence (at least in appearance)[1] over their loyalty to their fellow countrymen whom they fight alongside in battle.

Thus, by definition ancient hospitality revolved around cross-cultural interactions. Interactions unfolded and relationships were established between at least two people of different regions, often with different cultural norms. At times, these host and guest interactions simply renewed a previously founded relationship, perhaps a relationship that was forged by them or by their ancestors. On other occasions, the host and guest were distant relatives who may have been meeting for the first time (e.g., Abraham's servant and Laban in Gen. 24:15–27; Tobias and Raguel in Tob. 6:10–10:11). Frequently, however, the host and guest were complete strangers. As a result, the custom of hospitality provided a normative script for how people from alien cultures could, and perhaps should, proceed whenever they first encountered one another.

General Dynamics and Common Elements of Ancient Hospitality

Respectable hosts served ancient travelers according to well-established protocols by meeting travelers' two primary needs: provisions and protection. By supplying guests with provisions, the host met the essential needs of the traveler. By protecting guests, the host made

---

1. Because Diomedes ends up with the far superior set of armor after the gift exchange, some see this passage as another example of the Greeks outmaneuvering the Trojans in the *Iliad* through the use of cunning trickery. Regardless, the narrative logic of *Il*. 6.137–282 builds on and only makes sense in light of the value that ancient Mediterranean peoples placed on permanent hospitality relationships.

sure the guest had safe passage through the host's home region. We elaborate on both categories below.

Generally speaking, travelers or strangers located prospective hosts and requested hospitality in somewhat predictable patterns. First and foremost, travelers often began their search for a host in public places. For instance, a traveler might search for a hospitable host at a local well or town square (e.g., Gen. 24:17; Judg. 19:14–15; 1 Sam. 9:11–13; John 4:6–7). Wells afforded travelers an opportunity to get a drink of water for themselves or their animals while also encountering local residents in a nonthreatening environment. Similarly, travelers might discover potential hosts as residents passed through the center of a town. If possible, a traveler would ideally elect to stay with a relative, perhaps even a distant relative, as noted above (Malina and Rohrbaugh 1992, 297; see also Luke 1:39–40). In addition, it appears that travelers often sought out potential hosts whom they perceived to be of equal social rank as themselves (cf. Acts 16:15). Regardless, unless a resident volunteered to host the traveler after a casual encounter in a public place, the traveler would approach the outer gate or threshold of a house and shout out a greeting to the householder within the house. If a householder returned the greeting, the householder was welcoming the traveler to cross the threshold of the householder's home and become the host's guest. If the householder failed to return the greeting, the traveler knew to search elsewhere for a hospitable reception (see, e.g., Luke 10:5–6).

Exemplary hosts immediately began to assess and meet the needs of their guests, their companions, and their animals. Hosts generally offered guests the opportunity to bathe. This act of kindness varied by culture and according to the host's resources. As a result, bathing could range on the modest end from supplying the guest with water to wash his or her own feet to the more extravagant end where the host's servants bathed the guest's entire body. Afterward, exemplary hosts might supply their guests with new or perhaps dry clothes. Next, virtually all ancient texts mention hosts supplying their guests with a meal. In fact, ancient texts frequently portray exemplary hosts providing as lavish of a meal as they could possibly supply. Then, only after the traveler had been reinvigorated by means of an abundant meal, it was finally permissible for the host to ask the traveler personal or biographical questions—questions such as his or her name, home region, reason for traveling, and so on. These conversations provided the householder and perhaps the householder's family with a type of post-dinner entertainment as the guest described his or her travels while also relaying bits of news from other regions. Of course, hosts also provided sleeping accommodations for their overnight guests. Finally, as travelers departed their hosts' homes, the hosts routinely supplied their guests with supplies for the next leg of the travelers' journey (see, e.g., Acts 28:10).

In addition to provisions, ancient hosts also accepted the responsibility to protect their guests from those in the hosts' home region who might wish to harm travelers. Ancient writers frequently speak about people who exhibited inhospitality, violence, and abuse toward travelers, whether motivated by fear, prejudice, personal gain, or personal self-gratification. In contrast, exemplary hosts sought to protect and defend the travelers from their own neighbors. Hosts not only protected their guests while they were in the hosts' homes but generally escorted their guests out of the region, thereby providing their guests with safe passage out of the hosts' territory.

Finally, it is important to note that hosts and guests who practiced hospitality in antiquity assumed from the outset that the newly forged relationship was reciprocal in nature. The Greek terminology related to the custom of hospitality is instructive. The word *xenia* refers to the overarching custom of hospitality, but other Greek terms beginning with the *xen-* root were also employed when speaking of hospitality. In particular, the host and the guest were both identified as a *xenos*. Furthermore, the terminology for both parties was interchangeable. Similarly, the duties of both members in a hospitality relationship, and in particular a guest-friendship, were likewise interchangeable. When a traveler accepted hospitality from a host, that traveler also simultaneously bound himself or herself to provide equally generous hospitality to the host whenever the host traveled to the guest's home region. In essence, from the outset a standing invitation was established for the original host, or perhaps the host's family members or representatives (see, e.g., Matt. 25:34–40; Luke 10:16; Rom. 16:1–2), to receive hospitality in the guest's home. Both parties anticipated and essentially agreed upon reciprocal generosity whenever they inaugurated a hospitality relationship.

Risks Associated with Ancient Hospitality

Precisely because guests and hosts were often complete strangers to one another, the ancient custom of hospitality presented significant risks to both the guest and the host. In other words, there was nothing safe, easy, or cheap about the custom of hospitality in antiquity. Both the guest and the host were capable of exhibiting inhospitality. Both the guest and the host were capable of violating their counterpart's trust. As a result, both the guest and the host found themselves in highly vulnerable positions.

Because strangers were by definition unknown persons, travelers could never be assured of a positive reception by the people they encountered in a new region. Perhaps the dominant culture fostered a generally negative disposition toward outsiders, a manifestation of either fear or prejudice toward strangers. (In

this regard, see Paul's account of the Galatians' generous reception of him, even though he was a stranger who suffered from an illness; Gal. 4:13–15.) Or perhaps the residents of a region were inclined to take advantage of travelers for personal gain. Unlike Abraham's hospitality toward strangers in Genesis 18, Philo claims that the Egyptians displayed inhospitality (*axenia*) toward Abraham and his family (Philo, *Abraham* 107). Likewise, the Hebrew Bible depicts townspeople who desire to violently abuse strangers for their own sexual pleasure as examples of inhospitality (Gen. 19:1–23; Judg. 19:22–28). Additionally, Lycaon, the Arcadian king, exhibits extreme inhospitality when he kills a man from the Molossian race, mixes the man's remains into the meal being prepared, and attempts to feed the tainted meal to his guest, who turns out to be Zeus disguised as a human stranger (Ovid, *Metam.* 1.212–15, 226–44). In 3 John 9–10, a Christian man named Diotrephes is said to refuse hospitality to other "brothers" who do not align themselves with his influence.

When hosting strangers, householders likewise faced significant risks. Because hosts frequently knew little if anything about strangers' backstories, outsiders represented a potential threat to the well-being of hosts, their household, and their people group. For instance, strangers might be spies conducting reconnaissance for a foreign army (e.g., Josh. 2:1–22), or strangers might possess questionable character and therefore be capable of acting in dishonorable ways. For example, Herodotus claims that the Trojan War began after a guest (Paris) violated his host's (Menelaus) hospitality by literally running off with the host's wife (Helen) (*Hist.* 2.113–15, 120). Furthermore, potential hosts might wonder whether strangers who just arrived at their threshold were fleeing punishment for crimes committed in another territory. Consequently, welcoming complete strangers into one's household, even on a temporary basis, was a highly risky endeavor.

To mitigate these risks, ancient travelers frequently carried letters of recommendation to assure potential hosts of travelers' noble character or purposes. In essence, letters of recommendation from trusted individuals who may have been known by the potential host lessened the risk that potential hosts incurred (Malherbe 1983, 101–2; see Paul's comments about letters of recommendation in 2 Cor. 3:1–3).

It should also be noted that the custom of hospitality potentially required great sacrifices on the part of ancient hosts. Exemplary and magnanimous hosts used vital resources to host their guests. As a result, the custom of hospitality had the potential to be quite taxing on hosts. Often, ancient texts portray ideal hosts as those who lavish food, clothes, and gifts upon their guests at an unsustainable rate. For example, in Genesis 18:1–15 Abraham sees three strangers walking by his tent, extends hospitality to them, and prepares a great feast. In the process, he prepares more food than three people could reasonably eat in one sitting. For example, he asks Sarah to make bread using "three measures of choice flour," likely amounting to about thirty-six pounds of flour (Gen. 18:6). He also asks his servants to kill and prepare a choice and tender calf (18:7). On top of that he adds curds and milk (18:8). Similarly, Baucis and Philemon in Ovid's *Metamorphoses* 629–88 and the poor hunter in Dio Chrysostom's *Discourse* 7.1–22 are famous for their sacrificial hospitality. Despite extreme poverty in both instances, the hosts offer the very best of what they have to their guests. Similarly, Homer portrays King Alcinous and the Phaeacians' hospitality as so generous that they actually restore most of the wealth that Odysseus lost to Penelope's suitors, who consumed his household while he was away (Homer, *Od.* 13.47–53, 63–125). In short, these literary examples illustrate how magnanimous expressions of ancient hospitality in antiquity had the potential to strain hosts' resources.

This fiscal strain on hospitable hosts multiplied exponentially if guests elected to stay for long periods of time or if numerous guests relied on a host's hospitality in a relatively short timeframe. In fact, it is difficult to say how long a typical guest anticipated staying with a host. As previously mentioned, some hospitality encounters lasted only as long as it took to prepare and eat a meal together (e.g., Gen. 18), while many included an overnight stay. Some Greek and Roman texts, however, depict months-long stays by some guests, especially if the host was a wealthy landowner and if the relationship between the host and guest morphed into a guest-friendship. Regardless, in an early Christian context that encouraged the practice of evangelism and pilgrimage, some Christian hosts who lived along well-traveled roads were likely inundated with requests for hospitality. As a result, the author of the Didache (late first or early second century) seeks to limit the number of days Christian guests can stay with Christian hosts. The author prohibits Christian guests from staying more than two days. A three-day stay is permitted only if there is a true need (Did. 12.1–2). The author even declares that any prophet or apostle who stays more than one day, unless there is a legitimate need, is a false prophet whom Christians should avoid (11.4–6). These restrictions suggest that early Christian travelers may have overwhelmed some Christian hosts, particularly those who lived along thoroughfares. The Didache's instructions constitute a corrective measure.

In short, most ancient travelers likely experienced fear and trepidation as they requested hospitality from an unknown householder, and most ancient householders likely experienced anxiety and hesitancy when they extended hospitality to unknown travelers. It is safe to say that many people in antiquity may have preferred to avoid hospitality encounters. Hosts risked far more than they received in the interaction, and guests hoped that the person they appealed to for help would in fact help them rather than harm them.

Common Motivations Guiding Ancient Hospitality

The previous statements beg the question of why any host would take on the risk of extending hospitality to a stranger in the ancient world. While Ladislaus Bolchazy (1977, i) believes he can document as many as five motivations for the extension of hospitality in antiquity, the most commonly cited motivation revolved around the belief that the gods cared about and monitored the care of strangers. Zeus, in particular, was often hailed as the "God of Hospitality." In ancient Mediterranean literature, Zeus and the other gods routinely take on incognito appearances as strangers in order to test householders' responses to strangers who request hospitality.[2] Then, if the gods deem householders to be inhospitable, they frequently punish the negligent householders. For instance, Jupiter (or Zeus) destroys Lycaon's house and turns Lycaon into a wolf after he attempts to feed human remains to his incognito guest (Ovid, *Metam.* 1.231–44).

Alternatively, when the gods deem householders to be hospitable, they frequently reward them. This belief was explicit in the Greek and Roman cultures. For example, Telemachus hosts an incognito Athena disguised in the form of a man named Mentes in Homer's *Odyssey* 1.102–324. In the context of Telemachus's generous hospitality, Athena provides the necessary direction Telemachus needs to learn more about the status and location of his father. Similarly, Baucis and Philemon are rewarded richly for the rest of their lives after they sacrificially serve their guests.

Unbeknownst to them, their guests turn out to be Jupiter (or Zeus) and Atlas, whose appearances have been disguised (Ovid, *Metam.* 8.618–724).

While the belief that the gods policed the practice of hospitality was not the only reason ancient hosts cared for travelers, it certainly was the most prominent one. As a result, ancient householders frequently sought to honor the gods and curry their favor by providing provisions and protection for strangers who traveled outside of their home territories. Consequently, the practice of hospitality in Mediterranean antiquity was intimately linked with one's efforts to please the gods in Greek and Roman contexts.

Similar beliefs existed in the Hebrew and Christian cultures as well. For example, Abraham and Sarah are rewarded with news of the upcoming birth of their son after they unknowingly host three strangers closely associated with the Lord (Gen. 18:1–15). Centuries later the author of the book of Hebrews likely reminds early Christians of Abraham and Sarah's encounter with the Lord's emissaries. The author exhorts Christians "to show hospitality to strangers, for by doing that some have entertained angels without knowing it" (Heb. 13:2). Similarly, when Paul recounts his initial reception by the Galatians, he notes that their generosity was extended to him "as an angel of God, as Christ Jesus" (Gal. 4:14). And when Jesus teaches about the separation of the sheep and the goats in Matthew 25:31–46, he indicates that the Son of Man will consider whether those standing before him at the judgment have responded with hospitality or inhospitality toward the strangers they encountered.

Finally, Paul exhorts his readers in Romans 12:9–13 to show love to others as service to the Lord. In the process, Paul caps off his illustrative list by beseeching the Roman Christians to "extend hospitality to strangers" (12:13). Yet, he does not merely ask them to extend hospitality to strangers (*xenia*). Rather, he exhorts

---

2. Literary depictions of these instances where the gods are disguised as strangers or travelers are referred to as theoxenies; see Jipp 2013, 77–78.

them to extend hospitality to strangers that is marked by and motivated by love (*philoxenia*).

Works Cited

Arterbury, Andrew. 2005. *Entertaining Angels: Early Christian Hospitality in Its Mediterranean Setting*. New Testament Monographs 8. Sheffield: Sheffield Phoenix.

Bolchazy, Ladislaus J. 1977. *Hospitality in Antiquity: Livy's Concept of Its Humanizing Force*. Chicago: Ares.

Ferguson, Everett. 2003. *Backgrounds of Early Christianity*. 3rd ed. Grand Rapids: Eerdmans.

Herman, Gabriel. 1987. *Ritualised Friendship and the Greek City*. Cambridge: Cambridge University Press.

Jipp, Joshua W. 2013. *Divine Visitations and Hospitality to Strangers in Luke-Acts: An Interpretation of the Malta Episode in Acts 28:1–10*. Leiden: Brill.

Malherbe, Abraham J. 1983. *Social Aspects of Early Christianity*. 2nd ed. Philadelphia: Fortress.

Malina, Bruce J., and Richard L. Rohrbaugh. 1992. *Social Science Commentary on the Synoptic Gospels*. Minneapolis: Fortress.

Reece, Steve. 1993. *The Stranger's Welcome: Oral Theory and the Aesthetics of the Homeric Hospitality Scene*. Ann Arbor: University of Michigan Press.

52

Meals and Symposia

Paul B. Duff

Meals and Symposia in the Greco-Roman World

Human beings eat not only to survive but also to acknowledge their identity and their place in the world. The way one ate, with whom one dined, and with whom one refused to dine mattered a great deal in the Greco-Roman world. Like formal meals in the contemporary world, Greco-Roman banquets were highly ritualized. They could serve any number of purposes. Such banquets could, for example, function as social events, as club banquets, as dinners honoring one or more gods, as wedding feasts, as funerary banquets, or some combination of the above. But regardless of the purpose, in its simplest form, the Greco-Roman banquet consisted of three components: the meal itself (the *deipnon*), a libation, and a symposium (Smith 2003, 27–31). Ancient diners typically reclined throughout the three stages. Of course, there were some variations in the ancient patterns. For example, women sometimes sat rather than reclined during the meal (sitting was usually reserved for subservient people or slaves). Jewish banquets and some banquets held by Jesus

followers included a blessing over wine prior to the *deipnon* (cf. Did. 9.2–4). But despite minor variations here and there, the tripartite structure—*deipnon*, libation, symposium—remained stable for centuries.

The Deipnon

The Greco-Roman banquet was opened by the *deipnon*—a Greek term that simply means "supper" or "meal." During the *deipnon*, the main course was served, which typically consisted of bread and vegetables. In the case of more lavish banquets, fish or meat would be served. Condiments such as *garum* (a fermented fish sauce) were typically available to the diners as well. As already noted, diners reclined during the *deipnon*, usually on couches along the three outer walls of a dining room (*triklinos* in Greek or *triclinium* in Latin). The seating arrangement—that is, who reclined next to whom—was significant. Honored guests were placed in the most desirable spots, often next to the host. They would receive food of the choicest quality and quantity. Others would receive the fare according to their status or the whim of the host. The satirist Lucian of Samosata, in his work *On Salaried Posts in Great Houses*, depicts a fictional resident philosopher of a prominent household who complains of his treatment at a lavish *deipnon* hosted by his employer. He is, he claims, "pushed off into the most unregarded corner and . . . merely witness[es] the dishes that are passed, gnawing the bones like a dog if they get as far as [him], on the tough mallow leaves with which the other food is garnished, if they should be disdained by those nearer the head of the table" (*Merc. cond.* 26 [trans. Harmon 1921, 457, slightly modified]).

Ironically, despite hierarchical dining arrangements, formal meals were often touted as the means to create a sense of commonality and community by breaking down social boundaries. Hosts of these banquets (unlike the host of Lucian's fictional banquet mentioned above) were expected to be unstinting. The Jewish sage Ben Sira encourages generosity, insisting that such is in the hosts' self-interest: "People bless the one who is liberal with food, and their testimony to his generosity is trustworthy" (Sir. 31:23). Furthermore, the sage warns, should hosts be ungenerous, they would ultimately pay a price for their miserly behavior: "The city complains of the one who is stingy with food, and their testimony to his stinginess is accurate" (31:24). Guests, on the other hand, were expected to focus on the potential for fellowship created by the meal and not on the food itself. Ben Sira admonishes them:

> Are you seated at the table of the great?
>> Do not be greedy,
>> and do not say, "How much food
>>> there is here!" . . .
> Do not reach out your hand for every-
>> thing you see,
>> and do not crowd your neighbor at
>>> the dish. (31:12–14)

Instead:

> Eat what is set before you like a well
>> brought-up person,
>> and do not chew greedily, or you will
>>> give offense.
> Be the first to stop, as befits good
>> manners,
>> and do not be insatiable, or you will
>>> give offense.
> If you are seated among many persons,
>> do not help yourself before they do.
>> (31:16–18)

The philosopher Plutarch likewise insists that selfish behavior contradicts the communal spirit of the shared feast: "Grabbing, snatching, and elbowing among the guests do not . . . make a friendly and convivial prelude to a banquet; such behaviour is boorish and crude and often ends in insults and angry outbursts aimed not only at fellow-guests, but at waiters and at hosts" (*Quaest. conv.* 644a [trans. Clement 1969, 191]).

Of course, at banquets of Greco-Roman clubs or associations, good behavior and fellowship among the diners were also expected. Many such associations were religiously oriented; they were specifically created to honor one or another of the gods, and their banquets provided a venue for such worship. One scholar has described the dual function of such religiously oriented banquets as "honoring the gods [and] feasting with friends" (Harland 2003, 55).

The importance of banqueting within religiously oriented associations is emphasized by the fact that some groups built their own dining facilities. A group dedicated to the god Dionysus, whose members called themselves the "dancing cowherds," built a sizable dining hall in Pergamum, which was big enough to hold seventy diners (Harland 2003, 78–79). Another association dedicated to the same deity, whose members called themselves the Iobakchoi, constructed a large dining facility in Athens, near the acropolis. An inscription laying out the rules and regulations of that association tells us that the group dined together once a month as well as on the days of festivals dedicated to Dionysus. All members were expected to attend the banquets and were fined if they did not appear (*IG* 2² 1368, 42–44, 96–102 [trans. Kloppenborg and Ascough 2011, 246, 247]).

The Libation

At the end of the *deipnon*, the food tables were taken away, and a libation, a drink offering of unmixed wine, was made to the *agathos daimon* (the good spirit), while the guests sang a paean (i.e., a hymn of praise). Then the wine was mixed (in the Greco-Roman world, wine was usually mixed with water before serving), and the first cup was ladled out. This was accompanied by a toast to Zeus, the Savior (*Dios Sōtēros*). The leader poured a few drops of wine onto the floor and took a sip of the wine. The leader then passed the cup to the next diner, who also pronounced the name of the deity, took a sip of the wine, and passed it on. After the cup had been passed to everyone, the libation came to a close (Klinghardt 1996, 100–105).

The Symposium

The end of the libation signaled the beginning of the symposium. In contemporary parlance, a symposium is usually conceived to be a relatively formal affair during which weighty matters are discussed by serious people. However, the Greek term *symposion* can simply mean a drinking party, and that is literally what took place during the symposium of a banquet. But, of course, drinking was not the symposium's only activity. At social meals, serious conversation was encouraged, and professional entertainment was often presented. Musicians, singers, and/or dancers were sometimes hired for this portion of a banquet. Obviously, as the wine flowed, the guests' inhibitions would weaken, which could, in turn, result in rowdy behavior of one kind or another. The above-mentioned satirist, Lucian of Samosata, lampooning the symposium of a wedding banquet, tells of drunken guests hurling insults, throwing drinking cups, flinging wine, pulling beards, and fist-fighting (Lucian, *Symp.* 30–35). At such boisterous symposia, *hetairai* (prostitutes) would sometimes appear, looking for customers. Sometimes flute girls, hired for musical entertainment, took on the usual duties of the *hetairai*. Luke 7:36–50 provides an example of such a woman at a banquet: when Jesus dines with a Pharisee named Simon, a woman, "a sinner," arrives and enters the banquet unchecked, likely during the symposium. But, unexpectedly, she has not come to ply her usual trade. Instead, she has come to anoint Jesus.

The symposia at banquets of religious organizations offered diners the opportunity to honor their deity in various ways. Of course, as usual, wine was served, but other important activities also took place. Sometimes hymns were sung, either by members of the association or by singers hired for the occasion. At other times, a sermon might be delivered. The Athenian Iobakchoi inscription states that "the priest . . . shall give the discourse about the god, which the former priest Nikomachos inaugurated out of his zeal" (*IG* 2² 1368, 111–16 [trans. Kloppenborg and Ascough 2011, 247]).

But hymns and sermons were not the only activities that might take place at religiously oriented symposia. A theatrical performance could be staged or a sacred dance performed. A stone monument discovered in northwest Turkey and now housed in the British Museum (no. 1890, 0730.1) provides an example of the latter.[1] It depicts a reclining group of diners watching a dance performance. In the center of the room a woman dances, accompanied by two musicians, one on either side of her.

1. https://www.britishmuseum.org/collection/object/G_1890-0730-1.

On her left, a figure plays a double flute, and on her right, a percussionist accompanies her. Farther off to her right, a slave mixes wine in a large vat. Above the diners watching the dancer and musicians, three overly large figures also observe the dance performance. These figures represent the gods Zeus, Artemis, and Apollo, for whom the performance was obviously intended. Each of the deities holds a libation cup, indicating that they, as well as the human observers, are participants in the symposium (Harland 2003, 56–57).

Since religiously oriented symposia included wine, trouble could also occur during these ceremonies. In order to avoid such, some associations outlawed certain things that could give rise to friction among the diners. For instance, the regulations of an association dedicated to Zeus Hypsistos state: "It shall not be permitted for any [members of the association] to . . . make factions or to leave the brotherhood of the president for another, or for people to enter into one another's pedigrees at the banquet or to abuse one another at the banquet or to chatter or to accuse one another" (lines 10–17, in Roberts, Skeat, and Nock 1936, 40–42). In the regulations of the Iobakchoi, a similar prohibition appears:

> Now if anyone begins a fight or is disorderly or takes another's place or insults or abuses someone else, the person abused or insulted shall produce two of the *Iobakchoi* as sworn witnesses [testifying that they heard the insult or abuse]. The one who committed the insult or abuse shall pay to the treasury twenty-five light drachmae, or the one who was the cause of the fight shall either pay the same twenty-five drachmae or not come to any more meetings of the *Iobakchoi* until he pays. (*IG* 2² 1368, 73–84 [trans. Kloppenborg and Ascough 2011, 247, slightly modified])

An officer of the Iobakchoi association was designated to enforce the rules:

> The officer in charge of order shall be chosen by lot or be appointed by the priest, bearing the thyrsus of the god for anyone who is disorderly or creates a disturbance. And if the thyrsus be laid on anyone—[and] the priest or the *archibakchos* ("chief bacchant") approves—he shall leave the banquet hall. If he refuses, those who have been appointed by the priests as bouncers [lit., "horses"] shall take him outside the door. (*IG* 2² 1368, 136–44 [trans. Kloppenborg and Ascough 2011, 248])

Meals and Symposia among Early Jesus Followers

Social dining with nonbelievers was controversial among early Jesus followers because of the possibility of eating meat that had previously been sacrificed to Greco-Roman deities (*eidōlothyta*). In the mid-first century, Paul tells the Corinthian Jesus followers that, in most cases, they can "eat whatever is set before you without raising any question on the ground of conscience" (1 Cor. 10:27, although he offers significant qualifications of this position throughout 1 Cor. 8 and 10). A half century later, the author of the book of Revelation excoriates Jesus followers who eat *eidōlothyta* (Rev. 2:14–15, 20). But the controversy did not end there. Justin Martyr's *Dialogue with Trypho* informs us that some Christians continued to consume sacrificial meat in the mid-second century, although Justin insists that they were heretics (35).

The earliest account of a formal meal attended by Jesus followers appears in 1 Corinthians 11, where Paul narrates an account of Jesus's last meal that he had previously presented to the group: "On the night when [the Lord Jesus] was betrayed [he] took a loaf of bread, and when he had given thanks, he broke it and said, 'This is my body that is for you. Do this in remembrance of me.' In the same way he took the cup also, after supper, saying, 'This cup is the new covenant in my blood. Do this, as often as you drink it, in remembrance of me'" (1 Cor. 11:23–25). As is evident, this meal took the form of the standard Greco-Roman formal meal. The consumption of bread represents the *deipnon*. "After supper" (that is, after the *deipnon*), the symposium followed, and it was opened by a variation of the libation—in this case, the words of Jesus over the cup.

The next earliest account of a formal meal among Jesus followers also comes from 1 Corinthians. It suggests that Jesus followers assembled for a formal meal in much the same way that other associations did. While we do not know much about the way that individual household assemblies worshiped, 1 Corinthians tells us that the various smaller household assemblies would gather together periodically for a meal. We know this because Paul mentions the "whole *ekklēsia* coming together in the same place" (14:23, my translation; cf. 11:20). This "coming together" for a meal (see also 11:17, 18, 33) also appears to have followed the standard pattern of Greco-Roman banquets (McGowan 2014, 30–31). Paul refers to the *deipnon* portion of the Corinthian banquet ("the Lord's *deipnon*" or "the Lord's supper") in 1 Corinthians 11:20, whereas his reference to the "whole *ekklēsia* coming together in the same place" in 14:23 points to the symposium portion of the banquet (Smith 2003, 200–201).

The Deipnon

Given the financial status of the early Jesus followers in Corinth (Friesen 2004; Longenecker 2010, 220–58), it is unlikely that any one particular householder provided the food for the *deipnon* of the Corinthian meal. Rather, it is probable that the meal took the form of an *eranos*, what we might call a potluck (Lampe 1991a, 1–5; 1991b, 198–201). In other words, each individual, or perhaps each household, brought its own food, while the host of the meal provided assorted condiments. Unfortunately, it seems that such an arrangement resulted in

rivalries surfacing (1 Cor. 11:18). While Paul expected that the food would be shared equitably, this was not the case. Paul consequently accuses the Corinthians of showing contempt for the *ekklēsia* by humiliating "those who have nothing" (11:21–22). In an attempt to modify the behavior of the Corinthians, the apostle warns that "all who eat and drink without discerning the body, eat and drink judgment against themselves" (11:29). In short, those who participate in the meal without showing concern for the larger community—that is, the body of Christ—bring condemnation on themselves.

The Libation

Paul does not explicitly mention or allude to the Corinthian libation during his discussion of the meal (1 Cor. 11:17–34). Rather, it is simply assumed. Perhaps the libation consisted of Jesus's words over the cup in the tradition quoted by Paul in 11:25. Or perhaps the libation was more extensive, like the prayer of thanksgiving following the communal meal described by the Didache, a prayer that states in part:

> We thank you, holy father,
> For your holy name,
>   which you made to dwell in our
>   hearts
> And for the knowledge and faith and
>   immortality,
>   which you made known to us
>   through Jesus your servant.
> To you be glory forever. (Did. 10.2
>   [trans. Niederwimmer 1998, 155])

Unfortunately, we can only speculate on the words that were recited during the libation portion of the Corinthian meal. However, we can be relatively sure that such a libation took place because in 1 Corinthians 10:16 Paul refers to "the cup of blessing that we bless." This phrase is not redundant, as it first appears. Rather, the act of blessing the cup points to the libation (Klinghardt 1996, 309).

The Symposium

There is little doubt that the worship service of early Jesus followers took place during the symposium of their festive meal. This is supported by two things. First, there is a curious passage in Ephesians, which seems to connect a worship service with wine drinking, obviously a fundamental activity of any symposium. The passage states, "Do not get drunk with wine, for that is debauchery; but be filled with the Spirit, as you sing psalms and hymns and spiritual songs among yourselves, singing and making melody to the Lord in your hearts, giving thanks to God the Father at all times and for everything in the name of our Lord Jesus Christ" (Eph. 5:18–20). Although Ephesians comes from a later time than 1 Corinthians (and was possibly written by a different author), this passage nevertheless suggests that wine drinking accompanied early worship services. Or to say it another way, worship occurred during the symposium of a communal meal.

A second reason for supposing that the worship service took place during the symposium of the Lord's Supper comes from 1 Corinthians 12, where Paul speaks metaphorically about the Corinthians' reception of the Spirit. There he asserts that "we were all made to *drink* of one" (12:13, my emphasis). This figurative language almost certainly points, metaphorically, to the drinking of wine at the Corinthian symposium (Smith 2003, 202–3).

What specific activities took place during the symposium of the Corinthian meal? In 1 Corinthians 14, Paul mentions prophesying, hymns, teachings, revelations, speaking in tongues, and interpretation of tongue speech (14:26). Although Paul discourages speaking in tongues, he does not prohibit it. All the other above-mentioned activities were acceptable as long as order was maintained. Order, not least because of the presence of wine, could easily devolve into chaos. To combat that threat, the apostle urges:

> If anyone speaks in a tongue, let there be only two or at most three, and each in turn; and let one interpret. But if there is no one to interpret, let them be silent in church and speak to themselves and to God. Let two or three prophets speak, and let the others weigh what is said. If a revelation is made to someone else sitting nearby, let the first person be silent. For you can all prophesy one by one, so that all may learn and all be encouraged. (14:27–31)

Ultimately, Paul insists that order is key: "God is a God not of disorder but of peace" (14:33).

The Christian Meal in the Second and Third Centuries

By the end of the first century, the Eucharist (as the ritual was known in the Didache) became more formalized than it was in Paul's time. Although the meal still retained the traditional Greco-Roman tripartite structure, standardized thanksgiving prayers over both bread and wine prior to and following the *deipnon* began to gain prominence. This is made evident by the fact that the Didache's focus is on prayers of thanksgiving, both before and after the *deipnon* (Did. 9 and 10). It pays no attention to the actual *deipnon* or symposium of the meal. Their presence is merely assumed.

By the middle of the second century, the Eucharist began to diverge from the tripartite pattern of the Greco-Roman banquet. The role of the assembly leader was expanded, and the ceremony began to take on its own formal structure. According to Justin, on Sunday "all who live in cities or in the country" assembled, at which time, either "the memoirs of the apostles" (i.e., the Gospels) or the writings of the prophets were read. Exhortation by the leader would follow, after which the assembly would rise and pray. Then bread, wine, and water (to be mixed with the wine) were brought to the leader, who offered prayer and thanksgiving over them. Those assembled would then add, "Amen." Only after all of this would the bread and wine be distributed to the people. Deacons would subsequently take a portion to congregants who were unable to attend (*1 Apol.* 67 [trans. Dods and Reith 1885, 186]). Clearly, as Justin's narrative indicates, a more standardized eucharistic ritual started to take the place of the traditional *deipnon*, libation, and symposium. Tripartite eucharistic meals probably still took place, but only within subgroups, like family or patron-client groups.

Works Cited

Clement, Paul A., trans. 1969. *Plutarch: Moralia*. Vol. 8, pp. 1–281. LCL 424. Cambridge, MA: Harvard University Press.

Dods, Marcus, and George Reith, trans. 1885. *Ante-Nicene Fathers*. Vol. 1, *The Apostolic Fathers, Justin Martyr, Irenaeus*, edited by A. Roberts, J. Donaldson, and A. C. Coxe. New York: Christian Literature Publishing Company.

Friesen, Steven J. 2004. "Poverty in Pauline Studies: Beyond the So-Called New Consensus." *JSNT* 26: 323–61.

Harland, Philip A. 2003. *Associations, Synagogues, and Congregations: Claiming a Place in Ancient Mediterranean Society*. Minneapolis: Fortress.

Harmon, A. M., trans. 1921. *Lucian*. Vol. 3. LCL 130. Cambridge, MA: Harvard University Press.

Justin Martyr. 2003. *Dialogue with Trypho*. Translated by Thomas B. Falls. Revised and edited by Thomas P. Halton and Michael Slusser. Washington: Catholic University of America Press.

Klinghardt, Matthias. 1996. *Gemeinschaftsmahl und Mahlgemeinschaft: Soziologie und Liturgie Früchristlicher Mahlfeiern*. Texte und Arbeiten zum neutestamentlichen Zeitalter 13. Tübingen: A. Franke.

Kloppenborg, John S., and Richard S. Ascough. 2011. *Attica, Central Greece, Macedonia, Thrace*. Vol. 1 of *Greco-Roman Associations: Texts, Translations, and Commentary*. BZNW 181. Berlin: de Gruyter.

Lampe, Peter. 1991a. "The Corinthian Dinner Party: Exegesis of a Cultural Context (1 Cor. 11:17–34)." *Affirmation* 4: 1–15.

———. 1991b. "Das korinthische Herrenmahl im Schnittpunkt hellenistisch-römischer Mahlpraxis und paulinischer Theologia Crucis (1 Kor. 11, 17–34)." *ZNW* 82: 183–213.

Longenecker, Bruce W. 2010. *Remember the Poor: Paul, Poverty, and the Greco-Roman World*. Grand Rapids: Eerdmans.

McGowan, Andrew B. 2014. *Ancient Christian Worship: Early Church Practices in Social, Historical, and Theological Perspectives*. Grand Rapids: Baker Academic.

Niederwimmer, Kurt. 1998. *The Didache: A Commentary*. Translated by Linda M. Maloney. Edited by Harold W. Attridge. Hermeneia. Minneapolis: Fortress.

Roberts, Colin, Theodore C. Skeat, and Arthur Darby Nock. 1936. "The Guild of Zeus Hypsistos." *HTR* 29: 39–88.

Smith, Dennis E. 2003. *From Symposium to Eucharist: The Banquet in the Early Christian World*. Minneapolis: Fortress.

53

Coins and Culture

David H. Wenkel

Coins—with their symbols, images, and inscriptions—invite interpretation. One particularly promising method of qualitative interpretation views ancient coins as cultural texts that projected a world of meaning to their original audience and culture (Wenkel 2017, xv). Understanding imagery on coins as a form of discourse is an established part of numismatic literature (Howgego 1995, 87). One of the most poignant ancient examples of the call to interpret coins is found in Jesus's dialogue with the Pharisees who question him about paying taxes to Caesar (Matt. 22:15–22; Mark 12:13–17; Luke 20:20–26). Jesus asks them to bring him a silver denarius and says to his opponents, "Whose likeness and inscription is this?" (Matt. 22:20 ESV). It is noteworthy that this coin likely had a bust of the emperor (either Augustus or Tiberius) and inscriptions proclaiming his divinity. Determining the exact coin used in biblical references is mostly conjecture based on other available information (Hendin 2007, 191). When Jesus's opponents answer that they understand the coin to be

"Caesar's," they are left marveling at Jesus's wisdom. Such questions must continue to motivate us to ask: What signs and symbols are these? What did they mean, and how did they function?

Coins as Cultural Texts

Coins are cultural texts; they are part of ancient material culture, along with objects such as pottery, weapons, and utensils. The academic study of numismatics (or coinage) covers items such as coins, medals, stamps, tokens, and seals. These material items can be subjected to a range of *quantitative* studies about their composition of alloys, weight, metal purity, production quality, and so on. Yet coins are also products of human phenomenological expression and can also be studied through *qualitative* methods typically found in the social sciences. This is important because of the strong connection between coinage and religion ever since coins began to be used for currency around the seventh century BCE in Asia Minor (Williams 2007, 163).

The concept of coins projecting a symbolic world of meaning provides a method for qualitative analysis that can be integrated into biblical studies, archaeology, and ancillary disciplines. Whereas speech between two people utilizes the context of a common frame of reference, coins have no such benefit. Like written documents, they are fixed acts of communication that require interpretation. According to this model, the art and science of interpreting coins is an act of explicating how a world of meaning is projected or unfolded *in front of it* (Ricoeur 1981, 140). This addresses the critical question: Where is meaning located? Those who would engage with the projected world of meaning in any given coin must engage with the symbols, images, and inscriptions on it. These communicative elements work together as they project meaning, and this allows them to function as more than the sum of their parts.

This approach also offers a method for historical and cultural analysis as coins can be considered along three horizons: (1) the world *in front* of the coin: those who used the coinage as a monetary instrument; (2) the world *of* the coin: that which was projected by the communicative power of the coin's qualities; and (3) the world *behind* the coin: people in power who exercised choice in producing the coin. The next three sections introduce these dimensions in further detail, drawing attention to the salient points relevant for interdisciplinary analysis.

One preliminary task for understanding coins and culture is establishing proper dating. This is complicated by the fact that some coins have dates, and some do not. Dates were offered not for the sake of the people but to communicate the power and status of certain reigns. Additionally, there was no standard numerical dating system. The Roman Empire's use of time and calendars defies easy characterization (Feeney 2007, 7, also 156). The dating of coins is further complicated by the fact that

they are objects that may have been in use for decades. The very presence of dates is evidence that coins were used by those in power to structure the frame(s) of time and the identity of those who used the coins (Howgego 1995, 7).

A second preliminary task for understanding coins and culture is determining geographical location. One may also have to face the reality that once a coin has been removed from its archaeological context (i.e., other material culture), it is almost impossible to determine its original historical location with precision. For interdisciplinary biblical studies, the world in front of the coin(s) was the people of the entire Roman Empire. Despite being united by an empire, one location to the next could have vast differences between them, even within the same time frame. There were significant differences between the eastern and western sides of the empire. This is why the local *polis* was the fundamental structure of social cohesion. Alternatively, one might consider the *regions* or *provinces* in which coins circulated, which was the framework of the apostle Paul (Bartholomew 2011, 129).

The World in Front of the Coin

Understanding the cultural function of coins in the ancient world requires a consideration of their implied readers, those who used them as stores of value for buying and selling. These people should be understood as the "readers" of the coins, even if one concludes that they were functionally illiterate. Epigraphic material culture such as inscriptions or legends in antiquity are not a reliable means of determining literacy because of their symbolic function, although this is not exclusive of their literary features (Botha 2010, 45). Because coins are expressions of culture or everyday life, they cannot be fully objectified or reduced to mechanistic operations (Vanhoozer 2007, 22). Coins require the pursuit of understanding within the social dynamics of people, including their institutions, relationships, values, struggles, and beliefs. This section directs those who would understand coins and culture to consider the axes of the particular and the universal.

Understanding coins and culture requires consideration of the particular. This means the pursuit of understanding coins must consider particular circumstances, localized contexts, and unique situations. For example, some coins seem to have appeal to the changing hairstyles of women and feature prominent women such as Livia (wife of Augustus), Antonia (daughter of Marc Antony and Octavia), Agrippina Senior (wife of Germanicus), and Agrippina Junior (wife of Claudius). Another particular dimension to consider is the fact that high-ranking soldiers were one of the major recipients of government payments. Thus, the implied readers of these coins may have been men who would have understood the imperial policy and political nuances communicated through their symbols. Considerations of target audiences such as soldiers must be balanced with numismatic models of coin frequency and distribution.

Understanding coins requires consideration of universal human conditions and complex human relationships. This is important lest we imagine that the ancients stood around interpreting coins as we find in the conflict between Jesus and the Pharisees over taxes. Most of the time, coins were simply part of everyday life, and their communicative importance was relative to the importance of religious conflict, Roman subjugation, and other factors. Other universal aspects of the human condition to consider include (1) issues of trust as they relate to currency, (2) fear of death in relation to war and robbery, (3) taxation, and (4) religion. For example, Josephus describes people swallowing gold coins as they sought to escape the Roman army (*J. W.* 5.420–22). The topic of religion is especially important as it relates to the inseparable aspects of public life and civil religion under the Roman emperor.

The relation of Jews toward coins was regulated by the Mosaic law as mediated by scribes, priests, rabbis, and the Sanhedrin. The concept of "blood money" is described in the account of Judas Iscariot's reception of thirty pieces of silver for betraying Jesus—money that could not be brought into the temple treasury (Matt. 27:5–7). It is important to note that the act of paying taxes was not merely a financial transaction, but when given to the temple in Jerusalem, it was a cultic act of Yahweh worship (e.g., Mark 12:41–44; Luke 21:1–4). Paying taxes was a communicative act with theological and social implications (Wenkel 2017, 75). In the case of the Pharisees seeking to trap Jesus with the question about paying taxes (discussed above), they are hoping to charge him with apostasy and breaking the law of Moses by telling people to give money to a man who claims to be divine and/or to use a coin with images that profane God.

The communicative power of coinage may have increased in the midst of conflict. For example, some theorize that the author of Mark (12:13–17) may be mentioning the denarius to "force his Roman reader to think of the local coin with which they were familiar" and not the one that Jesus actually looked at (Incigneri 2003, 195). By the time the first readers of Mark's Gospel would have read of this denarius, "it would have had the new emperor and the IUDEA CAPTA inscription on it" (195). Whether this theory is true or not, it supports the broader claim that conflict increased interest in the interpretation of coins in their original context. Inhabitants of the Roman Empire may have held any number of coins from different rulers making different claims. The abundance of messages may have had the effect of canceling each other out. Some have described the dampening of communicative power due to familiarity, as new coins may not have even been noticed (Esler 1995, 240). But wars, oppression, and conflict drew attention to a coin's projected symbolic world. In other words, it is possible to overinterpret or under-interpret coins if one does not consider the wider cultural context in which they were used.

The World of the Coin

The world of the coin is a projection of the sum of its communicative features; it unfolds a world that invites people to live in it or in light of it. This means coins are not neutral historical objects but cultural texts. Each coin is a "text" that functions as a "discourse fixed by writing" (Ricoeur 1981, 145). When applied to coinage, this definition must be expanded to include the symbiotic relationship between its substance (metal type), inscription, and image on both sides. This means that understanding the world of a coin means translating inscriptions and identifying images (Wenkel 2017, 5). Once this preliminary work is done, one can pursue understanding coins as cultural texts. This section casts a wide net and introduces basic concepts related to Roman and Jewish coins in the first century CE.

The Roman currency system was composed of six base denominations: (1) gold aureus, (2) silver denarius, (3) sestertius, (4) dupondius, (5) as or assarion, and (6) quadrans (Sutherland and Carson 1984, 3). (The Greek system used a drachma, referenced in Luke 15:8–10, which was roughly equivalent to a denarius.) The Roman currency system used the denarius as the standard coinage of the Roman Empire, excepting Egypt. It was equal to a day's wage and was also the typical coin used to pay soldiers. The silver content of these coins remained relatively constant through the reigns of Augustus, Tiberius, Caligula, and Claudius (Butcher and Ponting 2011, 558). The silver Tyrian half-shekel (half-tetradrachma) was the medium of payment for the annual temple tax in Jerusalem. This coin featured the head of the Tyrian god Melqart on one side and an eagle on the other side. Although the law of Moses forbade the use of images in

Yahweh worship (e.g., Exod. 20:4), the Tyrian half-shekel was used for the temple tax because its silver content was purer than that of other coinage.

Roman coins used a wide variety of symbols, most of which communicated patronage through military victory (Wenkel 2017, 104). These images included busts of the emperor on one side and military symbols on the other, indicating that the victory was a divine sign that the emperor was chosen by the gods. The emperor's virtues were personified by the appearance of various gods. These gods may not have even been depicted in any cultic function except on coins (Williams 2007, 156). Temples and their architecture also appeared on many Roman coins, perhaps to associate the emperor with the divine. The laurel wreath was a traditional Roman image of victory that was appropriated by Augustus for himself. Other military images included the *quadriga* or four-horse chariot to proclaim the might of the Roman military. The images and inscriptions often projected a symbolic world characterized by emperor worship, Roman mythological religion, communal identity, patronage, and politics.

The Roman province of Judea used two contemporaneous currency systems, the imperial currency system and a Jewish provincial currency system. There were a variety of smaller fractional copper or bronze coins called prutah or lepton (two pruta made a quadrans) minted in this provincial system. These coins were often poorly made, reflecting a crude style, and were sometimes off-center. Smaller denominations were important because they enabled merchants to make small transactions in local markets. This may have led to the practice of weighing large amounts of smaller coins on scales to account for their value. These coins rarely pictured any humans or animals out of deference to the Mosaic law and rabbinic customs, especially before the revolt in 66 CE. The Roman procurators likely supported this out of a desire to keep the peace and avoid uprisings such as the scene at Paul's arrest in the temple (Acts 21:27–36). After 70 CE, they did mint coins with imperial portraits, similar to those of Rome or Greek cities (Esler 1995, 248).

The Iudaea Capta series will be of special interest for those in biblical studies, as these Roman coins were specifically designed to communicate Judea's submission to Rome. These imperial and provincial coins had imagery that projected a world in which Jews were humiliated and subjugated. The imperial series was targeted to those living in Rome but was likely rare compared to other coins in circulation (Elkins 2019, 128). One particularly poignant image features a Roman centurion with a spear standing over a subjugated Jewess who personified the nation (Wenkel 2017, 72). Such imagery degraded the Jews and elevated Rome, its generals, and its gods (Esler 1995, 248; Elkins 2019, 118). On one coin from Titus, an image of Winged Victory appears with a shield and a palm tree with the inscription *Ioudaias Ealokuias* (Judea Captured).

The World behind the Coin

The world behind the coin references the people who function as authors by exercising the prerogative of choice in its creation and using coinage as a medium to transmit propaganda. Such people may be regarded as authors who wrote (or influenced) the message communicated through the production of coinage. This involved making coins to influence a wide range of people to take a particular course of action, hold a certain attitude, or conform to a set of standards (Evans 1992, 1). In addition to coins, the Romans used music, uniforms, games, and processions as tools of communication (Evans 1992, 4). This section considers the world behind the coin with special attention to the concept of those in power as "authors" of coins who exercised choice over these cultural texts.

The Roman emperor was effectively the "author" of all Roman public coinage. He was the "regulator of its system of production at the imperial mint in Rome" (Williams 2007, 157). This is particularly true of the silver and gold coins minted with the name of the emperor. The Senate and its power were represented by the appearance of "SC" ("Senatus Consulto") on the reverse side of almost all bronze coins. Local mint locations included Carthage and Corinth (operating 44 BCE to 69 CE). Imperial mints were located in Pergamum (administrative capital for the province of Asia), Lugdunum (modern-day Lyon, France), and Rome, as well as others.

The magistrates in charge of the treasury would have approved any changes to the model used for casting the coin. Scholars theorize (but cannot definitely prove) that official likenesses of the emperor always came from Rome (Breglia 1968, 8). The images on coins may have been used for personal and local political agendas. The political agendas may have been relatively local or small when compared with the size of the empire. Some coins would have impressed only a small group of people. The office of "mint master" was often held by young Roman noblemen who took advantage of the opportunity to create honor for their family name and publicize their achievements (Zanker 1988, 12).

Cities and states also functioned as authors when they received approval to mint coinage. This is sometimes called city coinage. The ability to mint coinage was a public display of honor and power, as well as an act that provinces such as Judea pursued. All coins minted in Judea (Palestine) would be city coinage. These city coins were characterized by (1) bronze or copper content, (2) small denominations, and (3) localized circulation (Wenkel 2017, 160). We do not know much about the governmental approval process. Sometimes cities sought permission from the emperor or from other Roman officials to mint coins (Chancey 2004, 103).

What united Roman imperial coins with more regional city coins was the context of patronage and power operating in the social system of benefaction (euergetism). The emperor functioned as the benefactor of the Roman Empire because he was at the top of the benefaction pyramid. Those in power gave gifts to those below them, thus ensuring the loyalty of their subjects in civic affairs. The gifts given by benefactors could be peace, prosperity, land, victory, or money. All of the good things that people experienced in daily life were attributed to one's benefactor. The emperor was the distributor of good things, and consequently his name or likeness was on civic buildings, statues, and coins. In return, the populace was to show reciprocity and honor to those in power above them locally and ultimately to the emperor in Rome. Those who received benefaction were bound by the system to give back, either monetarily or through honor and/or worship.

Conclusion

Coins are cultural texts that call out for understanding. Answering the call of numismatic interpretation requires pursuing understanding with context. There was no uniform culture or even a uniform approach to wealth and money in the first-century Mediterranean milieu. The methodology proposed here applies a phenomenological approach to the interpretation of coins. In an empire as vast as the Roman one, coins offered access to vast communicative powers because of their ubiquity and importance as financial instruments. Models of interpretation must be flexible to accommodate a wide range of social dynamics, including religious sectarianism, the life of soldiers, and even interest in women's hairstyles. Approaching coins as cultural texts enables one to appreciate their communicative power, the role of those in power who made them, and the lives of those who used them in everyday life.

Works Cited

Bartholomew, Craig. 2011. *Where Mortals Dwell: A Christian View of Place for Today*. Grand Rapids: Baker Academic.

Botha, Pieter J. J. 2010. *Orality and Literacy in Early Christianity*. Biblical Performance Criticism 5. Eugene, OR: Cascade Books.

Breglia, Laura. 1968. *Roman Imperial Coins: Their Art and Technique*. New York: Praeger.

Butcher, Kevin, and M. Ponting. 2011. "The Denarius in the First Century." In vol. 1 of *Proceedings of the XIVth International Numismatic Congress: Glasgow 2009*, edited by N. Holmes, 557–68. Glasgow: International Numismatic Council.

Chancey, Mark A. 2004. "City Coins and Roman Power in Palestine." In *Religion and Society in Roman Palestine: Old Questions, New Approaches*, edited by D. R. Edwards, 103–12. New York: Routledge.

Elkins, Nathan T. 2019. "Publicizing Victory: The Frequency and Audience of Flavian 'Judaea Capta' Coins from the Imperial Mints." *Israel Numismatic Research* 14: 117–30.

Esler, Philip F. 1995. "God's Honour and Rome's Triumph: Responses to the Fall of Jerusalem in 70 CE in Three Jewish Apocalypses." In *Modelling Early Christianity: Social-Scientific Studies of the New Testament in Its Context*, edited by P. E. Esler, 239–58. London: Routledge.

Evans, Jane DeRose. 1992. *The Art of Persuasion: Political Propaganda from Aeneas to Brutus*. Ann Arbor: University of Michigan Press.

Feeney, Denis. 2007. *Caesar's Calendar: Ancient Time and the Beginnings of History*. Berkeley: University of California Press.

Hendin, David. 2014. "Jesus and Numismatics: The Importance of Coins in Reconstructing Jesus and His World." In *Jesus Research: New Methodologies and Perceptions*, edited by J. H. Charlesworth, B. Rhea, and P. Pokorny, 190–200. Grand Rapids: Eerdmans.

Howgego, Christopher. 1995. *Ancient History from Coins*. Approaching the Ancient World. London: Routledge.

Incigneri, Brian J. 2003. *The Gospel to the Romans: The Setting and Rhetoric of Mark's Gospel*. BibInt 65. Leiden: Brill.

Ricoeur, Paul. 1981. *Hermeneutics and the Human Sciences: Essays on Language, Action and Interpretation*. Edited and translated by J. B. Thompson. Cambridge: Cambridge University Press.

Sutherland, C. H. V., and R. A. G. Carson. 1984. *Roman Imperial Coinage*. Vol. 1, *From 31 BC to AD 69—Augustus to Vitellius*. London: Spink and Son.

Vanhoozer, Kevin J. 2007. "What Is Everyday Theology? How and Why Christians Should Read Culture." In *Everyday Theology: How to Read Cultural Texts and Interpret Trends*, edited by Kevin J. Vanhoozer, Charles A. Anderson, and Michael J. Sleasman, 13–60. Grand Rapids: Baker Academic.

Wenkel, David H. 2017. *Coins as Cultural Texts in the World of the New Testament*. T&T Clark Biblical Studies. London: Bloomsbury T&T Clark.

Williams, Jonathan. 2007. "Religion and Roman Coins." In *A Companion to Roman Religion*, edited by J. Rüpke, 143–63. BCAW. Oxford: Blackwell.

Zanker, Paul. 1988. *The Power of Images in the Age of Augustus*. Ann Arbor: University of Michigan Press.

54

Race and Ethnicity

Eric D. Barreto

Racial and ethnic discourses were a critical component of the ancient world's imagination about peoples and places, communities and lands, identities and histories. To interpret the New Testament is to encounter a body of texts whose concerns about race and ethnicity often differ from modern assumptions but sometimes mirror the underlying dynamics that continue to fuel how we narrate and practice belonging, identity, and community today. That is, in the New Testament we do not find texts ignorant of or uninterested in concerns about race and ethnicity. Indeed, these texts are participating in sophisticated and striking ways with the larger ethnic discourses of their own time. The primary characteristic of antiquity's imaginations about race and ethnicity is complexity. Nonetheless, students of the New Testament must seek to engage these ancient discourses and practices in order to engage in exegesis, whether historical, literary, and/or theological.

In addition, however, thinking about race and ethnicity is not just the concern of the historian of antiquity. How today's readers think about and interpret race and ethnicity matters very much still in our understanding and interpretation of the New Testament, for unspoken assumptions about such identities can color and too often distort the complex ways these ancient texts deal with questions that continue to press on us as contemporary readers of these texts. That is, to study the New Testament's grappling with race and ethnicity is to invite scholars to examine their own assumptions too, especially when such assumptions have underwritten oppression and exclusion.

Defining Race and Ethnicity

We face a challenge immediately. Defining what we mean by race and ethnicity is incredibly difficult. We tend to use the terms in Western cultures, particularly in the United States and Western Europe, as if the terms are self-evident; we are certain we know what we mean when we refer to race and ethnicity. Usually, these notions of race and ethnicity focus on skin color, facial features, and other visible markers of identity. That is, embodiment and ethnicity are intertwined. However, whether in antiquity or even today, a line between certain embodiments and a particular racial identity tends to be far more complicated than clear. There is more to the negotiations of race and ethnicity that we and ancient people alike undertake than is evident at first glimpse or on the surface of a person's skin. The first task, then, is to reject easy assumptions about the shape of race and ethnicity in the New Testament. Studying race and ethnicity in these ancient texts requires a careful deconstruction of modern assumptions about identity in order to avoid thoughtlessly importing modern conceptions into our analysis of ancient texts.

What, then, exactly are race and ethnicity? How do we identity racial and ethnic discourses in the interpretation of the New Testament texts? In my own research, I have worked out of the following definition, which I will explain further in the rest of this section:

> Race or ethnicity is a socially constructed, discursive, pliable claim to be a group of people defined around myths of putative commonality of kinship or ancestry including origins, language, culture, religion, geography, and other organizing principles. An indispensable qualification of this definition is that an ethnicity—while asserted by its members to be natural, inherent, and unchangeable—is in practice malleable and even mutable. (Barreto 2010, 29–30)

The definition is necessarily complex, but we can break down its parts. First, notice that I will be using the terms "race" and "ethnicity" largely interchangeably, for they belong to a similar class of identification. In a number of academic and public discourses, race and ethnicity are sometimes distinguished, but for this essay's purposes they address the same constellation of ideas and embodiments. Second is that race and ethnicity are socially constructed; they are a fiction we construct and in which we live and make sense of the world

and our neighbors. In earlier scholarship and often in public imagination, race is assumed to be an objective, measurable reality. Whether by classifying facial features, skin pigments, or genetic inheritance, race is tangible, biological, and thus real. This position is known as the *primordialist* account of race and reached a terrible nadir with the Nazi project's attempt to make concrete the distinction between supposedly superior and inferior races, an intellectual and political project that culminated in the disaster of genocide in the Holocaust. That history is a vital reminder that how we account for our neighbors and our differences is a weighty matter full of ethical import. The study of the notions of race and ethnicity in antiquity and today brings us to the heartbeat of questions about belonging and power.

Among scholars, the primordialist approach has given way to *instrumentalist* accounts that contend that race and ethnicity are social fictions that cultures concoct. Instrumentalists argue that ethnicity is not a given but a constructed, malleable, and changeable ideological organization of peoples and communities. Race is not really measurable as an objective reality attached to bodies or genes or skin color but can only be described in the discourses and cultural practices in which race is both created and practiced, nurtured and configured. That does not mean, however, that they are not "real"; race and ethnicity profoundly shape the world, and these social fictions have very real consequences.

The definition I forwarded, however, tries to take one further step by identifying the ways that primordialist accounts of race and ethnicity remain evident in both antiquity's and today's accounts of race and ethnicity. While it is clear that race and ethnicity are socially constructed, one of the key markers of such discourse is the interplay between primordial and instrumental perspectives as well as between "fixity" and "fluidity." That is, we will frequently find that ancient texts and modern ideas tend to imagine race and ethnicity as both real *and* imagined, unchangeable *and* mutable. Race is often seen as natural and inherited in how we talk about it, even as practices around ethnic identity exhibit a great deal of flexibility and construction.

Last, notice that race and ethnicity *draw on* but are not defined by any one of a number of cultural markers: language, dress, rituals, myths of origin, a geographic home, a common name, and so on. None of these individually *constitute* racial or ethnic identities. Physical difference may be a *marker* of race and ethnicity but does not establish it. Such an insight runs contrary to many assumptions people in the Americas and Europe alike hold about race, specifically the assumption that race is largely a matter of phenotypical facial features. Skin color or facial features are thus characteristics associated with particular ethnic identities, not the source or reason for the construction of these identities. Thus, students must look carefully to the complex ways racial and ethnic identities are built, tested, reconfigured, and reimagined in various times and spaces.

Defining race and ethnicity will remain a challenge for any student of the New Testament. First, analyzing the complexity of ancient notions of race and ethnicity means delving into the confounding intersection of primordialist and instrumentalist expressions. Second, the scholar will always and inevitably be required to confront the weight of contemporary assumptions about racial and ethnic identity that will seek to shape our reading of these ancient texts. In short, studying race and ethnicity in the New Testament is always an act of reconstructing ancient patterns of belonging while also rediscovering and reanalyzing the contemporary notions of race and ethnicity we have breathed in and been nurtured by, often via subtle and largely invisible influences. The task here is significant, but the possibilities of exegetical, theological, and ethical payoffs are equally robust.

Race and Ethnicity in the New Testament

The texts of the New Testament confront, function within, grapple with, and seek to reimagine racial and ethnic identities regularly. The texts of the New Testament emerge from a cultural setting in which ethnic discourses were prevalent and contributed significantly to the formation of communal identities. The ways to analyze race and ethnicity in the New Testament are thus multiple and complex (Nasrallah and Schüssler Fiorenza 2009; Hockey and Horrell 2018). Thus, we could broach questions about the imperial use of Judean identity as a slur (Park 2019), the place of Gentiles in Paul's theological imagination in Romans (Johnson Hodge 2007), the formation of exilic identities in Hebrews (Kaalund 2020), the logics of migration and exile in 1 Peter (S. T. J. Smith 2016; Ok 2021), or a womanist reading of Revelation (S. T. Smith 2014). Here, however, I will focus on several examples from Acts that illuminate but do not exhaust the diverse ways that notions of race and ethnicity shaped the texts of the New Testament but also the plural ways that writers of the New Testament lived in and sought to reconfigure ancient imaginations about difference, belonging, and the shape of community.

The narrative of Acts is populated by the diverse peoples of the ancient world. As Jesus's disciples follow his call to be "witnesses . . . to the ends of the earth" (1:8), they encounter the multiplicity of ancient racial and ethnic identities. As the disciples follow Jesus's call to the ends of the earth, they unavoidably encounter questions about human difference, especially along lines of race and ethnicity.

First, we encounter the pluriformity of ancient Judaism at the very beginning of Acts. In the Pentecost scene in chapter 2, Acts records the geographical, linguistic, and cultural expanse of people gathered in Jerusalem (2:5–11). Often called the Table of Nations by scholars, this list of places and identities represented by the Jews gathered at Pentecost reflects the realities of a life of diaspora and exile for Israel. While the origins of the list or the sources on which Luke would have relied are heavily disputed in the scholarship, more clear is that the Table of Nations points to the linguistic and cultural diversities contained within the ethnic term *Ioudaios*—that is, "Jew" or "Judean."[1] Moreover, that the Spirit empowers Jesus's disciples to proclaim the good news in multiple languages in all their particularity suggests something of Luke's perspective on racial and ethnic difference; such differences are at the center of the life of these communities of followers of Jesus (Barreto 2018). At Pentecost, the plurality of languages and ethnic identities is not an obstacle to belonging but an ingredient to the vitality of these communities.

Second, Acts introduces us to an Ethiopian eunuch in 8:26–40, whose multiple identities pose both an exegetical and interpretive challenge. For African American interpreters, the presence of an African, a Black person, S. E. Porter and A. W. Pitts in the context of the narration of the earliest days of the followers of Jesus provides an important corrective to the Eurocentric tendencies of too many interpreters (Martin 1989). The eunuch's striking presence in this narrative further suggests that the racial and ethnic vision of Acts is both wide and diverse. Moreover, queer readings of this text have led to vital exegesis that names the

1. There has been a rich and important scholarly conversation about the best way to translate the Greek term *Ioudaios*. Although the term is traditionally translated as "Jew," some scholars have argued that "Judean" is preferable because of the ethnic character of the identity being named. That is, in order to communicate clearly that Judean is akin to other ethnic identities in antiquity—like Roman or Greek—we avoid importing modern assumptions about Judaism as a religious identity with ethnic inflection. In the ancient world, Judean identity was associated with a people and a place, like other ethnic identities such as Roman or Greek. Other scholars have disagreed, contending that "Jew" remains the best translation as it continues to link ancient and modern communities gathered around the faith of Israel. For a brief introduction to these questions of translation and interpretation, see Reinhartz 2022.

ways that gender, sexuality, race, and ethnicity intersect in important ways (Burke 2011). That is, to study race and ethnicity in the New Testament is also to wrestle with other forms of identity at one and the same time.

Third, at the end of Acts 21, we find an example of Paul's own negotiation of ethnic identity. Paul finds himself in legal trouble, as he often does in these closing chapters of Acts. Here, an aggravated crowd has drawn the attention of a Roman tribune seeking to pacify a crowd turning riotous. The Roman tribune, however, is puzzled by the source of all this unrest and has Paul brought into the barracks. In that process, Paul speaks to this Roman tribune *in Greek*, further confusing the tribune, who seems stunned that Paul can speak Greek. It remains unclear why the tribune is confused by Paul's linguistic abilities, but he does, for some reason, now conclude that Paul is not an Egyptian revolutionary disturbing the Roman peace. Paul is indignant at this false charge and displays his ethnic credentials in 21:39. Then Paul code switches, turning from a Greek-speaking Roman tribune to speak "Hebrew" to his fellow Jews at the beginning of chapter 22.

Notice the different ways Paul identifies himself in Acts 21:39 and 22:3. When speaking to his Roman captor, Paul highlights that he is "a citizen of an important city"—namely, Tarsus. In contrast, when he is speaking to his ethnic kin in 22:3, Paul's Tarsian citizenship is subsumed under his Jewish ethnic credentials as a student of Gamaliel and as a Jew of zealous faith.

What is going on here? How do we make sense of Paul, within the span of just a few verses, identifying himself in two different languages in two very different ways? Paul's code switching is not deception but strategy, not two-faced lies but a tactic of the colonized. Paul's cultural and linguistic dexterity uses the tools of empire (the privileges granted to the citizen, the imposition of the empire's language on other communities, the frailties of an empire's "justice" system) against the empire itself. His ability to switch between languages and ethnic credentials is a tool of survival.

And then there's one more wrinkle to this story, a wrinkle about the privileges of being able to claim an imperial ethnic identity. Paul's speech in Hebrew eventually fails to pacify the crowds, so the Roman tribune turns to a weapon of empire to figure out what is going on: torture (Acts 22:24). Paul stops the mistreatment by asking if it is legal for a Roman to be treated in this way. The tribune is stunned once again! The tribune says he bought his citizenship for a great deal of money (22:28a); how is it that Paul is a citizen? Paul declares, "I was born this way!" (my translation of 22:28b). I was born not just a *citizen* but a Roman in a fuller sense than the tribune's purchased papers. Paul is suggesting he is the true Roman in this scene, not the tribune.

This passage is another instance (cf. Acts 16:35–40) in which Paul's complex ethnic identities as both Jewish and Roman do not necessitate resolution. Despite the way that most modern translations opt for "Roman citizen" in places where Luke's Paul uses only the Greek term for Roman, Paul here is not creating a clear distinction between his Roman *citizenship* and his Jewish *ethnicity*. Instead, he is claiming to be both Jewish *and* Roman, without one ethnic title diminishing the authenticity and import of the other. He can claim both identities without one diminishing the other.

These are but a handful of examples demonstrating the value and utility of noting the functions of race and ethnicity in our reading of the New Testament. Additional examples could extend far beyond the scope of this essay. The underlying argument is this, however: the New Testament's literary and theological imagination is coursing with racial and ethnic discourses that we neglect much to our detriment and often because scholarship has not paid sufficient heed to those who experience racial and ethnic identities as a daily—and often times—challenging reality.

Race, Ethnicity, and Contemporary Interpreters

Our focus thus far has been trained on antiquity, on the ways ancient people imagined race and belonging, ethnicity and identity. However, I want to highlight here two other ways that race and ethnicity shape the interpretation of the New Testament today.

First is how minoritized scholars in particular have highlighted the interested, invested character of all readings.[2] In doing so, such scholars criticize the tendency in some historical-critical approaches to erase the identity of readers and historians in striving toward objectivity. Such an erasure of the scholar and the reader will necessarily occlude how unspoken assumptions—especially around whiteness, colonialism, and patriarchy, among other forces—effect and even predetermine the kinds of reading practices such purportedly objective scholars will embrace, with potentially disastrous results for minoritized communities in particular. From the perspective of scholars like Fernando Segovia, there is no form of reading that is wholly objective and thus divorced from the particularities of place and identity (Segovia 2000). This is yet another way that students of the New Testament must consider the shaping power of race and ethnicity. For readers in majority cultures, the temptation will be to universalize their experiences and assume that biblical texts have a singular meaning. For readers in minoritized cultures, the temptation will be to diminish the immense contributions people of color and colonized communities have made to the reading and interpretation of the Bible because some contend that such interpretations lack objectivity and are thus a form of eisegesis. In both cases, noting the

2. The scholarly literature in minoritized biblical criticism is extensive and growing exponentially; it is a fecund part of the field of biblical studies. One helpful introduction to the work is Bailey, Liew, and Segovia 2009. See also Blount 2007; Felder 2021; Sechrest 2022; and Vena and Guardiola-Sáenz 2022 (among many others).

power race and ethnicity have to shape not just how ancients read these texts but also how contemporary readers engage is an opportunity to engage in New Testament scholarship more fully, critically, and rigorously.

Second, and no less important, are the racialized assumptions about Jews and Judaism that frequently and disastrously course through New Testament scholarship and interpretation alike (Levine 2007). The most egregious of such racialized readings of the New Testament were practiced in the scholarship that provided theological and biblical justification for the persecution and mass killing of Jews in the Holocaust. Such readings continue today in the thinking of white nationalists in the United States, for instance, who conclude that the Bible grants white folk superiority over those who are not. Less subtle but no less pernicious are the common caricatures of first-century Judaism uttered by preachers and scholars alike: that Judaism was a nationalist, ethnocentric, law-bound faith, while Christianity represents its universal, race-free, grace-filled opposite (Buell 2005). Also destructive is the common tendency to identify Pharisees as the ultimate hypocrites, a conclusion too easily and frequently mapped upon Jewish neighbors today (Sievers and Levine 2021).

And here we have only begun to scratch the surface of interpretive possibilities. The hermeneutical questions about race and ethnicity proliferate in scholarship today. For instance, Susannah Heschel has detailed the ways biblical scholarship, academic theology, and Nazi ideology intertwined in order to buttress a deadly racial "science" (Heschel 2010). In theology, Willie Jennings points to the ways racist imagination about land, place, Judaism, and the racialized other have infected theological work at a fundamental level; the moment Christian theology removed God-talk from a people and a place, it created a vacuum filled by colonial ideologies of racism (Jennings 2011). In his commentary on Acts, Jennings further points

to a reading that invites the reconstitution of belonging and love across difference (Jennings 2017). Angela Parker contends that theologies of biblical infallibility are themselves deeply inflected around questions of whiteness (Parker 2021). Lisa Bowens has collected and studied the ways African American preachers interpreted Paul's letters in life-giving ways in a context where those same letters were (mis)used to buttress slavery and segregation (Bowens 2020). Also wrestling with parallel questions is David Horrell's attempt to disentangle the interpretation of the New Testament and whiteness (Horrell 2020). All this is to suggest that the field of New Testament studies is in various ways contending with questions long left fallow, perhaps precisely because the field is only now reflecting the diversity of an ever-changing world.

Conclusion

In the New Testament and perhaps more broadly among scholars today as well, race and ethnicity are narrated more than measured, assumed more than argued. Asked to define and clarify what they mean by race and ethnicity, students and scholars alike run into a litany of obstacles, primary among them the reality that racial and ethnic discourses so often masquerade as natural and given rather than the constructed and pliable fictions they actually are. But the stakes of these questions are not solely definitional or even historical; the question before us is not just an accurate denotation of key terms or even a historically accurate account of the New Testament's accounts of racial and ethnic difference. No, the stakes are clearly much higher as the contemporary world encounters the lasting effects of racism, colonialism, and other forms of oppression. That the texts of Scripture were implicated in these processes is undeniable. The question that remains is whether and how interpreters of the Bible will advance these destructive projects or find ways to illuminate a way of justice, peace, equity, and wider belonging.

Works Cited

Bailey, Randall, Tat-siong Benny Liew, and Fernando F. Segovia, eds. 2009. *They Were All Together in One Place? Toward Minority Biblical Criticism*. Semeia Studies 57. Atlanta: Society of Biblical Literature.

Barreto, Eric D. 2010. *Ethnic Negotiations: The Function of Race and Ethnicity in Acts 16*. WUNT 2/294. Tübingen: Mohr Siebeck.

———. 2018. "Whence Migration? Babel, Pentecost, and Biblical Imagination." In *Latinxs, the Bible, and Migration*, edited by Efrain Agosto and Jacqueline M. Hidalgo, 133–47. The Bible and Cultural Studies. Cham, Switzerland: Palgrave MacMillan.

Blount, Brian K., ed. 2007. *True to Our Native Land: An African American New Testament Commentary*. Minneapolis: Fortress.

Bowens, Lisa M. 2020. *African American Readings of Paul: Reception, Resistance, and Transformation*. Grand Rapids: Eerdmans.

Buell, Denise Kimber. 2005. *Why This New Race? Ethnic Reasoning in Early Christianity*. New York: Columbia University Press.

Burke, Sean D. 2011. "Queering Early Christian Discourse: The Ethiopian Eunuch." In *Bible Trouble: Queer Readings at the Boundary of Biblical Scholarship*, edited by Teresa Hornsby and Ken Stone, 175–89. Atlanta: Society of Biblical Literature.

Felder, Cain Hope, ed. 2021. *Stony the Road We Trod: African American Biblical Interpretation*. 30th anniversary edition. Minneapolis: Fortress.

Heschel, Susannah. 2010. *The Aryan Jesus: Christian Theologians and the Bible in Nazi Germany*. Princeton: Princeton University Press.

Hockey, Katherine M., and David G. Horrell, eds. 2018. *Ethnicity, Race, Religion: Identities and Ideologies in Early Jewish and Christian Texts, and in Modern Biblical Interpretation*. London: T&T Clark.

Horrell, David. 2020. *Ethnicity and Inclusion: Religion, Race, and Whiteness in Constructions of Jewish and Christian Identities*. Grand Rapids: Eerdmans.

Jennings, Willie James. 2011. *The Christian Imagination: Theology and the Origins of Race*. New Haven: Yale University Press.

———. 2017. *Acts: A Theological Commentary on the Bible*. Belief Series. Louisville: Westminster John Knox.

Johnson Hodge, Caroline. 2007. *If Sons, Then Heirs: A Study of Kinship and Ethnicity in the Letters of Paul*. Oxford: Oxford University Press.

Kaalund, Jennifer T. 2020. *Reading Hebrews and 1 Peter with the African American Great Migration: Diaspora, Place, and Identity*. LNTS 598. London: T&T Clark.

Levine, Amy-Jill. 2007. *The Misunderstood Jew: The Church and the Scandal of the Jewish Jesus*. New York: HarperOne.

Martin, Clarice. 1989. "A Chamberlain's Journey and the Challenges of Interpretation for Liberation." *Semeia* 47: 105–35.

Nasrallah, Laura, and Elisabeth Schüssler Fiorenza, eds. 2009. *Prejudice and Christian Beginnings: Investigating Race, Gender, and Ethnicity in Early Christian Studies*. Minneapolis: Fortress.

Ok, Janette H. 2021. *Constructing Ethnic Identity in 1 Peter: Who You Are No Longer*. LNTS 645. London: T&T Clark.

Park, Wongi. 2019. *The Politics of Race and Ethnicity in Matthew's Passion Narrative*. Cham, Switzerland: Palgrave Macmillan.

Parker, Angela N. 2021. *If God Still Breathes, Why Can't I? Black Lives Matter and Biblical Authority*. Grand Rapids: Eerdmans.

Reinhartz, Adele. 2022 (last accessed Oct. 24). "Jew/Judean (Word Study)." Bible Odyssey. https://www.bibleodyssey.org/articles/jew-judean-word-study/.

Sechrest, Love Lazarus. 2022. *Race and Rhyme: Rereading the New Testament*. Grand Rapids: Eerdmans.

Segovia, Fernando F. 2000. *Decolonizing Biblical Studies: A View from the Margins*. Maryknoll, NY: Orbis Books.

Sievers, Joseph, and Amy-Jill Levine, eds. 2021. *The Pharisees*. Grand Rapids: Eerdmans.

Smith, Shanell T. 2014. *The Woman Babylon and the Marks of Empire: Reading Revelation with a Postcolonial Womanist Hermeneutics of Ambivalence*. Minneapolis: Fortress.

Smith, Shively T. J. 2016. *Strangers to Family: Diaspora and 1 Peter's Invention of God's Household*. Waco: Baylor University Press.

Vena, Osvaldo D., and Leticia A. Guardiola-Sáenz, eds. 2022. *Latinx Perspectives on the New Testament*. Lanham, MD: Lexington Books / Fortress Academic.

The Household

55

Household Structure

JUDITH M. GUNDRY

I n a Greco-Roman milieu, the household refers to the property and family of the head of the household, which generally included a man's wife, their biological or adopted unmarried children, other blood relatives, slaves and their families, former slaves, and other dependents.[1] The head of the household was the eldest man or, in the case of a widow or unmarried heiress, the eldest woman.[2] The

families belonging to a household might all live under one roof (Huebner 2010, 75–77). Elite Roman households also included nonresident clients. Roman and Jewish households were virtually identical in terms of "structure, ideals and dynamics" (Cohen 1993, 2).

The household was the "primary site of production, reproduction, consumption and the intergenerational transmission of property and knowledge undergirding production" (Saller 2011, 116).[3] Most households had slaves to perform essential labor for the household (Glancy 2002, 42–45). How to deploy the abilities of men, women, and children; how many children to produce and raise; how to regulate the consumption of food and other goods; and how to educate the young were all matters decided within the family.

The New Testament writers formulated instructions to the various members of the household on their responsibilities to each other in

---

1. The Greek and Latin words for "household" are *oikos/oikia* and *domus*, respectively. They are not limited to the father-mother-children triad. The Latin term *familia* in common parlance referred to *agnati*, those from the same *domus* related by blood through males, who were in the *potestas* of the *paterfamilias* (Saller 1984, 337–38). The *familia* included the wife in marriage by *manus*, but in free marriage, the wife was treated as part of her father's *familia*, even though she resided in the *domus* of her husband (339).

2. In the New Testament, male heads of households are Crispus (Acts 18:8), Philip (Acts 21:8), Aristobulus (Rom. 16:10), Narcissus (Rom. 16:11), Stephanus (1 Cor. 1:15–16), Caesar (Phil. 4:22), Onesiphorus (2 Tim. 1:16), and Archippus (Philem. 2). Women who were probably heads of households are Peter's mother-in-law (Mark 1:30), Martha (Luke 10:38; John 11:1), Dorcas (Acts 9:36, 39), the mother of John Mark (Acts 12:12), Lydia (Acts 16:13–15, 40), Phoebe (Rom. 16:1–2), Chloe (1 Cor. 1:11), and Euodia and Syntyche (Phil. 4:2–3).

3. "Slaves dominated, and virtually monopolized, large-scale production in both the countryside and the urban sector" and "provided the bulk of the immediate income from property . . . of the élites, economic, social, and political" (Finley 1960, 79–82).

light of these functions of the household. The earliest of these instructions are found in 1 Corinthians 7 and Philemon. Later, the early Christians created the household-duty codes (*Haustafeln*) in Colossians 3:18–4:1; Ephesians 5:21–6:9; 1 Timothy 2:8–15; 5:1–2; 6:1–2; Titus 2:1–10; 3:1; and 1 Peter 2:11–3:12 (hereafter, "the household codes"). First Corinthians 14:34–35 is similar to the household codes and will thus be treated here as belonging to this genre. Finally, Jesus's teaching in Matthew 10:34–37; 19:27–29; 23:9; Mark 3:33–35; 10:28–30; 13:12–13; Luke 12:51–53; 14:26; 18:28–30; and John 19:26–27 deals with religious authority in the household.

Purpose and Governance of the Household in New Testament Paraenesis

Household Codes in the New Testament

The household codes in the New Testament instruct wives to be subject to, to respect, and to love their husbands and to clothe themselves modestly, appropriately, and with a gentle and quiet spirit; children to obey their parents; and slaves to obey their masters in singleness of heart, not only when observed, and to serve with goodwill, as to the Lord. These instructions have been traced to a Hellenistic tradition "on household management" (*peri oikonomias*) that goes back to Aristotle. He defined household management as "ruling" over a wife, children, and slaves—based on the (assumed) naturally superior abilities of the free adult male—and as creating wealth (*Pol.* 1259a40–b11). The household codes emerged relatively late in early Christianity, probably to address social tensions with outsiders by demonstrating compliance with widely accepted social norms for household roles (Balch 1981).[4]

However, the authors of the household codes omit key parts of Aristotle's form of household management: natural differences as the basis for unequal household roles, wealth creation as part of household management, and the relevance of household management to the city.[5] Such substantive divergences from Aristotle's ideas about household management and other topics were characteristic of the Hellenistic reception of Aristotle (Gundry 2024).

Aristotle distinguished between three types of rulers in the household (Blythe 1989, 1): "political" rule over a wife,[6] "kingly" rule over a child, and "despotic" rule over a slave, based on the differences between these three (*Pol.* 1259b1–11). In *Epitome of Stoic and Peripatetic Ethics*, Arius Didymus explained and adapted Aristotle's teaching within a Stoic framework:

> The man is the ruler of the household according to nature; for the deliberative faculty is worse in a female, it does not yet exist in children, and is altogether absent in slaves. [Thus] the wisdom pertaining to the household being concerned with the administration of the house and the persons within it properly belongs to a man. This encompasses the role of the father, the husband, the master (of slaves) and the acquisition of resources; for the household needs necessities. (149.5–12 [trans. Tsouni 2018, 59])

---

households, and capture young women" (2 Tim. 3:6–7), "overthrow whole households by teaching things which they ought not" (Titus 1:11), and are "disobedient to parents" (2 Tim. 3:2). The baptismal formula of Gal. 3:28 is thought to have inspired the early Christians to reject the subordinate household roles expected of wives, children, and slaves.

5. For Aristotle, the household provided the foundation for the city by supplying everyday necessities so that the citizens of the *polis* would be free to pursue "the good life," which completes the human being (*Pol.* 1252b31).

6. Aristotle, however, went on to contradict himself by describing the male as a natural ruler over the female in the interest of the accomplishment of the household's purposes.

---

4. An apologetic purpose has been detected in the requirement that wives submit to their husbands to "win" those who are unbelieving (1 Pet. 3:1) and to ward off "reviling" (1 Tim. 5:14) and "blaspheming the word of God" (Titus 2:5) and in the critique of teachers who "enter

Didymus described rule over a wife as "aristocratic," not "political," and rule over siblings as "democratic" (148.14–21). The neo-Pythagorean philosopher (Pseudo-)Callicratidas disagreed, however, stating that the husband's rule is "political," not "despotic" or "guardian," for political rule fosters happiness in the household by eliciting the wife's admiration and love for her husband (Thesleff 1965, 106 [trans. Balch 1992, 397]).

The authors of the household codes do not use the philosophical terms for distinct types of rule over a wife, child, and slave but instead describe these types of rule in their admonitions to husbands, fathers, and masters.

How to Rule over a Wife

In Colossians 3:19 and Ephesians 5:23, husbands must "love" their wives and "not be embittered against" them.[7] The command to "love" one's wife (in scholarly lingo, "love patriarchalism") is not particularly new, since Aristotle and his intellectual heirs thought husbands should rule in their wives' interests as well as in their own interests for the common advantage. But in contrast to the Aristotelian tradition, the author of Ephesians prescribes imitating Christ's *self-sacrificial* love as "the head of the *ekklēsia*": "Husbands, love your wives, as Christ loved the *ekklēsia* and delivered himself up for her, that he might set her apart, having purified her by the washing of water with the word" (Eph. 5:23–27). A parallel is found in one of Xenophon's Socratic dialogues, where Ischomachus tells his wife: "[Of all the] duties particular to you that are pleasant to perform . . . the most pleasant experience of all is to prove yourself better than I am, to make me your servant" (*Oec.* 7.41–42 [trans. Marchant and Todd 2013, 455]). To rule over a wife does not exclude becoming her servant in both Xenophon and Ephesians. This notion is implicit in Aristotle's prescription noted above that a man should rule in a "political" way over a wife. For in political rule, the ruler's role is not fixed, and there is "interchange" between the ruler and the ruled, who must rule for equal periods, demonstrating that they are equal (Aristotle, *Pol.* 1255b23). (Although interchange is characteristic of political rule, it is not actually practiced by the husband Aristotle depicts, who is "continuously" in the same relation to the female; see, further, Gundry 2024.)

The command in Ephesians 5:21 to "submit to each other" can be interpreted to mean "wives, [be submissive] to your husbands" (5:22) and "husbands, love your wives, as Christ loved the church and gave himself for her" (5:25).[8] On this interpretation, there are distinct ways of being submissive among wives and husbands as equals.

In 1 Peter 3:7, husbands must "live according to knowledge with the female as one who is a weaker vessel and show [a wife] honor insofar as [you are] joint heirs of the gift of life." The two main clauses are synonymously parallel. The "knowledge" that informs how to "live with the female" is that the husband and wife are "joint heirs of the gift of life." The phrase alludes to 1 Peter 1:3–4, where believers inherit a "living hope"—that is, "the incorruptible and undefiled and unfading inheritance that is kept for you in heaven" and is obtained through faith in God (1:5, 7, 9, 21; 5:9).

"The female" as "a weaker vessel" may allude to the inferior female role as a "helper" for the male (Gen. 2:18) in sexual reproduction (1:28).[9] That role was fraught with pain and suffering as a result of the fall: "I will make great your toil and many your pregnancies. With hardship shall you have children. Your turning is to your man/

---

7. Unless otherwise indicated, all Scripture translations are my own.

8. Some take the command "be submissive to each other" (Eph. 5:21) to mean that wives should submit to their own husbands, children to their own parents, and slaves to their own masters.

9. In 1 Thess. 4:4, "vessel" refers either to a wife as a container for male seed or to the male sex organ.

husband, and he shall rule you [sexually]" (3:16 [trans. Myers 2013, 102]). Ancient Jews thought that God gave men wives as sources of children to succeed them after they died: "Therefore, have I given them [men] wives also that they might impregnate them, and beget children by them, that thus nothing might be wanting to them on earth. But you were [formerly] spiritual, living the eternal life, and immortal for all generations of the world. And therefore, I have not appointed wives for you" (1 En. 15.5–7 [trans. Nickelsburg and VanderKam 2012, 36–37]). The statement alludes to the notion that progeny ensured a man of an "ongoing, post-mortem existence" (Rothstein 2016, 272n22), based on the fluid boundary between the individual and the familial group in ancient Mediterranean societies (Levenson 2006, 114). This notion is ubiquitous in ancient Near Eastern sources. The psalmist refers to children as an "inheritance from the Lord" (Ps. 127:3), alluding to the promise of descendants. The "incorruptible and undefiled and unfading inheritance that is kept for you in heaven" (1 Pet. 1:4), however, rendered this function of wives obsolete, as implied by the command to "live according to knowledge with the female"—the knowledge of a surpassingly great inheritance—and "show [a wife] honor insofar as [you are] joint heirs of the gift of life" (3:7).

The corresponding role of a wife is illustrated by Sarah in 1 Peter 3:1–6: "Let wives be subject to their own husbands . . . as Sarah obeyed Abraham by calling him lord" (in Gen. 18:12). According to some Second Temple Jewish texts, in fulfillment of the promise to Abraham that he will have a son from his wife, Sarah conceived Isaac *without* Abraham's help, based on Genesis 21:1–3: "Yahweh visited Sarah as he had said, and Yahweh did to Sarah as he had spoken. Sarah conceived, and bore Abraham a son in his old age . . . Isaac" (Holtz 2017, 23–82, 115–33). If this interpretation is assumed by the author of 1 Peter, Sarah was subject to Abraham by calling him "lord" *rather than*

by being impregnated by him as "a weaker vessel" to bear his seed. Early Christian wives are thus to subject themselves to their husbands by respectfully addressing them instead of by bearing them children.

The author of 1 Corinthians 14:34–35—probably not Paul—enforces the husband's authority to teach his wife, using the following admonitions: "Let the wives be silent in the assemblies, for it is not permitted for them to speak, but let them be submissive, just as the law says. And if they want to learn anything, let them ask their own husbands at home, for it is a shame for a wife to speak in the assembly." The teaching role of the husband was a reflection of the significant age gap between husbands and wives (some ten to fifteen years) in a Greco-Roman milieu. According to the neo-Pythagorean philosopher (Pseudo-)Callicratidas, "It is necessary therefore that the husband should be the . . . preceptor of his wife . . . in teaching her such things as it is fit for her to know," and "virgins [young wives] are easily fashioned, and are docile; and are also naturally well disposed to be instructed by, and to fear and love their husbands" (Thesleff 1965, 107 [trans. Balch 1992, 397]). The early Christian assemblies were designed to "instruct" and "build up" others (1 Cor. 14:19, 26) so that "all may learn and all may be exhorted" (14:27–33).[10] We can assume, then, that the early Christian husband's role as his wife's preceptor was undermined by this practice. The second-century apocryphon Acts of Paul and Thecla illustrates the threat to men's control over their virgins posed by an early Christian teacher such as Paul. When Paul came to town,

10. Priscilla and her husband, Aquila, were active in the founding of the assemblies in Corinth and probably taught in those assemblies. Priscilla is mentioned before her husband, Aquila, often in the New Testament (Acts 18:18, 26; Rom. 16:3; 2 Tim. 4:19; contrast Acts 16:19), suggesting that her role was more prominent than his. The tradition of early Christian wives like Priscilla as teachers in the assemblies may have occasioned the admonitions in 1 Cor. 14:34–35.

the virgin Thecla sat unmoved for days, listening to his teaching of "deceitful and various things," and was impervious to the cries of her fiancé, Thamyris (Acts Paul Thec. 8–10, 16). Paul's teaching of celibacy convinced Thecla to break off her engagement and follow in Paul's footsteps. Similarly, Titus 1:11 refers to men who "overturn whole houses" with their teaching. Women's access to education apart from their husbands' firm control also led to men's being "conquered by female fury"—skilled women debaters—according to the Roman moralist and historian Valerius Maximus:

> If each man of us . . . had established that the right and authority of the husband should be held over the mother of his own family, we should have less difficulty with women in general; now, at home our freedom is conquered by female fury, here in the Forum it is bruised and trampled upon. . . . They want freedom, nay license . . . in all things. . . . If they are victorious now, what will they not attempt? . . . As soon as they begin to be our equals, they will have become your superiors. (Valerius Maximus, *Fact. et dict.* 3.8.6 [trans. Bailey 2000, 325])

The admonitions in 1 Corinthians 14:34–35 may have been occasioned by the same problem for early Christian husbands—namely, being "conquered by female fury" at home or in the assemblies—hence, the restriction of wives to passive learning in the assemblies and active learning at home from their husbands. These admonitions conflict with 1 Corinthians 11:4–5, 10 and appear to reflect a very different social context. In addition, the earliest Greek manuscripts place them either after verse 33 or after verse 40. For these reasons, verses 34–35 are regarded by many interpreters as a non-Pauline interpolation (e.g., Payne 2009, 217–67).[11]

The injunction in 1 Timothy 2:11 to women to "learn in quietness with all subjection" assumes passive learning by wives in the assemblies. The author excludes women teachers in the assemblies—"I do not permit a woman to teach or exercise authority over a man" (1 Tim. 2:12)[12]—based on the created order in Genesis 2–3: "For Adam was formed first, then Eve. And Adam was not deceived. But the woman was deceived and fell into transgression" (1 Tim. 2:13–14). By implication, since wives were much younger than their husbands, wives were more susceptible to deceitful teaching. With age, however, "older women" acquired the ability to teach "younger women," for Titus is instructed to teach that "older women . . . be teachers of what is good, that they might train the young [women] to be lovers of husbands, lovers of children, soberminded, pure, good household managers, subject to their own husbands, in order that God's word might not be blasphemed" (Titus 2:3–5). Timothy's mother and grandmother are remembered as examples of unfeigned faith (2 Tim. 1:5). "Younger widows" who pledged not to marry (and, implicitly, not to come under their husband's tutelage) are described as "idle," "gossips and busybodies, saying things they ought not," those who "go from house to house," and in some cases, "have turned aside toward Satan"; so they are required to "marry, bear children, and rule the household" (1 Tim. 5:11–15).

These later restrictions on women's active roles in the early Christian assemblies and the requirement that younger widows marry imply that the earlier assemblies were relatively effective in training women.

---

11. Alternatively, some hold that these verses are authentically Pauline and prohibit only interruptive speaking by wives or their evaluation of their own husbands' prophecies.

12. The precise meaning of the term *authentein* in 1 Tim. 2:12 is debated. Some argue that it has a pejorative sense and that the author of 1 Timothy does not prohibit neutral or positive uses of authority by women in the assemblies.

How to Rule over Children

In Colossians 3:21 and Ephesians 6:4a, fathers must not "embitter" their children and so "discourage" or "anger" them. Harsh discipline of children by fathers is in view. Roman citizen fathers had vast, state-sanctioned legal power over all members of the household (*patria potestas*, or "the power of the father"), which extended to all aspects of household life—economic, social, and religious. The power over the life and death of the children was in the father's hands. This power lent itself to abuse through harsh discipline. Nevertheless, there were constraints on the exercise of *patria potestas*, and "a balance . . . between harsh discipline and indulgent permissiveness" toward children was encouraged (Chen 2006, 20–28). In Greco-Roman writings, the stereotype of the tyrannical father is infrequent. In Ephesians 6:4b, fathers are required to "nourish [their children] with the instruction and discipline of the Lord." A parallel is found in Plutarch, where the Elder Cato educates his son for the purpose of "moulding and fashioning his son to virtue" (Plutarch, *Cato Maior* 20.9 [trans. Perrin 1914, 363]). "The instruction and discipline of the Lord" (Eph. 6:4b) that nourishes the child may refer to teaching *about* the Lord or to teaching *like* the Lord's. In the Gospel of Mark, Jesus welcomed the little children to come to him after his disciples rebuked those bringing the children, and Jesus blessed the children and taught that whoever wants to enter God's reign must become like a little child (Mark 10:13–16), perhaps providing an example for early Christian fathers of how to "nourish" their own children. The term also appears in Ephesians 5:29–31, where "nourish" is synonymously parallel to "take care of" and antithetical to "hate": "No one has ever hated his own body; rather, one nourishes and takes care of it, just as Christ does for the assembly, for we are members of his body." In Genesis 2:24, the son is one with his parents until he leaves and is "joined to his wife, and the two shall become one flesh." To "nourish" one's children with "the instruction and discipline of the Lord" is thus equivalent to treating *oneself* with care, and to use harsh discipline on one's children is equivalent to "hating" *oneself*. (The same argument is used in Eph. 5:29–31 for treating a wife with care rather than harshly.)

In the Pastoral Epistles, to qualify for the role of overseer of the *ekklēsia*, a man must "lead" or "manage his own household well" and keep his children "in subjection, with all reverence"; for the man who "does not know how to lead/manage his household" is unable to "take care of God's *ekklēsia*" (1 Tim. 3:2–5), which is "God's household" (3:15). The additional criterion of having raised "believing children" who are "not accused of loose or unruly behavior" (Titus 1:6), echoes the father's role to "nourish them with the instruction and discipline of the Lord" in Ephesians 5. Other qualifying traits for the role of overseer are being "given to hospitality," "a lover of good," "sober-minded," "fair," and "self-controlled," while disqualifying traits include being "self-pleasing," "easily angered," and "violent," which evoke the tyrannical father (Titus 1:7–8). The young pastor Timothy is told to "let no one despise your youth" (1 Tim. 4:12), alluding to the potential for abuse of *patria potestas* in the "household of God." Moreover, Timothy *may* "exhort"—though "not rebuke"—an "older man" (1 Tim. 5:1).

How to Rule over Slaves

In Colossians 4:1 and Ephesians 6:9, masters must grant their slaves "what is just and equal [or fair]," "do the same to them" as they do to their masters, and "stop threatening." These requirements replace despotic rule with the golden rule, "Do unto others as you would have them do unto you." In despotic rule, the ruler acts solely in his own interests and disregards those of the slave. Hence, the slave's obedience had to be extracted with threats. Slaves might derive some benefits from their relationships to masters, but if so, it was purely coincidental. The household codes' requirements to grant slaves what is just and equal, or fair, and do to slaves what they do to masters and stop threatening are incompatible with despotic rule and imply that it must be replaced with an antithetical form of rule: acting in the slave's interests and returning good to the slave for the good done to the master. The basis for this new type of rule over slaves is the common identity of the master and slave as "slaves" of the same "Master" in heaven, who is "impartial" and makes no distinction between the slave and the master on earth when recompensing them for their service (Col. 4:1; Eph. 6:8–9).[13] As the Master's "slaves," the master and the slave are equally under obligation to serve each other. Their status in the household is different, but their obligations in the household are the same.

Instruction on Household Duties in 1 Corinthians 7 and Philemon

First Corinthians 7 and Philemon, which predate the household codes, refer to the same three household pairs—the husband and wife, the parent and child, and the master and slave—as well as to unmarried men and women (including virgins [i.e., young women of marriageable age] and widows).[14] Paul advises the unmarried that they will do "better" or are "more fortunate" if they remain as they are, unless they "burn" with sexual desire and "lack self-control" and hence "must" marry as a way to satisfy their desire (1 Cor. 7:7–9, 36–38, 39–40). Paul wishes that all might be

like him, however—that is, unmarried by virtue of having a "gift of God" for the celibate life (7:7). Paul does not prefer celibacy because he thinks sex is wrong or tainted by evil desire. Rather, he operates with a stereotype of marriage as an all-consuming vocation to "devote care to what belongs to the world" and strive to "serve" a wife or a husband as a means of obtaining lasting happiness or a greater good (7:33–34). In ancient Mediterranean societies, people married to reproduce, and they sought to ensure that their children would survive them and to accumulate wealth to pass on to their heirs, so that their family line might not die out. Even though the individual man or woman would inevitably die, they aspired to continue their earthly existence through their progeny, as noted above. Such hopes represented by fruitful and productive households are illustrated by the Roman historian Velleius Paterculus's description of the adoption of Tiberius to succeed Augustus: "There sprang up once more in parents the assurance of safety for their children, in husbands for the sanctity of marriage, in owners for the safety of their property, and in all men the assurances of safety, order, peace, and tranquility; indeed, it would have been hard to entertain larger hopes, or to have them more happily fulfilled" (*Roman History* 2.103.4–5 [trans. Shipley 1924, 265]). But from Paul's perspective, there was no need for marriage and procreation as a way to secure an afterlife or, for that matter, as a requirement to secure the future of Augustus's empire, which depended on numerous fruitful marriages. For "the form of this world is passing away" (1 Cor. 7:31) and is being replaced with a "new creation" (2 Cor. 5:17), starting with the community of those who are "in Christ." The unmarried person is free to "devote care to the Lord's possessions [i.e., his people]" and to "strive to serve the Lord" and to "be consecrated both

---

13. In 1 Pet. 2:18–24, only slaves are addressed and told to be subject to their masters, both the good and the unjust, and to work "as for the Lord, not for human beings," just as Christ committed himself to the righteous Judge while suffering for doing good.

14. An expanded discussion of my comments here on 1 Cor. 7 can be found in Gundry 2024.

in body and in spirit" (1 Cor. 7:32–34)[15] in the overlap between the ages (1 Cor. 10:11).[16]

The married man who is a Christ believer finds himself with one foot in both worlds: "He is divided" between two incompatible vocations (1 Cor. 7:34). Given what time it is (the end time!), it is far better to be "constantly devoted to the Lord in a manner free from distraction" and to marry only for the sake of "seemliness," or sexual propriety (7:35), not for the sake of procreation and patrimony. Cynic philosophers viewed marriage similarly, as a distraction from the philosophical life, given the inescapable obligations of the married man. The Cynic philosopher Crates tried to avoid these obligations by marrying a fellow Cynic, Hipparchia, but she was less devoted to the philosophical life than Crates expected (Diogenes Laertius, *Vit. phil.* 6.97). From Paul's perspective, celibacy represented a similar choice not to be sucked into a lifestyle that required intense effort and devotion in order to attain the prize: an earthly afterlife through well-funded progeny (Rothstein 2016, 272n22; see also Levenson 2006, 114).

Furthermore, in light of the apocalyptic tradition that the first will be last and that the fruitful wives will be deeply unfortunate in the last days by virtue of being more exposed to suffering and death than the barren and childless,[17] Paul warns that some who marry "will have affliction" (1 Cor. 7:28). He is sparing the Corinthian women from this fate by endorsing the decision to remain as one is as "better" (7:26–28, 36–38) and declaring that even the widow is "more fortunate" if she

remains unmarried, despite the obvious socioeconomic disadvantages for widows (7:40).

In addition to its significance for the individual afterlife, the establishment of a household with many children and property represented hope for the city. In *Epitome of Stoic and Peripatetic Ethics*, Arius Didymus describes the aim of the married man and woman as follows:

> If . . . marriage brings the increase that is wished for . . . the children grow up and, coming together in pairs, another household comes into being and so a third and a fourth, and from these a village and a city. (148.5)

> The male comes together with the female driven by a desire for procreation and the preservation of the family, for each desires procreation. (148.19–21)

> The household comes to be from the coming together for a single purpose and the forethought of everyone toward a single advantage. (149.4)

> A city consists of a number of such persons which is adequate for a self-sufficient life . . . such that the city is neither wanting in fellow-feeling nor readily despised and is provided with the things necessary for life without shortage and so adequate for defending itself against foreign invaders. (150.5–9 [trans. Tsouni 2018, 59])

The household as a baby-making factory in this first-century CE Stoic adaptation of Aristotle's form of household management provides the backdrop against which to interpret Paul's silence about procreation in 1 Corinthians 7. It is not as though Paul does not like children (cf. 1 Cor. 7:14: "Your children . . . are consecrated," probably a cultic metaphor referring to people who are reserved for God's purposes, despite being outside the cult). It is that he does not see children as a means to an end for their parents' goals, entailing the multiplication of households and the acqui-

15. Paul is referring to the "chaste" woman's freedom from childbearing, which was a hindrance to engagement in the Lord's work.

16. Paul's affirmation of women's freedom to choose celibacy has been described as "a severe infringement of the right of the *paterfamilias*" (Schüssler Fiorenza 1983, 225).

17. Mark 13:14–20 par. Luke 23:29; Gospel of Thomas 79; 2 Bar. 10.13–16.

sition of descendants. Nor is childlessness a problem in the face of death from Paul's point of view, for he expected that at the resurrection of the dead they would be raised *incorruptible* (15:52). Given the eschatological irrelevance of procreating children, preserving them, and educating them for their roles in the household, there was no need to include instructions in 1 Corinthians 7 to children and parents on their household duties.

Just as Paul's eschatological convictions told him that there was no need for the Corinthians to establish households in order to procreate, so also these convictions meant that there was no need for dutiful household slaves to increase the productivity of the household. In 1 Corinthians 7:21, Paul writes, "If you were called while enslaved, do not pay attention, and if you are rather able to be free, make use [of it]." The admonition "do not pay attention,"[18] or do not assiduously fulfill one's obligations as a slave, is precisely the opposite of the requirement to "obey your masters" given in the household codes (Col. 3:22–25; Eph. 6:5–8; 1 Pet. 2:18–25). Paul's admonition to slaves not to pay attention is paired with the admonition "rather, if able to be free, make use [of it]" (1 Cor. 7:21). The absence of a direct object of the verb requires the interpreter to supply one. Most supply the direct object "freedom." The obligation to use freedom to serve the Lord without the duties of a slave is implied (although freed slaves had obligations to their former masters). In 1 Corinthians 7:22, Paul states that the one who was called while a slave is "a freedperson belonging to the Lord," with duties to the Lord that should now be fulfilled, just as the one who was called while free is "Christ's slave" and obligated to serve him.

In 1 Corinthians 7:30, "those who buy" are admonished to "be, as it were, like those who

do not possess." In Aristotle's schema, wealth creation was an essential part of household management and, for some, the most important or only part. For example, the Epicurean philosopher Philodemus writes in Περὶ οἰκο- νομίας ("On Property Management"), "We shall discuss, then, not how one can live well at home but what attitude one must take up both with regard to the acquisition and the preservation of wealth, concerning which property management and the property-management expert are in fact conceived specifically, (and we shall do so) without contending at all with those who prefer to make other meanings underlie the terms" (trans. Tsouna 2012, 33). Slaves were essential household property, insofar as they performed most of the work in the household. Paul's admonition to "be, as it were, like those who do not possess" may refer to the manumission of slaves. For in utopian communities such as the unmarried Essenes and the Therapeutae, the members had no private property and owned no slaves, in the interests of creating a harmonious community of equals and fictive siblings (Philo, *Contempl. Life* 13, 16–17; Josephus, *Ant.* 18.20–21). Paul exhorts the propertied in Corinth (including slave owners) to imitate these utopians. First Corinthians 7:30 is thus the flip side of verse 21b.

In the letter to Philemon, Paul writes that he has sent back Onesimus, Philemon's slave, and "if you have me as your partner, receive him as me" (Philem. 17). For he is Paul's "child," whom he "begat in chains" (Philem. 10). Paul gives no instructions to Philemon on his duties to his slave or to Onesimus on his duties to his master. Indeed, it is *Philemon's* "obedience" (Philem. 21) that Paul "requests" (Philem. 9), given his right to "command" Philemon to do "the appropriate thing" (Philem. 8), which was to manumit Onesimus: "He was parted from you for a while, so that you might have him forever no longer as a slave but beyond a slave, as a beloved brother, mine especially, but yours

---

18. The NRSV translation, "do not be concerned about it," does not conflict with the obligation to "obey" and results in a much less countercultural interpretation.

even more both in the flesh [household] and in the Lord" (Philem. 15–16). Paul promises to pay the price of Onesimus's manumission and make restitution for any wrongs to Philemon (although none are specified), and he reminds Philemon of his debt to Paul for "yourself" (Philem. 18–19), thus making up for any lack of resources on Paul's part. Presumably, Philemon would suffer economic loss by manumitting a slave who was "useful" (the meaning of "Onesimus"), so that Onesimus might continue to be useful to Paul "in chains," no longer on Philemon's behalf but as a freedman (Philem. 11). Paul writes, "I am confident of your obedience and know that you will do even more than I say" (Philem. 21). How could Philemon refuse to pay his debt to Paul and even go above and beyond, thus securing his own honor, based on the cultural expectations associated with reciprocal gift-exchange (Barclay 2015)? What Paul was asking of Philemon was, of course, poor wealth management. But it was the price of Paul's continuing "partnership" with Philemon in the gospel work. Since Paul refers to his coworkers as "brother" (1 Cor. 1:1; 2 Cor. 1:1, 13; 12:18; Phil. 2:25; 1 Thess. 3:2; see also 1 Cor. 15:6), perhaps he means to add Onesimus, "the beloved brother," to this group of coworkers who were free to come and go in their work for the gospel. In short, the letter to Philemon as a request for the manumission of an early Christian slave, in obedience to Paul as repayment for his gospel ministry, demonstrates that Paul expected early Christian slave owners to let go of their "property" at the expense of their household wealth for the benefit of the Lord's work. Paul demanded obedience not of the slave but of the master.

In 1 Corinthians 7, Paul prescribes the following duties for husbands and wives. With respect to the sexual relationship, they have the same duties. Each must "have [in a sexual relationship]" their own wife or husband (7:2), "render what is due" to their wife or their husband (7:3), and "not defraud each other,"

with an exception for sexual abstinence "by agreement for a suitable period,"[19] after which they must "be together again, lest Satan tempt you on account of your lack of self-control" (7:5). These shared obligations are based on the premise that neither the husband nor the wife "exercises the right over" their own body to the exclusion of the other, and conversely, each "exercises the right over" the other's body (7:3). With respect to the marital relationship in general, they have the same duties. Each "devotes care . . . striving to serve" a wife or a husband (7:33–34). Marriage is a "yoke" that they share (7:35). With respect to divorce, they have the same obligations. The husband "is bound to a wife" and the wife "is bound to a husband" (7:27, 39). Neither may "divorce" their spouse, unless they are married to an unbeliever who wants to divorce, in which case both the husband and the wife must "permit [the unbeliever] to divorce" (7:10–16). Should the unbelieving husband or wife choose to remain in the marriage, they can be "consecrated" by the believing wife or husband (7:14), portending their salvation by the believing spouse (7:16).

The identicality of the duties of husbands and wives in 1 Corinthians 7 is striking. Likewise, Paul's omission of the terms "male" and "female" from his discussion is remarkable, since his general preference for celibacy is based on the baptismal tradition in Galatians 3:28, which contains these terms: "In Christ . . . there is no 'male and female'" (Schüssler Fiorenza 1983, 211). Paul apparently omits them here so as to avoid evoking the Hellenistic tradition of household management in which the *male* is by nature better equipped to *rule* and the *female* is by nature suited to *be ruled* (Aristotle, *Pol.* 1252a32–b6). Paul's use of parallel formulations for husbands' and wives' duties in 1 Corinthians 7 is also striking. Why does he go

19. The phrase "the period suitable for conception" appears in Soranus, *Gyn.* 1.61, where sexual abstinence during the period suitable for conception is recommended to those who do not want to procreate.

to so much trouble, instead of addressing them jointly, which he rarely does in this chapter? He repeats himself without adding anything new (Wire 1990, 79–80).[20] Finally, Paul's use of euphemisms for sexual roles is also striking: "exercise the right over the body," "render what is due," "not defraud," and "please" or "serve." It is plausible that Paul uses these expressions as synonyms for "rule" and "be subject," which are euphemisms for the male and female roles in sexual reproduction, respectively (see above). Paul applies both equivalent terms or expressions indiscriminately to husbands and wives, implying that rule and subjection in the marital partnership are not associated with a particular sex but are roles that either sex may exercise. Since Paul understands the marital partnership to provide an acceptable solution to sexual "burning" for both men and women, it will not do for only one partner to "exercise the right over the body" of the spouse and for only one partner to be obliged to "render what is due" and "not defraud."

By ascribing both roles to the husband and wife equally, in synonymously parallel formulations, Paul effectively calls for political rule in the marital partnership, or the type of rule that alternates from one partner to the other. In (Pseudo-)Callicratidas's treatise *On the Happiness of Households*, political rule over a wife is required for the sake of the happiness of the household, which other forms of rule inhibit:

> But he [the husband] does not rule over her [the wife] with a despotic power: for he is diligently attentive to her welfare. Nor is his rule of her entirely of a guardian nature; for this is itself a part of the communion [between the husband and wife]. It remains, therefore, that he rules over her with a political rule, according to which both the ruler and the ruled establish [as their end] the common advantage.... Those husbands... that rule their wives despotically are hated by them, [and] those that rule them with a guardian authority are despised by them. For they appear to be, as it were, appendages and flatterers of their wives. But those that rule them politically are both admired and beloved. (Thesleff 1965, 106 [trans. Balch 1992, 397])

Political rule here consists in exercising the same function of ruling: "[*They*] establish the common advantage." That advantage is not defined, but it probably alludes to determining whether to procreate and how many children to have, a question in which the wife had a distinct interest as the child bearer. To exclude a wife from such decisions resulted in the husband's being hated or despised, while to include a wife in such decisions resulted in the husband's being admired and loved. If, then, the goal is to maintain the happiness of the household, wives must codetermine with their husbands what is their common advantage. As the saying goes, "Happy wife, happy life!" While (Pseudo-)Callicratidas refers only to the husband as "the ruler" and to the wife as "the ruled," we should not conclude that these are their *only* roles, given the statement "[*They*] establish the common advantage."

In summary, Paul's instructions about the household in 1 Corinthians 7 and Philemon imply that there was no need for households to be structured so as to produce legitimate children and wealth, as in ancient Mediterranean societies generally, based on unequal partnerships of men and women, free and slave, and mature and immature. These relationships had solely temporal value and should be structured accordingly. Husbands and wives exercised the same rights and had the same obligation to serve each other. Natural differences between male and female were unimportant

20. The instruction to divorced women in 1 Cor. 7:11a ("but if she is divorced, let her remain so, or be reconciled to her husband") lacks a parallel for divorced men. The joint instruction to unmarried men and widows in 1 Cor. 7:8 is expanded only for widows in 7:39–40. Antithetical parallelism is used in verse 34a ("and he is divided") and verse 34c ("that she might be consecrated both in body and in spirit").

to the purpose of their relationship. Children were reserved for God's purposes and should be treated accordingly. Slaves should be manumitted by property owners, and if not, slaves should not pay close attention to their duties and should make use of freedom, if they are able to be free, and devote themselves undividedly to serving the Lord. It was unnecessary to establish new households except for purely temporal purposes. The "shortened" time left in the present age required this revised structure of the household.

Religion, Authority, and the Household in the New Testament

The ancient Mediterranean family was intolerant of religious diversity, which reflects the household's dependence on divine favor for its survival and prosperity, so as to provide hope of an earthly afterlife through one's descendants and race or nation, as indicated above. For this reason, people were expected to marry within their own religious group and transmit their religious beliefs and traditions to their children. Religious authority in the household resided with the husband and father. It is illustrated by Joseph and Aseneth, an expansion of the biblical story of the Jewish patriarch's marriage to an Egyptian woman named Aseneth, who abandoned her gods and converted to Judaism before marrying a Jewish monotheist. In a Greco-Roman milieu, wives were expected to adopt their husbands' gods and not import other religious rituals and beliefs into the household.[21] The early Christians did not diverge from this norm, even though they placed no hope for the future in the earthly household. Paul instructs the Corinthian widows that they are free to marry "only in the

21. Plutarch wrote that the Roman wife was expected to worship only the household gods of her husband and to "shut the front door tight upon all queer rituals and outlandish superstitions," which do not please the gods (*Mor.* 140d [trans. Babbitt 1928, 311]).

Lord" (1 Cor. 7:39), presumably so that they will avoid pressure to engage in idolatrous household rituals. In early Christianity, when the head of a household converted and was baptized, the rest of the household converted and was baptized as well in some cases (Acts 10:44–48; 16:11–15, 25–34; 18:11; 1 Cor. 1:16).

Jesus's so-called anti-familial teaching (Matt. 19:27–29; Mark 10:28–30; Luke 14:26; 18:28–30) envisions the breakup of families as a result of conflicting responses to Jesus's message as something that he in fact came to do: "I came to bring a sword" or "division" (Matt. 10:34–36; Luke 12:51–53). The saying draws on Micah 7:6–7, where a son, daughter, or daughter-in-law rises up against a man who "will look to Yahweh" and "wait for the God of my salvation" (cf. Jub. 23.16, 19). Jesus's ability to divide the family makes him an alternative to the Jewish father, who had the authority to determine the religious beliefs and practices of the family. Hence, Jesus taught his disciples: "Do not call anyone on earth your father, for [you have] one [father], your heavenly Father" (Matt. 23:9; cf. Mark 3:33–35; 10:30 par. John 19:26–27). Jesus predicted that his disciples would be "hated" by their own family members and, in turn, must "hate" or reject their own family members or must "not love mother or father . . . son or daughter more than me" (Mark 13:13; Matt. 10:37)—that is, not demonstrate obedience to the religious authorities in the household who rejected him. As a result of their disobedience, Jesus's disciples will be expelled from their households and disinherited as apostates, implicitly to preserve God's blessing on the family. In Mark 13, Jesus goes as far as to warn that such apostates will be put to death by their own: "Brother will deliver up brother to death, and the father his child. Children will rise up against parents and cause them to be put to death" (13:12). The stakes could not be higher for the household as a source of hope for the individual and the nation.

In 1 Corinthians 7, Paul addresses husbands and wives who are married to an unbeliever (assumed to be a polytheist) and have unbelieving children (7:12–16). These Corinthians, by implication, have converted to faith in Christ not as part of a household but as solitary individuals, resulting in a violation of the norm of religious endogamy. They may have wanted to divorce their polytheistic spouses, and the polytheistic spouses may have wanted to divorce the newly minted Christ followers, based on that norm. Paul instructs them: "If the unbeliever wants to divorce, let him/her divorce. For the brother or sister is not bound to such ones. Rather, God has called you to peace. Do you know, wife, whether you will save your husband? Do you know, husband, whether you will save your wife?" (7:15–16). Conversely, if the unbelieving husband or wife "agrees to live together," then the Corinthians are bound to remain in the marriage: "Do not divorce! . . . For the unbelieving husband is consecrated by his wife, and the unbelieving wife is consecrated by the brother. For otherwise, your children would be 'unclean'; but as it is, they are consecrated [by the Christ believer]" (7:12–14).[22] Paul's justification for remaining in an interreligious marriage is difficult to interpret. A plausible interpretation is that he understood the unbeliever's willingness to live with a Christ believer to imply that already God had begun to redeem these unbelievers from idolatry, just as God had first "consecrated" the Corinthians to God and then "called" them (1:2). Similarly, in Romans 11:16 those who do not believe are "consecrated," since they are one with believers who are "consecrated." The salvation of the unbelieving spouses and children is on the horizon (Fee 2014, 332–33; cf. Rom. 8:29–30). The Corinthians' households will then be united in faith in one God and one Lord Jesus Christ, and there is thus now no need to divide these households based on different religious identities or practices. Similarly, in 1 Peter 3:1, early Christian wives with unbelieving husbands are encouraged to "be submissive" to them, so that they might "win" them by their respectful behavior.

To those who left their "household, or brothers, or sisters, or father, or mother, or wife, or children, or fields for my name's sake"— thus giving up the hope that these households represented—Jesus promised that they "will receive a hundredfold now in this time houses, brothers, sisters, mothers, and fields, with persecutions, and in the age to come eternal life" (Mark 10:29–30; similarly Luke 18:29; cf. Matt. 19:29). The fictive household that replaces the earthly household in anticipation of "eternal life" in the age to come has no "fathers" but only "brothers, sisters, mothers, and fields"; for fathers represent opposition to the heavenly Father and his representative, Jesus.

In short, Jesus came to abolish earthly households (people and property) as alternative sources of eternal life by proclaiming that it was a free gift from the heavenly Father to those who followed Jesus as God's Messiah. The father's authority to determine the religious identity of the household came into dispute as a result of Jesus's calling of disciples. Despite being deprived of their earthly source of hope by being expelled and disinherited as apostates, they would receive far bigger and better fictive households, not based on consanguinity, than those they had given up. Paul assumes the same for Christ believers who are divorced by their unbelieving husband or wife. But those who are not divorced by their unbelieving spouse may take comfort in the thought that the tolerant unbelieving spouse "is consecrated" to God by the Christ believer, who is "consecrated" to God, and that their children "are consecrated" to God, so that eventually they will also be saved, and the household will be united in faith in one God.

22. Alternative translations for "is consecrated" are "is ritually pure," "is morally sanctified," "is licit for marriage," and "is a saint"; see Gundry 2024.

Works Cited

Babbitt, Frank Cole, trans. 1928. *Plutarch: Moralia.* Vol. 2. LCL 222. Cambridge, MA: Harvard University Press.

Bailey, D. R. Shackleton. 2000. *Valerius Maximus: Memorable Doings and Sayings.* Vol. 1, *Books 1–5.* LCL 492. Cambridge, MA: Harvard University Press.

Balch, David L. 1981. *Let Wives Be Submissive: The Domestic Code in 1 Peter.* Society of Biblical Literature Monograph Series 26. Chico, CA: Scholars Press.

———. 1992. "Neopythagorean Moralists and the New Testament Household Codes." *ANRW* 2.26.1: 381–408.

Barclay, John M. G. 2015. *Paul and the Gift.* Grand Rapids: Eerdmans.

Blythe, James M. 1989. "Family, Government, and the Medieval Aristotelians." *History of Political Thought* 10: 1–16.

Chen, Diane G. 2006. *God as Father in Luke-Acts.* New York: Peter Lang.

Cohen, Shaye, ed. 1993. *The Jewish Family in Antiquity.* BJS 289. Atlanta: Scholars Press.

Fee, Gordon D. 2014. *The First Epistle to the Corinthians.* NICNT. Grand Rapids: Eerdmans.

Finley, Moses I., ed. 1960. *Slavery in Classical Antiquity: Views and Controversies.* Cambridge: Heffer.

Glancy, Jennifer A. 2002. *Slavery in Early Christianity.* Oxford: Oxford University Press.

Gundry, Judith M. 2024. *Women, Gender, and Sex in the End-Time: Household Roles in 1 Corinthians 7.* WUNT. Tübingen: Mohr Siebeck.

Holtz, Gudrun. 2017. *Jungfrauengeburt und Greisinnenbegurt: Zur Rezeptionsgeschichte von Gen 21,1f im antiken Judentum und im frühen Christentum.* Biblisch-Theologische Studien 172. Göttingen: Vandenhoeck & Ruprecht.

Huebner, Sabine R. 2010. "Household Composition in the Ancient Mediterranean—What Do We Really Know?" In *A Companion to Families in the Greek and Roman Worlds,* edited by Beryl Rawson, 73–91. Malden, MA: Wiley-Blackwell.

Levenson, Jon D. 2006. *Resurrection and the Restoration of Israel: The Ultimate Victory of the God of Life.* New Haven: Yale University Press.

Marchant, E. C., and O. J. Todd, trans. 2013. *Xenophon: Memorabilia, Oeconomicus, Symposium, Apology.* Revised by Jeffrey Henderson. LCL 168. Cambridge, MA: Harvard University Press.

Myers, Carol. 2013. *Rediscovering Eve: Ancient Israelite Women in Context.* Oxford: Oxford University Press.

Nickelsburg, George W. E., and James C. VanderKam. 2012. *1 Enoch: The Hermeneia Translation.* Rev. ed. Minneapolis: Fortress.

Payne, Philip B. 2009. *Man and Woman, One in Christ: An Exegetical and Theological Study of Paul's Letters.* Grand Rapids: Zondervan.

Perrin, Bernadotte, trans. 1914. *Plutarch: Lives.* Vol. 2, *Themistocles and Camillus, Aristides and Cato Major, Cimon and Lucullus.* LCL 47. Cambridge, MA: Harvard University Press.

Rothstein, David. 2016. "Hezekiah's Prayer and Childlessness: Variant Forms of a Tradition, as Reflected in LXX, Josephus, and Rabbinic Sources." *ZAW* 128: 267–83.

Saller, Richard. 1984. "'Familia, Domus,' and the Roman Conception of the Family." *Phoenix* 38: 336–55.

———. 2011. "The Roman Family as Productive Unit." In *A Companion to Families in the Greek and Roman Worlds,* edited by Beryl Rawson, 116–28. Malden, MA: Wiley-Blackwell.

Schüssler Fiorenza, Elisabeth. 1983. *In Memory of Her: A Feminist Theological Reconstruction of Christian Origins.* New York: Crossroad.

Shipley, Frederick W., trans. 1924. *Velleius Paterculus: Compendium of Roman History, Res Gestae Divi Augusti.* LCL 152. Cambridge, MA: Harvard University Press.

Thesleff, Holger. 1965. *An Introduction to the Pythagorean Writings of the Hellenistic Period.* Acta Academiae Aboensis 30.1. Åbo: Åbo Akademi.

Tsouna, Voula, trans. 2012. *Philodemus, "On Property Management."* Writings from the Greco-Roman World. Atlanta: Society of Biblical Literature.

Tsouni, Georgia, trans. 2018. "Didymus' Epitome of Peripatetic Ethics, Household Management, and Politics: An Edition with Translation." In *Arius Didymus on Peripatetic Ethics, Household Management, and Politics: Text, Translation, and Discussion,* edited by William W. Fortenbaugh, 1–67. Rutgers University Studies in Classical Humanities 20. New York: Routledge.

56

Sexuality

WILLIAM LOADER

"Sexuality" is a broad term that includes sexual orientation, sexual desire, and sexual behavior. As such, it belongs in discussions of households and marriage, dealt with in the chapters that precede and follow this chapter. As marriage is about more than sex, so sexuality is about more than marriage. This chapter deals more broadly and in overview with sexuality beyond marriage and the household.

Behind the scenes of the New Testament is first and foremost the world of Jewish cultural norms. The Jesus movement can scarcely be said to have been an innovator in relation to sexuality. Its focus was elsewhere. We may assume that it continued to operate with Jewish norms even when, like other Jewish movements, it found itself sometimes in contexts dominated by Greco-Roman cultures.

Sexuality in Genesis 1–3 and Its Interpretations

It is appropriate to start this overview at the beginning—with the Genesis creation stories. They make it plain that sexuality is an aspect of how God created humankind. Just like the animals and plants, humans are to reproduce (Gen. 1:28). God makes humankind (Hebrew 'adam) male and female (1:27). Being made in God's image (1:26) is related primarily to their unique role in being commissioned to rule God's creation (1:28).

Readers of this story in the world of the New Testament would then go on to read a second account of creation, which they would have seen as throwing more light on the event. The original human being is male, not both male and female, as a literal reading of Genesis 1:27 might suggest. The man ('adam) is formed like a clay model from the dust of the ground ('adamah, more than just a neat word play), and God breathes life into him (2:7). Reversing the order of Genesis 1, the passage continues with an account of God's creating a garden of plants and fruit-bearing trees (2:8–9) and making animals to keep the man company.

So far, the man lacks "a helper as his partner" (Gen. 2:20). God puts him to sleep, extracts a rib, and makes out of it a partner for the man. God makes woman (*'ishshah*) and brings her to the man (*'ish*, another neat word play). The passage continues: "Therefore a man leaves his father and his mother and clings to his wife, and they become one flesh" (2:24). The coming together includes sexual union, part of God's intent in creation, and thereby they become new kin, the likely emphasis of the word "flesh." The focus here is companionship and togetherness, including sexual intimacy.

As the first story highlights the role of sexuality for reproduction, so the second highlights oneness expressed in sexual union. Read together and in the light of actual experience in a pre-contraceptive age, the latter would be closely associated with reproduction, not least in creating new kin. The added emphasis in some versions of the two becoming one may also reflect an understanding of the origin of sexual attraction—namely, the two parts rejoining—although this is not explicit. It would form a positive parallel to what Plato has his character Aristophanes depict as negative—namely, that Zeus, offended by human insolence, took one of the first human beings, who was both male and female, and cut it down the middle, so that ever since the male and female halves have sought to rejoin (*Symp.* 189–93).

Sexual themes return in the account of sin in the garden of Eden in Genesis 3. Not the sin itself but the consequences touch on the theme. Accordingly, the story depicts God declaring, "I will greatly increase your pangs in childbearing; in pain you shall bring forth children, yet your desire shall be for your husband, and he shall rule over you" (3:16). This appears to explain women's desire (or enhanced desire?) for sexual intercourse with their husbands as part of the punishment for Eve's sin. There is a connection between their sexual desire and being ruled by their husbands, who would keep them safe through the journeys of pregnancy and childbirth and keep their sexual desires under control.

Genesis 1–3 in the Greek translation (the Septuagint, the Bible of the early church) reproduces the stories with some subtle changes (Loader 2004, 27–59). It makes the creation of woman match the creation of man, by repeating "Let us make" from 1:26 instead of "I will make" in 2:18 and by echoing in 2:20 the language of likeness (1:26). The result was that readers could see a two-level hierarchy: as man is made in God's image, so woman is made in man's image. Thus, Paul could write that man "is the image and reflection of God; but woman is the reflection of man" (1 Cor. 11:7).

The Greek was not able to reproduce the neat word plays of the Hebrew. It loses, then, the use of *'adam* both for "humankind" and for "a man" (which thereby become a man's name), as well as the man being formed from *'adamah* (the ground), and the wordplay of *'ishshah* (woman) and *'ish* (man) in Genesis 2:23–24. More significantly, it translated "clings to" in 2:24 by a word that means literally "shall be joined to," leaving it open to the question: Who, then, did the joining? The anecdote in Mark 10:9 about Jesus's response to divorce has him imply that God does the joining as people have sexual intercourse. The Greek word used for "flesh" rarely carries the notion of kin, unlike the Hebrew word it translates, so that readers would have seen it much more in terms of two bodies coming together in sexual union. This is why Paul can use Genesis 2:24 to warn against becoming one flesh with a prostitute (1 Cor. 6:16).

The Greek translation also provided new possible understandings of sin in the garden. Confronted by God over her sin, Eve exclaims: "The serpent tricked me, and I ate" (Gen. 3:13). The Greek translated "tricked" by a word that can simply mean "tricked," but, unlike the Hebrew, it can also mean "seduced," including "sexually seduced." Some did read Eve's sin in those terms. Thus, Paul tells the Corinthians that he wants to present them as a pure virgin to Christ and does not want them to be seduced like Eve (2 Cor. 11:2–3; cf. 1 Tim. 2:14). It is read similarly in the Jewish apocryphal text 4 Maccabees (18:8). Such readers would see women's propensity for being seduced and seductive as warranting their subjection to male control as in Genesis 3:16, where the Greek renders "desire" by a word meaning "return" or "refuge." The Hebrew word for "desire," *teshuqah*, was so similar to the word for "return," *teshubah*, that they became interchangeable, which probably accounts for its translation by the Greek word *apostrophē*, meaning "return" (the related verb is used similarly in 3:19 of the man's return to the ground) but also "refuge." It could refer, then, to her constant returning and becoming pregnant or its effect: placed in safe keeping under her husband's control.

Age disparity at marriage, where most men were around thirty and marrying women generally half their age, reinforced the notion that women's sexual desire needed to be controlled (Loader 2013, 32–47). Younger and less experienced, such women were deemed less able to control their sexuality. Male logic usually took the next step, concluding fallaciously that women are inferior to men. The Greek version of woman's creation, noted above, fitted this widely held prejudice. Plato suggests that women were men who had failed in their former life and had been reincarnated as female. If they continued to fail, they would one day be reduced to being snakes on the ground (*Tim.* 42b, 91a). Aristotle also saw women as imperfect versions of the male (*Gen. an.* 737a28).

The author of 1 Timothy draws on Genesis 3:16 to support his instruction that women "learn in silence in full submission" and not teach or have authority over men, because Eve sinned first (2:11–15). They should keep to the security they have through bearing children and being in submission to their husbands. Paul passes on similar instruction about restricting women's leadership (1 Cor. 14:33–35), though he clearly knows that in the movement, as in wider Jewish and Greco-Roman cultures, there

were exceptions and women could often undertake significant forms of agency (1 Cor. 11:2–16; Rom. 16:1–12). The danger of women's sexuality was deemed a major factor rendering them unsuitable for leadership.

Within Jewish literature of the period, including that of the early Christian movement, we do not see women demonized, such as being blamed (as in later Gnostic thought) for the perpetuation of the physical, which trapped the divine light in human bodies. Women were God's creation, even if at a lower level than men. Women's sexuality was dangerous but not demonic. It was part of how God made men and women. Marriage was the appropriate place for sexual fulfillment as part of God's order.

Sexual intercourse was central to the bond of oneness, hence Paul's use of Genesis 2:24 about becoming one flesh to warn against being joined with prostitutes. Only Sibylline Oracles 1–2 is an outlier, as it limits the interaction between Adam and Eve simply to conversation. By contrast, the Jewish book known as Jubilees merges the creation stories, deleting the command to multiply but expanding the account of woman's creation. Adam, seeing coupling among the animals, wants this for himself. God agrees, makes woman, and brings the man to her (Jub. 3.1–7), reversing the sequence of events in Genesis 2:22 (Loader 2007, 236–48). Sexual union in companionship rather than procreation is the focus. This strongly positive account of sexual relations finds its echo in Josephus's account of creation (*Ant.* 1.27–51; Loader 2011a, 265–70), who otherwise makes procreation paramount.

Sexuality in Second Temple Literature and the New Testament

Much in biblical law pertaining to sexuality carries no moral overtones. Provisions for purification after menstruation, childbirth, and seminal emission during intercourse (Lev.

12:2–8; 15:2–30) were not about sin. Sin would be to fail to follow the appropriate procedures regarding impurity. By the first century CE, Jews became increasingly sensitive to purity issues, reflected in the abundance of immersion pools and additional scruples such as ritual washing of hands (e.g., Mark 7:1–5). Ritual purifications before entering a temple were not uniquely Jewish. Some Jews, such as the sectarian authors of the Damascus Document and Temple Scroll found in the Dead Sea caves, sought to extend sacred space beyond the temple to the whole city of Jerusalem, imposing purity requirements on all who entered and forbidding sexual relations and nakedness (usually forbidden in sacred places) in the city (11QTª/11Q19 XLV, 11–12; CD XII, 1b–2a; Loader 2009, 10–27, 166–67).

Jubilees depicts the garden of Eden as a sanctuary and adjusts the sex life of Adam and Eve accordingly. They were created and copulated before entering the garden and after leaving it but not while in it (Jub. 4.26; 8.19). Jubilees applies such abstention also to sacred times, forbidding sexual intercourse on the Sabbath (50.8; similarly, CD XI, 5; 4QDᶠ/4Q271 5 I, 1–2). Paul reflects a similar stance when, in defending marriage, he allows an exception for couples to abstain from sexual intercourse for the sake of prayer, understood as entering sacred space and time (1 Cor. 7:5).

More significantly, it appears that Paul shared with others in the emerging church the view that the age to come would be without sexual activity. Mark has Jesus declare: "When they rise from the dead, they neither marry nor are given in marriage, but are like angels in heaven" (12:25). This is not about weddings but about sexual relations. Being "like angels" reflects the view that resurrection bodies will be different but probably also that heaven's space will be holy, sacred space. Revelation depicts 144,000 people as celibate, "who have not defiled themselves [ritually, not morally] with women" (14:4), joined by thousands of others (7:4–9), who would also become celibate, reflecting the understanding expressed in Mark 12:25 that heavenly being is of a different order and the principle that nakedness and sexual relations were forbidden in sacred space. The more common Jewish understanding was that the age to come would not be sexless but would be marked by abundance and fertility (Loader 2014).

The assumption that the age to come would be sacred and sexless would have led some to decide to live now as they would then. This was true of Jesus, John the Baptist, and Paul. Since Paul also believed that Christ would soon return and the new age would soon begin, he thought it was not an ideal to have sexual relations with women and marry (1 Cor. 7:1), offering advice to the betrothed and the widowed in this light, and giving instructions about how fathers should treat daughters accordingly (7:8–9, 17–40; Loader 2012, 182–214). Some apparently went further to require that all remain celibate and so abandon their marriages. Paul found he had, therefore, to defend marriage and to assert that those who chose to marry were not sinning (1 Cor. 7:28, 36). While aware of the dangers of uncontrolled desire, Paul never deems desire demonic but urges its expression in the proper place—namely, marriage (Ellis 2007; cf. Martin 2006).

While Paul's personal choice was to remain celibate, he resisted the notion that this should apply to all (1 Cor. 7:7). Matthew, similarly, has Jesus mention that some are called to celibacy, to be in that sense eunuchs for the kingdom of God, but then the qualification is added that this was not a rule for all (19:10–12)—a qualification that clearly addresses a similar misunderstanding that Paul addressed. Jesus's saying mentions men born eunuchs (i.e., impotent) and eunuchs made so by castration. They were not without sexual feelings. Some were notoriously active with women and men. Hence Wisdom's counter: "Blessed also is the eunuch whose hands have done no lawless deed" (3:14).

Paul warns against engagement in prostitution (1 Cor. 6:12–20; Loader 2012, 166–82), including as a danger when married people lived in self-imposed celibacy (1 Cor. 7:2). Prostitution was common in the Roman world. It also was not unknown in Jewish communities, through figures such as Rahab and Tamar in Jewish Scripture. Tamar, for instance, plays that role incestuously with Judah as a lesser evil than intermarriage with men from other nations, winning her acclaim in Jewish literature (Gen. 38:12–30; see LAB 9.5–6; Loader 2011b, 264–69). Prostitutes were probably included among the "sinners" present in part as entertainment at toll collectors' men's parties. Antipas has his stepdaughter dance at his men-only party (Mark 6:21–24). Jesus's presence at such parties evoked consternation, as did his allowing himself to be a recipient of such a woman's affection (Mark 14:3–9; similarly, Luke 7:36–50). Driven to prostitution sometimes through poverty, such women (or women deemed unworthy or demon possessed, like Mary Magdalene) found their way into the Jesus movement, which, led by Jesus, refused to write them off (Luke 8:1–3).

While Roman rules for men forbad adultery with fellow citizens, they cast a blind eye to sex with slaves, prostitutes, and foreigners. In Romans 1:18–32 Paul seizes on sexual profligacy to establish common ground with those in Rome who would be listening to his letter, many of whom would be Jews or converts to Judaism, as well as Gentiles, all of whom would now embrace common Jewish abhorrence of the depravity of the wider world (Loader 2012, 293–326; Loader et al. 2016). In typically perceptive style, Paul writes not just of sins but of the psychology of distorted minds that have perverted understandings of God and therefore of themselves and their sexuality. In their senseless, darkened, unfit minds (Rom. 1:21, 28), their passions have turned to people of their own gender. Informed by Genesis 1:27, he shared his listeners' assumptions that God made humankind male and female, heterosexual (Loader 2017; 2021b, 349–77; 2022, 101–19). Anything other than that had to be perversion, unnatural, other than how God made people, just as sex with animals and the Watchers' sex with human women was sin. Their deed led to the birth of the warring giants, out of whose corpses evil spirits arose to plague humanity (1 En. 6–16; Loader 2007, 8–53). Such sexual deviance had dire consequences.

In Plato's *Symposium*, Aristophanes's etiology of sexual desire explains not only heterosexual desire, as noted above, but also gay and lesbian desire, as those sliced in half by angry Zeus have even after sought reunion: male-male, female-female (189–93). Like Plato, the Jewish author Philo, informed also by Genesis 1:27, rejects this theory (*Contempl. Life* 50–63). Plato claims (wrongly) that not even animals engage in same-sex behavior (*Leg.* 836c) and deplores it as endangering the propagation of the species through wasted and misplaced semen, grounds also for condemning male self-pleasuring (sometimes called Onanism, based on Gen. 38:9), sex with slaves and prostitutes, sexual gratification for its own sake, and contraception (*Leg.* 838e–839a). Female sexual self-pleasuring is not addressed in extant literature.

Fulfilling the biblical command to be fruitful and multiply (Gen. 1:28) allied well with the widespread emphasis on procreation. Neo-Pythagorean and some later Stoic philosophers sometimes advocated the extreme view that sex must never be for pleasure but solely for procreation (Loader 2012, 91–94). Like Plato, whose views tended in that direction (*Leg.* 783–85), Philo nevertheless concedes that sexual intimacy is still to have its place in companionship when partners have advanced beyond childbearing age (*Spec. Laws* 3.35).

As a Jew, Philo cannot deny that desire and pleasure are also God's creation, but he assigns their role to enhancing the chances of conception (*Creation* 161; Loader 2011a, 56–66), an insight now better understood as the positive effect of orgasm mobilizing sperm to reach its goal. (In the Genesis Apocryphon 2.9–10, Bitenosh attributes the conception of her resplendent child, Noah, to their experience of heightened orgasm.) One common understanding of procreation was that the man planted the seed in the woman, who nurtured it in her womb, the seed effectively seen as the egg—far from our current understanding (Aristotle, *Gen. an.* 727a29–30). Another was that both male and female produced semen, the gender of the child depending on who produced the most (Hippocrates, *Genit.* 6, followed by Plato and reflected in Sarah's producing seed in some texts of Heb. 11:11).

With high levels of infant mortality and deaths of women in childbirth (Loader 2012, 102), concern about survival of the species or the male line was not as bizarre as it may seem. It generated legends and stories of miraculous conceptions, from Sarah's conceiving in her nineties (Gen. 17:17) to Mary's conceiving as an act of divine creation as a virgin (Matt. 1:18; Luke 1:26–31). This elevated Mary's status, but only much later did people idealize virginity above motherhood and speculate that Jesus's siblings must have been only his cousins. Luke depicts Anna the prophetess as a widow who did not remarry, a *univira* (a woman of only one husband; Luke 2:36–37), but women who remarried were not deemed inferior. At most, we sometimes read of disapproval of men who went from marriage to marriage, probably for economic benefit (Ps.-Phoc. 205–6).

In Romans 1 Paul does not use the argument about procreation and wasted semen, but he does assume other common arguments. While male and female genitalia did not indicate inequality, the female genitalia were sometimes seen as the inverse version of the male genitalia (Galen, *Usu part.* 14). Inequality between the sexes rested on other assumptions and was serious. To be effeminate (*malakoi*, Paul's term in 1 Cor. 6:9 referring to passive partners, usually called *kinaidoi*) and to be penetrated was to make oneself inferior, like a woman. True manhood was to be strong, to penetrate, including by bedding other males, as Paul's term for active partners, *arsenokoitai*, indicates (Loader 2012, 326–34). Paul's Roman addressees would have given their ready consent to any condemnation of abandoning how God created males naturally to be and of the emotional excess that produced homosexual deviance. This consent would have included people in imperial circles (Brownson 2013, 157) and possibly Stoic circles (Swancutt 2004, 43, 70–72).

Like other Jews of the time, such as Philo and Pseudo-Phocylides, Paul also extends the prohibitions in Leviticus 18:22 and 20:13 of men engaging in sex with other men (especially taking the passive role) by applying them to all such activity by both men and women (Rom. 1:26–27; cf. Philo, *QG* 2.49; *Virtues* 20–21; *Heir* 274; Ps.-Phoc. 190–92). Such behavior between women was widely deplored, even in the Greco-Roman world (Brooten 1998, 29–60; Williams 1999, 233–34). Paul cites it first (Rom. 1:26, though some deny a lesbian allusion in that verse; e.g., Swancutt 2004, 63; Brownson, 2013, 207–8) and then deals with the men (1:27).

Paul's condemnation addresses not only abusive exploitation (such as same-gender pedophilia or sexual abuse of slaves) but also mutual consenting relations, men "consumed with passion for one another" (Rom. 1:27; Loader 2021a, 265–79). Jesus's stark warning that men causing little ones to stumble should be drowned with a millstone round their neck (Mark 9:42) probably referred originally to pedophilia in his community, and in Mark's context the words are used to warn believers against the same (forewarning what has recently been exposed, to the shame of many churches). Paul does not cite Sodom as an instance. The Sodomite men wanted to rape Lot's male guests, unaware they were angels (Gen. 19:4–11)—a story generalized later to depict them as sexually promiscuous and as seeking sex with men, hence the term "sodomy" for male anal penetration (Philo, *Abraham* 133–41). Such gross violation finds its echo in the terrible story of the rape of the Levite's concubine in Judges 19.

Paul's stance on same-gender relations was for his addressees uncontroversial (Loader 2018). It made sense given his assumptions and, like his views on women, has come into question primarily as people have become aware that some people are indeed born with ambiguous genitalia, intersex, and others with inner orientations not matching their outer equipment.

Works Cited

Brooten, Bernadette J. 1998. *Love between Women: Early Christian Responses to Female Homoeroticism*. Chicago: University of Chicago Press.

Brownson, James V. 2013. *Bible, Gender, Sexuality: Reframing the Church's Debate on Same-Sex Relationships*. Grand Rapids: Eerdmans.

Ellis, J. Edward. 2007. *Paul and Ancient Views of Sexual Desire: Paul's Sexual Ethics in 1 Thessalonians 4, 1 Corinthians 7 and Romans 1*. LNTS 354. London: T&T Clark.

Loader, William. 2004. *The Septuagint, Sexuality and the New Testament: Case Studies on the Impact of the LXX in Philo and the New Testament*. Grand Rapids: Eerdmans.

———. 2007. *Enoch, Levi, and Jubilees on Sexuality: Attitudes towards Sexuality in the Early Enoch Literature, the Aramaic Levi Document, and the Book of Jubilees*. Grand Rapids: Eerdmans.

———. 2009. *The Dead Sea Scrolls on Sexuality: Attitudes towards Sexuality in Sectarian and Related Literature at Qumran*. Grand Rapids: Eerdmans, 2009.

———. 2011a. *Philo, Josephus, and the Testaments on Sexuality: Attitudes towards Sexuality in the Writings of Philo, Josephus, and the Testaments of the Twelve Patriarchs*. Grand Rapids: Eerdmans.

———. 2011b. *The Pseudepigrapha on Sexuality: Attitudes towards Sexuality in Apocalypses, Testament, Legends, Wisdom, and Related Literature*. Grand Rapids: Eerdmans.

———. 2012. *The New Testament on Sexuality*. Grand Rapids: Eerdmans.

———. 2013. *Making Sense of Sex: Attitudes towards Sexuality in Early Jewish and Christian Literature*. Grand Rapids: Eerdmans.

———. 2014. "Sexuality and Eschatology: In Search of a Celibate Utopia in Pseudepigraphic Literature." *Journal for the Study of the Pseudepigrapha* 20: 43–67.

———. 2017. "Reading Romans 1 on Homosexuality in the Light of Biblical/Jewish and Greco-Roman Perspectives of Its Time." *ZNW* 108: 119–49.

———. 2018. "Homosexuality in the New Testament." Bible Odyssey. http://bibleodyssey.org/en/passages/related-articles/homosexuality-in-the-new-testament.

———. 2021a. *Jesus Left Loose Ends: Collected Essays*. Adelaide: ATF Press.

———. 2021b. *Sexuality and Gender: Collected Essays*. WUNT 458. Tübingen: Mohr Siebeck.

———. 2022. *Sex, Then and Now. Sexualities and the Bible*. Eugene, OR: Cascade Books, 2022.

Loader, William, Megan K. DeFranza, Wesley Hill, and Stephen R. Holmes. 2016. *Two Views on Homosexuality, the Bible, and the Church*. Edited by Preston Sprinkle. Counterpoints: Bible and Theology. Grand Rapids: Zondervan.

Martin, Dale B. 2006. "Paul without Passion: On Paul's Rejection of Desire in Sex and Marriage." In *Sex and the Single Savior: Gender and Sexuality in Biblical Interpretation*, 65–76. Louisville: Westminster John Knox.

Swancutt, Diana M. 2004. "Sexy Stoics and the Rereading of Romans 1.18–2.16." In *A Feminist Companion to Paul*, edited by Amy-Jill Levine with Marianne Blickenstaff, 42–73. London: T&T Clark.

Williams, Craig A. 1999. *Roman Homosexuality: Ideologies of Masculinity in Classical Antiquity*. Oxford: Oxford University Press.

57

Marriage and Divorce

Alicia D. Myers

Marriage was an assumed part of life for free/freed men and women in the New Testament world, whether they were Jewish or Gentile.[1] These familial, sexual, and economic relationships were crucial to create social continuity and stability, forming the location for producing legally acknowledged children who could inherit wealth and preserve traditions. So ubiquitous was marriage that enslaved people also had long-term monogamous relationships, even though they could not own property or produce heirs. When New Testament writers engage with the concept of marriage, they enter well-worn territory, offering interpretations of practices as well as exploiting its symbolic value as a metaphor.

---

1. This topic overlaps with others in this collection. For more information, I encourage readers to explore the chapters on women in the ancient Mediterranean world (chap. 29), masculinities (chap. 30), household structure (chap. 55), sexuality (chap. 56), widows (chap. 58), and slavery (chap. 60).

Marriage: Practices and Ideals

At the base level, marriage was an economic relationship focused on the production of heirs, legitimate children who could inherit their parents' property (Grubbs 2002, 81; Satlow 2001, 21; Loader 2013, 51–53). Roman law reflects this emphasis in designating as legitimate (*iustum matrimonium* or *iustae nuptiae*) only those marriages between free or freed Roman citizens since only they could own property to pass on to their children. Roman children were under the power (*potestas*) of their father until his death, potentially making fathers influential for marriage arrangements. Fathers, however, often died early on in a child's life since men generally married in their late twenties and started producing children only after that point. Women (and girls) married approximately ten years younger, in their late teens, and would be under the authority of a male guardian after a father's passing. Given the low life expectancy of the Roman world, Richard Saller estimates that between 20 and 30 percent of Roman men would still have a living father at the time of their marriage, while about half of women would (Saller 1987, 33; Shaw 1987, 43). Free Roman males, therefore, probably had greater freedom in choosing their partners, although mothers also had a significant say, even though their power was unrecognized in Roman law (Dixon 1988, 65–67).

Roman law dictates that all partners must agree to a marriage: the man, the woman, and the woman's father (Justinian, *Dig.* 23.3.5; Grubbs 2002, 82; Hylen 2019, 69; Ilan 1996, 84). Again, although unrecognized in law, mothers also influenced these decisions. Beginning in the late Republic, marriages *sine manu* (without hand) became the dominant practice. *Sine manu* marriages meant a woman did not shift her *potestas* from her father to her husband upon marriage (Dixon 1988, 44–47; Grubbs 2002, 20–23). This means that once a wife's father died, she functioned with a great deal more independence even though she was technically under male guardianship after her father's death (Hylen 2019, 67–68). Male guardians played largely symbolic roles, and Roman wives owned property in the form of dowries given at marriage as well as inherited wealth. Even though husbands could use dowries for investments, they had to return equivalent amounts if they divorced for reasons other than a wife's adultery. Even then, husbands returned a portion of the dowry. Roman wives, therefore, had some degree of agency and functioned as patrons, property owners, and *paterfamilia* over households after their fathers' or husbands' deaths (Hylen 2019, 69). Women in the New Testament reflect this context, reportedly owning businesses and households (Luke 10:38; Acts 12:12; 16:14; 18:2–3). Women not identified by husbands or fathers may also have had financial independence, such as Mary "the one called the Magdalene" and Susanna in Luke 8:2–3, both of whom helped to fund Jesus's ministry "from their own possessions" (my translation; see also Matt. 28:1;

Mark 15:40; 16:1; John 19:25; cf. Paul's descriptions of women coworkers in 1 Cor. 1:11; Rom. 16:1; Phil. 4:2–3).

Marriages orchestrated by the aristocracy were the most controlled by Roman law, particularly with Emperor Augustus's reforms in 18 BCE and 9 CE (Grubbs 2002, 83–87; Milnor 2005, 140–43). Issuing the *Lex Iulia et Papia Poppaea* (Laws of Julia and Papia Poppaea), Augustus sought to control whom noblemen and women married in order to retain wealth and power among the elite. Although elites disliked Augustus's intrusion into their private lives, these laws lasted until the fourth century (Tacitus, *Ann.* 3.25–28; Milnor 2005, 143–51). Augustus's legislation awarded men and women for marrying and penalized them for singleness, even if they had been widowed. Since children were the expected outcome of marriage, Augustus conveyed the status of *ius liberorum* to couples having three or four children, officially releasing women from any lingering male guardianship and allowing men to bequeath a greater portion of their wealth to wives (Grubbs 2002, 37–43; Hylen 2019, 72). The honor associated with this title is shown by its bestowal on powerful women and men even when they did not meet the requirements (Milnor 2005, 152–53).

Augustus's changes came as he ushered in Rome's imperial era (31 BCE). To smooth the transition, Augustus presented himself as the savior of traditional Roman values through legislation, building projects, and his personal life (Milnor 2005, 52–53). As the model of ideal Roman masculinity, Augustus was portrayed as the "father of the country," while his wife, Livia, came to represent marital harmony (*concordia*) and sexual purity (*pudicitia*). Rebecca Langlands traces Livia's portrayal of *pudicitia* through her dedication of a shrine to Concordia on the Capitoline Hill in Rome as well as through statues, coins, and personal appearance (Langlands 2002, 37–77; cf. Flory 1984; Milnor 2005, 53–64). *Pudicitia* was the Roman virtue and goddess of sexual morality (Langlands 2002, 31). For women, sex was confined to marriage. Men, too, ideally had sex only with their wives, though it was accepted that men also exploited enslaved people (Glancy 2006, 21–24; Hylen 2019, 79). Paul's admonitions on sexual self-control to the men of Corinth largely correspond to the ideal morals of Roman culture (1 Cor. 5–6). A woman showed self-control and *pudicitia* through modest dress (covering her body and wearing veils), the industrious pursuit of household management, and loyalty to her family even at the cost of her personal dignity (Parker 1998; Hylen 2019, 43–57; cf. 1 Cor. 11:2–16; 1 Tim. 2:8–15; 5:10–16; 1 Pet. 3:3). Not only did this display of *pudicitia* bring a wife status and influence, but it reinforced the masculine performance of her husband. Augustus's reforms effectively legitimatized married women's presence in public spaces and granted wives greater power, even as they punished those who lived outside these norms.

Men and women in lower classes often followed the model of the elites. Lower-class couples, however, had more freedom in choosing their partners since less was at stake in their alliances. For those who were connected to aristocratic families through patronage, however, approval from patrons could affect their choices. Lower-class couples often married later, men in their thirties and women in their mid-twenties (Saller 1987; Shaw 1987). Enslaved people and noncitizens likewise participated in long-term partnerships, which they termed "marriages" even though Roman law classified them separately as *contubernium* ("cohabitation"; Grubbs 2002, 143–45). Mixed marriages between non-elite Roman men and their slaves were allowed, so long as enslaved women were freed beforehand. Women slaveholders, however, were never allowed to marry either their slaves or their former slaves. Judith Evans Grubbs explains the double standard as part of the larger Roman program to enforce

male dominance. Marriage was to be between "social equals" to ensure a husband's power in the relationship (Grubbs 1993, 126–30; Hylen 2019, 73). A wife to whom a husband was beholden (e.g., for wealth, connections, or freedom) was undesirable, though Plutarch, at least, allowed for some exceptions (Nikolaidis 1997, 81).

Although noncitizens were not technically bound by Roman laws, Susan Hylen suggests that most cultures assimilated to these norms with a few notable regional differences (Hylen 2019, 76). Egyptian law, for example, permitted the marriage of siblings to keep wealth in a single family. Jews also tended to follow Greco-Roman norms but adjusted them in light of Torah, especially Genesis 1–2. Thus Jews emphasized marriage because of God's command to "be fruitful and multiply" rather than doing so necessarily out of loyalty to imperial reforms (Gen. 1:27–28; Ilan 1996, 105–7; Satlow 2001, 58–61; Loader 2013, 9–19). Jews also forbade marriages between slaves and free persons and strongly discouraged marriage to non-Jews (Satlow 2001, 133–47; Loader 2013, 81–87). Exceptions were made for Jewish men to marry women proselytes, as long as the men were not from a priestly class (Ilan 1996, 211–12; Loader 2013, 88–91). Jewish women also married Gentile men, because of both capture during war and living in a shared context. Thus, Acts reports Timothy's mother being Jewish, even though his father was a Gentile (16:1–4). Some also read 2 Corinthians 6:14–15 as Paul's preference for Christian endogamy, but the passage is unclear, and such a reading contradicts his instructions in 1 Corinthians 7:12–16 (Barton 2017).

Like the Romans, Jewish families in positions of civic power sought to retain their power by limiting marriages to one another (Ilan 1996, 69–79). Aristocratic families, such as the Hasmoneans and Herodians, arranged marriages between cousins and often uncles to nieces. Marrying nieces, however, was a hotly debated topic, with different Jewish groups coming to different conclusions on whether the practice violated incest laws from Leviticus 18 (Loader 2013, 41–42). The Pharisees argued that these marriages were permitted, while the Qumran sect forbade them. John the Baptist reflects this stricter interpretation when he condemns Herodias's marrying Herod Antipas while her former husband, Herod's half brother, was still alive (Matt. 14:1–5; Mark 6:17–18; Luke 3:18–19). John accuses her and Herod of incest and perhaps also adultery; the latter is also how Jesus presents remarriage after divorce (Matt. 5:31–32; 19:9; Luke 16:18; cf. 1 Cor. 7:10–11).

Jews, at least in theory, also maintained the practice of levirate marriage, which dictated that a brother marry his brother's childless widow to ensure the continuity of the family line (Deut. 25:5–10). The Sadducees' famous query to Jesus concerning the widow married to seven brothers reflects this tradition (Matt. 22:23–33; Mark 12:18–27; Luke 20:27–39). Scholars question how often levirate marriage was practiced in the first century, however, since it contradicted incest laws (Lev. 18:16; Ilan 1996, 153; Satlow 2001, 186–89; Weisberg 2009). When practiced, levirate marriage was probably performed for economic reasons and may have resulted in polygyny (Loader 2013, 51).

Roman and Jewish writings both portray a consistent idealization of harmonious and affectionate marriages. Roman inscriptions show praise for loving wives, such as the lengthy praise for Turia left by her grateful husband (*Laudatio Turiae* [*CIL* 6.1527, 31670, 37053]; cf. Hemelrijk 2004). The wisdom author Ben Sira likewise praises marriage to a good wife, writing, "A friend or a companion is always welcome, but a sensible wife is better than either" (Sir. 40:23). Plutarch also advises couples to live in harmony, having "all things in common," including property and children, but also sharing meals, friendships, and laughter (*Conj. praec.* 29.142a–b; 34.143a). Although women were consistently deemed inferior in

Roman and Jewish contexts, husbands were not to be domineering or violent toward wives and children. Similar to advice in New Testament household codes, Plutarch admonishes a husband to "control" a wife by considering her feelings rather than through force (*Conj. praec.* 331.142e; cf. Eph. 5:25–31; Col. 3:19). While violent and tragic marriages certainly existed in the first century (as they do today), the ideal was a peaceful marriage that brought joy and fulfillment to both partners and their families (Ilan 1996, 57–60; Hylen 2019, 73–76; cf. Satlow 2001, 237–48).

Divisions: Infertility, Adultery, and Divorce

Although marrying only once was praised, divorces were expected in Roman society in cases of infertility, adultery, and incompatibility. Rabbis encouraged divorce for couples not having children after ten years, and Augustus's legislation penalized childless couples. While couples did divorce due to infertility, those who remained together could be praised for their devotion and affection for one another (Ilan 1996, 111–14; Grubbs 2002, 188–89; cf. Luke 1:5–7).

Adultery, however, was a different matter. Augustus's reforms required husbands to divorce unfaithful wives or else be charged as pimps (Grubbs 2002, 84; Hylen 2019, 81). Laws against adultery reached back to the beginnings of the Roman Republic, where adultery (*adulterum*) was defined as a man (i.e., free, male citizen) having sex with another man's wife. The seduction of a virgin or child was prosecuted as *stuprum* rather than adultery, regardless of the man's marital status; any woman having illicit sex was also guilty of *stuprum* (Grubbs 2002, 19, 84). When Augustus issued the *Lex Iulia de adulteriis coercendis*, he reinforced these definitions and required that unfaithful wives be divorced to prevent confusion over inheritance. Both men and women could potentially suffer death for their crime, but most were divorced and perhaps exiled instead (Tacitus, *Ann.* 2.85). While wives could not accuse husbands of adultery in court, they could divorce them for their impropriety (Grubbs 2002, 63, 84).

Jewish laws regarding adultery were similar. As with Roman moralistic literature, Jewish sources issued warnings against the wicked wife, which focused on her unfaithfulness and deception (Ilan 1996, 60–62). Such perceptions are also seen in developing interpretations of Genesis 3, where Eve comes to take on the blame for human sin in a manner similar to Hesiod's Pandora (Myers 2017, 24–30). Numbers 5 records the "test of bitter waters" for husbands to use to expose a suspected wife. Traveling to the temple and witnessed by a priest, the wife was to drink water that had been tainted with dirt from the grounds. If she died immediately (or even sometime later in an unexpected way), God had judged her as guilty; if she lived, she was innocent. Rabbinic reflections on these practices were written after the destruction of the temple in 70 CE, leading to doubts about whether these tests were carried out in the Second Temple period (Ilan 1996, 135–41). If, however, a wife was caught in adultery or a husband had irrevocable proof, Jewish men were expected to divorce.[2] Jesus's admonition allowing husbands and wives to divorce in the case of adultery in Matthew 19:9, therefore, reflects cultural practices (Loader 2013). Similar disdain for adultery surfaces in uses of the marriage metaphor throughout the New Testament, as discussed below (cf. Heb. 13:4).

Unlike his larger context, however, Jesus's instructions limit divorce to situations of adultery only. William Loader (2013, 71) argues that divorce after adultery was mandated and ubiquitous in the first century, and as such, it should be assumed in all of Jesus's teaching, including in Mark 10:11–12, where he seems

to outlaw divorce altogether. If Mark's record is accurate, however, Jesus's teaching against all divorce contrasts Roman and Jewish norms that emphasized producing children with clear paternity. Jesus himself was the child of debated paternity, which Mark also does not address. The addition of birth narratives in Matthew and Luke clarifies Jesus's origins, showing divine paternity and thus freeing Mary from accusations of unchastity (Loader 2013, 45). The fact that debate continued, however, is reflected in John 8:41 when the crowd implies Jesus is the child of "fornication" (*porneia*). *Porneia* is a broad word, but it refers generally to any unsanctioned sexual activity and makes its way onto many vice lists in the New Testament (Acts 15:20; Gal. 5:19; Eph. 5:3; Col. 3:5; 1 Thess. 4:3).

Jesus's teaching on marriage, as well as his own singleness, reflects his controversial disinterest in believers' creation and maintenance of households. Rather than having households with children, believers were to be "children" in God's kingdom by trusting God as their Father and letting go of worldly affairs (Osiek and Balch 1997, 132–33; Myers 2017, 70–74; Knust 2019, 524–28). Paul echoes this teaching in 1 Corinthians 7:25–40, and it is further developed in apocryphal Acts, which portray sex and children as distracting for those truly committed to Christ (Acts of Paul and Thecla; Acts Thom. 12, 13; Acts Andr. 14–16; Myers 2017, 134–44). Most believers, however, continued to marry and have children, since both were culturally expected and often desirable. Moreover, without the conversion of a father or guardian, a woman would have little say in preventing her marriage for the sake of her family. Paul acknowledges this reality in 1 Corinthians 7, even though he sees marriage as a lesser lifestyle. Paul similarly does not encourage divorce, but he allows it if an unbelieving partner chooses to depart (7:10–16) and perhaps in cases of adultery (Loader 2013, 75–77). Like 1 Peter, Paul sees marriage as an avenue for converting an unbelieving spouse

---

2. Jesus's mercy for the woman caught in adultery in John 7:53–8:11 is unusual, but it could reflect a concern also voiced by later rabbis that men should be punished alongside women (cf. Ilan 1996, 138).

and household (1 Cor. 7:12–16; 1 Pet. 3:1–2; cf. Barton 2017).

No part of the New Testament permits divorce for reasons of political intrigue and power. Jesus also forbids remarriage after divorce (Matt. 19:9; Mark 10:11–12; cf. 1 Cor. 7:15, 39–40; Knust 2019, 523–24). Yet among aristocratic Romans, divorce and remarriage were relatively common tools for creating and dissolving alliances. Both Augustus and Livia had multiple marriages before their coupling, and such facts did not prevent their representing Roman ideals of family and marriage. Tal Ilan (1996, 147) argues that divorce, other than for adultery, was often too expensive for most Jews since it required a wife's dowry either to be returned or to be sacrificed to a divorced husband. Rabbis, however, assumed divorce (Satlow 2001, 183), and Hylen (2019, 80) suggests divorces were largely left unrecorded since no official documentation was required. Women as well as men could initiate divorces, though it was more socially acceptable for men to do so (Grubbs 2002, 187; Hylen 2019, 81; cf. Ilan 1996, 145–47); women's fathers could also initiate divorces until the middle of the second century (Grubbs 2002, 196).

Marriage as a Metaphor in the New Testament

Since marriage was such an important, and often assumed, part of people's lives in the Roman world, it is not surprising that the New Testament and early Christian writings use marriage as a metaphor to describe fidelity, reconciliation, and even salvation (Solevåg 2013; Knust 2019, 530–32). The marriage metaphor in the New Testament and Christian literature is rooted primarily in Jewish traditions, though they also correspond to Roman ideals. Marriage, adultery, divorce, and remarriage were common images used in the prophetic books of the Old Testament, most notably Isaiah, Jeremiah, Ezekiel, and Hosea (Weems 1995; Satlow 2001, 42–50). As in the prophetic books, New Testament authors use the marriage metaphor to chastise unfaithful audiences, especially when they are tempted by idols or alternative teachings. In Matthew and Mark, Jesus accuses people of being part of an "adulterous generation" to emphasize their unfaithfulness to God, which inhibited their ability to accept Jesus as God's Messiah (Matt. 12:38–39; 16:1–4; Mark 7:17–23; 8:34–9:1). Paul describes the Corinthians as Jesus's promised "bride," whom Paul is to present as "spotless" to her groom. He fears their return to old practices, perhaps including idolatry, risks tainting their reputation as well as their future marriage (2 Cor. 11:1–5). Revelation, however, presents the heavenly Jerusalem as Jesus's bride rather than the believers themselves (Rev. 19:6–10; 21:1–22:7).

Implicit in these descriptions is a presentation of marriage as salvation. Paul makes the connection explicit in Romans 7:1–3, explaining the Romans' freedom from previous laws now that Christ died and was resurrected. Ephesians develops the metaphor further by blending a discussion of household rules with an explanation of Jesus's relationship with the church, his bride (5:25–33). According to Ephesians, husbands imitate Christ in sacrificing themselves to love their wives, while wives remain submissive, which conforms with general Roman-era expectations (Myers 2017, 130–34; cf. Col. 3:18; Titus 2:4–5; 1 Pet. 3:1). First Timothy 2:8–15 similarly presents marriage, and especially its expected outcome of childbirth, as salvific for women (Solevåg 2013, 96–100; Myers 2017, 124–30). Unlike the Gospels and earlier Pauline teaching, 1 Timothy and Titus encourage marriage and restrict church leadership to those married only once (1 Tim. 3:1–2, 11; Titus 1:6; cf. Lee 2021, 128–29). First Timothy 4:1–5 goes so far as to say that those teaching against marriage are false prophets. Paul perhaps faced similar controversy in Corinth since he defends marriage as appropriate for believers, even if it is not the highest good (1 Cor. 7:1–7). Marriage, according to Paul, helps believers maintain the self-control that befits followers of Christ by limiting sexual expression to marriage. The conflict between 1 Timothy and Titus with Paul's earlier writings is one reason why many scholars believe these letters were written by later disciples rather than Paul himself.

Conclusion

As the above overview shows, marriage was a common but complicated part of the New Testament world. Overall, New Testament authors reflect general Roman practices informed by and adapted through Torah interpretations. Jesus participated in debates about marriage and divorce from his time period, taking a more extreme position against divorce than most of his contemporaries while also expressing the ubiquitous condemnation of adultery. Christians continued to struggle with questions about marriage long after, and later Pauline tradition shows a development of thought toward more positive conclusions. Nevertheless, that later apocryphal works still idealize virginity and sexless marriages shows that Christians took different sides on the issue. All these works, however, continue to condemn adultery and sex outside of marriage. By picturing believers as the bride of Christ, Christian authors feminize believers to encourage obedience. Whether, and how, this metaphor is helpful for contemporary believers remains up for debate.

Works Cited

Barton, Stephen C. 2017. "Sanctification and Oneness in 1 Corinthians with Implications for the Case of 'Mixed Marriages' (1 Cor. 7.12–16)." *NTS* 63: 38–55.

Dixon, Suzanne. 1988. *The Roman Mother*. Norman: University of Oklahoma Press.

Flory, Marleen Boudreau. 1984. "*Sic Exempla Parantur*: Livia's Shrine to Concordia in the Porticus Liviae." *Historia* 33: 309–30.

Glancy, Jennifer A. 2006. *Slavery in Early Christianity*. Minneapolis: Fortress.

Grubbs, Judith Evans. 1993. "'Marriage More Shameful Than Adultery': Slave-Mistress Relationships, 'Mixed Marriages,' and Late Roman Law." *Phoenix* 47: 125–54.

———. 2002. *Women and the Law in the Roman Empire: A Sourcebook on Marriage, Divorce, and Widowhood*. Routledge Sourcebooks for the Ancient World. London: Routledge.

Hemelrijk, Emily A. 2004. "Masculinity and Femininity in the 'Laudatio Turiae.'" *Classical Quarterly* 54: 185–97.

Hylen, Susan E. 2019. *Women in the New Testament World*. Essentials of Biblical Studies. Oxford: Oxford University Press.

Ilan, Tal. 1996. *Jewish Women in Greco-Roman Palestine*. Peabody, MA: Hendrickson.

Knust, Jennifer W. 2019. "Marriage, Adultery and Divorce." In *The Oxford Handbook of New Testament, Gender, and Sexuality*, edited by Benjamin H. Dunning, 521–38. Oxford: Oxford University Press.

Langlands, Rebecca. 2002. *Sexual Morality in Ancient Rome*. Cambridge: Cambridge University Press.

Lee, Dorothy A. 2021. *The Ministry of Women in the New Testament: Reclaiming the Biblical Vision for Church Leadership*. Grand Rapids: Baker Academic.

Loader, William G. 2013. *Making Sense of Sex: Attitudes towards Sexuality in Early Jewish and Christian Literature*. Grand Rapids: Eerdmans.

Milnor, Kristina. 2005. *Gender, Domesticity, and the Age of Augustus: Inventing Private Life*. Oxford Studies in Classical Literature and Gender Theory. Oxford: Oxford University Press.

Myers, Alicia D. 2017. *Blessed among Women? Mothers and Motherhood in the New Testament*. Oxford: Oxford University Press.

Nikolaidis, Anastasios G. 1997. "Plutarch on Women and Marriage." *Wiener Studien: Zeitschrift für Klassische Philologie und Patristik* 110: 27–88.

Osiek, Carolyn, and David L. Balch. 1997. *Families in the New Testament World: Households and House Churches*. The Family, Religion, and Culture. Louisville: Westminster John Knox.

Parker, Holt N. 1998. "Loyal Slaves and Loyal Wives: The Crisis of the Outsider-Within and Roman *Exemplum* Literature." In *Women and Slaves in Greco-Roman Culture: Differential Equations*, edited by Sandra R. Joshel and Sheila Murnaghan, 152–73. London: Routledge.

Saller, Richard P. 1987. "Men's Age at Marriage and Its Consequences in the Roman Family." *CP* 82: 21–34.

Satlow, Michael L. 2001. *Jewish Marriage in Antiquity*. Princeton: Princeton University Press.

Shaw, Brent D. 1987. "The Age of Roman Girls at Marriage: Some Reconsiderations." *JRS* 77: 30–46.

Solevåg, Anna Rebecca. 2013. *Birthing Salvation: Gender and Class in Early Christian Childbearing Discourse*. BibInt 121. Leiden: Brill.

Weems, Renita J. 1995. *Battered Love: Marriage, Sex, and Violence in the Hebrew Prophets*. Overtures to Biblical Theology. Minneapolis: Fortress.

Weisberg, Dvora E. 2009. *Levirate Marriage and the Family in Ancient Judaism*. Waltham, MA: Brandeis University Press.

58

Widows

Timothy J. Murray

There are two reasons why it is important for any student of the New Testament to know about widowhood in the first century CE. The most obvious is that widows appear frequently in the New Testament; we encounter them at least once in every major group of writings (the Gospels; Acts; the Pauline, Pastoral, and Catholic Epistles; and Revelation). The second reason is that widows were so numerous that they must be accounted for in our historical imagination if we want to understand the social context in which the New Testament was written.

Sources

The most important sources pertaining to widowhood in our period can be organized into three groups. First, we have the demographic evidence provided by epigraphic sources (from across the Mediterranean) and census returns (from Roman Egypt), which have informed us about birth, death, and divorce rates and the ages at which people married. These are particularly important for estimating the num-

ber of widows in society and reconstructing generalized life cycles for women. The second group of evidence is legal material, whether that be Roman law (largely preserved in Justinian's *Digest*), surviving legal documents (e.g., the Babatha archive), or other law codes from the ancient world. These help us understand the legal and economic consequences of widowhood but also illuminate what the main social concerns surrounding widowhood were for society in general. Finally, we have a range of literary sources, from personal letters to philosophical treatises, which inform us about how widows were thought of and portrayed in the first century and what (if any) moral assumptions existed as to how widows should be treated.

When working with these sources, it is important to remember that most of the legal and literary documents we have were written by, and primarily concern, the wealthy strata of society. This leaves us in the inescapable situation of being able to say considerably more about widowhood for the elite (or, at least, those who owned significant property) than widowhood for the non-elite (or the unpropertied), despite the latter group far outnumbering the former. For ordinary widows we necessarily have to work with inference and supposition for the relative lack of direct evidence. As we shall see, it is likely that the experience of widowhood was considerably different depending on the social and economic status of the woman concerned.

The Number of Widows in Society

In 1994, a major study by Jens-Uwe Krause estimated that approximately 30 percent of the female population in the ancient world were probably widows (Krause 1994, 1:73). This figure has achieved widespread acceptance as being a reasonable estimate that is applicable across the Roman Mediterranean (Bagnall and Frier 1994, 170–73), although it seems likely that the rate would be a bit lower among elite women (McGinn 1999, 623–25). The high number of widows is primarily explained by mortality rates and the average age at which people married.

The overwhelming majority of freeborn women would have been married (Saller 2007, 91), usually to an older man; the average age gap was around ten years, perhaps reducing to seven among the elite. Mortality rates were high, so this age differential meant most marriages lasted less than twenty years (Krause 1994, 1:73), and much of the time husbands predeceased their wives. There were likely to be not only many widows, then, but many *young* widows who were still of childbearing age, making remarriage both common and complex, as we shall discuss. Marriages were not always ended by the death of a spouse; divorce was also a relatively common phenomenon and could place the woman in similar social and legal circumstances. Either way, the fragmentation of the family created considerable numbers of both widows and orphans: "In a context of high mortality, women who lived

through their child-bearing years must have had on average five or six children in order to maintain the population. A plausible guess is that one-third to one-half of those children survived to age ten, and those surviving ten-year-olds could expect on average an additional 35 or 40 years of life" (Saller 2007, 91).

Demographic modeling suggests that only approximately 20 percent of children would have reached adulthood with both parents still living (Saller 2007, 91). This leads us to one final demographic point: most women had lost their fathers by the age of twenty (McGinn 2008, 26–27), meaning that significant numbers of widows would be without husband, father, or adult children.

The Vulnerability of Most Widows

It is perhaps easy for those of us living in societies with a responsive police force to overlook the sheer physical dangers to widows who were without the protection of a husband. For some, strong social networks with neighbors and extended family embedded them in a close-knit community that would have offered them considerable protection, but those who were more socially isolated and/or managing their own small households must have been far more insecure. In fact, we may say that the degree to which any particular widow was vulnerable depended a great deal on her networks and socioeconomic status; for the majority, the most important factor would be whether she had another household to which she could belong following the end of her marriage.

Most of our evidence pertains to the legal and economic vulnerabilities of widowhood. To understand the position of widows, it is crucial to know that Roman law of this period dictated that when a couple married their possessions were not mutually owned but were kept (legally) strictly separate. If a married man died, it was his children who tended to inherit his property and wealth, rather than his wife. If she was to inherit anything substantial, it would most likely be from her father, not from her husband. Furthermore, the husband was under no legal obligation to provide for his wife out of his own resources; for this reason, a dowry might be provided at marriage by the woman's father (which would become her property when her father died). The legal principle was that the dowry came under the control of the husband (providing the resources from which he would support his wife) but remained the property of the wife.

The situation of a widow upon the death of her husband was, therefore, that she usually had no legal claim to her husband's possessions other than the return of her dowry. If the dowry was adequate, then it might offer substantial protection from destitution and good prospects for remarriage, but a poorer widow without a dowry, or with only a small one, faced ruin. Her prospects depended on a number of factors.

If she had children with her deceased husband, then they usually stood to inherit from his property. If they were preadult, then she would be required to get a male tutor to manage their inheritance until they came of age. This might provide her with greater security for her household, as it would generally be recognized that the mother was the best person to care for such children. If her father was still alive, then she might well return to his household before seeking remarriage; if she had adult children, then one of her sons would be expected to care for her in his household. If, however, her father was dead and her children were not yet of age, then she might have no alternative household to return to, leaving her either to lead a household herself or, if they were willing, to live within her deceased husband's family. Given her legal position, this latter option would depend on the quality of relationships with her in-laws and their willingness to take responsibility for her. It is easy to imagine how important age was in

such circumstances—widows who were young enough to bear children may well have caused a level of anxiety due to their sexual availability, but on the other hand they may have been physically able to contribute to the labor of the household. In contrast, older widows were less of a risk but also a greater drain on resources. Such widows faced the "double marginality" of old age and gender (Parkin 2003, 246). Widows compelled to lead their own household would face severe difficulty as they had very few options for generating any income. Those with skill in a trade, few young children, and some meaningful social connections would perhaps have had the best chances. But even if a widow was capable of productive work, this was no guarantee of sufficient income, especially if she had numerous dependents or her vulnerable position was exploited by others. No doubt widows in these kind of situations were most at risk of being forced into prostitution (McGinn 2004, 70).

Finally, we should also note the social vulnerability of widows. If they had no adult male to act on their behalf, widows would have had to do more in public than was normal for women at the time. One example would be taking legal action: although women could represent themselves in court (Grubbs 2002, 270), this was usually done only if there was no male relative to do so for them, and they faced greater restrictions than men. Engagement in trade or with public officials may have been necessary but could raise suspicions about their propriety and leave them open to abuse.

It should be clear that for those with few resources, who stood to inherit little, widowhood could well deprive a woman of the means of subsistence. If she had a household to which she could belong (a father or an adult son), then she may have been saved from the worst suffering, her prospects becoming aligned with the rest of the household. If she did not, she was left remarkably vulnerable, and most widows must have faced severe hardship. No wonder that those with prospects of remarriage usually sought to do so.

The Opportunities for Some Widows

For the relatively few women who had substantial resources, widowhood may not have placed them at risk of much suffering but rather increased their independence and presented them with opportunities. The typical scenario would be where a woman had inherited significant wealth from her father. Upon widowhood, she would be legally independent (under the authority of neither father nor husband) and self-sufficient. If she was also the primary beneficiary of her husband's will, then she might wield great wealth and social influence (Dixon 1988, 66). If she did have children, she might control the inheritance and thus secure power over them while she lived.

Some have suggested that the improved sociolegal position of wealthy women in the first century contributed to a cultural movement of "new women" who used their autonomy to pursue a vigorous social life in ways that contrasted with traditional values—for example, by being more present in public life or by nonmarital sexual relationships (Fantham et al. 1994, 280–93; Winter 2003, 15–38). Although the "new woman" is perhaps best understood as a literary construction rather than a historical reality (Murray 2018, 215–17), we have plenty of evidence showing elite women commanding significant wealth in this period, and in such cases widows may have preferred not to remarry. The resultant lack of children became a big enough problem among the Roman elite that it likely lay behind Augustan marriage legislation that incentivized remarriage and childbearing (Grubbs 2002, 83–84).

Remarriage

Evidence from Roman Egypt suggests that remarriage was common (Huebner 2013, 97–106; Rathbone 2006, 101–5), which is no surprise given that remarriage provided the best chance of security for most widows, both in the present (by the provision of a husband) and in the future (by the support of her children). Young widows with a dowry presumably found it easiest to remarry, as they could conceive children and contribute labor to the household; widows past childbearing age would rarely have been able to remarry.

Remarriage may have been necessary for many, but it could be complex. If a widow had children, she may often have had to leave them in her deceased husband's household when she remarried, creating emotional suffering and complex webs of obligation. This is reflected in the two major legal concerns about remarriage: the dowry and inheritance. Roman jurists developed detailed provisions to ensure that property was maintained by the correct parties. Particular attention was given to ensuring that children from the first marriage inherited appropriately from their deceased father's estate rather than seeing his property subsumed into the household of the second marriage.

As discussed above, self-sufficient women may have chosen not to remarry, which presented both a demographic and a cultural concern. Given high mortality rates, it was important that women who could bear children did so. The fear that the Roman senatorial class was not reproducing itself led Augustus to pass a series of laws (the *Lex Iulia et Papia Poppaea*) that penalized those of childbearing age who refused to remarry and rewarded those who had more than three children. Remarriage was expected within two years but not before ten months after the death of the husband (to ensure clarity about the paternity of any child). Culturally, the decision not to remarry was sometimes seen as undermining the stability of the household and challenging the traditional roles of women, which were largely domestic. This context helps us understand the various ways widows were spoken about in our period, as we shall see.

Care for Widows

The vulnerability of widows in the ancient world is perhaps best evidenced by the range of sources expressing concern for their well-being. Across the ancient Near East, gods and kings claimed to be particularly concerned that widows receive justice (Stol 2016, 275–78; Galpaz-Feller 2008). Among these sources are the Jewish ones, in particular the biblical laws that wrestle with two major issues: the provision of subsistence to poor widows and levirate marriage, which sought to maintain the woman in her deceased husband's family (Adams 2014, 51–58). It is difficult to say whether this heritage found any concrete expression in the care of widows by Jewish communities in the first century, but it is perhaps unlikely (Murray 2018, 90–135). Laws protecting the rights of widows are also found in some of the Greek tradition (Cudjoe 2010).

In the Roman world there was no "public" provision for widows. There were no social security systems of any kind, and benefactions by wealthy individuals were not for the relief of the poor. Nor was there any legal requirement for relatives to care for widows before the second century CE. Protection for widows was primarily found in the widespread cultural expectation that just as parents care for their children when they are growing up, so children should care for their parents when they are old. This reciprocity was one of the fundamental moral expectations across Greco-Roman culture and was part of what was encompassed by the Greek virtue *eusebeia* and its Roman equivalent *pietas* (Murray 2018, 33–55, 204). Adult children were expected to take on the care of their elderly parents, and to refuse to do so would have been disgraceful. Nonetheless, before the second century this was a matter of social and moral pressure rather than legal

obligation. The only time a person was legally required to provide for a widow was when they controlled her dowry.

Care for widows was thus a private matter that was expected of children. Whether a widow would receive any help depended, therefore, on whether her children survived, whether they had the means to help her, and whether she had succeeded at impressing on them the obligations of reciprocity.

Widows Portrayed

Widows regularly served as an archetypal example of poverty and insecurity, but their representation in literary sources could extend beyond this to either vilification or praise. Positive portrayals of widows focused on their virtue, diligence, social propriety, sexual purity, and religious piety. The sexual ideal was embodied by the *univira* (*monandros* in Greek)—a woman who had only had sex with her husband and remained unmarried after he died, forever devoted to his memory and the upbringing of his children. As we have seen, this was a choice available only for self-sufficient women, but the image of the virtuous older widow served as a literary model for "good" widows.

Negative portrayals broadly tend in two directions. First we have the figure of the *anus ebria*, the old drunken woman, portrayed not just in literary sources but also in sculpture; although a literary stereotype, it likely reflects something of the social reality (Hemelrijk 2016, 901). Second, younger widows in particular could be portrayed as socially disruptive and sexually dangerous. Such characterizations are often polemical and usually, but not exclusively, concern wealthy widows (for further discussion, see McGinn 2008, 30–34).

Historical Complexities

There are three complexities that must be particularly borne in mind when thinking about widowhood in our period. First, a significant amount of our understanding is informed by Roman legal sources, but it is not clear how relevant this law was for the majority of people. Although Roman law was egalitarian in principle, there are questions about its accessibility (who could afford access to legal process), its enforceability, and its applicability to those spread across the empire who were not Roman citizens (for references, see Murray 2018, 48–51). For example, the collection of documents that has come to be known as the Babatha archive shows a variety of different legal processes being used by the same woman (see Czajkowski 2017; Esler 2017).

Second, we have little way of knowing the extent of regional or ethnic variations in both legal and cultural practices regarding widows. There are some things we can be more confident about (e.g., the moral virtue of supporting parents in old age was common), but others less so (e.g., the importance and function of the dowry).

Finally, as Christianity developed we see the appearance of "virgins who are called widows" (Ign. *Smyrn.* 13.1), which should caution us not to assume too quickly that a "widow" is actually a widow in Christian sources from the end of the second century onward.

Issues Emerging in the New Testament

We will conclude this chapter by briefly indicating where some of our discussion may begin to inform the study of the New Testament. First, we see widows portrayed as poor or facing injustice, or the moral imperative to care for such women (Mark 12:42–43; Luke 7:12; 18:3–5; Acts 6:1; James 1:27). We also find the pious widow Anna at the temple (Luke 2:36–37) and widows especially gathered to mourn, a religious and social function (Acts 9:39, 41).

Particularly interesting is 1 Timothy 5:3–16, where the author addresses a problem concerning widows at some length. Reconstructions

vary (see Murray 2018, 196–222), but the passage touches on many issues we have explored in this chapter: discussion about the moral obligation for children to support their parents (including the language / verbal form of *eusebeia*); a positive portrayal of virtuous older widows who qualify for support; a negative portrayal of younger widows who refuse to remarry; and, above all, clear concern for the right ordering of households and the proper allocation of resources (Barclay 2020).

Works Cited

Adams, Samuel L. 2014. *Social and Economic Life in Second Temple Judea*. Louisville: Westminster John Knox.

Bagnall, Roger S., and Bruce W. Frier. 1994. *The Demography of Roman Egypt*. Cambridge: Cambridge University Press.

Barclay, John M. G. 2020. "Household Networks and Early Christian Economics: A Fresh Study of 1 Timothy 5.3–16." *NTS* 66: 268–87.

Cudjoe, Richard V. 2010. *The Social and Legal Position of Widows and Orphans in Classical Athens*. Athens: Centre for Ancient Greek and Hellenistic Law.

Czajkowski, Kimberly. 2017. *Localized Law: The Babatha and Salome Komaise Archives*. Oxford: Oxford University Press.

Dixon, Suzanne. 1988. *The Roman Mother*. London: Croom Helm.

Esler, Philip F. 2017. *Babatha's Orchard: The Yadin Papyri and an Ancient Jewish Family Tale Retold*. Oxford: Oxford University Press.

Fantham, Elaine, H. P. Foley, N. B. Kampen, S. B. Pomeroy, and H. A. Shapiro, eds. 1994. *Women in the Classical World: Image and Text*. Oxford: Oxford University Press.

Galpaz-Feller, Pnina. 2008. "The Widow in the Bible and in Ancient Egypt." *ZAW* 120, no. 2: 231–53.

Grubbs, Judith Evans. 2002. *Women and the Law in the Roman Empire: A Sourcebook on Marriage, Divorce and Widowhood*. London: Routledge.

Hemelrijk, Emily. 2016. "Women's Daily Life in the Roman West." In *Women in Antiquity: Real Women across the Ancient World*, edited by Stephanie Lynn Budin and Jean MacIntosh Turfa, 895–904. London: Routledge.

Huebner, Sabine R. 2013. *The Family in Roman Egypt: A Comparative Approach to Intergenerational Solidarity and Conflict*. Cambridge: Cambridge University Press.

Krause, Jens-Uwe. 1994. *Witwen und Waisen im Römischen Reich*. 4 vols. Stuttgart: F. Steiner.

McGinn, Thomas A. J. 1999. "Widows, Orphans, and Social History." *JRA* 12: 617–32.

———. 2004. *The Economy of Prostitution in the Roman World: A Study of Social History and the Brothel*. Ann Arbor: University of Michigan Press.

———. 2008. *Widows and Patriarchy: Ancient and Modern*. London: Duckworth.

Murray, Timothy J. 2018. *Restricted Generosity in the New Testament*. WUNT 2/480. Tübingen: Mohr Siebeck.

Parkin, Tim G. 2003. *Old Age in the Roman World: A Cultural and Social History*. Baltimore: Johns Hopkins University Press.

Rathbone, Dominic. 2006. "Poverty and Population in Roman Egypt." In *Poverty in the Roman World*, edited by Margaret Atkins and Robin Osborne, 100–114. Cambridge: Cambridge University Press.

Saller, Richard P. 2007. "Household and Gender." In *The Cambridge Economic History of the Greco-Roman World*, edited by Walter Scheidel, Ian Morris, and Richard P. Saller, 87–112. Cambridge: Cambridge University Press.

Stol, Marten. 2016. *Women in the Ancient Near East*. Translated by Helen and Mervyn Richardson. Berlin: de Gruyter.

Winter, Bruce W. 2003. *Roman Wives, Roman Widows: The Appearance of New Women and the Pauline Communities*. Grand Rapids: Eerdmans.

59

Household Worship

CAROLINE JOHNSON HODGE

A family gathers around a stone altar in the courtyard attached to their house. They have each stopped their work for a few moments, on this Kalends day (the first day of the month), to honor the gods of the household. They bring offerings of incense and cakes to place on the altar, parents and children both reciting prayers to the deities that watch over their health and their livelihoods.

A woman in her eighth month of pregnancy passes through the reception area of her house. She pauses at a niche in the wall and reaches out to touch a bronze figurine of Aphrodite, the deity who protects women in childbirth. This gesture, which she repeats daily now, serves as her petition to the goddess for a healthy delivery and her own survival of the birth.

An enslaved man steps out of the bakery where he works, headed on an errand for his owner. On the busy street corner he stops at a small niche in the wall dedicated to Silvanus. Here he leaves a few kernels of grain, whispers a quick prayer, and continues on his way.

All of these scenes (which are historically imagined, based on literary and material evidence)

represent household worship in the Roman period. These rituals reflect the widespread beliefs of people living at this time that myriad powerful beings could influence life for good or for ill; therefore, it was critical to supplicate and thank the gods for their gifts related to all facets of life, including food, health, work, and reproduction.

In cities and towns around the Roman Empire, similar interactions with the gods took place in public squares, in civic ceremonies that were organized and supervised by officials with some degree of political power. These might include public sacrifices to the deities that belonged to that particular city, preceded by processions and followed by a shared meal.

More commonly, interactions with the divine occurred in smaller spaces, with fewer people, and incorporated gestures or speech into the activities of daily life, such as in the scenes sketched above. This was household worship in the Roman period, a pervasive, adaptive, and practical collection of actions intended to supplicate the gods and other powerful beings regarding daily life concerns.

Although it shared some characteristics with civic cult (similar understandings of the gods and similar rituals, for example), domestic cult was characterized by several features that set it apart.

Features of Household Worship

One of the most common traits of household worship was its variability. This is a critical starting point for understanding household worship: it defies simple definition. A study of the literary and material evidence for household worship in this period makes clear that there was no doctrine or uniform practice for domestic rites. Instead, it seems that households improvised their own worship, depending on their particular needs and activities (Bodel 2008, 260–62). Assemblages of statuettes found in different locations suggest this: the assortment of deities honored differs from place to place, from house to house. Similarly, there could be different groups of worshipers, or perhaps individuals within a household, who might adapt their worship practices to their space or responsibilities, such as slaves in the kitchen, or the pregnant woman imagined above (Foss 1997, 218; George 1997; Bodel 2008, 265).

A second feature of household worship is its integration into daily life. Although there were special occasions such as the Kalends or other holidays, quotidian activities also occasioned interactions with deities. For example, the gods were honored when lamps were lit at the end of the day or when a small libation was poured at the beginning of a meal. Simply entering and exiting the house could be accompanied by a gesture asking for protection or luck (Frankfurter 1998, 132). Thus household rituals, unlike official, civic rites, could be performed by many members of the household, including not only the head of the household but also subordinates such as women, enslaved people, and children.

A third feature of household worship is that it was not necessarily confined to the concrete borders of the house; we find evidence of these devotions in other contexts as well, such as tombs, neighborhood shrines, and shops. Indeed, we might conceive of Roman-period domestic religion as a "cluster of concerns and orientations" related to family and household rather than as rituals that necessarily take place in a particular space (Frankfurter 2017, 7). These concerns might relate to familial continuity, production of goods (including food), marriage, protection, and so on. A good example of household worship extending beyond the physical confines of the house is caring for the dead. Mortuary rituals often began in the household itself with preparation of the body, then proceeded to a tomb for burial, and then continued in the following days, months, and years as household members honored the deceased family member at regular intervals (Toynbee 1971, 43–50). The tomb became the site of family gatherings, offerings, and meals, as though it was an extension of the household.

A final feature of household worship is that it is implicated in power dynamics, both those internal to the household and those related to wider society. Within a given household unit, ritual activity was shaped by hierarchical relationships: as humans honored the divine, subordinate household members in particular also honored the head of the household. Indeed, belonging to a household as a wife, child, slave, or dependent meant obedience and loyalty to the gods of the master/father/husband (Johnson Hodge 2010, 7). This expectation could potentially create tension because wives and slaves especially were responsible for enacting household rituals. Recognizing how this might destabilize power relationships, Cato warns slaves not to initiate their own rituals but only to do so at the request of the master (*Agr.* 143.1); likewise, Plutarch admonishes a wife to worship only her husband's gods and to close the door to others (*Conj. praec.* 140d).

These authors recognize the patriarchal power dynamics of household worship—and worry that these might not always be followed.

In the context of wider society, household worship was sometimes treated with suspicion. As we have seen, these practices were ubiquitous, available to many, often unsupervised, and subject to adaptation and improvisation. These features drew censure from civic officials and literate elites who were invested in public rituals and the power structures they supported (Frankfurter 2005, 265–66; Bowes 2008, 44–48). A famous example is Plato's objection to household cult, which he perceives as a haphazard mode of worship, especially by women and the sick: "No one shall possess a shrine in his own house: when anyone is moved in spirit to do sacrifice, he shall go to the public places to sacrifice, and he shall hand over his oblations to the priests and priestesses to whom belongs the consecration thereof" (*Leg.* 909d–e [trans. Bury 1967–68]). These suspicions were echoed by Roman-period writers, who identify certain cults as foreign and superstitious (Bowes 2008, 44–98). For example, Cicero advises, "Let no one have the gods separately, either new gods or foreign gods, unless publicly adopted. Privately let them worship those gods whom they have received as duly worshiped by their fathers (or ancestors: *patres*)" (*Leg.* 2.19 [trans. Bodel 2008, 250]).

As these warnings from elite writers signal, household cult practices were less contained and less observed than civic cult and were therefore difficult to define and to control. Rooted in household concerns, these rites served as the means through which families, neighbors, and shopkeepers communicated with the powerful beings that influenced their lives.

Archaeological Snapshots of Household Worship

To get a more concrete sense of how people interacted with the gods in their daily lives, it is helpful to look at specific examples, snapshots of three well-preserved sites: Karanis (Egypt), Ephesus (Turkey), and Pompeii (Italy). The aim is not to construct a comprehensive picture of household worship across the Roman Empire, an endeavor that would be nearly impossible given both the variability of this mode of worship and also the unevenness of the surviving evidence. Instead we will examine specific examples in three geographical regions of the Mediterranean basin, noting the features of household worship discussed above.

Karanis

The ancient village of Karanis, located fifty miles southwest of Cairo, was founded in the third century BCE and flourished as a producer of grain in the Roman period (Gazda 1978, 9). Excavations of Karanis have yielded rich information about domestic life there, with numerous houses having been unearthed and studied (Boak and Peterson 1931; Husselman 1979). Among the finds are numerous figurines, niches, lamps, and incense burners that indicate household worship.

A variety of deities and other beings are represented in this material, including Serapis, Isis, Aphrodite, Harpocrates, praying figures (orants), horses, and fertility figures. Isis appears in various forms, including as Thermouthis, a snake goddess responsible for harvesting grain; Isis-Thermouthis appears on two reliefs in Karanis, bearing a female torso and the tail of a snake (Gazda 1978, 13–14, 35; Yandek 2013, 86). Multiple terracotta figures in the form of praying women were found in houses in Karanis (see fig. 59.1; also Allen 1985, 137, 414–57). One seated figure is interpreted either as a worshiper bringing offerings of fruit and grain or as a deity herself (her iconography being reminiscent of Demeter; Gazda 1978, 13, 42; Yandek 2013, 71). A variety of representations of Harpocrates, standing for fertility and rebirth, were found in both houses and civic

University of Michigan Library Digital Collections

Fig. 59.1. Terracotta figures of women praying

spaces in Karanis, where he was popular in the Roman period (Gazda 1978, 14, 54, 64).

It is likely that these figurines were placed in niches in the walls of Karanis houses (Gazda 1978, 60). Excavators delineate two types of niches found at Karanis: utilitarian spaces used for storage and characterized by a lack of decoration, and more elaborate spaces, marked by fluted columns and shell motifs, among other things. These latter examples were likely used as shrines or altars (Husselman 1979, 47, 73).

In addition, a number of clay lamps and incense burners, indicating rituals associated with lighting and offering, were found in the remains of domestic Karanis (Yandek 2013, 56, 60, 80–81). The interpretation of these objects is supported by documentary evidence from Egypt: letters written to family members mention the rituals that these objects evince. For example, in one letter Apollonia and Epons ask their sisters at home to "please light a lamp for the shrines and spread the cushions" (*PArthen* 60 [trans. Frankfurter 2012]). And Aelius Theon tells his brother that he makes an offering for his niece before Serapis (*POxy* 3992).

The domestic finds at Karanis illustrate a household cult concerned with themes of fertility, protection, and agriculture. Indeed, in several cases, similar figures were found both in houses and in granaries, evincing the importance of agricultural production and the easy flow of devotion between domestic and work spaces. Connections to civic cult are also found

in this evidence, with figures in houses echoing those found in temples. One bronze statuette, featuring a mix of the characteristics of Serapis, Zeus, and Amun, is thought to imitate a monumental statue from the North Temple, now lost (Gazda 1978, 14, 53).

Ephesus

In the heart of Ephesus, an ancient harbor city on the west coast of Asia Minor (modern-day Turkey), a series of well-appointed houses was built into a hillside stretching up from the famous library and theater. Based on their location, the quality of their building, and their decoration, it is clear that these were the domiciles of the elite of the city. Called Terrace Houses or Slope Houses by excavators and scholars, these structures offer a wealth of information about household worship in these elite families. In the second half of the third century CE, an earthquake leveled these structures, after which time they were uninhabitable (Zimmermann and Ladstätter 2011, 41, 53). As is often the case, an ancient tragedy yields a treasure for modern archaeologists who have excavated the well-preserved remains of these toppled homes. We turn our attention to a few of the finds in Terrace House 2, an area that includes seven separate living units (43).

As in Karanis, also in Terrace House 2 excavators unearthed statuettes, niches, altars, and paintings. *Thymiatēria*, multipurpose cult furnishings that served as altar, lamp, and incense burner all in one, were located at entrances and work spaces (the latter of which were often accessed by multiple residences). These were decorated with busts of deities such as Serapis or Dionysius (Zimmermann and Ladstätter 2011, 53–54), who protected and cared for the occupants and their shared workshops.

In one case, a *thymiatērion* was found together with three bronze statuettes representing Isis Panthea, Sarapis, and Athena. Based on the different dates of these pieces, archaeologists surmise that the last resident of this house had assembled this grouping (Rathmayr 2006, 108–9), most likely according to the particular needs of the family and household. A blend of Greek and Egyptian deities characterizes this assemblage.

In one residential unit archaeologists have traced the renovation of an entrance hall into a small sanctuary dedicated to cult worship (Fugger 2017, 206–8; Rathmayr 2006, 112; Zimmermann and Ladstätter 2011, 126). Two funerary reliefs decorated this room, and a third was located in the adjoining room; each of these depicted the deceased (possibly ancestors) reclining at a meal surrounded by figures who are likely members of the household. By incorporating the funeral reliefs into the cult space of the house, the occupants marked their connection to past generations, deceased family members who had joined the realm of powerful beings who might influence the lives of the living.

A *thymiatērion* also occupied this room, as did a painting of a snake winding up the wall opposite the reliefs. Interpreters associate this image with protective deities, either the *agathos daimon* (the good spirit) from the Greek tradition or the *genius loci* (guardian of place) that we find in Vesuvian sites (Fugger 2017, 207). Strategically located so as to be seen from the entrance to the residence as well as the courtyard, the serpent likely served an apotropaic function (meaning it warded

off evil) for the household and its various activities (Zimmermann and Ladstätter 2011, 126).

Pompeii

The eruption of Mount Vesuvius in 79 CE, a catastrophic event for all nearby inhabitants, has resulted in an extraordinary trove of material evidence of first-century life on the Italic peninsula. The pyroclastic flow from the volcano buried the surrounding landscape within minutes and preserved for us a snapshot of life on that fateful day. Excavations of houses and neighborhoods help us understand something about household worship in the Campanian town of Pompeii. In the sampling that follows, we will see evidence of the worship of *lares*, *penates*, and *genii*, household deities that are typical of this region. There is some fluidity in what these beings represent: *lares* have been interpreted as spirits of ancestors and also as spirits of place; *penates* have been described as the gods of pantry and also, more generally, as the particular gods of a given household; and the *genius* is a guardian or spiritual personification of the head of the household (Flower 2017, 1–2; Orr 1978, 1569–75).

In the household shrine of the House of the Red Walls (VIII.5.37 Pompeii; see fig. 59.2), we find the familiar feature of an assemblage of deities, as well as paintings of *lares* and a *genius* (Boyce 1937, 77, plate 31; Van Andringa 2009, 258–59; Flower 2017, 50–52). This shrine took the form of an aedicula, a niche framed by columns on the side and an architrave and pediment above. This particular niche, rather than being recessed into a wall, protruded out from the wall, sitting on a masonry base. Within the aedicula stood a collection of bronze figurines, likely the *penates* or particular gods of the household (Apollo, Asclepius, Mercury, Hercules, and, flanking these, twin *lares* on either side) along with a bronze lamp (see fig. 59.3; also Boyce 1937, 77).

Fig. 59.2. Aedicula shrine in the House of the Red Walls
(VIII.5.37 Pompeii)

Fig. 59.3. Aedicula shrine in the House of the Red Walls
(VIII.5.37 Pompeii), with figurines in situ and paintings visible

As with the Terrace House 2 collection, the figures in this assemblage are of different sizes and quality, a characteristic consistent with the practice of householders creating their own groupings. The back of the niche features paintings of two *lares* on either side of a *genius*, who offers produce and a libation over an altar. Located in the atrium (a central room for visiting and conducting business), this shrine made a clear statement about the piety of the householders.

A kitchen painting in another Pompeiian house helps us imagine the rituals that might have taken place at such a shrine. In the house of Sutoria Primigenia, the whole household is depicted at worship, flanked by two outsized *lares* who, by their Phrygian hats, may offer protection especially to enslaved and freed-people (see fig. 59.4). The husband and wife make the offering at an altar, while enslaved members of the household stand at attention, attired in similar tunics, and gesturing their prayer in unison (Van Andringa 2009, 253–56; Flower 2017, 58; Giacobello 2008, 100, no. 28). This painting communicates the ideology of household worship, the leadership of the head of the household and his wife, and the obedient worship of subservient members. The adjoining wall of this corner shrine features a painting of a snake near an altar in a garden, as well as an actual niche recessed into the wall, as though the live members of the Sutoria Primigenia household might mimic the painting by making their offerings.

We find similar features in neighborhood shrines in Pompeii, indicating that the mode of household worship extended into neighborhoods and shops as well. One altar on Via dell'Abbondanza was located in an alley next to a shop (I.11.1). The scene on the wall, which can just be made out with the paint that remains, is of two *lares* pouring wine into buckets next to an altar with a snake in between them (Flower 2017, 154, plate 18; Frölich 1991, 308, F). Below this scene is a stone altar, on which were discovered the charred remains of half a chicken, indicating a sacrifice had recently been offered. Scrawled on the wall next to the painting (perhaps by a passerby?) is the phrase

Johannes Eber

Fig. 59.4. Kitchen painting in the House of Sutoria Primigenia (I.13.2 Pompeii)

"by the holy Lares, I ask you . . ." (*CIL* 4.8426 [trans. Flower 2017, 154]). These neighborhood shrines, although they vary greatly in size and shape, are often installed at crossroads (*compita*) and might be frequented by shopkeepers, shoppers, and residents of that neighborhood. Sometimes an inscription or a graffito accompanied these crossroads shrines, where it was likely to be seen by many (Flower 2017, 149).

Christians and Household Worship

When the cult of Christ developed in the first century CE, the household figured prominently in its gatherings. Our earliest evidence comes from Paul, who refers to meetings of the *ekklēsia* in households (e.g., Rom. 16:5; 1 Cor. 16:19; Philem. 2). Communal rituals such as the Eucharist (originally a regular meal) and baptism occurred in households, as did the reading of Scripture, prayer, and singing (Bradshaw 2002; McGowan 2014). Although followers of Christ may also have met in shops, gardens, or

barns, the household was a formative context for communal worship in the early centuries.

Like their families and neighbors, however, early Christians also participated in less formal modes of worship in the household, creating something akin to household worship described above (Johnson Hodge 2013). For example, followers of Christ signed themselves with the cross as a protective gesture. Tertullian explains that this should be done throughout the day: when putting on shoes, walking through the door, bathing, eating, and so on (*Cor.* 3). Sometimes this gesture included a ritual blowing into the hand before signing the body. The moist breath captured in the hand recalled baptismal water and carried a similar sanctifying power (*Apostolic Tradition* 41.14; Tertullian, *Ux.* 2.5.3). Some Christians brought home bread from the communal ritual of the Eucharist to eat at home throughout the week (Bowes 2008, 54–56). Early church manuals also prescribe proper prayer routines at home (certain times of the day, certain places in the house), indicating that this was a regular practice (Bradshaw 1982, 23–71; Bowes 2008, 53–54). Thus those who followed Christ, like those around them, created ritual space in the household for their new cult (Cianca 2018).

As the church developed into a public, imperially backed institution in the fourth century and beyond, officials grew suspicious of worship in homes and leveled the same critiques we see from the elite writers discussed above. Christian household worship endured, however, giving believers the opportunity to adapt their practice to their particular circumstances (Bowes 2008). This mode of Christian worship, rather than standing out as unique and new, shared a common vocabulary and adaptability with the wider tradition of household worship in the Roman period.

Works Cited

Allen, M. L. 1985. "The Terracotta Figurines from Karanis: A Study of Technique, Style, and Chronology in Fayoumic Coroplastics." PhD diss., University of Michigan.

Boak, A. E. R., and Enoch Peterson. 1931. *Karanis, Topographical and Architectural Report of Excavations during the Seasons 1924–28*. Ann Arbor: University of Michigan.

Bodel, John. 2008. "Cicero's Minerva, *Penates*, and the Mother of the *Lares*: An Outline of Roman Domestic Religion." In *Household and Family Religion in Antiquity*, edited by John Bodel and Saul M. Olyan, 248–75. Malden, MA: Blackwell.

Bowes, Kimberly. 2008. *Private Worship, Public Values, and Religious Change in Late Antiquity*. Cambridge: Cambridge University Press.

Boyce, George K. 1937. *Corpus of the Lararia of Pompeii*. Memoirs of the American Academy in Rome 24. Rome: American Academy in Rome.

Bradshaw, Paul F. 1982. *Daily Prayer in the Early Church: A Study of the Origin and Early Development of the Divine Office*. New York: Oxford University Press.

———. 2002. *Search for the Origins of Christian Worship*. Oxford: Oxford University Press.

Bury, R. G., trans. 1967–68. *Plato in Twelve Volumes*. Vols. 10 and 11. Cambridge, MA: Harvard University Press. http://www.perseus.tufts.edu/hopper/text?doc =urn:cts:greekLit:tlg0059.tlg034.perseus-eng1:10 .909d.

Cianca, Jenn. 2018. *Sacred Ritual, Profane Space: The Roman House as Early Christian Meeting Place*. Montreal: McGill-Queen's University Press.

Flower, Harriet I. 2017. *The Dancing Lares and the Serpent in the Garden: Religion and the Roman Street Corner*. Princeton: Princeton University Press.

Foss, Pedar. 1997. "Watchful Lares: Roman Household Organization and the Rituals of Cooking and Eating." In *Domestic Space in the Roman World: Pompeii and Beyond*, edited by Ray Laurence and Andrew Wallace-Hadrill, 197–218. JRASup 22. Portsmouth, RI: Journal of Roman Archaeology.

Frankfurter, David. 1998. *Religion in Roman Egypt: Assimilation and Resistance*. Princeton, NJ: Princeton University Press.

———. 2005. "Beyond Magic and Superstition." In *Late Ancient Christianity*, edited by Virginia Burrus, 255–84. A People's History of Christianity 2. Minneapolis: Fortress.

———. 2012. "Religious Practice and Piety." In *The Oxford Handbook of Roman Egypt*, edited by Christina Riggs, 319–36. Oxford: Oxford University Press.

———. 2017. "The Spaces of Domestic Religion in Late Antique Egypt." *ARG* 18–19, no. 1: 7–23.

Fröhlich, T. 1991. *Lararien- und Fassadenbilder in den Vesuvstädten: Untersuchunges sur "volkstümlichen" pompejanishcen Malerei*. Mitteilungen des Deutschen Archaeologischen Instituts, Roemische Abteilung, Ergänzungsheft 32. Mainz: Philipp von Zabern.

Fugger, Verena. 2017. "Shedding Light on Early Christian Domestic Cult: Characteristics and New Perspectives in the Context of Archaeological Findings." *ARG* 18–19, no. 1: 201–35.

Gazda, Elaine. 1978. *Guardians of the Nile: Sculptures from Karanis in the Fayoum (c. 250 BC–AD 450)*. Ann Arbor: University of Michigan Press.

George, Michele. 1997. "Servus and Domus: The Slave in the Roman House." In *Domestic Space in the Roman World: Pompeii and Beyond*, edited by Ray Laurence and Andrew Wallace-Hadrill, 15–24. JRASup 22. Portsmouth: Journal of Roman Archaeology.

Giacobello, Frederica. 2008. *Larari pompeiani: Iconografia e culto dei Lari in ambito domestico*. Milan: LED.

Husselman, Elinor. 1979. *Karanis Excavations of the University of Michigan in Egypt, 1928–1935: Topography and Architecture; A Summary of the Reports of the Director, Enoch E. Peterson*. Ann Arbor: University of Michigan Press.

Johnson Hodge, Caroline. 2010. "'Holy Wives' in Roman Households: First Peter 3:1–6," *Journal of Interdisciplinary Feminist Thought* 4, no. 1: http:// escholar.salve.edu/jift/.

———. 2013. "Daily Devotions: Stowers's Modes of Religion Meet Tertullian's *ad Uxorem*." In *"The One Who Sows Bountifully": Essays in Honor of Stanley K. Stowers*, edited by Caroline Johnson Hodge, Saul M. Olyan, Daniel Ullucci, and Emma Wasserman, 43–54. Providence, RI: Brown Judaic Studies.

McGowan, Andrew. 2014. *Ancient Christian Worship: Early Church Practices in Social, Historical, and Theological Perspective*. Grand Rapids: Baker Academic.

Orr, David G. 1978. "Roman Domestic Religion: The Evidence of the Household Shrines." *ANRW* 2.16.2: 1557–91.

Rathmayr, Elisabeth. 2006. "Götter- und Kaiserkult im privaten Wohnbereich anhand von Skulpturen aus dem Hanghaus 2 in Ephesos." *Römische historische Mitteilungen* 48: 103–33.

Toynbee, J. M. C. 1971. *Death and Burial in the Roman World*. Ithaca, NY: Cornell University Press.

Van Andringa, William. 2009. *Quotidien des dieux et des hommes: La vie religieuse dans les cités du Vésuve à l'époque romaine*. Rome: École française de Rome.

Yandek, Amy C. 2013. "Pagan Roman Religious Acculturation? An Inquiry into the Domestic Cult at Karanis, Ephesos and Dura-Europos: The First to Fifth Centuries CE." PhD diss., Temple University.

Zimmermann, Norbert, and Sabine Ladstätter. 2011. *Wall Painting in Ephesos from the Hellenistic to the Byzantine Period*. With contributions by Mustafa Büyükkolancı, Renate Pillinger, Andreas Pülz, Barbara Tober, and Johannes Weber. Istanbul: Ege Yayınları.

60

Slavery

Katherine A. Shaner

I, Tertius, the one who wrote this letter [under the master], greet you all [in the Lord]" (Rom. 16:22).[1] Tertius, whose voice is heard in this "I" statement of Paul's letter to the Romans, is one of the very few voices of enslaved people in our ancient sources. Tertius (whose name means "Third") was likely a trained scribe whose enslaver was part of the earliest Christ-following communities in the northern Mediterranean (Cadwallader 2018). Most epistolary writers in the Roman Empire of Paul's time used such enslaved scribes to do the physical work of writing—preparing ink, constructing writing utensils, writing legible letter shapes, understanding format and style for different kinds of writing, smoothing out arguments, organizing ideas, not smudging the ink before it dries (Haines-Eitzen 2000). Cicero, for example, speaks of the collegial work he does with his enslaved scribe, Tiro, and is distressed when Tiro's illness prevents him from doing that work (*Fam.* 16).

Indeed, most of the New Testament was likely the product of the physical work of enslaved scribes, even though most interpreters ascribe singular authorship to each book (Moss 2024). This single historical fact attests not only to the complexity of studying slavery in New Testament contexts but also, more mundanely, to the ubiquity of enslaved labor in every aspect of ancient life (and the study of ancient life).

Slavery in the Roman Empire was a complex institution that involved nearly every aspect of everyday living (Shaner 2018, xvi–xix). The varieties of slaveholding ideologies, geographic and economic circumstances, and means of enslavement attest to an institution that both devalued enslaved people and highly valued the labor, skill, and efficiencies that enslavement produced. Thus, one finds within the institution of Roman slavery a broad range of experiences. Moreover, contradictions between hope for freedom (manumission) and masters' power of life and death over their slaves illuminate the conundrum of navigating capricious power dynamics. Skilled labor was often del-

1. Unless otherwise noted, all Scripture translations are my own.

egated to highly trained enslaved people, while some of the most difficult and dangerous work was pawned off on disposable slaves. Across the spectrum of the institution, some slaves enjoyed relative privilege and wealth, while others worked in appalling conditions. In previous generations, scholarship connected to the New Testament focused on the better-attested plight of the privileged and wealthy slaves (i.e., imperial slaves, domestic slaves in large houses, managerial slaves, skilled slaves; see Bartchy 1992, 65–73; D. Martin 1990, 30–42). The experiences of these enslaved people are better attested precisely because they or their enslavers could afford the durable materials that preserved their names and occupations (Meyer 1990; Shaner 2018, 154n40). Basing the experience of enslaved people mentioned in the New Testament on this limited experience erases the exploitations and horrors of ancient slavery, even among early Christ-following communities (Callahan, Horsley, and Smith 1998). Even if they had access to wealth and privilege, all ancient enslaved people bear in their persons the social stigma of enslavement. This stigma followed slaves and former slaves throughout their lives.

Language of Slavery

English-language translations of early Christian texts often toggle their vocabulary for slavery between connotations of enslavement and connotations of service—with the latter understood as an almost noble kind of humility. These different connotations for Greek words that denote or imply slavery completely change the power dynamics within any given text. Even if a servant has little autonomy, translating Greek terms for enslavement with the term "servant" rather than "slave" downplays the violence and dishonor associated with enslavement in both ancient and contemporary contexts (C. Martin 1990). Part of the difficulty comes in the variety of vocabulary associated with enslavement. The most common Greek word for an enslaved person is *doulos/ē*, with *douloō* as the verbal expression. This word in the Greek world always signals the legal, social, and physical condition or action of enslavement. In other words, a *doulos* is always a slave, someone who slaves (*doulei*) or does the work of a slave. Examples of this vocabulary in the New Testament are myriad, including Philemon 16 and Luke 17:7–10.

Yet early Christian texts, including New Testament texts, often indicate the slavery system or the presence of enslaved people through more subtle vocabulary. For example, Matthew 8:6–8 uses the word *pais* or "boy" to identify a slave of a centurion (cf. Luke 7:7). Some commentators suggest that this term may signal that the person in question is a child or a young boy, perhaps even the centurion's son. Yet the infantilizing of enslaved people was not invented in the American South. Calling an adult enslaved man "boy" was commonplace in the Roman world (Hatter 2021, 102–19). Such infantilizing designations were not gender limited. Women were also designated as "serving girls." More often enslaved women, like Woman Babylon in Revelation 17:1–7 (see also 1 Cor. 6:15–16), were designated as *pornai* ("whores" or "prostitutes"), a term that most often indicates masters' sexual use of slaves or even profit from slaves' sex work (see Glancy and Moore 2011; Glancy 2024, 72–83).

Vocabulary that designates specific work for enslaved people is not limited to sex workers. In Luke, for example, the character of the enslaved manager (*oikonomos*) appears (Luke 12:41–48; 16:1–9). Paul also uses this term in the context of his own relationship with God in 1 Corinthians 4:1–2, extending the metaphor of his apostleship as enslavement to God. While the term leaves some ambiguity about enslaved status (not every manager is necessarily enslaved), in the social world of the first century CE wealthy masters who owned multiple large houses often appointed an enslaved manager at each site, giving that manager access to resources for maintaining the household.

Enslaved people were often recognized as such by their names. One way of ensuring their subordination was to name them with diminutives, with names signifying luck or success, or simply with a number (C. Martin 2005, 229). Some enslaved people were named according to a quality their master wanted in them. Onesimus (Philem. 10), for example, means "useful" (Solin 1996, 2:465). Syntyche and Euodia (Phil. 4:2) mean "good luck" and "sweet smell," respectively (Solin 1996, 2:228, 447–48; Marchal 2015, 141–46). Names that designate numbers, such as Secundus, Tertius, Quartos, are also common names of enslaved people (see, again, Rom. 16:22; Solin 1996, 1:152–53). While the possibility always exists that those named in the text were eventually freed, the evidence for their freedom is as elusive as evidence for their enslavement. Since slavery as a marker of status stays with a person for life (even if one becomes a freedperson), readers of Paul's letters must reckon with the possibility of enslavement as much as the possibility of freedom (Schüssler Fiorenza 2009). Additionally, early second-century Christian texts are divided about manumitting enslaved people using Christ-community funding (Harrill 1995, 158–92). Some texts instruct communities to use their funds toward freeing enslaved people (*Didascalia* 18.4.2; Herm. Mand. 8.10). Other texts suggest that such a practice should be curbed lest it bankrupt the community (Ign. *Pol.* 4.3).

Enslaved Work

The kinds of work that an enslaved person would do depended on their enslaver's labor needs. Some slaves lived in large urban households working as maids, gatekeepers, washers, pedagogues, bookkeepers, and religious practitioners. Some slaves lived on rural plantations

and worked as animal caretakers, field workers, harvesters, and horticulturists (Roth 2007). Some slaves worked in heavy industry such as quarrying, mining, infrastructure construction, and metallurgy (Joshel 2010, 166–214). Others attended to public needs like bathhouse maintenance, latrine cleaning, theater productions, temple functions, gladiator shows, and civic hospitality (Luciani 2022). Still others were representatives of the Roman emperor, serving as his proxy far from Rome and enjoying significant economic, social, and political resources, albeit at the whims of their imperial owner (Flexsenhar 2020, 1–26). There were few sectors of life where slaves were not present (Glancy 2024, 60–64). The primary work done by most enslaved people was physical labor (building, moving supplies, mucking animals, cleaning, manufacturing, etc.). But slaves were also skilled workers: cartographers, scribes, accountants, cooks, tailors, leather smiths, potters, managers (Bond 2016). Skilled work required a significant number of enslaved people in antiquity to be highly trained, and thus their value was located in their skill set.

Many processes of daily living that are automated in contemporary life were "automated" in antiquity through enslaved labor. Such skilled workers would have been trained since childhood for these tasks. For example, the skill of drawing letter shapes and combining them to make words was not an easy process. Certainly, there were no computers or typewriters, but there were also no ready-made pens, mass-manufactured ink, quick-drying paper, or even standardized spelling resources. Enslaved people were often trained in the technical aspects of writing, such as paper preparation, pen construction, and ink formulation. Enslaved workers also took dictation, physically writing the words of the person who would "sign" the document (Haines-Eitzen, 2000, 53–75; Moss 2021).

Whether they knew how to write or had other technical skills, enslaved people with this kind of training would have been extremely valuable to their masters. Not only did they do their master's writing, but they could also be hired out to others on a fee-per-service basis. In the New Testament, Paul's letters show many signs of this process of writing. In Romans 16:22, Tertius interrupts the end of the letter to identify himself as the writer and greet the communities. In Philemon 19 and Galatians 6:11, Paul interjects into the letter that he has written these verses with his own hand—presumably, his less-careful script would have been discernible. Paul likely used enslaved secretaries in writing his letters. In addition, enslaved scribes likely copied many early Christian texts, including the Gospels, for distribution (Moss 2024, 19–114).

Sources of Slaves

Slaves came from a variety of sources. The most common source was children born to enslaved mothers. These children were slaves of their mothers' owners, regardless of their paternity. Since slaves could not legally marry, enslaved children were born outside of the patrilineal system, even if their fathers were known. The sexual availability of slaves to their masters also meant that some of the master's slaves were his own offspring—a fact that raised anxieties among some early Christian writers who worried about inadvertent incest (e.g., see Justin Martyr, *1 Apol.* 27; Clement of Alexandria, *Paed.* 3.3.21).

A thriving slave trade is well attested around the Mediterranean rim, especially in Amphipolis, Delos, and Ephesus. In Amphipolis, the grave stone of a slave trader named Timotheos illustrates his trade with an image of enslaved people chained together below his own portrait (Dunchêne 1986). Delos and Ephesos inscriptions name a *statarion* or slave market in the city, although the exact building and location cannot be verified (Trümper 2009; see also Bradley 1987b). Prisoners of war were sold

as slaves, often connecting conquered ethnic groups, such as the Judeans, with slavery. Infant exposure (the practice of abandoning unwanted or unhealthy newborn babies) also generated young slaves for the markets. Kidnapping by slave-trading pirates is attested in inscriptions from the Aegean Islands and in novels and plays (Harris 1999). Slave traders, whether considered kidnappers or businesspeople, were not people of high repute. In the "vice list" in 1 Timothy 1:9–10, the writer included slave trading as a business to avoid (compare Rev. 18:13; see Harrill 2006, 119–44). At the same time, Paul did not hesitate to use slave-buying and slave-selling metaphors as an illustration for the Corinthians' relationship with God (1 Cor. 7:21–24). Limited instances of self-sale are also attested in the Roman Empire. For example, 1 Clement says that "many have delivered themselves to slavery and provided food for others with the price they received for themselves" (1 Clem. 55.2). Unfortunately, some influential scholarship from the twentieth century vastly overstated the importance of this fact for understanding the institution as a whole and Christians' relationship to it more specifically (see Bartchy 1973, 46–48, for a discussion of this scholarship).

Yet even the more "positive" experiences of enslavement, or examples of enslaved people who manipulated the system for their advantage, were all part of a system of social control. Masters manipulated this same system, with the sociopolitical and legal backing of the Roman Empire. Because of the structures of reward and punishment systems, especially the reward of manumission, enslaved persons were likely to comply with the master's wishes for the sake of rewards like gratitude, familial ties, relief from physically punishing work, and even the promise of freedom (Bradley 1987a, 47–112). When these manipulatory techniques failed, masters always had recourse to physical violence. Crucifixion is just one example of such recourse. The Romans intended the practice to serve as a deterrent through the strategic public display of violence and torture.

Violence and Slavery

Slavery at its core in the ancient world was a violent institution. Legally and sometimes practically, enslavers held the power of life and death over their slaves. Enslaved people (regardless of gender) were sexually available to their masters as morally neutral outlets for sexual practices (Glancy 2024, 72–77). Beatings, extreme physical danger, and unsustainable work practices were part of daily life for many enslaved people—especially those in heavy industrial contexts like mines, quarries, and construction (Shaner 2024, 110–14). Slaves were physically marked or constrained as a condition of their enslavement. Some enslavers tattooed their slaves. Some enslavers used containment devices, including heavily fortified *ergastula* (or slave prisons), iron arm and leg shackles, metal collars, and other physical restraints (Glancy 2024, 14–15). In Roman courts, testimony from enslaved people could be admitted only if it was gathered under torture (Glancy 2005).

New Testament texts reflect some of these extremes of violence in their depiction of slaves. Mark 12:1–9 (esp. vv. 2–5) depicts a landowner sending enslaved representatives to collect rent from the tenants. Each successive slave is beaten, tortured, and/or killed. This violence, while bracing to the reader, does not illicit a moral lesson in the parable until the son is treated as a slave. While the allegorical nature of this parable is clear within Mark (see parallels in Matt. 21:33–46 and Luke 20:9–19), the inevitability of violence against enslaved people is also clear. First Peter 2:18–19 also explicitly names suffering and beatings as part of enslaved experience when the writer advises, "Slaves, accept the authority of your masters with all deference, not only those who are kind and gentle but also those who are harsh. For it is a credit to you if, being aware of God, you en-

dure pain while suffering unjustly." The writer continues that God approves even more of the one who endures unjust suffering. These two examples of the assumption of violence suggest that enslaved people were understood as fundamentally different from free people—a difference that belies deep ideological entrenchments regarding slaves and slavery in the social network of the ancient world.

Ideologies of Enslavement

Across literary, documentary, and instructional texts apart from the Christian tradition, a variety of ideologies about the value of enslaved people existed. One of the most cited is the theory of natural slavery. This line of thought perpetuated the idea that slavery was innate for some people. Just as some were naturally born women or men, some were naturally born slaves. A person's capacity for virtue was correlated to this natural state. For example, Aristotle's *Politics* argues that individuals' capacity for virtue should determine how power is distributed (1.1259b22–25). Naturally slavish persons fall to the bottom of such a hierarchy because they possess only enough virtue to obey their masters (1.1260a30–35). Slaves are therefore living tools in the hands of their masters. In turn, Aristotle argues, a master displays his own fullness of virtue in the orderly management of his household dependents, including slaves (1.1252a25–30).

Yet even for Aristotle this kind of natural slavery was not only about an individual's legal status. Natural slavery intertwined with concepts of ethnicity and gender. For example, Greeks did not exhibit the same naturally slavish tendencies as barbarians, because all Greeks were by nature not slaves. In addition, among enslaved barbarians gender hierarchies did not exist, since their slavish tendencies automatically placed them lower on the social hierarchy than even enslaved Greek women (Garnsey 1996, 107–27).

Many early Christian texts such as the household codes (Eph. 5:21–6:9; Col. 3:18–4:1; Titus 2:1–10; 1 Pet. 2:18–3:7) and church orders (*Didascalia*; 1 Tim. 3–6) operate on similar logic, suggesting that those with the most virtue prove as much when they successfully control those without. Those without leadership virtues fulfill their natural vocation through their enslavement—and/or their gender roles, depending on the text at hand.

A second ideological position suggested that slavery was not an inevitable physical condition for certain persons but an inner orientation resulting from a lack of philosophical discipline. Stoic philosophers, for example, argued that enslavement is an inner condition regardless of a person's physical reality. Thus, those who cultivated inner freedom could never be truly enslaved. Those who were legally free, if they were enslaved to their passions, did not experience true freedom. For example, Arrian reports that Epictetus (who was himself a former slave) criticized those who pursued political power rather than correct philosophy, calling such ones "slaves" (Arrian, *Epict. diss.* 4.1.3). While this ideological position advanced the idea that enslaved persons, just like free persons, can make choices about their inner disposition, the dissociation of enslaved bodies from philosophical or cognitive functions kept intact the master's legal right to an enslaved person's body.

Paul's letters indicate some familiarity with this particular theory of enslavement (although not through direct citation of any one Stoic philosopher). Especially in Romans, Paul argues that a person's obedience is the equivalent of enslavement, whether to sin or to righteousness (6:15–23). Paul then uses this idea of enslavement to delineate the difference between fleshly bodies and spiritual bodies (8:1–11), suggesting that setting one's mind on things of the spirit proves a person's freedom from enslavement to sin (8:12–17). In both Paul's thought and Epictetus's, this view of slavery depended on the alterability of slave/free status.

Manumission

Manumission, or the practice of legally freeing an enslaved person, was a frequent occurrence in the first and second centuries. A person who was formerly enslaved, whether originally freeborn or not, was legally designated as a freedperson. Many methods of manumission existed. For example, some enslaved people were manumitted after a certain time of service while their former master still lived, frequently after a slave turned thirty years old. Some purchased their own freedom, or their relatives purchased freedom for them. Some were manumitted in their owner's last testament (Zelnick-Abramovitz 2005, 61–129).

Most freedpersons were obligated, however, to their former owners through multiple conditions placed on them through manumission contracts (Zelnick-Abramovitz 2005, 184–207). While some former slaves drew a measure of social prestige from their former owners (e.g., imperial freedpersons), most continued in their work with their former owners. In Delphi, near Athens, throughout the Apollo temple complex, *paramonē* (or manumission inscriptions) cover the walls of the theater and temple. These and many inscriptions in other cities indicate that the god purchased enslaved people for freedom, but at the price of lifetime obligation to their former owners (Zelnick-Abramovitz 2005, 207–62). This formulation of manumission suggests that little changed for enslaved people other than their legal status. In 1 Corinthians 7:21–24, Paul formulates the community's relationship to God in much the same way as the Delphi *paramonē* inscriptions. Paul writes: "Were you a slave when called? Do not be concerned about it. Even if you can gain your freedom, make use of your present condition now more than ever" (7:21).

Although manumission raised a former slave's social status, the designation of freedperson carried with it the *macula servitutis*, or "stain of slavery." Freedpersons always carried a stigma associated with their past that made them suspicious at best (Mouritsen 2011, 10–35). This stigma marked freedpersons, particularly those with access to wealth, with stereotypical expectations, such as ostentatious taste in both dress and living. Trimalchio, the bombastic wealthy freedperson in Petronius's *Satyricon*, is just one example of this stereotype at work in ancient literature (*Sat.* 76; Fitzgerald 2000, 87–88). While it is tempting to suggest that freed slaves in the Roman world became autonomous and self-sufficient (men), this suggestion assumes that enslavement was a neatly delineated status. Yet this assumption about manumission does not address the experience of manumitted slaves who carried both the stain of their slavery and obligations to their former owner into their manumitted lives.

Evidence and Frameworks

If the preceding picture of the institution of slavery in the Roman Empire is complicated, the ways in which scholars approach the study of slaves and slavery in antiquity is equally so. One of the difficulties in studying ancient slavery is the lack of evidence that fits scholarly expectations. Few, if any, first-person narratives exist. Archaeological evidence focuses on owners and institutions rather than laborers. Spaces dedicated only to slave quarters either have not survived or did not exist as we expect. Yet the ubiquity of enslavement in the ancient world leaves open the possibility that every material piece of the ancient world involved enslaved people in its production. Every text through its transmission and production potentially has some evidence to add, even if the words on the page do not explicitly discuss slavery.

Masters had power; slaves did not. Wrestling with this fact as interpreters of the ancient world requires attention to the power dynamics of ancient relationships and institutions—in addition to analysis of power dynamics in contemporary scholarly perspectives. Texts,

inscriptions, images, and spaces most often reflect the perspective of enslavers, property owners, and legal masters. This master-perspective rhetoric constructs slavery as a form of total domination, dishonored objectification, natal alienation, and indeed "social death," as Orlando Patterson (1982, 13) puts it. This definition of slavery, while correct in its characterization of slavery from masters' perspectives, leaves no possibility for enslaved persons to transmit their presence in history. Yet their presence is not disputed, and the master perspective is readily admitted.

The threat of social death and systematic natal alienation were strategies that masters used as a way of asserting dominance over the people they enslaved. In fact, this threat kept the Roman slavery system in place. Nonetheless, even this threat cannot fully erase the presence of enslaved people from ancient texts—their mention is a reminder of their existence and ubiquity, even as masters' perspectives attempt to obscure such presence. Critical rhetorical imagination asks what any piece of ancient evidence (literature, documents, materials, spaces) can tell us about enslaved reality as an underlying structure to the social, political, economic, and religious structures of the ancient world—including, and perhaps especially, early Christians within that world.

Works Cited

Bartchy, S. Scott. 1973. *Mallon Chrēsai: First-Century Slavery and 1 Corinthians 7:21.* Atlanta: Scholars Press.

———. 1992. "Slavery (Greco-Roman)." *ABD* 6: 64–79. Edited by David Noel Freedman. New York: Doubleday.

Bond, Sarah E. 2016. *Trade and Taboo: Disreputable Professions in the Roman Mediterranean.* Ann Arbor: University of Michigan Press.

Bradley, Keith. 1987a. *Slaves and Masters in the Roman Empire: A Study in Social Control.* New York: Oxford University Press.

———. 1987b. "On the Roman Slave Supply and Slave-breeding." *Slavery and Abolition* 8: 42–64.

Cadwallader, Alan H. 2018. "Tertius in the Margins: A Critical Appraisal of the Secretary Hypothesis." *NTS* 64: 378–96.

Callahan, Allen Dwight, Richard A. Horsley, and Abraham Smith. 1998. "Introduction: The Slavery of New Testament Studies." *Semeia* 83–84: 1–18.

Dunchêne, Hervé. 1986. "Sur la stèle d'Aulus Caprilius Timotheos, Sômatemporos." *Bulletin de correspondance Hellenique* 110: 513–30.

Fitzgerald, William. 2000. *Slavery and the Roman Literary Imagination*. Cambridge: Cambridge University Press.

Flexsenhar, Michael. 2020. *Christians in Caesar's Household: The Emperors' Slaves in the Makings of Christianity*. State College: Penn State University Press.

Garnsey, Peter. 1996. *Ideas of Slavery from Aristotle to Augustine*. Cambridge: Cambridge University Press.

Glancy, Jennifer A. 2005. "Torture: Flesh, Truth, and the Fourth Gospel." *BibInt* 13, no. 2: 107–36.

———. 2024. *Slavery in Early Christianity*. Minneapolis: Fortress.

Glancy, Jennifer A., and Stephen D. Moore. 2011. "How Typical a Roman Prostitute Is Revelation's 'Great Whore'?" *JBL* 130, no. 3: 551–69.

Haines-Eitzen, Kim. 2000. *Guardians of Letters: Literacy, Power, and the Transmitters of Early Christian Literature*. Oxford: Oxford University Press.

Harrill, J. Albert. 1995. *The Manumission of Slaves in Early Christianity*. Tübingen: Mohr Siebeck.

———. 2006. *Slaves in the New Testament: Literary, Social, and Moral Dimensions*. Minneapolis: Fortress.

Harris, William V. 1999. "Demography, Geography and the Sources of Roman Slaves." *JRS* 89: 62–75.

Hatter, Jonathan Jess. 2021. "Slavery, the Enslaved, and the Gospel of Matthew: A Narrative, Social-Scientific Study." PhD diss., Loyola University.

Hezser, Catherine. 2005. *Jewish Slavery in Antiquity*. Oxford: Oxford University Press.

Joshel, Sandra R. 2010. *Slavery in the Roman World*. Cambridge: Cambridge University Press.

Luciani, Franco. 2022. *Slaves of the People: A Political and Social History of Roman Public Slavery*. Stuttgart: Franz Steiner Verlag.

Marchal, Joseph A. 2015. "Slaves as Wo/men and Unmen: Reflecting upon Euodia, Syntyche, and Epaphroditus in Philippi." In *The People beside Paul: A Philippian Assembly and History from Below*, edited by Joseph A. Marchal, 141–76. Atlanta: Society of Biblical Literature.

Martin, Clarice J. 1990. "Womanist Interpretations of the New Testament: The Quest for Holistic and Inclusive Translation and Interpretation." *Journal of Feminist Studies in Religion* 6: 41–61.

———. 2005. "The Eyes Have It: Slaves in the Communities of Christ-Believers." In *Christian Origins*, edited by Richard A. Horsley, 221–39. Minneapolis: Fortress, 2005.

Martin, Dale B. 1990. *Slavery as Salvation: The Metaphor of Slavery in Pauline Christianity*. New Haven: Yale University Press.

Meyer, Elizabeth A. 1990. "Explaining the Epigraphic Habit in the Roman Empire: The Evidence of Epitaphs." *JRS* 80: 74–96.

Moss, Candida R. 2021. "Between the Lines: Looking for the Contributions of Enslaved Literate Laborers in a Second-Century Text (*P. Berol.* 11632)." *Studies in Late Antiquity* 5: 432–52.

———. 2024. *God's Ghost Writers: Enslaved Christians and the Making of the Bible*. New York: Little Brown.

Mouritsen, Henrik. 2011. *The Freedman in the Roman World*. Cambridge: Cambridge University Press.

Patterson, Orlando. 1982. *Slavery and Social Death: A Comparative Study*. Cambridge, MA: Harvard University Press.

Roth, Ulrike. 2007. "Thinking Tools: Agricultural Slavery between Evidence and Models." *Bulletin of the Institute of Classical Studies, Supplement* 92: iii–171.

Schüssler Fiorenza, Elisabeth. 2009. "Slave Wo/men and Freedom: Some Methodological Reflections." In *Postcolonial Interventions: Essays in Honor of R. S. Sugirtharajah*, edited by Tat-siong Benny Liew, 123–46. Sheffield: Sheffield Phoenix.

Shaner, Katherine A. 2018. *Enslaved Leadership in Early Christianity*. New York: Oxford University Press.

———. 2024. "Slaves of the Gods or Enslaved to the Gods? Enslaved Labour and the βασιλεία τοῦ θεοῦ." *RRE* 10: 107–26.

Solin, Heikki. 1996. *Die stadtrömischen Sklavennamen: ein Namenbuch*. 3 vols. Stuttgart: Franz Steiner.

Trümper, Monika. 2009. *Greco-Roman Slave Markets: Fact or Fiction?* Oakville, CT: Oxbow Books.

Zelnick-Abramovitz, Rachel. 2005. *Not Wholly Free: The Concept of Manumission and the Status of Manumitted Slaves in the Ancient Greek World*. Leiden: Brill.

61

Literacy and Education

Teresa Morgan

The Writings of Early Christianity

We cannot begin an essay on literacy and education without noting that the New Testament is a collection of writings. This fact is so obvious that it tends to hide in plain sight, but in the world of the first century it was far from self-evident that any new religious initiative would generate many texts, much less that texts would become central and authoritative in it.

Across the Gentile Mediterranean and Near East, established cults tended to generate a certain amount of practical writing, especially from the late archaic period (around the 6th c. BCE) onward. For example, sacred laws, ritual calendars, records of offerings, or thanksgivings for prayers answered often survive at cult sites because they were inscribed on stone. Some oracular shrines preserved questions asked or answers given, and we also hear about independent collections of oracles, such as the Sibylline Oracles at Rome. New cults of the Hellenistic and Roman imperial periods, such as that of Serapis in Hellenistic Egypt, could follow this traditional model. Some, however, like the popular and widespread cult of

Mithras, generated, as far as we can tell, very little writing at all.

Many of the types of religious writing we associate with Judaism and Christianity, if they existed in the Gentile world, were not closely linked with cults. Stories about the gods and their interactions with human beings appear in literature from epic and drama to learned miscellanies like Pliny the Elder's *Natural History* or Athenaeus's *Deipnosophists*. Theological speculations about the creation of the world, the nature of the divine, or the duties of human beings to the god(s) were developed mainly by philosophers, largely independently of their cultic affiliations. The vast majority of artists and intellectuals, if not all, would also have practiced conventional forms of piety, and we have no reason to think they were insincere. But thinking and writing about the gods was not necessarily closely linked to any religious practice, nor answerable to any religious authority.

Judaism, unsurprisingly, offers more models for early Christian writing. Most significantly, we think of most of the writings of the Jewish Scriptures, and many non-scriptural writings, as having been created in a context of piety and sometimes of worship. Jewish writings offer generic models for early Christ confessors who want to record and reflect on the life of Jesus as savior of God's people, and the lives of his followers, or to describe divine revelations, compile collections of Jesus's sayings or miracles, or explore the theological implications of the "good news" of God's kingdom. (The model for early Christian letters, though, as for letters in Hellenistic Jewish literature, probably lies in the administrative and diplomatic letters that circulated constantly around Near Eastern, Hellenistic, and later kingdoms, and the letters and exhortations written by philosophers to friends and followers.)

Even within Israelite religion and ancient Judaism, however, the written word was not always equally important. Before the Babylonian exile of 597–539 BCE, the cult and temple(s) of Yahweh in Israel probably functioned very like Gentile cults of the region, largely by oral transmission of tradition with the aid of some inscriptions. The creation of large-scale portable writings—the Torah, Prophets, Psalms, and history books—probably began during the Babylonian exile, when Israelites had no temple in which to worship and maintain tradition, and continued after the return of 539, when they were grappling with the theological implications of the destruction of Jerusalem and the temple and life under foreign rule. Many of the writings composed or compiled in the following centuries were written in the diaspora, by Jews reflecting on tradition at some physical, and sometimes intellectual, distance from Jerusalem. Among the distinct groups that developed during the later Hellenistic period in Israel, the community (or communities) of the Dead Sea Scrolls, which had withdrawn from temple worship and mainstream religious life, produced a good deal of writing, but others, notably the Pharisees and Sadducees, apparently did not. In the early Roman Empire, meanwhile, diaspora Jews wrote much less, and

less varied, literature than they had during the Hellenistic period.

Even within Judaism, therefore—although, by the first century, the books of the Law and the Prophets were integral to Jewish religious life and identity—there was not always and everywhere a strong impulse to produce new religious writing. In addition, though literacy levels in the Roman Empire were high for a preprinting society, literacy was not the norm. It was therefore far from a foregone conclusion that Christianity would become a "religion of the book," and we may wonder why Christians so early produced a good deal of writing, which quickly became important and authoritative in churches.

There are probably several reasons. Jewish or God-fearing Christ confessors were, from a very early date, in conflict with many other Jews and sometimes ejected from synagogues, so they were distanced from an important inherited focus of identity, religious practice, and community life. After 70 CE, the Jerusalem temple had been destroyed, and Christians did not (or were not supposed to) attend Gentile places of worship or rituals. In some places and times they were pressured or persecuted by the political authorities, so they could also feel marginalized in relation to political and civic life. Perhaps most significantly, early Christian communities were small and widely scattered, and it was evidently important to them to keep in touch, not least to support and encourage each other. All these factors, together with the example of Jewish writings and the opportunity of literacy, may have encouraged early Christians to seek to capture in writing their story, their understanding of God and what God had done through Christ, their future hopes, the evolving organization of their communities, and their views on how those communities should order themselves and live in the present time, and to share those writings among themselves for support, encouragement, religious formation, and the strengthening of churches and the church. Their writing habit would have momentous consequences for the nature of Christianity as a faith.

Literacy in the Roman Empire

We can only estimate levels of literacy in the Roman world, or communities within it. Pre-exilic, and probably (though decreasingly) postexilic, Israel and her diaspora communities are sometimes characterized as "scribal cultures." In such cultures, which were typical of the ancient Near East, literacy was a skill of a specific group, in the service of the political and religious authorities (Schams 1998; Jamieson-Drake 2011). Most Jews, therefore, as members of Jewish communities, need not have been able to read or write. As members of Hellenistic and Roman society, however, it is likely that many Jews who were not scribes were literate.

Among Gentiles, literacy probably increased steadily from the archaic period onward (Bowman and Woolf 1994; Harris 2001; Kolb 2018). It served different purposes among different groups. The aristocratic or wealthy did not need to be able to read or write for practical purposes, having slaves to do it for them, and, even under the Roman Empire, some probably could not. With wealth, position, and leisure, however, went high culture, and, from the classical period (around the 5th c. BCE) onward, some of its productions were composed to be read as well as performed. To take part in elite culture, the wealthy and aristocratic increasingly learned to read and write.[1]

Under the Roman Empire, the aristocratic or wealthy also, increasingly, needed to read and write to play their part in local and imperial administration. The empire had the largest and most complex bureaucracy of any Western society to date, in which a significant section of society played some part, often on a voluntary or *noblesse oblige* basis. Much of this administration was conducted in writing, and many people therefore needed at least the elements of literacy (Schubert 2018). Those engaged in trade, meanwhile, or professions such as banking, medicine, and engineering, probably also found it practically convenient to be able to read and write, while soldiers were taught the elements of literacy in the army (Speidel 2018).

It has been estimated that male literacy under the empire may have been as high as 20 percent, though female literacy would have been significantly lower (Enos and Petermann 2014). Some people learned to read and write by being apprenticed, for instance, to someone whose work required literacy or by being trained as a slave accountant or secretary in a large household. Many, however, learned the elements of literacy, together with elements of Greek or Roman culture, by being taught the curriculum of "ordinary" or "general education," *enkyklios paideia*.[2]

Literate Education in the Ancient World

Enkyklios paideia developed in the Macedonian kingdoms of the early Hellenistic world. Our earliest evidence comes from Egyptian papyri in Greek from the third century BCE and includes fragments of teachers' handbooks and student exercises. From that time to the end of antiquity, evidence survives of *enkyklios paideia* from Egypt to Britain and from Syria to Gaul on papyrus, fragments of pottery, wooden or waxed tablets, strips of bark, and in literary texts such as Pseudo-Plutarch's *On the Education of Children,* Quintilian's *Training of an Orator,* and collections of rhetorical exercises or *progymnasmata* (Kennedy 2003).

---

1. It is also possible that some could read but not write, since reading might be regarded as culturally desirable but writing as a banausic skill.

2. See Morgan (1998) and Cribiore (2001), along with Bloomer (2011), on the transplantation of this kind of education to Rome in the late Republic.

In some ways, *enkyklios paideia* looks surprisingly familiar to anyone educated in the modern Western world, because it is the ancestor of medieval literate education and the liberal arts, and so, indirectly, of modern school education and the humanities. It had, from an early date, a clear curriculum, which, as far as we can tell, was not designed or enforced by any authority but remained remarkably stable for several centuries. Students began by learning to read and write letters of the alphabet; then syllables, monosyllabic words, disyllables, trisyllables, and so on; and then simple sentences. Much of their early reading was drawn from classical Greek or, later, golden-age Latin authors, especially Menander, Euripides, and Homer, and Greek orators and historians, Virgil, Horace, and Cicero. Sometimes students read substantial passages, or even complete texts, but often "literary" texts consisted of single lines or couplets taken from poems or plays. These often had some moral point, and sometimes multiple moralizing one-liners were put together to create a moral anthology or "gnomology": "Letters are the beginning of wisdom. Life without a livelihood is no life. Revere the old, the image of the god."[3]

Alongside learning to read and write went simple arithmetic and geometry. Once students could read and calculate, if their families could afford to continue to educate them, they were introduced to Greek or Latin grammar. This was not the grammar of everyday spoken Greek or Latin but that of classical Attic Greek or late Republican literary Latin. A minority of students then learned the elements of rhetoric and more advanced mathematics. Rhetorical handbooks were popular under the principate and themselves attest to a well-established curriculum of exercises, which include turning proverbs into fables and vice versa, paraphrasing

a passage of literature, arguing for or against the plausibility of a story, composing a speech of praise or blame (usually about a person), drawing a comparison between two persons or things, and writing a speech as someone else (usually a famous character from myth or history).

Some students went on to study more advanced rhetoric with a professional rhetorician. Some well-known rhetoricians in this period held "chairs" of rhetoric funded by cities or emperors; some were also active in public and political life, while others were essentially teachers and entertainers (Suetonius, *Grammarians and Rhetoricians*; Philostratus, *Lives of the Sophists*). Some students, in addition or instead, studied philosophy or mathematics with philosophers, some of whom were also high-profile public figures. At this level, education was for the wealthy, and it often involved the student's traveling abroad to a famous center of learning such as Athens, Alexandria, or Beirut.

Although the curriculum of *enkyklios paideia* was very stable, in other ways it looks very unlike a modern education system. There is no sign that literacy-based education was compulsory for children anywhere in the ancient world, though surviving inscriptions suggest that one or two individual Greek cities did make provision for children to receive education of some kind (e.g., SIG^3 578 [Teos, 2nd c. BCE]). There was no standard age at which children went to a teacher. No dedicated school buildings have been identified: teaching took place in any convenient public or private space, from a city gymnasium or public library to a private house or a village crossroads. There was no accreditation of teachers, whose only authority came from their demonstrable knowledge of the curriculum. As a result, teaching was sometimes regarded as a low-status activity: as the Greek proverb says, "He's either dead or teaching letters" (Zenobius 4.17, my translation; see von Leutsch and Schneidewin 1839, 88).

---

3. Sayings of Menander; the beginning of an alphabetical gnomology, *PBour* 1.169–76 (4th c. CE), my translation.

Enkyklios paideia not only taught people the elements of literacy and numeracy but also acculturated them to a degree into the Greek or Roman culture that dominated the Hellenistic and Roman Mediterranean and Near East. It equipped them to look as if they belonged to the privileged classes, and it was used for that purpose by subjects of the Hellenistic kingdoms and Roman Empire of all ethnicities, backgrounds, and legal statuses, including Jews and early Christians.

Education in Judaism and Early Christianity

In contrast with the relatively abundant evidence for *enkyklios paideia* and with later Judaism, there is relatively little evidence for Hellenistic and early Roman Jewish education, and it has been relatively little studied.[4] We do, however, have a little evidence for education in very early Christian communities: communities such as those that developed and made the earliest use of Christian traditions, oral or written, and in which what became New Testament texts were created. Since what we find is rather different from our picture of *enkyklios paideia*, and since many early Christians were Jewish, it seems likely that early Christians borrowed their style of teaching from Jewish communities.[5]

Jesus and the apostles are remembered as teaching by preaching in synagogues, private houses, or open spaces (Matt. 4:23–5:1; Mark 2:2; Luke 4:16–21; 24:25–27; Acts 8:6–35; 13:16–41; 17:22–31). In several cases, teaching includes interpretation of the Scriptures. By the time the authors of 1 and 2 Timothy and Titus were writing, it was possible to refer to *pistos ho logos* ("this trustworthy word/teaching"; e.g., 1 Tim. 1:15; Titus 3:8) or *hē kalē parathēkē* ("this rich trust," meaning the teaching that had been entrusted to an individual or community; 2 Tim. 1:14). The teachings handed down as from Jesus or the apostles, whether orally or in writing, were already acquiring authoritative status.

In early churches, teaching is always said to come ultimately from God, through the commandments, the Scriptures, and the Christ event (e.g., 1 Clem. 2.8; Pol. *Phil.* 2.2; Did. 1.2), and from Jesus, who, in his earthly life, taught by precept and example (1 Clem. 13.1–2; 2 Clem. 6.1; Ign. *Eph.* 9.2).[6] After Jesus and the apostles, the most important human teachers, by word and example, are local community leaders (1 Pet. 5:3; Ign. *Rom.* 1.1–2; Pol. *Phil.* 5.1–2). Female community leaders may have had responsibility for teaching women and children: in the Shepherd of Hermas (Herm. Vis. 2.4.3), Hermas is instructed to write and send a "little book" to Grapte, who will use it to teach widows and orphans in another city,[7] while the apocryphal Acts of Paul and Thecla (10.15) shows Thecla instructing other women. There were also traveling teachers who, not being personally known to communities, needed to be treated with respect but caution. The Didache tells its community to receive such teachers but to test them, recognizing that there are false teachers, just as there are false prophets (11.1–2; cf. 2 Pet. 2:1–3, 10–21; Jude 4–16).[8]

---

4. See Zurawski 2016, 1–19; Zurawski and Boccaccini 2017. On sectarian education at Qumran, see McCready 2019. Gemeinhardt 2020 explores three second-century Christian authors describing their educational formation.

5. First Clement (21.8) makes the first explicit reference to "Christian education." The writer exhorts the Corinthians, "Let us teach the young the teaching [*paideia*] of the fear of God. . . . Let our children share the teaching that is ours in Christ" (21.6, 8, my translation).

6. In early texts it is extremely rare for the risen or exalted Christ to teach, as he does later (e.g., in some of the Nag Hammadi writings), but (e.g., at 1 Clem. 22.1) the writer tells the Corinthians that Christ speaks to them through his Holy Spirit.

7. Proctor 2021 discusses the importance of books and reading in Christian education and the construction of authority.

8. James 3:1–2, 5–6 warns that "not many of you should become teachers," because those who teach are

Early writings also envisage community members as teaching each other, not least by reproving each other where they see sin (e.g., Heb. 5:12; Did. 4.3; 15.3). Male householders are sometimes told to teach their own households, especially their wives and children (Did. 4.9; Herm. Vis. 1.3.1; cf. 1 Clem. 1.3). All community members are also learners, who have a responsibility to pay attention to teachers, teachings, and examples; to consider and confess their transgressions; and to imitate Christ and the longsuffering of fellow Christians, especially under persecution. Last but not least, all the early, biblical and extrabiblical, Christian writings that survive, explicitly or implicitly, seek to teach: in the first place, individuals and individual communities, but also, potentially, any number of others, as writings were shared among communities. An affirmation by the writer of the Letter to Diognetus can stand as a motto for all early Christian writings: "Having become a disciple of the apostles, I am becoming a teacher of the nations" (11.1, my translation).

The lack of detail in early references to education in Christian communities suggests that it was a routine part of community life. It was evidently embedded in communities' organizing structures and practices, and, like the teaching of Jesus and the apostles, and also like *enkyklios paideia*, it probably took place both in community gatherings and one-to-one, in the open, in urban or rural settings, or in private houses. It focused on what God was believed to have done and made possible through the Christ event, the interpretation of Scriptures, the earthly teaching of Jesus, how Christians should live together in the present time, and the nature of their ultimate hope. Hebrews 6:1–2 mentions what was taught to catechumens, in particular: "repentance from dead works and

trust in God, instruction about baptisms and laying on of hands, resurrection of the dead and eternal judgment" (my translation). There is no obvious distinction between what is taught to adults and what is taught to children except in relation to ethics, where different groups within the community are often given different advice: for example, children should be obedient to their parents, young men continent, wives obedient to their husbands, husbands respectful to their wives, and so on (e.g., 1 Cor. 7:1–11, 25–40; Eph. 5:21–6:9; Col. 3:18–24; Pol. *Phil.* 4.2–6.3; Did. 4.11; Barn. 19.7). One thing early Christian sources do not tell us is how many, or how, community members were taught to read and write, or if that kind of education took place in churches at all. Since both Jews and Gentiles became Christians, however, and most, especially in the early years, were adult converts, we can assume that some were literate and had been taught by traditional Jewish methods or by *enkyklios paideia*.

The Language and Education of New Testament Authors

Even if we assume, along with almost all scholars, that all the texts of the New Testament were composed in Greek, we know so little about most of the writers that we cannot even be sure whether Greek was their first language. Paul, coming from Tarsus, and the Johannine writers, based in western Asia Minor, were almost certainly first-language Greek speakers, but the writer of Matthew's Gospel, for instance, if he was based in Antioch, could have been a first-language Aramaic speaker or bilingual.

Nor is it easy to tell how much education these writers had, or of what kind. In principle, none of them needs to have been literate: they could have dictated to scribes (as Paul probably did, though we know that he could also write, since he adds "this greeting in my own hand" to the end of 1 Corinthians [16:21, my

---

held to a high standard of behavior and may fall short, and also because the tongue is a powerful weapon that must be used with care.

translation]). It is, however, likely that most, probably all, were literate. Most New Testament texts are substantial and complex, and they show knowledge of literary forms from history to biography, paraenesis, apocalypse, and more. It must be theoretically possible that a person could learn to compose, say, a Gospel or set of acts purely by hearing the Jewish Scriptures and listening to public performances of histories or biographies, but it is much more likely that the writers had a degree of literate education. If so, then those who were Jews (as almost all, if not all, New Testament writers were) may well have had both some Jewish education and some Greek *enkyklios paideia*. How much Greek education they had doubtless varied (Mark's Greek, for instance, is relatively simple; that of Hebrews noticeably more literary), but all of them use Greek fluently and effectively for their varied purposes. We should probably assume that they reached at least the level of elementary rhetorical training. It is worth noting that if this is the case, then they will have encountered classical Attic grammar. All, however, write some form of Koine, the everyday form of first-century Greek. They choose to communicate what they have to say in the plain language of everyday life, which would have been most accessible to the greatest number of people, whether listening or reading. This in itself attests to the significance of texts in Christianity, from a very early date, with which we began.

Works Cited

Bloomer, Martin. 2011. *The School of Rome: Latin Studies and the Origins of Liberal Education*. Berkeley: University of California Press.

Bowman, Alan, and Greg Woolf, eds. 1994. *Literacy and Power in the Ancient World*. Cambridge: Cambridge University Press.

Cribiore, Raffaella. 2001. *Gymnastics of the Mind: Greek Education in Hellenistic and Roman Egypt*. Princeton: Princeton University Press.

Enos, Richard Leo, and Terry Shannon Petermann, eds. 2014. "Writing Instruction for the 'Young Ladies' of Teos: A Note on Women and Literacy in Antiquity." *Rhetoric Review* 33: 1–20.

Gemeinhardt, Peter. 2020. "Teaching the Faith in Early Christianity: Divine and Human Agency." *Vigiliae Christianae* 74: 129–64.

Harris, William V. 2001. *Ancient Literacy*. Cambridge, MA: Harvard University Press.

Jamieson-Drake, D. W. 2011. *Scribes and Schools in Monarchic Judah: A Socio-Archaeological Approach*. 2nd ed. Sheffield: Sheffield Phoenix.

Kennedy, George A. 2003. *Progymnasmata: Greek Textbooks of Prose Composition and Rhetoric*. Leiden: Brill.

Kolb, Anne, ed. 2018. *Literacy in Ancient Everyday Life*. Boston: de Gruyter.

von Leutsch, E. L., and F. G. Schneidewin. 1839. *Corpus Paroemiographorum Graecorum*. Göttingen: Vanderhoeck & Ruprecht.

McCready, Wayne O. 2019. "Education in the Sacrospace of Qumran Judaism." In *Religions and Education in Antiquity: Studies in Honour of Michel Desjardins*, edited by Alex Damm, 55–75. Leiden: Brill.

Morgan, Teresa. 1998. *Literate Education in the Hellenistic and Roman Worlds*. Cambridge: Cambridge University Press.

Proctor, Travis W. 2021. "Books, Scribes, and Cultures of Reading in the Shepherd of Hermas." *Journal of Ecclesiastical History* 30: 1–19.

Schams, Christine. 1998. *Jewish Scribes in the Second-Temple Period*. Sheffield: Sheffield Academic Press.

Schubert, Paul. 2018. "Who Needed Writing in Graeco-Roman Egypt, and for What Purpose? Document Layout as a Tool of Literacy." In *Literacy in Ancient Everyday Life*, edited by Anne Kolb, 335–50. Boston: de Gruyter.

Speidel, Michael A. 2018. "Soldiers and Documents: Insights from Nubia; The Significance of Written Documents in Roman Soldiers' Everyday Lives." In *Literacy in Ancient Everyday Life*, edited by Anne Kolb, 179–200. Boston: de Gruyter.

Zurawski, Jason. 2016. "Jewish *Paideia* in the Hellenistic Diaspora: Discussing Education, Shaping Identity." PhD diss., University of Michigan.

Zurawski, Jason, and Gabriel Boccaccini, eds. 2017. *Second Temple "Paideia" in Context*. Berlin: de Gruyter.

62

Death and Burial Practices

DANIEL L. SMITH AND WILLIAM L. POTTER

As they pondered death, some first-century Jews were convinced not only of its certainty but also of its absolute finality. Josephus notes that the Sadducees believed that body and soul were both destroyed in death (*Ant.* 18.16; cf. *J.W.* 2.165; Acts 23:8). Others, including the Pharisees and Essenes, expected resurrection and an afterlife. Josephus observes that these fellow Jews and their Greek neighbors shared some beliefs, such as the notion of rewards for the pious and punishments for the wicked (*J.W.* 2.156). Popular Epicurean philosophers, however, aligned with the Sadducees in their skepticism about such posthumous recompense. Still, those who believed in resurrection appear to have outnumbered the skeptics, at least among Second Temple Jews (Bauckham 1998; see also chap. 34 under the heading "Jewish Afterlife").

In addition to holding beliefs in common, first-century Jews and other inhabitants of the Mediterranean world also shared high mortality rates. While life expectancy can be difficult to calculate, census records from Roman Egypt suggest that the majority of people died before reaching their twenty-fifth birthday (Bagnall and Frier 1994, 104). A thirty-year-old male might have a total life expectancy of fifty-five years, but less than 6 percent of the population could expect to reach the age of sixty (Bagnall and Frier 1994, 100). Ancient inhabitants of the Mediterranean world were all too familiar with death.

Corpses and Purity

Death renders bodies into corpses. In the Second Temple world, corpses constituted powerful sources of impurity (Thiessen 2020, 98–99; on purity more generally, see chap. 38 of this volume). As the Scriptures familiar to Jesus and Paul make clear, corpse impurity was highly contagious, spreading not only through direct touch but also through proximity: "This is the law when someone dies in a tent: everyone who comes into the tent, and everyone who is in the tent, shall be unclean seven days" (Num. 19:14). The Hebrew word translated as "tent" is translated in the Septuagint with the Greek word for "house" (οἰκία, *oikia*). For Second

Temple Jews, then, the act of setting foot in a house where someone had died would render the one who enters unclean. Moreover, that impure person could transmit their status to others for seven days.

Corpse impurity was easy to contract but difficult to remove. Numbers 19:18–19 prescribes a sprinkling of the impure on the third and seventh days of their impurity, and these instructions are echoed and expanded in the Temple Scroll, which adds a washing on the first day (11Q19 XLIX, 16–21). The person who touched the bearer of corpse impurity would become impure, but the stakes were lower. According to the Temple Scroll, they could wash and be considered pure by evening (11Q19 L, 8–9).

The potency of corpse impurity generated various practical responses. For instance, priests were instructed to avoid corpse impurity entirely, with exceptions made only for immediate family members (e.g., his own parents, children, brothers, or virgin sisters; see Lev. 21:1–3). Regulations for the high priest were even more strict, banning contact or proximity with any corpse, even that of his own mother or father (21:11). Additionally, corpses were to be buried properly in designated cemeteries outside of and apart from human dwelling places. The Temple Scroll goes so far as to specify the establishment of one cemetery for every four cities (11Q19 XLVIII, 13–14). Last, we find aqueducts running through the cemeteries of both Jerusalem and Jericho, supplying at least one ritual bath (Hachlili 2005, 10; cf. m. Yad. 4.7). This archaeological evidence would support the Temple Scroll's practice of first-day washing by those who came into contact with corpses (cf. Tob. 2:9).

Burial Practices

Given the contagious character of the corpse, timely and careful burial of the deceased was a priority. Deuteronomy stipulates that even a cursed person should be buried before nightfall (21:23), and Josephus includes in a list of Mosaic legislation the requirement not to leave a corpse unburied (*Ag. Ap.* 2.211; cf. *Ant.* 4.265). While Josephus emphasizes the piety of the Jews by noting their strong regulations requiring timely burial (*J.W.* 4.317), practices of proper burial and prohibitions against leaving even one's enemies unburied held sway throughout the Mediterranean world. Hellenistic and Roman sources also make provision for the proper burial of one's enemies who fall in battle (Kurtz and Boardman 1971, 247–58). The limits of the obligation to bury are explored by Sophocles in his *Antigone*. After Polynices (Antigone's brother) dies in an attempted coup, King Creon forbids his subjects to mourn or bury Polynices. Defying this order, Antigone honors her brother with burial. When she is caught and brought before Creon for punishment, she argues that universal, divinely instituted precepts required her to bury her brother. Creon counters that a traitor should not be honored by burial. However, in the end, Antigone's choice to honor even the treasonous Polynices proves the more laudable, as the unwritten divine law requiring burial outweighs the human prohibitions imposed by Creon. Sophocles's drama attests to an enduring social norm requiring the burial of even the most odious persons. Against this backdrop, Jesus's command to "follow me" in place of burying one's own father stands out with even more striking contrast (Matt. 8:21–22 // Luke 9:59–60).

Despite the universal protocol requiring burial of the dead, a range of geographic, cultural, and economic factors affected the practices performed between biological death and deposition in a grave. They also determined the location of the grave, its architecture, and the manner in which one was buried therein. Finally, these factors determined if and how one was mourned and commemorated after the burial was complete. John's Gospel, for instance, describes the burial of Jesus as following the customs common to his fellow Jews (19:40).

From Death to the Grave

In Judea during the Second Temple period, funeral rites were supposed to take place on the same day that the person died (Hachlili 2005, 480). This is at variance with wider Hellenistic culture, which prescribed an additional day for the viewing of the corpse, called the *prothesis*, during which time ritual lamentations were performed around the body (Alexiou 2002, 6–7). Despite Second Temple Jewish convictions about the polluting nature of the corpse, immediate family members had to risk close proximity to the dead, since funeral practices involved washing the corpse with water. Family and close relatives were primarily responsible for the arrangement and cost of the funeral. In the later Second Temple period, burial societies emerged that shared the cost of funeral arrangements for their members, thus alleviating some of the family's financial burden. Given the central role of the family and the vital need to be buried, great anxiety surrounded the thought of dying in a foreign place, cut off from relatives who might provide for the proper burial procedures (cf. Kurtz and Boardman 1971, 247–59). However, there is no evidence from the Second Temple period for the later Jewish practice of having one's remains returned from abroad to be buried in the land of Israel (Hachlili 2005, 470).

After the body was prepared for burial through washing and anointing with unguents (e.g., John 19:40; Acts 9:37; cf. Mark 16:1 // Luke 23:56–24:1), it was placed on a bier and processed from the deceased's home to the burial location. It is one of these processions that Jesus interrupts outside of Nain (Luke 7:11–15). Further lamentations and eulogies were offered on the way to the grave and during the deposition of the body in the tomb. In

the wider Hellenistic world, gifts were often offered to the dead for use in the afterlife. The most well-known example of this practice is the placing of coins on the eyelids of the deceased as payment to Charon, who ferries departed souls safely across the River Styx. In Judea, the grave goods tended to be ordinary items, such as a cooking pot or wooden vessel, and functioned to retain a connection to the departed or served as a mourning strategy. Oftentimes the offered grave goods were damaged, perhaps suggesting an economic restraint on displays of lavish mourning (Hachlili 2005, 484–85).

Location and Method of Burial

The archaeological evidence from Palestine (Jerusalem and Jericho primarily) suggests that burials occurred outside of the city, with many tombs cut into hillsides. These facades, which opened into the burial chamber, tended to be plain but could also be ornamented. Extended families often owned the burial chamber, which held multiple individual graves. Depending on whether the tomb needed to be accessed for another burial, these chambers could be covered with a removable stone or sealed with stone and plaster to make the entrance blend in with the surrounding hillside (Hachlili 2005, 63–64). Readers of the New Testament will be more familiar with the former option, as both Lazarus (John 11:38) and Jesus (Matt. 27:60 // Mark 15:46) were buried in tombs covered with large but removable stones.

The burial chamber itself consisted of a central recess where the deceased would be laid, surrounded on three sides by raised benches. Along the walls behind these benches, two types of tombs could be found. The most common was the loculus, a simple rectangular chamber hewn perpendicularly into the rock wall (Hachlili 2005, 55–69). These recesses were roughly the size of an adult, suggesting that they were used for primary burial. Later rabbinic sources stipulate both the size and the arrangement of loculi (m. B. Bat. 6.8; b. B. Bat. 100b–101a). The archaeological evidence seems to correspond to these sources, but the driving force of loculus size remained the pragmatic needs based on the size of the coffin. Several loculi might be cut into the chamber walls, and there is evidence that successive generations reused the same burial chamber. Additional loculi might be hewn as needed, working in a counterclockwise direction from the entrance. This tomb architecture enabled individuals to be buried separately within the same family-owned tomb (Hachlili 2005, 57).

The second type of tomb is the arcosolium. Similar to loculi, arcosolia were hewn into the sides of the burial chamber. However, unlike loculi, arcosolia were cut as a niche parallel to the chamber wall around waist-height and featured an arched roof. These types of tombs may have been used by more prominent or wealthy families, or they may have been reserved for the more prominent members of a given family. While they were often used for primary burial, arcosolia could also house ossuaries, which held the bones gathered for secondary burial. There are also examples of Second Temple burial chambers with both loculi and arcosolia (Hachlili 2005, 69–72).

Both loculi and arcosolia existed in wider Greco-Roman burial culture. The two tomb types can be found, for instance, in the Roman catacombs. However, what distinguished the Judean loculi and arcosolia was the layout of the burial chamber with its characteristic recessed central pit surrounded on three sides by benches with loculi or arcosolia cut into the walls.

Rare but striking monumental tombs housed the remains of Second Temple elites (Hachlili 2005, 29–43). Several examples survive from the Kidron Valley at the foot of the Mount of Olives, east of Jerusalem. These monumental tombs also featured underground burial complexes with loculi or arcosolia for the individual burials, so they too were likely owned by wealthy families—rather than single prominent individuals. Unlike the more common chambers hewn into the hillside, however, these tombs featured above-ground monuments exhibiting a unique synthesis of Greco-Roman and Egyptian architectural motifs, such as pyramids and Doric columns (Hachlili 2005, 29).

At the other end of the economic spectrum, some Jews buried their dead in graves that left no lasting architectural remains. Since an expensive tomb carved into the rock was not always an option, the lower classes likely buried their dead by digging trench graves or pit graves in the soil. While little evidence of such graves survives, the limited number of rock tombs available to the total population suggests the widespread use of graves that were not carved or hewn but rather dug (Magness 2011, 156–57).

Changes in Burial Practices in the Second Temple Period

The architecture of Second Temple burial chambers is distinctive. First Temple period rock-cut tombs also featured benches on which corpses would be laid for primary burial, along with a central pit for gathering the decomposed bones. However, these tombs lack the characteristic loculi or arcosolia of the Second Temple period (Hachlili 2005, 66). The introduction of loculi and arcosolia in the Second Temple period may have been due to the influence of Persian, Greek, or Roman cultural forms. Loculi tombs are found prior to the Second Temple period in regions neighboring Judea (67). On the other hand, the use of loculi in family-owned burial complexes may have fulfilled a new social need for individual burials in a family tomb (69). Regardless of its origins, throughout the Second Temple period the architecture of tombs remained consistent. The three tomb types (loculi, arcosolia, and monumental) are widely attested from the first century BCE to the first century CE. The methods of burial, on the other hand, exhibited clear developments over the course of the Second Temple period.

Prior to the Second Temple period, Judean burials took place in two phases. First, the body was laid out on the benches cut into the rock wall. Then, after sufficient time had elapsed, the decomposed bones were transferred to a central pit that also contained the bones from the community's previous burials. The archaeological evidence conforms to passages in the Old Testament that speak of one's bones being "gathered to one's fathers," a striking example being Joseph's request for his bones to be taken from Egypt to Canaan to be buried with his ancestors (Gen. 50:24–25; Josh. 24:32).

The introduction of loculi tombs in the Second Temple period marked an innovation in Judean burial practices. Loculi tombs housed individual burials, usually in wooden coffins or stone sarcophagi. Unlike the earlier practices, these burials were not followed by secondary burial, and the bodies were simply left in the burial receptacle (Hachlili 2005, 517–18). This shift from communal bone heaps to individual burial in coffins may reflect the emergence of a belief in an afterlife in which the self persists as distinctive from one's community. This shift may also have occurred due to intercultural interaction with Hellenistic ideas about the individual person. The use of loculi within a family burial chamber facilitated these individual burials while also retaining the importance of being buried near one's kin.

However, secondary burial reemerged later in the Second Temple period, with bones being gathered in a communal receptacle or left unburied in a communal heap after decomposition had occurred. Finally, stone containers known as ossuaries were employed for secondary burial of the bones of the deceased. Ossuaries might contain the bones of a single individual, or the bones of

multiple individuals might be placed in the same ossuary.

These three burial methods overlapped, but they appear to represent successive stages in the development of Second Temple burial practices. That loculi and arcosolia were used first for primary burials in coffins is evident from the fact that these niches were cut for the size of a coffin rather than for an ossuary. Given the cost associated with creating a tomb, when secondary burial became the norm in the later Second Temple period, the human-sized loculi were simply repurposed to store the smaller ossuaries for secondary burial. Ossuaries only followed more communal bone receptacles, being introduced in Jerusalem around 20 BCE before spreading to the wider region (Hachlili 2005, 520). Ossuaries used for secondary burials became the norm and persisted into later antiquity.

Mourning and Commemorating the Dead

Rituals of mourning and commemorating the dead began during the burial process. In the wider Hellenistic world, it was common to hire professionally trained women mourners who would perform ritual lamentations on behalf of the deceased and their family. Performed during the procession to the grave, these lamentations also communicated one's death to the wider public. Though Josephus highlights the responsibilities of close relatives in Jewish funerary practices (*Ag. Ap.* 2.205), their role could include hiring professional mourners, such as the flute players mentioned in Matthew 9:23. Another common Hellenistic practice was the serving of a graveside meal for those in attendance at the funeral, a custom that persisted into later antiquity (Samellas 2002, 281–86). Hellenistic and Roman burial customs also appointed times during the year when relatives were supposed to return to the grave to celebrate these graveside meals (Kurtz and Boardman 1971, 146–48). The material evidence from Judea, however, suggests that these types of meals were not practiced.

Jewish burial customs and tomb architecture discouraged mourning beyond the immediate events of primary or secondary burial. Sirach, for instance, advises restraint in times of mourning. After the dead are laid to rest, the bereaved should not dwell on their memory but should instead move forward with their own mortal life (Sir. 38:16–23). In 1 Thessalonians, Paul encourages a similar restraint from grieving, though he grounds this exhortation in the assurance of future resurrection rather than the certainty of one's own mortality (4:13–18). Such an outlook may explain the absence of graveside meals or recurring mourning rites among Jewish communities. Second Temple tomb architecture also tended to discourage later mourning, as the tombs would be sealed with stones and sometimes plastered over. While the central recess allowed for mourning practices during the burial itself, reentry after the burial had concluded would have been difficult. A rare exception is the so-called Goliath tomb in Jericho, which possessed a courtyard or "mourning enclosure" that may have been used as a place to grieve or memorialize the dead. A similar architectural feature at the Nabatean tomb in Petra was the site of annual commemorative meals on behalf of the deceased (Hachlili 2005, 10). The courtyard in the Goliath tomb may have served a similar purpose or may have simply provided a larger space for gathered mourners during the burial process itself. Its large size suggests a public rather than familial use (60).

In addition to mourning rituals, commemorative practices both preserved the legacy of the deceased and served as a coping mechanism for the bereaved. Two primary methods existed for commemorating the deceased: inscriptions and the tombstone (or *nefesh*). Funerary inscriptions most commonly feature the name of the deceased and their relation to the person who wrote the inscription (Hachlili 2005, 163–234).

They also often give the deceased's occupation or some other notable achievement. However, not all inscriptions were intended for public consumption. There are many examples of inscriptions written on the inside of an ossuary or facing the rear of the loculus. Moreover, the burial chambers were often sealed and rarely visited, so the likelihood of others reading these inscriptions was slim. Funerary inscriptions, therefore, were more often ways to fulfill one's social obligations to the deceased or to cope with their passing, rather than to secure their memory for future generations.

A more certain method of commemoration was through the use of a *nefesh*, a pyramidal tombstone (Hachlili 2005, 339–53; compare Kurtz and Boardman 1971, 218–46). These were employed primarily by the wealthier citizens of Second Temple Palestine, but the practice was also used among the lower classes as well. The *nefesh*, like similar monuments in Greco-Roman contexts, both marked the location of a grave and provided a means of commemorating the deceased. Perhaps Jesus has such memorials in mind when he refers to the adornment of the "graves of the righteous" in Matthew 23:29. Often these monuments contained commemorative inscriptions lauding the achievements of the deceased and garnering them a form of social immortality.

Works Cited

Alexiou, Margaret. 2002. *The Ritual Lament in Greek Tradition*. Oxford: Rowman & Littlefield.

Bagnall, Roger S., and Bruce W. Frier. 1994. *The Demography of Roman Egypt*. Cambridge: Cambridge University Press.

Bauckham, Richard. 1998. "Life, Death, and the Afterlife in Second Temple Judaism." In *Life in the Face of Death: The Resurrection Message of the New Testament*, edited by Richard N. Longenecker, 80–95. Grand Rapids: Eerdmans.

Hachlili, Rachel. 2005. *Jewish Funerary Customs, Practices and Rites in the Second Temple Period*. JSJSup 94. Leiden: Brill.

Kurtz, Donna Carol, and John Boardman. 1971. *Greek Burial Customs*. Ithaca, NY: Cornell University Press.

Magness, Jodi. 2011. *Stone and Dung, Oil and Spit: Jewish Daily Life in the Time of Jesus*. Grand Rapids: Eerdmans.

Samellas, Antigone. 2002. *Death in the Eastern Mediterranean (50–600 A.D.): The Christianization of the East; An Interpretation*. STAC 12. Tübingen: Mohr Siebeck.

Thiessen, Matthew. 2020. *Jesus and the Forces of Death: The Gospels' Portrayal of Ritual Impurity within First-Century Judaism*. Grand Rapids: Baker Academic.

Scripture Index

Old Testament

Genesis

1–2 270, 454
1–3 446
1:16–18 278
1:26 445, 446
1:27 445, 449
1:27–28 454
1:28 433, 445, 449
2–3 435
2:2 162
2:7 445
2:8–9 445
2:18 433, 446
2:20 445, 446
2:22 447
2:23–24 446
2:24 436, 446, 447
3:16 446, 447
3:19 447
5:24 21, 277
6:1–4 272, 282, 283
6:5–7 284
6:5–8 283
6:9–22 283
9:4 306
12–25 132
16:7–14 282
16:15 172
17:1 250
17:17 450
18 397
18:1–6 402
18:1–15 405, 406
18:6 405
18:7 405
18:8 405
18:12 434

19:1–23 404
19:4–11 450
21:1–3 434
21:2 172
21:9–10 172
22:1–19 162
22:15–19 282
24:1–67 164
24:15–27 402
24:17 403
24:40 282
28:12 282
32:1 282
32:3 282
37–50 132
37:35 277
38:9 449
38:12–30 449
39:1–6 164
49:9–10 189
49:10 188
50:24–25 495

Exodus

3:1–6 282
5:3 169
7:1–13 297
7:3 297n3
7:14–11:10 298
11:9 297n3
12:1–13 311
12:22 313
13:9–13 309
14:19 282
15:26 299
16:23 310
17:8–9 169
20 230

20:4 418
20:24 230
23:20–23 282
29:38–42 350
30:7–8 350
30:7–10 350
30:10 315
31:12–17 310
31:14 302, 310
33:2 282
34:11–17 214
34:15–16 212
34:22 313, 314

Leviticus

1–7 348
1:3 349
1:4 348
1:5 349
1:9 349
1:11 349
2:1 349
2:2 349
2:3 349
2:4–7 349
2:14 349
3:2 349
3:2–5 349
4:1–5:13 349
4:3 189
4:4 349
4:5 189
4:5–7 349
4:7 350
4:10 350
4:11–12 350
4:16 189
4:24 349

4:25 350
4:30 350
4:34 350
5:5 349
5:11–13 349
5:14–6:7 350
5:16 350
6:1–7 350
6:26 350
6:30 350
7:1–2 350
7:1–7 350
7:2 350
7:3–5 350
7:6 350
7:11 306
7:12–15 349
7:14 306
7:15–16 349
7:16–17 349
7:28–36 349
7:37–38 351
8:15 350
9:9 350
11–15 213
11:44–45 302
12 303, 352
12:2–8 447–48
12:8 303, 398
13 252
13–14 252, 303
13:47 304
14:1–32 352
14:34 304
15 303
15:2–30 448
15:31 306
16 350
16:1–8 311

17:8 214
17:10 214
17:11 351
17:13 214
18:22 450
19:9–10 395
19:23 171
19:31 277
19:34 214
20:2 214
20:6 277
20:7 302
20:13 450
20:23–26 212
20:26 302
20:27 277
21:1–4 304
21:7 212n2
21:15 212n2
21:16–23 248
21:17 251
21:19 251
22:18 214, 348
22:32 302
23 311
23:4–14 311
23:6–8 350
23:9–11 312
23:9–14 350
23:15 313
23:15–21 313
23:16 313
23:17 313
23:21 313
23:26–31 315
23:26–32 350
23:33–36 350
23:33–43 314
23:34 314
23:40 314
23:42–43 314
25:35–38 392

Numbers

5:1–4 303
5:5–8 350
5:7 350
6:6–7 304
10:9 162
10:10 349
12:12 306
12:15 252
13:31–33 283
15:38 309
18:11–13 303
19:1–12 304
19:11–20 304

19:13 306
19:14 491
19:18–19 492
19:20 306
20:14 282
20:16 282
22:22–23 282
24:17 162, 188, 191

Deuteronomy

5 230
6:4 259
6:9 309
7:3–4 212, 214
10:18–19 395
11:18 309
11:20 309
14:28–29 397
15:1–5 395
15:7–11 395
16:9–12 313
16:16 311
18:9–22 288
18:11 277
18:15 189
20:2–5 162
21:10–14 214
21:23 492
22:12 309
23:3–8 214
24:19 395
25:5–10 455
26:12–15 397
29:3 297n3
30:11–20 325n5
32:16–17 286
32:36 164
32:39 298n7

Joshua

2:1–22 404
7:22 282
24:32 495

Judges

3:21–22 252
4:9 164
5:24 164
6:11–27 282
9:7–15 137n1
19:14–15 403
19:22–28 404

Ruth

1:1 134

1 Samuel

1:12 163
2:2 305
9:11–13 403
16 132
17:4 251
21:1–6 162
28:3–25 277

2 Samuel

5 132
5:8 251
7:12–13 188
7:12–14 189
7:14 162
11 109
12:1–7 137, 141, 142

1 Kings

2 109
6:1–22 270

2 Kings

2:3–12 277
5:7 306
14:9–10 137n1
17 228, 232
17:24–41 232
17:29 232
19:22 305
19:35 282

1 Chronicles

21:15–16 282
35:11 350

2 Chronicles

8:13 311
35:11 350

Nehemiah

8:13–18 314
8:15 314

Esther

9:20–22 315

Job

1:1–22 164
1:6 283
1:12–21 283
1:13 164
1:22 164

2 298n8
2:1 283
2:7–10 283
7:4–6 252
18:13 306
38 269

Psalms

1:1 250
2 189
2:2 162
2:7 162
6:5 277
7:15 253
11:4 302
11:4–7 277
27:12 163
30:9 277
34:7 282
35:6 282
38:11 163
40:6 161
41:9 163
42:3 163
44:22 326
51:17 351
69:7 326
69:21 313
69:25 163
71:22 305
78:2 138
78:41 305
78:49 282
78:69 270
79:2–3 163
80:8–17 137
88:10–12 277
91:11 282
95:11 162
96:5 286
106:16 302
110:4 189
112:9 400
115:17 277
118:22 141
127:3 434
148:2 282

Proverbs

1:1 134
8:22–31 162
21:13 397
26:27 253

Ecclesiastes

1:4 20
9:14–18 137

Isaiah

1:1   134
1:4   305
2:6   396
3:24–26   163
5:1–7   137
5:8–9   396
5:11–13   396
6:9–10   140
7:1   292
8:1   292
8:18   297n3
8:19   277
9:1–2   161
11:1–2   188
11:1–5   162, 189
12:3   315
14:9–11   277
19:14   163
24:21–23   278
25:8   20
26:19   20
26:20–21   278
37:36   282
42:1   162
42:1–4   161
45:1   189
49:6   212, 275
51:17–23   163
56:3–7   212
58:1–7   396
61:1   189
65:17–25   276
65:18   276
65:20   20
66:15   279
66:23   212

Jeremiah

1:6   163
13:1–14   137
17:21–24   310
23:5   189
24:1–10   137
31:1–22   275
31:31–34   162, 276

Ezekiel

18:7–8   396
22:16   302
34:23–24   189
36:25–27   276
37   20, 277
37:21–22   275
37:26–27   276
37:26–28   275

39:7   305
40–48   272, 275
43:23–24   349
44:23   302
47:1   315

Daniel

2:31–45   137
4:27   396
7   22
7:9–14   162
7:13   21
7:13–14   188, 189
7:18   21
7:27   21
8:16   284
9   21
9:21   284
9:25–26   189
10:13   20, 284
10:20   20
10:21   20, 284
11:5–14   20
11:45   20
12:1   20, 284
12:2   277
12:2–3   20
12:3   278
12:11   21
26:19–21   277

Hosea

6:6   162

Joel

2:28–32   314

Amos

5:21   396
5:24   396
5:26–27   162
7:1–9   137
8:10   164
9:11   189
9:14   188

Micah

4:2   212
5:2   189
6:8   250
7:6–7   442

Habakkuk

1:17   161
2:15   161

Zechariah

1:12   282
3:1–5   283
4:14   189
5:1–11   282
6:1–8   282
9:9   189
14:8   315

Malachi

4:5   189

New Testament

Matthew

1:1   189
1:18   450
1:18–25   285
1:23   164
2:1–12   134
2:1–16   296
2:1–18   179
2:1–22   185
2:12–20   164
2:13–15   285
2:19–23   44
2:22   183n5, 185
3:10   138
3:13–17   271
3:33–35   442
4:2–3   385
4:11   285
4:12–17   164
4:13   69
4:15–16   161
4:23   69
4:23–25   66, 69
4:23–5:1   488
4:24–25   65, 67
4:25   61
5:1–7:29   164
5:3   119, 386
5:3–12   118
5:10   329
5:23–24   352
5:29–30   253
5:31–32   455
5:38–48   393
5:43   118
5:43–44   57
6:1–4   392, 398
6:1–18   396n2
6:2   70
6:2–4   395
6:5   70
6:9–13   155
6:11   385

6:22–23   253
6:24   386
7:5   87
7:6   216
7:15–20   342
7:24–27   143
7:28–29   171
8:1–4   252
8:14–17   164
8:21–22   492
8:28   65
8:28–34   65
8:29   67
8:34   67
9:5   251
9:18–26   208
9:23   495
9:33   286
9:35   69
10   229
10:2–4   275
10:5   227
10:5–14   208
10:10   195
10:30   442
10:34–36   442
10:34–37   432
10:37   442
11:4–5   382, 384
11:23   280
11:23–26   270
12:1   385
12:1–8   162
12:2   310
12:18–21   161
12:22–32   286
12:24   286
12:28   286
12:38–39   457
13   140
13:3–9   141, 143
13:11   336n7
13:33   141, 142
13:34–35   138
13:36–43   285
13:44   139, 141, 142
13:47–50   118
13:53–58   69
13:54   69
14:1–5   455
14:1–12   185
16:1–4   457
16:24   329
16:27   285
17:1–8   271
17:14–18   286
17:24   385
17:24–27   82

18:8–9 253
18:10 284
18:17 216
18:23–25 386
18:23–35 142
18:24 140
19:9 455, 456, 457
19:10–12 253
19:23–24 386
19:27–29 432, 442
19:28 275
19:29 443
20:1–16 384
21:9 163
21:12–13 199
21:12–17 81
21:28–32 142
21:32 384
21:33–45 142
21:33–46 383, 480
22:15–22 385, 415
22:16 118n4
22:19–23 91
22:20 415
22:23 277
22:23–33 455
23:9 432, 442
23:21 7
23:29 496
24:1–4 82
24:24 297n3
24:29–31 268, 285
25:31 276
25:31–46 398, 406
25:34–40 404
25:41 285
26:19 82
26:20–25 163
26:26–29 118
26:58–60 163
27:5–7 417
27:55 163
27:60 493
28:1 453
28:5 285
28:18–20 229
28:19 213
35:31–46 398

Mark

1:2–3 282
1:7 134
1:9–11 271
1:10 268
1:13 285
1:14 134
1:15 280
1:17 134

1:21 69
1:21–22 69
1:21–28 70
1:22 171
1:30 431n2
1:38–39 69
1:40–45 252
1:41 305
1:45 51
2:2 488
2:9 251
2:27 310
3:1 310
3:1–6 70, 310, 341
3:6 118n4
3:8 51
3:14–19 275
3:23–27 138
3:33–35 432
4 140
4:10–12 140
4:11 336
4:26–29 138
4:41 341
5 44
5:1–20 65, 66, 322
5:2 65
5:7 67
5:10 310
5:13 149
5:14 67
5:15 342
5:15 341
5:18 310
5:20 61, 65, 67
5:21–43 295
5:36 341
5:38–43 208
6 244
6:1–2 69
6:1–6 69
6:2 69
6:8 195
6:8–11 208
6:14–29 134, 185
6:17–18 455
6:17–20 134
6:20 341
6:21–24 449
6:21–29 244
6:48–56 263
6:50 341
6:52–53 118
6:60–44 244
7 44
7:1–5 448
7:3–4 213
7:4 213

7:4–9 448
7:17 138
7:17–23 457
7:24 51, 52
7:24–30 286
7:31 66
7:31–37 65, 66
7:31a 51
7:31b 51
7:34–35 295
7:36 66
7:37 67
8:15 118n4, 185
8:22–26 253
8:23–25 208
8:27 51
8:34 134
8:34–9:1 457
8:38 189, 285
9:2–8 271
9:42 450
9:45–48 253
10:9 446
10:11–12 456, 457
10:13–16 436
10:17–31 398
10:21 134
10:23–25 386
10:28 134
10:28–30 432, 442
10:29–30 443
10:45 352
10:46–52 253
10:47 189
10:52 134
11:1–11 315
11:8 315
11:15–17 199
11:18 341
11:32 341
12:1–9 480
12:1–12 141, 143, 383
12:10 85, 141
12:13 118n4
12:13–17 385, 415, 417
12:18–27 455
12:25 448
12:25–29 448
12:31 118
12:41–44 82, 417
12:42–43 45
13 442
13:1–27 276
13:9 70
13:9–13 134
13:12 442
13:12–13 432
13:13 325, 442

13:14–20 438n17
13:22 191, 297n3
13:24–27 268
13:27 285
13:32 285
14:1 311, 312
14:3–9 449
14:4 448
14:12 313
14:14–15 94
14:17–21 163
14:17–25 312
14:21 315
14:26 152
14:36 119
14:53 7
14:54–56 163
14:62 189
15:40 163, 453
15:46 493
16:1 453, 493
16:8 341
23:9 325

Luke

1:1–4 127, 134
1:5 185
1:5–22 352
1:7 237
1:19 284
1:26 51, 284
1:26–31 450
1:26–38 285
1:32–35 119, 189
1:36 237
1:39 51
1:39–40 403
1:46–53 398
1:46–55 155, 156
1:46–79 162
1:52–53 398
1:68–79 155
2:1–20 134
2:4 51
2:4 51
2:7 398
2:8–20 285
2:11 51
2:14 155
2:22 307
2:22–24 398
2:22–38 82
2:29–32 155
2:36–37 45, 450
2:39 51
2:41–51 82, 134
3:1 185

3:1–2 43, 45, 50, 127
3:7–14 398
3:9 138
3:13 386
3:18–19 455
3:19–20 185
3:21–22 271
4:2–3 385
4:14–15 69
4:15 69
4:16 69
4:16–20 310
4:16–21 189, 488
4:16–30 69
4:18–19 382, 384
4:23 138
4:24–27 164
4:25 385
4:29 51
4:31 51
4:31–32 69
4:31–37 286
4:41 286
4:43–44 69
5:12–15 252
5:17–26 251
5:23 251
5:29 51
5:30 171
6:6 69
6:6–11 70
6:13–16 275
6:17 52
6:20 386
6:20–21 398
6:21 385
6:24–25 398
6:42 87
6:47–49 143
7:2–5 224
7:5 69
7:7 477
7:11–12 51
7:11–15 493
7:11–17 164, 208
7:12 45
7:22 295, 382, 384
7:24 282
7:36–37 51
7:36–50 410, 449
7:41–43 386
8:1–3 449
8:2 286
8:2–3 453
8:10 336n7
8:26–39 65, 286
8:27 65
8:28 67

8:34 185
8:35–36 67
8:39 67
8:40–56 208
9 229
9:2–5 208
9:3 195
9:7–9 185
9:10 51
9:17 385
9:28–36 271
9:37–43 286
9:39 45
9:41 45
9:51–56 227
9:52 51, 282
9:59–60 492
10 229
10:5–6 403
10:5–7 402
10:15 270
10:16 404
10:25–37 142, 227
10:30–37 57
10:38 431n2, 453
11:1–11 82
11:3 385
11:5–8 143
11:14 286
11:15 286
11:34–36 253
11:37–41 398
11:38 213
11:41 395
11:47 326
12:8–9 285
12:13–34 398
12:14 163
12:16–18 385
12:16–21 142
12:22 385
12:33 395
12:41–48 477
12:51–53 432, 442
13:10 69
13:14 70
13:21 141
13:31 185
14:1 51
14:1–6 252
14:12–14 392, 398
14:16–24 142, 143
14:21 382, 384
14:26 432, 442
15 140
15:8 91
15:10 285
15:11–32 140, 142, 393

15:24–26 385
16:1–9 477
16:13 386
16:18 455
16:19–22 380
16:19–31 398
16:23 280
17 229
17:7–10 477
17:11–19 227, 393
18 140
18:1–9 143
18:3–5 45
18:14 139
18:24–25 386
18:28–30 432, 442
18:29 443
19:1–10 252, 386, 398
19:5–6 51
19:8 386
19:43–44 7
19:45–47 199
20:9–19 383, 480
20:17–18 162
20:20–26 385, 415
20:27–39 455
21:1–4 417
21:16 13
21:20–24 7
21:25–28 268
21:37–37 82
22:24–27 399
22:30 275
22:39 54
22:54 163
23:7–12 185
23:15 185
23:29 438n17
23:49 163
23:56–24:1 493
24–47 229
24:13–35 402
24:25–27 488
24:44–45 160
24:53 82

John

1 151
1:1 261
1:1–3 260
1:1–18 135, 152, 262
1:29 313, 352
1:36 313
1:38 134
1:41 134
1:42 134
1:51 285

2:1–11 245
2:3–11 295
2:6 73
2:13 312
2:13–16 199
2:13–22 81
2:14–22 164, 341
2:16 82
2:19–21 275
2:21 85
3:13 189
3:13–14 138
4 229
4:1 213
4:1–42 227
4:6–7 403
4:48 297n3
5:1–16 251
5:14 251
6:4 312
6:5–14 295
6:16–20 295
6:59 69
7:1–13 315
7:2 315
7:7 268
7:10–14 82
7:14–36 315
7:37 315
7:37–39 352
7:37–8:20 315
7:53–8:11 244, 456n2
8:12 315
9:2 253
10 138
11:1 431n2
11:17–44 208
11:38 493
11:38–44 295, 300
11:47–50 300
11:55 312
12:4–6 399
12:13 163
12:31 268
12:35–36 118
12:36–43 164
13:29 399
13:34–35 57
15:18–19 268
15:20–21 329
18:20 69
19:14 313, 352
19:14 313
19:25 453
19:26–27 432, 442
19:28–30 313
19:31 313
19:40 493

20:12 285
20:28 260

Acts

1–7 52
1:1 127
1:8 329, 424
1:12–15 94n1
1:15–16 164
1:16–20 163
2:10–11 223
2:43–47 398
2:46 57, 82
3–4 251
3:1 352
3:1 82
3:1–10 295n1
3:2–10 395
3:11 82
4:27 185
4:32–35 118, 398
4:32–37 199, 386
5:12 82, 295n1, 297n3
5:19–20 285
5:25 82
5:40 325
5:41 329, 330
5:42 82
6:1 45, 384
6:1–7 57
6:5 52, 223
6:8–7:60 324
6:9 52, 69n1
7:2–53 127
7:55–56 189, 271
7:56 269
8 229
8:3 325
8:4–25 227
8:6–35 488
8:9–13 296
8:9–24 208
8:13 295n1
8:26–40 47, 425
9 52
9:2 250
9:2 70
9:8–27 67
9:17–18 295n1
9:20 70, 90
9:29 12
9:30 88
9:36 395, 431n2
9:37 493
9:39 431n2
10:1–4 398
10:1–48 95
10:2–4 395

10:3–8 285
10:18 329
10:22 223
10:28 216
10:30–31 398
10:31 395
10:34–11:18 127
10:44–48 442
11–14 52
11:2–3 216
11:13 285
11:19 53
11:20 12
11:26 53, 260
11:27–30 382
11:28 385
12 184
12:1–23 185
12:3 325
12:5–11 424
12:7–11 285
12:10–17 94n1
12:12 431n2, 453
13 52
13:1 185
13:4–12 295n1
13:5–6 90
13:6–9 208
13:13 90
13:14–15 70
13:16 223
13:16–41 127, 488
13:26 223
13:43 223
13:44 70
14 52
14:1 70
14:8–18 263
14:11 263
14:12–13 82
14:13 89
15:8–9 216
15:20 456
15:23–29 147
15:35 52
15:39 52
16:1–4 454
16:8 52
16:11–12 91
16:11–15 95, 442
16:12–40 52
16:13 54, 310
16:13–15 431n2
16:14 52, 56, 223, 453
16:14–15 54
16:15 94, 403
16:16–19 293
16:17 368

16:19 87, 434n10
16:22 368
16:25 151
16:25–34 95, 442
16:29–34 94
16:34 94
16:35–40 426
16:37–38 224
16:38 368
16:40 94, 431n2
17:1 91
17:1–4 70, 97
17:4 223
17:7 94
17:10 310
17:10–12 70
17:15–34 52, 264n11
17:16 88
17:16–34 31, 52
17:17 54, 70, 223
17:17–18 87
17:22–23 82
17:22–31 54, 488
17:23 89
17:24 89
17:28 155
17:28a 156
17:29 90
18 52
18:1–3 54, 98
18:1–8 97
18:2 52
18:2–3 56, 453
18:3 88
18:4–7 70
18:7 90, 94, 223
18:8 94, 431n2
18:11 442
18:18 88, 434n10
18:19–21 52
18:22 52
18:23 52
18:24 52
18:26 70, 239, 434n10
18:37 329
19 89
19:1 52
19:8 70
19:8–10 52
19:9 54
19:11–12 295n1
19:21–20:1 155n6
19:23–37 82, 84
19:24 89
19:29 87
20:1–2 91
20:1–6 52
20:6 314

20:7–12 54, 295n1
20:17 52
20:21 13
20:34–35 54
20:35 391
21:1–7 52
21:3–6 402
21:8 431n2
21:23–26 7
21:26–30 82
21:27–36 419
21:35 325
21:39 224, 369, 425
22:3 425
22:5–11 67
22:20 13, 329
22:21–22 216
22:24 426
22:25–29 224
22:27–28 369
22:28a 426
22:28b 426
23:1 370
23:6–10 198
23:8 277, 491
23:25–30 147
23:26 369
23:27 224
23:35 185
24:17 395
25:10–12 369
25:13–26:32 185
25:23 52
25:31–46 395
26:12 67
26:14 155
26:20 13, 52, 67
26:25 342
26:26 50, 51
26:28 260
27:9 315
27:12 88
28 52
28:7–9 295n1
28:10 403
28:12 88
28:13–14 402
28:13–16 91
28:14–16 53
28:15 54
28:30 54, 98
28:31 127, 128
28:31–33 324
32–35 295n1

Romans

1:1 147
1:1–4 149

1:3 189
1:6–7 147
1:7 52, 147
1:15 52
1:18–32 205, 298n6, 449
1:18–4:25 148
1:21 449
1:26 341, 450
1:26–27 450
1:27 450
1:28 343, 449
1:28–32 343
1:29–31 342n4
3:1–2 9
4:12 250
4:23–24 173
4:24–25 149
5:3–5 342n4
5:14 173
5:25–33 457
6:1–2 10
6:1–14 276
6:4 250
6:15 457
6:15–23 481
6:17 173
7:1–3 457
7:14 342, 344
7:14–25 342
7:22 343
7:22–23 343
7:23 343
7:24 343
7:25–8:2 343
8:1–11 481
8:3–11 276
8:4 250
8:5 342
8:12–17 481
8:17 329
8:18–24 276
8:23 312
8:29 13
8:37 330
9:5 260
9:6 216
10:7 269
10:9–10 149
11:16 443
11:25 336
11:26 275
12:1 54
12:1–2 267, 394
12:2 343
12:3–8 56
12:5 341
12:8 399
12:9–13 406

12:13 406
12:17–19 341
13:11–12 19
15:14–32 382
15:18–19 53, 295n1
15:19 297n3, 300
15:22 53
15:25–28 205
15:25–29 399
15:25–32 393
15:26 207
15:27 399
15:31 393
16:1 88, 96, 453
16:1–2 56, 148, 239, 404,
    431n2
16:1–12 447
16:3 94, 434n10
16:3–5 96, 98
16:3–16 148
16:5 94, 473
16:5–17 52
16:7 56
16:10 431n2
16:10–11 94, 97
16:11 431n2
16:16 148
16:22 148, 476, 478
16:23 52, 87
16:25–27 148, 205
20:1–2 91
26:22 479

1 Corinthians

1:1 147, 148, 440
1:2 96, 443
1:3 147
1:4–9 147
1:11 56, 453
1:15–16 431n 2
1:16 94, 95, 442
1:18–15:58 148
1:26 52
2:1 336
2:6 286
2:8 286, 287
3:16–17 54, 85
4:1–2 477
4:9 285
4:11 385
4:11–12 384
4:12 54, 207
4:13–21 344
4:17 145
5–6 454
5:7 313
5:7–8 352

5:9–11 342n4
5:11 13
6:2 275
6:3 285
6:9 450
6:9–10 342n4
6:12–20 449
6:15–16 477
6:16 446
6:19–20 54
7 432, 440, 442, 456
7:1 448
7:1–7 457
7:1–11 489
7:2 440, 449
7:2–6 342
7:3 440
7:5 440, 448
7:7 437, 448
7:7–9 437
7:8 441n20
7:8–9 448
7:10–11 455
7:10–16 440, 456
7:11a 441n20
7:12–16 95, 443, 454, 457
7:14 438, 440
7:15 457
7:15–16 443
7:16 440
7:17–40 448
7:19 16
7:21 439, 481
7:21–24 479, 481
7:22 439
7:25–40 489
7:26–28 438
7:28 438, 448
7:29 19
7:30 439
7:31 24, 286, 437
7:32–34 438
7:33–34 437, 440
7:35 438, 440
7:36 448
7:36–38 437, 438
7:39 442
7:39–40 437, 441n20, 457
8–10 84
8:1 89
8:4 84, 89
8:5 261
8:6 56, 259
8:10 89
9:1–18 207, 393
9:24–27 87
10:6–13 173
10:11 438

10:14 312
10:16–17 216
10:17 56
10:20–21 266, 286
10:25 89
10:27 411
11:1–16 239
11:2–16 293, 447, 454
11:7 446
11:10 285
11:17 412
11:17–34 399, 412
11:18 412
11:20 412
11:21–22 412
11:23–25 412
11:23–26 149
11:23–32 312
11:25 412
11:29 412
11:32 412
11:33 412
12 300, 413
12–14 293, 297
12:2–3 149
12:4–11 295n1
12:7–11 204
12:9 299
12:12–26 394
12:12–27 56
12:13 413
12:27–31 295n1
12:28 299, 399
13:1 285
13:14 448
14 292
14:19 434
14:23 412
14:23–36 96
14:26 151, 413, 434
14:27–31 413
14:27–33 434
14:33 413
14:33–35 447
14:33–36 293
14:34–35 432, 434
14:34–36 239
14:35–36 434n10
15 19, 24, 245
15:3 352
15:3–4 160
15:3–8 149
15:6 440
15:10 343
15:12–32 205
15:16 19
15:20 19
15:20–23 312

15:24–25 276
15:24–28 189
15:29 297
15:33 155, 156
15:35–49 278
15:50–52 297
15:52 439
16:1 207
16:1–4 393, 399
16:2 57
16:8 314
16:13 342
16:15–17 95
16:19 54, 94, 98, 473
16:21 148, 489
16:23 382
19:10–12 448

2 Corinthians

1:1 147, 440
1:3–11 147
1:13 440
1:16 52
1:23 52
1:23–2:11 145
2:12 52
3:1–3 405
3:18 344
4:4 286
4:11 329
5:7 250
5:17 273, 344, 437
6:4–8 342n4
6:14–15 454
6:14–7:1 284
6:16 85
7:5–16 145
7:9–10 341
8–9 382, 393, 399
8:1–2 383
8:5 394
8:9 394, 399
8:13–14 399
8:13–15 394
8:16–17 52
9:1 207
9:6–11 399
9:8–11 399
9:9 396n2
9:13 399
10:10 249
11:1–5 457
11:2–3 447
11:5–15 207
11:8–9 207
11:14 285
11:23–25 325

11:23–33 324
11:27 207, 384, 385
11:28–29 341
11:32 52, 67
12:1–10 269, 271
12:7 283, 285
12:11–18 207
12:12 295n1
12:14–18 52
12:18 440
12:20–21 342n4
13:1 52

Galatians

1:2 96, 148
1:6 148
1:8 285
1:13–14 6
1:17 52, 67
2–3 119
2:1–10 205
2:9 85
2:10 57, 382, 399
2:11–12 216
2:20 343, 394
3:1 148
3:13 10
3:22 344
3:28 56, 432n4, 440
4:3 269
4:8–11 269
4:9 269
4:13–15 404
4:13–16 249
4:14 406
4:21–31 139
4:22–26 171
4:24 171
5:2–4 8
5:6 16
5:16 342
5:16–21 342
5:16–25 341
5:17 342, 344
5:17–21 342
5:19 342, 456
5:19–21 342
5:22 342
5:22–23 342, 342n4
6:7–10 399
6:11 148, 479
6:15 273
6:18 148

Ephesians

1:2 147
1:3–14 147

2:2 266
2:20 85
2:21 85
4:21–24 266
4:26 341
4:26–27 341
4:27 266
4:31 342n4
5:1–2 339
5:3 456
5:6 207
5:6–11 118
5:9 342
5:14 152
5:18–20 413
5:19 151, 153
5:21 433, 433n8
5:21–6:9 432, 481, 489
5:22 433
5:23 433
5:23–27 433
5:25–31 455
5:29–31 436
5:30 56
6:4a 436
6:4b 436
6:5–8 439
6:8–9 437
6:11 266
6:12 266

Philippians

1:1 52, 147, 148
1:3–6 147
1:3–11 147
1:7–8 148
1:11 342
1:12–26 148
1:13 325
1:27 370
1:29 329
1:30 330
2:1–4 148
2:2–4 342n4
2:5–11 156, 245
2:6–11 149, 151, 152,
    152n4, 153n5, 154
2:9–11 245
2:10b 269
2:12–13 343
2:13 343
2:17–19 148
2:25 440
3:2–11 369
3:5 9
3:10–12 344
3:13–14 330
4:2 478

4:2–3 431n2, 453
4:4 330
4:8 342n4
4:10–18 52
4:10–20 394, 399
4:15–16 207
4:21–22 148
4:22 52, 369, 431n2
4:23 148

Colossians

1 153n5
1:1 148
1:1–2 52
1:3–8 147
1:7 52, 53
1:15–20 149, 151, 152
2:1 52
2:4 205
2:8 31, 205, 269
2:14–15 287
2:18 205
2:20–23 207
3:1–10 276
3:5 342, 456
3:15 56
3:16 151, 153
3:18 457
3:18–24 489
3:18–4:1 432, 481
3:19 433, 455
3:21 436
3:22–25 439
4:1 437
4:12–13 52
4:13 52
4:15 90, 94
4:15–16 52
4:16 147
4:18 148, 325

1 Thessalonians

1:1 52, 96, 148
1:2–10 147
1:6 324
1:8–9 329n17
1:9–10 149
2:1–12 393
2:2 52
2:9 53
2:14 325
2:15 326
2:17 148
3:1 52
3:2 440
3:3–4 324
3:6–10 148

3:11–13 147
4:3–5:11 148
4:4 433n9
4:11 53, 54
4:13 341
4:13–18 285
4:16–17 19
4:17 19
5:3 322
5:4–5 118
5:27 147
16:21 148

2 Thessalonians

1:1 52, 148
1:6–10 285
1:7 285
2:1–12 277
3:17 148
3:18 148
4:3 456
7:5–16 148

1 Timothy

1:3–7 207
1:4 205
1:7 205
1:9–10 479
1:15 488
2:8–15 432, 454, 457
2:9 342
2:11 435
2:11–15 239, 447
2:12 435, 435n12
2:13–14 435
2:14 447
3–6 481
3:1–2 457
3:2 342
3:2–5 436
3:11 457
3:15 436
3:16 149, 152, 153n5
4:1–5 457
4:12 436
5:1–2 432
5:3–16 45, 57, 384, 399
5:10–16 454
5:11–15 435
5:14 432n4
5:17 436
6:1–2 432
6:3–5 207
6:3–10 399
6:10 386
6:11 342
6:17–19 399

2 Timothy

1:16 431n2
1:16–17 52
2:11–13 149, 155
2:20 91
3:2 432n4
3:6–7 432n4
3:11 52
4:3–4 207
4:19 148, 434n10
4:20 52
4:21 52
4:22 148

Titus

1:6 457
1:7–8 436
1:11 432n4
1:12 155
1:13–14 205
2:1–10 432, 481
2:3–5 435
2:4–5 457
2:5 432n4
2:13 260
3:1 432
3:8 488

Philemon

1 148, 325
2 431n2
4:22 431n2

Hebrews

1:5 162
1:6 163
2:2 285
2:14–16 352
3:7–4:10 162
4:4–5 162
4:14 352
4:14–16 353
5:12 489
6:1–2 489
6:20 353
7:14 189
7:25 353
8:1–5 85
8:13 162
9:7 353
9:24–25 352
9:24–26 353
9:26 352
9:28 352
10:5 163

10:5–7 161
10:19–20 353
10:34 325
11:11 450
12:25–29 276
13:2 406
13:3 325, 397
13:4 456
13:6 163
13:11 353
13:16 398
13:22 149
13:23–25 149

James

1:1 149, 275
1:6–8 342
1:12 330
1:14–15 341
1:27 45, 384, 398
2:2–7 96
2:14–17 398
3:1–2 488n8
3:5–6 488n8
5:13 151

1 Peter

1:1 149
1:3–4 433
1:4 434
1:5 433
1:7 433
1:9 433
1:21 433
2:1–3 488
2:5 85
2:6–8 162
2:10–21 488
2:11–3:12 432
2:18–19 480
2:18–24 437n13
2:18–25 439
2:18–3:7 481
2:21–23 329
3:1 432n4, 457
3:1–2 457
3:1–6 434
3:3 454
3:7 433, 434
3:9 341
3:18–22 272
3:22 285
4:16 53, 260
5:3 488
5:9 433
5:12 149

2 Peter

1:1 260
1:1–2 149
1:6 342
1:12–15 149
1:16–18 271
2:1–3 207
2:4 270, 280
2:4–5 272
2:4–9 285
3:1–13 273
3:5–13 276
3:10–12 280
3:15–16 205

1 John

1:7–9 353
1:7–2:2 353
2:1–2 353
2:12–14 155
2:15–17 268
3:16 399
3:17 398
4:1–5 268
4:1–6 207
4:9–10 353

2 John

7–9 207

3 John

9–10 404

Jude

4–16 207
6 285
9 284
14–15 269

Revelation

1:1 285
1:9 329
1:10 57
1:11 52
1:13 189
1:18 280
2–3 86
2:1–3:22 147
2:2 207
2:8–11 52
2:9 8
2:10 330
2:12–17 52
2:13 13, 84, 89

2:14–15 411
2:18–29 52
2:20 207
2:20–23 293
3:1–6 52
3:7–13 52
3:9 8
3:12 85
3:14 329
3:14–16 52
3:14–22 52
4–5 85, 151, 276
4:1 269, 271

4:1–5:14 162
5:5 189
5:6–14 352
5:11–12 285
6:9 325n3
6:12–17 276
6:14 273
7 276
7:1–2 285
7:11 285
8:2–13 285
9 269
9:20 286

11:19 271
12:7 285
12:8 285
12:9 285
14:17 271
15:3–4 155
16:14 286
17:1–7 477
17:6 325n3
18:3–5 386
18:11–13 91
18:13 479
19:6–10 457

20–22 276
20:1–3 285
20:7–10 285
20:9 109
21 118
21–22 276
21:1 273, 276
21:1–22:5 162
21:1–22:7 457
21:5 344
21:9–27 275
22:16 189, 285

Ancient Writings Index

Old Testament Apocrypha / Deutero-canonical Books

Note: For 2 Esdras, see 4 Ezra under Old Testament Pseudepigrapha.

Judith

8:9–11 238
8:33 164
13:18 164
14:10 215, 223

1 Maccabees

1:1–5 326
1:20–23 326
1:41–51 225
1:41–64 326
2:32–38 214
4 326
4:11–17 326
4:13 12
5:15–21 326
7:16–17 163

2 Maccabees

3:35–40 328n15
4 160
4:13 12
5:17 327
5:20 328
5:25–26 214
6:1–2 225
6:1–11 326

6:2 232
6:11 214
6:12 327
6:18–31 326
6:21–22 327
6:28 326, 327
6:30 329
7:6 164
7:9 326, 328
7:11 326, 328
7:14 278, 328
7:18 327
7:23 326, 328
7:24 327
7:29 328
7:32 327
7:37 326
8 328
9 328
9:24b–25 328n14
9:32 328n14
10 326
10:6–8 315
10:22 315
12:11–18 328n14
14:46 328
15:9 160
15:36 315

3 Maccabees

33:3–7 213

4 Maccabees

1:1 326
1:11 327n10, 328
4 160

4:15–26 326
5:38 328
6:10–11 329
6:27 326
6:30 326
7:22 326
7:38 328
8:2 328
9:8–9 328n14
9:18 328
9:31 329
10:20 329
11:12 327n11
11:20 329
11:21 328
11:27 328
12:3–5 327
12:14 329
16:21 328n16
16:25 328
17:5 328
17:11–12 329
17:12 328
17:22 329
18:8 447
18:10 160

Sirach (Ecclesiasticus)

3:30 396
7:10 396
12:2 392
12:3 396
14:12 280
17:27–28 277
29:11–12 397
31:12–14 409

31:16–18 409
31:23 409
31:24 409
35:3–4 397
36:13 275
38:2 299
38:9 299
38:13–14 299
38:16–23 496
40:2 396
40:23 455
41:5–13 277
42:23 455

Tobit

1:3 396
1:6–8 396
1:13 164
1:19–2:14 164
1:22 164
2:6 164
2:9 492
4:7–8 396
4:9–10 397
4:12a 212
4:12–13 164
6:9–12 164
6:10–10:11 402
12:8 397
12:9 392
14:5–6 216

Wisdom (of Solomon)

1:14 280
11:9–10 326
13–15 84

Old Testament Pseudepigrapha

Apocalypse of Abraham

19 270

2 Baruch

10.13–16 438n17
24.1 278
25–32 276
29–30 276
30 278
30.2 276
40 276
44.15 279
50–51 278
50.2 278
51.1–12 278
54.19 22
70 276
73 276
73.1 276
73.1–74.4 276

3 Baruch

270, 276

1 Enoch

1–36 21, 269, 272, 277, 279
1.9 269
5.7–9 276
5.8–9 276
6–16 449
6.1–8 283
6.7 283
7.1–6 283
8.1–3 283
9.6 283
10.1–22 284, 285
10.21 276
14 270, 271
15.5–7 434
15.8–12 284
18.13–16 278
20.2 280
22 22, 278
22.13 278
22.14 276
25.1–7 276
25.6 278
37–71 21, 189, 279
41 269
45.4–6 276
45.5 278

46 189
51.5 278
53.3–5 279
58.3 278
61.14 276
61.14–16 278
63.1–7 276
72–78 269
72–82 22, 269
84.2 276
84.2–7 276
85–90 22, 273
89 138
90.19 275
90.28–29 275
91.5–10 276
91.11–17 273
91.12 275
91.13 275
92–105 199
92.4 276
93 + 91.11–17 22
93.1–10 273
95.3 275
98.7–8 278
103.8 279
104.1–6 278
104.2 22, 278
104.4 22
104.7 278
105.2 276

2 Enoch

8–9 276
10.1–3 279
40.13 278
53.2 278
61.2–3 278
70.10 276

4 Ezra

4.41 280
6.6 280
7 276, 278
7.32 278
7.32–38 278
7.50 24
7.88–99 276
7.97 278
7.117–18 22
8.52 276
12–13 276
12.32 189
13 22, 189
13.36 275
13.39–40 275

Joseph and Aseneth

6.2–8 343
12.8 138n4

Jubilees

1.1–26 313
1.20 284
1.22–24 276
1.26–27 276
1.29 275, 276
2.1–4 283
2.17–22 310
2.29–30 310
3.1–7 447
4–5 272
4.26 273, 275, 276, 448
5.12 276
6.14 350
7.21 283
7.21–25 284
7.27 284
8.19 271, 448
15.25–34 9
15.33 284
22.16–17 213
23 276
23.3 276
23.16 442
23.19 442
23.30–31 278
30.13–15 212
32.18–19 275
50.8 310, 448

Letter of Aristeas

106 213
310–11 169

Liber antiquitatum biblicarum (LAB)

3.10 276, 278
9.5–6 449
13.7 314
25–29 164
50.5 163
56.6 163

Life of Adam and Eve

19.3 343

Psalms of Solomon

2.20–21 163
4 275
8.14–16 163

11 275
17 189
18 189

Pseudo-Phocylides

190–92 450
205–6 450

Sibylline Oracles

3.56 276
3.652–56 189
3.702–4 275, 276
3.710–23 275
3.715–24 216
3.781–95 276
4.181–82 278
4.186 280
5.420–27 275

Testament of Abraham

12 278

Testament of Benjamin

6.1 284
7 284

Testament of Dan

5.10–11 284

Testament of Job

18.6–8 138n4

Testament of Judah

25.3 284

Testament of Levi

1–3 271
2.7–8 270
3.1–10 270
18 189
18.12 284

Testament of Moses

10 276

Testament of Naphtali

3.2–3 284

Testament of Reuben

4.8 284

Rabbinic Literature

Babylonian Talmud

Avodah Zarah

36b 213
64b 215

Bava Batra

10b 400
100b–101a 494

Sanhedrin

36b 216
93b 191

Shabbat

13a 213
17b 213
86b 314

Sukkah

51b 69

Yevamot

22a 216

Jerusalem Talmud

Shabbat

15d 72

Ta'anit

4.8 191
68d 191

Lamentations Rabbah

2.2 191

Mishnah

Bava Batra

6.8 494

Hagigah

2.5 213

Menahot

5.7 349, 350
9.7 350
9.7–8 349
13.11 349

Pesahim

1–3 311
1–5 312
4–6 311

5.5–6 350
7.13–8.8 311
8 311
8.8 213
10 311
10.1–7 312
10.8 312

Qiddushin

4.1 212
4.1 216
4.6 216

Sanhedrin

4.2 216

Shabbat

8 310

Sotah

6.3 162

Sukkah

3.8–16 314
4.9–10 351
5.2 315

Yadayim

4.7 492

Yoma

315

Zevahim

5.5 349
5.7 349

Nega'im

14.8 350

Pe'ah

4.18 397

Tosefta

Demai

2.1 216

Menahot

10.12 349

Qiddushin

5.1 216

Shabbat

1.14 213

Sukkah

2.3 314
4 213

Apostolic Fathers

Barnabas

16.1–10 85
19.7 489

1 Clement

1 52
1.3 489
2.8 488
2.18 488n5
11.1 489
13.1–2 488
21.6 488n5
21.8 488n5
22.1 488n6
55.2 479

2 Clement

6.1 488

Didache

1.2 488
1.5 209
4.3 489
4.9 489
4.11 489
9 413
9.2–4 408
10 413
10.2 412
11 209
11.4–6 405
11.5 209
11.6 209
11.12 209
12.1–2 405
12.6 209
14.1 57
15.3 489

Ignatius

To the Ephesians

9.1 85
9.2 488
15.3 85

To the Magnesians

7.2 85

To the Philadelphians

7.2 85

To Polycarp

4.3 478

To the Romans

1.1–2 488

To the Smyrnaeans

13.1 465

Martyrdom of Polycarp

3.2 325

Polycarp

To the Philippians

2.2 488
4.2–6.3 489
5.1–2 488

Shepherd of Hermas

Mandate(s)

8.1 478

Vision(s)

1.3.1 489

New Testament Apocrypha and Pseudepigrapha

Acts of Andrew

14–16 456

Acts of John

60–61 54
62–68 54
72–86 94

Acts of Paul

3.23–27 54
11.1 54, 94
20.9–12 54

Acts of Paul and Thecla

3 249
8–10 435
10.15 488
11.1–2 488
16 435

Acts of Thomas

79 438

Pseudo-Clement

Homilies

4.1 54

Recognitions

4.6 54
5.36 54
7.2 54
7.38 54, 94

Greek and Latin Works

Anonymous

Anthologia Palatina

11.154 55n6
11.156.3–4 55n6
11.279 55n6
11.430 55n6

Appian

Mithridatica

6.39 368

Apuleius

De deo Socratico

6.2–3 266
7.4 266
9.1–2 266

Aristotle

Analytica posteriora

83a34–35 27

De anima

15.411a 262

De caelo

1.10–12 279

Ethica nicomachea

1104a33–b1 341

De generatione animalium

727a29–30 450
737a28 447

Physica

3.807b 251
6.811a 253

Politica

1.1252a25–30 480
1.1259b22–25 480
1.1260a30–35 480
1252a32–b6 440
1252b31 432n5
1255b23 433
1259a40–b11 432
1259b1–11 432

Arnobius

Adversus nationes

6.1 54

Arrian

Epicteti dissertationes

2.9.20 223
4.1.3 481

Augustine

De civitate dei

4.31 220
6.11 215n5, 224

Basil the Great

Destruam horrea mea

3.30 400

Cassius Dio

Historia Romana

2.103.4–5 437
2.126.1–4 318
60.17.5–6 366, 369
63–65 36
66.7.2 225

Cato

De agricultura

143.1 468

Cicero

De divination

1.10 290

Epistulae ad familiars

16 476

Pro Flacco

28.66 221
28.68 221
28.69 221

De haruspicum responso

9.19 318
13 292

De legibus

2.19 469
2.22.9 207
2.25 95
2.40.11 207
234 57

De natura deorum

1.1 260
1.39 261
1.50 262n8
2.6 263
2.7 261
3.2.5 318
3.5 263, 264

De oratore

1.44.197 365
3.221–22 253

De provinciis consularibus

5.10 221

In Verrem

2.4.81 318

Clement of Alexandria

Paedagogus

3.3.21 479
3.12.93 395

Quis dives salvetur

32 398

Cornutus

Theologiae Graecae compendium

31 171

Cyprian

De opere et eleemosynis in toto 400

Diodorus Siculus

Bibliotheca historica

34.1.1 221
34.1.1–2 221
40.3.3 220
40.3.6 220

Diogenes Laertius

Vitae philosophorum

5.1 27
6.38 31
6.39 31
6.97 438
6.103 31
7.108 342, 343
7.110–11 340
7.116 340
7.127 344
7.134 261n6
7.183 29

Dionysius of Halicarnassus

Antiquitates romanae

1.9.4. 366

De Thucydide

27–28 124

Ennius

Annales

F619 95

Epictetus

Diatribai

2.24.41 369

Euripides

Medea

1074–80 343
1078–79 340

Eusebius

Commentarius in Psalmos

23.597 400

Historia ecclesiastica

3.5.5 67
6.4.2 191

Praeparatio evangelica

9.21.14 170
9.29.16 170

Gaius

Institutiones

1.1.16–21 367
1.12 367

1.55 365
144 368
190–91 368

Galen

*De alimentorum
facultatibus*
6.749 385

*De propriorum animi
cuiuslibet affectuum
dignotione et curatione*
7.30.16–31.6 342

De usu partium
14 450

Gregory of Nazianus

Orationes
8.12 400

Gregory of Nyssa

*Orationes viii de
beatitudinibus*
44.1208 400

Herodotus

Histories
1.27.50 402
1.69.3 402
1.91 290
2.104 43
2.113–15 404
2.120 404
3.91 43
4.39 43
7.89 43

Hesiod

Opera et dies
121–29 285–86
122–23 265
342–51 390

Theogonia
105 262
277 262

Hippocrates

Epidemiae
2.5.1 249

Genitalia
6 450

Homer

Iliad
1.100a 169
1.180 173
1.180–81 173
1.222 265
6.115 265
6.137–282 402, 402n1
21.17a 169
24.602–4 173

Odyssey
1.102–324 402, 406
3.487–93 402
10.773–74 263
11 277
13.47–53 405
13.63–125 405
17.484–87 263
19.416–17a 169

Horace

Carmina
3.6.5 318

Sermones
1.6 367
1.9.70 221

Iamblichus

De mysteriis
1.8–9 262

John Chrysostom

*Homiliae in epistulam ii
ad Corinthios*
61.533 400

Homiliae in Genesim
5.4 395

Josephus

Against Apion
1.1 125
1.47–52 122
1.50 16, 123
1.50–52 55
1.130–36 212

2.74–75 84
2.79–96 221
2.112–14 221
2.123 223
2.148 221
2.173–74 367
2.193 79
2.205 495
2.210 214
2.211 492
2.218 278

Jewish Antiquities
1.1 125
1.5 126
1.7 123
1.27–51 447
1.73 283
1.73–76 284
1.156 16
3.32 385
3.179–87 271
3.227 349
3.230–32 350
3.264 252, 306
3.276 212
4.265 492
6.67–71 115
6.342 133
7.104 63
9.279 228
9.288–91 228
11.285 215
11.302 228
11.302–47 79
11.306–12 228
11.341 228
12.145–46 213
12.146 213
12.148–53 224
12.257 228
12.416–19 224
13.171–73 115
13.172 117
13.254–56 79
13.257–58 223
13.318 63
13.393–97 63
14.74–76 63
14.110 223
14.144–55 224
14.190–95 368
14.191–98 224
14.213–16 215, 368
14.213–67 224
14.225–27 368
14.241–46 368
14.242 57

14.256–67 368
14.285 213
14.306–22 224
14.381–89 181
14.403 179, 180, 181
15.8–10 181n3
15.183–93 181
15.217 64, 182
15.267 183
15.281 183
15.351–58 64
15.371–79 117n4
16.27–30 224
16.150–59 179, 183
16.162–65 215
16.162–73 224
16.271–94 182
16.335–55 182
17.28 184
17.272 190
17.273 251
17.273–76 190
17.278–79 251
17.278–84 190
17.285 183
17.289 200
17.320 64
18.3 278
18.3–9 190
18.4 277
18.16 491
18.18–22 115
18.19 117
18.20–21 439
18.23–25 190
18.29–30 231–32
18.30 38
18.31 38
18.65–84 207
18.82 223
18.83–84 222
18.85–87 190
19.300–311 69
19.328–34 184
19.356–59 38
20.17–47 223
20.38–48 215
20.97–98 190
20.105–24 38
20.118–24 232
20.125–36 38
20.169–70 190
20.179–81 197
20.195 38
20.205–7 382
20.218 197
20.219 200
20.259 44

Jewish War
1.1–2 123
1.6–8 123
1.11 36
1.11–12 122
1.13 123
1.31–33 79
1.62–63 79
1.88 64
1.129 63
1.155–57 63
1.282–85 181
1.327 181
1.355 181
1.366–85 64
1.396 182
2.14 277, 278
2.14–15 278
2.56 190
2.60–64 190
2.65 183
2.86 183
2.94 183
2.95–98 183
2.118 190
2.119–61 115, 198
2.129–30 117
2.129–31 213
2.129–33 117
2.137–38 213
2.137–39 117
2.139 117
2.143–44 117
2.147 115
2.150 213
2.156 491
2.162–64 198
2.164–65 197
2.165 491
2.181 184
2.204–17 184
2.247–48 200
2.261–63 190
2.266–70 196
2.285–92 69
2.293–329 39
2.408–556 39
2.427 386
2.433–34 190
2.442 190
2.445 190
2.458–59 64
2.461 64
2.461–80 64
2.463 64
2.466–80 64
2.478 64
2.487–98 225
2.521 223

2.559–61 225
3.446 61
3.446–47 61
4.317 492
4.503–13 190
4.574–76 190
5.184–287 271
5.194 213
5.222–23 80
6.312–13 191
7.29–31 190
7.36 190
7.44–45 211–212
7.45 214
7.153–55 190
7.367 64
7.423–32 79
18.106–8 184
420–22 417

The Life
8–9 134
13 367
16 38
28–29 39
42 65
276–303 69
341–42 61
410–11 61

Justin
Historiae Philippicae
36.2.11–15 220

Justinian
Digesta
1.1.6 366
23.3.5 453

Justin Martyr
Dialogus cum Tryphone
122–23 216

First Apology
27 479
31.6 191
66.4 337
67 57, 414

Second Apology
2 95

Juvenal
Satirae
3.166 384
6.153–60

6.508–91 205
14.96–98 215n5
14.96–106 223
14.106–7 214

Lactantius
Epitome divinarum institutionum
38.7 333

Lucan
De bello civili
5.173–75 291

Lucian
Alexander
1.1–2 130
1.3 132

Demonax
1–2 132, 134

Fugitivi
13 384
17 384

Gallus
1 384

De mercede conductis
26 409

De morte Peregrini
27 205
29 205

Philopseudes
16.3–7 206

Quomodo historia conscribenda sit
2 123
22 124
44 124
50 124
52 127

Symposium
30–35 410

Lucretius
De rerum natura
2.1105–72 279
3.455–58 280

5.91–109 279
235–415 279

Marcus Aurelius
Meditationes
8.48 343

Martial
Epigrammata
1.1 55
4.7 221
7.30 221
7.82 221
7.88 55
8.3 55
11.3 55
11.94 221
14.184–92 55

Minucius Felix
Octavius
8.4 54
9.2 56
32.1 54

Origen
Contra Celsum
3.55 94, 98
6.24 337
8.17.19 54
8.25 286
121–29 286

Exhortatio ad martyrium
45 266

Homiliae in Genesim
7.2 172
7.3 172

Ovid
Ars amatoria
1.75–76 221
1.413–16 221

Metamorphoses
1.212–15 404
1.226–44 404
1.231–44 406
8.618–724 406
8.626–724 397
629–88 405

Persius

Satirae
5.176–84 221

Petronius

Satyricon
76 482
102.13–14 221
frag. 37 221

Philo

Against Flaccus
126, 225

Allegorical Interpretation
1.2 170
1.33 170
1.101 170

Hypothetica
1–18 115
4 117
10–12 117
18 117n4

On Dreams
1.141 264
1.233 263

On Flight and Finding
157 170

On Giants
1.6 266
1.6–16 264

On Planting
113 171

On Rewards and Punishments
152 223

On Sobriety
31 170
62 170

On the Change of Names
234 349

On the Confusion of Tongues
1–15 169
14 171

On the Contemplative Life
13 439
16–17 439
50–63 449

On the Creation of the World
3 370
7 370
142–43 370
157–70 343
161 449

On the Embassy to Gaius
143 69
155–56 367
299–306 38
312 69

On the Life of Abraham
107 404
133–41 451

On the Life of Moses
1.1–2 132
1.29 133
1.158 133
1.158–59 133
2.216 69

On the Posterity of Cain
1 171
7 171
32 170
49–50 171

On the Preliminary Studies
3 171
74 168

On the Special Laws
1.51–53 223
1.154 197
1.197–99 349
1.199 349
1.227 350
1.234–37 350
2.62 69
2.145 350
3.35 449
3.63 213
3.205–6 213

On the Virtues
20–21 450
102–3 223
182 223

Questions and Answers on Genesis
2.49 450
4.2 263

That Every Good Person Is Free
2.81–82 69
75–91 115
86 117
121–24 172
122 173
125 173

That the Worse Attacks the Better
32 170

Who Is the Heir?
274 450

Philodemus

De libertate dicendi
20.24–25 340
36.20 340

Plato

Apologia
22b–c 288
27c–d 265

Cratylus
398a–b 265

Leges
10.899b 262
783–85 449
836c 449
838e–839a 449

Phaedo
107d 265

Phaedrus
66c–67a 262
244a 288
246a–b 340
247c–248a 262
249 280

Respublica
7.535a 135
10.614–15 280
554d–e 342
620e 265

Symposium
189–93 446, 449
201e–204a 285

Theaetetus
176b 26

Timaeus
1 131

Plautus

Aulularia
1–39 95

Mercator
834–37 95

Pliny the Elder

Naturalis historia
2.22 262
5.18.74 61
5.66 43
5.73 115
13.46 222
13.2171–89 146
28.27 263
28.28 263
30.11 221
33.134–35 367

Pliny the Younger

Epistulae
3.18.9 55
5.10.3 55
10.96 325
10.96–97 151
10.96.9 52

Plutarch

Alexander
1.1–2 130
1.3 132

Cato Maior
20.9 436

Conjugalia praecepta
29.142a–b 455
34.143a 455

140d   468
331.142e   455

De defectu oraculorum
416d–f   265

Demetrius
1.4–6   131

De Iside et Osiride
25   285
26   285

Moralia
140d   442
360e   285
361a–c   285

Quaestiones convivales
2.10.2   374
644a   409

Quomodo quis suos in virtute sentiat profectus
76e–f   344

Timoleon
1   131

De virtute morali
451e–f   342

Porphyry

De abstinentia ab esu animalium
2.39   265
2.42   265

Pseudo-Aristotle

Physiognomonica
810a.25–29   251
814a   251

Quintilian

Institutio oratoria
3.7.21   222

Seneca the Elder

Controversiae
4 pref. 10   242n1
10.5.21   57

Seneca the Younger

De beneficiis
1.3   389
1.4.2   393
2.10.4   393
2.17   389
2.18.5   397
4.28   390

De clementia
1.1.8   319
2.6.3   397

Epistulae morales
41.3   262n7
75.8–16   344
88.37   55n6
95.47   221

De ira
1.9.4–1.10.1   340
1.14.1   340

Soranus

Gynaecia
1.61   440n19

Stobaeus

Anthologium
3.32.11   259n3

Strabo

Geographica
12.7.18   57
16.2.2   44
16.2.35   220
16.2.36–37   220

Suetonius

Divus Augustus
25.3   369
31.1   292
76.2   221

Divus Claudius
25.4   222
25.44   53n3

Divus Julius
84.5   220

Nero
16.2   53

Tiberius
36   222

Tacitus

Annales
2.85   456
3.25–28   453
12.43   385
15.44   325
15.44.2–5   53
15.45.1–2   38

Historiae
1.78   366
2.68   12
5.1–13   36
5.3.1–5.5.2   222
5.5.1   223
5.5.1–2   223
5.5.5   222

Tatian

Oratio ad Graecos
15   265

Tertullian

Apologeticus
15   54
40   324

De baptismo
5.1   337

De corona militis
3   473

De spectaculis
13   54

Ad uxorem
2.5.3   473

Theophrastus

De causis plantarum
5.4.3   297
5.4.4   297

Thucydides

History of the Peloponnesian War
2.68   12

Valerius Macimus

Facta et dicta memorabilia
1.1.1a–b   264
3.8.6   435

Velleius Paterculus

Historia Romana
2.126.1–4   318

Vitruvius

De architectura
1.7.1   82

Xenophon

Hellenica
6.1.2–4   402

Oeconomicus
7.41–42   433